THE HISTORY OF THE
BRITISH FILM

1918–1929

by Rachael Low and Roger Manvell

The History of the British Film, 1896–1906
The History of the British Film, 1906–1914
by Rachael Low
The History of the British Film, 1914–1918
by Rachael Low

THE HISTORY

OF THE

BRITISH FILM

1918 – 1929

by

RACHAEL LOW

LONDON

GEORGE ALLEN & UNWIN LTD

PRINTED IN GREAT BRITAIN
in 10 on 11 point Plantin
BY BILLING AND SONS LIMITED
GUILDFORD AND LONDON

ACKNOWLEDGEMENTS

As with previous books in this series I have, over the years, received much valuable assistance in my research from the British Film Academy, the British Film Institute and the National Film Archive, as well as from the many film makers of the twenties whom I have interviewed, to all of whom I am greatly indebted. Acknowledgements must also be made to the Stills Department of the National Film Archive for many of the illustrations and, through the Stills Department, to the Hepworth family for those from films by Cecil Hepworth. I must express my gratitude also to the many others who supplied me with illustrations. Finally, my special thanks are due to Ernest Lindgren, George Pearson and Baynham Honri for their unfailing encouragement and help.

CONTENTS

A*

CONTENTS

LIST OF ILLUSTRATIONS

(dates are those of Trade Show)

LIST OF ILLUSTRATIONS

CHAPTER ONE

Artistic and Critical Theory in the Twenties

It was during the 1920s that people started treating the film seriously in Britain. The writer John St Loe Strachey was a founder member of the Film Society formed in London during the twenties and, as editor of the *Spectator*, was an early sponsor of serious articles about the cinema. He said at the Stoll Picture Theatre Club in 1924:

'One of the things which have attracted me to the cinema is the fact that it has enabled us to witness the birth of a new art—an opportunity that has not previously arisen for many generations. . . . Nobody is consciously developing the cinema; it is developing itself.'[1]

There was much truth in this. The cinema illustrated the historical process of invention and discovery, whereby the problems posed at any existing stage of knowledge and achievement point the way to their own solution. Changes in technique were suggested by the exigencies of production, and new methods were indicated by the very problems that arose. There was a great difference between the ordinary film of 1919 and that of 1929. Even in England, where few outstanding film makers could survive during the twenties, film making was pushing its exponents forward. The primitive stages of a new art could indeed be examined by highly civilized contemporaries, not for the first time for many generations as Strachey had suggested, but for the first time in history. Eric Elliott, in his book *Anatomy of Motion Picture Art*, wrote:

'. . . *it is the only new one mankind has ever known*. The other arts evolved with Man himself, and were ready only when he was ready.'[2]

By the end of the decade the new mastery of technique, and the possibilities it revealed, had earned an entirely new respectability for the cinema. The Society of Cinema Veterans, formed in 1924, was open to people who had entered the industry before 1903 when the film had been new and disreputable. The formation of the Society was the trade's proud claim to have come of age. But it was much more important that a new generation of young people, born since the cinema and taking its existence for granted from childhood, were also coming of age and approaching it with open minds. During the twenties not only was it increasingly accepted by the middle classes but a growing, if small, number of upper middle class and university-educated people committed themselves to it as film makers and as critics. The advance in the art of film making took place at the same time as a significant improvement in the social and cultural standing of the film.

In 1929 the sudden arrival in Britain of the commercial sound film from America checked this. Showmen and audiences had always wanted, and welcomed, any form of sound accompaniment. But to the new theorists, recorded sound seemed to destroy the very limitation which was thought to be the essential mainspring of film art. Undoubtedly the fluidity of expression which the silent film had recently achieved was impossible with the early sound apparatus. Many of the new enthusiasts were repelled by the clumsy and crude sound films which resulted. Indeed, had the sound film arrived five or ten years earlier the serious public attracted by the flowering of the silent film would not have existed. It was natural that for a while antagonism to the sound film seemed greatest among those who were most serious about the film. It is interesting in this connection that in replies to a contemporary questionnaire 50 per cent of the men and 30 per cent of the women were in favour of the talkies, but only 19 per cent of the section described as 'people of prominence'. The setback, however, was only for a short while. The new intellectuals of the cinema were not to be so easily discouraged.

The temporarily hostile reaction to sound was to be found in the work of a new group of serious writers on the cinema. Early struggles towards the formulation of aesthetic and critical standards can be traced to the work of this group, which represents an interesting effort to understand the nature of the new art while it was still in its primitive stages.

After the war there was an air of change and rebellion among the young, symbolized by the girls' short hair and skirts and what one of our local film stars described as 'the Jazz':

'I think the Jazz expresses the feelings of the public at the present time better than anything else. After four years of war weariness it is only natural that everyone wants relaxation—the one desire is to dance, and what better than the Jazz to express the exultant feeling now abroad?'[3]

The film trade by this time had a great idea of its own importance. Big talk about its technical marvels, the speed of its growth and its tremendous influence was commonplace. *The Bioscope*, an influential trade paper, even referred to the cinema in 1919 as the Church's 'legitimate competitor in moulding the character of the nation'[4] and a film executive wrote in 1926 that the cinema was the 'most potent single factor in modern life'.[5] It was true that the social status of the film was considerably higher than it had been before the war. The Stoll Picture Theatre Club, for example, which had been formed about 1919, assembled for discussion many people with a more serious approach towards the film and its speakers included not only the film censor and ex-journalist T. P. O'Connor and the journalist Hannen Swaffer, but even well-known writers like Hilaire Belloc and G. K. Chesterton and the critic St John Ervine. The Film Society was formed in 1925 with a most distinguished list of founder members (see page 34). Royalty, as well as the progressive intelligentsia, accepted the film. Queen Mary and George V were circumspect, visiting the Marble Arch Pavilion in 1924 to see a worthy British film of the battle of Zeebrugge, but other members of the family were less formal. The Prince of Wales charmed the trade by unexpectedly dropping in to the London Pavilion to see *Covered Wagon*, for example, and agreeing to attend the first presentation of the British film *Reveille*. It was said that Prince George had seen *Foolish Wives* three times, and the Duke and Duchess of York took a party to an ordinary showing of *Beau Geste* at the Plaza in 1926. No less than nineteen members of the Royal family were said to have seen *Ben Hur* when it was on in London. A few years later *The Film in National Life* could say, in fact,

'A fellow of an Oxford College no longer feels an embarrassed explanation to be necessary when he is recognized leaving a cinema.'[6]

These were signs of the times but there was still massive hostility from much of the social and intellectual establishment. An article in *The Bioscope* in 1919 gives point to some of this opposition:

'Has the time not come for the public to recognize that pictures can be made to fulfil a nobler purpose than merely to afford an opportunity of witnessing absurdity carried to imbecile excess, salaciousness smugly masquerading as a problem play, flagrant and disgusting immorality veneered with a thin coating of pinchbeck virtue, dramas as vapid as newspaper feuilletons, and thrilling adventures which far transcend the comparatively feeble exploits of Spring Heeled Jack and other worthies?'[7]

The critic Ernest Betts, devoted though he was to the serious cinema, wrote in 1928:

'. . . chiefly as a result of American films, a large part of the world, and especially the youthful world, now has a cabaret outlook, full of feeble passion, Woolworth glitter, and trumpery heroics. . . .

'But there is a difference between entertaining a man by making him drink and entertaining a man by making him drunk. The American film has doped the world with rotten juices. By a strength of purpose which is staggering and its one superb virtue, it has flung at us, year by year, in unending deluge, its parcel of borrowed stories and flashy little moralities.'[8]

Criticism from outside the industry was even more damning. Augustus John wrote in *The Actor* in 1922 and was quoted in the *Bioscope*:

'The film writers, never out of their shirt-sleeves, are day and night engaged in boiling down more and more novels, reducing them to the pap-like consistency considered acceptable to the edented jaws and tired stomachs of the crowd. All this devoted labour results in a perpetual out-pouring of reels intended to attract, comfort and subdue the humblest, the commonest, the most universal level of intelligence in the land.'[9]

Gordon Craig, the great stage director, was quoted on the cinema in 1922:

'Smears all it touches. Enslaves the mind of the people. Rules the people as in ancient days a degenerate Church ruled them. Is the brat of yellow journalism.'[10]

General Booth of the Salvation Army spoke of films:

'. . . most disgusting and absolutely unfit for public exhibition.'[11]

and the poet John Drinkwater stated the cinema

'. . . has no existence at all as an art'.[12]

The theatre critic James Agate, the theatrical producer Basil Dean and St John Ervine were all known to be critical, although Agate made an exception in the case of Chaplin's film *The Circus* and Dean was soon to engage in film production himself when the arrival of sound film led to something more like stage production. Many writers had a rather ambivalent attitude to films, contempt for film makers and audiences being mingled with appreciation of the fees paid by production companies. Edgar Wallace, many of whose books were filmed and who later became involved in film production himself, wrote in a pamphlet published privately after the war and reviewed in the *Bioscope*:

'The difference between the book, the play and the photo or cinema play lies in the educational equipment of the consumer.'[13]

Writers who ventured into the studios sometimes had reason to raise their eyebrows. Compton Mackenzie has written in his autobiography:

'Meanwhile, Ideal Films had been going ahead with turning *Sinister Street* into a film. I was taken to see some of the "rushes". To my consternation I was shown Lord Saxby in full regimentals of the Welsh Guards, bearskin and all, riding along a country lane to have tea with Mrs Fane.
' "But look," I protested to the two little Jewish brothers who were managing Ideal Films, "a Colonel in the Guards would not go to tea in the country dressed up like that. He must be in mufti."
'The two Rowsons smiled.
' "What you must try and understand, Mr Mackenzie, is that the cinema audience wants rómance. We must give them rómance. There's no rómance in a suit of dittoes".'[14]

Arnold Bennett, writing in the magazine *Close Up* later, was more sympathetic to the problems of film making. He criticized not so much the story-telling technique, which was in fact quite highly developed by 1927 when he wrote, but the deplorable stories themselves:

'All the new stories, contributed *ad hoc*, are conventional, grossly sentimental, clumsy, and fatally impaired by poverty of invention. The screen has laid hands on some of the greatest stories in the world, and has cheapened, soiled, ravaged, and poisoned them by the crudest fatuities.'[15]

Bennett was shortly to write an original scenario for the film *Piccadilly*. Meanwhile, suggesting that the producer should seek someone with the gift of creating character and contriving events in terms of the screen, this middle-aged master added:

'Useless for him to go to established and therefore middle-aged masters of literary narration. To all these distinguished artists the screen is still a novelty. The film medium does not come naturally to them because they were not familiar with it in their formative years.'[16]

George Bernard Shaw refused to have anything to do with the cinema until the sound film arrived, when he became sufficiently interested to grant a couple of filmed interviews. H. G. Wells was more tolerant, openly admiring the work of Chaplin and allowing several of his own novels to be filmed but resisting many requests to write especially for the cinema. One of his sons, however, worked in the industry during the twenties and Wells himself became a founder member of the Film Society, and, after the arrival of sound, published a book purporting to be the idea for a film script (see page 242).

Wells's son was one of the new type of educated young people entering the industry and changing it, to some extent, from within. Lord Asquith's son Anthony Asquith, Lord Swaythling's son Ivor Montagu, and Edward Craig's son Edward Carrick were others. At least a dozen new young members of the industry in the later twenties were from universities, a number of them from Cambridge. Several of them had been at Cambridge together in the early twenties. Grouped round Harry Bruce Woolfe of British Instructional Films, George Pearson of Welsh–Pearson and the editing firm of Ivor Montagu and Adrian Brunel, most were keen members of the Film Society and had more in common with the new school of critics and theoretical writers than with other members of the trade. These young people were rebels against both the cultural snobbery of their elders and the vulgarity and ignorance of much of the trade. The latter, which had always contained an element yearning for artistic respectability, both welcomed the new tone and at the same time resented it. Art, to the more naïve of the pioneers, had meant Shakespeare, beauty and a little moral uplift. Instead of these, however, the new young people had obscure theories about light, rhythm and montage and were talking and writing enthusiastically about films of dubious box-office value. Foreign films which were often sombre, even shocking, were held up for admiration. There must have been many showmen who agreed with the correspondent who wrote to *The Bioscope* about the brilliant and daring Russian film *Bed and Sofa*:

19

'It is pitiably futile that such an artist as Room should be expected to paint a beautiful picture with no materials save a palette knife—and *mud*.'[17]

At all events, writing about films became more and more important. There was, of course, a flourishing trade press (see page 37) and a fan press. But the national and daily press also took more and more notice of films. Important papers with regular film correspondents in 1919 were the *Daily News*, which later became the *News Chronicle*, with E. A. Baughan; the *Evening News* with W. G. Faulkner, who left and went into the film trade in November 1921 and was succeeded by Jympson Harmon; and the *Westminster Gazette*, with Macer Wright. Other papers began to include reviews and information, at first often as a side line to dramatic criticism. Iris Barry, previously critic on the *Spectator*, joined the *Daily Mail* in 1925. The *Daily Express*, *The Times*, and G. A. Atkinson on the *Daily Telegraph*, frequently gave news and criticism. Walter Mycroft wrote for the *Evening Standard* and the *Illustrated Sunday Herald*. Ivor Montagu, after writing for *The Observer*, where he followed Angus Macphail, joined *The Sunday Times* at the end of 1927 and was followed on *The Observer* by C. A. Lejeune in 1928. Both Macphail and Montagu had written for *Granta* when at Cambridge. Lejeune, having started as critic on the *Manchester Guardian* in 1922, wrote for a wide, educated and liberal public, and with Iris Barry was one of the first real film critics. Most of the weeklies were slower to take regular notice of the cinema, although the *Bystander* had a feature called 'Picture Plays as seen from the Stalls' in 1923. Such papers as the *English Review*, *Saturday Review*, *Fortnightly Review*, *London Mercury*, *Drawing and Design*, *Illustrated London News* and *New Statesman* noted the phenomenon from time to time with varying degrees of friendliness. Even *The Studio* reviewed several films of particular interest for their sets or design. There were also occasional broadcasts from 2LO, including some by G. A. Atkinson in 1923, and a series of six talks on *The Art of the Cinema* by Anthony Asquith in 1927.

A few books on the cinema were also published, including manuals of film production, books of criticism and a handful of more ambitious theoretical works.

The handbooks or how-it-is-done type of books were designed more to interest and amuse the public than to instruct those entering the industry, although there were virtually no teaching books and they may have been used as such. The days when an amateur could read one of these books and feel equipped to start his own production company were over. But although not really for professional use these little books give an insight into the practices and attitudes of ordinary commercial production at the time. Particularly helpful are *The Film Industry* written by Davidson Boughey in 1921 and *Kinematograph Studio Technique* by L. C. MacBean in 1922, both of which are frequently mentioned in the later chapter on film production techniques. Of greater interest at this point are books by two screen writers, *The Modern Photoplay and its Construction* by Colden Lore in 1923 and *Writing for the Screen* by Arrar Jackson in 1929, both of whom, as writers, were concerned with the planning of the film as a whole. Of greater interest, also, is the 1928 publication *Through a Yellow*

Glass by Oswell Blakeston, a critic and associate editor of *Close Up* and later co-producer of an experimental film.

Most of the books of criticism were works of hearty condescension. Their tone was interested but lighthearted, at equal pains to claim the cinema as an art and to avoid being thought stuffy or serious. Iris Barry's bright and chatty *Let's Go to the Pictures*, in 1926, for example, took a realistic stand:

'It seems to me that the best way to help progress is not by condemning cinematography off-hand, but by seeing for oneself what the cinema's function and its virtues are, and then by patronizing those films which most nearly reach one's ideal. If enough people support the better type of pictures, and stoutly demand more and still finer ones, they will get them.'[18]

Despite the obvious concern to avoid a highbrow appearance the best of these writers, if they were faithful to a sufficiently high standard, could perform a very useful task of popularization. But not all were as careful as Iris Barry. The American Gilbert Seldes, in *The Seven Lively Arts* in 1924, permitted himself to be timidly outrageous by approving things already widely accepted such as the genius of Chaplin, whom for some reason he preferred to call by his French title 'Charlot'. When he ventured into something more theoretical his ignorance of the processes of production and of developments in France, Germany or Russia led him to some rather strange conclusions: that in comedy the 'secret of pace [is] in the projector', that film is 'movement governed by light' and that the 'serious moving picture' was 'a *bogus* art'. *This Film Business* by Rudolf Messel in 1928 and *Films: Facts and Forecasts* by L'Estrange Fawcett in 1927 were in a similar vein of general enthusiasm. Fawcett's book, in particular, was an example of a type of criticism that seems to be peculiar to films, genuinely appreciative of the better films but at the same time over-reasonable about the commercial justifications for the worst.

Running with the hare and hunting with the hounds, this type of writer hesitated to offend his public by saying that rubbish was rubbish, yet would not yield place to the highbrow in his clamorous admiration of more *avant-garde* films. The aggressively positive pose of 'I'm as intellectual as anybody, personally, of course, but let's keep our feet on the ground', the ready forgiveness of pot-boilers and the ability to see a mysterious artistic discipline in the need to please all of the people all of the time showed more enthusiasm than discrimination. One such critic was even able to describe *Potemkin* and *Hindle Wakes*, a meretricious British popular success, as 'equally absorbing'.

Selection is as much part of the process of art appreciation as it is of artistic expression itself, and those who displayed such a jolly willingness to compromise were not likely to push the artistic advancement of the film very far. But a more discriminating attitude was beginning to appear even then. Ernest Betts, a contributor to *Close Up* who had been a film critic from 1922, produced a book called *Heraclitus, or the Future of Films* in 1928 which said firmly:

'. . . for art does not, and cannot, appeal to everybody, whatever people may say about the Old Vic, and B.B.C. concerts and native dances in South Africa.'[19]

The possibility that different types of films and film makers might find greater freedom if the mass audience split into groups with varying tastes was already being recognized in the appearance of the film society and repertory cinema movements. And an essential part of these movements was the growth of a more advanced level of writing about films.

Thus Betts' flippant, breezy and discursive little book claims boldly on its first page

'. . . this is to be, at least in part, an aesthetic or "highbrow" study concerning films which are works of art'.[20]

Most of the serious writers of this type were connected with *Close Up*. This was a monthly magazine printed in Switzerland as an international venture by Pool from July 1927 until 1933. Its historical importance is very great despite its small circulation. It was edited by Kenneth Macpherson. One associate editor was Blakeston, who also contributed criticism to the *Architectural Review* and collaborated on an experimental film, *Light Rhythms*, with the American photographer Francis Bruguière. The group of writers which grew up addressed the magazine, and a few books, to each other and a small circle of film initiates. The other assistant editor was Winifred Ellerman, under the professional name of Bryher, whose book on the film problems of Soviet Russia was also published by Pool in 1929. Another frequent contributor was Robert Herring, whose work also appeared in the *London Mercury* and *Drawing and Design*, and who produced a book of stills called *Films of the Year 1927–28*, which was published by *The Studio*. Ernest Betts, Jean Prévost and Ivor Montagu appeared in its pages, and also works by the writers Gertrude Stein and Dorothy M. Richardson. Eric Elliott, another *Close Up* writer, produced an ambitious theoretical book called *Anatomy of Motion Picture Art* published by Pool in 1928.

Close Up rarely had a good word to say for a British picture, but enabled its readers to keep in touch with the far more important developments taking place in films abroad, especially in Germany, France and Russia. It was particularly important as a source of information concerning films in Russia, as widespread opposition to the new political régime kept Russian films out of the British cinemas. Its characteristic literary style was affected, fashionable writing in an elliptical, casual manner. Sentences sometimes lacked verbs, capitals were used for emphasis, 'one' did this and 'one' did that, typographical errors and split infinitives were cheerfully disregarded. The text was peppered with such remarks as 'What rot', 'Oh, its a mess' and even '*quien sabe?*' or '*va bene*'. But the pretentious and precious tone of much of the writing can readily be forgiven for the passionate commitment to all that was best in the film. The style has dated, and years later it is easy to see the pitfalls into which theory led. But the magazine undertook an important job which it did without compromise, that of building up a nucleus of cineastes devoted to the development of the art of the film. Some of these were film makers who brought a new seriousness to their work within the commercial framework, some were soon to be making films outside this framework in the documentary movement, and some were critics or merely spectators who were stimulated to seek, and support, better films.

There were a few other writers, equally earnest, who were not associated primarily with *Close Up*. Betts' *Heraclitus, or the Future of Films*, published in 1928, was one of a series with titles by some serious and even distinguished writers. *Parnassus to Let*, by Eric Walter White, was published by Leonard and Virginia Woolf at the Hogarth Press in 1928. It was strongly criticized by *Close Up*, which found it ignorant and obscure, referring to it as

'a little essay on (I suppose) rhythm and the cinema.'[21]

Meanwhile young Paul Rotha was at work on his monumental book *The Film Till Now*, which appeared in 1930, a critical account of the cinema which was to introduce several generations of serious cinema goers to the subject, and to prove one of the greatest single factors in the growth of a new attitude.

Outside the mainstream of critical writing were three books which had little practical effect but which were significant of a growing desire to understand the real nature of the film medium. One was a new edition, published here in 1922, of an American book of 1916 called *The Art of the Moving Picture* by the popular poet Vachel Lindsay. The second was *The Mind and the Film* by Gerard Fort Buckle, published in 1926. And the third was the Pool publication in 1928 by Eric Elliott, *Anatomy of Moving Picture Art*.

The book by Vachel Lindsay, which probably had nothing like the influence he claimed for it, was an extraordinary attempt to establish the artistic credentials of the film by categorizing it in terms of the other arts. His main theme was an elaborate systematization of films into six classes, as Photoplays of Action, Intimate Photoplays, and Motion Pictures of Fairy Splendour, Crowd Splendour, Patriotic Splendour and Religious Splendour. The Action Photoplay was defined as Sculpture-in-Motion, with references to moving bronze, wood and stone; the Intimate Photoplay was likened to Painting-in-Motion; the Motion Picture of Fairy Splendour was Furniture, Trappings and Inventions in Motion; the Motion Picture of Crowd Splendour was Architecture-in-Motion with special reference to landscape; so was the Motion Picture of Patriotic Splendour, with special reference to mural paintings, and the Motion Picture of Religious Splendour with special reference to architecture. The four categories of Splendour Photoplays had two characteristics. Firstly they were out-of-doors, a definition which included large sets; and secondly they were concerned with the meaningful movements of inanimate things. The picture of Action, Intimacy and Splendour were further identified with the colours red, blue and yellow.

Steeped in the other arts and a Museum background which stressed the visual and plastic arts of painting, sculpture and architecture, Lindsay called on producers to seek inspiration only in these arts. He was fascinated with the power that films could exercise over the senses, and ignored their intellectual content almost entirely. In this he was like many of the more esoteric critics coming after him, who overlooked the simple truth that however great the appeal to the emotions or senses, if a film offers nothing to the mind it will in the end be boring. He regarded films as pageants, even as tableaux. As a result he felt that they should be short, as 'a one-hour programme is long enough for anyone', and an individual film should not exceed twenty minutes. He saw the cinema as a place where people conversed as they watched the images on the screen. Believing this, he could regard a trite film like Trimble's short *Battle Hymn of the Republic* as a greater achievement than Griffith's *Birth of a Nation*, and some of his other preferences were equally unusual. Lindsay, in fact, had no interest in film technique as later understood and made no contribution to its understanding. He was a popular poet, and his style was free-swinging, roistering and uproarious. The book is a panegyric, full of froth and self-display but bursting with praise and enthusiasm for film, and is a brave attempt to inspire others with his own joyful faith in it. It did show occasional insight. He referred, for example, to the 'noble managerial mood' which could make 'an artistic photoplay . . . the product of the creative force of one soul', and foresaw the emergence of individual style among directors. But on the whole, despite the rhetoric, his highly personal vision of the film could be of little real service to the cause of artistic development.

Buckle's book, which was written between 1921 and 1926, was a very different matter. It was a laboured attempt to isolate film technique, as an art, from the technological aspect of film making. Buckle felt that the best way to do this was to approach the subject from the psychological angle, and the bulk of the book was what he called a treatise on the psychological factors in the film, largely irrelevant psychological and even physiological material. Buckle himself wrote the scripts of several rather unsuccessful silent films, but although more knowledgeable than Lindsay about how films were made he seems to have lacked the poet's vision and enthusiasm, while sharing his propensity for making categories and misleading analogies, and for laying down laws. Although the title of the book refers to the mind, and although he stated on Page One that the 'primary duty of a film is to tell a story' he, like Lindsay, over-emphasized the visual nature of the film. The most important part of the book was the treatment of what he called Photographic Aids to the Mind. Here he discussed the techniques of cinematography almost as though the brain was capable of receiving visual stimuli, but not of thinking. He began with a misstatement of the theory of persistence of vision, in which he implied that the retinal impression was retained not for a fixed period, but until it was superseded by the next one. He then elaborated on this as if a retinal impression was the only consequence of the image. Again and again it was assumed that the spectator's mind would be doing what the film image was doing: if the picture faded the mind would experience 'complete loss of the thought movement', slow motion cinematography would cause slow thought, overuse of leisurely fading would even produce a 'state of coma'. In fact, of course, what the mind would be doing was to observe that fading or slow movement was being presented before it, and interpreting its significance. It was as a corollary to Buckle's mechanistic view that despite his good intentions he undervalued the very aspect of film in which he claimed to be most interested, the part played by the mind. What both he and Lindsay ignored was that besides being visual, the film occupied time. Because of this it was necessary to provide the mind with something to think about at the risk, quite simply, of being a bore. Leisurely fading produces not a coma, but a spectator who is thinking about something else. But their complete lack of interest in film content, and therefore in film structure, made it unlikely that either of them would discover the truth. Buckle's short and inadequate treatment of structure, in fact, simply came to the rather perfunctory conclusion that what he called balance and continuity should be determined on the floor of the studio. This was too much for J. D. Williams, the film producer who wrote his preface. Williams, a practical man, groped his way through the fog of pseudo-scientific argument and emerged to state politely but firmly that in fact the structure of the film should 'be determined before the studio floor is reached'.[22]

The terminology of film technique was still fluid at the time that Buckle tackled the subject, and the written works of Pudovkin and Eisenstein had not yet elucidated it for others. Buckle did realize that film technique was more than the technical information contained in the manuals. But his attempt to work the fundamentals out for himself came to some disappointingly obvious conclusions. It was rather an anticlimax to be told that a good film story was a good story which did not lose by being translated into a film.

Eric Elliott, who seems to have been unfamiliar with the work of the Russians, came much nearer to a modern understanding of film technique than Lindsay or Buckle in his *Anatomy of Motion Picture Art* in 1928. Showing the same tendency to codify and name with quaint terms, he was a far more sympathetic and perceptive observer. He was somewhat hampered by his basic assumption that

'Dramaturgy, Histrionism and Pictorial Craft are the established foundations of screen technique.'[23]

Worried by the debate as to whether photography was an art, he had already come to the conclusion that there was art in the arrangement of the material, and only the means of reproducing it were mechanical. Fortunately he did not pursue this, but discovered that

'. . . the cinema's peculiar values in *continuity* are independent of any refinement in the single scenes.'[24]

Anticipating the Russian use of the term 'plastic material', he decided

'. . . *action, acting* and *pictures* became more or less elementary values, parts of photoplay construction, materials for a superior ensemble.

'Usually, the changing of scenes is intended to elucidate the plot of drama; but beyond that is the finer purpose of arranging scenes not for mere incident's sake, but to interpret, compare and reflect the transitive expressions latent in those scenes.'[25]

Accordingly Elliott devoted an important chapter to what he decided to call the principles of continuity:

'There may be thousands of scenes in the complete photoplay. They, in turn, become factors in a larger scheme of composition. To avoid confusion with the still-picture term we do not speak of this larger scheme as composition. Technically it is termed CONTINUITY.'[26]

At this point the prevailing habit of naming and classifying ran riot, and he distinguished various types of episodes besides those for purely narrative purposes. There might be episodes of incurrence, intensive or passive, objective or subjective; or they might be episodes of recurrence or concurrence, either of which might be cumulative.

'By these arrangements we are able to obtain unlimited effects by COMPARISON.'[27]

Comparison comprised contrasts, similes and reflections, and could be of five orders: remote, successive, incurrent, parenthetic or appended. As a result of this Elliott finally concluded that film most nearly resembled music, and described its design as

'ENSEMBLE—the concinnity of detail to detail, scene to scene, motif to motif— a symphony of images, weaving in Time, Space and Motion, and pictures by Light.'[28]

It is clear that the decade from the end of the war until 1929 was a time of enqiury about the cinema's artistic significance. But as yet there was no accepted approach among those convinced that it was an art, and the only thing they had in common was a determination to establish its claim to serious attention. It was for this reason that all of them sought to establish in what way, exactly, the film was a creative art different to others.

It was not even easy to decide who the artist was. During the twenties specialization of function inside the studio separated the work of producer, director, the writer or writers of various types, lighting cameraman, designer, actor and editor. And while each became a skill with some creative scope of its own, final responsibility for the artistic conception of the film as a whole was not always as clear as it might be. The creative importance of the director was more or less accepted, but it could not escape notice that the actual influence exercised by the director in any particular production set-up could vary according to the temperament and talents of the actual people involved. It was the fact that film production was a group activity which made many sceptical of whether it could possibly be an art at all. Possibly it was ignorance of film-making procedures which made the multiplicity of skills so confusing to outsiders in their efforts to locate creative responsibility. One director warned them:

'Be quite sure of your ground—technically. Don't blame the lighting when the print is poor; the acting when the situation is false; the director when the script is at fault. And when you are bored with a film, don't *always* think you have put a finger no the trouble by suggesting "judicious cutting".'[29]

Perhaps it is not the critic's job to discuss the contribution of different people in such detail, but to assess the work as a whole. But with no clear idea of which function was responsible for the film as a film, only the most superficial criticism was possible. Hence the desire to place artistic responsibility, also, involved an attempt to define the qualities which made the film a medium of expression on its own. If it was more than a mere conglomeration of the skills of the actor, the writer, the set designer and the cameraman, what was it? Why was the film maker anything more than a stage producer working under extra limitations to make a silent photographed record of his work?

This idea, that a film was a photographed record of other forms of art, had indeed been the earliest way of looking at it. The desire to claim artistic status for the film had arisen before this elementary view had been superseded. Above all, art was identified at first simply with photographic beauty, and this unsophisticated view lingered into the twenties in the Victorian sentimentality of some early British producers. A first step towards a deeper understanding was taken by those who felt that the film, visual and largely wordless as it was, must tell its story in visible activity and that the art of film making lay in devising stories which could be told purely in visual terms. This was taken to mean in terms of action, and the results of this over-simplification were all too obvious in many British films of the twenties. No time was wasted, in this school of film making, on the establishment of mood or setting, on characterization, or on the subtlety of personal relations.

'The Film Play is pre-eminently the vehicle for stories rich in incidents and action.'[30]

Fawcett wrote that the director

'. . . must translate every phase and scene into action, and no matter what sort of action it is, the treatment must be lively in order to appeal to the modern audience.'[31]

He even referred to a film being

'. . . representative of modern life—its movement, rapid change of scene, speed, sharpness of detail, plain straight-forward expression.'[32]

But the busy little films which sped through their complicated plots managed to be strangely dull. The more thoughtful, while accepting that the film could only convey what had been externalized in visible objects and actions, realized that this need not imply ceaseless activity. Incidental but 'telling' incidents, symbolic shots, and in fact the whole technique of the expressive 'little touch' which gathered strength in the early twenties was a more subtle and leisurely development of the original idea of externalization. It is significant that films employing this technique were among the first to elicit favourable comment from more serious observers. Stage business, in the actor's sense of the term, could be adapted to film narrative and be more expressive than Fawcett's 'rapid change of scene, speed, sharpness of detail. . . .' But it was still accepted that, since the camera could show only external things, the power of the film itself to suggest abstract ideas was very limited.

At the other extreme to those who tussled with the idea of overt action were those *avant-garde* critics who all but ignored the story in favour of light, movement and rhythm, visual patterns moving in two-dimensional space and in time.

'Light speaks, is pliant, is malleable. Light is our friend and god. Let us be worthy of it. Do not let us defame light, use and waste brilliant possibilities, elaborate material, making light a slave and a commonplace mountebank.'[33]

'Think what you have. First of all pure form, every single attribute of photographic art, miracles to work in tones and tone depths, light, geometry, design, sculpture . . . pure abstraction all of it. Then this not static but with all the resources of movement, change, rhythm, space, completely fluid to the will of the artist. Then miracles to work again with trick photography, infinite possibilities of suggestion, contrast, merging, dissociation; whole realms of fantasy, states of mind, of emotion, psychic things, to symbolize not in the limit of one special moment of time, but in all the ebb and flow of their course, their beginning and their end. Not only have you mastery over the outward manifestation, but over the inner and inmost working too.'[34]

Some pinned their hopes on light, some on movement. But all were preoccupied with the use of visual and temporal composition for a direct aesthetic assault on the senses. In this they were as exclusively concerned with visual values as their opposite numbers who thought only of visible action. And whilst the simpler view ignored the aesthetic appeal to the emotions, the more highbrow critics tended to underestimate the importance of a narrative thread or subject to engage the mind.

Strangely enough the highbrow critics of the twenties were merely restating in a more sophisticated way the eccentric position taken by Vachel Lindsay, with his purely sensual aesthetic of the visual and plastic arts in motion. Betts stressed movement. He wrote:

'Heraclitus it was who first perceived that all life consisted of, and tended towards, change and change is the first principle of all cinematography. . . . The film is unique among the visual arts in postulating a perpetual fluidity or becoming as the basis of the conception.'[35]

An Essay on the Cinema in Herring's book of stills in 1928 maintained that, although a story was used to set the flow of images in motion, the essence of the matter was not the story but the design and rhythm, representing the visual and the time or motion elements. The experimental work of Francis Bruguière was cited for having 'perhaps carried it further than anyone else; by means of triple-exposure and parti-coloured make-up, he has obtained a form capable of expressing simultaneously the most evanescent shades of feeling, the most conflicting currents of thought.'[36]

And Eric Walter White in *Parnassus to Let*, seeking to free cinema from the drama and painting from which he believed it had sprung, treated it as a form of poetry, and asked if

'the basis of cinematic metre is caesural and not accentual? that rhythm is built up by motion and emotion deployed from shot to shot?'[37]

White's questions suggest a new interest in the way that shots of different duration related to each other, and produced different reactions in the spectator. But from the interesting instances of rhythm, which he went on to describe, it is clear that he was considering only the effects of rhythm, properly understood, as a periodical or regular metrical flow. In a way, contemporary use of the word rhythm in this connection was as unfortunate and misleading as the word montage which became so popular at this time. Just as montage became identified with the montage sequence, and emphasized quick impressionistic cutting rather than the creative importance of the whole edited structure, so the word rhythm drew attention to the emotional impact of regular and particularly of accelerating passages. This obscured the fact that it was the duration of all shots and their relationship to each other, whether it involved regular patterns or not, that were to be considered.

Most of these writers, despite their sincerity and occasional insight, were one-sided in their approach, and the critical theory of the time was full of unresolved questions. The answers, for those who cared to hear, finally came with the publication in 1929 of a number of essays and lectures by the great Russian director Pudovkin, under the title *Pudovkin on Film Technique*. As their translator Ivor Montagu wrote, the analysis of principle had so far been the work

'of aestheticists, who have approached the problem of filmic expression from the perceptual, not from the creative, standpoint.'[38]

But the ideas of the film makers Kuleshov and Dziga Vertov, developed in Soviet films and above all in the work of Pudovkin and Eisenstein during the middle twenties, had gradually begun to circulate among British film intellectuals despite the barriers put up by political prejudice. They were first expressed coherently in these fragments by Pudovkin.

Three short passages explain the core of these views:

'Kuleshov maintained that the material in film-work consists of pieces of film, and that the composition method is their joining together in a particular, creatively discovered order. He maintained that film-art does not begin when the artists act and the various scenes are shot—this is only the preparation of the material. Film-art begins from the moment when the director begins to combine and join together the various pieces of film. By joining them in various combinations, in different orders, he obtains differing results.'

'But the combination of various pieces in one or another order is not sufficient. It is necessary to be able to control and manipulate the length of these pieces, because the combination of pieces of varying length is effective in the same way as the combination of sounds of various length in music, by creating the rhythm of the film and by means of their varying effect on the audience. Quick, short pieces rouse excitement, while long pieces have a soothing effect. . . .

'To be able to find the requisite order of shots or pieces, and the rhythms necessary for their combination—that is the chief task of the director's art.'[39]

Pudovkin emphasized the fact that film production was a group activity, and was able to fit the director's creative function into this. He was the

'commander-in-chief. He gives battle to the indifference of the spectator; . . . in order to attain a unified creation, a complete film, the director must lead constant through all the numerous stages of the work a unifying, organizing line created by him.'[40]

At last a group of practising film makers, whose creative imagination was accompanied by an intellectual grasp of the subject, had been able to state the nature of the medium and stake an articulate claim for it as a form of artistic expression. The actor, the designer and the lighting-cameraman had gradually taken over different aspects of the creative illusion of reality, and superficially the director seemed to have little function except to unite them. But according to the Russian view their share was simply the preparation of the visible, or plastic, material. In a famous example it was demonstrated how a neutral shot of an actor's face could seem to express different feelings according to the content of the shots which came before and after it. The primitive view of the film maker as an illusionist, using the tricks of cinematography to give the appearance of reality to things that had never actually happened, had been transformed. The film maker's power of illusion lay in creative editing. The vision of reality was that selected by whoever decided the structure of the film. It was true that the camera could show only behaviour and visible objects, as others had realized, but the film itself as an edited structure could suggest ideas and abstractions with great freedom. The art of the film maker lay in the creative power of constructive editing, controlling both content and form, which used the order and the pace in which the plastic material was presented both to convey the idea, and to act directly on the emotions of the viewer. When Pudovkin had stated in 1927 that editing was the foundation of film art he had brought into harmony the visual and temporal patterns, on the one hand, which had so greatly occupied the aestheticists, and the externalization into acts and objects on the other, which had seemed the only problem to the popular theorists.

Did any of these writers, other than Pudovkin, have any real influence? If the function of aesthetics and the critic is to assist in the cultivation of taste, to help others to discriminate between good and bad and to enjoy the best, their task was just beginning. There were mistakes and confusions, as there were bound to be in an entirely new field. There were writers who felt that if they gave something a name they had explained it, and that they could establish the true function or 'duty' of an art as though it were a game to be played according to agreed rules. At their worst, there was the critic's besetting sin of turning an observation of successful practice into an imperative, transforming the fact that something is usually done into a rule that it must be done. Even Iris Barry, in a burst of zeal, wrote:

'I ask then: critics arise, invent terms, lay down canons, derive from your categories. . . .'[41]

An easy trick of the mind turns a canon from a statement into a command, forgetting that it is the nature of the creative imagination to ignore commands. But what all these writers except perhaps Buckle had, above all, was the ability to communicate their enthusiasm. Sometimes, looking at the films for which they made such great claims, this enthusiasm seems almost inexplicable. It must have taken a great deal of faith to see the possibilities of greatness in the primitives of the new art. Such faith certainly had an effect, if only a marginal one, in creating a larger public for it. But it was for the artist, rather than the critic, to discover the real nature of the film and to turn it into a medium of expression for the creative imagination. For the development of film technique we must turn to the film industry, with all its faults.

CHAPTER TWO

Exhibition and the Public

(I) RELATIONS WITH THE PUBLIC

The film industry was anxious to please everybody. 'Give them Joy', advised the *Bioscope* in 1922:

'There are certain things in film entertainment that can always be relied upon to please, such as romance presented with sincerity. It may be far-fetched, but it must not be sloppy. Baby scenes always get over. Even the lowest mental types always enjoy peeps into "furrin' parts" if they are not prolonged. All stories must end happily. There's no need to bother about logical or artistic endings. People don't go to cinemas to study logic or art. They want to be cheered up. Therefore, see you get humour into your programme. Broad humour, not coarse or vulgar, is safest, because it appeals to the majority, but vary this line with occasional light humour.

'And don't neglect the tragic. Folks like to know that other people get into trouble as well as themselves. Women especially love a good cry. But the end must strike a happy note.'[1]

But many in the business took a cynical view of their public and would have agreed with an American screenwriter who said

'. . . production generally is crippled by the mentality of greater America'.[2]

A British renter advised in 1927

'. . . appeal to the primitive emotions rather than to the reasoning faculties'.[3]

and one of the scenario editors wrote brutally

'. . . roughly sixty per cent are women; and even if a woman is devoid of teeth, has a carcass which rattles like a box of dominoes as she walks, and wears elastic-sided boots and red flannel, she is still enough of a woman to simper at an emotional close-up, even if she simpers in secret.'[4]

There is little serious information on tastes, and it must be assumed that the showmen were right and the films actually booked were those the majority wanted, although every now and then someone would raise the alarm that the cinema was dying because the films were so bad. In 1924 the *Daily News* held a

32

Favourite British Film Stars poll which put Betty Balfour and Alma Taylor at the top, followed by Gladys Cooper, Violet Hopson, Matheson Lang, Fay Compton, Chrissie White, Stewart Rome, Owen Nares and Ivor Novello.[5] But English players were of small importance compared with the Hollywood stars, and Betty Balfour and Ivor Novello, the only British players to be included in most popularity polls not confined to British actors (e.g. in Birmingham in 1924 and in the *Daily Mirror* in 1927), were described by the critic Iris Barry as our only two stars.[6] A poll with 10,500 entries held in 1925 to discover which types of film were popular showed society drama at the top, followed by comedy drama, Western drama, comedy, costume drama and war drama. Interest films were low on the list.[7] There was some excuse for this as the latter, even *The Epic of Everest* in 1924, were usually unskilfully made and dull. The short, well-made *Secrets of Nature* films were a popular exception. In 1927 and 1929 Sydney Bernstein, more intelligent than other exhibitors, delved deeper into audience preferences with two questionnaires. The second of these was to be issued to 250,000 cinemagoers. Results, however, were broadly similar to those of the earlier polls. The first showed among other things that whereas men and boys preferred adventure, followed by comedy and then society drama, women and girls put it the other way and preferred society drama and then comedy and adventure. With both, costume and war drama and melodrama were less popular. On the other hand 80 to 90 per cent liked the news reels. As before Betty Balfour and Ivor Novello, this time joined by Matheson Lang, were the only British stars. By the time of the second questionnaire in 1929 most of the stars in favour were different, yet Betty Balfour, although now appearing in a different type of part, was still high on the list.[8]

It was realized that all audiences were not the same, yet the mainstream of the commercial cinema depended more and more on finding the lowest common denominator. Books were published to appeal to circles of almost limitless variety, the theatre catered to many different tastes, and the feeling grew that the exhibition structure for films was not sufficiently elastic. Even *The Bioscope* as early as 1919 suggested that different cinemas might specialize in different types of film.[9] In 1920 Adrian Brunel was associated with an early attempt to form a Cinemagoers' League to make articulate the demands of a new and more discriminating public. The foundation of the magazine *Close Up* in mid-1927 to encourage the showing of more progressive films was very important. As the editorial pointed out:

'. . . there is a minority of several million people to whom these films are tiresome, a minority that loves the film, but has too much perception, too much intelligence to swallow the often dismal and paltry stories and acting set up week by week before it on the screen. This minority has got to have films it can enjoy, films with psychology, soundness, intelligence . . . how much more charming and easy if we—the minority—could just walk into a theatre, one particular theatre, haphazardly as the majority wanders into its many theatres, knowing we would see films which, even if we did not always like, would be stimulating to mind and perception.'[10]

In London a few cinemas began to show some of the more advanced imported films. The Holborn Cinema, Marble Arch Pavilion and New Gallery did so, and later the Academy Cinema. The Davis family embarked on a regular policy of showing unusual films at the Shaftesbury Avenue Pavilion Cinema at the same time as the formation of *Close Up*. This ran successfully as a repertory or specialist cinema for two years, showing among other films *Waxworks, Warning Shadows, Jeanne Ney, The Nibelungs, Vaudeville, The Student of Prague, The Street, Gosta Berling, Tartuffe, Cinderella, Berlin* and *The Last Laugh*. Stuart Davis wrote:

'The repertory audience is composed, I find, roughly of three different classes: the intelligenzia, the intellectual amateur who likes to follow new art movements, and the ordinary, average middle-class business man who doesn't go to the cinema as a rule because he does not like the fare provided for "the masses".'[11]

Much of the trade was in favour of such specialization at the time, feeling that the prestige of these films was good for the cinema as a whole, but there was little scope for them outside London.

The other way of showing films of minority interest was in film societies. The earliest of these seem to have been formed for amateur production rather than exhibition, and it is significant that they were formed at Oxford and Cambridge by the generation of undergraduates which in a few years was to bring a more cultivated approach into commerical production.* The Film Society itself, whose importance can hardly be over-estimated, was formed in London in 1925. It was founded by Ivor Montagu and Hugh Miller and run by the film critic Iris Barry. It numbered amongst its celebrated founder members Lord Ashfield, Anthony Asquith, the film critic G. A. Atkinson, Lord David Cecil, Edith Craig, Roger Fry, J. B. S. Haldane, Julian Huxley, Augustus John, E. McKnight Kauffer, J. M. Keynes, the film writer Angus Macphail, George Bernard Shaw, John St Loe Strachey, Lord Swaythling, Dame Ellen Terry, Ben Webster and H. G. Wells. The Council included Iris Barry, Sidney Bernstein, Frank Dobson, Hugh Miller, Ivor Montagu, Walter Mycroft, and Adrian Brunel. The Society intended to show films not otherwise available in the belief that there was a large serious minority audience which, with critics and film makers, would like to keep abreast of new developments in film making. Jibes from the ignorant that the Society studied freaks and failures died away as the industry found that it did not compete with the ordinary cinemas, but supplemented them. A few films, amongst them *Berlin, Tartuffe, Waxworks* and Reiniger's *Cinderella*, were shown at cinemas after their Film Society reception, and the film trade's persistent interest in artistic respectablity was even flattered a little by its existence. The first Scottish Film Society began in Glasgow at the end of the decade, and soon there were others, although the movement was hampered at first by the

* The Cambridge Kinema Club was formed in 1923 by Peter Le Neve Foster, who wrote and directed the half-reel *The Witch's Fiddle* in 1924, and later the 800-foot *The Wizard of Alderley Edge* for Manchester Film Society in 1927; an Oxford group was also planning production in 1924.

fact that licensing regulations and their offshoot, censorship, were applicable to film society shows as well as to cinemas. All the same, a serious public for the silent film was growing during its last few years, and the influence of the London Film Society in this was very great.

The trade's pleasure in having a small arty fringe, as long as it was harmless, was part of its ambivalence at this time. Fearful of competition from any source, even from radio after 1923 or from greyhound racing after about 1927, and usually scornful of anything regarded as highbrow, many in the industry nevertheless seem to have regretted that the marvels and success of the cinema had not yet obtained much artistic and social prestige. Early encouragement for the idea of an Academy or Institute was part of a hunt for dignity. As early as 1920 the views of Thomas Ince in America on the need for a serious Academy were reprinted here with approval.[12] In 1922 the Faculty of Arts was formed as part of a larger movement 'to develop the arts and crafts of the country as a national asset' and included a plan for diplomas and medals for British films of outstanding merit, and this received considerable support from the trade. It formed the Kinema Art Group, later called the Faculty of Cinema Art, which was registered in January 1927. In a way it was the trade's approach to the same problem as that faced by the Film Society, 'to provide a central organization giving facilities for the study of cinema art', and aimed at co-operation, the exchange of information, training and what was later called Film Appreciation as well as the foundation of a film museum.*

Gradually there were other signs of academic recognition and encouragement. The Royal Photographic Society inaugurated a Kinematograph Group at the Royal Society of Arts in 1923. Abroad an organization called The Friends of the Cinema was offering an annual medal for 'advance of cinematographic art'[13] and the American Academy of Motion Picture Arts and Sciences had been formed. An International Congress of Motion Picture Arts was held in New York in 1923. French trade bodies organized an international Congress of Cinematography in October 1923, which was attended by a British contingent drawn mainly from the Cinematograph Exhibitors' Association and which discussed such practical matters as taxes, educational films, insurance premiums, authors' rights and technical and electrical questions.

Outside the trade a British Empire Film Institute was set up in 1926, its director J. Aubrey Rees, with an inaugural dinner under the chairmanship of Lord Asquith. Its motive was patriotic rather than artistic, its aim to 'promote and develop public interest in British films throughout the world . . .', but it would also

'. . . act as a Bureau of Information with regard to British and other Films, British Film Producers and Users, Educational Institutions, Churches, Schools

---

* In 1919 the official war films were kept in the Imperial War Museum. The preservation of films presented technical problems, and in 1924 the post of Government Cinematograph Adviser was created and the films put in his care at His Majesty's Stationery Office. The idea of preserving other types of film for posterity received little support.

and other organizations and persons interested in or concerned with Cinematography.[14]

The trade was sceptical:

'. . . Laudable objects, to be sure, but—I can't find among the sponsors the name of anyone, however familiar to the public, who is known to have made a special study of the film business, except that of Sir John Ferguson.'[15]

and *Close Up* was frankly scornful:

'Equally moving is the announcement of the British Empire Film Institute (slogan: More British Films on British Screens) that "all over the world films from other countries are shown whose tone is, at least, not beneficial to the interests of the British Empire". Among its aims, these bright jewels: to rouse a patriotic feeling sufficient to prevent the scandal of British Films being actually excluded from the great majority of film houses here and elsewhere . . . to confer Awards of Merit for films of Imperial value, *to break down prejudice*, to attract better brains to the industry.

'Now what more could anybody ask? With this sort of feeling if we cannot produce the most exquisite and subtle masterpieces there must be something radically wrong with us.'[16]

Nevertheless the Institute did not give up, but began acquiring the nucleus of a film archive with Ponting's polar films and, having started a book library, planned a film library as well.

In 1926 the French National Committee of Intellectual Co-operation organized yet another Congress, this time under the patronage of the League of Nations. The Faculty of Arts, Authors' Society and British Empire Film Institute sent representatives, and the Film Society sent Ivor Montagu, Adrian Brunel, Iris Barry, Walter Mycroft and Angus Macphail. The C.E.A. sent only three representatives but, although the *Bioscope* sneered at the Congress's 'pious resolutions', the three trade representatives found the Congress interesting and advised the C.E.A. to take the one next year at Berlin more seriously. In 1928 the League of Nations recognized an International Institute of Educational Cinematography set up at Rome.[17]

None of this, however, did anything to meet the far more important need for organized training in film production. *Close Up* had pleaded for a Cinema University in 1927.[18] And in 1929 the American J. D. Williams, known for his grandiose schemes both sides of the Atlantic, proposed the formation of an Academy with a teaching staff. He hoped this could be self-supporting through the distribution of its experimental films, and even more optimistically that it could be attached to Oxford or Cambridge University:

'. . . something more than the Parliament of British Cinema, that it might be the British National Research Laboratory of Cinema Art . . . the incubating ground of Youth, as the meeting place for Experience, as the testing place for theory'.[19]

The renter G. W. Pearson suggested that each production company should contribute £1,000 a year towards its expenses. There was premature enthusiasm from some who were dazzled by hopes of academic glory, a cautious preference for apprenticeship schemes from others, and guarded meanness from those who would have to foot the bill. The Chairman of the Federation of British Industries Film Group emphasized the huge capital that would be needed and the pitfalls of an educational system dependent on selling its products, and like many other grand schemes it sank without trace.

While part of the trade pursued respectability like a will o' the wisp, showmanship and publicity made contact with the public in a more practical way. The trade was well served with trade papers.* These were augmented in the early part of the decade, when publicity was for brand names rather than for individual films, by elaborate house organs sent periodically by film publishers not only to the press and exhibitors but also for sale on the bookstalls.† They contained the photographs, news and gossip later described as press hand-outs, and the desire to exploit the press for free and apparently spontaneous publicity was undisguised:

'. . . publicity that is not paid for, by which I mean, of course, news paragraphs. . . .'[20]

One leading article suggesting a weekly radio chat about films appears to be based on the assumption that similar 'inspired paragraphs' were the basis of dramatic and music criticism.[21] Like studio handouts, posters stopped advertising film brands and began to advertise individual films in the early twenties. With elaborate illustrated Trade Show synopses and front-of-the-house displays the stills photographer became an important technician in the studio. E. Gordon Craig's firm Winads provided simple trailers from the mid-twenties and National Screen Service was registered in May 1928 to provide a rather more elaborate type of trailer. The joint managing directors were W. Brenner from the parent company in New York and Paul Kimberley, previously with Hepworth's. With these changes also came stunts, personal appearances and tie-ups with commercial products and local shops as well as occasional trouble over 'tasteless' posters, which contrived to suggest that some films were more daring than they actually were. One notorious publicity stunt caused an outcry in 1925. When the European Motion Picture Company imported *The Phantom of the Opera* from America they somehow managed to have it escorted from Southampton docks by a contingent of soldiers. So great was the public's anger at this that the

* There were three main weeklies: *Kinematograph Weekly* was edited by Frank Tilley and *The Cinema* by Sam Harris: *The Bioscope* was founded, edited and owned by John Cabourne, with his review editor J. H. Beaumont, and followed an independent policy with growing difficulty. Cabourne died in January 1929.

† House organs included the *Idealetter, Jury Box, Pathé News, Hepworth Picture Play Magazine, British Actors Film Company Brochure,* Phillips' *The Flashlight* and Stoll's *Editorial News.*

Cinematograph Exhibitors' Association banned the film amongst its members and European was persuaded to substitute another film for those who had booked it. The ban remained in force until Carl Laemmle himself induced the C.E.A. to lift it in November 1928, the violence of the reaction a reminder that the search for publicity could over-reach itself.

Meanwhile the showmen were complacently abrogating some of the functions of the film maker, in preparing

'the minds of the audience to receive in the appropriate mood the story that is to be unfolded'[22]

by means of 'American presentation methods', or elaborate staged prologues and accompaniments. In the first instances, admittedly, they were the work of the film maker himself.

'For the first time in this country there will be shown to the British public a film which is presented in a specially designed artistic setting. . . . *Broken Blossoms* will form the only feature, and will be presented three times daily. The entire theatre will be decorated in the Chinese manner, and the Chinese attendants will form a feature in the auditorium. The screening of the film will be preceded by a Prologue in which the two leading characters will appear in one of the scenes from the film, and after the lowering of the curtain the film will be presented, followed by an enacted epilogue. Every care will be taken to present *Broken Blossoms* in the same manner as presented by Mr David Wark Griffith at its original presentation in New York.'[23]

'Suspended from the proscenium were cages of singing birds which were heard at tense moments in the action.

'In the prologue were employed nine actors who mimed a scene laid in a Buddhist temple which was disclosed as the curtain rose to three notes of a gong. Perfume floated out to the auditorium from censers swung by Chinese incense bearers. After the preliminary action, a Chinese singer chanted a litany, standing in an amber spot light, and, with another note of the gong, the curtain fell to be followed immediately by the screening.'[24]

There were a large number of such prologues in the super cinemas from 1921 until about 1925. A 'barefoot ballet' by the Margaret Morris dancers prefaced Hepworth's *Pipes of Pan* at the Alhambra Trade Show, and with his *Comin' thro' the Rye* in the same year a prologue called *A Picture of 1860*, and described as a 'tabloid version of the story played in pantomime behind a gauze curtain by the leading artists,'[25] ran at a number of theatres. There were other forms of build-up, ranging from Paul Whiteman and his band appearing with Lupino Lane's *A Friendly Husband* in 1923 to Elgar himself conducting the prologue to Samuelson's deplorable film *Land of Hope and Glory* at an Armistice Day show in 1927. Many exhibitors were extremely proud of their work and began to feel that they contributed to the artistic success of the film. After 1926 some showmen also interspersed their programmes with variety turns. But voices began to be raised against this, especially when not only the super cinema but ordinary ones also were involved, and even more when elaborate staging was suspected of disguising an inferior film. Castleton Knight went a little far in his arrangements for opening the London Palladium as a cine-variety house in 1928:

'The stage curtains parted, Reg. Foort, the well-known cinema organist, lulled the house to silence with the opening bars of "The Lost Chord", and then a spotlight traced De Groot standing before a transparent background, on which was seen "the golden gates".

'His music! Then the gates opened as the one hundred performers took up the harmony, which swelled into a terrific crescendo, as dazzling light fell upon a crystal fountain playing in the background. Then the fountain disappeared as "The Lost Chord" gave place to "The Blue Heaven", and suddenly the symphony died, it was gradually merged into syncopation, and an elevator rose at the back of the De Groot party, bearing Teddy Brown and his band, furiously working out the same melody according to more popular and more modern conceptions of musical entertainment.

'But greatest of all was the rendering by De Groot and players of Tschaikowsky's "1812", with organ accompaniment, and with a tableau of choristers dressed as Russian peasants singing the refrain. It beggars description, though when four trumpeters appeared in the stage-side boxes I felt it was rather too much. . . .'[26]

(2) THE EXHIBITION COMPANIES

The increasing elaboration and respectability of the picture show was accompanied by the evolution of a highly capitalized modern industry. Lord Burnham said at a Cinematograph Exhibitors' dinner in 1920:

'The High Financiers of the world are flocking into the Cinema industry. Formerly it was difficult, I believe, to raise even a small capital for a cinema enterprise. Today, if you ask for a million you get half a million oversubscribed.'[27]

According to F. W. Ogden Smith some £15 million was invested in exhibition by 1914. By 1927 the President of the Board of Trade, replying to a Parliamentary question, put it between £30 and £50 million, and in 1929 an anonymous estimate put it as high as £70 million.[28] Certainly greater capital had been available for exhibition long before the quota legislation became probable, and big business had appeared early in this sector of the industry. At first, single cinemas run by local exhibitors had obtained their small capital from local businessmen in private companies or perhaps from local renters, but gradually as bigger cinemas became profitable backing was available from banks and insurance companies, and the 1927–28 edition of the *Blue Book*[29] listed fifty-three public limited liability companies connected with cinema exhibition, with an authorized capital of over £11 million.

The financial structure of exhibition during the twenties had changed in two important ways. The dependence on private capital tended to be replaced by the growth of public companies, and the enormous number of small firms were rationalized at first by horizontal combination into circuits, and finally by vertical combination of the largest circuits with renting and production interests. Similar integration was taking place in many sectors of British industry at the time. Sir Alfred Mond spoke of this in the *Daily Mail* towards the end of the period:

'There is apparent in Britain at the present time a distinct tendency towards large scale amalgamations. . . . These are necessary to enable it to deal on terms of equality with similar organizations being formed on the Continent, and already formed in America. . . . The combinations of industry taking place are being literally forced upon us, and, although many people may not like them, they will have to come if Britain is to maintain its place in the commercial and industrial future of the world.'[30]

The inducement to form circuits lay in their organizational and booking advantages. The better runs and barring terms (see page 76) secured by groups of cinemas made competition difficult for the remaining independents, and as renters could and did refuse to deal with co-operative groups of cinemas many small exhibitors were compelled either to form proper circuits or sell out to existing ones. This trend accelerated as the decade wore on, and meanwhile the specialized nature of the industry encouraged vertical combination. Especially as the quota prospects brought capital into renting and production firms did they seek control of an assured exhibition outlet. Such integration was slow here in comparison with that in America, where large circuits linked to producer-renters already existed by 1920. But large impersonal combines did not please the older showmen in Britain. Sir Walter Gibbons, the theatrical impresario, complained on resigning from General Theatres Corporation in 1928 that

'I am now definitely finished with the theatrical and film business unless any specially tempting offer in the future causes me to reconsider my decision. The new régime thinks that theatres can be managed by boards of directors consulting on every point and by banks, but the great days of the theatre were the days of big personal figures whose decision was absolute.'[31]

The growth of circuits can be illustrated by companies listed in *Kine Year Book* from the war to the early thirties. The following account was compiled from the *Kine* directories for 1918, 1921, 1927, and 1931. During the war, in 1917, there were 90 circuits in Britain with 429 cinemas. 27 per cent of these circuit halls, or 114, were in a mere 8 large circuits of 10 or more each; the average size of these was 14 cinemas against the average of 4 in the rest of the circuits. The largest circuit was Albany Ward's, with its head office in Weymouth and with 28 cinemas in the south-west. The only circuits based in London were Biocolour Picture Theatres and the Central Hall Circuit of Wandsworth, most of the others being local circuits in the provinces.

Circuits in 1917

Albany Ward Circuit (Weymouth)	28
Biocolour Picture Theatres (London)	10
Broadhead's Theatres (Manchester)	17
Central Hall Circuit (Wandsworth)	12
Eastern Counties Electric Theatres (Norwich)	10
Glasgow Corporation Public Halls (Glasgow)	13
George Green Circuit (Glasgow)	12
Thomas Thompson (Middlesbrough)	12

By the immediate post-war period, in 1920, both the number of circuits and the number of cinemas in them had increased considerably to 157 circuits and 787 cinemas. About the same percentage of the circuits as before had the same percentage of the cinemas, that is to say 27 per cent of the circuit halls or 213 cinemas were in 12 large circuits of 10 or more halls; their average size was bigger than that of the larger circuits before. The average size of the many smaller circuits continued to be 4 cinemas. Again most of the circuits were regional, but two of the biggest were national in scale with headquarters in London. These were Provincial Cinematograph Theatres with 33 and Biocolour with 25.

Circuits in 1920

Award Circuit (Bristol)	26
Biocolour Picture Theatres (London)	25
Broadhead Theatres (Manchester)	17
Green's Film Service (Glasgow)	12
Haigh & Son (Liverpool)	14
A. B. King Circuit (Glasgow)	18
Levy Circuit (Birmingham)	14
New Century Pictures (Leeds)	13
Thomas Ormiston (Motherwell)	11
P.C.T. (London)	33
Scottish Cinema & Variety Theatres (Glasgow)	20
J. F. Wood's Circuit (Liverpool)	10

By 1926 the figures show some consolidation. The number of circuits had temporarily fallen from 157 to 139, and the number of circuit halls they comprised had gone up proportionally less from 787 to 856. The percentage of the circuits which could be considered large, with 10 halls or more, had gone up to 11 per cent; the percentage of circuit halls in these larger groups had also gone up, to 33 per cent. The average size of the mass of circuits was still small, with 5 halls, and the average size of the larger circuits was still not very big at 15 halls; but it is significant that one much larger circuit, excluded from this average,

THE HISTORY OF THE BRITISH FILM

had appeared. This was Provincial Cinematograph Theatres, which had grown from 33 cinemas in the previous list to 75. There were still only three circuits with headquarters in London, P.C.T., Biocolour and Savoy Cinemas, all the others still being regional.

Circuits in 1926

Bradford Cinemas (J. F. Wood) (Liverpool)	14
Biocolour Picture Theatres (London)	17
Broadhead's Theatres (Manchester)	16
E. C. Clayton (Sheffield)	13
Eagle Picturedromes (Wigan)	11
J. F. Emery's Circuit (Manchester)	14
George Green (Glasgow)	13
E. Haigh (Liverpool)	11
A. B. King (Glasgow)	18
A. G. Matthews (Glasgow)	10
New Century Pictures (Leeds)	19
Thomas Ormiston (Motherwell)	22
P.C.T. (London)	75
Savoy Cinemas (London)	10
Scottish Cinema & Variety Theatres (Glasgow)	24

The position in 1930, although strictly speaking out of our period, shows clearly how this trend developed under the influence of the sound film and quota legislation. The number of circuits had gone up again, back to 167, but this represented not consolidation as before but a much greater inclusion of previously independent halls. The larger circuits of 10 halls or more now numbered 23 or 14 per cent, and they had as much as 52 per cent of the circuit halls, which was a big increase on the previous 33 per cent. Not only had combination into circuits taken a big step forward, but it showed a trend to bigger circuits. Whereas the average size of the small circuits was more or less unchanged at 5, and the average size of the larger circuits other than the outstanding ones still 15, there were now two giants. These were first A.B.C. with 118 halls and secondly G.B.P.C.–P.C.T. with 296. Together with the appearance of the huge circuit had come nation-wide organization from London, where renting and exhibition could most easily be merged, and as many as ten other circuits besides the two giants had their headquarters in London.

Circuits in 1930

A.B.C. (London)	118
Sidney Bacon's Pictures (London)	31
Cambria & Border Cinemas (Wrexham)	12
Cinema House (London)	10
E.C. Clayton (Sheffield)	12
County Cinemas (London)	13
Eagle Picturedromes (Wigan)	11
J. F. Emery's Circuit (Manchester)	15
Federated Estates (London)	12
G.B.P.C. (London)	200

A. B. King (Glasgow)	25
H. D. Moorehouse Circuit (Manchester)	38
Thomas Ormiston (Motherwell)	11
P.C.T. (London)	96
Regent Enterprises (Liverpool)	10
Shipman & King (London)	10
George Singleton (Glasgow)	13
Standard Cinema Properties (Birmingham)	14
Thompson's Enterprises (Middlesbrough)	15
J. F. Tidswell (Leeds)	12
Union Cinema Company (London)	13
United Picture Theatres (G.B.P.C.) (London)	17

Details of the remarkable growth of the two large circuits shows how the process took place. Associated British Cinemas was the creation of John Maxwell. He had entered exhibition in 1912 and later moved into renting, and by 1923 was chairman of the new firm of Wardour Films together with Arthur Dent and J. A. Thorpe. This successful firm took its first abortive flutter in production with Maurice Elvey in 1926 under the name of M.E. Productions. Early in 1927 a huge new public company, British International Pictures, was floated to acquire and enlarge the recent British National producing set-up with its studio at Elstree. Maxwell, Dent and Thorpe were on the Board, and distribution was to be effected through Wardour. A big public issue was made in November 1927, and Sir Clement Kinloch-Cooke and J. D. Bright joined the Board. In December Maxwell took part in arranging a merger between First National and Pathé, and had reached a position of considerable power in renting and production. The quota legislation had been passed and British production now had some security of market. Plans to ensure a regular distribution circuit were in the air. At the end of January 1928 A.B.C. was registered quietly as a private company with a capital of £50,000, with J. E. Pearce as managing director, controlled by B.I.P. and having an entirely new circuit of 29 cinemas scattered over the country. In November 1928 Associated British Cinemas was registered as a public company with a capital of £1 million. B.I.P. had a controlling interest and Maxwell was Chairman, with Pearce as managing director and Kinloch-Cooke and Bright on the new Board. The object of the new company was to acquire other circuits besides the original 29 halls, including Scottish Cinema and Variety Theatres, which had 24 in 1927–28. A.B.C. was further expanded in January 1929 to a capital of £2 million. By this year it had 88 cinemas, and was ready to grow considerably during the next few years.

The organization of G.B.P.C. was an even bigger operation. The firm of Gaumont's in Britain had been started in 1898 by the brothers A. C. and R. C. Bromhead, to distribute the films made in France by the firm of Léon Gaumont. They also started production at a studio at Shepherd's Bush, but renting was the more important part of the business. In December 1922, after some eighteen months of negotiation, the Bromheads bought out the French interests in the agency and it became an entirely British firm, continuing production at Shepherd's Bush for several years.

Like others, Gaumont's moved into exhibition in 1927 when the coming of the quota was leading to reorganization in the industry. Gaumont–British Picture Corporation was registered as a public company in March 1927 with a capital of £2,500,000 and the backing of the Ostrer brothers, Maurice and Isidore, whose city firm had already taken an interest in the film industry. It was essentially an amalgamation formed to control the Bromheads' firm of Gaumont: Ideal, a renter and producer formed in 1920 and run by the Rowson brothers and Edward Russell: W. & F. Film Service, a renting firm formed in 1919 by C. M. Woolf and handling mostly American productions including the popular films of Harold Lloyd: and the Biocolour circuit of E. E. Lyons. The new firm was to acquire immediately 21 cinemas, including the 15 Biocolour halls which had already been bought by the Ostrers as well as four in London said to be worth £550,000 and owned by the Davis family, who had been in the exhibition industry since 1908.

Biocolour, which was the basis of the G.B.P.C. circuit, had been one of the earliest of the big circuits. It was a private company run by E. E. Lyons and had been sold to a syndicate which included the Ostrers in November 1926. The next step was the formation of Denman Picture Houses out of several other circuits of similar size. D.P.H. was registered as a public company in March 1928 with a capital of £1 million and links with G.B.P.C., with the Bromheads on the Board. It already included New Century Pictures of Leeds, a pre-war company run by Sidney Carter which in 1927 had 19 cinemas, and National Electric Theatres with 9. By April 1928 D.P.H. had 96 cinemas and the Board included not only the Bromheads, H. A. Micklem, C. M. Woolf and Simon Rowson representing G.B.P.C., but also a number of exhibitors like Thomas Ormiston, the Hyams, A. J. Gale, E. E. Lyons, Thomas Thompson and Sidney Carter whose small circuits had been absorbed. Before long it had over 100 halls and a capital of £4 million.

The next action was to take over General Theatres Corporation, an unexpected but happy acquisition. Sir Walter Gibbons, as managing director of this company which had an authorized capital of £2 million, had embarked on a policy of buying both theatres and cinemas early in 1928. His Board was distinguished, but not representative of the film trade, and perhaps because of its inexperience in films there was a very poor response to its public issue of shares. Gibbons had indignantly resigned in the spring of 1928. The company was taken over and reorganized by G.B.P.C. Only George Black of the original Board remained, and he was joined by the Bromheads and Stephen Gordon in August.

The foundation of Gaumont–British in size, if not in time, was Provincial Cinematograph Theatres. This was one of the earliest public companies in the business, founded before the war and expanded to its capital of £1 million in early 1919 with an issue which was heavily oversubscribed. 1919 was a big year for P.C.T. and at the end of it Lord Beaverbrook bought a £400,000 share in the company. He also acquired a large holding in Pathé, and at the same time in February 1920 bought £300,000 of the £500,000 associated company of Associated Provincial Picture Houses, of which F. A. Adams of P.C.T. was the managing director. P.C.T. also acquired the circuit of Albany Ward in the West

Country, although this remained more or less separate and temporarily regained its independence in 1923. P.C.T. made another big issue in March 1920, bringing it up to £3 million, and this was once more oversubscribed. Lord Ashfield joined as Chairman of the Board with Beaverbrook and Adams, and the company had direct control of 33 cinemas. Further reorganization followed in 1923 and Will Evans became managing director. During the next few years more halls were gradually acquired. In 1926 there were 79, 37 of them under direct control, 11 in A.P.P.H., 19 under Albany Ward and 8 others; in 1928 there were 93, 44 direct, 15 in A.P.P.H., 27 under Ward and 12 others; and in 1930 there were 97, 49 direct, 16 in A.P.P.H., 26 under Ward and 17 others.

In February 1928 the Standard Film Company was registered as a holding company for P.C.T. and First National–Pathé. It was a private company, with a capital of £300,000 and with Beaverbrook and his associates Ashfield, Jury, A. P. Holt and Will Evans on the Board. It took over control of P.C.T. and there was another successful issue of capital.

Later in 1928 a bombshell exploded with a battle between G.B.P.C. and A.B.C. for the control of P.C.T. The upshot of this was that Beaverbrook and Ashfield withdrew from much of their interest in the film trade, control of First National–Pathé was sold to Maxwell, and P.C.T. fell to G.B.P.C. In February 1929 the latter expanded once more, its capital going up to £3,750,000 and, with control of P.C.T., it now had 287 cinemas. These included the Tivoli as its London showplace, acquired by P.C.T. from Metro–Goldwyn when the latter's new cinema, the Empire, was ready in 1928. Meanwhile Gaumont–British had stepped into production, acquiring a big holding in Michael Balcon's important new production outfit Gainsborough in April 1928. Woolf and Maurice Ostrer were on the board of the latter company. At this stage the G.B.P.C. Board included the Bromheads and the Ostrers, but in August 1929 both the Bromheads resigned and the field was left open for the Ostrer brothers, C. M. Woolf and Will Evans to continue expansion of the large new combine.

As the shape of a modern industry emerged, so did a degree of self-awareness and the beginnings of political activity. The Cinematograph Exhibitors' Association, although its membership still did not cover all exhibitors, had grown from 1,600 members in 1919 to 2,882 in 1928.[32] W. Gavazzi King was its outspoken and energetic General Secretary until he retired at 70 in 1926, when he was replaced by his Assistant Secretary since April 1921, W. R. Fuller. The officials, Presidents and Councils of the C.E.A, gave active leadership in many of the acrimonious controversies affecting exhibitors during this period of change, over issues such as the model contract, barring and tied houses; block, blind and advance booking and the quota; co-operative booking; pre-release runs; percentage booking; entertainment tax; and labour troubles. (See Chapter III). But there was considerable divergence of interest between the circuits and the independents, especially in the late twenties, and some suspicion of the centralized London leadership. Both regional and other breakaway movements appeared occasionally,* but on the whole there was apathy among the majority of small

* E.g. The Manchester breakaway in 1922 and the proposed Sussex Small Exhibitors' Protection Society in 1927.

exhibitors, who were roused only by occasional outbursts of emotion. It proved difficult to mobilize them for effective action.

There seems to have been a vague idea that the size and importance of the exhibition industry entitled it to more respect, even power, than it had. A Report by Blake, Bromhead and Rowson for the newly formed Cinematograph Trade Council in June 1923 which discussed how to improve the trade's relations with the public even suggested that space in the papers should be bought for articles about films by 'public men', and that public relations paragraphs should be supplied to the press as news. The general attitude to Parliament, also, was somewhat naïve. Appeals were made to the so-called power of the screen as though it could be wielded in the interests of the film trade, and as though Parliament existed to represent organized interests as in a syndicalist system, rather than geographical constituencies under a party system. A. E. Newbould, President of the C.E.A., stood for Parliament for the West Division of Leyton as an Independent Liberal in November 1928, but many in the business seemed to feel that he was standing on behalf of the film industry. He was defeated by a Coalition Unionist, and *The Bioscope* consoled its readers with some artlessness:

'After all, Parliament only makes the laws, and it is the local bodies that are charged with carrying them out.'[33]

Newbould's successful opponent, however, died and he sportingly entered the 'Parliamentary Handicap' again for the by-election of March 1919, which he won. He sat until 1922. The less sophisticated expected him not only to act as an authority on exhibition matters in the House of Commons but to be accountable to the industry for his actions, and there was some indignation when he voted for an amendment regretting the omission from the King's Speech of any intention to nationalize the coal industry.[34] Old-fashioned individualists for the most part, many small showmen were natural Tories and not only disapproved of nationalization but even failed to make use of the potential sympathy of the Labour Party for cheap popular entertainment. The most determined effort to influence Parliament in their own interest was the campaign to reduce Entertainments Tax (see page 48) but they were unable to mobilize a majority under a Conservative Government. When remission did take place in 1924 it was under a Labour administration. The first steps in political education were taken when *The Bioscope* remarked with surprise that

'It is not giving any secrets away to state that the Trade's partial success in connection with the last Tax Campaign was largely brought about by MPs who derived no financial benefit, or even desired it, for the assistance that they gave.'[35]

(3) THE CINEMAS

The picture show, the object of all this activity, was established as part of the economic and social structure of the country by the end of the war in 1918.

Early estimates of the number of cinemas vary because different people defined them variously as permanent cinemas with daily shows, as permanent cinemas even if shows were only on certain days of the week, or as all halls having occasional shows even if used for other things as well. A figure of only 3,500 has been quoted for 1915 as the number of those listed in *Kine Year Book* excluding public hall cinemas[36] (*The Factual Film* by the Arts Enquiry); but it is doubtful whether such an exclusion is valid for this period as public halls still played a considerable part in providing facilities for picture going. The figure of 4,000 to 4,500 given by a 1917 Report by the National Council of Public Morals would probably give a fairer picture. Boughey in 1921 spoke of 4,000 cinemas in the United Kindgom and, although his figures were not always reliable, this agrees with those listed in *Kine Year Book,* which still included even the once-weeklies, although by 1921 these were certainly declining in relative importance. Gradually the smaller and occasional shows died out and bigger cinemas replaced them, fewer in number but with more seats. The Federation of British Industries told the Moyne Committee in 1936 that there had been some 3,000 cinemas in the United Kingdom by 1926, and the *Bioscope British Film Number* of 1928 quoted 3,760. The Rowson pamphlet of 1934, which is usually taken as the first reliable body of statistics concerning the British film industry,[37] estimated that there were 4,305 cinemas open six days a week, intermittent shows having by then ceased to be part of the mainstream of exhibition, with a total of 3,872,000 seats. This estimate was said to be based on *Kine Year Book, The Cinema Buyers' Guide* and the records of the four big sound installation companies. This sounds more likely than the figure of 5,000 commercial cinemas in the United Kingdom given by *The Film in National Life* in 1932.

Simon Rowson said in 1927 that 14 million people, or 20 million attendances, yielded £30 to £35 million a year at the box office.[38] But these figures included many people who went twice a week or even more often, and in their desire to expand their sales, many exhibitors seemed to have regarded the whole population as a field for exploitation, their ideal being a state in which everyone went to the pictures at least twice a week.

In fact the percentage of people who went twice a week did seem to be increasing. According to the two questionnaires organized by Sidney Bernstein, in 1927 $33\frac{1}{2}$ per cent of the cinema-goers questioned went once a week and $47\frac{1}{2}$ per cent twice, whereas by 1929 only $23\frac{1}{2}$ per cent went once a week and as many as 60 per cent went twice.[39]

Admission prices and the normal length of time each film ran at any particular cinema reflected this fact, with programmes aimed at an unselective, low-income audience going regularly several times a week. Cheap seats and several changes of programme a week were essential to this. The general pattern did not change very much during the period. At first a three-day run was most usual, shows beginning at 5.30 or 6 p.m., although many cinemas also had two or three matinées a week. According to Rowson, although the six-day run had made some headway by 1934, three-day runs were still more numerous; and although the key house with runs of two to four weeks or even more had appeared at the top of the scale, the large number of small houses served a small local population where the twice-weekly patrons were still necessary to make a profit, and there were still cinemas with even more than two changes a week.*

The price structure also resisted change. The increase in cinemas with medium prices and a few high-priced key houses left the lower prices of 4d to 1s 6d more or less unchanged, despite proposals in 1920 for a 6d or 9d minimum. The highest prices in 1920 were 11s 6d at the Marble Arch Pavilion, 21s at the West End Cinema, Coventry Street, and 10s 6d at the Regent Street Poly, but some cinemas even continued to have seats for 2d. The larger super cinemas which began to occupy the best residential areas in London and the provinces had seats from 4d to 2s 4d or even 3s 6d, with the higher range of 1s 3d to 5s 9d or even 8s 6d confined to West End or show-case cinemas.

The low price level contributed to the mean standards of many cinemas, with badly paid labour, inferior presentation and a poor choice of films. But despite C.E.A. efforts to change this many small showmen who relied on their poorly-paid twice-weekly patrons refused to co-operate. When Entertainments Tax remission came in 1924 many cinemas even lowered their prices.

Entertainments Tax, which had been introduced as a wartime measure, was blamed for many of the cinema closures and must have contributed to the difficulties of the humble semi-amateur occasional shows. After the war there was a small remission of tax on the cheapest seats and by 1920 it stood thus:

Seats under 2d . . .	No tax
Seats 2d–2½d	½d tax
Seats 2½d–4d	1d tax
Seats 4d–7d	2d tax
and up to 2s tax on seats of 10s 6d to 15s.	

Exhibitor groups such as the C.E.A., Provincial Entertainments Proprietors' and Managers' Association, Entertainment Protection Associates, Theatrical Managers' Association and the Society of West End Managers campaigned throughout the twenties for abolition or at least remission of tax on both theatre and cinema tickets. A C.E.A. deputation led by A. E. Newbould, at that time a Member of Parliament, went to the Chancellor in May 1921; it accepted the fact that the tax was probably permanent but asked for some rearrangement. The Chancellor refused. Early in 1922 the C.E.A. and the renters decided to press for abolition in the cinema industry alone and formed a Cinema Tax

---

* Sunday opening was not a live issue during this period. Some local authorities allowed it and some did not, but there was little active demand for it by either trade or public. The Labour Party was generally in favour of it as it was entertainment for people who worked during the rest of the week, but some unions, which had found that despite regulations Sunday opening did in many cases lead to a seven-day working week, were opposed to it. Records of a couple of ballots in 1927 are of limited value as the voters were self-selected. But the *Manchester Evening News*' open ballot, so-called, gave 215,643 against Sunday opening and only 30,078 in favour, and a referendum in one Manchester ward of nearly 20,000 people, of whom about half voted, gave approximately 70 per cent against and 30 per cent for Sunday opening.

Victor McLaglen as Dick Turpin.

Top right: Betty Blythe in Wilcox's *Chu Chin Chow*, 1923.

Bottom right: Henry Edwards and Chrissie White on the left, in *John Forrest Finds Himself,* 1920.

Top Left: Lily Elsie and Gerald Ames in Elvey's *Comradeship* in 1919.

Centre Left: A. V. Bramble shooting *Wuthering Heights* on location in 1920.

Bottom Left: Betty Compson and Clive Brook in Cutts' *Woman to Woman* in 1923.

Top Left: Owen Nares and Gladys Jennings in Kellino's *Young Lochinvar* in 1923.

Centre Left: Ivy Duke and Guy Newall in *Fox Farm* in 1922.

Bottom Left: George Robey as Widow Twankee in Sinclair Hill's *One Arabian Night*, 1923.

Abolition Committee, with an organizing committee which included F. E. Adams, F. R. Goodwin, A. J. Gale and Frank Hill. They lobbied MPs and obtained another hearing from the Chancellor, but again with no results. In April 1923 Baldwin's Budget, after yet another deputation, still gave no relief. MPs who had connections with the entertainment industry became active at the Committee stage of the Finance Bill, some pressing for abolition and some for an alternative scale of taxes suggested by Sir Walter de Frece, MP. Both were decisively beaten as the Government felt that the entertainment industry was simply sharing the general depression of the country and had no case for special treatment. The politically inexperienced trade was dismayed to find that many whom they had supposed to be their friends voted on party lines and failed to support them.

Hopes rose again as a change of government became imminent, since it was known that the Labour Party was sympathetic to the remission of tax. An Entertainments Tax Abolition League was formed and its deputation met the Labour Chancellor, Philip Snowdon, in March 1923.

When Entertainments Tax remission finally came in 1924 it gave considerable relief to small exhibitors but was otherwise something of an anti-climax. Tax was removed from seats up to 6d in price and reduced on those up to 1s 3d as from June 2, 1924. The concessions were made on the understanding that they would be passed on to the public in the form of cheaper seats.

The Labour Government was soon replaced by another Conservative administration in which Winston Churchill as Chancellor soon received the usual deputations seeking more concessions. Every year the Budget aroused new hopes, only to disappoint them. When in 1926 a motion to reduce the scale of the tax was tabled in the House of Commons the Chancellor's reply was that this was inadvisable as it would cost the Revenue £1,350,000 a year. The tax seemed immovable. And when in 1929 the prospect of another change of government encouraged fresh approaches even Snowdon no longer favoured immediate remission 'in view of the serious state into which the present Chancellor has got the national finances.'[40]

There had been no new cinemas built during the war and large queues in 1918 and 1919 led many to believe that there was room for up to another two thousand cinemas in the United Kingdom. In fact, as general economic depression set in the queues disappeared and it was bigger and better cinemas, rather than more of them, that were needed. The cosy Bijou and Biograph closed, and were replaced by the grander Pavilions and Metropoles. At first the restrictions on luxury building presented difficulties, but capital was diverted into the conversion of stores, hotels, older cinemas, legitimate theatres and music halls. By the time restrictions eased and big new cinemas could be built the audiences were slackening. Meanwhile legitimate theatres were converted as skating rinks had been before the war, and the upstart entertainment was often accused of killing the theatre.

Many legitimate theatres and music halls were taken over as supers or pre-release theatres. The Capitol in New Oxford Street had made its intentions clear in 1919:

'As every film is to run so long as there is a public demand for its retention in the programme, the Capitol will introduce a new innovation in regard to the run that a film may enjoy.

'It will, in fact, be the premier motion picture theatre in every sense of the term, for films will have their initial screening there before they appear in the programme of other picture theatres.[41]

The renter discovered early that if in order to give publicity and good presentation for a special film he gave his own pre-release run, he could skim the profits and, by puffing the picture, could even put up its eventual price. It was suspected before long that this treatment was employed to build up unremarkable films, the renter's expenses on the pre-release run being made up later by inflated prices for the ordinary runs. *Broken Blossoms,* put on at the Alhambra early in 1920, had been seen by 96,782 people by April; *Fabiola* was seen by 20,000 at the Stoll in its first three days, and *Orphans of the Storm* by 63,000 at the Scala during its 1922 run; Harold Lloyd's *For Heaven's Sake* took £6,033 in its first seven days at the Plaza in 1926; *Ben Hur* took as much as £5,128 even in its forty-fourth week in London. The renters tactlessly announced the huge crowds drawn to these shows, and the large sum taken at the box office, in their trade publicity. There was much resentment, especially among showmen with large cinemas in parts of London other than the West End, who had been accustomed to securing genuine first runs. Matters were made worse by the renter's deliberate exploitation of the long delay there would be before the film was allowed to appear at any other theatre.

As building restrictions eased, conversions ceased and super cinemas were built. By 1928 a West End pre-release run was the normal practice and the *première*, also, was becoming a popular way of launching a film, having appeared first in the guise of an evening Trade Show. The old Empire theatre in London was taken over by Goldwyn in 1921, and the New Empire in Leicester Square was opened by Metro–Goldwyn in November 1928. In the meantime the Tivoli, Strand, had been opened by Metro–Goldwyn in September 1923 on the site of the old Tivoli theatre which they had bought in May 1919. The Tivoli was later acquired by Provincial Cinematograph Theatres and used by Gaumont–British. The Capitol, Haymarket, which had been planned in 1919, was finally opened by the Clavering brothers in February 1925. The New Gallery, which had been a P.C.T. theatre even before the war, had been rebuilt by July 1925. Famous–Lasky, a company which also had theatres in Manchester and Birmingham, opened the Plaza in February 1926 and the Carlton in March 1928. Universal had Rialtos in both London and Leeds. The Regal, Marble Arch, was opened in November 1928, and the Marble Arch Pavilion was opened by Gaumont–British by 1928.

When the pre-release run began to take place in the provinces as well as London it made a farce of expensive first runs and objections were raised in the C.E.A. Because it was associated with the big American renters the question became confused with patriotism but the real issue for other showmen was the same whether the pre-release cinema was American or British. Mention was made of the first American producer to buy a cinema in the provinces at Leeds, at a C.E.A. Branch Meeting in 1925. In October of that year Lt. Col. Levita unsuccessfully suggested that the L.C.C. should license only entirely British cinemas. And at a Birmingham meeting of the C.E.A. it was decided that:

'. . . in view of the fact that the members of this Association welcome and are willing to show the films of all producers on a basis of merit, the General Council desires to place on record its considered opinion that there is grave danger to the interests of the exhibitors if cinema theatres be controlled by producers or renters, and therefore recommends that a committee be appointed to ascertain the interest of producers and/or renters in the exhibition side of the industry.'[42]

Matters came to a head in 1926 when Famous–Lasky acquired the Futurist and Scala in Birmingham for seven years (see page 84). Birmingham exhibitors wished to boycott renters who competed with them in this way and the General Council decided to bring this to the notice of other branches. But Famous–Lasky put out a Manifesto dated February 10, 1927, claiming first that the Birmingham opposition came from people who did little business with them at the best of times, and second that they had only proposed to use one of the cinemas in question.[43] The boycott was impracticable and agreement was soon reached with J. C. Graham of Famous–Lasky. But provincial pre-release continued to be a matter of concern to exhibitors.

While the large pre-release theatre was the subject of controversy the ordinary cinema itself was becoming bigger and grander. According to *The Film in National Life* one thousand cinemas were built between 1924–25 and 1931–32, especially after 1926.[44] The few 2,000- and 3,000-seaters were mainly in London and a few other large cities. Most were of medium size. Rowson in 1934 said 71·4 per cent had 1,000 seats or less and the average size was 900. There were larger ones, however, and Bernstein's new Cricklewood cinema in 1919 was to seat 3,800, the West End Capitol planned one with 4,000 seats, and the East Ham Premier 5,000.[45] Many had lounges and restaurants, and more care was given to seating, lighting and projection. Boughey claimed that projection was powered by electricity in all the better halls by 1921:

'The old method of turning the mechanism by hand has long since given place to a power-driven projector in all places where electric current is available. The hand-drive is still used, however, as a standby in case of sudden break-down.'[46]

Much was made of the improved architecture, especially in the West End and the larger London cinemas like the Shepherd's Bush Pavilion. The sculptor Frank Dobson and designer Komisarjevsky were said to be associated early in 1927 with Bernstein's cinema building, and the *Kine Year Book* of 1929 refers proudly to the contemporary cinema's 'beauty of architecture'. Inside, there were impressive entrance halls and elaborate curtains and coloured lights. Apart from the façade, however, the outside of the buildings was usually, in fact, as bleak as a warehouse, and the backs and sides of the new buildings disfigured many small towns. After 1928 atmospheric *décor* enlivened the inside. The American John Eberson, described as the originator of atmospheric cinemas in America, was over here in December 1927. The 1927 *Kine Year Book* already spoke of Paramount's Plaza as an 'Italian Renaissance kinema' and Charing Cross Road Astoria as a 'fine Pompeian conception'. The Alexandra Cinema, Aldershot, reconstructed as the first atmospheric cinema in England in June 1928, showed on its walls a 'courtyard and garden in the Italian style with an Alpine background'. Another early atmospheric cinema was the Lido at Golders Green, with romantic Venetian *trompe-l'oeil* murals surrounding the audience.

The costs of film hire in these cinemas naturally differed widely according to the age of the film, that is to say whether it was its first run, second run and so on down the scale to the end of its circulation, and also according to the rank of cinema and the duration of the run. Very approximately 20 to 25 per cent of the expected box-office receipts seems to have been considered a fair profit for the renter, but the charge was made as a flat rate, descending with the age of the film and other considerations, not as a percentage of actual receipts. In 1920 £30 was spoken of as normal for a three-day run for a feature, but as a general figure this is misleading. In 1925 Associated–First National's booking prices for five classes of film for various runs was said to descend all the way from £300 for a first run to £3.[47] A big popular cinema in a good district could afford an early run and would pay at a rate very much higher than a small, old hall in a sparsely populated area, putting in films that had already gone the rounds of the better cinemas. A special case was Chaplin's two-reel *The Idle Class* offered in October 1921, just after the success of his film *The Kid* and his much publicized visit to England in September. Film Booking Offices offered it at £2,800 for a two months' booking, £2,000 for four weeks or £500 for a week. This offer exhibitors were urged by the C.E.A. to resist as outrageous, but the bigger cinemas must have felt that for such a film it was worth while. But this was exceptional. The issue was further complicated by the existence of block booking, in which the price of individual films fell if they were booked in company with a large number of others. A leader mentions a small exhibitor accustomed to paying £5 to £25 for his features in 1924 being offered a bargain of twelve for £50.[48] Few British producers had a large enough output to be able to offer blocks. (See Chapter III for booking practices.) British films, which had to cover their costs in this country, were also more expensive to book than those from America. An ordinary British picture at £200 a week in 1926 was said to compare with an American super at £70, and one exhibitor complained of being asked 150 per cent more for British films.[49]

Sir Michael Balcon, addressing the British Kinematograph Society, later said that in 1920 a good film would have received about five hundred bookings and yield renters' receipts of £12,000. Assuming this to be in the region of a quarter of box office takings this would indicate a gross of some £48,000, an approximate estimate which seems fairly accurate. British films earned far less and a British film of 1920 like *Nothing Else Matters*, which had cost £7,000 to make, was considered to have done very well to have made £30,000 at home and abroad. Several years later Elvey's great success, *The Flag Lieutenant*, was said to have received £50,000, making it somewhat more profitable than earlier British films. Yet next year a letter mentioned a British film costing £6,000 to produce and grossing only £12,000. And even in 1927 Simon Rowson said that the British cinemas normally yielded renters' receipts of only £7,000 to £10,000.[50]

(4) EDUCATIONAL USE OF THE FILM

The idea that films might have more than entertainment value appeared early. It will be remembered (see Volume III) that in 1917 the National Council of Public Morals had set up a Cinema Commission of Enquiry. This appointed two Committees to study the matter of film and education: the Psychological Research Committee which included Professor Charles Spearman as Chairman and Professor Cyril Burt; and the Cinema Experiments Sub-Committee which was to deal with projectors, processes and films.

There were, in fact, very few films that could be described as educational in any but a very general way. After the war Sir Richard Gregory addressed the British Association in 1919 on the value of film in education and was later connected with Joseph Best in the founding of a company to make films to accompany text-books. The Macmillan Educational Film Company was registered in May 1920 as a private company with a capital of £2,300. But the trade, pointing proudly to the educational value of such films as Ponting's record of Scott's expedition or the many small travel and industrial films, was not really interested in making specialized films for classroom work.

The subject continued to arouse interest outside the film industry, however. In 1921 the London County Council set up an Education Sub-Committee to study the question. Then in July 1923 the Imperial Education Conference set up a large Committee to study it further under the Chairmanship of Lord Gorrell. This Committee included people from all branches of the trade and from outside it, including F. W. Baker, the Bromhead brothers, A. J. Gale, Edward Godal, A. G. Granger, Richard Gregory, Cecil Hepworth, Sir Sidney Low, E. V. Lucas, George Pearson, Simon Rowson, Sir Oswald Stoll, E. G. Turner and J. Brooke Wilkinson.

The *Report on the Use and Value of the Cinematograph in Education* was published by this Committee in June of the following year. It was strongly in favour of the use of film in education, which it urged the Board of Education to adopt, claiming that satisfactory equipment was available and that more use was being made of films in schools and special educational shows than had previously been thought.

The Film in National Life, however, later referred to this Report as inconclusive. But early next year, 1925, came the Report of the Cinema Commission of Enquiry set up earlier by the National Council of Public Morals, called *The Cinema in Education*. The terms of reference of the Psychological Research Committee had been very wide, covering the durability of impressions made by film, a comparison with other methods of instruction, future development in the production and use of educational film, its possibilities for cultivating aesthetic appreciation and evidence as to what had already been done. Very limited experiments had been carried out, resulting in the unremarkable conclusion that 'the cinema has, from every point of view, a well-marked advantage for Educational purposes.'[51] Meanwhile the Experiments Sub-Committee had optimistically sought a projector which would be portable, cheap, easy to manipulate and capable of stopping at any frame for examination, a projector meeting the requirements of local authorities for exhibition in schools without licence or special permit, giving a brilliant and well-defined picture by electric light or any other means, and capable of use as both a film projector and a magic lantern. They had viewed some sixteen projectors ranging in price from £10 to nearly £100, but could find no one projector embodying all these requirements.

As a result of these reports the President of the Board of Education announced in the Commons that he was

'. . . disposed to think that its proper place and function as an instrument of instruction cannot yet be defined. No doubt films of a general character, illustrating scenery, natural history, wild or primitive life, agricultural, commercial and industrial operations and other activities of our complex civilization may serve a very useful purpose in supplementing and providing a background for the instruction given in the schools, and in augmenting its significance and interest; such films would be education in the widest sense for adults as well as for children. But so far as concerns the use of films as a means of specific instruction in the classroom, at a cost not out of proportion to its value, the results of my enquiry have been generally speaking, negative; and while there is no doubt a fairly wide field for educational experiment, I do not think that the time has yet arrived when it is possible to make specific recommendations on the subject.'[52]

Next year, 1926, the L.C.C. Education Sub-Committee of 1921 published its Report. This gave qualified approval but maintained that little was yet known of the film's potential use in a strictly educational sense. *The Film in National Life* later summed it up:

'. . . was doubtful whether cinematography had made much progress in its use for educational purposes. It was difficult to bring films into real relation with class syllabuses, and the limitations of the cinematograph within the scope of subject appropriate to an elementary school were more narrow than was at first supposed. Reviewing all circumstances, therefore, including the high cost of projectors and the limited number of films, the Committee saw no grounds for advising the Council to depart from the policy of encouraging private enterprise in out of school displays of a high quality, but would hesitate to propose any policy which might involve expenditure on equipment or attendance at displays in school time.'[53]

British Instructional Films had formed an Educational Department in

November 1925 to provide suitable films for educational use, and the head of this department, Mary Field, replied sharply to the L.C.C. Report that it was out of date and ignored the real use that was already being made of films in many schools. The claim, which referred to seven projectors in London schools, was not impressive. In October 1927 British Instructional started a series of partly educational film shows at the Kingsway Hall in conjunction with the London County Council. But this company, with its *Secrets of Nature* and other well-made factual films, was the only one seriously tackling the problem of providing suitable material. Even so their programmes were mainly selections from news, conventional travel and interest films and such expedition or other films which happened to be suitable, together with the *Secrets of Nature* films, many of which were compiled from earlier material. Stoll's also started educational shows, the first given at the Stoll Picture Theatre on a Saturday in April 1929 before an audience of teachers, but as the company did nothing to produce suitable films itself this may be seen more as a form of prestige publicity than as a constructive step in the field of educational cinematography. Bernstein's Saturday morning shows for children which started in March 1928 were for entertainment only.

There were real difficulties in the way of using film for true educational purposes. For one thing, no one was certain how far films could aid in teaching. It was felt that as one of a teacher's functions was to respond to students' progress, and modify his pace accordingly, an impersonal demonstration like that of a film was of limited value; and whereas general interest films might stimulate children's curiosity and illustrate their lessons, film lectures as such seemed more suitable for higher and technical education than for schools. Meanwhile, although sub-standard projectors and non-flam film did come into use during the twenties, the expense and inadequacy of the equipment available made the outlet for specialized films very small. This discouraged production and resulted in a vicious circle, in which the few people interested in making educational films made them only if they were also suitable for commercial showing in the cinemas.

A change took place after 1929. In November of this year a Commission on Educational and Cultural Films was set up by a Conference of educational and scientific organizations, largely on the initiative of the British Institute of Adult Education and the Association of Scientific Workers. The Commission, whose terms of reference were even wider than those of previous investigations, did not produce its great Report, *The Film in National Life*, however, until the early thirties.

(5) CENSORSHIP

At the end of the war the system of censorship in Britain which had begun in 1912 was firmly established. Censorship certificates were issued by the British Board of Film Censors, a body set up by the film industry itself to safeguard its interests against the effect of differing regulations all over the country, and were widely required by local authorities as a condition of licenses issued under the Cinematograph Act of 1909. This Act, however, was primarily concerned with fire precautions, and neither the Board nor the Licensing authorities had been entrusted by Parliament with authority to limit freedom of expression by censorship. Freedom of expression was officially still controlled only by the laws relating to libel, sedition, obscenity and blasphemy, except in the case of stage plays, which were subject to some control by the Lord Chamberlain's office.

The British Board of Film Censors consisted of the President, the Rt. Hon. T. P. O'Connor, to whom was left the final and complete responsibility for the passing or rejection of films; four Examiners appointed by him, who except for the Secretary J. Brooke Wilkinson were anonymous and had no contact with the film trade; and a Committee elected by the different branches of the trade which, however, merely held discussions on general principles and policy. Monthly lists of the films passed were sent by the Board to licensing authorities and the C.E.A. O'Connor died in November 1929 and was replaced by a former Home Secretary, the Rt. Hon. Edward Shortt.

Licences were issued under the Cinematograph Act of 1909 by County and County Borough Councils, which could also delegate this duty to Justices, Watch Committees and Borough, Urban and Rural District Councils. The number of licensing authorities in the country was put by *The Film in National Life* in 1932 at seven hundred. The 1915 Report of the Board of Film Censorship said that thirty-five of the licensing authorities in the country had notified the Board that they had inserted in their licenses a stipulation that only films passed by the Board were to be exhibited. This saved them the trouble of viewing films themselves and silenced most local critics of the cinema. The first post-war Report, in 1919, stated that a large proportion of the licensing authorities had adopted the Board's certificate in this way, and the system spread further during the twenties. At the same time the certificates acquired both greater authority and greater precision.

Exhibitors were still harassed by the differing standards among local authorities, and the Cinematograph Exhibitors' Association wished to make the Board's certificates universally acceptable. After the war the bad publicity attracted to the cinema as a whole by so-called propaganda, or 'health propaganda', films about sex caused concern to the Cinematograph Exhibitors' Association which sought to reinforce the Board's power to ban them. The C.E.A. suggested that after a date to be agreed with the Kinematograph Renters' Association no film should be shown by C.E.A. members unless it had passed the Board. The K.R.S. took no action, so in January 1920 the C.E.A. acted on its own and resolved that its members should not show films that had not passed the Board. Later in the year it expelled several members who had done so, and in October an Educational and Propaganda Committee was appointed to urge the authorities to strengthen and uphold the Board.

The authority of the Certificates was greatly increased by the Brentford case. It still appeared possible in 1920 for an exhibitor to show uncertified films without the express consent of the licensing authorities. This was tested in the case of Ellis *v*. Dubowski in 1921. The Middlesex County Council had included in its licences in 1920 the stipulation that cinemas should not show films without a Board certificate. A Twickenham exhibitor showed a film about the Armenian atrocities called *Auction of Souls*, a film which had been widely shown and had not in fact caused much trouble elsewhere despite its lack of a censorship certificate. A case was brought against them in 1921 for contravening the conditions of the licence, and it was dismissed. It was held that to stipulate that cinemas should not show uncertified films would have been acceptable had it been a reasonable stipulation, but that in this case the condition was not reasonable, as there was no appeal from the Board's decisions; it was *ultra vires* for the licensing authority to delegate its final responsibility for the decision in this way. It was maintained, however, that the stipulation would have been all right had it been in the form of a prohibition to show films not so certified except by the express consent of the licensing authority.

Later in 1921 the Theatres and Music Halls Committee of the London County Council recommended the adoption of the following clauses in licences:

(1) That no film, other than photographs of current events, which has not been passed for Universal or Public Exhibition by the British Board of Film Censors shall be exhibited without the express consent of the Council.

(2) That prior to the exhibition of a film passed by the British Board of Film Censors a reproduction of the Certificate of the Board be legibly exposed to the audience.

(3) That films passed by the Board for Public Exhibition be only exhibited to adults.

(4) That nothing in the forgoing shall be deemed to relieve the licensee of his personal responsibility for any films shown which may, in the opinion of the Council, be detrimental to the public.[54]

The Board pointed out that Clause 3, that even films passed by it as suitable for public exhibition should only be exhibited to adults, was quite beyond its scope, and the L.C.C. accordingly held a conference of the trade, the Board, the Home Office and the Lord Chamberlain's office, at which it was decided that films passed thus by the Board should only be exhibited to adults provided that this condition should not apply in the case of a child accompanied by its parent or *bona fide* guardian. This was later accepted by the General Meeting of the L.C.C., which defined a child as anyone under sixteen years of age. Other licensing authorities followed suit. Morever, in future it was accepted that a film not certified by the Board could only be shown if the express consent of the licensing authority was obtained.

This gave the decisions of the Board almost legal force. But in June 1923 a Conference of licensing authorities was called by the Home Office to discuss the absence of uniformity in accepting this system. It was agreed that the Secretary of State should recommend all licensing authorities to adopt the Dubowski clause, and in July a circular letter went out to this effect. In the 1926 Report it was stated that most authorities now included the condition in their licences.

But by the end of the period a certain number of licensing authorites still did not impose it and a Home Office letter of December 16, 1929 to all licensing authorities strongly recommended them to do so.

Further controversy centred round the system of issuing two classes of certificates, U and A, for films suitable respectively for universal and adult audiences. By early 1925 this needed strengthening. Many of the most bitter critics of the cinema for its supposedly harmful effects on young people were ignorant that this system existed. The National Council of Women had wanted stricter censorship of films shown to the under-sixteens several years before, and during 1926 the Board received three important deputations, from the National Association of Head Teachers, the London Public Morality Council and the L.C.C., all concerned with this problem. There was further agitation in 1928 and some authorities wished to go further than the model rules recommended by the Home Office and ban young people under sixteen from the cinema unconditionally.

The proportion of films given a certificate for adult audiences declined very sharply from 57 per cent in 1919 to 20 per cent in 1928, according to the Board's Reports. The Board put this down to the willingness of the film publishers to accept its ruling not only in making changes to films already produced but also in the original planning of the scenario. The Board's certificate was important enough to be considered by the film makers during production, especially after the coming of sound at the end of the period. The difficulties of cutting a film with sound-on-film, to say nothing of sound-on-disc, at first seemed to present them with a choice between banning or certifying films in their entirety. In some cases a cut silent version was passed and the sound version banned. Before the Board acquired sound projection facilities of its own they found it necessary to study the script with the film. By the end of 1929 they had installed sound equipment, but even so the 1929 Report was able to state that, owing to the greater difficulty of cutting sound film,

'. . . in the case of British Producers, it is becoming quite a common procedure to discuss a proposed production with the Board and submit the dialogue before commencing work in the studio'.[55]

It is difficult but not impossible to form a general picture of what was cut out. Owing to the secrecy under which the work of the Board was conducted there is little information as to individual cuts. One useful source of information, however, is the annual list of reasons for cuts made during the year which was given in the Board's printed Reports. The cumulative effect of these is to outline the attitude and standards of the censors. In a way it is more revealing than the occasional statements of principle, which are unexceptionable generalizations.

The Board's stated priciples were recapitulated, for example, in the first post-war Report in 1919:

'They are guided by the main broad principles that nothing should be passed which is calculated to demoralize an audience, that can teach methods of, or extenuate crime, that can undermine the teachings of morality, that tend to bring the institution of marriage into contempt, or lower the sacredness of family ties. Objection is taken to incidents which bring Public Characters into contempt, when acting in their capacity as such, together with subjects which might be calculated to wound the susceptibilities of foreign people. The question of religious observances is very carefully considered, also subjects which are calculated to foment violent social unrest. That while it is impossible to exact poetic justice always overtaking evil-doers, the Board has considered it essential that no halo should be placed round the heads of the delinquents or criminals.

'Subjects dealing with the "triangle" theme are numerous and very frequently require the most careful consideration, owing to the complicated nature of the story. It has been found in some cases that while involving departure from virtue, such films do not necessarily suggest actual depravity, and there is, of course, a distinction to be drawn between errors caused by love, even if guilty love, and the pursuit of lust. The Examiners always endeavour to eliminate any manifestations of the latter character. Situations have been depicted in which it was sought to attain dramatic interest by representing characters bearing abnormal relations, e.g. a brother and sister unknown, making love to each other. Such situations are considered repugnant, and alterations have been insisted upon which remove the unwholesome complications.

'The betrayal of young women is a question which depends upon the treatment; when the subject is treated with restraint, it seems impossible to exclude it as a basis for a story. Objection, however, is taken when the treatment is such as to suggest that a girl is morally justified in succumbing to temptation in order to escape sordid surroundings or uncongenial work.

'One of the most difficult subjects with which the Board has had to deal is the question of crime. There is a great temptation to produce "crime" films in the undoubted fact that, as with the kindred arts of the drama, the novel, and the newspaper, it is abundantly demonstrated that stories of crime make a strong appeal to the imagination of the Public, especially to the less educated sections. When a story of crime is accompanied with the further elements of daring adventure, of romance, and of mystery, there are the elements of a popular success. It is also true that to young people, especially boys, with their ingrained instinct for adventure, uncorrected by experience of life, such "crime" films make a special appeal, and it may be added, a dangerous appeal.

'These "crime" films threatened to become a serious danger to the reputation of the cinema. The Examiners for a while found themselves flooded with films, in some cases running to twenty episodes or parts, in which inhuman monsters, using all kinds of mysterious methods of assassination, were to be shown, week by week, over a lengthened period of time. The Board found the evil assuming such proportions, from the cumulative effect of these serial films, that a strong stand was necessary, and the following regulations were laid down and communicated to the Trade:

(1) No Serial dealing with crime will be examined in future except as a whole.

(2) No Serial in which crime is the dominant feature, and not merely an episode in the story, will be passed by the Censor.

(3) No film will be passed in which the methods of crime are set forth and form the chief theme. This rule is applied even in cases where at the end of the film retribution is supposed to have fallen on the criminal; and equally when the detective element is subordinate to the criminal interest, or when actual crime is treated from the comic point of view.

'In defining "crime" for the purposes of Censorship it is necessary to discriminate between stories calculated to familiarize young people with theft, robberies and violence, leaving them to conclude that such are normal incidents, and on the other hand, stories which deal with "costume" crime, such as cowboy films, Mexican robberies, etc. It is felt that the latter incidents are regarded simply as dramatic and thrilling adventures with no connection whatever with the lives, or probable experiences, of young people in this country.

'In endeavouring to check indecorum in dress, no figure is passed in which the dress appears to be meant to be indecent or suggestive.

'Considerable difficulty has arisen in respect to a special class of films which have been termed "Propaganda" films. . . .'[56]

General principles mean little unless we know how they are applied. Most of the individual reasons given for cuts occurred repeatedly, year after year. Crime was always a sore subject. Crime as a dominant theme was disliked, and sympathy for a criminal, extenuation of crime, successful crooks and of course the detailed exposition of criminal methods, as well as suicide and drug taking, were cited frequently. Morbid, brutal or horrific scenes and wilful lingering on suffering were often mentioned, cruelty especially to animals, children or women, realistic and gruesome murders or fights, dead bodies, executions, torture, 'painful scenes of lunacy' and the effects of venereal disease and medical operations were considered unsuitable matter for films designed for entertainment. In 1928 bull-fights caused some annoyance.

The Board had taken a stand about crime films as early as 1917. In 1923 they cut the American *Oliver Twist*, censoring the matron kicking an old woman on the workhouse floor, Fagin showing Oliver how to pick pockets, and the murder of Nancy. In 1925 it was found necessary to issue a warning letter to the trade recapitulating its position, and a further warning was added later about a new tendency to enlist sympathy for criminals as victims of circumstance and a tendency

'. . . to hold up the recognized authority of the law either to odium or ridicule'.

Apparently all this did not stem the flood of crime films and both warnings were repeated in 1928. In November 1926, also, a letter to the trade had noted

'. . . a tendency on the part of some producers to issue films depicting organised knuckle fights with the consequent brutality . . .'

and it was observed that, as such fights were illegal in England, the Board intended to ban films of them in future. Again this seems to have been swimming against the tide, and the Report for 1928 once more noted a tendency to produce incidents of prolonged and gross brutality, in which drastic cuts had to be made during the year.

As for indecency or indecorum, the Board was very conscious that it was in this area that the cinema was likely to attract its most implacable critics. During the early part of the period, trouble was caused mainly by what were called propaganda films. The word was not used at the time to describe reforming or revolutionary pleading, which was summarily dismissed as 'Bolshy'. But there were a number of films at this time described euphemistically as health propaganda and said to be about 'certain diseases', 'race suicide', 'illegal operations' and so on. Such were Samuelson's *Damaged Gods* (1919), *Open Your Eyes* (1919) which was said to be made with the blessing of the American Public Health Service, a film about venereal diseases called *End of the Road* (1919), *and Unmarried* (1920), made for the National Council for the Unmarried Mother and her Child. The Board defined its attitude in a circular letter which was reprinted in the 1919 Report:

'. . . produced for the purpose of influencing public opinion, or enlisting sympathy, on certain subjects. . . . The Board has consistently refused to issue their Certificate for these films, even though, in some cases, there was nothing indecorous in the pictures. . . . The Board has no criticism to offer on the purpose of these films; some of them may be useful, and in certain cases, even necessary. . . . In the opinion of the Board, these films should be exhibited in Halls specially taken for the purpose where securities could be taken for choosing the audience which are impossible in the ordinary cinema. . . .'[57]

Another cause of complaint in the 1919 Report was the increase in swearing in sub-titles. This

'. . . gives a bad tone to the whole story while failing to add to the impressiveness or farce [*sic*] of the script. As it is impossible to make an arbitrary limit of the extent to which the use is advisable, it is thought that the only course is to rule out entirely all such language and expressions. . . .'

A letter from T. P. O'Connor instanced 'Damn', 'Go to Hell' and 'the damned'. In 1925 the Board also found occasion to deprecate 'alien idiomatic phrases calculated to debase the purity of the English language' and

'. . . a growing habit with actors of both sexes to divest themselves of their clothing on slight or no provocation'

and

'. . . dances, especially in cabaret and similar scenes, which are of a nature that cannot be considered decorous or even decent'.

61

In connection with cabaret, the 1919 Report spoke with disapproval of a new form of

'. . . Back Stage Drama . . . a continuous succession of them is subversive, tending to inculcate a lower outlook, and to invest a life of irregularity with a spurious glamour'.

In 1923 the Board had trouble with films based on books described in their Report as notorious.

'A book may be objectionable, though widely circulated, if . . . the moral of the story is a glorification of free love. And even if the film be purged—and a great part of the time of the Examiners of the Board is taken up with the task of purging films of undesirable scenes—the fact remains that the book on which it is founded and with which it is associated, may be of a pernicious tendency, and therefore ought not to get additional publicity by its title being associated with the film. . . . Its position would be indefensible if it could be properly charged with allowing the film to be the advertising agency for demoralizing literature.'

The film to which this refers seems to have been that written by Marie Stopes with Walter Summers and originally entitled *Married Love*, after her book, but subsequently changed first to *Maisie's Marriage* and finally issued in May as *Married Life*. Another 'sensational' title which had to be changed was Cutts' *Cocaine*, finally trade shown as *While London Sleeps* (1922). *Afraid of Love* (1925), an English film made by an unimportant company to capitalize on the notoriety of a recent legal case of non-consummation of marriage and featuring one of the people concerned, the Hon. Mrs John Russell, was accompanied by 'undesirable' posters and had been serialized in a newspaper. Even a cut version aroused opposition in the C.E.A. *A Modern Dubarry*, a film made in France by Alexander Korda, was shown here in 1926 and criticized solemnly in *The Bioscope* under the heading 'Salacious Pictures'.

De Mille's *King of Kings* (1927) was in a different category. This was not submitted to the Board at all as the latter consistently refused to allow the materialized figure of Christ to be shown. It had been passed by both the London County Council and the Middlesex County Council by November 1927, on condition that it should be shown alone and the players not given any publicity, imparting a sort of reverence by treating it differently from other entertainment films. It was shown in December at Covent Garden, and many licensing authorities subsequently passed it. It was stated in *The Bioscope* in April next year that 80 per cent of the cinemas in the country were at liberty to show it. Nevertheless, it aroused strong emotions and violent controversy, in which the Board prudently did not take part.

Anything provocative was suspect and, as an over-all description, scenes dealing with immorality. Extenuations of either marital infidelity or the 'sacrifice of a woman's virtue' were common objections, 'first night scenes', men and women in bed together (1926), excessive drunkenness whether treated seriously or comically, and in 1929 'outrageously indecent exhibitions disguised under would-be morals'. Such objections beg the question of what is excessive or undesirable, terms which occur frequently. Mere reference to orgy scenes carried 'to excess', 'equivocal' bedroom and bathroom scenes, 'provocative and sensuous' exposure of a girl's legs (1925), women in 'alluring or provocative' attitudes leave much room for disagreement. The objections are full of loaded words like 'indelicate', 'indecorous', 'impropriety', 'immodest', 'equivocal' or 'outrageous'. No guidance is given as to the extent of 'unbridled and illicit passions', 'offensive vulgarity and indecent gestures' and 'salacious wit'. People have always differed widely as to where to draw the line. Possibly modesty forbade more detailed definition, but the result was sadly open to subjective interpretation.

The vagueness and discretionary nature of censorship standards is often defended on the grounds that these are interpreted in the light of prevailing public opinion, and can therefore change as public opinion changes. Two inherent characteristics of censorship as an alternative to legal controls over freedom of expression, however, appear to be firstly that the change is always made at the rate of those sectors of society least willing to change, serving by its very nature as a drag, and secondly that banning the representation or discussion of anything produces a misleading impression that it does not exist. The history of film censorship shows both these features.

To be fair, in the absence of much detailed evidence we cannot often tell how reasonably the interpretation was made, and much cut material may well have been crude and inartistic. But the result of cutting out things that are 'not nice' was to imply that they do not happen. Not only crimes committed by children, and drug-taking, but even 'oppressive treatment of natives' and the 'horrors of warfare' did not exist for the screen. They were not content to suppress inflammatory political subtitles, 'incitement to class hatred', and the advocacy of free love and contraception, but also any mention of 'antagonism of Capital and Labour'. Finally the logical outcome was to ban 'reference to controversial or international politics' and indeed, of any social problem. Furthermore, drunkenness among women, brutality to women, fights between women, prostitution and procuration, 'illegal operations', brothels, rape, confinements and puerperal pains were apparently not just to be banned if 'excessive' but were actually not to be mentioned at all. Girls were not made drunk or seduced; incest and white slave traffic did not exist. This unhealthy attitude of chivalry-by-ignoring is reflected in the words of a Home Secretary of the twenties, Sir William Joynson-Hicks.

'One side of this question, and one of terrible and far-reaching importance, is the effect of films produced either in America or in this country and exhibited in India and in the East, showing the white woman as an object of degradation. There is no room here to elaborate this aspect of the question, but it is undoubtedly essential that all nations which rule in Eastern countries should see to it that the pride and character of their womanhood is maintained unimpaired.'[58]

Probably the most stultifying group of objections was that designed to protect existing authority and the social establishment. The result of such prohibitions can only be to stifle protest and the discussion of any injustice, however real. The institution of marriage, it goes without saying, was not to be disparaged, nor was any suggestion of collusive divorce to be allowed. Further, the 'unauthorized use of Royal Names, Public Characters and well-known members of Society', 'lampoons on the institution of the Monarchy', and in 1928 and 1929 even mere reference to the Prince of Wales, were banned. The Board would not tolerate 'holding up the King's uniform to contempt or ridicule', 'bringing discredit on British uniforms', 'scenes in which British officers and officials in India and elsewhere shown in invidious circumstances' or, final horror in 1926, 'white men in state of degradation amidst native surroundings'. Women had a special duty; 'equivocal situations between white girls and men of other races' became a frequent objection and 'reflection on wife of responsible British official stationed in the East'. 'British social life held up to ridicule' was not allowed, nor was impugning the honour of members of the medical profession, 'misrepresentation of prison life, and the holding up of constituted authority to odium', 'attacks calculated to undermine the administration of the Law', criticism of the Police Force, 'police official leading a double life', 'libels on the British nursing profession' and even 'workhouse officials shown in an offensive light' or a 'minister of religion in equivocal situations'. Finally in 1928 and 1929, when *Potemkin* and *Mother* had at last reached England, soldiers and police were not to be shown firing on a defenceless populace.

Those producing and marketing films were subject to the usual laws concerning obscenity, sedition, libel and blasphemy. Were they such a wild, licentious and seditious lot that they required this extra machinery to control them? The answer lies in the purpose for which the Board has been set up, and which was simply to avoid expensive delays and difficulties owing to the rules different local authorities might impose as a condition of granting licenses. The anonymous men who executed the censorship were doubtless aware that many of the world's great works of art had been about serious and controversial subjects, banned by them as suitable matter for films. But they did not regard the film at that time as a serious medium of expression, nor was it their aim to facilitate its development as such, but simply to protect it as a profitable and innocuous form of family entertainment. The fact that films banned by them were in fact, in all but a few cases, denied any exhibition at all was not their intention.

In terms of its own purpose, the British Board of Film Censors succeeded very well. It had a high reputation for integrity, and exercised its power with admirable independence of the trade interests which supported it. On the whole its decisions enjoyed a growing loyalty among renters and exhibitors alike, and managed to disarm most of the likely pressure groups. And as a result the films which circulated in Britain at this period, especially those made in Britain, were of limited and trivial content, suitable only for a largely uneducated and ignorant audience. As more serious films began to arrive, they suffered the same fate as the saucy, the sadistic and the morbid.

So far we have been discussing the censorship of films which, except for *King of Kings,* were of little individual importance and were often deliberately sensational. If censorship had been confined to such films, the deliberations about whether one could say damn in 1925, show a man and woman in bed together or only on a divan, or whether the wife of a Britisher abroad could be less than perfect would have been merely ridiculous, stupid cuts in stupid films for stupid audiences. But it is clear, although exact information is sparse, that many of the best films of the day, almost all imported, were cut in the same spirit and for the same purpose. The result was to discourage variety and seriousness in film making and deny to intelligent people the right to see serious attempts to use the cinema for something better. To some extent the very poverty of imagination in British film production, and the early contempt in which it was held, may have been due to the fact that people simply did not know what could be done, and in fact was being done abroad, with the film medium.

Chaplin's *A Woman of Paris* (1923), Dupont's *Variety* (1926, shown in Britain as *Vaudeville*), *Metropolis* (Lang, 1926) and *The Love of Jeanne Ney* (Pabst, 1927, shown in Britain in 1929) were among the outstanding films which were passed by the Board only after cuts had been made in the spirit outlined above. Eric Walter White, whose interest in the idea of rhythm in film construction made him especially sensitive to the impertinence of interfering with the cutting of a finished film, complained in his book *Parnassus to Let* in 1928 of the mutilation of many films in this way. The contents of Karl Grune's *The Street* (Germany 1923) is described in the Museum of Modern Art *Film Index*:

'. . . omnipresent poverty in the slums of a post-war German city as the cause of crime and prostitution'.[59]

which must have required rather a lot of adjustment to fit into the Board's view of the world, but even the cut version was attacked at a C.E.A. meeting by an exhibitor who complained that it should never have been 'certificated' and that it was a film he would not like to take his wife to see. . . .[60] *The Joyless Street* (Pabst, 1925) was banned, and *The Tragedy of the Street* (Rahn, 1927) banned at first but passed with cuts for the Avenue Pavilion in London late in 1929. *Bed and Sofa* (Room, 1927), like many others, was shown at the Film Society.

Such films, like the Russian *Mother* (Pudovkin, 1926), *End of St Petersburg* (Pudovkin, 1927), *Battleship Potemkin* (Eisenstein, 1925) and many others, were shown at the Film Society in the late twenties, but had difficulties with the censor even for this limited circulation. On the whole they were films which made little direct appeal to the British public or the showmen, being of interest mainly to the nucleus of more serious cinema enthusiasts beginning to form around the London Film Society and the Avenue Pavilion but very thin on the ground outside London.

Lacking the appeal which the health propaganda films of the early twenties made to the prurient, these films would hardly have caused a run on the cinema by rowdy or lewd audiences and the censorship machinery for protecting the trade's reputation was invoked from timidity in the face of pressures real or imagined. The sinister nature of such pressure began to give concern. The D. W. Griffith film *America* (1924) about the war of independence was considered offensive to Britain. But considered by whom? When first banned by the Board, it was said to be 'on the wish of a high authority', although a cut version called *Love and Sacrifice* prepared after a visit to England by D. W. Griffith was passed later. But the most important, and most distasteful, censorship cases of the decade were those of *Potemkin*, *Mother* and Herbert Wilcox's *Dawn*.

Dawn (1928) was the story of Nurse Edith Cavell, played by Sybil Thorndike. At the time many people in favour of letting bygones be bygones wrongly assumed that the film would not only revive painful memories of the war but also portray the Germans in a crudely insulting way. The Foreign Secretary, Sir Austen Chamberlain, declined to see the film, and his secretary wrote to Wilcox of his feeling of 'repugnance to its production'.[61] It was later said that he had warned O'Connor of his disapproval even before he had heard from the German ambassador. Whichever came first, pressure seems to have been exerted on the Board by both the German ambassador and the Foreign Secretary, and it decided in February not to give the film a certificate. The film was a well made, dignified and by no means hostile account, hardly worthy of the words of either the American writer H. L. Mencken on the one hand:

'I assume that the picture is swinish and abominable but I am unalterably against any effort to stop its showing.'

or of George Bernard Shaw on the other:

'You have a most moving and impressive incarnation of that heroine by our greatest tragic actress whose dignity keeps the whole story on the highest plane. It has been told by a young film poet who has been entirely faithful to his great theme.'[62]

The controversy was sensationally treated in the papers and led to some discussion of censorship in the Commons, during which Sir Austen, 'speaking as an English gentleman', described it as an 'outrage on a noble woman's memory to turn for purposes of commercial profit so heroic a story'.[63] The profit aspect of it certainly bothered many, and to appease them part of the proceeds were devoted to charity. For despite the Board's rejection many, if not most, local licensing authorities to whom it was submitted gave their consent and it was shown all over the country. In April the L.C.C. passed it by 56 votes to 52, subject to certain conditions. All this publicity must have been gratifying to the producers.

The film, although it marked a new maturity in Wilcox's work, was not a masterpiece and the incident is significant chiefly because of the suspicion of backstairs foreign influence. Far more important was the interference in our right to see two of the greatest silent films ever made, by two artists whose influence on the meduim was of enormous importance in the development of the film. *Potemkin* was made in 1925 and *Mother* in 1926, but by the end of the twenties they had only been seen here at the Film Society in London. The Board had turned *Potemkin* down because it had a bearing on recent 'controversial' events, the Russian revolution of some ten years before, although the incident portrayed actually took place in 1905. It was turned down by the L.C.C. and the Middlesex County Council. *The Bioscope*, aware that it had done well at the box office in America, and hearing that it would not offend the 'most anti-Bolshevik alive', was indignant. According to Ivor Montagu's account the agent, Film Booking Offices, was about to submit it to other local councils when they received intimidating visits from the special department of Scotland Yard. Not wanting trouble, they decided to drop the matter. Two Members of Parliament, James Maxton and L. A. Plummer, wrote on behalf of the *New Leader*, the organ of the Independent Labour Party, to the Home Secretary, Joynson-Hicks, on February 2, 1929, asking him to permit F.B.O. to lend the film for a private show to some MPs and others, their purpose being to win the support of influential people for the removal of the prohibition on films banned for political reasons. Joynson-Hicks replied that he was unable to comply. Montagu later maintained that the *New Leader* missed the point of this reply, which was that Joynson-Hicks literally could neither give nor withhold permission, as it was not in his prerogative to do so, and that the film could have been shown in a trade theatre without permission from anyone. However, the hint of disapproval was enough to deter the renter, who would take the matter no further, and the Government was able to claim that the film had been banned by the trade's own action.

    Mother, made in 1926, was banned by the Board on the ground

'. . . that its scene was Russia, that its action concerned a strike, and that forces of order were depicted firing on a mob'.[64]

After protest this ground was altered to

'. . . cover rather the tenour of depiction of scene and action than the scene and action themselves'.[65]

The Bioscope reviewer, seeing the film at the Film Society in 1928, rather strangely found it a dull and conventional melodrama, and was puzzled about the censorship:

. . . though it has been banned by the Censor on political grounds, it failed to evoke in me a desire to rush out and burn down Regent Street'.[66]

There were continued protests, as a result of which the President of the Board said that although he personally agreed that the film would probably do no harm and indeed might do good, his view was not shared by many members of the public nor, significantly, by the Government, and he would therefore not pass it.

The disadvantages of the system of self-control were now beginning to show. Laws, decided however imperfectly after discussion in Parliament, are subject to the democratic control of Parliament and ultimately, through this, to public opinion. But the British Board of Film Censors, much though it was to be commended on the seriousness with which it took its work, had imperceptibly assumed the position of an oracle and the custodian of society's moral sense. There was never, to do it credit, any hint that it was not fully independent of the trade interests which had set it up. But it was utterly dependent for its continued effectiveness on avoiding trouble with articulate pressure groups. In fact it was sensitive not so much to public opinion as to the strength of groups organized to impose their own taboos on a largely passive public. Its best hope of fulfilling its own purpose was to avoid trouble with the intolerant or the powerful, and it could be trusted to come down on the side of the *status quo* on every political and social issue. The cinema was trying to grow up, and was now ready to try a little elementary comment on the controversial world around it. The Board, as the result of its curious history, was in a position to prevent this.

Ivor Montagu stressed that the three films were banned not on the ground that they were subversive or seditious, but because they were controversial in the eyes of the Board, or more likely in what the Board believed to be the eyes of the Government. Worse, censorship of the film as a means of controversial expression existed not as a result of Parliamentary decision but more or less as an accident, in the hands of people whose qualifications for the work were unknown and whose activities were subject to no formal control by society. Perhaps worst of all was the fact that it operated not only against public shows but also private. Since the Board could not sanction films for specific shows as the Lord Chamberlain could plays, it 'must handicap payment by the film of serious attention to the problems of life',[67] and the film society and specialist or repertory cinema movements were greatly hampered.

Joynson-Hicks quoted with approval the Cardinal Archbishop of Westminster:

'No silly prating about the necessity of elucidating problems, or that "to the pure all things are pure", or that the claims of art must be satisfied, which we frequently hear, can change the moral law, or alter the fundamental facts of human nature."[68]

Unfortunately great power was exercised at this point by people whose contempt for the film was equalled only by their ignorance of it. Joynson-Hicks himself had great influence over film censorship during the twenties as Home Secretary. He clarified his attitude to censorship in his pamphlet called *Do We Need a Censor?* in 1929, after he had become Lord Brentford. In an inept attempt to reach fundamentals he equated censorship with any form of legal action against criminals, and even referred to the arrest of a murderer as an act of censorship. In fact censorship, depending on unwritten rules applied in advance of wrong-doing by a discretionary authority, is a radically different form of control to law, where punishment is exacted only after the breach of known rules has been established by an open trial, with rights of defence and appeal. But the misleading analogy is not unusual. A serious American writer many years later wrote:

'The mechanics of the penal code are inadequate to prevent the exhibition of such pictures in as much as prosecutions cannot be made until after the "damage" has been done.'[69]

But a murderer, also, cannot be prosecuted until after the 'damage' is done and the laws against libel are, presumably, as effective in preventing libels as laws against murder in preventing murder. The ability to treat a would-be utterer of libel differently from a would-be murderer and to censor, or prevent, him is a practical matter. He announces his intention, whereas a murderer rarely does so. But many people who would be horrified at the idea of government without the rule of law in any other sphere of life will accept this breach of it. Perhaps this is partly because of the difficulty of defining the minutiae of such things as pornography in advance. Indeed, attempts to do so have a way of sounding pornographic themselves or, worse still, ridiculous. Nevertheless, there seems little to recommend a system in which matters admittedly difficult of definition and agreement were left to the discretion of a body uncontrolled by, and not responsible to, any organ of public control and operating under imprecise directives about matters of taste.

Doubts began to appear as to whether the system was satisfactory, and what alternatives were possible. No one at this time suggested that a total absence of censorship and a reliance on ordinary law instead was desirable. Even Ivor Montagu conceded that regulations for the ordinary commercial cinema should be more stringent than those for plays because of the nature of the audience. His objection was to such controls being applied indiscriminately to films not in the mainstream of commercial cinema. The question seemed to the opponents of the Board to be whether some form of official censorship might not prove more broad-minded and more subject to democratic control. It was probably realized that any attempt to do away with censorship entirely in show business was likely to lead to some form of self-censorship like that of the Board because of the investment involved. Eric Walter White, considering the vicissitudes of imported films, wrote in 1928:

'Perhaps a solution of these difficulties would be for the League of Nations to set up an international board of censors that should pass all films or cause them to be modified, once and for all.'[70]

Even the Board itself considered the possibility of a third class of certificate in October 1927, to cover films which, although not family entertainment, should not be banned entirely. In March 1929 *Close Up* organized a petition to help bring about a revision of the system. Two major complaints in the petition were the mutilating cuts made in foreign films and the high customs duties which made it difficult to import films which were of interest only to minority audiences. It was asked that third category of certificate, neither A nor U, should be created for films of artistic, scientific and educative value; that such films should be entitled to a rebate of customs duties and reduction of entertainment tax: and that the board of censors should include people qualified to distinguish films of this calibre. The Parliamentary elections of that year, holding out the promise of a more liberal attitude from the Labour Party, led to some delay, after which several attempts to raise the matter in the Commons met with disappointing failure.

The shortcomings of the system seemed too obvious to be tolerated for much longer. Montagu concluded with admirable optimism:

'Power without responsibility is the negation of English Constitutional principle. Realisation of the position—must lead to its revision.'[71]

But the democratic processes work slowly, and the system was to remain firmly in control for some time to come. The triviality of film content was unchanged. As the Commission on Educational and Cultural Films was to report in the early thirties:

'Plain vulgarity may do little harm. It is the steady stream of third-rate films passed for "Universal Exhibition" which is the danger, with its sentimental and sham-emotional standards of value applied to unreal people.'[72]

CHAPTER THREE

The Film Trade

At the end of the war there was still a large number of renters, most of them independent private companies operating in comparatively small provincial territories, making their own choice of the many films offered by film publishers in London. During the next decade this situation changed completely. The open market, with its many small films of varying age, disappeared entirely. The situation which had emerged by the end of the period was one in which a comparatively small number of large renting firms, national in scale and with large capital resources, handled a much smaller number of films which were, however, longer and more individual in character. The renters were linked in several ways to the producers. Some, especially the American ones, were agencies or subsidiaries of production companies. A few of them became sponsors of British or joint British-foreign production, partially financing films which would be handled by them on completion. This trend greatly increased with the coming of quota legislation in 1927, when American renters began to sponsor production in British studios to make sure of the British quota they were now obliged to handle. The outstanding features of development in renting during the twenties was its growing concentration in the hands of a small number of prosperous and powerful firms, and the predominance among these of the subsidiaries of big American companies.

This concentration in the hands of a few large and powerful companies can be seen if we study the identity of the renting companies, and the number of films handled by each firm at the beginning, middle and end of the period.*

For the year of December 1919 to November 1920 *Kine Year Book* lists 64 renting firms, offering 891 new feature films. Of the 64 firms we may say that 17, each handling 15 films or more in the year, were important; and these firms handled no less than 74 per cent of the total number of films. But as much as 65 per cent of the total was actually handled by no more than nine major firms in this list, each with 29 films or more.

Butcher's F.S.	23	Ideal	14
Film Booking Offices	40	Jury	76
Famous–Lasky F.S.	89	L.I.F.T.C.	29
Fox	67	Pathé Frères Cinema	24
Gaumont F.H.S.	37	Phillips Film Co.	17
General Film Renting	19	Stoll Film Co.	22
Goldwyn	26	Vitagraph F.H.S.	51
Granger's Exclusives	17	Walturdaw	50
		Western Import	62

* Information for this section is taken from the *Kine Year Books* for 1921, 1927 and 1930.

Some of the renters in this list were anxious to specialize in British films. Butcher's, an early company founded and run by F. W. Baker, remained a private company throughout the period and handled British productions of different makes, including many Hepworth films; their first American picture was not announced until 1924. Gaumont's included their own British films with some imported ones. Ideal was incorporated in 1921 (capital £172,500) to market the films of the Ideal production firm, and Stoll's also had a renting subsidiary. Jury and Walturdaw continued to handle British films along with others, and Granger's Exclusives and General Film Renters were new companies founded to distribute British films. G.F.R. began as a private company. G.F.R. (1920) was founded in February 1920 with a capital of £60,000 to take over Barker Motion Photography and the earlier G.F.R., and with a contract for films of the G. B. Samuelson production company. Granger's Exclusives was started towards the end of the war by A. G. Granger, also with pro-British declarations. Granger's, like G.F.R., had production contracts which included one with Samuelson. It is unfortunate that the efforts which were being made to provide outlets for British films had such poor material to handle, confirming the vicious circle of small output and poor distribution facilities.

Firms handling American films, on the other hand, prospered. The six large firms handling American films, in most cases those of their parent companies, were Film Booking Offices, Famous–Lasky, Fox, Goldwyn, Vitagraph and Western Import, and they accounted for 38 per cent of the total number of films; in fact five of these firms had about half of the films we have mentioned above as being in the hands of the seventeen important companies. The Famous–Lasky Film Service had begun life in February 1915 as J. D. Walker's World Films and was reformed in March 1919, with a capital of £20,000, under its chairman and managing director from America J. C. Graham; they handled the much sought-after American output of Famous Players–Lasky and occasioned one of the greatest block-booking controversies with their '104 Policy', by which they contracted to supply a block of 104 films over a period of a year. Film Booking Offices was incorporated in October 1919 with the large capital of £100,000, its directors being Sir Edward Hulton, W. C. Jeapes, A. and A. Clozenberg and F. A. Enders as managing director. Fox Film Company had been incorporated in 1916 during the war, Vitagraph as far back as 1912, and Goldwyn's was registered in June 1920 as a private company with a capital of £50,000. Big business was taking shape. Not only was Sir Edward Hulton in Film Booking Offices, but another newspaper magnate, Lord Beaverbrook, had also entered renting with a share in Pathé in February 1920. Both these discerning tycoons were interested in renting rather than exhibition, and in handling imported rather than British films, a comment on the profits to be expected from making or distributing British films. But two firms that were going to be important in providing backing to British production before long, Wardour and W. & F., were quietly established during this period, although neither yet handled British films. W. & F. Film Service, with a capital of £10,000, was founded by S. Freedman, D. Tebbitt, J. Hagen and C. M. Woolf in February 1919, and Wardour Films, with £50,000, by John Maxwell in September 1919.

There was considerable anxiety about the supposed intention of American firms to open branches in Britain, or even to go further and start production here. After a while any casual visitor or location seeker was suspected of forming a company in England. Even a rumour that United Artists contemplated renting their popular films directly to exhibitors here was heralded in *The Bioscope* as the beginning of an invasion.

A number of the larger renters had branches in provincial cities, especially Birmingham, Leeds, Liverpool, Manchester and Newcastle, and in addition there were many small local renters serving small areas.

The organization of renters for their mutual advantage in the Kinematograph Renters' Society was easier and more successful than the organization of the many exhibitors in the C.E.A., and was intensified by the concentration of renting during the twenties. After some agitation in the northern counties just after the war, about half a dozen provincial branches were formed with small local memberships. But this was bound to become less important as the trade became concentrated into a few companies of national scope, and the branches became fewer and smaller during the decade. In 1920 there were 33 members of the K.R.S., or 63 members if we include members of provincial branches. These included all the important firms handling 15 or more films each, except Goldwyn's. Famous–Lasky, the largest renter of all with 89 films, had joined late in 1919.

By 1926 the number of films had fallen from 891 to 709, partly because of the generally depressed state of the industry and partly because of the gradual disappearance of the short, mass-produced film in favour of fewer, longer, individually advertised films. The number of firms renting the films had fallen from 64 to 43, and the growing concentration was clearly seen. Instead of the 9 major firms with 29 films or more, 8 less important firms with 15 to 28 films and 49 small firms with less than 15, there was a much clearer division of the market into 15 large firms each handling 20 films or more, and 28 much smaller firms with outputs of less than 10 films each. The 15 larger firms handled 562 or nearly 80 per cent of the total number of films, and whereas most of them had from 20 to 50 films, two companies, European and Famous–Lasky, had over 50 each.

Butcher's	24	Ideal	29
European	55	Jury–Goldwyn	33
Famous–Lasky	64	Pathé	33
F.B.O.	26	P.D.C.	29
First National	47	Stoll	25
Fox	49	Wardour	43
Gaumont	48	Western Import	22
		W. & F.	35

This was the nadir of British production and Butcher's, Stoll and Gaumont now handled very few British films, Ideal and Jury none. However, New Era was registered in August 1923 as a private company, with a capital of £10,000 and with H. Bruce Woolfe, E. Gordon Craig and C. L. Buckle on the Board, to handle the new British Instructional Films output. These films, although distinctive, were few in number. The only one of the big companies which had a considerable number of British productions was W. & F., with a number of important films made by Gainsborough under various financial arrangements. But with Harold Lloyd, Snub Pollard, Our Gang and many others on their lists, W. & F. were not dependent on their British films. G.F.R. and Walturdaw had been wound up by 1924. Wardour, which was now national in scale, and from September 1924 had Arthur Dent (previously of Waverley Films), as Sales Manager, had no British films at all.

The vast majority of the films came from America. The big American companies Famous–Lasky, F.B.O., Fox, Jury–Goldwyn and Western Import, together with two big newcomers First National and European, and the smaller Warner–Vitagraph, provided as much as 44 per cent of the total number of films. They were, moreover, the most popular films. Jury–Metro–Goldwyn, as it was later called, was formed by a merger first of Metro–Goldwyn early in 1924, which was joined by Jury in August. Its authorized capital was £200,000 and the managing director Sam Eckman. Sir William Jury retired in 1927 at 57.[2] With films like *Greed*, *The Merry Widow* and the Jackie Coogan productions they had little need for British films, and Jury's pro-British policy died out. Producers Distributing Company was incorporated with £10,000 capital in August 1925, primarily to distribute the films of Cecil De Mille. The old firm of Vitagraph was reconstituted as Warner Brothers Pictures in November 1926 under a British managing director, Arthur Clavering. Associated First National was formed as an entirely British concern in 1921 to take over the distribution here of the pictures of First National of America made by Ince, Max Sennett, Vidor, the Talmadges, Buster Keaton and Charles Ray. European Motion Picture Company was established in 1923 to handle the large output of Universal, Carl Laemmle's company.

As for the K.R.S., there were now 31 London members, or 48 members including those of the provincial branches, which had become less important. The London membership was more or less the same as before, with minor changes, mostly among the small firms. Goldwyn now belonged, as Jury–Metro–Goldwyn, and the K.R.S. at last included all the bigger firms with twenty or more films a year except Fox and the large new firm of European. The former, with 49 films, had previously been a member.

The independent renter of the early twenties, who had tried to choose the best pictures from all sources, had already declined by 1924. Branches of American firms, whether technically British firms or not, handled only the imported films of their parent companies. As early as January 1923 P. A. Powers, managing director of F.B.O. in the United States, was reported to have said that the big American producers' sales organizations would finally oust British renters, and that British producers would eventually have to distribute through American firms.

By the period from December 1927 to November 1928 the number of renting firms had fallen again to 36. The number of films suggested the end of the depression and had risen slightly to 722, but was not up to the 1920 figure because of the changed nature of production.

The pattern of distribution had become clearer. 84 per cent of all the films were handled by 14 large renters, each with 18 films or more. But as much as 33 per cent of all the films were actually in the hands of three American companies, two of them fairly new, European, First National–Pathé and Paramount, which had previously been Famous–Lasky. It was conspicuous that these three firms dominated the market with 86, 76 and 75 films respectively. The other 11 of the larger firms were considerably smaller with from 18 to 48 films each.

Butcher's F.S.	19	Jury–Metro–Goldwyn	37
European	86	Paramount	75
F.B.O.	21	P.D.C.	42
F.N.–Pathé	76	Wardour	38
Fox	47	Warner	27
Gaumont	48	W. Import	18
Ideal	46	W. & F.	30

The domination of the market by American films and those handling them was very noticeable. British films were beginning to be adopted by these companies for quota purposes, although the process had only just begun. Butcher's handled a few. First National–Pathé, which had been incorporated in December 1927, handled a few films made by agreement with them or under their auspices in the United Kingdom. Gaumont had the output of Gaumont–British and a few other British or joint British–foreign films. Ideal had the Edgar Wallace films being made by British Lion. Paramount early acquired a few British films with some prestige, those of Welsh–Pearson and British National, and Wardour and W. & F. were about to be integrated with British International Pictures and Gainsborough respectively. European had as yet no British films.

By 1928 the K.R.S. had 34 London members, or 47 members including London and the provincial branches. The London membership included every important renter handling 18 or more films, with the large and noticeable exception of European with its 86 films. The number of the London renters had thus not changed much since 1920, although the personnel had changed a little. The over-all fall in membership was due to the decreasing importance of provincial branches, which in turn reflected the centralization of renting. Throughout the twenties it was a comparatively small and controllable fraternity, whose deliberations were less wild, anarchic and exciting than those of the exhibitors but considerably more to the point.

The renters, indeed, occupied a key position in the film industry and had secured virtual control of it by the end of the twenties. In the following chapters we shall watch this come about, and with it the domination of the British market by American interests. It is not suggested that there was any malevolent intention. But the expensive and elaborate nature of film production and its retail outlet, the cinema, were such as to put decisive power in the hands of the middlemen. And their interests were naturally somewhat narrower than those of people who were beginning to see the great potential of the film as an art and a means of communication.

The large output of America, which had already more than covered its cost at home, flooded the British market at prices, and with a publicity, which local producers could not match. By the practices of block booking and advance booking renters inadvertently killed the earlier British production structure. Perhaps much of it deserved to die. But the booking abuses, the fate of so many British producers, and the renters' indifference to voluntary trade schemes to remedy the situation, led directly to the quota legislation of the later twenties. And this, while attempting to regulate the industry, soon led to further degradation. The Quota Quickie of the thirties was the renters' cynical reply to attempts to rehabilitate British film production. At the same time renters' advances, and the distribution they were able to assure, were the only means of survival for British production of any sort. The more enlightened companies were responsible for financing a small number of good films. But it is not in the nature of an industry organized on such lines to favour experiment or variety, and the monotonous dictatorship of a mass market made it less and less possible for independence to appear.

While the producers' dependence on the renter increased, so did that of exhibitors. The contracts by which renters agreed to bar the showing of their films for periods, and over areas, which depended on the bargaining strength of the cinema, meant that a profitable hall, which could afford to book an early run and bar its competitors over the maximum area and for the maximum time, was in a position to impair its competitors' bargaining power permanently thereby. As the successful cinemas grouped into circuits to secure better terms and in the later twenties were finally integrated with the renters, the latter successfully refused to deal with booking co-operatives which independent exhibitors tried to form in self-defence. In this way was laid down the rigid pattern of exhibition which was familiar to later generations of cinema-goers, with the same films being shown repeatedly all over the country, first in comfortable and expensive cinemas and then down the scale until they ended, scratched and cut but cheap, in the flea pits. Films which could not expect the maximum public did not find favour in the first place with the powerful combines controlling production, exhibition and distribution; but had they been produced at all they would soon have found too few independent cinemas of reasonable status and price to make even a modest showing. The independent cinema, able to take a more varied selection of films loosely known as repertory, was able to exist tenuously only in London. It was as though, in the world of books or music, nothing but the popular novel or song of the day were ever available. While film societies and a few cinemas were testing the possibility of minority audiences, the exhibition strait-jacket of the large circuits was generally accepted as the only possible structure.

Enough has been said already to indicate that in international trade, also, the situation was dominated by the enormous volume of American film imported into this country. Before the war London had been a world clearing house for the large mass of open market films, many of them imported in negative form and printed here for foreign buyers, giving a large export figure against smaller imports. London was a distributor of whole foreign outputs, imported for a round sum and sold over a period of months. Early in the war, as part of the McKenna Duties, an import duty had been imposed of 1s 3d a foot on blank film, 1d on positive and 5d on negative. This combined with other factors to destroy London's position as a world market. It became advantageous to import a positive rather than a negative unless five or more copies were going to be printed. The war situation itself made it impossible for London to continue being the printing and clearing house for the Continental market. Meanwhile there was a shift from an open market for many small films to the fewer, individually-known films, with publicity for the producers and even for the film rather than for the middleman's brand. Big American producers began to set up their own retail outlets, not only in England but in other European countries. After the war ended fluctuating exchange rates added to the difficulties facing small British agents who bought outputs in bulk for gradual sale to other countries. Foreign countries also imposed import regulations, and it became a general practice for films to be imported in negative form to the country of distribution and printed there. Many films brought to Britain stayed in the Bonded Film Stores until sent to destinations abroad, and did not appear in our trade figures.

Nevertheless, immediately after the war people were optimistic and thought that the pre-war position would return. British producers expected to export once more. It was pointed out at a meeting held to consider the question in 1919 that whereas £800 was a normal return on a British film sent to America and £5,000 an exceptionally high figure, from £3,000 to £15,000 might be sent back to the United States for one of the many American pictures in the United Kingdom. A number of firms set out to capture markets abroad, but many of the films sent were second-rate. Granger's *Call of the Road* (1920), *Unmarried* (1920) and *Weavers of Fortune* (1922), for example, were not representative of the best in Britain and were already out of date in 1923 when a mutual exchange was arranged with the French firm Films Le Grand in 1923.[3] Godal disposed of *Nobody's Child*, *A Sinless Sinner* and *Queen's Evidence* in America in 1920, films which could only deal another blow at British prestige.[4] W. A. Northam went to America in 1919 to show British pictures which, according to his bitter complaint on his return, nobody even came to see, but an American correspondent sadly replied that his offerings were of 'a school of production which was considered very good in this country about nine or ten years ago'.[5] G. B. Samuelson not only got a showing on Broadway for *The Elder Miss Blossom* (called *Choosing a Wife* in U.S.A.), where it was considered slow, but boldly went on to California to produce half a dozen films in an attempt to create an international link. The idea may have been praiseworthy, but the films could do little for the British reputation. Phillips Film Company, which specialized in export, did comparatively well in America with the B. & C. *12.10*. The Ivy Duke–Guy Newall film *The Bigamist*, Stoll's *Adventures of Sherlock Holmes*, Hepworth's *Alf's Button* and *The Amazing Quest of Mr Ernest Bliss*, and British Instructional's *The Battle of Jutland* were among a few better British films which were exported with comparative success, and Harley Knoles himself took

Carnival over to America in 1921 to ensure its showing. Hepworth also went to America, and his company as well as Stoll's attempted to set up a permanent sales organization there. Alliance, too, negotiated an early distribution contract with First National Exhibitors' Circuit in America.[6]

But this school of British production was deservedly on the point of collapse at home. The new style of producer also visited America with his new films, but discovered that tripper methods of sales promotion were not good enough. More consistent and aggressive export methods were needed, with titling and adaptation for different tastes and a knowledge of what each market needed, as well as a regular supply of films. In this Britain was hampered by the smallness of her output and the small capital of her producers. An ill-advised habit of using faded stars from Hollywood to give the films export appeal ignored the fact that great films make stars, not the reverse.

A great deal was heard of the unfairness of other countries. But other countries, especially America, in fact did not need our films, despite the kind and patronizing assurances from visitors such as Eugene Zukor, William Fox and Goldwyn who came to reconnoitre the advantages of producing here in the years immediately following the war. We *do* want your pictures . . . if they are any good, of course . . . which unfortunately they aren't. '. . . what a wonderfully rich, untapped vein of material you have . . .' as one visitor said politely.[7] Untapped indeed, with so many producers confined by their own tastes, and what they believed to be their audiences' tastes, to stilted society drama. But in the absence of a film so outstanding that it could turn the tide and create a demand where none had existed before, there was little reason for American cinemas to put on British films. It disappeared altogether as huge combines of circuits, renters and producers took over the American market. Formal distribution agreements with these were the only hope for British exporters. A suggestion made in 1924 that British producers might combine to form a joint distribution organization in America was ignored.

Meanwhile changes were taking place in the rest of the world. Other countries began to take German pictures again soon after the war, and Pola Negri's *Passion*, for example, was a box office hit in America during 1921. The German Kontingent system of legalizing the import of only a small ratio of what they produced at home was started in 1920. In Britain the import ban on German films had been dropped early in 1920, but in December 1921 the C.E.A. was still arguing, with some emotion, whether British cinemas should take German films or maintain the ten-year ban they had unwisely imposed in 1918, and a decision was not reached until well into 1922. *Dr Mabuse*, *The Golem* and *The Cabinet of Dr Caligari* were seen here during the next year and by the mid- and late-twenties German films had considerable prestige in Britain. A number of British production firms obtained production and distribution contracts with German firms during the next few years.

France had taken its own steps to deal with the problems of American imports and had imposed a 20 per cent *ad valorem* import duty. In the same year America itself, discussing the Fordney Tariff Bill, had considered a 20 to 30 per cent *ad valorem* duty on films going into the States, although this had been successfully opposed. Britain clung to the idea of the Empire as an alternative market

to America, and removed the import duty on Empire films in March 1919.
But both as a source of films and as a market for them, the Empire proved to
be something of an illusion.

In 1924 the McKenna Duties were lifted by the Labour Government, a move
not welcomed by the film printers, who since their imposition had built up a
printing business estimated by Brooke Wilkinson at some 250,000 feet a week.[7]
The duties were reimposed in 1925 by Winston Churchill, as Chancellor, when
the Conservatives returned to power.* The import duty had no doubt played
its part in the decline of London as a world market. But the situation had moved
far beyond that, and the market was by now overwhelmingly dominated by
American imports. Churchill said in reply to a Parliamentary Question in 1927
that about £3 million was paid for foreign films every year. As the *Moyne Report*
later said:

'By the year 1923 British production had revived to a degree that made it possible
for about 10 per cent of the films exhibited in Great Britain to be British made;
but it subsequently declined again in face of foreign competition and in 1926
the proportion of British films shown over the country as a whole appears to
have been not more than 5 per cent. The actual proportion of exhibitions of
British films on the screen at that time was probably well below 5 per cent owing
to the larger percentage of exhibition dates secured by American films through
the system of blind and block booking.'[8]

Consideration of remedies for the worsening situation went beyond the
imposition of a small import duty. As early as 1923 a 33⅓ per cent import tax
on American imports had been suggested by a Conservative MP, Sir Arthur
Holbrook[9] but had been turned down by the Board of Trade on the grounds
that it would upset the exhibitors. When the McKenna duties were reimposed
The Bioscope considered the possible value of an import tax as high as 10s or £1
a foot, but rejected it on the grounds that it would encourage bad quality British
production.[10] It was seen that any heavy import tax would make imported films
much more expensive without necessarily increasing British production, and a
Kontingent or Quota system was suspected as a shelter for home mediocrity.
Nevertheless it became obvious that something had to be done. The talk caused
some anxiety in America, where according to a statement by Will Hays 25 to
30 per cent of the total revenue came from the foreign markets.[11]

Some pinned their hopes on the principle of Reciprocity. There had long been
an optimistic belief that it would actually pay American producers to have
reciprocal agreements with the best British firms. In 1926, during the year
granted to the trade by the Home Office to sort out its own problems (see page
94), Thomas Ormiston worked hard to get his Reciprocity Plan accepted. It
was submitted to the industry's Joint Trade Committee in June.[12] It was a
five-year plan for films, each having a production cost of at least £10,000, to be
handled by American firms in the ratio of 1 to every 25 American films distributed

* A jump in imports during this year was largely due to imports of raw stock during the
two months' grace before the duties came into effect again.

79

here; the producer was to receive a third of the gross rental receipts in America and Canada. British producers were opposed to the plan, and the renters were divided. T. C. Elder and Michael Balcon, having had some experience of the American market, did not regard it as a practical solution. The plan was supported only by E. E. Lyons, Simon Rowson and T. A. Welsh, the latter adding the proviso that there should be a British distributing agency in America.

Meanwhile individual distribution and production contracts which included some measure of reciprocity between certain English and foreign firms, chiefly American and German, increased in number from about 1924 onwards. *Woman to Woman*, whose distribution in America and other countries was arranged by Balcon, was one of the new modern type of big feature film which could be expected to stand on its own merits, and was followed by *The Rat* and *The Passionate Adventure*. In spite of some success Balcon became sceptical about the value of American distribution and later favoured links with German companies instead. Wilcox and Maxwell, both of whom retained their confidence in the American market, were others of the new style of tycoon who, armed with important productions, set out to prove them in America. But in general the prestige of British films abroad was so low that even when quota legislation was introduced in 1927 to remedy the situation at home, few were bold enough to tackle the question of British exports.

The concentration and power of the renters, and the domination of the market by the Americans, were factors in an economic situation which finally brought government intervention into the film industry on a large scale. The central difficulty of British film production was, and has remained, its peculiar liability to American competition. It was during the twenties that this, and its commercial consequences, led to the first attempt to bolster production by State action. Problems set by trade practices in the twenties and the solution attempted in the quota legislation of 1927 continued to be relevant decades later.

The home market was in a state of conflict throughout the twenties, with renting and exhibiting struggling for control. We have seen that neither side was fully united. Small exhibitors' interests were not the same as those of larger firms or circuits, and among the renters the interests of the large and powerful American companies were not the same as those of British or independent renters. The interests of British producers were apparently irrelevant, but owing to factors which were not strictly economic they complicated the issue at certain stages. The controversial issues of the day evolved out of the general movement to push film prices up, and to get the free-for-all of the open market organized into a stable system in which the strong got stronger and the weak got weaker. Conflict centred round the renters' desire to enforce sharing terms and stiff barring contracts, and also to cream the market by holding pre-release runs with shop-window cinemas and tied houses. The renters' most powerful weapons were the booking of films far in advance, often unseen, and often in blocks which might contain only one or two productions really wanted by the showman. The exhibitors' and producers' resistance included an attempt to reduce the number of films on the market by means of an import tax; the efforts of Ormiston, Lord Beaverbrook and others to secure trade agreements; the British Film

League's campaign to promote British films; and finally, when all else failed, the movement for legislation to prevent the outstanding booking abuses and to compel the trade to handle a legal quota of British films.

After the war, films were sold to dealers by the makers on a flat rate or, in the case of many American films, handled by the maker's agency in this country. The renter then put them on the market on an exclusive basis, with territorial rights which were sold to different dealers or exhibitors all over the country. Trade shows were held by the firm issuing the film, whether in London or in the various territories, but films were also booked on the basis of systems of marking by the C.E.A. and others which were heartily disliked by the K.R.S. in early years. The old open market was more or less dead except for short films.

The cost of film production had gone up a great deal since before the war and higher returns were necessary. There was much resistance to putting up the price of cinema seats, but some realignment of the price structure was inevitable. Controversy and struggle over model contracts and barring, percentage booking, tied houses and the practice of blind and advance booking and block booking were complicated by resentment of the big American interests' intrusion into the British market, but all were basically aimed at getting a better price.

The Stoll–Goldwyn dispute of 1919 was limited in its repercussions, but it showed the way the wind was blowing, and illustrates both the raising of film prices and the growing power of the American firms. The desirable Goldwyn Star films were productions in the new post-war manner, expensive to make and widely advertised. The American firm estimated that 80 per cent of the receipts of their films came from the United States, 10 per cent from the United Kingdom and another 10 per cent from the rest of the world. Thus their profit from British exhibitors, although relatively small, was not a matter of indifference to them. In the summer of 1918 they were offering 18 films, to be released in the next film season of September 1918 to August 1919. In December 1918 and February 1919 they signed agreements with Stoll whereby the latter acquired sole United Kingdom rights in return for 60 per cent of the gross profits, paying £10,000 in advance. In January Stoll proudly announced the 18 films and began to take bookings. During 1919 the films began to be available, but Goldwyn explained that production had been delayed by the 1918/19 'flu epidemic and the last 6 films would not be available under the current agreement. Stoll was obliged to announce this fact and cancel the contracts on these six films. They later claimed that these were worth £41,000, adding that they had hoped final bookings might total £60,000. It was being said openly that Goldwyn was finding receipts from the United Kingdom exhibitors too low in view of the greatly increased cost of production. Stoll and the exhibitors who had booked the films were angry, and had the support of both the C.E.A. and the K.R.S. In December 1919 the C.E.A. recommended a boycott of the 6 films in question.

Jeffrey Bernerd of Stoll went to America and was offered the 6 films as part of a new agreement, with others, for the 1919/20 season. But according to a cable, later quoted in court, Goldwyn now wanted, for 49 pictures, the sum of £220,000 as well as £58,000 for the prints; assuming that this represented the previous share of 60 per cent, it implied total receipts of £464,664, whereas

Stoll claimed that they could not, in fact, expect more than £296,500 in all. They maintained that Goldwyn's action was a manoeuvre to put the price up for the 6 films already covered by contract. They claimed these at the earlier price, and refused to sign.

Goldwyn agreed that the films would be more expensive but denied that this was the reason they had been delayed. Early in 1920 the peace was rent by acrimonious correspondence and press statements, with Stoll, the K.R.S. and the C.E.A. on one side, and Goldwyn, coldly holding all the cards, on the other. That most difficult weapon, the boycott, was declared in February 1920. But by May the C.E.A., doubtless aware that solidarity was never strong among its members and that the films were exceptionally tempting, was losing interest. Goldwyn was bound to win, for not only did they have films that people wanted, but in June they quietly moved into the British distribution market and registered their own company (registered capital £50,000). After this, opposition died away and the embargo was lifted in July. A legal action was brought in 1923 and settled out of court.[15]

It was true that production costs had risen a great deal, especially in America and more had to be wrung out of the exhibitors. Simply to put the flat rate up would make films too expensive for the less prosperous cinemas. One logical answer was percentage booking, or payment by results as it was called at first, but this made very slow headway.

We have seen in the Goldwyn–Stoll case that the producer might let a renter have his film for a lump sum worked out as a percentage of his estimated take or as a straight percentage. It was a short step to a percentage basis for cinemas, and pre-release runs in big London cinemas or theatres were normally on this basis. Reports were arriving from America after the war that payment by results was even being asked of ordinary exhibitors, who might be required to pay the renter a proportion of their box office take instead of a flat rate.

It was pointed out in favour of this that if producers were more involved in a film's success at the box office their work would improve. An item in *The Bioscope* in 1920 said that the 50–50 principle was now being adopted by some renting houses.[14] By 1923 it was said that Associated First National had taken to percentage booking and that Jury, among the English renters, was in favour of it.[15] Nevertheless, the system was not yet usual and Balcon, speaking later of the twenties as a whole, said that bookings were made on a 'highly competitive flat figure basis, sharing terms being unknown.[16] This is confirmed by L'Estrange Fawcett's account in 1927.[17] Percentage booking was discussed throughout the period, with renters largely in favour of it, but with bitter opposition from many exhibitors. As *The Bioscope* somewhat awkwardly phrased it:

'. . . in disclosing to the renter the money-earning propensities of one's hall, one is creating a rod for one's own back.'[18]

Apart from not wanting to disclose their own takings and cut down the profit which everyone dreamed of making on an exceptionally good buy, exhibitors feared that renters would prefer to do business with more profitable halls and, like so many other new ideas, it would go against the small man. The C.E.A. Branches fought the idea and at a General Council meeting it was described as 'vile and abominable'.[19] Exhibitors, much given to passing resolutions in favour of boycotts and co-operation, lacked cohesion and rarely kept them. The system gained ground. Finally, when sound films arrived and were both expensive and speculative, renters found it much easier to persuade exhibitors to accept sharing terms. As it happened, sound films did well. But it was too late for exhibitors to return to the former system.

Thus, during the twenties as the open market died, percentage booking was very gradually taking its place. At the same time, out of the old 'exclusive' film there developed an elaborate system of bars on how long, and over how wide an area, other exhibitors were to be barred from showing the film. These were written into the contract and the more profitable and powerful the cinema signing the contract, the bigger the bars they were able to secure. This made model contracts the subject of bitter wrangling.

Negotiations between renters and exhibitors were found to follow common patterns, and in February 1919 the K.R.S. published a Model Contract regulating such things as the method of cross-overs, dates of dispatch, and time and place bars. A seven days bar was suggested. The C.E.A. did not approve of the renters' Model and after discussion it was decided to operate their own provisional contract for a year. Meanwhile the C.E.A. Scottish Branch prepared their own version of a contract incorporating a two weeks bar. In March 1920 a new K.R.S. draft was produced. Then in May a new C.E.A. version was discussed by a Joint Committee of the C.E.A. and K.R.S., but the exhibitors' modifications were rejected by the K.R.S. and in July the C.E.A. published its own Fair Clauses Contract which it instructed members to use. The barring period was left blank. The K.R.S. itself refused to accept this, although the Scottish renters and Jury, Goldwyn and Vitagraph, not at that time members of the K.R.S., were prepared to consider agreement. A short period of chaos in renting ensued. In September this was resolved by a Joint Meeting at which the version preferred by the Scottish renters and the exhibitors was recommended. Later on several model contracts existed side by side, the Fair Clauses Contract of the C.E.A., the K.R.S. draft contract and a Simultaneous Signature Contract used by Associated First National.[20] At the end of 1924 a New Standard Contract was formally adopted by the C.E.A. and the K.R.S.,[21] but its use was by no means universal.

In the second half of the twenties, discussion of barring became more open, and it was clear that this was the main reason for the continual dissension over contracts. It could also be seen that time and distance bars, successfully sought by first-run and prosperous cinemas, were having the effect of perpetuating the differences between them and the less successful. Once negotiated, bars tend to be maintained, and to perpetuate or reinforce the advantages or disadvantages which had led to them in the first place. They thus give formal shape to the pecking order of cinemas, and the traditional division into good-class halls and flea pits. This was especially so after 1927, when the growth of the circuits reinforced barring to lower the bargaining power of the small independent. Renter's bars, by which shop-window runs were held in London and even some other big cities, were also greatly resented. As we have seen, the wide publicity and the announcement that it would be months before there would be another chance to see the film attracted many of the ordinary exhibitors' potential customers to such shows and left the former fuming about unfair competition.

The tied house, or pre-release cinema tied to a big renter, was another aspect of the stratification of halls by bars and contracts, and one more way in which renters maximized their own receipts. Their argument that the prestige of such shows was helpful publicity for the later bookings was regarded with deep suspicion by ordinary showmen. The Famous–Lasky dispute over this in 1919 caused a furore. It showed the desire of the big American producers to get more out of exhibition by moving into it themselves if necessary, and at the same time demonstrated the fear that many small and disorganized British exhibitors had of the Americans, the renters, and the circuits. In the middle of 1919 a new million pound company with a large circuit called Picture Playhouses was in process of formation. Its capital was to be 90 per cent British, and five of the seven directors were British. But its directorate interlocked with that of Famous–Lasky in the persons of J. C. Graham and C. A. Clegg.[22] The obvious link with the Famous Players' American productions and the expected output of Famous–Lasky's English studio caused an almost hysterical outburst among some English exhibitors, who feared their own access to the films would be affected. Famous–Lasky Film Service assured them that the only formal connection they had with the proposed circuit was to provide them with a constant supply of pictures, and that other cinemas would continue to be served as before. But there was a genuine fear of trusts and unfair competition, and in the arguments that followed the position of P.C.T., and its former link with the London Film Company (see Volume III), was not ignored. As usual a boycott was suggested but, also as usual, the disunity of exhibitors made such a thing impossible. At all events by the end of 1919 the proposal for a circuit had been dropped. Famous–Lasky was in trouble again later. At the end of 1926 Paramount, as it was then called, acquired two cinemas in Birmingham, Sol Levy's Scala and Futurist Cinemas. Once again the hint of danger crystallized opposition, and once again the exhibitors talked wildly about boycotts. But this time there was no question of a circuit, and in fact Paramount used only one of the cinemas, and that one as a showcase. There was no real danger of an American invasion of exhibition. Most big American firms had pre-release cinemas in London by the end of the twenties (see page 50), and there was little reason for American producers or renters to seek further participation in ordinary British exhibition, which was already completely dominated by their films.

Exhibition was setting into a caste structure of first-run cinemas, circuits of good-class halls, and independents. Eventually the better cinemas were drawn into the vertical integration that was going on, and their supply of films was centralized. But during much of the twenties the position was still unresolved and many showmen, still not yet gathered into circuits, could see the weakness of their position and wondered if co-operative booking might be a possible answer.

It seemed that a First National Exhibitors' Association had been formed in

America largely to get films at a better rate from the renters who were trying to increase their share by percentage bookings. In September 1920 unsuccessful efforts were made to form a similar association of some thousand members in Great Britain and Ireland.[23] In 1922 a First National Circuit was planned in England by David P. Howells, the London representative of Associated First National of America and associated with the American company.[24] These were more like loose circuits than true co-operatives, and had neither sufficient capital backing nor support from renters. But in 1927 a genuine move towards co-operative booking was made. The apparent effort of Paramount to get a foothold in exhibition in Birmingham, the imminent threat of the two growing circuits associated with P.C.T. and A.B.C., and the sight of powerful vertical combines in America operating drastic time and place bars drew attention to the insecurity of isolated British exhibitors. In November 1927 the General Council of the C.E.A. considered a proposal by Thomas Ormiston to establish a co-operative booking circuit. It was claimed that the object was not so much to keep booking prices down as to prevent the takeover of the better cinemas, leaving the rest in a hopeless position. The latter felt that acting in concert would bring their bargaining power into line with that of the circuits. It was suggested that halls of three classes, A, B and C, should contribute capital in proportion to their classification at £50, £100 or £200 each; they should get interest on this at 10 per cent, and all other profits should be divided on a basis of dividends upon film hire. The group should be controlled by a Board of Directors, one to be elected from each of the principal exchange areas and three from an agreed list of non-exchange areas. Bookings should be negotiated by a small committee, and film hire should be 25 per cent of takings. Some sort of machinery was required to avoid unnecessary competition in big pictures, and it was essential to the scheme that members should not book any picture which the circuit had failed to negotiate with the renters.[25]

The commercial circuits already in formation were hostile to the scheme. But even more important was the attitude of the K.R.S., from whose members the bulk of the films would have to come. It announced immediately that its members would refuse to deal with such a combination,[26] and its refusal successfully stopped any co-operative of exhibitors either then or at any other time. Ormiston bravely but unconvincingly maintained that film supply could be maintained direct from America. But the scheme was impracticable both because of the obdurate refusal of the K.R.S. to deal with such a co-operative and because of the small exhibitors' fatal disinclination to combine, preferring to slog on or sell out. Many years later the *Monopolies Commission Report* of 1966 quoted a K.R.S. recommendation still in force:

'. . . recommend to members that agreements for licensing the exhibition of films in any cinema should not be entered into or negotiated with any person already undertaking the booking of films for another cinema or cinemas unless all the cinemas concerned are under the same control or unless such person himself possesses the control of the first-mentioned cinema.'[27]

The renters already held all the cards, and in February 1928 the scheme was officially dropped by the C.E.A.[28]

Meanwhile, as the twenties progressed, certain practices of the renters had emerged as the chief causes of distress in the rest of the industry. These were blind booking, booking for long periods in advance, and block booking. The practices were interlocked. After the war the large renters had offered films for periods longer and longer in advance, and therefore in many cases unseen or even unmade, and frequently in blocks consisting of one or two desirable and highly publicized films together with a large number of indifferent productions. The more desirable films tended to be those of large well-known firms, usually American. As a result many exhibitors were fully booked up for periods up to eighteen months or more ahead. Smaller independent producers, a category which included most British firms, consequently found a growing difficulty in securing any bookings at all; they had to wait a long time even for these, locking their small capital up in films not yet shown. In this way it incidentally damaged British film production, and it was this fact which attracted public attention at last to the economic troubles of the industry and led to the first national effort to find a solution by legislation.

Few people had much to say openly in favour of blind or block booking or advance booking. With one voice they declared their disapproval, but each claimed that he had to do what everyone else was doing. To some extent exhibitors resented having to take films they did not like in order to get those they did, and having to book without seeing the films, but it must be assumed that their gains on the plus films usually made the minus films worth while; and in any case a few duds did not drive away their patrons, many of whom were habitual rather than selective. For the lazy or out-of-the-way showman it was not unlike the old system of contracting with a renter to supply regular programmes, which had also been booked unseen on the renter's reputation. Their polite sympathy with the British producer was verbal only and their regret at not having room for occasional British films somewhat unconvincing, considering British prices and quality at the time. Stoll, Walturdaw, Gaumont, G.F.R. and Butcher's were said to block book, and all specialized in brands of British films. Famous–Lasky with their 104 Policy, Vitagraph and Western Import were among those accused of extremes of block and advance booking, but most big firms worked the same way, however informally. Hepworth in 1919 and 1920 did his best as an individual to attach a six-month release date to his films, and in 1921 Goldwyn's announced that they would not block book or accept bookings before trade shows; later they stopped their trade shows for four months in order to shorten the existing gap. But most renters, like exhibitors, found the system simply a modern substitute for their old function of supplying regular programmes to their customers. They had even less real interest in independent British production than exhibitors had.

So when the question of block booking was raised at the K.R.S. Council Meeting in July 1919 it was briefly dismissed by R. C. Bromhead, who maintained that the remedy was in the hands of exhibitors. The latter, according to him, had in America quite simply refused to book more than three months ahead.[29] But next month, when the K.R.S. Council attempted a small measure of relief and resolved that films should not be booked before their trade shows, Jeffrey Bernerd of Stoll immediately warned that if this was enforced the larger firms would leave the K.R.S. and join others, like Famous–Lasky, who practised blind booking outside its ranks.[30]

For the K.R.S. no more controlled all renters than the C.E.A. did all exhibitors. None of the affected interests, in fact, were sufficiently united to control their members. As for the producers, a number of whom had divided loyalties as they were also large renters, they had no combined representation on the economic front. The Kinematograph Manufacturers Association, which had been formed before the war and was responsible for setting up the Censorship Board, was an association for the makers of equipment and film laboratories rather than of film producers. In the autumn of 1921 the Kinema Club was formed with premises open early in 1922 and a large membership of producers, but as a social club rather than a professional association.* Another association of British film producers was also formed in early 1922 by a group which included Manning Haynes, Fred Paul, Will Kellino, Donald Crisp, Hugh Croise, A. V. Bramble, F. Martin Thornton and the moving spirit and President, Percy Nash. Nash was followed by George W. Pearson and later Maurice Elvey, but few of the better directors seem to have supported it. It was called the British Association of Film Directors, and although its original aims were more those of a professional guild than of an industrial association, it later took some part in the quota discussions simply because there was no more suitable organization to represent the producers.

By the mid-twenties it seemed that first impressions that booking problems could be tackled by trade agreements and voluntary action were too optimistic, owing to the anarchic state of the trade, and that government action might be needed. Legislative help was not a new idea. A view strongly held at the end of the war was that there were too many films for the number of cinemas. The enormous American output flooded over here and was accommodated further and further into the future by advance booking. As cinemas were still well patronized at this early period, it appeared likely that the provision of more cinemas would take up the surplus and ease this pressure. In fact, however, as big modern cinemas opened during the ensuing years the smaller old ones closed. The alternative was to reduce the number of films. In 1921 Simon Rowson, for example, in a privately issued pamphlet, was urging a reduction in the number of films, a process in which his own prolific firm of Ideal was hardly helping. Meanwhile the K.M.A. had held a big meeting in October 1919 to consider whether the government might impose an import tax which could be expected to reduce imports. The C.E.A. and K.R.S. were invited to a joint trade conference which was held early in 1920, but with no result.[31]

Discussion now turned to ways of checking booking abuses, without legislation if possible. Later in 1920 a conference of Scottish exhibitors was urged by the exhibitor Alex B. King to consider how to stop block booking. Thomas Ormiston

* The Club made a film at studios in Walthamstow, *The Crimson Circle*, Trade Show October 1922, directed by George Ridgwell.

put forward a scheme, which they adopted and submitted to the C.E.A. for discussion. This included a ban on booking until after the local trade show, a ban on the booking of reissues, graduated time limits on booking dates to bring the gap down to three months from the trade show, and a system of deposits and disciplinary fines.[32] Ormiston's plan, which tackled forward rather than block booking, was greeted by *The Bioscope* as the solution.

During the next few months F. E. Adams of P.C.T., E. E. Lyons of Biocolour and Lord Beaverbrook also became interested in the problem of forward booking. Adams and Lyons expressed their disapproval of the Scottish scheme, and early in April Beaverbrook invited all exhibitors to a meeting at the Hyde Park Hotel in London. It was resolved by the comparatively small number present that exhibitors should not make bookings for the period after August 31, 1922, pending an agreement to limit the waiting period between trade show and release to six months; other recommendations included a 25 per cent reduction in film prices. The booking stop was felt by many to be an attempt to steam-roller the vast mass of exhibitors, and some were not too happy about Beaverbrook's ambiguous position as a renter-exhibitor or the attempt to bypass the C.E.A. *The Bioscope*, which on other occasions was known to lament the lack of strong leadership, was nevertheless very critical of Beaverbrook and even went so far as to refer to him as 'Cromwell Redivivus'. Sir Oswald Stoll, as a renter-producer, was opposed to the plan. Nevertheless the General Council of the C.E.A. at an emergency meeting endorsed the conclusions of the Hyde Park Hotel meeting and many exhibitors favoured Beaverbrook rather than the Ormiston Glasgow scheme, which although similar and very practical lacked the recommended price reduction.

A meeting was quickly held at the Connaught Rooms on May 5, 1921, for the exhibitors to meet the renters and discuss the Beaverbrook proposals. The renters came determined to get the proposals withdrawn until they had had time to consider them. It was at this meeting that William Friese-Greene, the old and impoverished inventor, died dramatically after making a passionate plea that they should not insist on this withdrawal. It was resolved to ask the C.E.A., K.R.S., and K.M.A. each to appoint five members to consider the proposals.[33] Needless to say the choice of the C.E.A. and K.R.S. personnel aroused some difficulties because of the double interests of so many leading figures in the trade. It was finally done with much delay and vituperation. The producers were represented, quite unsuitably, by the K.M.A. Several important renters remained aloof but the committees were finally ready for talks, with Beaverbrook acting as mediator. A Joint Trade Committee held an Advance Booking Conference, and in August published a complex and controversial agreement with provisions to abolish blind and block booking, speed up trade shows and form a film registration committee, all without the need for legislation.

Even had such things been possible on a voluntary basis, the agreement depended on all three parties being able to secure unanimity among their members. This was impossible, except perhaps for the K.M.A., whose action mattered least. The C.E.A. held a postal vote, as a result of which they found 1,349 members for the plan and 830 against it, and these figures accounted for only some of the exhibitors. It was hardly likely, with such a lack of enthusiasm, that restrictions on exhibitors would be enforceable. The death blow was dealt to the scheme by F. C. Graham of Famous–Lasky, who in September wrote both to Frank Hill of the K.R.S. and to Beaverbrook saying that Famous–Lasky would disregard the agreement. In reply Beaverbrook realistically washed his hands of the problem.[34] By October the effort to tackle the general economic structure of the industry from within had clearly failed.

By restricting the market block booking, blind booking and advance booking had had a very adverse effect on British production; activity was now transferred, for a while, to an attempt to promote this. Neither the K.M.A. nor the Directors' Association was designed to fight for the commercial survival of the British production industry, but there was, now, an important attempt to get British producers to combine in their own economic interests. This was the British National Film League.

By 1921 it was realized that the small British firms, trade showing their few films haphazard, might well show several in one week and then no more for weeks or months. Exhibitors, subject as they were to the booking pressure and never knowing when to expect British films, could hardly be expected to keep dates free for them. It was hoped by seven or eight British producing and renting firms that if they co-ordinated their activities so that there was a regular, if small, flow of British films, and at the same time drew attention to them by a joint publicity campaign, they might establish a regular booking pattern and even reduce the time between trade show and release date to about six months.

Thus the British National Film League was formed in November 1921. Its stated aims were to encourage the production and exhibition of British-made films, to eliminate blind and block booking, to shorten the interval between the trade show of a film and its release and to develop an effective publicity service. The promotion of a closer and more sympathetic understanding between the British film industry, the press and the public was its over-all intention.

The League arranged a programme of films to be trade shown at the rate of one a week from June 1922, each to be released six months later. They hoped that exhibitors would keep a place for them. There was to be joint publicity and a joint committee to judge the films and keep them up to standard, but it shows how bad things had become that a body organized at the end of 1921 should be talking about release dates in 1923. The films, moreover, were of disappointing quality.*

The League, of which A. C. Bromhead and F. W. Baker were alternating chairmen, next planned a British Film Week. The idea was to secure as many bookings as possible in the same week for a group of British films, to arouse interest in British production. The C.E.A. agreed to support this and it was announced in July 1923 that successive British Film Weeks would be held in seven areas.[35] Ideal and Stoll had previously held aloof largely because the size of their output enabled them to get distribution independently, but they now joined the scheme and by September 15 firms belonged. By November the number was over 20.

* Films included in the League's programmes are indicated in the Film Index.

The Weeks were originally planned for the autumn of 1923. Then a luncheon was held to launch them on November 14, 1923, at which the Prince of Wales was the guest of honour, and which included

'. . . leading members of the diplomatic corps, Colonial and Dominion representatives, the shining lights of the stage and screen, the world of art and letters, Members of Parliament, legal luminaries, civic dignitaries, the Army and Navy, and practically everyone who matters in the social scale.'[36]

Five hundred people came, and flattering speeches were made. It was good prestige publicity not merely for British films but for the cinema as a whole. Interest was reflected in the press and on 2LO. The trade press supported it, and C.E.A. branch meetings were addressed all over the country by Victor Davis.

But owing to difficulties over booking dates there were repeated postponements, and the Weeks themselves did not take place until February and March 1924. By this time much of the attention aroused by the campaign had been dissipated. Even in July 1923 many exhibitors had complained that they had few free bookings left. The postponements and the extra costs of the publicity added to their disappointment when the films proved to be of poor quality. A list of 195 features and shorts was published in October 1923. Only some 25 of these were new features and they aroused little enthusiasm. American firms dutifully sent telegrams of good wishes, but Carl Laemmle also pointed out that concentrating films in one week did nothing to increase output.[37] Nor did it do anything to improve them. On the contrary, as Paul Rotha later said, it simply protected bad films.[38] The only service it might have performed would have been to create a new demand for British films by focusing attention on them. But for this to succeed, the films needed to be good.

'In 1924, a publicity campaign was launched to help the British film. This campaign was perhaps the worst thing that could have happened. By extravagant articles from eminent hands in the Press, by debates in both Houses, by libellous accounts of foreign methods, by reported scandals about American stars, by a tremendous stirring of agitation amongst the public, the latter was browbeaten into a state of receptivity for British films. For months the Press told the public how good the British films then in the making were going to be. After all this publicity, with the public hypnotized into readiness to applaud the worst picture in the world because it was British, the promised films came, one by one.'[39]

And there they were at last, including some of the worst productions of a depressed industry.

The move to mend the economic ills of the trade now took on another look. It was gradually accepted that legislation was necessary, and people began to discuss the possibility of enforcing by law the showing of a minimum quota of British films in every programme. The legal abolition of practices like block and advance booking were to be incorporated in this legislation.

Actually the time between trade show and release seems to have shortened a little on its own. An analysis of 210 films trade shown between January and the end of April in 1926 showed that 62 per cent had only from five to seven months to wait, 26 per cent six months; only 26 per cent had a delay of more than seven months. But the occasional assertions that block booking was dead were clearly not correct. Flagrant cases came to light every now and then. Associated First National offered 52 three-day bookings at once,[40] and W. & F. were accused of offering Harold Lloyd's *Girl Shy* with a mammoth block of 33 two-reelers, 26 one-reelers and 4 features in 1924.[41] Carl Laemmle's special pleading for Universal was most ingenuous:

'These Universal Attractions will be released in groups. This method is being used because I wanted to concentrate on production and on building up the show-value of the individual pictures in each group.'[42]

Self-help through the British National Film League having failed, the search for a solution to the trade's problems now shifted to the idea of a quota. The plight of the British producer, and with it the booking abuses which bedevilled the film industry as a whole, engaged the attention of Parliament. It was felt that if a share of screen time was not going to be granted to British films voluntarily, perhaps it would have to be provided by legislation. Lord Burnham in the Lords in May 1925 suggested that the time had come for block booking to be stopped by law, an idea ridiculed by *The Bioscope* as impossible. Discussion of the industry's difficulties moved into a new phase, as a result of which the quota legislation of 1927 came into being. Nevertheless, in the end *The Bioscope*'s cynicism proved justified.

In 1921 the renter Lionel Phillips had already written to *The Bioscope* pointing to New Zealand as the first country to require cinemas to show a certain proportion of British films. His argument was the cultural–commercial one based on the importance of British prestige and the belief that trade follows the film. He summed up the economic arguments for protection of film production. He pointed out that the cost of prints was so small in comparison with the initial cost of production that films were peculiarly suitable for dumping, giving an enormous advantage to the country with the biggest guaranteed or home market.[43] During the next few years it gradually became accepted that the problem was basically an economic one. Rowan Walker, General Secretary of the British National Film League, suggested Entertainments Tax remission for exhibitors who showed a proportion of British films.[44] Watson Hartley, managing director of Photographic International Ltd., wrote bitterly about the Americans, advocating the showing of a quota of British films and citing the American immigration quota as a precedent.[45] In actual fact the idea was not new. Sidney Morgan had suggested it in 1917 (see Volume III). It was known that Germany had instituted its Kontingent system after the war linking imports with home production, and that by the mid-twenties renters in Germany had to handle one German film for every foreign one.

By early 1925 the Board of Trade was studying the economic situation of the industry, the practices of block, blind and advance booking, the difficulties of

British production and the rarity of British films in the cinema. It would seem, however, that they had consulted neither the Cinematograph Exhibitors' Association, the Kinematograph Renters' Society, the Cinematograph Trade Council nor the British National Film League at this stage.

It was in May of the same year that the depressed state of British production was debated in the House of Lords and questions were asked in the Commons.[46] The Lords were kind to the film, but puzzled. On an undisclosed basis it was estimated that the proportion of British pictures exhibited in Britain fell from 25 per cent in 1914 to 10 per cent in 1923, and to 2 per cent in 1925. Because of the industrial, educational and political importance of the film it was proposed by Lord Newton that a Departmental Committee should study this alarming state of affairs, but this was turned down because of the Board of Trade's current activity and another study which was being conducted simultaneously by the Federation of British Industries.

The F.B.I., like the Board of Trade, was studying the question without formal consultation with the big trade bodies.[47] Its motive was also the cultural–commercial one. It was more concerned with the question of production than anything else, and through contact with the British Association of Film Directors had set up a Film Manufacturers' Committee which included Colonel Bromhead, T. A. Welsh, Simon Rowson, Cecil Hepworth and T. C. Elder. In June an important letter appeared in *The Telegraph* which was signed by such assorted celebrities as Robert Bridges, Dawson of Penn, Edward Elgar, Thomas Hardy and Gordon Selfridge. This emphasized the general anxiety, stressing the cultural importance of the film and requesting a public enquiry into the plight of the industry.

In August the Government requested the F.B.I. to report its findings, but the latter preferred to wait for the trade's own proposals. The C.E.A., meanwhile, had sent a delegation to the United States to study conditions there. At the annual summer conference in June, T. A. Welsh had spoken in favour of a central national studio. At the same time the delegation made its report and a sub-committee was appointed to produce a scheme, which was ready for submission to a special joint committee of all three bodies by September.[48] At the request of Philip Cunliffe–Lister, the Conservative President of the Board of Trade, a Trade Committee was appointed to receive this and report on it to the Board of Trade.

At the end of October two schemes were ready, that of the F.B.I. and that of the C.E.A. The Federation scheme was reported to be for a quota of $12\frac{1}{2}$ per cent, rising to 37 per cent. But the big plan was that prepared for the C.E.A. by its President, Thomas Ormiston, and Welsh. This recommended a quota, to apply to renters on October 1, 1926, and to exhibitors on January 1, 1927, starting at 10 per cent and rising to a maximum of 25 per cent by June 1929. A Board of Trade authority was to be set up as a safeguard against worthless British pictures, renters buying but not using films, and an insufficient volume of British production. Foreseeing a shortage of British talent and the importance of star publicity, it was conceded that a 'British picture' might have a producer or one top star not domiciled in Britain. The companies, however, must be *bona fide* British-owned and -controlled producing companies. To placate exhibitors, blind booking was to be legally abolished, and it was assumed that block-booking would therefore also disappear in time. The Committee was also in favour of a national studio.[49]

Even these easily-evaded provisions had a very mixed reception from the industry. The safeguards were immediately attacked by exhibitors, and a revised version was soon issued. In this it was suggested that if there were too few good British pictures the date of operation of the quotas might be postponed; there was also a proviso for disallowing British films for quota purposes if they were not of a sufficiently good standard of production and entertainment value. An authority to decide these question was to be set up by the trade itself, subject to the Board of Trade's approval. An exhibitor was to be able to stand out of his quota obligations if he could satisfy this authority that he could not pay the price, or prove that films were not available 'having regard to the usual methods of business in the district'. A renter, also, was to be able to stand out if the price of the films was prohibitive owing to shortage of supply. The Board of Trade was to have powers to deal with foreign attempts to corner British production, cinemas, studio facilities, artistes or authors. Small renters were to be allowed to combine for quota purposes. Some attempt was made to deal with the problem of block booking, but the provision of a national studio was now left to be the subject of later study.

This revised scheme was passed by a full Joint Committee of the Cinematograph Trade, and was referred back to the C.E.A. and K.R.S. The C.E.A. Council and a meeting of all renters, although not of the K.R.S. itself, accepted it. The Board of Trade impatiently waited for the scheme to be accepted by the rank and file of the C.E.A.

While arguments about quality, talent and enterprise, and their economic basis were continuing in the branches, the vast majority of exhibitors were slow to understand these new ideas and were easily aroused by the fear of State control and Government interference. One of the most vocal opponents of any quota was the exhibitor E. E. Lyons of Biocolour:

'. . . films which are not at present made, of which there is no proof they ever will be made, and if they are made, there is no proof they will possess that entertainment value demanded by the public, or that they will be able to be hired at a proper commercial price. . . .'[50]

Perhaps the most telling argument in favour of this scheme of the trade's was that if the exhibitors rejected it the Government would impose a scheme of its own and, after a visit to Cunliffe-Lister, Ormiston wrote to the exhibitors warning them of this. The C.E.A. then held a referendum. But to the Council's dismay a majority of the 50 per cent or so who bothered to vote was against the Ormiston scheme. Some of its fiercest opponents were big and influential exhibitors. The scheme was referred back once more to the sub-committee, now enlarged by the addition of some of its critics, especially Lyons, Will Evans of Provincial Cinematograph Theatres, T. C. Elder and A. George Smith. Lyons brought forward an interesting scheme of his own for the exhibitors to raise £100,000 for production, the C.E.A. to act as renter.

Meanwhile Cunliffe-Lister intimated that the Government could not wait much longer and the F.B.I. decided to go ahead and present its own plan. In a *Bioscope* leader entitled 'Fiddling While Rome Burns' it was suggested that the area of agreement within the C.E.A. had now shrunk to include only the plan for a national studio and the abolition of block booking. The K.R.S. refused to agree to any plan covering only these aspects of the problem.

The F.B.I. bill was made public in February 1926, suggesting a quota rising from 12½ per cent to 37 per cent in three years. It was planned to set up a registration authority, and to make it illegal to show unregistered films; a film would only be registered if the person presenting it for registration was also renting a British quota.[51]

Alarm at this alternative to the earlier scheme spread through the trade in general and the C.E.A. in particular. An informal committee convened by Simon Rowson of Ideal asked for a year's grace, and the President of the Board of Trade announced that quota legislation would be delayed for one final year in the hope that the trade would be able to agree on a scheme of its own. It was announced that there would be no subsidy for production, but that legislation against blind booking would be introduced if the trade requested it.

The Joint Committee floundered on, but virtually the only thing now generally accepted was the need to abolish blind booking, and the proposed new C.E.A. bill was aimed only at this. It was suggested that the producer should register films when complete, and have a Trade Show; a Registration Committee of three to six people should be appointed by the President of the Board of Trade from C.E.A., K.R.S. and Association of Kinematograph Manufacturers panels; its decisions should be subject to an appeal to the Board of Trade; and provision should be made for penalties of six months prison or £20 a day. This attenuated scheme was accepted by the C.E.A., which decided to present it to the Board of Trade if a K.R.S. scheme was not forthcoming.[52]

Even this modest proposal offered little help to British producers, who had hoped that release dates would be shortened. Meanwhile the feeling was growing that even if a home market were assured to British films it might not be large enough to make production economic, and some form of reciprocity with American firms was also needed to open the American market to them. The Joint Committee discussed this with American interests but the F.B.I., foreseeing American production in this country, deplored it. Finally the C.E.A., trimming its sails, held a plebiscite on the immediate abolition of blind booking by law and in July 1926 got a vote of 1,704 in favour, with 198 diehards against it. Recognizing that this was all they could achieve, they proceeded to frame a scheme embodying this alone.[53]

It had to be recognized that the trade discussions had broken down, and the Joint Committee was dissolved. Welsh had already resigned from it as he was unable to accept any State compulsion, and Lyons, carrying the free trade banner, was loud in opposition to legislation of any sort. The deep division within the C.E.A. could no longer be contained, and when its bill against blind booking was published there was no general agreement with it, although it was decided to go ahead and present it to the Board of Trade.

Meanwhile the K.R.S. decided to prepare a plan for voluntary action sanctioned by the threat of boycott, despite the obvious fact that neither the exhibitors nor the renters were sufficiently organized to make such a threat credible. The F.B.I. also began to revive its own proposals again. In September the Government was finally informed that the trade as a whole could not agree on a scheme.

A new voice now entered somewhat fortuitously into the discussions, that of the Imperial Conference. An idea persisted that the answer to the big American home market was to treat the Empire as a home market for Britain. This was in harmony with the general theory of imperial preference current at the time, but was not realistic in its application to films. The first reliable estimates of the numbers of cinemas were those of the Moyne Committee in 1934, when it was stated that there were some 14,500 cinemas in the U.S.A. with ten million seats, and 4,300 cinemas in Great Britain with 3,872,000 seats, whereas the Empire as a whole including Great Britain had 7,900 cinemas and 5,593,000 seats. Although these figures relate to a few years later on, they give some idea of the proportions involved, and suggest that even if British films had secured a stranglehold on those Empire cinemas normally showing English-language films, it would still only have given them a market a little over half the size of the American home market. Nor was it at all likely that Britain could have secured such a stranglehold, with American films already firmly entrenched as they were.

The imperialists were bemused by a dream of Empire films spreading wholesome imperial sentiments. The projection of an ideal British image attracted people who knew little about the film industry. At the Imperial Conference of October 1926 such eminent speakers as Mackenzie King of Canada, Bruce of Australia and Peter Coates of New Zealand referred to the possibilities of the Empire as a market, and the General Economic Sub-Committee appointed by the Conference

'. . . drew attention to the small proportion of films of Empire origin shown in Great Britain and Northern Ireland and the other parts of the Empire. The Sub-Committee attached great importance to the need for a larger production within the Empire of films of high entertainment value and sound educational merit and to their increased exhibition throughout the Empire and the rest of the world. They suggested a number of measures by which Empire Governments could assist at that end. These included:

Effective customs duties on foreign films.
Ample preference or free entry for films produced within the Empire.
Legislation for the prevention of blind and block booking.
Imposition of requirements as to the renting or exhibition of a minimum quota of Empire films.'[54]

The result was to wrench attention back from purely commercial problems of the exhibitors like blind booking, which were of little interest to the Imperial

Conference, to the cultural and economic implications of the decline of British production. It is difficult to overestimate the amount written and spoken about the importance of films as a commercial traveller. Imperial Conference and F.B.I. circles were also greatly influenced by the fear of American monopoly, which was part of a more general problem and applied to such other commodities as cars. The Conference received a memorandum from the F.B.I., which recommended an immediate quota of 12½ per cent, estimating that whereas some 90 British pictures would be needed in a year the production of as many as 115 was feasible. According to *The Bioscope* this was an overestimate, and the scheme was not popular in the trade. Fuller of the K.R.S. issued a memorandum in opposition to it.

In November 1926 the Conference issued a Report called *Exhibition Within the Empire of Empire Cinematograph Films*. This noted the enormous importance of the cinema as an 'instrument of education in the widest sense of that term', and gave specimen figures showing the small percentage of Empire films shown in Great Britain and Northern Ireland, Australia, New Zealand and Canada. The Conference deplored this and the consequent misrepresentation of the Empire abroad; it listed certain tariff preferences in various parts of the Empire, but noted that they had been of little use in promoting production. The sub-committee had considered various methods of getting good entertainment films circulated in the Empire and outside, including customs duties on foreign films, preference for Empire films, legislation against blind and block booking, and quotas. It recommended that governments should look into these methods, stressing the need for real and competitive exhibition value and effective distributing arrangements throughout the Empire. Finally the Conference resolved thus:

'The Imperial Conference, recognising that it is of the greatest importance that a larger and increasing proportion of the film exhibited throughout the Empire should be of Empire production, commends the matter and the remedial measures proposed to the consideration of the Governments of the various parts of the Empire, with a view to such early and effective action to deal with the serious situation now existing as they may severally find possible.'[55]

As a result of the lack of agreement within the film industry, it was on the deliberations of the Imperial Conference that the eventual legislation was based. By the end of 1926 the Board of Trade was drafting a Bill based on this Report. Early in the new year Blake and Ormiston led deputations to Cunliffe-Lister to inquire about its proposed provisions. Silence descended, but the imminence of protection was said to be revitalizing the industry already both in expanded production and in the attraction of capital and enterprise, leading to greater integration in the industry as a whole. Protagonists of the Bill thought a 5 per cent quota would be the starting point and that this would not be much higher than that already existing in practice. But warnings that protection leads to inferior quality were already heard, opposition being especially fierce among exhibitors in Manchester, traditional home of free trade.

The Bill was finally presented in March 1927. It emerged from Committee in July and passed its third reading in November, was debated in the Lords in December and became law. Statutory Rules were issued by the Board of Trade in January 1928 and an advisory Committee appointed with Sir Alexander F. Whyte as Chairman; A. C. Bromhead and H. Bruce Woolfe represented the producers; T. C. Elder and Simon Rowson the renters; Blake, Gale, Ormiston and Hewitson the exhibitors; and, as outsiders, Mrs Philip Snowdon, G. R. Hall Caine, Sir Robert Blair and St John Ervine.[56] At the end of June the C.E.A. General Council protested at the appointment of Ormiston, Gale and Blake to represent the exhibitors because they all had large renting interests as well. It was not possible for Cunliffe-Lister to dismiss them. Two of them resigned immediately but Gale, resentful of what seemed like jealousy from the C.E.A. Council, demanded a C.E.A. ballot; F. H. Davis, F. H. Cooper and E. Trounson were elected by the members, and to general relief Gale resigned at the end of December. The renters' quota came into operation in April 1928 and that of the exhibitors in October.

The Act was called the Cinematograph Films Act of 1927. It was to start on January 1, 1928, and continue in operation for ten years. The stated aim was to restrict blind and advance booking and to secure the renting and exhibition of a certain proportion of British films. Part I, intended to check advance and blind booking, limited rental agreements to films which had been registered under the Act and eventually to six months in advance. Part II dealt with the registration of films with the Board of Trade, registration to be linked with Trade Show or pre-release show. Part III defined the quota as a renter's quota of $7\frac{1}{2}$ per cent for the year ending March 31, 1929, rising to 20 per cent in 1936–38, and an exhibitor's quota of 5 per cent for the year ending September 30, 1929, and rising to 20 per cent for 1936–38. Part IV dealt with definitions and interpretations, especially of what was a British film; and the setting up of the Advisory Committee mentioned above, which was to advise the Board of Trade and which was to consist of 2 representatives of the film makers, 2 of the film renters, 4 of the exhibitors and 3 members with no pecuniary interest in the industry, of whom one was to be Chairman. It should be noted that production companies were described as 'British companies', not 'British-controlled companies' as some people had wanted, a fact which left the door open for foreign-controlled companies. Renters and exhibitors were required to be licensed, and it was stipulated that the Board of Trade could allow combinations of renters for quota purposes.

There was considerable hostility to the new legislation. The Labour Party had originally been opposed to the Bill, and although the National Association of Theatrical Employees was in favour of it the Manchester opponents continued to be active. Earl Russell, in the Lords' debate, had given a more sophisticated exposition of the misgivings about quality, and the lack of a quality guarantee was widely criticized. There were many who foresaw shoddy production. G. B. Shaw was quoted by *The Bioscope*:

'My contempt for it deprives me of speech.'[57]

THE HISTORY OF THE BRITISH FILM

H. G. Wells, as well as the Beaverbrook paper the *Daily Express*, showed vigorous disapproval. Even the City Correspondent of the *Daily Chronicle* felt it worth pointing out that a quota would encourage quantity but not quality. It was, in fact, quite possible to see clearly what was wrong with the system before it was tried, and many did so. Herbert Wilcox was a producer who felt he could stand on his own feet, and he described it as un-British,[58] but many British producers looked forward with pleasure to an easy time. A. E. Bundy, more thoughtfully, maintained that the health of British production could not be improved without an effective scheme of world distribution. Reaction in America was not merely unfavourable but even incredulous. Will Hays came over to Europe early in 1928 to discuss the English, French and German restrictions.

Throughout the negotiations different groups of people had been seeking different objectives. The Act was a compromise, which in the end served none of them.

On the one side were the F.B.I. and the producers. The F.B.I. Film Group under the Chairmanship of the Deputy Director of the Federation, Sir Charles Tennyson, included Michael Balcon, A. C. Bromhead, A. E. Coleby, T. C. Elder, F. A. Enders, John Maxwell, George Pearson, Dinah Shurey, Bruce Woolfe and W. M. Borrodaile. The F.B.I. had in 1925 been in contact with the B.A.F.D., whose Secretary at the time was the same Sidney Morgan who had originally suggested a quota system in 1917, and the B.A.F.D. itself was in favour of a 25 per cent quota. The producers took their stand on neither altruism nor patriotism but on the theory that lack of talent and poor quality were economic phenomena, which could only be overcome by special measures designed to ensure an adequate market. A letter from Morgan in *The Bioscope* in 1925 suggested that the size of the market was so crucial that even had British films been outstandingly good, and widely booked in Britain, the home market was so small that they might still not have been economically viable.[59]

But the backing for British producers provided by the F.B.I. had been due to the concern for the industrial and political repercussions of poor British production, rather than to concern for the producers themselves. As an industry, and an employer of capital and labour, film making was still small and its fate insignificant. A letter to Ormiston from Col. the Hon. Vernon Willey, President of the F.B.I., made it clear that the F.B.I. was interested solely because the disappearance of British films affected the prestige of Britain, and therefore of British industry as a whole. They were far-seeing in their suggestions for semi-official loan capital and a studio which, however, came to nothing. Later a further step away from the purely trade interest and towards the ideological interest had been taken when the Imperial Conference were persuaded that the matter deserved their attention. The cultural unity and strength of Britain and the Empire seemed to require a strong film production industry, and ideas of preference and protection were in the air. After the war the idea of imperial preference to help industries whose existence seemed necessary for the strength of the Empire was current, and the reimposition of the McKenna duties by the Baldwin Government of 1924 led Imperialist circles naturally to think along similar lines for the cinema. The possibility that something rather different was needed where art and fashion were concerned was dimly recognized, but the quota was a first attempt to find a solution.

The renters, certainly very much affected by the changes proposed in their habits of block, blind and advance booking and the prospect of having to handle British films, said little. Coolly negotiating from a middleman position of great power, as renters they were not really affected by the plight of British production and indeed, owing to the predominance of American interests, were actively hostile to the latter. George Smith of Vitagraph, chairman of the K.R.S. in 1925, was quoted in the Lords as saying that there was, in fact, no British film industry to protect, a fact which he put down simply to lack of initiative.

To the exhibitors, on the other hand, the British film industry meant themselves. What they wanted was help in solving their booking problems, and the fact that booking practices had damaged British production was, despite some crocodile tears, quite incidental to them. Conventional laments about the Americanization of our youth had no economic motivation and also rang a little false. True, it was possible that if British production disappeared, American films might go up in price; but this was unlikely as the expensive, few and bad British films already provided little effective competition. Besides having no real economic reason to care about British production many of these exhibitors, mostly small businessmen, had been free traders all their lives and their natural reaction was to protest that art cannot be legislated, and that British films should be booked on their merits. The debate throughout was on a distressingly low level and there was little understanding of the complex connections between economic prosperity and quality. Exhibitors were naturally reluctant to see their access to American films tampered with and they used old-fashioned *laissez-faire* arguments against any government interference, continuing to claim that voluntary action by exhibitors was all that was necessary. They were, however, prepared to favour government capital and studios to help the producers, as this did not affect their own interests. The attitude is summed up in a petition to Parliament presented in the autumn of 1927 by P.E.P.M.A.:

'The object of the Cinematograph Films Bill now before your honourable House has been stated by supporters of the Government to be to promote the making of British films for the purpose of propaganda, commercial, religious, social and political, but our object is to provide the best entertainment the world affords.

'The Cinematograph Films Bill, if passed into law, will deprive us of the free choice of films for our programmes, and in doing so, interfere seriously with our endeavour to meet the wishes and taste of the public. In place of the popular films, of which the Bill will deprive us by the quota proposals in increasing quantity for the next twelve years, films of British production are to be forced upon us, but there is no guarantee whatsoever that an adequate number of these, suitable in quality and price to enable us to comply with this portion of the Bill and also to satisfy our patrons, the public, will be forthcoming. The substitution of the judgement of the Board of Trade for our own, even when assisted by that of an Advisory Committee, on the question of the films to be exhibited in response to public demand, appears to us an act that will, in practice, prove highly detrimental to our business and distasteful to the public.

'Further, the Bill in this respect, as also in its entire provisions, aims at taking away our constitutional right as British citizens to freely contract and trade in the industry in which we are engaged, and alternatively imposes heavy penalties upon us for exercising that which hitherto has been our lawful right and the right of every other citizen.'[60]

Ormiston, as President of the C.E.A., took a more enlightened view than many other exhibitors and, friendly to British production, realized that a quota was necessary; he would have been glad to see a studio scheme put into effect also. The eventual legislation was similar to his own scheme of October 1925, and throughout the discussions he tried to persuade his colleagues that the industry needed more than the mere abolition of booking abuses. In this he received explosive support from Gavazzi King, now seventy and the grand old man of the C.E.A., who clearly realized that co-operation and integration were vital to withstand American domination and at the 1926 C.E.A. Conference had upbraided the rank and file for their excessive individualism. Powerful exhibitors, however, resisted legislation. Lord Ashfield, Chairman of P.C.T. and a former President of the Board of Trade, went so far as to suggest that a voluntary undertaking to book British would suffice,[61] and Sir Oswald Stoll, as an exhibitor-producer, maintained throughout the view that he had expressed at the annual general meeting of Stoll Picture Productions in 1925:

'Unless British pictures can get their costs back in the home market by a Government scheme or a private scheme, willingly supported by exhibitors, it seems to me that the British film industry is doomed.'[62]

He did not change this attitude, and although as a producer he did want practical help for production he maintained that legal protection could only produce bad quality, and that the Act left an opening for foreign companies to form subsidiaries here to use our quota time. He was right on both counts. It is ironic that his confidence that merit should stand on its own feet came from the production, and incidentally the block booking, of some of the worst of British films, films which had helped to bring British production into contempt. Stoll production, in fact, brought costs and profits into line by cutting costs, tacitly accepting the impossibility of increasing home receipts. But the resulting quality was so poor that it accelerated the decline in popularity of the British film, suggesting perhaps that there was more to the problem than a simple business equation. The remedy suggested by Stoll in preference to a quota was a Reel Tax of 1s a day on all foreign films exhibited, the proceeds to be put back into production and used 'for making up losses on British pictures, judged to be good ones'. Like other interesting and advanced suggestions, this one was ignored at the time.

The new legislation now began to show what sort of an effect it would have. As far as booking abuses were concerned, although both producers and exhibitors later claimed that blind booking had been partly stopped, we have it on the authority of the Moyne Committee in 1934 that

. . . the full measure of benefit expected from the provisions abolishing blind booking has not been attained owing to various methods of evasion which have been practised.'[63]

The Act had tried to restrict advance booking to six months but this was said by the *Moyne Report* to have been only a qualified success. Forty years later another writer was more explicit:

'Exhibitors are statutorily forbidden to book a film before it has had a trade show and more than six months in advance of a proposed cinema screening. The law has been avoided by the practice of what is called in trade jargon "pencilling-in" dates for the showing of films well over six months in advance. The Federation of British Film Makers has alleged, regarding films in which Rank or A.B.C. have an investment, that "it is generally understood that provisional [*sic*] dates are often pencilled in for them well before they are finished, or their quality known. Such a practice would of course reduce the number of dates available to distributors of other films, though what is pencilled in can always be rubbed out in favour of a better work.'[64]

Block booking had not been tackled directly, as it was felt that its disappearance would follow the abolition of blind and advance booking. But here again it seems that the problem had been underestimated. Forty year later, also, the Monopolies Commission was to state:

'We accept that distributors do not impose an explicit condition to the effect that an exhibitor may not book one film without also taking another; some exhibitors themselves said that no condition is put in writing. On the other hand we have no doubt that, when a distributor has a particularly attractive film to offer, he will do his best to take advantage of it by seeking to persuade exhibitors to book some of his less attractive films as well; an exhibitor in a weak bargaining position may feel that he has no alternative but to give way to such pressure if he is to secure the more popular films that he needs in order to attract sufficient custom. Distributors admitted as much, and defended it as a reasonable commercial practice.'[65]

So much for the exhibitors' aim, the prevention of booking abuses. What about the expansion of production sought by the producer and the Imperial Conference? Money flowed into the industry as soon as the quota was reasonably likely, and many new producing companies were registered. Output expanded very noticeably. Rowson later said that of the long films (i.e. 3,000 feet or more) registered as renters' quota under the Act in the first years of its operation, April 1, 1928, to March 31, 1929, 550 were foreign and 128 British, a high figure due to the backlog waiting to register; in the second year, April 1, 1929, to

March 31, 1930, there were 96 British films to 506 foreign, and the proportion of British films rose thereafter. Rowson estimated that in these first two years there was an excess footage of 230 per cent and 70 per cent of British long films registered over quota requirements, and he gave the footage of British long films required by the quota, and footage actually registered, as:

	Required	Registered
April 1, 1928–March 31, 1929	276,000 ft	909,000 ft
April 1, 1929–March 31, 1930	370,000 ft	624,000 ft
April 1, 1930–March 31, 1931	474,000 ft	803,000 ft[66]

Short films, however, were a different matter. The Act:

'. . . did not provide a separate quota for shorts; on the contrary it contained clauses which proved to be weighted against the documentary film in particular. Under the ruling of the Act no films depicting wholly or mainly news or current events, natural scenery, industrial or manufacturing processes, no scientific and natural history films, and no educational films were eligible for quota unless "of special exhibition value" (which proved to be a very ambiguous phrase). Many short films, including most documentaries, were automatically excluded on these grounds and therefore received no protection against foreign shorts nor against being crowded out by feature films. As a result, the registered footage of short films produced in Britain dropped from 170,000 feet in 1929 to 68,000 feet in 1935.'[67]

Thus it would seem that British feature production did expand a great deal as a result of the quota. But there were two important qualifications to its apparent success. Firstly, quality was disappointing. Secondly, after a while the nationality of much of the new production was not British in the sense intended by the framers of the Act.

The immediate reaction of large renters was to acquire existing films, or the films of existing companies of good repute. Small independent renters began to combine as renters or renter-producers, and big American renters began to adopt films. The First National–Pathé combination intended to produce their own; Fox, Paramount and Allied Artists moved in quickly to acquire British films, and later Warner, Jury–Metro–Goldwyn–Mayer and the P.D.C. followed. Films by reputable companies like Welsh–Pearson, British Instructional and British Lion were in high demand, but lesser known brands also began to find a market. Here is a list of twenty early films with their producers and the firms distributing them for quota, in the order of their trade shows:

Huntingtower (Welsh–Pearson), Paramount	T.S.	2.28
Madame Pompadour (B.I.P.), Paramount		4.28
Tip Toes (British National), Paramount		5.28
Love's Option (Welsh–Pearson), Paramount		9.28
S.O.S. (Strand), Allied Artists		12.28

Spangles (British Filmcraft), Paramount	12.28
Three Passions (St George), Allied Artists	12.28
The Flying Squad (British Lion), Warner	2.29
Adventurous Youth (Pall Mall), Warner	2.29
The Lost Patrol (B.I.F.), Fox	2.29
Little Miss London, Fox	3.29
Runaway Princess (B.I.F.), J–M–G	3.29
Sacrifice (B.I.F.), Fox	3.29
Inseparables (Whitehall), Warner	3.29
Clue of the New Pin (British Lion), P.D.C.	3.29
Chamber of Horrors (B.I.F.), P.D.C.	3.29
Celestial City (B.I.F.), J–M–G	3.29
Auld Lang Syne (Welsh–Pearson–Elder), Paramount	4.29
Power Over Men (British Filmcraft), Paramount	4.29
Silver King (Welsh–Pearson–Elder), Paramount	6.29

Most of these films were considered good quality British films. The *Moyne Report* stated:

'We were informed that in one or two cases foreign-controlled companies distributing foreign films in this country did, at the outset, make genuine attempts to comply not only with the letter but with the spirit of the requirements of the Act that a certain percentage of British films should be acquired by renters for the purpose of renting to exhibitors.'[68]

But, as its critics observed, there was no quality clause in the Act as this was considered too difficult to define:

'The Act of 1927 did not stipulate that registration for renters' quota should be dependent on the attainment of reasonable quality in the film in question. It was provided merely that inability to comply with the quota on account of the character of the British films available might be regarded as a reason beyond the control of the renter or exhibitor excusing him, in effect, from his statutory obligation.'[68]

Thus before long, no serious attempt was being made by renters to find good quality films to comply with their obligations:

'It was admitted, however, even by the renters themselves, that in recent years the spirit of the Act has not, speaking generally, been given effect. In order to obtain the requisite length of British film to satisfy the renters' quota, the majority of foreign-controlled renters appear to have made arrangements for the production of British films at the minimum of expense, regardless of quality. Such films were not in a position to attract exhibitors, save in so far as they needed the films to satisfy their quota and indeed they were not, in the main, worthy of exhibition. It was admitted by the renters in evidence before us that the majority of the films made for them to enable them to satisfy their quota obligations are worthless and remain in their offices largely unsold and unused.'[68]

Under the quota legislation a British company was a company registered under the laws of any part of the Empire, the majority of the directors of which were British subjects. As *The Film in National Life* put it:

'A "British" film is a film made by a British subject or a British company in a studio within the British Empire, and from a scenario written by a British subject. With a margin of discretion allowed to the Board of Trade, 75 per cent of salaries and wages must be paid to British subjects, exclusive of the remuneration of one foreign actor or producer.'[69]

But the *Kine Year Book* of 1928 admitted:

'It would be too much to claim that this provision effectually bolts and bars the door to any development of an alien interest in our film industry.'[70]

There was no case before 1930 of an American production company working in England, but the trade was all in favour of bringing over foreign celebrities to brighten up the new British pictures. *Kine Year Book* said:

'The last Commons debate had made a long desired concession on the subject of the director's nationality which the super-patriots had insisted upon in Standing Committee "C". A point which had been ceaselessly laboured by the Trade was admitted, and Sir Philip Cunliffe-Lister expressed the opinion that the best interests of British film production would be served by allowing British film producers to call upon unlimited talent in the production of their films.'[70]

At first some American has-beens came over to be our visiting talent, and a number of British emigrants who had failed to reach the top in Hollywood. More important, the British film writers upon whose encouragement the Act had laid such stress did not appear.

'In the period which has elapsed since the Act of 1927 an adequate supply of British scenario writers has not become available. British film production has accordingly been limited through this provision in its capacity for expansion.'[71]
The 'quota quickie' which disgraced British production in the thirties had its genesis here. At first, as renters who did not normally handle British pictures looked around for genuine British productions, the term quota film began to be applied to the latter, sometimes when still in production. Before long the term was used for a film made specially to fulfil quota obligations, or at best because the quota provided a sure market. Betts, writing in *Close Up* as early as November 1927, also referred disparagingly to 'quickies' in a different sense:

'. . . directly after the Films Bill had been outlined he was deluged with offers to come in with men to make "quickies". A "quickie" is an old film with a few modern sequences inserted."[72]

In June 1928 a Gaumont advertisement said

'Not Quota Pictures, but Big British Pictures available for Quota.'[73]

and next month the General Council of the C.E.A. when discussing European Motion Pictures' quota pictures noted very severely that 'any old films' were being brought in for quota purposes. In the same month *Close Up*, citing three B.I.P. films as particularly bad British productions, referred to them as 'quota pictures'. And an item in *The Bioscope* of March 13, 1929, described a £4,000 'quickie' as a

'. . . four-reel subject . . . made in a week's intensive work using unwanted scraps from other films, disengaged sets from any studio, all kinds of ingenious economies and working a star under terrific pressure for a day or day-and-a-half.'[74]

Finally, as the *Moyne Report* was to make clear, the term referred to

'. . . production of cheap British films, made at the lowest cost, irrespective of quality, by or at the order of foreign-controlled renters solely to enable them to show formal compliance with those provisions of the Act which relate to the renters' quota. Such films, known as "quota quickies" from the speed at which they are made, have tended to bring British films into disrepute.'[75]

Final assessment of the results depends on your standpoint. Simon Rowson, a renter-producer whose own output at Ideal during the early twenties had suggested a complete indifference to quality, took a rosy view in his 1934 pamphlet. He claimed that the growth in British footage was attributable to the British renters, answering the need to stimulate first-class British production:

'British film production might never have been, but for the determination, courage and enterprise of the British renting companies.'[76]

Balcon, on the other hand, as one of the best producers, was bitter. Of the money raised for production after the quota legislation, he said:

'Most of the money, incidentally, was raised for Distributing and Exhibiting companies who never failed to quote on their prospectuses the British films they had distributed or exhibited. These were *their* films, as ever—*their* achievement, perpetuating the domination of the primary producer by other trade interests.'[77]

Certainly the quota did make room on the screens for British films of a sort, and thus did bring capital into the production industry, both directly and also indirectly by stimulating the vertical combination which organized distribution outlets. But it also led straight to the disastrous decline in quality which had been clearly foreseen by so many people. Since the film industry is not a major capital or labour user like steel, coal or shipbuilding the Government and F.B.I. circles were probably mistaken in thinking that their primary objective was a great increase in the size of British output. Their real cause for concern was the way in which American standards rather than British ones, both social and commercial, were being propagated all over the world and even in Britain itself. By the quota they achieved a larger output of film, but of film which was even less highly regarded than before, and did nothing to spread a British image. It happens sometimes that in matters of taste or fashion outstanding quality, even in quite small amounts, can set a trend. A small output of very high quality can sometimes become the highly-sought and fashionable thing, leaving production to expand naturally in response to a real demand. A few British films of fine quality might well have tipped the balance. But there was nothing in the legislation designed to encourage quality, no training schemes, awards or incentives, no subsidised loans or studio facilities. Even reliable safeguards against a drop from the already low standards of quality had been neglected. Disregarding all economic experience, quality was expected to improve of its own accord simply because a protected market had been provided.

CHAPTER FOUR

Producers in the
Early Twenties

There were some hundreds of film producers in Britain during the twenties. From the basic facts of their careers, from looking at those of their films which still survive, from things written and said about them and their associates both at the time and since, from meeting some of them or people who knew them, and from what many of them have written either then or later it is possible to estimate their positions in the production scene and see how this changed during the period. In general the picture is one of unfounded optimism after the war when the old guard of producer expected to return to much the same sort of production as before 1914, and a gradual decline from 1920 to 1924 or 1925 during which they were almost all forced out of business and a new, more modern, type of producer began to appear. The latter realized the need for bigger capital resources and better distribution, but found that British film production was only just economically viable. The quota legislation of 1927 designed to remedy this situation brought capital into the industry. As production expanded, not always wisely, it was further disrupted in 1929 by the arrival of commercial sound film production.

Optimism lasted for several years after the war despite a frosty reception from both critics and box office and the difficult situation created by booking abuses (*see* Chapter III). Even in 1923 *The Bioscope* wrote, absurdly,

'The world dominion of the British Super Film may well prove the outstanding feature of 1923.'[1]

The difficulty which British producers found in marketing their films was put down to many things, among them overproduction, unfair competition from America and the wickedness of renters, but the producers blindly continued to think in terms of meagre backyard production, albeit expanded to the scale of the mansion-type studio. The important producers of the early twenties were Hepworth, Gaumont, Welsh–Pearson, Ideal and Stoll, all of them small in comparison with American firms. Of these Hepworth and Gaumont had started before 1900 and Pearson, as an individual producer, almost as early. Ideal and Stoll had been formed during the war and were somewhat larger, but their conception of film making was equally old-fashioned. Meanwhile Harry Bruce Woolfe of British Instructional Films, Michael Balcon of Gainsborough and Herbert Wilcox all successfully began making films of a completely different character during the very years when the older firms were finding things difficult. British Instructional and Gainsborough showed their ability as soon as they started and Wilcox by 1925, although their true importance did not emerge until slightly later. The largest company of all during the twenties and the one which most nearly approached the Hollywood ideal, British International Pictures, did not appear until the second half of the decade.

Amongst the early companies Hepworth and Ideal most clearly typified the old school of film making and had disappeared completely as regular producers by the middle of the period, although Ideal still existed as a renter. Henry Edwards, whose separate brand of film within the Hepworth organization had showed great promise, survived the crash but did not continue to develop as a director as might have been hoped. Gaumont remained in business after a period of difficulty, and at the end of the period combined with Balcon's firm Gainsborough as the basis of a big film empire. Stoll more or less withdrew from production, a huge output of mediocre films to its credit. Welsh–Pearson, relying on the work of George Pearson, appeared largely unaffected by the crisis in production but succumbed later when, against his advice, it was slow to adopt the production of sound films.

The trouble with the older companies was that, faced with difficulties in getting capital or a wide market, they allowed themselves to think that films financed cheaply on a pre-war scale could survive in the post-war world. The higher cost of the films coming over from America meant, in fact, a completely different style of production. It was no good Col. Bromhead of Gaumont writing that the quality of British films was now up to standard

'. . . having regard to the cost of production. Naturally, one cannot expect a £5,000 film to compare in elaborateness with a £25,000 picture.'[2]

The £5,000 picture was almost dead. The old days when features were films of three to five reels put out under brand names, and selling on the reputation of the brand, were gone. Features of seven reels or more, fewer in number and each one advertised as an individual work and booked as such, replaced them. Dominated by their think-small mentality and limited by their small studios and inadequate capital, British film makers were apt to appeal to patriotism on the part of showmen and audiences to get them out of their difficulties. At the same time stars and film makers from abroad, usually from America, were frequently used to give the film greater popular appeal.*

Thus, whilst the old guard were finding their difficulties too much for them during the early twenties, their failure coincided with the successful growth of a new type of producer. The new men thought and planned on a bigger scale. Consequently, although they had to contend with the same tightness of capital

---

* Foreign visitors who worked in British studios at this time included writers Ouida Bergere, Margaret Turnbull and Eve Unsell; directors John Stuart Blackton, Herbert Brenon, Michael Curtiz, Donald Crisp, George Fitzmaurice, Fred Leroy Granville, Duncan McRae, Walter Niebuhr, the Canadian John S. Robertson and Tom Terriss; cameraman Nicholas Musuraca; players Lionel Barrymore, Betty Blythe, Betty Compson, Marjorie Daw, Marie Doro, Josephine Earle, Bernhard Goetzke, Wanda Hawley, Sessue Hayakawa, Charles Hutchison, Alice Joyce, Werner Krauss, Mae Marsh, Anna Q. Nilsson, Jane Novak, Seena Owen and Bryant Washburn.

and the same distribution difficulties, and tried the same shifts of foreign talent, foreign backing and distribution links, they were able to lay solid foundations during the worst years of the production slump. The successful new producers were serious in purpose and deliberate in direction, and the old days of small catch-penny operations and the unsophisticated amateur were over.

Immediately after the war the Hepworth Company was ready for expansion. Paul Kimberley had joined the firm as general manager in 1918 and former members of the staff returned from the war, among them Geoffrey and Stanley Faithfull, cameraman and stills photographer, and director Gaston Queribet. The leading players Violet Hopson and Stewart Rome left to join Broadwest, but James Carew, Eileen Dennes and others became members of the stock company and Anson Dyer joined the organization to make cartoon films. Hepworth Picture Plays was formed in April 1919 with a capital of £100,000 and during the summer bought a large house at Weybridge, Oatlands Park Estate.

The intention was to expand the Walton studio and use the house and grounds at Weybridge for settings. For the next few years Hepworth maintained a small and disciplined stock company and most of his films featured Gwynne Herbert, John MacAndrews, Gerald Ames and Lionelle Howard as well as Eileen Dennes and James Carew and of course his star, Alma Taylor. According to his autobiography the company's greatest artistic strength lay in the work of Chrissie White, Alma Taylor and Henry Edwards, and it is true that the two girls were the only English heroines other than Betty Balfour, and to a lesser extent Joan Morgan, who could be described as film stars. Henry Edwards and Chrissie White, however, played in a separate brand of Hepworth–Edwards films directed and usually written by Edwards himself. These were referred to by Hepworth as a series of productions made side by side with his. Edwards, who was also a director of the parent company, emphasized in later years that his work was not subject to Hepworth's control.

Henry Edwards seemed at this time to have it in him to be not merely competent but outstanding as a film maker. He became a director of the new Hepworth company when it was formed in 1922, and from the end of the war to the collapse of the company worked on his own independent series of about sixteen films featuring himself and Chrissie White, whom he married in November 1922. Charles Bryce was his cameraman. One of the most important of these films was *The City of Beautiful Nonsense* (Trade Show November 1919), based on a Temple Thurston novel. This was a sentimental story about a girl who realized her true duty was to marry for love, not for money. A review of this early film gives an idea of Edwards' style:

'Effects are obtained quietly, easily and powerfully by a calm, orderly statement of the facts of the story, touched here and there by poetic embellishments such as the voyage of the toy boat of thoughts sailing in the dreamer's imagination from Kensington Gardens to the golden waters of Venice. Deft and imaginative to a degree are these stylistic flourishes. Thus, the hero's mental struggle between the allurement of his bed and a lover's appointment is cleverly illustrated by a wavering dissolve, in which the scene of the meeting finally predominates. In the invention of pictorial idioms, Mr Edwards displays the utmost technical dexterity and originality, which mark him as one of the most individual producers of the day. He is fond, too, of symbolistic touches, introduced gracefully and without labouring the point, such as the heroine's movement to bar her lips from the man she loves with the hand which bears the ring of her "duty" engagement.'[3]

His films had much in common with those of Hepworth. Although they had different cameramen they used the same technical facilities and stock company and shared the same middle-class outlook and sentimental approach, as well as a pleasure in lovely English scenery, well photographed. The sweet and lovable Chrissie White was a perfect English heroine and like Alma Taylor was a contrast to the low-life *gamine* of Pearson's Betty Balfour. But despite his closeness to Hepworth, Edwards' early films had considerable individuality. He had given up writing original stories, although he did his own adaptations as well as directing and acting. He took his stories from very varied sources and preferred more exciting and unfamiliar settings than Hepworth. His acting background provided him with a sense of structure and pace which Hepworth lacked, and an interest in characterization. As an actor, also, he delighted in the 'little touches' so greatly admired in his films. These were the cinematic equivalent of stage business, and were his imaginative contribution to the development of visual story telling. In this inventiveness he was far ahead of Hepworth or even Pearson, and probably excelled in Britain only in the work, a few years later, of Hitchcock and Asquith. Less theoretical than Pearson and without his thoughtful approach to theme, he did attempt one conscious experiment in film narrative in *Lily of the Alley* (Trade Show February 1923), his only original scenario at this time, which was made entirely without subtitles. It would seem that this film was not the first to be made without titles* but when interviewed Henry Edwards clearly believed that it was, and there is no reason to suppose that he was aware of any others at the time. It was outstanding more as a brave attempt, however, than as a success, and *The Bioscope* criticized the way the self-imposed limitation had led to some rather far-fetched ways of conveying simple ideas which could have been explained more easily by titles, and some desperate attempts at conversation through gestures and pictorial allusions.

Edwards was financially involved in the failure of the main company but unlike Hepworth he found continued backing for further films, on which he worked variously as actor, director and producer. Ultimately, however, he turned more and more to acting. The early promise of a genuine feeling for the medium which would make him one of the few highly creative directors of the silent cinema was not fulfilled.

Hepworth's own films almost all featured Alma Taylor, whose warm, sympa-

* In *Anatomy of Motion Picture Art* Elliott mentions several films without titles which he believed pre-dated it: *The Old Swimming Hole*, undated; *The Audacious Mr Squire*, which was actually trade shown eight months after *Lily*; *The Rail* or *Shattered*, and *Warning Shadows*, which were made in Germany in 1921 and 1922 respectively and do not seem to have been shown in England when *Lily* was made in 1922.

thetic personality suited him, and were all adaptations, mostly by Blanche MacIntosh until she left the company in 1922. *The Nature of the Beast* (Trade Show early 1919) and *Sunken Rocks* (Trade Show August 1919) were the last of an uneasy collaboration with the novelist Temple Thurston during the war. *Sheba* (Trade Show October 1919) by Rita, *The Forest on the Hill* (Trade Show December 1919) by Eden Philpotts and *Anna the Adventuress* (Trade Show February 1920) by E. Phillips Oppenheim, were all favourites of Hepworth himself. His own films were few in number and, apart from some mild travel and interest shorts, each was intended to be an important work in the modern manner, but he was not really in tune with the post war spirit in film production. In his autobiography[4] he wrote later that there

'. . . was a pressure in the air which we did not understand and we worked on as best we could in spite of it.'

All seemed well on the surface and his next film appeared to him in later years to be the most completely successful he had ever made. This was *Alf's Button* (Trade Show May 1920) and was adapted by Blanche MacIntosh from a novel by W. A. Darlington of *The Daily Telegraph*. It was a comedy, and completely uncharacteristic of Hepworth's work. It concerned a soldier with a magic button giving him control over a genie who granted his wishes, and it featured the cinema's power to show sudden appearances, disappearances and transformations. Although the film was slow and episodic, the burlesque war story suited the post-war mood and it was an outstanding popular success, even making the novel a best-seller, so much so that Darlington wrote a play based on it which ran for months at Prince's in 1924. Part of its success was due to the performance of the stage comedian Leslie Henson. According to Darlington, Hepworth would not accept any comic ideas from Henson but

'Hepworth, essentially a serious-minded man, was the only film director who saw that, given the original ridiculous situation, the more gravely the adventures of Alf with his button were treated the funnier they became.'[5]

and Hepworth had a similar explanation:

'You may invent the maddest idea of which your brain is capable but if you state it clearly at the beginning and go on to develop it on sane and logical lines, keeping true to the one impossibility and letting every situation grow naturally out of it, just as if it were a sane and sound premise, you will find that it will be accepted and enjoyed without question in spite of its primary absurdity.'

After this film's successful trade show Paul Kimberley, who was at this time running a renting organization called Imperial Film Company, devised a joint scheme to distribute Hepworth films instead of selling them outright to other renters. *Alf's Button* was to be the first. A distribution set-up was secured here and in America where Hepworth, who visited the United States with Alma

Taylor at the end of 1921, claimed that his films sold well. Production seemed to flourish. He directed most of his own films, with some assistance from Queribet, Ames and Dewhurst for the less important productions. All his own films starred Alma Taylor except *Wild Heather* (Trade Show September 1921), which he made with Chrissie White when Henry Edwards was away in 1921. Again, all were adaptations and most from sentimental novels. *Helen of Four Gates* (Trade Show September 1920) was from a novel by Mrs E. Holdsworth, and he considered it one of his best, though not one of the most popular. Others were *Mrs Ericker's Reputation* (Trade Show December 1920) by Thomas Cobb, *The Tinted Venus* (Trade Show April 1921) by F. Anstey, and *Tansy* (Trade Show December 1921) by Tickner Edwards. Early in 1923 *Mist in the Valley* (Trade Show March 1923) was shown, and then *Strangling Threads* (Trade Show September 1923), from the play *The Cobweb* by Leon M. Lion and Naunton Davies, and finally *Comin' thro' the Rye* (Trade Show November 1923) from the novel by Helen Mather. Of all his films this last was the one he prized most dearly. It is a sign of his unadventurous approach to the question of story that both this and *Strangling Threads* were remakes of his own earlier successes.

His films appeared to be popular and his reputation was at its peak. He wrote in his autobiography that he put everything that he had in him into *Comin' thro' the Rye* and was puzzled later that he could have worked so cheerfully on this, his best and most important film, while financial disaster was so near.

During the last few years work had started on the new studio space, and the old studio had been shut for about six months in 1922 while the company was reformed. A row of six big daylight stages was planned, sharing dressing rooms, carpenters' shops, scene docks and other departments, with electric generators for auxiliary arc lighting. But meanwhile the booking difficulties were strangling British film production. Block and advance booking kept capital locked up in films for as long as eighteen months, and Hepworth found that to maintain his own renting organization was too expensive. It was announced that from August 1923 his films would be handled by Ideal. It was no longer a suitable time to float a production company, as the difficulties suffered by British producers were already causing alarm, but the company was too far committed to the expansion of its studio to withdraw and in any case it was felt that their films did make modest profits once they secured distribution. Planning to treble their output, they had appealed to the public in March 1922, the prospectus putting their profits at £7,614 for 1919, £10,734 for 1920 and £13,921 for 1921. The issue, however, was badly undersubscribed.

Hepworth speaks in his book of

'. . . seemingly unreasonable failure bearing down with cruel insistence upon the very peak of my greatest success.'

Plans for expansion had been abandoned as a result of the unsuccessful bid for capital, yet he seems to have felt that with films like *Comin' thro' the Rye* he could not fail. It was released in conjunction with the National Film Weeks scheme and the firm's publicity representative called for support on grounds

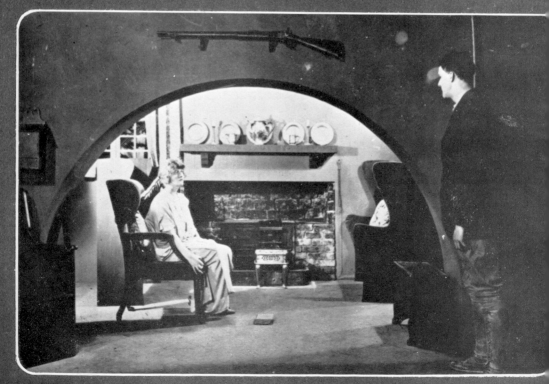

both of patriotism and of loyalty to one of the oldest firms in the business. Sentiment carried little weight, however, and the film did not save the company. A receiver was appointed to wind it up in June 1924, and according to Hepworth himself, in an interview many years later, the business was sold at the bottom of the production slump for as little as £4,000.

It should be remembered that while Hepworth was being pushed out of business others, like Balcon and Bruce Woolfe, were just beginning, and his financial collapse cannot be blamed entirely on external economic factors. He was not a businessman by temperament and was somewhat out of date in both business methods and film style. He did not seek backing for further production and, perhaps to his disappointment, other firms did not press him for his services as a director. He busied himself with the stage presentation of an elaborate mime designed as a prologue to *Comin' thro' the Rye*. He and Alma Taylor made one more film together in 1926, the melodramatic *House of Marney* (Trade Show January 1927) for Archibald Nettlefold, the uncongenial personality who had acquired his studio, but the experience must have been an unhappy one and he does not mention it in his reminiscences. Instead he speaks of *Through Three Reigns*, a compilation of his own early news items concerning the Royal family, which he says he put together and exhibited himself when all the trouble was over. Block booking delayed its release and 'meantime, "Sound Pictures" burst like a bomb', and it was a failure.* After this he retired from feature production and returned to the technical side of photography, printing and developing amateur roll films.

Hepworth and Pearson were the two important British producers of the early twenties. Both were squeezed out of this position in their fifties, and both wrote autobiographies in later life. It is interesting and sad to compare their difficulties. Hepworth's book contains much searching for his mistakes, with a dryness that only partly conceals considerable hurt and bitterness. Proud and reserved, his reaction to the rebuff was to withdraw from the struggle. Pearson's sweet-natured humility and enthusiasm enabled him to accept disappointment more easily, learn new ways and adapt himself to a more modest rôle in sound films, quickie production, and later even documentary, and in the end to retain the devotion and respect of many younger film makers although he was no longer a prominent producer.

Hepworth's most positive contribution to the British film was a measure of dignity and respectability and a feeling that cinema was more than a vulgar money-making novelty. A meticulous and careful worker in firm control of his studio and employees, his films were always well photographed and presented. He was intensely idealistic and patriotic.

---

* Actually a Hepworth compilation called *Through Three Reigns* was trade shown in July 1922, before the crash. A second one compiled by Will Day for Gaumont using film by Lumière and R. W. Paul as well as Hepworth and called *Royal Remembrances* was trade shown in November 1928 and held for immediate release by Gaumont in February 1929; this may well have been partly made about 1925 and held over because of booking difficulties.

'It was always in the back of my mind from the very beginning that *I was to make English pictures, with all the English countryside for background and with English idiom throughout.*'

They were nice stories about nice people, cosy, traditional and even a little smug. Members of his company felt that they were the aristocrats of film making. A photographer and artist himself, his emphasis was always on visual interest, and above all the well-photographed beauty of England. Perhaps his most interesting advance was towards the use of settings not only for their pictorial beauty but for their mood significance, almost as forces shaping the destiny and expressing the character of those involved. The mood tended to be monotonously mild and sentimental, but nevertheless in this he was ahead of most other producers. Even years later many still thought of the visual aspect of films mainly in terms of the so-called production values of spectacular and unusual settings.

His films had two highly individual characteristics. First, he preferred to fade out of every shot and into the next instead of cutting. This he felt

'. . . created a feeling of smoothness—avoided the harsh unpleasant "jerk" usually associated with change of scene . . .'

and although he did add that

'. . . in a long smooth sequence, an unexpected jerk may be dramatically important and then it can be used with redoubled effect . . .'

he felt that this should be employed but rarely. Fading was already widely used to imply a lapse of time. Hepworth's fades were too quick to imply a false time relation, but they undoubtedly slowed the film down to the point of tedium. Secondly, a

'. . . soft vignetted edge all round the picture was much more aesthetically pleasing than a hard line and the unrelieved black frame . . . it is produced by a carefully adjusted little frame just in front of my lens, which, being so close is entirely out of focus and merely gives a pleasing soft edge to the picture.'

Speaking of visual values he sums up:

'Always . . . I have striven for beauty, for *pictorial* meaning and effect. . . . Much of my success, I am sure, is in the aesthetic pleasure conveyed, but not recognized, by the beauty of the scene and generally mistaken for some unknown other quality in the film.'

This obsession with film as a pictorial art and a search for beauty took precedence over the dramatic or narrative interest in his work. His lack of stage antecedents made him, like Pearson, a contrast to many English pioneers whose work was stagey and unsuitable. When the early feature of about three thousand feet had arrived and longer stories were necessary, he had felt that stage plays were not the best material, and had tried to write stories himself. Although he gave this up he continued to feel strongly that film stories should be specially written. He always preferred to work in the open air and, when indoor work was necessary, preferred daylight if it were possible. In fact when he did use sets they tended to lack verisimilitude. He had strong views about make-up, and his own players wore little or none, which was unusual at this time.

'It is in the tiny interstices in the skin around the eyes that all changes of expression are registered. If this is so, it would seem to be bad practice to fill up those tiny interstices and almost invisible wrinkles with grease-paint. It is robbing the artists of their best means of telling the story.'

But though his lack of theatricality was of value in some ways he lacked the warm and sympathetic handling of actors, interest in the externalization of character and emotion, or the dramatic inventiveness which made Henry Edwards and Pearson so alive to the possibilities of the film. Of actors, he wrote:

'I was able to tell each actor where he was to stand, what his movements were to be and when, and give some indication of necessary gestures. . . . Then the scene was rehearsed quietly and gently. . . . In those silent days the director was able to give a great deal of help by quiet prompting while the scene was actually in progress . . .'

and again:
'I knew from experience that some of them come to the peak of their endeavour after, say, ten rehearsals, while others boil up after three. Also that if they once pass the peak, you never get such good work out of them again in that scene. So the "early boilers" had to be tactfully asked to stand aside for a bit while the "simmerers" were poked up a little and all brought to the boil at the same time.'

Yet a player who knew him well said many years later that in handling actors he was 'as cold as a fish' and Hepworth repeatedly said to the author that the function of the camera was simply to turn, and allow the actors to behave suitably in front of it. He was vehement about the impertinence of teaching actors their job. When an actor went on the floor he was able to tell him where

'. . . to stand at the beginning of the scene, where and at what cue he was to move and, of course, what he was to portray, *not* how he was to portray it—that was his business, not mine: I am not an actor.'

Not only did he feel this reticence, but apparently he did not think in terms of the little touches and devices, which pushed forward the use of cutting and story structure as a result, which came naturally to Edwards for characterization and associative reference. He relied heavily on mime to convey character and emotion, and since he left so much to the actors the results here were not always happy. The technique seemed to suit Alma Taylor, with her delicacy and poise and the tranquil reality she projected on the screen. The following note on her performance in *Sheba*, from *The Bioscope*, says a lot about both her and about Hepworth:

'It is indicative of the play's haphazard construction that the most moving incident in the story is one which has practically no direct dramatic importance, and which derives its value solely from the exquisite beauty and delicacy of its treatment by player and producer. This memorable little scene shows Sheba's first realization that she has been accorded the gift of motherhood. Seated among the rising corn, bathed in the bright spring sunshine, she understands suddenly that she also is destined to have her share in the universal fruitfulness of Nature. Fear, wonder, and finally, triumphing joy succeed each other in her soul as she kneels there with the new life of the earth stirring around her.

'The knowledge of a great mystery about to be revealed is in her eyes as she raises them from the book she had been reading, and one can almost hear the whispering of her heart while she grasps its significance. As an isolated moment, this is, perhaps the greatest piece of acting Alma Taylor has ever done, whilst it typifies perfectly Cecil Hepworth's unique art as the poet producer, who can write lyrics with his camera.'[6]

His inventiveness was in cinematography engineering rather than in film technique. Here he was a genuine innovator, and made interesting and valuable improvements in processing, and in the early days of lanterns and the Vivaphone had taken out several patents. In more specifically camera technique his inventiveness lent itself to double photography in *Anna the Adventuress*, the appearances and disappearances of *Alf's Button* and later on an interesting seven-minute take, in very long shot, of a sheep dog at work in *Tansy*. But there was none of the wild and enterprising improvisation by which Pearson, for example, contrived to suggest the things he could not show.

His contrast to Pearson was probably greatest in his attitude to the story, which further led the latter to the idea of a theme. It is true that Hepworth felt that stories should be written specially for the film. But although he had devised his own little made-up enacted films from his pioneering film *Rescued by Rover* in 1905 onwards he did not, after his original screen story for *The Basilisk* in 1914, want to write them himself. On the contrary, he fell in with the current fashion of adapting novels, in his case contemporary novels, and although he had considerable influence over the adaptation, the script itself was prepared by and formally acknowledged to his scenario writer Blanche MacIntosh. He explained:

'When I read a book or saw a play or studied a synopsis, there came into my mental vision a fairly detailed and consecutive pattern of what the film would be like. That pattern stuck in my head and gradually crystallised out into a definite form, while the working scenario was being prepared for me.

'The next step was to complete the crystallisation process. I chewed the scenario over bit by bit, suggested alterations and discussed them and finally I took it home and lived with it. . . .

'I re-transcribed every word of it myself, chewing over every line in my mind, cutting out and rearranging the pieces as seemed to me to be best and stopping and forcing myself to visualize every little scene as it was to appear on the screen. I even estimated its length and jotted that down on the paper. So when I went on the floor I knew exactly what I wanted. . . . I wrote in every sub-title and every spoken title which was to appear in printed words on the screen. The actors were instructed to use this wording where it occurred. . . .'

Having finished his scenario, he felt that the final construction of the film was fixed.

'I have always held the view that the editing should be done in the original script, before ever an inch of it goes under the camera.'

It is here, in the matter of editing, that the inelasticity of his attitude was probably at its most damaging. In his view the function of the editor was to doctor or tighten up the already constructed film:

'None of my films had ever been "edited". Editing in film production means, broadly, cutting out unnecessary pieces and joining in and rearranging others to get the best effect.

'I never saw a single "rush"—never had anything to do with any of the scenes after they were photographed until they were all joined together in their proper order with all the titles and sub-titles in place—in short, the whole thing completely finished.'

This was the time when the great Russian film makers were revolutionizing the concept of film structure with the idea that the very changes from one shot to another, and the tempo of the cutting, could have dramatic and emotional impact of their own, and that the juxtaposition of different shots could itself convey meanings not inherent in the isolated shots themselves. It is a question of definition whether this complex of ideas is called editing, montage, or simply film structure, and if Hepworth used the word editing to refer merely to the mechanical task of cementing the bits of film together, and resented any interference with his film structure at that stage, he was simply following the custom of many of his contemporaries. Nevertheless it is true that his film structure remained very elementary and his rigid definition of editing, and the very disinterest he showed in it, were likely to prevent any extension of his film technique. He could even write many years later, speaking of sound films:

'Two figures arguing heatedly would probably be best built up in excitement by cutting sharply backwards and forwards from one to the other. Even there I would rather, for the sake of smoothness, keep them both in view in one longer shot and allow the expressions of both faces to be studied together.'

He was inhibited by the set of rules he had built up for himself: not to cut, not to interfere with the actors, not to use make-up or artificial lighting if he could avoid it, not to make alterations during shooting or editing, not to see the rushes. Within this dead-end he proceeded aloofly on his own lines. It is hard not to conclude that the great regard in which he was held by the trade and by much of the British film public was more a tribute to his personal integrity than to any great vitality in his work.

The other large company formed before the end of the war which gave up production entirely during the slump of 1923–24 was Ideal. This was a company of a very different type. Formed much more recently, it was large and impersonal, and sprang more from the businessman's demand for films to rent than from the film maker's desire to make them. The different motivation showed clearly in the product.

The Ideal Film Company, under its managing director Simon Rowson, the renter, had started production during the war with a fairly large output of theatrical films, mostly made by Maurice Elvey and Fred Paul at the old Neptune studios at Boreham Wood, Elstree. When the war ended production was at a standstill and the studios were leased to British Lion, a private company whose managing director was David Falcke. A. V. Bramble, previously in the theatre, was engaged as producer, and a handful of films were rapidly made. The first, *A Non-Conformist Parson* (Trade Show March 1919), was a sordid story of a provincial parson whose career was ruined by his wife, and was adapted by Eliot Stannard from a novel by Roy Horniman. *The Bioscope* was strangely delighted with it and the review is of interest as a sign of the optimism there was in the British film industry just after the war:

'. . . Mr A. V. Bramble, who shows that he possesses a quality that is very near genius . . . it is his personal contribution to the film—his instinct for character in details, his mastery of dramatic tempo, his extraordinary psychological insight—that is, in our opinion, mainly responsible for the brilliant result upon the screen. Quite in the Griffith manner is his method of character revelation by vivid flashes. Until one grows used to his style there seems some jerkiness in the action. There are no pauses. Point after point is made with rapid emphasis, and there are no long explanatory passages.'[7]

But by June of the same year British Lion was in financial trouble. According to the bankruptcy proceedings later their backer was 'a wealthy woman' who had at first ventured £2,000 but eventually lost £12,000 in the company. Ideal began to use the studio again themselves, taking over with it both Bramble and Fred Goodwins, an actor from the American stage who had joined British Lion as a producer. Early next year it was decided to expand both the renting and producing business, and the enlarged company was registered in May 1920 with a capital of £115,000. Meanwhile a building in the grounds was leased to Harry Bruce Woolfe who was already at work independently on what was to be the first British Instructional film, *The Battle of Jutland* (Trade Show September 1921).

For the next few years Ideal had a very large output, especially in 1921 when as many as eighteen films were trade shown. (Two films featured the actor who had played Christ in the American film *From the Manger to the Cross* in 1912, R. Henderson Bland.) Many directors worked for them, especially Bramble and later Denison Clift, both of whom made eleven films, with Goodwins, Meyrick Milton, Thomas Bentley, Jack Denton, Bert Wynne and later Duncan McRae, Georges Tréville, Edwin J. Collins, George Béranger, Frank Crane, Tom Terriss and at the end Henry Kolker. The most outstanding of these was probably Denison Clift, who was responsible for the only three Ideal films from this large output to be included later in the *World Film Encyclopedia*'s retrospective list, such as it was, of famous films. These were *A Woman of No Importance* (Trade Show June 1921) with Milton Rosmer and Fay Compton, *Sonia* (Trade Show September 1921) with Evelyn Brent and Clive Brook, and *This Freedom* (Trade Show April 1923) from a novel by A. S. M. Hutchinson with Fay Compton and Clive Brook. Clift, an American who joined Ideal as a promising young director at the end of 1920, stayed until the end of 1923 when he made *The Loves of Mary Queen of Scots* (Trade Show November 1923) with Gerald Ames and Fay Compton. This was called a Denison Clift Art Production and added greatly to his growing reputation. By 1925 he was working for de Mille in Hollywood, from which he returned in 1928. Bramble did not live up to the review of his first film and after *Shirley* (Trade Show April 1922) he made no more films for Ideal but worked on the live action sequences of Bruce Woolfe's second British Instructional war film, *Armageddon* (Trade Show November 1923). Subsequent to the collapse of Ideal's production in 1923–24, Bramble found occasional film work as an actor and also co-directed another war reconstruction film with Bruce Woolfe, *Zeebrugge* (Trade Show October 1924), and then in 1927 was engaged by the latter, now making feature films, to supervise the Asquith film *Shooting Stars* for British Instructional (see page 182). He himself seemed in his old age to feel that his best film was the Ideal version of *Wuthering Heights* (Trade Show July 1920) with Milton Rosmer, but there is every indication that this, like the rest of this make, was an old-fashioned production of very poor quality.

Like the output of the other large renter-producer in England, Stoll, the films were mostly adaptations of novels. But whereas the Stoll films were from contemporary or recent works, Ideal specialized in Victorian novels, typically those of Dickens, George Eliot, Thackeray, the Brontës, Disraeli, Oscar Wilde and Bulwer Lytton. Long complicated plots were told cursorily in films crammed with incidents and people but lacking any subtlety of treatment, the function of the script being taken so much for granted that mention was rarely made of the scenarists, usually Eliot Stannard or W. J. Elliott. In the same way the cameramen, Horace Wheddon and William Shenton, were rarely credited. Edwin Greenwood, who was described as Art Director of the company from 1919 to 1921, was from the theatre, and the visual concept of the films was entirely theatrical. The date of the stories, moreover, encouraged a hired fancy-dress appearance, executed cheaply and without imagination. The casts were enormous and included all the usual British standbys who appeared in film after film at this time, as well as a number of appearances from Warwick Ward, Mary Odette,

A. Harding Steerman, Mary Brough, Haidee Wright, Evelyn Brent, Olaf Hytten, Sydney Paxton and Daisy Campbell. The favoured leading men were Milton Rosmer and Henry Ainley, both in their forties at the time and heavily made up with stagey greasepaint. Later there seems to have been an attempt to bring production up to date. After a dinner in December 1920 at which the guests of honour were W. W. Jacobs, Dion Clayton Calthrop and Compton Mackenzie, stories by these writers were adapted for the cinema and also three by Arnold Bennett and one by A. S. M. Hutchinson. Clive Brook and Fay Compton, both young and modern, replaced the earlier leads, and to bring a little variety into production the pre-war favourite from America, Florence Turner, was engaged for two character parts, in Clift's *The Old Wives' Tale* (Trade Show December 1921) by Arnold Bennett, and Bramble's *Little Mother* (Trade Show March 1922); the comedian Laddie Cliff appeared as Arnold Bennett's *The Card* (Trade Show April 1922), and the American thrill-a-minute superman cowboy 'Hutch', Charles Hutchison, was engaged for two films: *Hutch Stirs 'em up* (Trade Show August 1923) and *Hurricane Hutch in Many Adventures* (Trade Show March 1924); and finally the American star Seena Owen, with Joan Morgan, appeared in the last Ideal film, *The Great Well* (Trade Show April 1924).

The volume of this output makes it necessary to treat it as important, yet few of the films are worth mentioning by name. It was mass production at its worst, the technique showing little if any advance on that of films made during or even before the war. Fewer films appeared in 1922 and 1923 and production was given up at the beginning of 1924, although after Ideal had merged with Gaumont–British in 1927, Meyrick Milton came back briefly to produce *His House in Order* (Trade Show February 1928), which was adapted from Pinero by Pat Mannock and directed by Randle Ayrton at Teddington, and featured no less a star than Tallulah Bankhead. It was said at the time that if the economies of such large-scale production, and the provision of capital sufficient to minimize the difficulty of delayed release dates, were unable to make production profitable, then no British company could stay in business. The wonder is that with such bad films the company managed to survive as long as it did, but this may have been because Ideal, like Stoll, was a big enough renting firm to carry some influence. This might explain some puzzling reviews in *The Bioscope*, which would mention bad acting, bad art direction, bad adaptation from a bad source, only to conclude that the film was a masterpiece.

The Welsh–Pearson company was about the same age as Ideal, although George Pearson himself had been making films for almost as long as Hepworth. The company was formed towards the end of the war by Pearson and T. A. Welsh with a capital of £6,000 and made three or four films a year during the early twenties. It survived the slump, and in fact the early and mid-twenties were probably the period of Pearson's greatest success. The company then continued to produce one or two films a year until finally defeated by the arrival of the sound film. Although it was a small firm, each of its films was treated as an important individual achievement and its small output was of far greater interest than the Ideal mass production. Thomas Welsh was Chairman and Managing Director and the unit was a stable one, with Emile Lauste as cameraman and laboratory technician until Percy Strong took over in 1923, assisted by Bernard Knowles, and Ernest Jones as scenic artist. The reason for the company's existence was plainly Pearson's own enthusiasm and creative ability, and the trade regarded him as a leader in thoughtful and artistic film making. Yet the choice of other directors like Thomas Bentley, F. Martin Thornton and later Fred Paul and T. Hayes Hunter for occasional extra films was strangely old-fashioned and undistinguished, and suggests an unnecessary timidity.

In 1919 the new studio was ready at Craven Park and their first post-war film, *Garryowen* (Trade Show January 1920), was finished there and shown in 1920. It was a racing story adapted by Pearson from the novel by H. de Vere Stacpoole and starred Moyna MacGill, Fred Groves and the stage comedian Hugh E. Wright, who had also been in in the last two Welsh–Pearson films. Feeling like Hepworth that films should be based on original stories rather than adaptations, Pearson now collaborated with Hugh E. Wright on the idea for his next film, *Nothing Else Matters* (Trade Show July 1920), a homely sentimental story about an old music-hall comic played by Wright. It was warmly received by the trade, in fact according to Valentia Steer it was so much liked at the trade show at the Alhambra that it was run through a second time.[8] Production and photography were admired, as they always were in Pearson's films, and he was rewarded by critical appreciation of the script and the story's special suitability for the cinema. Moyna MacGill was again the star, but two young actresses, Betty Balfour and Mabel Poulton, made their first appearances in small parts; as a comic skivvy Betty Balfour stole the show.

Pearson had now found a star and a style which were to characterize his work for several years. His films featured Betty Balfour as an exuberant Cockney urchin, roguish and with a heart of gold. She immediately became one of the very few British film stars, and in the mid-twenties had a very large following in England, equalled among British players only by Ivor Novello. She was able to register on the screen a charm and expression unequalled among the actresses in British films. In his films at this time Pearson permitted some pretty crude mime, especially from Hugh E. Wright, whose efforts to convey emotion were frequently grotesque. The script of *Squibs* even contains the direction 'he tells by his actions that he has shot a man'. But in Betty Balfour he had found a player of great delicacy. The association suited both of them, but her enormous box-office appeal gave Pearson himself a reputation for the commercial touch which may perhaps have been slightly fictitious. His own artistic development was to lead him along paths the trade would find more difficult to follow. His early films were handled by Jury's Film Service, and it was William Jury who in 1922 pressed him to turn the character of Squibs into a Betty Balfour series. This was immensely successful. When Gaumont secured exclusive rights to Welsh–Pearson films in 1923, Betty Balfour was an important part of the bargain, and in October 1924 they contracted to take ten films in five years in at least five of which she was to star.

The next film was *Mary Find the Gold* (Trade Show March 1921), another original scenario, this time with Betty Balfour as the star. The company had prospered and at the end of 1920 the capital had been increased to £20,000.

Mabel Poulton proved herself a useful actress also in *The Old Curiosity Shop* (Trade Show April 1921), for which Thomas Bentley was engaged as director, but after this she worked for other companies. In 1921 the first of the Squibs films confirmed the successful collaboration of Pearson and Betty Balfour. The title of *Squibs* (Trade Show September 1921), suggested by Eliot Stannard, was taken from a current music-hall sketch, but the story was original. It showed Betty Balfour as a little Cockney flower-girl with Fred Groves, Pearson's rather unromantic choice of leading man, as her policeman sweetheart. The pert, tender-hearted little heroine was such a success that the mixture of pathos, cheerful humour and sentiment in a low-life British setting trapped both her and Pearson for several years to come.

Mord Em'ly (Trade Show January 1922), and *The Wee MacGregor's Sweetheart* (Trade Show June 1922), both adaptations, followed in 1922, and in both she played similar tomboy parts. Jury meanwhile persuaded Pearson to follow up the success of Squibs and at last he and Hugh E. Wright collaborated on another script, *Squibs Wins the Calcutta Sweep* (Trade Show September 1922), which was an even greater success.

There were signs that the extreme ingenuousness of these stories and the careful but old-fashioned production was beginning to irk more sophisticated contemporaries, and that Pearson was becoming more interested in some mild experiment with narrative structure. He now made a more expensive film which in later life he regarded with particular affection, called *Love, Life and Laughter* (Trade Show May 1923); at first it was intended to call this film *Tiptoes*. This told a tragic story-within-a-story with an unhappy ending, but finished by flashing back to the original situation and providing an alternative, happy ending. The script and the original idea were both Pearson's and the film, with Betty Balfour as the chorus girl Tiptoes, was the first to be handled by Gaumont. *The Bioscope* was doubtful:

'Mr Pearson was evidently more concerned with the treatment than with the raw material upon which he set to work. . . . It is full of masterly touches, but, in the absence of a clearly-defined underlying idea, it tends to lack that unity of thought and feeling which is essential to great art. There are too many pretty fancies which have been introduced for their own sakes, and not because they help to develop the argument. . . . Apart from these considerations, Mr Pearson is to be complimented upon a production for the artistic equal of which one must go to the best French and Swedish pictures.[9]

Two more Squibs films followed in the same year, *Squibs, M.P.* (Trade Show September 1923), and *Squibs' Honeymoon* (Trade Show December 1923), which was the last of the series. They were the usual mild farces with a minimum of incident and a maximum of expressive detail, and were taken eagerly by Gaumont. But now Pearson was becoming more ambitious and in 1924 wrote and produced one of his more important pictures, *Reveille* (Trade Show June 1924), in which he attempted to show a slice of life rather than a plot. This, featuring Betty Balfour and Stewart Rome, was a diffuse story of how the war had affected a group of humble people, and dealt with a large number of characters in two periods in an anecdotal manner rather than the closely woven plot of the time.

Pearson was proud of the film, and attached much importance to the fact that he had deliberately set out to express a theme, which he described as the Victory of Courage, rather than to tell a story. Although the film was felt to be a little slow, the mood of sentimental patriotism suited the temper of the time and it was extremely successful both at the box office and with the critics. All the same these modest experiments were beginning to get Pearson the reputation, not very useful in the film industry, of being a highbrow.

At the end of 1924 British production as a whole was running into difficulties. At the same time Pearson's relations with Gaumont's were no longer so happy. He returned to conventional scripts and adaptations with another story from H. de Vere Stacpoole, *Satan's Sister* (Trade Show May 1925), this time backed and handled by W. & F. The contract with Betty Balfour was running out and her next film was made for Gaumont in France by another director, Louis Mercanton. Pearson was compelled to close his studio. He obtained backing from W. & F. to make *Mr Preedy and the Countess* (release date untraced) in France with his former star Mona Maris as leading lady, but the changed set-up does not seem to have suited him and he was reticent about this period in his reminiscences. Unlike most of his contemporaries, however, he was not beaten yet, whether by the economic difficulties of the British production industry or by changing fashions in film making.

At the other extreme to Welsh–Pearson, a company which was important because of the exceptional work of one man, was the company important by virtue of size alone. By far the largest producing company during the early part of the period was Stoll Picture Productions, and a greater contrast to Welsh–Pearson would be hard to find.

The company had begun production at the end of the war in a large house at Surbiton, and in 1919 produced *Comradeship* (Trade Show January 1919), a film about the Red Cross made by Maurice Elvey with the stage star Lily Elsie. Later in the year there were several sentimental films based on novels by Marie Corelli and Ethel M. Dell, and a stage success of 1913, *Mr Wu* (Trade Show October 1919). Both *Comradeship* and *Mr Wu* featured stage celebrities, the latter with Matheson Lang, an established stage actor who had created the part of Mr Wu on the stage before the war. The encouraging commercial success of these films, and the cancellation of the contract to handle the popular Goldwyn films from America (see page 81), made the theatre owner Sir Oswald Stoll decide to expand film production. Stoll Picture Productions, a public company with the large capital of £400,000, was registered in May 1920. Directors were Sir Oswald, J. D. Williams, Jeffrey Bernerd, W. S. G. Michie and T. C. Elder. Their chief producer was Elvey, who had been in the industry since before the war and was well known as a shrewd maker of successful box office films. Assisting him from September 1920 to October 1921 was Harold Shaw, who had been with the London Film Company before the war and was now past his best work, Sinclair Hill who joined as a young man in January 1920, F. Martin Thornton and René Plaisetty. The latter, who joined in July 1920 after making some films in Paris and his native America, was full of energy and new ideas and considered then to be potentially the most interesting of them, but his work suffered badly from the usual Stoll defects of dark sets, slowness and overweight casts. Cameramen were the Belgians Paul and Germaine Burger, J. J. Cox and Percy Strong. In charge of the art or scenic department until 1924 was Walter Murton. Although Murton was undoubtedly hampered by the parsimony of the company, which usually involved him in the use and re-use of stock sets, he was responsible for the characteristic appearance of countless Stoll films, heavily conventional, unimaginative, dark and unrealistic.

The company bought a former aeroplane factory belonging to the Nieuport Aviation Company at Cricklewood in June 1920, having decided that this would be a quicker and more economical way of acquiring studio space than altering the small building at Surbiton. This, however, was also kept in use and was taken over by British Instructional in 1923. The Cricklewood studio was to be ready for production by February 1921, but work on some films which needed big sets, such as Plaisetty's *The Yellow Claw* (Trade Show January 1921), started there immediately. The company now had the largest studio in England, not very suitable for film production perhaps, but equipped with some of the latest and best American and French lighting and camera equipment. They proceeded to demonstrate in the next few years that capital and equipment alone do not ensure the production of good films. As in the case of Ideal, the company existed to provide films as a commodity to be marketed. The reasonable desire to bring costs into line with expected profits was not accompanied by any real understanding of quality, and economy resulted in second-rate talent, mean mounting and above all feeble scripts.

It is sad that such good intentions went so wrong. Sir Oswald Stoll was a theatre owner rather than a theatrical impresario, but he was not unconcerned with what was shown on the screen and throughout the twenties was vociferous in the cause of wholesome British and Empire films, and the possibility of using the cinema for moral uplift. But the firm's supposed masterstroke, the mass purchase of film rights to contemporary British novels announced in January 1920 as the Eminent British Authors Series, turned out to be their undoing. It was a time when film makers were beginning to question whether it was better to adapt novels and plays or to write original scenarios. It was a common miscalculation that the size of a popular novel's public, as well as a sort of naïve appeal to patriotism, would ensure the success of a film. Hepworth, as we have seen, stuck closely to novels, and Pearson had trouble several times with his own original stories. Stoll counted heavily on the cash value of created reputations and even hoped to get contemporary popular writers to write novels with film adaptations in mind. Not all the books so purchased lent themselves to filming and the adaptation was perfunctory. But the businesslike spirit of the company demanded that once film rights were acquired they were to be used at all costs, and some of the resulting films were so bad that they had to be altered, or edited, again and again.

The output was enormous, but 'Stoll films are dull films'. The technical standard was better and the appearance more modern than in Ideal's output, and many were competently made and photographed. But good equipment could not overcome unsuitable stories mechanically adapted, poorly mounted in standard sets, edited and sometimes re-edited by cutters whose task was all too often to make the best of a bad job. It was a film factory without creative leadership.

In 1920 about a dozen films were released, most of them made by Elvey. The films were adaptations from such contemporary best sellers as Geoffrey Farnol, A. E. W. Mason, Ethel M. Dell, Olive Wadsley, Rita, Rafael Sabatini and Baroness Orczy. Casts were extremely large but undistinguished, with many smallish parts of roughly equal weight. The company also released some Ivy Duke and Guy Newall films, which were called Stoll films but were in fact independent productions, and during this year also the company ran into trouble over another which they advertised as a Stoll film, Louis Mercanton's *Call of the Blood*. Mercanton,* who was brought up in Great Britain but later took French nationality, was a director of considerable talent who made this film independently in 1920 with Phyllis Neilson-Terry and the then little known Ivor Novello; as a result of the dispute it was not eventually released until 1927. One of the successes of the year was Elvey's *At the Villa Rose* (Trade Show April 1920) based on A. E. W. Mason's novel and trade shown before the play, based on the same work, began its long run at the Strand Theatre.

In 1921 the number of trade shows doubled and the adaptations continued to pour out from works by E. Phillips Oppenheim, A. E. W. Mason, Artemus, Edgar Wallace, Robert Hichens, S. J. Weyman, Ethel M. Dell, A. Conan Doyle, Marie Corelli, H. G. Wells, Rita and Sax Rohmer. Casts lists were more over-crowded than ever. Only one film made by Sinclair Hill was shown this year. Harold Shaw left the company in October; and most of the films were made by Elvey backed up by Martin Thornton, René Plaisetty and later in the year by George Ridgwell. Some of the films were successful, Harold Shaw's version of *Kipps* (Trade Show January 1921) so much so, despite the strange miscasting of his wife Edna Flugrath as a young *ingénue*, that a second H. G. Wells novel, *The Wheels of Chance*, was filmed and George K. Arthur found work in Hollywood as a result of the first. Charlie Chaplin wrote of H. G. Wells' reaction to *Kipps* in *My Wonderful Visit* in 1922, repeated substantially in *My Autobiography* in 1964. He met Wells at the Stoll offices to see the first showing and:

'As the picture is reeling off I whisper to him my likes and dislikes, principally the faulty photography, though occasionally I detect bad direction. . . . Then Wells whispers "Don't you think the boy is good?"

'The boy in question is right here on the other side of me, watching his first picture. I look at him. Just starting out on a new career, vibrant with ambition, eager to make good, and his first attempt being shown before such an audience. . . . Wells nudges me and whispers, "Say something nice about the boy".'[10]

In the autobiography Chaplin writes:

* Mercanton died in 1932.

125

'As a matter of fact, the boy, George K. Arthur, was the only redeeming feature of the picture.'[11]

The Four Feathers (Trade Show May 1921) and *The Fruitful Vine* (Trade Show September 1921) were fairly successful and besides making a five-reel *The Hound of the Baskervilles* (Trade Show July 1921) featuring Eille Norwood as Sherlock Holmes, Elvey put out a series of 15 two-reel *Adventures of Sherlock Holmes* (Trade Show March 1921), the first of a number of two-reeler series made by Stoll. Two more Sherlock Holmes series, this time by Ridgwell, *Further Adventures of Sherlock Holmes*, 15 two-reelers of 1922, and *The Last Adventures of Sherlock Holmes*, 15 two-reelers (Trade Show March 1923) followed. In 1922 A. E. Coleby, whose *Froggy's Little Brother* (Trade Show November 1921) had been put out as a Stoll production, stayed with the company and showed two films made from original scenarios by himself, *The Peacemaker* (Trade Show March 1922) and *Long Odds* (Trade Show May 1922), but in general the company struggled on with the same unsuitable material and enormous casts. Some of the worst films disappeared for months whilst being doctored for the market.

A temporary and colourful visitor from the United States who hired a floor at Cricklewood about this time was John Stuart Blackton, a veteran of over twenty years in the American film industry. He came over early in 1921, the big man from the States who was going to show the British how to do things. Like all the more modern producers at the time he paid particular attention to lighting. He used a colour system, Prizma Color, for which he brought over a colour camera specialist, W. T. Crespinal, as well as his cameraman Nicholas Musurca. He was taken up by a number of bright young society people, among whom was Duff Cooper's wife Lady Diana Cooper, a society beauty with no great acting pretentions but a publicity value which was enthusiastically exploited by Blackton. As Lady Diana Manners she played the lead in *The Glorious Adventure* (Trade Show January 1922) in Prizma Color, and *The Virgin Queen* (Trade Show January 1923), some of which was shot at Beaulieu Abbey and which was partly in colour. Victor McLaglen in the first and Carlyle Blackwell in the second were her leading men. Blackton's other film in Britain, *A Gypsy Cavalier* (Trade Show August 1922), featured the heavyweight boxer Georges Carpentier with Flora le Breton. The films were ambitious costume spectacles with huge sets, crowd scenes, involved plots and enormous casts supporting the fashionable and celebrated leading players. The films were monumentally slow and dull and the use of colour disappointing, and despite society *premières* they were not especially successful. Blackton left England in early 1923, having given a display of showmanship, however, which may well have made an impression on a few rising young English entrepreneurs.

Back on the Stoll floor the experiences of 1922, when film after film had to disappear for alteration even though its publicity had already been issued, seem to have combined with the example of their showy tenant downstairs to produce a change of policy. Some more ambitious films of greater individuality were made in 1923, including several costume spectacles. Sir Frank Benson in

Ridgwell's *Becket* (Trade Show November 1923), from Tennyson's play first performed at the Lyceum in 1893, and George Robey as Sancho Panza in Elvey's *Don Quixote* (Trade Show December 1923) were more consciously literary than the earlier adaptations. Hill's *Indian Love Lyrics* (Trade Show July 1923) with Owen Nares, based on the song cycle by Amy Woodforde Finden; Elvey's *Guy Fawkes* (Trade Show September 1923) and *The Wandering Jew* (Trade Show May 1923), a long run of 1920, both with Matheson Lang indulging his delight in stage make-up; and Kellino's *Young Lochinvar* (Trade Show October 1923) with Owen Nares, all departed from pot-boiling modern novels, and all gave some scope for costume, spectacle, interesting locations and visual design. One of the few virtues of the Stoll output at this time was the excellent, and indeed frequently very beautiful, locations chosen if the subject allowed it, and much of these films was shot on location and provided relief from the studio, where the sets remained flimsy and shoddy even in the aspiring spectacles. Kellino joined in January 1923 after making *Rob Roy* for Gaumont. Both Hill and Coleby made a Robey film, *One Arabian Night* (Trade Show December 1923) and *The Rest Cure* (Trade Show November 1923) respectively; another Robey film, *Prehistoric Man*, was released in April 1924 with no announced Trade Show, and Coleby's *The Prodigal Son* (Trade Show February 1923, re-edited seven-reel version trade shown in April 1929 by Equity–British) based on Hall Caine's novel lasted over four hours and must have seemed tiring even to people used to Stoll films. Cast lists swelled similarly, and cameras were operated by Joe Rosenthal, D. P. Cooper and Basil Emmott as well as Cox. Coleby also started a series based on the Fu Manchu mystery stories by Sax Rohmer which was carried on next year by Fred Paul: *The Mystery of Dr Fu Manchu* by A. E. Coleby, 15 two-reelers (Trade Show May 1923); *Further Mysteries of Dr Fu Manchu* by Fred Paul, 8 two-reelers (Trade Show August 1924).

Like the Rowsons of Ideal and the Bromheads of Gaumont, Stoll had a strong renting organization through which he was for a time able to direct a large output of spiritless films on to the market. But by 1924 even this company was beginning to feel the difficulties of British film production. Their output must have contributed very largely to the poor reputation of British films. Stoll himself cared deeply about the British reputation, but he was not a man who cared, or felt that he should know, about film technique itself, and it seems likely that the poor quality prevailing in his company was due to ignorance rather than to indifference.

The Gaumont company, under its Managing Director A. C. Bromhead and his brother the General Manager R. C. Bromhead, was the only veteran company which survived the vicissitudes of the twenties and went on producing, although in changed form, in the thirties. Like some of the other companies, it was at first primarily a renting concern, run by people whose interest in films was as commercial commodities, and for long periods it did little to foster any real development in English production or the reputation of English films. Its production policy was unimaginative but businesslike, and output contracted to almost nothing during times of difficulty. Nevertheless a number of the commercially successful British pictures of the later twenties were Gaumont films.

The company remained in existence, and formed a most interesting and valuable production amalgamation with Gainsborough at the end of the period.

At the end of the war production was stagnant at the Shepherd's Bush studio. The film which reopened them was *The First Men in the Moon,* made in November 1918 by J. L. V. Leigh (release delayed). Will Kellino joined the company in March 1919 and made *The Fall of a Saint* (Trade Show January 1920). The company then began to think of reorganization and expansion, and Captain C. C. Calvert was also engaged. Two brands of film, Westminster and British Screencraft, were created for the two directors and ran until 1923, when Kellino left to join Stoll. In 1922 the Bromheads and their British associates bought the proprietary rights from the parent company in France, and from now on the Gaumont company in London was wholly British.

The British Screencraft series were made by Calvert with Basil Emmott, one of the best British cameramen of the twenties. In type they were contemporary melodramas, contemporary that is in subject matter rather than in style of production, hampered by over-involved plots but with a certain amount of production value, as it was beginning to be called. Individually the pictures were not important despite several appearances by the American Josephine Earle, a sophisticated former Vitagraph star now fading a little. Later some costume dramas were written for the series by Alicia Ramsey, with spectacular sets and location crowd work in an ambitious, but not altogether successful, attempt to give the series a more vital character. Of these *Bonnie Prince Charlie* (Trade Show November 1923) was the best known, and featured Ivor Novello and Gladys Cooper.

The Westminster brand was made concurrently by Kellino, with camera work by A. S. Aubyn Brown. Kellino's reputation was as a producer of homely comic films and he now turned out a number of get-rich comedies, often formula stories of the social embarrassment of lowly people who find they have suddenly risen in the world, a class comedy often popular in Britain. Perhaps the best known of his films was *The Fortune of Christina M'Nab* (Trade Show April 1921) with Nora Swinburne. Kellino left Gaumont to work for Stoll in January 1923, and the last Westminster film, *Claude Duval* (Trade Show April 1924), starring Fay Compton, was made by G. A. Cooper. In 1923 Kellino was working in Hollywood, but he rejoined Gaumont in 1928 after changes in the composition of the company. He was a careful, competent director, conscientiously trying to find out what was popular and repeat it.

Hitherto the company had kept up a fairly steady output but during the slump years of British production overlapping 1923 to 1926 its own output shrank, apart from news and mild travelogue and interest films, to very occasional or sponsored films. Shorts production was a great standby of British companies during the difficult years. Early in the twenties Gaumont had a popular series of one-reelers called *Around the Town,* and in 1926, like a number of other companies, they put out several series of shorts; *John Henry Calling,* 6 two-reelers (Trade Show May 1926) were made by Challis N. Sanderson featuring John Henry; and *Screen Playlets,* 6 two-reelers (Trade Show November 1926). The *Gaumont Special Comedies,* two-reelers made by Billy Merson, were made later in 1928. After a film made for Gaumont by the American Tom Terriss, with the American star Wanda Hawley, *Fires of Fate* (Trade Show July 1923), the company was joined by George A. Cooper in 1924. William Shenton was now their cameraman. Cooper, an undistinguished director who for a time acquired a slightly clever, arty reputation, made the melodramatic *The Eleventh Commandment* (Trade Show September 1924) with Fay Compton, Stewart Rome and Lillian Hall-Davis, and two other films featuring Jack Buchanan and Fay Compton. In 1926 Manning Haynes' *London Love* (Trade Show July 1926) with Fay Compton again and John Stuart, was very much admired. Meanwhile, as we have seen, determined efforts had been made to capture Betty Balfour from Pearson's films. She made *Monte Carlo* (Trade Show September 1925) for Louis Mercanton as an Anglo-French production for Gaumont before her contract with Welsh–Pearson had finished, but did not seem at home in this sophisticated society drama. She followed it with a weak film made by Cooper for Gaumont, and then with a better French Gaumont–Cinegraphic film made by Marcel l'Herbier, *Little Devil-May-Care* (Trade Show September 1927). *Cinders* (Trade Show September 1926) and *Monkeynuts* (Trade Show May 1928) were also made by Mercanton with Betty Balfour but handled by other companies.

A company which falls into a totally different category, which indeed stands entirely on its own, was successfully putting down roots during these early years which other firms found so dangerous. British Instructional Films was founded with a completely different approach to business. As a result the story of the company during the first half of the twenties is one of growth, commercial success and prestige, suggesting that even a small output, if of sufficiently high quality, could survive the apparently irresistible forces of economic deline.

The character of the company was determined by Harry Bruce Woolfe, who began by making films himself with an original method of production using compilation, animated maps and diagrams to tell the story of episodes in the war. Beginning as an actual film maker, he was afterwards drawn into the business and administration of the firm, distribution deals and take-overs, and later still into the production of fiction films. But he retained his concern over what the films were about, and his hold on reality, which can be discerned even in the later purely story films, and which contrasted with the hectic Hollywood dream-world seen, for example, in many of the B.I.P. films of the same period.

Bruce Woolfe had entered the film industry in 1910 as a provincial exhibitor. In August 1919 he and H. M. Howard registered British Instructional Films with a modest capital of £3,000. Working in an army hut at the old Neptune studios at Boreham Wood, Elstree, rented from Ideal, he set to work with the assistance of Sir George Aston on an animated model and map film telling the story of the battle of Jutland. Herbert Lomas joined him as cameraman early in 1921. *The Battle of Jutland*, which was three reels long, was trade shown in September 1921 and was distributed with success by Ideal.

To approach the commercial cinema with such a proposition must have been a labour of love, for at the time actuality filming virtually appeared only in news reels and some elementary interest films. The official feature actuality films of the war were being re-presented in 1920 as *The World's Greatest Story*, a series of 15 two-reelers trade shown in March by British Famous Films, which used the War Office material crudely reorganized and strung together with florid titles. And just after *Jutland*'s trade show Nash's old-fashioned melodramatic film *How Lord Kitchener was Betrayed* was shown.

Despite its unusual nature the Jutland film was both a critical and a commercial success, and by the end of 1921 the group at Elstree was preparing to do a second war film, this time with War Office help, about Allenby's campaign in Palestine. This was a longer and more ambitious film with re-enacted incidents directed by the veteran producer A. V. Bramble, as well as contour maps with moving discs, and passages from the large archives of official war actuality films.

Meanwhile British Instructional had become a centre for naturalists interested in cinematography and prepared a number of short nature films which were collectively known as the *Secrets of Nature*. Together with the renter E. Gordon Craig, British Instructional at first distributed these through the Regent company, and later formed New Era. This company started in September 1923 with a set of six more *Secrets of Nature* and in November of that year trade showed *Armageddon*, as the Palestine film was called. With a Royal *première* to provide a touch of showmanship, the film made a splash and confirmed the success of the new type of film. According to Bruce Woolfe it had cost only £3,000 to make and eventually took £18,000.

The excellence and popular success of the *Secrets of Nature* films was one of the few bright features of the British film industry during the twenties. Bruce Woolfe has described how the series began in 1922 between the showing of the *Battle of Jutland* and *Armageddon*. He

'. . . got in touch with Mr Charles Head, who at once started photographing the life history of a butterfly and the garden spider. It was about this time that Mr Edgar Chance was causing a good deal of comment by his discoveries of the habits of the cuckoo . . . the following autumn I had his cuckoo film and five others ready for showing . . . as time went on other duties claimed me and I handed over the preparation of these subjects to Mary Field. . . . We had been joined in our work by other well-known nature cinematographers, including Oliver Pike, Captain Gilbert, Walter Higham and Percy Smith. Gradually our horizon widened; Smith introduced his botanical subjects and later used the microscope to aid him in bringing to the screen some of Nature's secrets. . . .'[12]

During the autumn and winter of 1922 five sets were shown, each of six *Secrets of Nature* films. Each film lasted about eight to ten minutes and was about some phase of natural history in Britain—birds, insects, fish or plants. They were made for showing in the cinemas, where they were extremely well received. There was a small but continued output of them throughout the rest of the period, nearly a hundred being shown before the end of 1929.[13] Many contained earlier filmed material re-edited.

Other cameramen began to contribute, whether freelance or as members of British Instructional, with production by W. P. Pycraft and general supervision by Bruce Woolfe. The most important contributor was Percy Smith, who had started making films as a young man in 1907 when still working at the Board of Education. He made speed-magnification films of plant life, improvising automatic equipment to take shots at intervals of an hour which, projected at a normal speed, showed the process of growth speeded up some 96,000 times. Several Kinemacolor series were shown at the Scala in 1910, and in 1911 the earlier monochrome ones were shown at other cinemas. Meanwhile he had begun taking microscopic films in 1909–10, also with improvised equipment, although he was preceded in this by F. W. Martin Duncan. He had established a studio at Southgate but had given it up during the war. Under Bruce Woolfe's encouragement, however, he started work again, and both he and Martin Duncan did many plant, insect, underwater and microscopic films for British Instructional, using their early material.

Other cameramen included Charles Head, whose films of bird life, small mammals and insects were characterized by placid observation of the countryside and the homely details of everyday life. Edgar Chance, a scientist in search of evidence, knowing what he wanted to film before he began, gave a clear and detailed picture of his subject woven into a narrative. Walter Higham, on the other hand, was primarily an artist; interested in the visual beauty of his subjects, bird life and small animals, rather than in exposition, he shot a great deal of film and was relatively difficult to edit. Oliver Pike, who was an expert on bird life and filmed birds and small animals, was chiefly interested in giving information and had made many such films as early as 1907 to 1910. Captain H. A. Gilbert was more of a sportsman camera-adventurer who energetically took his heavy equipment on field trips on which he discovered his bird and animal subjects. Mary Field, who joined British Instructional in 1927 as Education Manager, took the less scientific subjects including zoo films, to which she added a touch of humour, as well as doing much of the editing of other films. Other contributors included H. N. Lomas, C. W. R. Knight, P. Chalmers Mitchell, George Southcoate and Maxwell Lefroy. Geoffrey Barkas was another member of the staff of British Instructional who helped in the preparation of the films. He had started film work, as a cameraman under Sydney Blythe with G. B. Samuelson, when he was working in Hollywood after the war, and then worked for Ideal with William Shenton and Horace Wheddon. In 1923 he went to Canada and made 7 one-reelers about the lumber industry which he sold to British Instructional for £5 on his return, and which they later released under the name of *Tall Timber Tales* (reviewed March 1925).

According to Bruce Woolfe the average cost of these films was about £500 and receipts just about covered their costs. This, however, was a remarkable record for such serious films which, in the absence of a sub-standard market or the use of films in schools, had to rely on theatrical showing. They were liked by both ordinary audiences and highbrows, and added a small but precious glow to the reputation of British film making. Rotha even went so far as to refer to them as the sheet anchor of the British film industry.[14]

It was characteristic of Bruce Woolfe that the *Secrets of Nature* films, cool, factual and not primarily poetic, should come out under his wing. He was a link in the chain of the factual film from the Charles Urban Trading Company and others of the early days to the documentary movement of the thirties, and the documentary narratives of even later. Because he was shrewd and businesslike he was able to make a success of intelligent film making at a time when few British companies could keep afloat at all. His integrity and hardheadedness were greatly respected in the trade, but he was cautious and possibly humourless, and was not a colourful figure. His leaning towards realism was pedagogical rather than artistic, and though his early work was contemporary with that of the great Russian directors it does not seem to have been influenced by them. All the same, although he was not an *avant-garde* intellectual himself, he assisted many who were in such practical ways as supporting the Film Society, and he eventually gathered together in his firm some of the brightest and best of the new generation of serious young film makers.

From 1923 until 1927 New Era handled the British Instructional films, and their profitability kept the company alive at a time when other British firms were failing. According to a prospectus during the latter year some of the war reconstructions were produced under contracts with the appropriate Departments which gave the company a fee in addition to the entire production cost, plus a percentage of the profits. The Stoll studio at Surbiton was taken over for their use and in 1924 the company was bought by Stoll for £20,000, Bruce Woolfe remaining in control.

Another of the important new figures in British production in the twenties was Herbert Wilcox. Like Michael Balcon and Bruce Woolfe he had an approach which was entirely modern, and like them he was successfully laying the foundations of an important production firm during the very years which proved fatal to older companies.

After the war Wilcox and his brother Charles entered the film distribution business in Leeds, setting up on their own as Astra Films for this purpose. *The Bioscope* described him:

'Young, slightly built and with an air of quiet gravity, Mr Wilcox impresses one as a singularly distinctive personality. What is almost an old-world courtesy of manner does not conceal his evident forcefulness of character.'[15]

In July 1920 they decided to embark on production in conjunction with the northern exhibitor H. W. Thompson, and *The Bioscope* announced a gigantic producing scheme. 'We shall, of course, continue to handle American pictures', said Wilcox.[16] Hiring a studio, they planned to film the stage actor Sir John Martin Harvey in one of his favourite stage parts in *The Breed of the Treshams* (Trade Show September 1920), a play first put on at The Lyric in 1905. Kenelm Foss was to be the director and Frank Canham the cameraman. Not surprisingly, the film was considered rather stagey. Foss continued to make Astra films, but the Wilcoxes now broke away and, with the backing of Rudolph Solomon, formed a new company. This was Graham–Wilcox, and was to produce pictures directed by Jack Graham Cutts, a northern exhibitor at that time seeking a way into film production. He had in fact already made a sensational-sounding film called *Cocaine* some while before, and after some censorship troubles this was retitled *While London Sleeps* and trade shown by Astra in July 1922. By this time his next film, *The Wonderful Story*, had already been trade shown in May, also by Astra, and was called the second Graham–Wilcox film. Wilcox refers to this film in his autobiography as his own first production.

Wilcox tells how he deliberately chose a simple homely story with few characters, which were played by Herbert Langley, Lillian Hall-Davis and Olaf Hytten, as he considered this type of story most suitable for the cinema and it was, moreover, possible to make it for only £1,400. The film was acclaimed by the critics and he sold it outright for £4,000, but it proved to be a box-office failure. For his second film, known as the third Graham–Wilcox production, he accordingly chose a more vivid story. This was *Flames of Passion* (Trade Show November 1922) and was also made by Cutts, at Islington, featuring Herbert Langley and with René Guissart as cameraman and Norman Arnold in charge of design. It was a lurid tale and at the finale the film burst into colour, described at the time as Prizma colour like the films made in the same year by John Stuart Blackton, also at Islington, but referred to by Wilcox in his book as Kinemacolor. This time Wilcox had used an American star, Mae Marsh. The film was a success and he even managed to sell it in America.

Cutts then made another successful film with Mae Marsh, *Paddy-the-Next-Best-Thing* (Trade Show January 1923), again with Guissart as cameraman and again made at Islington as a Graham–Wilcox film. It featured George K. Arthur once again and was from a Savoy Theatre success of 1920. It was an outstanding success, as good technically as the last one and with a better story, a warm-hearted romance about an Irish tomboy. In January Cutts and Wilcox visited America to promote its distribution. There is no doubt that the talent of this director was one of the stepping stones of Wilcox's career, as it was soon to be of Balcon's. However, Wilcox makes no mention of this film in his memoirs, and Cutts next appears working for Balcon on the latter's first production, *Woman to Woman* (Trade Show November 1923), which was also made at Islington and also featured an American star brought over for the purpose.

Wilcox had by now decided to direct his own films. He also wished to distribute them himself, and gave up the connection with Astra, which continued under the management of H. W. Thompson. Wilcox's films continued to be called Graham–Wilcox productions. He started with *Chu Chin Chow* (Trade Show September 1923), a film version of the long-running musical spectacle of the war years. According to his autobiography he paid £20,000 for the film rights, borrowed from his bank, and made the film under an agreement with U.F.A. of Germany under Erich Pommer. He kept the services of Guissart and Arnold, engaged Betty Blythe from America and made the film at the U.F.A. studios. It was only a moderate success, but in this first film many of his characteristics as a film maker can already be seen. It was an easily exploitable film with the borrowed publicity of a stage success; it was a costume spectacular; it was production with an international flavour, with its American star, the use of German studios and the search for distribution in America. But although Wilcox had profited as a showman from his experience hitherto and realized the value of these things as selling angles, he still had much to learn about film technique. He stuck so closely to his stage original that the film, eleven thousand silent feet of it at the trade show, even introduced the songs with subtitles containing the words. But although as a film it was heavy, its presentation managed to be a notable event worthy of a big impresario, and it later found its way into the *World Film Encyclopedia* List of Famous Films.

His next film, *Southern Love* (Trade Show January 1924), was made under difficulties in Austria and featured Betty Blythe again, with Herbert Langley, Warwick Ward and Liane Haid. It was not a success. But Wilcox now began to find his feet. His next film was *Decameron Nights* (Trade Show September 1924), from a play based on Boccaccio which had run for over a year at Drury Lane in 1922. He liked its story 'with overtones of sex'.[17] The account in his autobiography of the filming makes it sound extremely casual. He had secured another agreement with Pommer of U.F.A., under which U.F.A. were to provide the script, a German cast and 50 per cent of the finance, while Wilcox was to produce and direct, provide English and American stars and the rest of the finance. When Wilcox arrived in Germany with Lionel Barrymore, Jameson Thomas and Ivy Duke he found ready some spectacular sets of the East and Venice at the time of the Crusades, a cast which included Werner Krauss, Bernhard Goetzke and Hannah Ralph, but an unusable script, so he proceeded to shoot it off the cuff. This may well have been a better method than his previous stilted and literal adaptation of *Chu Chin Chow*, and although still somewhat slow and heavy, this time in the German manner, the film with its magnificent sets and crowd scenes was a spectacular success in both Britain and America, and to a large extent triumphed over its complicated and diffuse story and the impersonal handling of the large cast.

Wilcox was now ready to expand. Graham–Wilcox was left in the hands of Solomon, and Herbert Wilcox Productions was registered in March 1925 by Wilcox and E. A. Bundy with a capital of £500.[18]* In August 1925 Wilcox trade showed another mammoth film, a ten-thousand foot version of Sir John Martin Harvey's *The Only Way*, an adaptation of Dicken's *Tale of Two Cities* which was a favourite part of Martin Harvey's repertoire and had been revived frequently since first put on in 1899. This was filmed at Twickenham at a cost of £24,000, of which Bundy put up £11,000. It had some large sets and a prodigiously large cast but was crushingly slow, stagey and impersonal and studded with long subtitles. Nevertheless it had immense prestige and was a commerical success. It was given the distinction of being handled by an American distributor, First National, which gave a cash guarantee of £12,500 and, according to a subsequent lawsuit brought by Martin Harvey, the takings during the first two years were as much as £53,336.

Michael Balcon was a contemporary of Wilcox, and although the latter became a director, which Balcon never did, they were alike in many ways. They both

---

* Graham–Wilcox produced little after this: Thomas Bentley's *White Heat* (Trade Show September 1926) and Fred Paul's *Luck of the Navy* (Trade Show November 1927). In 1928 Solomon was to be involved in Edward Godal's plans for British Multicolour Film Corporation.

entered production from provincial renting during the very years when most of the earlier producers were closing down; both had a serious and professional approach to the film industry, and a showman's instinct for exploitation held in check well short of flamboyance; both had a far-sighted appreciation of the importance of capital backing, distribution tie-ups and the American market.

Balcon entered films in 1920. He formed a small renting firm in Birmingham called Victory in partnership with Victor Saville, and they held the local agency for W. & F., a renting firm recently formed by C. M. Woolf. Saville and Balcon came to London and started to make and handle advertising films. There they met Jack Graham Cutts, the same ex-showman who had recently made the Graham–Wilcox films for Wilcox. Early in 1923 they combined with John Freedman, and as Balcon–Saville–Freedman started production with Cutts as director. They managed to raise between £30,000 and £40,000, £7,000 of it in the form of a distribution advance from Woolf, and some of the rest from others associated with them in their Birmingham days such as Oscar Deutsch.[19] Their first film, *Woman to Woman* (Trade Show November 1923) was announced in May and finished by August. It was directed by Cutts and shot by Claude McDonnell, and like Cutts' previous films it was made at Islington. His last two films had starred the American Mae Marsh, and for this one Betty Compson was brought over from America at a salary of £1,000 a week, a very large salary for a British firm. Others in the film were Clive Brook and the American Josephine Earle. The film was a great success, the staging and photography were much admired and the story, about a wartime romance forgotten by a shell-shocked officer, was based on a stage success of 1921 and was considered very adult. Compared with other British productions of the time it was a lavish and sophisticated film.

The same team made a second film rather too hastily at Islington in the summer of 1923, *The White Shadow* (Trade Show February 1924), in order to make use of their expensive star before her return to the United States. They advertised 'The same Star, Producer, Author, Hero, Cameraman, Scenic Artist, Staff, Studio, Renting Company as *Woman to Woman*', but the results were sadly different. After this failure Woolf was unwilling to give them another distribution advance and the partnership broke up. Another Balcon–Freedman–Saville film, *The Prude's Fall*, was directed by Cutts in 1923 and shot by Hal Young, starring the American Jane Novak with Warwick Ward. It was based on a play of 1920 which had a long run with Gerald du Maurier, but as a film it was not well accepted and its release was delayed until 1925.

In February 1924 a new company, Gainsborough, was registered with capital of £100, and from now on Balcon's importance as a producer, with the accountant Reginald Baker at his side, was established. The next film, *The Passionate Adventure* (Trade Show August 1924) was once more made by Cutts and MacDonnell at Islington with an American star, this time Alice Joyce, playing with Clive Brook and Victor McLaglen, who attracted much attention. Adapted from a novel, the film was about the double life led by a man married 'in name only' who sought solace, oddly enough, by hanging around the East End dressed as a down-and-out. It was made by arrangement with Gaumont and was described as the third Balcon–Freedman–Saville film. It was also, however, the first film of a brand which was to become increasingly important in the later twenties, Gainsborough Pictures.

Alongside the larger early companies which failed, the ones that just survived, and the big new personalities who were building the important companies of the future, were many smaller enterprises. The little old-style companies, like Butchers, Barkers, I.B. Davidson, Harma, B. & C., and Samuelson were easily forced out of the game. There were a few with larger capital and a better appreciation of modern problems who were still unable to make production pay: Alliance, which superseded London Film Company and British Actors Film Company; Famous Players Lasky; and Anglo-Hollandia Granger. The only producer of any stature outside the London area was Sidney Morgan, whose small daylight studio beside the sea at Shoreham, with its small stock company, made a number of modestly successful films during the early twenties. Stanley Mumford was his cameraman and the leading lady his young daughter Joan Morgan. Using stories from novels, which the company adapted, they made inexpensive films of which perhaps the best known were *Lady Noggs* (Trade Show January 1920), *Little Dorrit* (Trade Show August 1920), *Two Little Wooden Shoes* (Trade Show September 1920), *A Lowland Cinderella* (Trade Show December 1921), *Lilac Sunbonnet* (Trade Show July 1922) and *Dicky Monteith* (Trade Show February 1922). There were in addition a large number of individuals, floaters who tried again and again to fit into some company or find a base from which to operate. There was the sad category of the talent that might have been; the talent that fought hard to stay afloat but was just too old-fashioned; and finally and most depressing of all the hard core, the no-talent, who persistently littered the production scene with rubbish and unfulfilled promises.

Butcher's Film Service had withdrawn from the K.M.A. by August 1918 on the grounds that they had ceased production, and during the following years they confined themselves to their original business of renting, although they backed many films with advances on distribution. The early studios at Woodlands, Whetstone, seem to have simply gone out of use after an unsuccessful attempt by two renting firms, Ashley Exclusives and Victory Motion Pictures, to take over and expand the firm which owned it at the end of the war, Famous Pictures. One of the best known of the early companies had been Barker Motion Photography, with a studio at Ealing. W. G. Barker himself retired from production, although he went on the *Renown* tour with the Prince of Wales as Admiralty Official Cinematographer in 1920. The company was taken over by his former assistant Jack Smith, but apart from an early version of *The Flag Lieutenant* (Trade Show September 1919), made by Percy Nash, and a few other melodramas, nothing was made and the studio was acquired in 1920 by General Film Renters to use for hire.

Another early company with a rough and ready style of production was that of I.B. Davidson at Leyton. After the war it continued to put out films directed by A. E. Coleby, a big, burly tough man who sometimes appeared in them himself, and photographed by D. P. Cooper. Two of them featured the boxer

Bombardier Billy Wells: *The Great Game* (Trade Show December 1918) and *The Silver Lining* (Trade Show November 1919), and another marked the first film appearance of Victor MacLaglen in *The Call of the Road* (Trade Show October 1920), bold and carefree and full of charm. Next year they made a backing and distribution arrangement with the renting firm of Grangers, and until the middle of 1924 their films were known as Granger–Davidson films. The *Fifth Form at St Dominic's* (Trade Show November 1921) was the last film made for Davidson by Cooper and Coleby, as the latter then joined the Stoll company, and the rest of the Davidson films were produced by A. H. Rooke and shot by Leslie Eveleigh. They included some sporting dramas and two more appearances by Victor McLaglen: *M'Lord of the White Road* (Trade Show November 1923) and *The Gay Corinthian* (Trade Show July 1924). The last few films were rented by Butchers.

Old-fashioned melodramas, conventional and sometimes sentimental, the films were nevertheless fast and full of action. They had racing, and boxing, crime and thrills, elopements, highwaymen and vengeance, and were usually low-life rather than society. Rooke's films, later, were more ambitious and had better casts, but the style of production was still somewhat casual and neither photography nor continuity were above reproach. They were popular enough in the cheaper cinemas but unable to compete with the new sophistication which was invading the whole industry, and the company collapsed at the end of 1924.

Another company of similar age and character was B. & C. This was the old British and Colonial Kinematograph Company, with studios at Hoe Street, Walthamstow. They had plans for expansion soon after the war under their new managing director Edward Godal. The idea was to break into the American market by using American directors and stars, and their first film was *12.10* (Trade Show about June 1919), a thriller directed by Herbert Brenon and starring Marie Doro. It had considerable success. Other films during 1919 and 1920 were directed by George Edwardes Hall, James McKay and George Ridgwell, one featuring Marie Doro, two José Collins and two Godfrey Tearle; and two adaptations from Balzac were made by Hall, featuring Yvonne Arnaud: *The Magic Skin*, (Trade Show January 1920) and *The Temptress* (Trade Show November 1920). The B. & C. output was small and Godal appreciated the importance of having a good director and well-known leading players, making each film a super in some respect, and getting distribution. In this the company was ahead of such a comparative giant as Ideal. Nevertheless it did not prosper, possibly because it had a leaning towards the tasteless and outrageous, but more likely because of the chronic shortage of capital. By late 1920 the studio was being rented briefly by Granger–Binger and in 1921 by H. W. Thompson. Then in 1923, under Julius Hagen's management, there were efforts to revive production with several series of shorts such as *The Romance of History, Gems of Literature* and *Wonder Women of the World* in 1922 and 1923 by Edwin J. Collins and Edwin Greenwood, *The Audacious Mr Squire* (Trade Show October 1923) by Greenwood with Jack Buchanan, and a film *The Heart Strings* (Trade Show October 1923) with Gertrude

E* 137

McCoy and Victor McLaglen. A last effort was made by presenting some short José Collins dramas in 1924 and *The Art of Love,* not put out until 1925. The films were not a success and this company, like others, was in the hands of the receivers by June 1924.

The final stages of the old Clarendon company were interesting as one of several abortive attempts by exhibitors to co-operate with each other to ensure a supply of films made in this country. Clarendon, with its studio at Croydon, had been taken over by Harry Maze Jenks, who did business as Harma. A few pictures were made in 1919 by F. Martin Thornton, but he later fell out with the company over his salary and left. James Reardon directed a few short comedies. During 1920 the company was reorganized with backing from some provincial exhibitors in the belief that the stranglehold of American films might be broken if production in England was actually owned by the exhibitors. Associated Exhibitors Film Company was registered in January 1921 with a capital of £150,000. Gavazzi King of the C.E.A. became one of the directors, but was later forced to resign by pressure from other exhibitors. Jenks' holding had been taken over by the exhibitor Thomas Thompson in 1920, and by the end of 1921 the Wilcox brothers, at this time seeking a way into production from the provinces, briefly became directors. A few rather poor Associated Exhibitors' films were made in 1921, mostly by A. H. Rooke with Leslie Eveleigh at the camera, but the venture was not a success.

Master Films was of more recent formation than Clarendon. Formed during the war, it moved to the studios at Weir House, Teddington, and until 1922 had a fairly large output of features and shorts, most of them produced by Percy Nash but also some by Bert Wynne, Edwin Collins and others, including their General Manager Harry B. Parkinson after the end of 1920. Many were handled at first by British Exhibitors Films and later by Butchers. Aiming at useable popular pictures, they underestimated their audience with silly sentimental or melodramatic scripts crowded with incidents and characters in the old-fashioned manner, slow, and in this unlike the Davidson pictures which, although primitive, kept up a brisk pace. *Won by a Head* (Trade Show July 1920), for example included a murder, two chases, a fire, a race and another death in its five reels. Production was cheap and careless, and reviews complained of horizons that swayed in unison with the decks, Norwegian seamen speaking French and other anomalies. Two which found their way into the *World Film Encyclopedia* list of Famous Films were *Daniel Deronda* (Trade Show May 1921) with Clive Brook and *Corinthian Jack* (Trade Show June 1921) with Victor McLaglen, both directed by their scenarist W. C. Rowden. Nash's *How Lord Kitchener was Betrayed* (Trade Show November 1921) was written by Norman Ramsey in connection with a newspaper feature in *John Bull,* which purported to reveal that Kitchener's intention to visit Russia was communicated to Berlin by Rasputin. This unfortunate stab at reality was described by *The Bioscope* as 'a silly and vulgar journalistic "sensation".'[20] In 1922 several sets of potted dramas in one or two reels were issued by Master–British Exhibitors, many of them featuring well-known stage players. They included Grand Guignol dramas, songs, and the so-called *Tense Moments With Great Authors, Tense Moments from Great Plays* and *Tense Moments from Great Operas*. Parkinson, formerly a renter, had registered Screenplays as a private company with a capital of £5,000 in February 1919. Working at Bertram Phillips' old studio at Cranmer Court, Clapham, with directors like Nash, Fred Paul and Bert Wynne, he was turning out short films by early 1921. He seems to have been one of the first to see shorts production as a solution for the hard-pressed British film industry, and justified it with a bold claim that normal film features were padded with unnecessary material, and that what the public wanted was a return to the old short drama.[21] After a while even this form of dramatic production was given up, and Master Films disappeared for good. From 1924 onwards Parkinson confined himself to the production of sets of interest shorts, usually of travelogue or show-business type (see page 291).

G. B. Samuelson, like Walter West, was a large-scale commercial producer who failed to survive the slump, at least with his previous standing. He is a particularly good example of a type of producer in the middle ranks of the British film industry, robust and enthusiastic but seriously underestimating what they were up against. It was no longer possible to keep afloat with a capital of a few thousand pounds, and there was a limit to the carelessness in production and the stupidity of the stories which even the most ignorant audiences were prepared to accept. Producing at Worton Hall Isleworth, usually as executive producer, he had Rex Wilson and Albert Ward acting as directors under him. His cameraman was Sydney Blythe, scripts were at first by Roland Pertwee and later by Walter Summers, and he had a regular group of players. These included Isobel Elsom and Owen Nares, with C. M. Hallard, Minna Grey, Tom Reynolds, Daisy Burrell and Campbell Gullan, with a few appearances by Haidee Wright and Sydney Fairbrother. Isobel Elsom was in almost all his films at first; then in 1920 Madge Titheradge played many leads together with Peggy Hyland, the British actress Samuelson had brought back from Hollywood, and Maudie Dunham; and from 1922 leading parts were taken by the former beauty queen Lillian Hall-Davis.

Samuelson started the post-war period well with an output of more than a dozen films in each of the two years 1919 and 1920, and an enterprising jaunt to Hollywood in early 1920 with partner H. H. Lorie, Butler and some of his staff to produce films at Universal City: *Love in the Wilderness* (Trade Show May 1920), *At the Mercy of Tiberius* (Trade Show May 1920), *Her Story* (Trade Show June 1920), *David and Jonathan* (Trade Show July 1920), *The Night Riders* (Trade Show July 1920) and *The Ugly Duckling* (Trade Show May 1921). This early effort by a British company to popularize British films abroad by a form of international production was carried out under a contract with the new firm of General Film Renters, a company formed in January 1919 by Denton Hardwicke, which over-optimistically envisaged fifteen films a year for six years. Until the end of 1921 all of the large Samuelson output was taken by either General Film Renters or Granger's. But Samuelson's financial position was clearly not stable and his operations became most involved. In November 1920, according to the trade press, Samuelson's was bought outright by General Film Renters, but after May 1921 Samuelson films ceased to be handled by them. Then in February 1922 British Super Films was registered with a capital of £50,000 to take over the company, but only three films appear to have been put out under this name, all made by Fred Paul: *Brown Sugar* (Trade Show July 1922), *If Four Walls Told* (Trade Show September 1922), and *The Right to Strike* (Trade Show July 1923), and handled by Jury. In November 1922 Napoleon Films was registered with a capital of £10,000 to exploit Samuelson films, and until the end of 1924 these were usually, but not always, called 'Napoleon' films. Reciprocity was formed, again with H. H. Lorie, in December 1924, with a capital of £1,000. At the beginning of 1925 Worton Hall studio seem to have been taken over and an old aeroplane hangar at Southall converted to a studio with one dark stage. Another small company, G. B. Samuelson Films, was formed by Lorie and Samuelson in July 1926 to rent Worton Hall and produce films, but it was wound up at the end of 1926. Its failure was innocently attributed by Samuelson himself to 'less successful production', expenses due to an accident, wrong development and damage to the film.[22] But it is no good operating on a shoestring if you are prone to accidents. Much of Samuelson's production took the form of shorts series such as *Twisted Tales*, *Milestone Melodies* and *Proverbs*. His last handful of films appear to have been produced between 1925 and 1928, under the Reciprocity banner. In February 1928 Worton Hall was sold to British Screen Productions. Like many others at the time, Samuelson made several sets of shorts in 1925 and 1926. But all these later manoeuvres did not save the firm. Although he continued to work in the industry, it is clear from his record of production that he was virtually finished as a major producer as early as the end of 1923, although like other ebullient optimists in the industry he would probably have been the last to agree.

To see why he was finished it is necessary to consider the films. A producer like Walter West for the most part chose less famous books to adapt, but chose them carefully to fit in with his own conception of a film story. As a result his films had a consistent character and comparatively simple plots. Samuelson tried to fly higher and often chose more famous, and sometimes much better, works of the most varied character, but with little regard for their suitability. He was ready to try anything, including the daringly unconventional. Brieux's long-running play of 1917 about venereal disease, *Damaged Goods* (Trade Show December 1919), received much notoriety from its censorship troubles, as did *Married Life* (Trade Show May 1923), a film said to be 'based on' Marie Stopes' *Married Love*. Amongst Samuelson's varied output were films with beauty queens Miriam Sabbage, *The Bridal Chair* (Trade Show July 1919), and Lillian Hall-Davis, the midget comedian Wee Georgie Wood: *Convict 99* (Trade Show April 1919), the former star Florence Turner in one of her favourite pathetic-unattractive parts: *The Ugly Duckling* (Trade Show May 1921), the American star Josephine Earle, *The Hotel Mouse* (Trade Show July 1923) and another American, Gertrude McCoy, in a travesty of a Napoleonic 'spectacular' which was a rough version of the old melodrama *A Royal Divorce* (Trade Show January 1923). *The Honey Pot* (Trade Show November 1920) and *Love Maggie* (Trade Show February 1921) were two directed by the American Fred Leroy Granville, starring Peggy Hyland. A third film made by Granville with Peggy Hyland was *Shifting Sands* (Trade Show December 1922) but this seems to have been made independently. A. A. Milne's *Mr Pim Passes By* (Trade Show April 1921) and Pinero's *The Magistrate* (Trade Show May 1921) were attempts to do something better, while *Tilly of Bloomsbury* by Rex Wilson was based on a novel *Happy Go Lucky* and a long-running play of 1919 by Ian Hay, featured such excellent actresses as Edna Best, Isabel Jeans and Helen Haye, and achieved a place in the *World Film Encyclopedia* list of Famous Films.

But even well-motivated stories which hung together could not overcome the crude and old-fashioned style of production. The creaky and economical mounting was particularly unfortunate because of Samuelson's fondness for spectacle and 'olden times'. The preference for 'high society' was also regrettable, for few of his company looked the part. And the inability to deal visually with his complicated stories laid a heavy burden on the titles, which were often ungrammatical and aroused many complaints from reviewers.

Samuelson's last films illustrate these faults and show how sadly he had failed to change with the times. Rider Haggard's *She* (Trade Show May 1925), with the Americans Betty Blythe and Carlyle Blackwell, was shot in a German studio. These were among the most advanced in the world and Samuelson was one of the first British producers to think of taking advantage of their facilities. Yet in its phoney, cheap-looking production, absurd over-acting and incredible slowness, *She* was years out of date. According to the report of a court action brought later by Betty Blythe, it was a 'financial disaster to Mr Samuelson.'[23] In 1927 and 1928, when British Instructional's new patriotic war reconstructions were already setting a new standard of realism and seriousness, he had three so-called patriotics. Of one of them, *Motherland* (Trade Show October 1927), *The Bioscope* said it was hard to believe that a scenario had been used in its production at all. Another was *For Valour* (Trade Show October 1928), and *The Bioscope*'s review of this may be quoted in full as a verdict on Samuelson:

'Though achievement is not commensurate with the ambition evinced throughout this production, it contains much likely to interest uncritical patrons. A considerable amount of padding of rather puerile nature alternates with scenes spectacular and stirring. Many details are ludicrous in their inaccuracy, such as John Bright's presence at a Conservative Cabinet Council, and a very hebraic Queen Victoria in her drawing room. . . .

'Production: Much behind the times.'[24]

All these companies continued to think of production in such humble terms that they had little chance of competing with new, modern companies. But there were several other firms which although small did have better capital and studio resources and yet still failed to make a success of production at this time. One of these was Anglo-Hollandia. In the early twenties Hepworth, Pearson, Stoll and others made much of their desire to produce films representative of Britain. Another attempt to exploit this 'Britishness' as a selling angle was made by a foreign company, Anglo-Hollandia. This was a Haarlem company, its managing director Maurice Binger, which possessed a studio in Holland but had a relatively small local market. Their own production *Joy* (Trade Show February 1920) was described ominously as unsophisticated. In July 1919 they announced that they would undertake printing for British firms. In mid-1920 it was announced that the London renting firm of Granger's Exclusives was to back their productions. Granger's had previously shown an interest in financing production with their independent venture *Unmarried* (Trade Show April 1920), a propaganda film made by Rex Wilson for the National Council for the Unmarried Mother and her Child with a worthy stage cast headed by Gerald du Maurier and Mary Glynne. The new productions were to be called Granger–Binger films, and the first of them was *The Little Hour of Peter Wells* (Trade Show August 1920).

The production unit was usually made up of either B. E. Doxatt-Pratt or Frankland A. Richardson as producer, Feiko Boersma as cameraman, and Anglo–Dutch casts headed by Adelqui Migliar and Zoe Palmer. *The Skin Game* (Trade Show January 1921), based on Galsworthy's successful current play and featuring Edmund Gwenn, Helen Haye and Mary Clare, was included in the *World Film Encyclopedia* list of Famous Films, as was *Blood Money* (Trade Show February 1921). Most of the films were based on novels and plays, although *Laughter and Tears* (Trade Show October 1921) and *Circus Jim* (Trade Show January 1922) were melodramas written with heavy parts for himself by Migliar, or Millar as he was known after April 1921. The Dutch studio was used, with pleasant Dutch exteriors bravely labelled 'Chelsea' or 'Kensington'. The B. & C. studios were used for a short while in 1920. The films were amateur-ish, slow and badly made, and the brand ceased when Binger died in April 1923. Granger's, under the London manager Arthur Backner, was still seeking a foot-hold in production and now backed I. B. Davidson films, which were then to be known as Granger–Davidson films. In September the Commonwealth Film Corporation was registered with a capital of £10,000 and early in 1924 Granger's showed a Granger–Commonwealth film called *The Money Habit* (Trade Show January 1924), made at Islington by Walter Niebuhr with Baron Ventimiglia at the camera and a better cast than usual, headed by Nina Vanna and Clive Brook.

An important attempt to make a success of production in England by providing adequate backing and studios, and distribution as well, was made soon after the war by the Famous Players–Lasky company of America. Famous Players–Lasky British Producers Ltd. was launched, and a former power station of the Metropolitan Railway at Poole Street, Islington, was leased later in 1919 and turned with some difficulty into a modern studio. It had two stages with a large floor area, workshops and offices, and up-to-date American equipment. The new company concentrated on good lighting, in which England now lagged far behind America. The managing director was J. C. Graham, but the general manager of the company in the United States, Milton E. Hoffman, was in charge for the first year. Adolph Zukor visited England in March 1920 and Jesse L. Lasky in June 1920.

The first films were *The Call of Youth* and *The Great Day* (both Trade Shows

November 1920), directed by the American Hugh Ford, shot by Hal Young. The former was from an original story by Henry Arthur Jones and the latter based on a G. R. Sims' melodrama. Ford was a Famous Players director of some experience and Mary Glynne, who starred in the first, was married to the actor Dennis Neilson–Terry and had already tried film acting for a smaller company. The results seem to have been disappointing. Next year there were three films by Donald Crisp: *Appearances* (Trade Show June 1921), *The Princess of New York* (Trade Show June 1921), and *Beside the Bonnie Briar Bush* (Trade Show November 1921), and two by Paul Powell, with various cameramen. The films appear to have improved technically. Next year there were two made by George Fitzmaurice: *Three Live Ghosts* (Trade Show March 1922), and *The Man from Home*, released June 1923, with A. Miller at the camera, and two by John Stuart Robertson: *Perpetua* (Trade Show May 1922) and *The Spanish Jade* (Trade Show August 1922) with Roy Overbaugh on the camera. All were adaptations. Anna Q. Nilsson, who had been a star for many years, was in *Three Live Ghosts*, and this was considered to be the studio's best production so far. All the same,

'. . . early in 1924 J. C. Graham announced that in the opinion of the American company the productions had failed to reach a quality comparable with those made in the States.'[25]

British shareholders were paid back and the studio and equipment were sold for very little to Michael Balcon and his associates (see page 166). This was, it is true, the beginning of the slump in British production. But the films had improved as the company settled down, and it is interesting to speculate why the American company decided to give up at this juncture, or indeed why they had ever come over to England at all. Their arrival coincided with the bitter controversy about American companies owning cinemas in Britain, and it was publicly stressed that the company was to be controlled by British capital and a British board, and that the films would be 'British-*made* pictures'. The aim was, they said, to exploit the characteristically British quality of the films. There may have been a desire to persuade well-known British writers to prepare original screen stories for them, but the only one to do so was Henry Arthur Jones, and his *Call of Youth* was not particularly successful. Crisp's *Beside The Bonnie Briar Bush* (Trade Show November 1921), a picture whose Scottish scenes were largely shot in Devon, might as well have been made in the United States, and the company seems gradually to have become resigned to the British weather and retired into the studio. They had also announced that they would start production with staff from America but that when the company was established these would hand over to British technicians. The American screen writers Margaret Turnbull and Eve Unsell stayed only about a year and several of the various directors were also temporary. Some of the remaining staff could be described as British, in a way, as producers Donald Crisp and Paul Powell, actor David Powell and cameraman Hal Young were all of British origin, although all had made good in America. But it would seem that financial backing, adequate studios and equipment and distribution arrangements were not the only obstacles to British production, and that the climate and the scarcity of first-class talent, particularly of writers, were of decisive importance.

With more than a touch of sentimentality *The Bioscope* announced after the war that one of the biggest and most respected of British companies, the London Film Company, was starting work again at Twickenham.

'The studio at St Margaret's has housed for a while certain sorrowful ghosts of past successes, but now once again, in the early sunshine that holds the first promise of a Peace spring, it is throbbing with busy life, and quick-footed people with keen smiling faces flash in and out, cameras whirr, and the gong is struck for silence every few minutes while busy "takes" are being made.'[26]

The few films made by L.F.C. in 1919 and trade shown in 1919 and 1920 suggest an extraordinary assumption that nothing had changed since 1914. Exactly as before, Harold Shaw and Fred Paul were directors, Bannister Merwin and Frank Powell wrote the scenarios, Fred Groves and many other old reliables were in the casts, and the films were handled by Jury. Shaw's work had deteriorated, his wife Edna Flugrath astonished and appalled the critics by taking unsuitable *ingénue* parts, and the work of the company seemed naïve and out of date. The only modern, serious and sophisticated note was struck by Einaar Bruun, whose first film in England was *Enchantment* (Trade Show April 1920) with the actor Henri Krauss, who was already well known in French films. Of the original company Ralph Jupp and George Loane Tucker died in 1921, Merwin in 1922 and Shaw in 1926. But by the end of 1919 rumour already said that the company was finished and the studio was to be bought by a big new company, Alliance.

Alliance was one of the earliest and most ambitious of the companies formed after the war, and was expected to remedy the chronic inadequacy of capital and studios here. Referred to as a 'million pound company', it was associated with the business tycoon Charles F. Higham MP, and its registration in October 1919 was accompanied by a spate of statistics and rumours about its network of cultural and financial connections. It seemed like an auspicious start. The Board included the theatrical manager Sir Walter de Frece, recently knighted, the publisher Walter Hutchinson, and the actors Gerald du Maurier and A. E. Matthews. The latter were already connected with the British Actors Film Company, on whom the new company proposed to draw for their supply of actors. It was intended to have a Consultative Literary Committee including the playwrights Pinero, Sims, Knoblock and Carton. First National Exhibitors' Circuit of America was to distribute the films, and several American directors were to be engaged. Harrow Weald Park Estate was to be turned into a 'British cinema city' at a cost of £70,000 and another £35,000 was to be spent on good American lighting. The ideas of technical quality were derived entirely from America.

A public issue took place in November and the prospectus outlined grandiose and optimistic production plans for an annual output of 26 five-reelers costing £4,750 each with expected returns of £5,800 in Great Britain alone; 26 two-reelers at £1,000 each with returns of £1,200; and 4 super productions at

£7,425 with returns of £8,500. These estimates were based on the successful films of the pre-war British Actors Film Company, in which they had acquired a controlling interest.

British Actors Film Company had been making films for several years at its small studio at Bushey. The chairman was the actor Charles Macdona, the general manager Gerald Malvern, and the managing director was the stage actor A. E. Matthews. Film directors were Wilfred Noy and Duncan McRae, and the scenario department was in the charge of S. H. Herkomer with the assistance of Adrian Brunel. In 1919 and 1920 they showed some dozen films, unsensational and rather old-fashioned dramas which did well enough in a modest way, although their prestige must have been damaged by a celebrated court case over Thomas Bentley's film *The Lackey and the Lady* (Trade Show March 1919). The already delayed trade show of this film in March 1919 was stopped by the renter who had contracted to handle it, H. J. Boam of Phillips Film Company, on the ground that it 'was not considered of a sufficiently high standard to place before the prospective exhibitors'.[27] Bentley eventually secured judgement in an action for slander in early 1920 but such publicity was not helpful. The company is interesting for appearances by McRae's wife, the American actress Gertrude McCoy, and by several actors who later became well known in films, A. E. Matthews himself, C. Aubrey Smith and Leslie Howard.

According to Brunel's autobiography, British Actors Film Company at this time wished to increase their capital to some £120,000 but were persuaded by Higham to merge with Alliance instead. Malvern himself later said in an interview that the firm had been prosperous in its small way and that he had opposed the merger, which he felt would be of advantage only to the newer firm in enabling it to claim credit for the British Actors' films, but that Lauri de Frece and Charles Macdona were persuaded by the former's brother Walter de Frece. The smaller company was taken over.

Harley Knoles was made managing director and Director General of production for Alliance, and the cameraman René Guissart was engaged at the high salary of £90 a week. The company was to make supers, large productions in the modern style based on books and plays, with the accent on spectacle and the picturesque. The former pageant-master Willie Davies, who already had considerable film experience, did some of the design and it would seem that a spectacular appearance was considered important. Casts were large, but unlike the Stoll and Ideal casts they contained some good actors and concentrated attention on a small number of leading players. These included Matheson Lang, Ivor Novello, Gladys Cooper, C. Aubrey Smith and Constance Collier, all of whom were familiar with film acting. The biggest and most important film was *Carnival* (Trade Show February 1921) by Harley Knoles, with Matheson Lang and Ivor Novello, from a stage success of the year before of which Matheson Lang was part-author. The production was lavish, with carnival scenes in Venice, balloons, lights, canals and throngs of people, but the reviews suggest that the story itself, which concerned an Othello-actor consumed by real-life jealousy, was told largely through the titles. The other two productions were *The Door that has no Key* (Trade Show March 1921) and *The Bohemian Girl* (Trade Show

May 1922), from the opera. The latter was romantic, beautiful to look at and shot with considerable invention, and was of added interest for a small appearance by the elderly Ellen Terry.

Meanwhile the company had quickly run into difficulties. The response from investors was not good and it was necessary for the underwriters to take up a large part of the stock. They could not finish their Weald Park Studios, and by February 1920 had bought the old Twickenham studio at a cost of £35,537. They spent another £22,750 on modern lighting for it. They were unable to finance British Actors Film Company as intended, and in April 1921 the latter company was wound up. By this time it was said that Alliance had already spent over £90,000 on production. In view of the misleading prospectus estimates and the small output to date, shareholders had been restive from October 1920 onwards and some of them now took court action. As it turned out *Carnival* was an outstanding production, extremely successful in the modern manner and by May 1921 was said to have already taken £43,000, but it was too late to establish confidence in the company, and although *The Bohemian Girl* was finished later in 1921 the company was wound up at the end of 1922. The studio was later sold for a mere £9,750. The London Film Company continued to exist as a printing business only, and the British Actors Film Company studio at Bushey was first used for hire and later sold. It was bought in 1927 by Randal Terraneau and G. Humphries for hire, and Bushey Studios was registered in February 1928 as a private company with a capital of £3,500.[28]

Alliance, which was considered at the time to be a sensational and extravagant company, attempted to introduce large scale and a modern style of production to Britain. The films were creditable and might well have succeeded in this. But the prospectus estimates had been in terms of old-fashioned production, whereas their actual operations were not. Already by 1919 it was quite impossible to finance a super production for as little as £7,500. Unfortunately the company was dominated by stage people whose admiration for American success was not backed by any real knowledge of the film industry, and who failed to appreciate the real difference between the type of films the British Actors had turned out, and the type of film they wished to make themselves.

Still further down the business scale were the loners, the individuals who floated from one production set-up to another, but for various reasons never seemed to find the niche they were seeking.

One of the biggest disappointments of the silent British film was the work of Guy Newall. Working with little capital in the small, oddly-shaped studio in Ebury Street, he made films which for a while seemed full of promise.

Newall was an actor who had done some work for the London Film Company before the war. In August 1919 he advertised a new brand, Lucky Cat comedy-dramas, which were to be 'very, very English'. George Clark, whom he had met during the war, was business manager, and for a short time Kenelm Foss as well as A. H. Rooke directed the films, with Bert Ford and Joe Rosenthal junior on the cameras and design by Charles Dalmon. The leading parts were taken by Guy Newall and Ivy Duke, whom he married in late 1922. Four Lucky Cat feature films were shown in 1919: *I Will* (Trade Show July 1919), *The March*

Hare (Trade Show August 1919), *The Double Life of Mr Alfred Burton* (Trade Show August 1919), and *Fancy Dress* (Trade Show September 1919). *I Will*, an original scenario by Foss, was much liked for its good-humoured story about a young Lord who tried to justify himself to his socialist girl friend, and for Newall's light-hearted acting. *The Garden of Resurrection* (Trade Show December 1919), directed by Rooke and loosely adapted by Newall from a Temple Thurston story, was the first film to be put out as a George Clark production. The plot, about a young man who almost killed himself for love of an Irish wench he hardly knew, was silly. The film was described as long and ragged. Yet the humorous film treatment of the characters and sincere playing by Newall and Duke aroused exceptional interest. It was rented by Stoll, who after this continued to handle the George Clark films.

In April 1920 Ducal Studios was registered with a capital of £70,000. In 1920 and 1921 four more features were put out, all of them based on novels and featuring Newall and Duke, one of them also directed by Newall. These were *The Lure of Crooning Water* (Trade Show January 1920), *Duke's Son* (Trade Show June 1920), *Testimony* (Trade Show October 1920) and *The Bigamist* (Trade Show August 1921). These films were still produced under considerable difficulties in the narrow, awkward studio at Ebury Street, but all were successful. Meanwhile a new studio was being built at Beaconsfield, with one dark stage of some 120 × 60 square feet, and George Clark Productions was registered in October 1920 with a capital of £50,000. The company went to Nice for production for seven months and the new studio was opened in May 1922. They continued with some short comedies and the same sort of feature film, the best of which were *Fox Farm* (Trade Show July 1922) and the last made by Newall, *The Starlit Garden* (Trade Show July 1923). In *Fox Farm* the lovely photography by Hal Young shows us the vanished English countryside of the twenties in a way that Hepworth talked about but failed to achieve. After this a couple of unimportant films were made at the studio by F. Martin Thornton and handled as Ducal films, and then production ceased. Guy Newall and Ivy Duke after this appeared separately, and Newall confined himself to acting. The studio was hired in October 1924 by Britannia to make a slightly disreputable film, *Afraid of Love* (Trade Show March 1925), and was then derelict until it was bought by the second British Lion company after the quota legislation.

The films of this charming and gifted couple, while the collaboration lasted, aroused the trade's admiring interest rather than its practical support. Put out with good publicity and an air of taste and elegance, they were not really showmen's pictures. The sets and lighting were good, despite the handicaps of the old studio, and were characteristically light and uncluttered. Both stars had screen presences. Ivy Duke played with a light touch and a faintly ironical air, and was indeed very English. Guy Newall, with an ugly and even a misleadingly coarse appearance, was sometimes somewhat miscast as a young aristocrat, but the delicacy of his playing and their combined realistic, shrewd and humorous observation of the interplay of personal relations was a refreshing contrast to the stock figures portrayed in most contemporary films. Nevertheless it seems that their ideas were better than their execution. Perhaps the choice of story was their weak point, indulging their interest in psychological subtlety and interrelations at the expense of action and finally slipping into melodrama to work out a plot. Like Henry Edwards, Newall's exceptional film sense was that of an actor, and though for a while it appeared likely to develop into an intelligent understanding of film making as a whole, the breaking up of the partnership seems to have put an end to this. It is worth adding that, as in other cases, the existence of better studio facilities were of little importance in comparison with the existence of the creative talent and drive, and work which had flourished in the bad old studio faded in the good new one.

In his early film career Adrian Brunel was also something of an individualist. After the war he was in the scenario department of British Actors Film Company at Bushey. When this company disappeared several members of it, amongst them Brunel, set up Minerva Films. This was registered in March 1920 with a capital of £10,000 and was originally, according to Brunel's autobiography,[29] the idea of the actor Leslie Howard. The Board included A. A. Milne, Nigel Playfair and C. Aubrey Smith, as well as Howard himself and Brunel, who was Director of Productions and Scenario Editor. The aim was to make short comedies based on comic plots rather than knockabout, using 'the charm of English settings, and the finished art of well-known English comedy actors'.[30] H. M. Lomas was cameraman until he joined British Instructional in March 1921, and the acting mainstay was Leslie Howard, already known for his work in some British Actors films and successful on the stage in 1920 in A. A. Milne's *Mr Pim Passes By*.

In October 1920 four two-reelers were trade shown by the renter Moss, written by Milne and directed by Brunel, featuring Leslie Howard and C. Aubrey Smith. These were *Bookworms*, *The Bump*, *£5 Reward* and *Twice Two*. Described as satires, they were extremely mild situation comedies. According to Brunel they were successful but, as shorts, were hardly profitable enough to keep the company in business. A year later he trade showed a three-reel comedy featuring Annette Benson and Miles Mander, *A Temporary Lady* (Trade Show September 1921). In December 1921 a new company was registered by Brunel and Sir Percy Sykes to make and exploit travel films, and they went to North Africa to shoot some film, both actuality and enacted. Next year, together with Miles Mander, Brunel formed Atlas Biocraft with £5,000 backing from financier Jimmy White, and at the end of 1922 was able to embark for the first time on an adequately financed feature film.

This was his first important film, *The Man Without Desire* (Trade Show December 1923), which was partly in modern dress and partly in costume. It was from a script by Frank Fowell based on an idea by Monckton Hoffe, and shot by Henry Harris in Germany and on location in Venice. It starred Nina Vanna and Ivor Novello, before the latter went to U.S.A. to work for D. W. Griffith. Novello had already made two films for Alliance and one for Gaumont and was an established film star, as well as having appeared on the London stage since 1921. The film, which was romantic and interestingly made, was a moderate artistic and commercial success. It began to look as if Brunel might be more than a dilettante and have something exceptional to offer. The film was handled by yet another small and short-lived company formed for the purpose, Novello–

Atlas Renters, which also showed film resulting from the African trip, a travel film *Moors and Minarets* (Trade Show December 1923) and a story film called *Lovers in Araby* (Trade Show May 1924) with Annette Benson and Miles Mander. At this time Brunel also worked the short comedy vein further with a string of facetious parodies or skits, inexpensive burlesques with punning titles which appealed especially to those in the film trade. He made *Crossing the Great Sagrada* and *The Pathetic Gazette* (both Trade Shows October 1924) independently at Bushey for about £90 each by using titles for about a third of the footage, library shots for another third, and shots of himself attitudinizing, as he called it, for the rest. Five more skits were commissioned early in 1925 by the renter C. M. Woolf and Michael Balcon at £150 each and again made at Bushey, *So This is Jollygood*, *The Typical Budget*, *Cut It Out*, *Battling Bruisers* and *The Blunderland of Big Game*. *Money for Nothing* was made privately for Woolf, at a cost of £65, to celebrate the first anniversary of the Shepherd's Bush Pavilion, and another private production was made in 1926 for £20 called *Love, Life and Laughter at Swaythling Court.*[31]

Swaythling Court was the home of Lord Swaythling, Ivor Montagu's father. Brunel made the acquaintance of Ivor Montagu through a mutual interest in the latter's creation the Film Society, and from this they began to edit foreign films for the English market. Brought into contact with the best foreign films, and especially with Russian concepts of film structure, they were in the van of the developing ideas of film technique. A number of young technicians who were to become well known in the film industry assisted them at one time or another, including Ian Dalrymple, Frank Wells, Angus Macphail, Sergei Nolbandov and Reginald Beck. The company Brunel and Montagu was registered in August 1927. By that time also Brunel's first film for Gainsborough, *Blighty* (Trade Show March 1927, see page 169), had been shown success fully and he seemed to be established as one of the more talented young British film makers.

Brunel and Newall both seemed capable of great things. Kenelm Foss, who was equally industrious for a few years, was similarly convincing at first. At the end of the war he and Arrigo Bocchi were working at the Catford studios for Windsor Films, a firm owned by Serra and Company. Late in 1918 and early in 1919 half a dozen films and shorts produced by Bocchi and variously written and acted by Foss were put out by Walturdaw, based on novels by romantic writers such as Elinor Glyn and Marion Crawford. At the same time Foss wrote a number of shorts for the comedian Bertie Wright, for New Agency. In March 1919 it was announced that the studios at Kew Bridge had been leased by Leon Comnen and Jack Clair, described as 'latterly cinematographers to the Serbian government'. Foss directed for them a set of six one-reel comedies: *Til Our Ship Comes in* (Trade Show June 1919) and *A Little Bit of Fluff* (Trade Show June 1919) with Ernest Thesiger and Bertie Wright in a stage adaptation from a long run of 1915. At about the same time he wrote the first four Lucky Cat films which were made at Kew, acting in one and directing two of them. While Bocchi was away in Italy, Foss attempted to take over the Catford studios and form a large company with grandiose plans—'Everyone employed there will be exclusively British'. But, as Foss put it later (in an interview) the money didn't materialize and Serra, the Marquis Guido Serra di Cassano, sued Foss and his associate H. J. Sutherland Mackay.[32] It appeared that they had agreed to buy the studio from Serra for £23,000 and had taken possession after paying £2,300, leaving the balance unpaid. The Catford establishment was sold early in 1920 to Walter West, and that was the end of the Windsor brand. Three more of the Bocchi–Foss films with Italian location sequences, complicated plots and many characters appeared later in 1919 as Walturdaw films. The only independent production from Foss was *The Joyous Adventures of Aristide Pujol* (Trade Show March 1920), which was directed and adapted by Frank Miller and featured Foss himself in a series of episodes designed to show his virtuosity as an actor. After this legal trouble was clearly on its way and Foss resigned on the grounds of illness.

But he had yet another iron in the fire. In August 1919 Reardon British Films had been registered with a capital of £30,000, working at Kew Bridge, and for them he had made *The Glad Eye* (Trade Show May 1920). This, which is not to be confused with Elvey's version of the same play made in 1927, was based on a mild marital farce which had enjoyed a long stage run in 1912 and featured Foss, who also directed and adapted it, and Dorothy Minto. By July 1920 Bocchi joined them. But the company made nothing more and was in liquidation by December 1921.[33] Foss had meanwhile seized another opportunity and become producer for Astra.

We have seen how he worked on *The Breed of the Treshams*, the ambitious film made by the Wilcox brothers and H. W. Thompson trading as Astra Films in 1920. After the Wilcoxes had gone their own way in the second half of the year, H. W. Thompson Productions was formed, in July 1921, and Foss began to make Thompson films for Astra to distribute. Working at the old B. & C. studios at Hoe Street, Walthamstow, Foss wrote and directed twelve films, all adaptations, some from sentimental writers like Ruby M. Ayres and Helen Mather, but mostly from melodramatic plays by Knoblock, Leon M. Lion, Tom Gallon and others. Tasteless and unsophisticated, the films sound as if they were made with a complete contempt for the audience, thin and false apart from a few good performances. Lionelle Howard and Mary Odette were his usual leads but several reputable stage actors also appeared, Cyril Maude playing his original part in *The Headmaster* (Trade Show January 1921) which had a long run in the theatre before the war, Zena Dare (*No. 5 John St* Trade Show December 1921), and Fay Compton (*The House of Peril* Trade Show February 1922) in others. Photography, which was usually acceptable, was by Frank Canham until later 1921 and then by the cameraman Jack Parker, who later went to British Instructional. Foss's last production was *The Romance of Old Baghdad* (Trade Show March 1922) with Matheson Lang, and it would appear that by now the tolerance of trade, press and public had worn very thin. After this he went abroad for a couple of years, and although there were signs in 1924 that he was interested in another company, they came to nothing. A stage actor originally, Foss was very active and persuasive for several years, with cultured and even *avant-garde* pretensions which were in the end not justified by his work.

As for Astra, later in 1923 they started to produce at St Margaret's, Twickenham. They later showed Fred Leroy Granville's *The Beloved Vagabond* (Trade Show October 1923) starring Carlyle Blackwell, a very popular romantic melodrama which had a long run on the stage in 1908, and *The Woman Who Obeyed* (Trade Show September 1923), a tasteful and opulent marital drama directed and written by Sidney Morgan, with Hilda Bayley and Stewart Rome and shot by Stanley Mumford. Morgan and Mumford made another film next year, *Miriam Rozella* (Trade Show March 1924), with Owen Nares and Gertrude McCoy. Morgan also directed Alma Taylor's first film away from Hepworth, *The Shadow of Egypt* (Trade Show November 1924), for which they went to Egypt. This was said by many to be Morgan's best film. His last production for Astra was *Bulldog Drummond's Third Round* (Trade Show October 1925) with Jack Buchanan. In 1926 two Elvey films appeared, one the immensely successful, *The Flag Lieutenant* (Trade Show October 1926), with Henry Edwards, a good strong story and a popular actor in a play which had enjoyed two long runs before the war.

There were several other producers, of whom Walter West and Bertram Phillips were typical, who were well-known characters in the trade and who fought long and bravely to remain in business, but were essentially old-fashioned and failed to adapt themselves to a more modern spirit.

Bertram Phillips had acquired an elementary studio under a railway bridge, Cranmer Court in Clapham, in about 1917, and made a number of films there with his leading lady Queenie Thomas and cameraman Percy Anthony. A handful of unimportant films were made after the war: *Rock of Ages* (Trade Show February 1919), *A Little Child Shall Lead Them* (Trade Show July 1919) and *Trousers* (Trade Show April 1920). Late in 1919 Queenie Thomas married, and although Bertram Phillips acquired a better 'mansion-type' studio at Thornton House, Clapham Park, it was reported later that it had been sold without having been used except for some short films. Early in 1923 it was said that Queenie Thomas was to make a comeback and a series of short comedies called *Syncopated Picture Plays* were made as well as four longer films with better casts, including two with Queenie Thomas playing opposite John Stuart. Considerable efforts were made to publicize her as a star. But this type of film making with poor technical resources, ridiculous stories and no real talent was weeded out by the production slump.

At the end of the war the astute and persuasive Walter West had returned from service in the Royal Flying Corps and his firm Broadwest started working again at the Wood Street, Walthamstow, studios. Early in 1920 it absorbed the Windsor studios at Catford. Until 1922 the firm operated at both studios, with a stock company headed by West's leading lady Violet Hopson and Stewart Rome, both formerly with Hepworth, and with Lionelle Howard, Gregory Scott, Poppy Wyndham and, in 1921, Clive Brook. The films were directed by Frank Wilson, Richard Garrick, George Dewhurst, Norman McDonald and Einaar Bruun, but Walter West, a big determined man, was very much the producer in charge and the films were characteristically his. Most of the scripts were adapted by Benedict James or Pat Mannock from novels. At this time all West's films were distributed by Walturdaw, on a working arrangement by which they guaranteed backing and distribution for long periods in advance.

The output was large and the films very similar to each other, but they were spirited showman's pictures and the many racing dramas were exciting and popular in their modest way. Although somewhat lacking in personality Violet Hopson was a star quite well known in Britain, slightly less popular than Betty Balfour, Alma Taylor, or Chrissie White. Production was smooth and the photography adequate, although conventional except where the exigencies of racing stories took them outdoors. The bleak suburban exteriors were real, even if mean and unattractive, and the cold open sky of the Downs familiar to home audiences. Uninterested in film technique though the company was, their film making was practical and uninhibited, and the racing and chases led them to use cutting, close-shots, travelling shots and even slow motion, as in *The Stirrup Cup Sensation*. The stories were as a rule simple and straightforward plots, unrealistic and contrived but not too grotesquely melodramatic, and spared the audience the high-emotion overacting which marred, for example, some of George Pearson's films. They created a world of their own, an imaginary society with people like the nice sensible heroine and the gentlemanly Stewart Rome moving through their familiar parts with no great emotion. It was a world peopled with guardians, profligate sons, concealed identities, girls delightfully learning to love their husbands-of-convenience and race-horse owners with their fortunes or their girl friends for ever at stake, their horses for ever in danger of nobbling. Three were Nat Gould adaptations: *A Great Coup* (Trade Show November 1919); *A Dead Certainty* (Trade Show April 1920), and *A Rank Outsider* (Trade Show November 1920), and two from Andrew Soutar: *Snow in the Desert* (Trade Show December 1919) and *The Imperfect Lover* (Trade Show October 1921). Probably the best-known films were *Kissing Cup's Race* (Trade Show January 1921) with Violet Hopson and Stewart Rome, based on a story by Campbell Rae Brown, which seems to have been handled by Butchers, and the American Norman McDonald's *Christie Johnston* (Trade Show October 1921). The latter, from Charles Reade, featured the American star Gertrude McCoy with Stewart Rome and Clive Brook and was unusual for West in being a costume adaptation. The only successful play used was *The Case of Lady Camber* (Trade Show August 1920) which had a long run at the Savoy in 1915.

In West's words he and his financial partner Broadbridge finally agreed to differ, and by September 1921 the company was in the hands of the receivers.[34] After this West produced on his own, with many of the same people and the same sort of film, put out as Walter West Productions or Violet Hopson Productions. These were made at Prince's Studio on the North side of Kew Bridge, later the site of the Q Theatre, and were made under a contract with Butcher which specified twelve films at a cost of up to the modest sum of £4,000 each,[35] although West in an interview gave the figure of £8,000. These included three more stories from Soutar, two of them with the former star Florence Turner: *Was She Justified* (Trade Show November 1922) and *Hornet's Nest* (Trade Show March 1923), and one with a big cast headed by Victor McLaglen, *In the Blood* (Trade Show November 1923). Violet Hopson continued to star in most of them, with Stewart Rome in 1922 and with James Knight in 1923, including two more from Campbell Rae Brown, *Son of Kissing Cup* (Trade Show August 1922) and

The Stirrup Cup Sensation (Trade Show September 1924). The completion of this last, however, was much delayed and Butcher's, who footed the bill, brought a court action against West, who by that time was bankrupt.[36]

After this West no longer ranked as an important producer. His own view, expressed in an interview, that he was ruined by the arrival of the sound film, must be questioned. He made few films after 1924. In 1925 he made a film for Stoll with Violet Hopson, *A Daughter of Love* (Trade Show February 1925), and another for Astra National with Juliette Compton, *Trainer and Temptress* (Trade Show September 1925), and six two-reel racing dramas at Islington for Gainsborough. These featured the famous jockey Steve Donoghue with Carlyle Blackwell, Miles Mander and June, and were shot by Hal Young. They were: *Riding for a King, Dark Horses, A Knight of the Saddle, Beating the Book, Come on, Steve* and *The Golden Spurs*. In 1927 West registered yet another company, Q.T.S., with a capital of £4,000, which was raised to £20,000 in August 1927. Q.T.S. made two melodramas at Islington, *Maria Marten* (Trade Show March 1928) and *Sweeney Todd* (Trade Show September 1928). These were marketed by Ideal, which by now was a subsidiary of Gaumont–British. They seem a curious choice for West, and out of keeping with the times. One must conclude that he was ruined not by the sound film or the difficulty of securing distribution, since this was amply provided by Walturdaw, Butcher and others, but by a more fundamental failure to keep up with the times.

At the very lowest level of film making there was no shortage of enthusiasm, although talent, imagination, luck and even common sense might be lacking. Individuals seeking capital, ingeniously making some modest film in the hope of impressing potential backers for the next one, forming or just talking about forming one small company after another and frequently going bankrupt themselves in the process, all these formed a small army of depressingly familiar names which acquired a professional ring simply through having been around so long. In the end the difference between them and some of the producers who succeeded was not so much in cheek, opportunism or talent as in their inability to think in big enough terms. Even when capital, studios and equipment were available they tried to produce on too small a scale.

The private firm of Lucoque which was registered early in 1915 with a capital of £6,000 became Artistic Films at the end of 1918, its capital having been increased to £20,000 at the beginning of the year. The firm was engaged in renting, but became known as the producer of Hugh Croise's *Three Men in a Boat* (Trade Show November 1920) from the novel by Jerome K. Jerome, made at the Ebury St Studio, and a series of popular adaptations by Lydia Hayward from stories by W. W. Jacobs which were directed by Manning Haynes and shot by Frank Grainger. They later used the Master studios at Teddington. The managing director of Artistic, until he resigned in September 1924, was George Redman. Lucoque registered another company with a capital of £6,000 in March 1920, Lucoque and Taylor, and after making a few unsuccessful films resigned from Artistic in early 1923. Production petered out, both companies were in liquidation by late 1925 and Lucoque was bankrupt. The firm had consistently made losses which were attributed to the shortage of working capital necessary for modern production. Lydia Hayward went to Gaumont, Croise produced more short films and Haynes made three rather more important features during the later part of the decade.

George Wilkinson Dewhurst was another producer who made fresh starts repeatedly throughout the twenties. Early in 1919 he showed an independent film, *The Home Maker* (Trade Show January 1919 and again April 1920), and later did some work for Broadwest. In June 1920 he was associated with a firm which had rights to the novels of Silas Hocking, several of which were made. In 1921 he was working for Hepworth, and later at Ealing made independently *A Sister to Assist 'Er* (Trade Show September 1922), from the late Fred Emney's music-hall sketch based on the Mrs May series by John le Breton, with Mary Brough and Pollie Emery. A company was formed to make short comedies at Ealing. Three independent films made partly in Germany followed: *The Uninvited Guest* (Trade Show July 1923), *The Evil that Men Do* (Trade Show August 1923), and *What the Butler Saw* (Trade Show October 1924). Later he remade *A Sister to Assist 'Er* (Trade Show September 1927) for Gaumont, and in 1928 assisted Harley Knoles to mend a film, *The Rising Generation* (Trade Show September 1928), which Hugh Castle claimed

'. . . gets near rock bottom. . . . That he got some sort of cohesion is a tribute to his ingenuity.'[37]

By 1927 the International Cinematograph Corporation was announcing plans for him to film the music-hall comic Harry Tate, and after this company was acquired by Filmophone. Harry Tate's famous sketch *Motoring* and some others were filmed at Cricklewood in 1929 by Dewhurst.

The difficulties of a rather old-fashioned producer who wished to produce independently on a small scale are illustrated even more clearly by Geoffrey Malins, who had been one of the official war cameramen. His company Garrick was registered as a private company with a capital of £10,500 in January 1919. Working at Stoll's Regent House Studio at Surbiton he made three films with his leading lady and partner Ena Beaumont. In 1920 he put out *Our Girls and Their Physique,* a series of 'health and beauty' shorts, and another series of dance lesson and comedy shorts, both featuring Ena Beaumont. Later he made some Rafael Sabatini films at Worton Hall for the Hardy Film Company, a short-lived firm formed by the Stoll studio manager Sam Hardy with Sabatini himself.* In 1921 Hardy put out more shorts, including *Ally Sloper's Adventures* featuring Ena Beaumont with Max Gionti (six two-reelers, reviewed August 1921). Still later he worked for Stoll, and throughout the twenties he kept hopefully forming small companies and announcing plans which came to little or nothing.

Perhaps this was better than the sad story of Gaiety Film Productions, for

---

* April 1921 to August 1922, capital £10,000. Sabatini wrote *The Scourge* in 1921 and Malins made a film of it; the book was then written and published in America as *Fortune's Fool,* and the film's name changed; the company was wound up and the film was placed with a renter in 1925, and finally was given another trade show in 1927. Rex Ingram's *Scaramouche* with Ramon Navarro was made in America from the same book in 1923.

which Sandground and Hinks raised £5,750 in 1919, rented a studio at Croydon to the company for £63 a year and made some films which nobody would book.[38] Or Fred Paul, another of the floaters who drifted from company to company: after the war he returned to work with the London Film Company, and when this closed he worked for Master–British Exhibitors Films, then for Samuelson. During 1920 he produced independently at Ealing two very old-style melo-dramas, *Uncle Dick's Darling* (Trade Show June 1922), and *The English Rose* (Trade Show November 1923). In the middle of the decade he worked for Stoll, being responsible for several series of shorts as well as some features. Later he made *The Luck of the Navy* (Trade Show November 1927) with Evelyn Laye for Graham–Wilcox and the *Dr Sin Fang* shorts (1928). At the end of the period his out-dated melodrama *The Broken Melody* (Trade Show October 1929) was the *coup de grâce* for the collapsing Welsh–Pearson Company (see page 163). He seems to have been accepted as a reliable professional by virtue of familiarity. The same could be said of many others, including M. A. Wetherell, who had acted in I.V.T.A. Films in South Africa and from 1923 onwards in British films. He tried his own hand at production in a rather unusual form with *Livingstone* (première September 1925) and *Robinson Crusoe* (Trade Show May 1927), and later made *The Somme* (Trade Show September 1927) for New Era, and *Victory* (Trade Show March 1928). An attractive figure in many ways, his good intentions were not realized by his films, which were naïve and roughly made.

CHAPTER FIVE

Producers in the
Later Twenties

There was a depression in British film production between the years 1924 and 1927, when the old guard of producers were weeded out and the ground was cleared for more highly capitalized companies with modern business methods and a modern style of production. During the next few years the industry was to be transformed, first by the quota legislation and then by sound film production.

Accurate statistics showing the rise and fall of production are not available. However, the table below has been drawn up on the basis of the Film List at the end of this book. It gives the annual number of trade shows of British feature films, with the total and average number of reels in them. Despite the various qualifications necessary to compile a set of figures spanning the whole period which are roughly comparable throughout, the over-all trend is very clearly shown. Production seems to have reached its lowest point at the very end of 1924 or the beginning of 1925. That this is so is confirmed by items in the press.[1] In February 1925 *The Bioscope* seemed cheered by the news that 5 film units

BRITISH FEATURE FILMS TRADE SHOWN DURING THE TWENTIES*

	No. of films	Appox. no. of reels	Average no. of reels per film
1919	103	545	5
1920	145	784	5
1921	136	748	5.5
1922	95	628	6.5
1923	75	484.5	6
1924	56	351.5	6
1925	45	295	6.5
1926	37	260	7
1927	45	333.5	7
1928	72	524	7
1929 Jan.–June	48	345	7
(rate per annum)	(96 p.a.)	(690 p.a.)	

* *Trade Show dates*, or failing these the first show or first run, are given in preference to production dates because they are ascertainable, whereas the latter rarely are. Consequently the figures show the output of a few months before; but this is complicated by the fact that the gap between production and trade show varied, sometimes being as much as 12 to 18 months or more in the early period and later falling to some 6 to 12 months. In cases where a film was reissued, or trade shown twice, it is classified under the earliest date only.

were at work, which implies that even fewer had been working recently. But in July 1926 14 studios were said to be in operation, and in June 1927 the stimulus given by the forthcoming quota legislation was already apparent with as many as 22 directors at work. It should be observed that after this the total number of reels, representing the actual volume of production, rose more steeply than the number of films owing to the greater average length of the films.

The large output of Stoll and Ideal in the earliest years and their subsequent decline was a factor of great importance in the slump. The combined output of these two companies was 17 per cent of the total in 1920, 30 per cent in 1921, 26 per cent in 1922 and 25 per cent in 1923. In 1925 Ideal marketed no films at all but Stoll alone had 17 or about 37 per cent of the total. Consequently its decline to five, with three joint foreign productions, in the 1926 Trade Show list was of crucial importance. Had Stoll maintained its previous output the 1926 total in Britain would have been virtually the same as that of 1925. Meanwhile firms like British Instructional, Gaumont, Gainsborough and Wilcox had been growing, and were soon joined by the giant British International Pictures. Thus by 1927, when Stoll had only 3 films, the gap caused by its virtual disappearance had been filled. All these new firms except B.I.P., incidentally, had held trade shows in 1926, or in other words had been working in 1925, some even in 1924, without succumbing to the difficulties which proved too much for the older companies. They owed neither their birth nor their early successes to the prospect of the quota legislation. Bruce Woolfe, Michael Balcon and Herbert Wilcox were, in fact, a new generation. There was much in *The Bioscope's* claim, often repeated, that the popular new pictures being produced just before the quota came into operation were the result of gradual changes which had started long before, and that the industry had cured itself. On the other hand an outside observer, Sir Sidney Low, had written in August 1926 that while producers needed masses of capital to build up a steady flow of good pictures, they were not likely to get it, because the City had no confidence in the industry.[2] There is no doubt that the quota made it easier for them to expand and at the same time provided an opening for many producers of inferior calibre.

The trouble was that quantity was not the only thing that mattered. As the Moyne Committee estimated later, only 5 per cent of the films shown in 1927 were British, as against 85 per cent to 90 per cent American,[3] the screen time achieved by most British films being far less than that of their American rivals

---

Feature Films are easily identified for the later years. For the earlier period, when categories were less distinct, they have been defined as films of 5 reels or more, except for certain shorter films known to have been generally regarded as features at the time.

Lengths have been given as closely as possible to the nearest half reel; where the length is not known, in the earlier films it has been assumed to be 5 reels and in the later 7. Lengths were sometimes changed; and the average for the year could be distorted by unusually long films like a seventeen-reel Stoll film in 1923.

As *British film production* and studio activity is the subject of this study it has been thought proper to include certain films produced partly in collaboration with companies abroad and others which never reached the cinemas, and also to omit a few films made purely as actuality or expedition films without studio connections, although they may be included in the Film List at the end of the book.

owing to their poor quality and unpopularity. A mean and meagre approach to film making lingered even when capital flowed into the industry. Paul Rotha wrote in 1929:

'It is not, moreover, as if British studios were insufficiently equipped or inadequately staffed. On the contrary, the technical resources of Elstree, Welwyn, Islington, and Walthamstow are as good as, if not better than, those of almost any other country in Europe. . . . The trouble lies in the way in which these excellent resources are employed. . . . The root of the trouble in this country lies in the conservative and narrow-minded outlook of the producing executives. There are not the men of broad vision, receptive to new theories and progressive ideas.[4]

It was obvious for well over a year that legislation was coming, and from the beginning of 1927 there was a great deal of movement in the industry, growth and reorganization of the companies already in existence and the formation of new ones with new financial alignments. When the quota Bill passed its third reading in the Commons in November 1927, 160 films, from 22 companies, were ready or nearly ready for quota purposes. There was a more confident search for capital, sometimes over-confident. The new type of company required big names on their Boards and on their staffs, and in their efforts to expand British production quickly many of them imported foreign talent, much of it from Germany. There were also a number of wild, grandiose schemes, and by the end of the decade when sound production caused a further upheaval there were signs of trouble and a number of the new groups were already in difficulties.

Among the big companies, we have already seen (see page 44) that Gaumont's was reorganized and formed Gaumont–British Pictures Corporation early in 1927, laying the foundation of a large and important vertical combination in the film industry. Gainsborough and British Instructional also increased greatly in importance. Gainsborough was reorganized in April 1928 as Gainsborough Pictures (1928), with production links with the new Gaumont–British company. British Instructional Films (Proprietors) was registered in May 1927 and began to build new studios at Welwyn early next year. Welsh–Pearson, although surviving, had somewhat changed in character and was already in difficulties when Welsh–Pearson–Elder was formed; the new capital issue was undersubscribed and it was unable to build the proposed new studio, but unwisely went ahead with a large programme of silent films. Stolls lingered on, but as a shadow of its former prolific self. Of the smaller units Hepworth's old studio was taken over by Nettlefold, a company of little interest except for a few films made by the comedian Walter Forde. Henry Edwards worked indefatigably as an independent producer and actor, and after the success of his film *The Flag Lieutenant,* made in 1926, formed the company of Strand with Julius Hagen. Herbert Wilcox, also after several years of producing and directing, formed a company of some importance with his brother and Nelson Keys in June 1927, British Dominions. But although, like Edwards, Wilcox undoubtedly found the quota helpful in obtaining capital, he already had several years of successful film making behind him. All these companies may be said to have been founded on the work of a few individuals. But the biggest company of the twenties, B.I.P., was a conspicuous example of the new type of large company based on a belief that if production facilities were provided in abundance the talent would be attracted to them. Its large and well equipped studios at Elstree were soon peopled with film makers of varying ability from all over the world, including some of the best from other British companies.

Meanwhile Whitehall, British Lion, British Filmcraft, British Screen Productions, British and Foreign, Blattner, and British Multicolor were the best of a rather doleful company of smaller firms formed towards the end of the twenties for a variety of reasons, all depending heavily on the new legislation to provide a market. Many other producers, strangers to the industry or hitherto unsuccessful in it, also tried to jump on the bandwagon, and it is perhaps not surprising that the quota, which tackled distribution outlets but not quality or talent, attracted some whose motive was all too clearly the making of money rather than the making of films.

The newly emerging industry had two significant characteristics. One was a new form of internationalism. One of the first films to be made abroad in collaboration with a foreign firm was probably George Dewhurst's *The Uninvited Guest*, an insignificant film made in Germany with British capital in 1923. After this a number of films were made partly or entirely abroad, usually in Germany or Austria with foreign stars and key technicians and also with foreign backing, in an attempt to secure distribution in other countries. With the quota the number of such links grew. At the same time more and more foreign stars and technicians came to swell the output of the new British studios, Continental visitors to a large extent replacing the Americans of earlier years.*

Another and more sinister feature of the production of the last years of the decade was the gradual appearance of films made solely to fill quota requirements. During the mid-twenties most of the output of the better British companies had found backing and distribution from such British renters as Wardour, W. & F., Butcher and Pro Patria, and this continued to be so. Thus, although the capital and operations of these companies now increased, it would hardly be fair to describe their output as quota production. But the American company Paramount also distributed five British films, in 1928, Allied Artists two, and First National–Pathé began production. Next year twelve British features were handled by the renting agencies of the big American producing companies of Paramount, Jury–Metro–Goldwyn, United Artists, Warner, Fox and Tiffany.

---

* The directors were G. V. Bolvary, E. A. Dupont, Alexandre Esway, Henrik Galeen, T. Hayes Hunter, Rex Ingram, Georg Jacoby, Louis Mercanton, Franz Osten, Lupu Pick, Arthur Robison and Tim Whelan; cameramen Werner Brandes, Karl Freund, Charles Rosher and Theodor Sparkhul; and art directors O. F. Werndorff and Alfred Jünge; players Tallulah Bankhead, Monty Banks, Carl Brisson, Syd Chaplin, Mady Christians, Lili Damita, Pauline Frederick, Dorothy Gish, Lars Hanson, Lilian Harvey, Antonio Moreno, Nita Naldi, Anny Ondra, Lya de Putti, Paul Richter, Will Rogers, Nadia Sibirskaia, Blanche Sweet, Alice Terry, Olga Tschechova, Virginia Valli and Anna May Wong.

Most of these were still made by the well-established older British producers with a few from the newer companies Strand, Whitehall, British Filmcraft, British Lion and B. & D. Most, in fact, were made by people who had been in production for years. But the promotion of films by renters purely for quota purposes was already beginning to appear. Fred Bernhard of the firm British Exhibitors Films announced his intention to produce here on behalf of Tiffany as early as March 1927. F. A. Enders of F.B.O. announced on his return from the United States in April that he would make pictures for the quota, and *This Marriage Business* was made at Shepherd's Bush in 1927. J. V. Bryson of European was quoted as saying that they would make a quota film in 1928. In the same year *Afterwards* was made at Bushey by a Hollywood director, Lawson Butt, for A.P.D., and Rex Ingram made *The Three Passions* as a quota picture for Allied Artists. *Adventurous Youth* was a Warner's quota picture shown early in 1929. Finally Arthur Clavering, British branch managing director for Warner's, floated Foremost Productions to make Warner's quota pictures, of which *Sir or Madam*, made at B.I.P. with a mixed German and English team, was the first.

The twenties ended with the bustle of company formation, much of it involving grand schemes and impressive financial arrangements but little actual production. There were optimistic estimates of the proposed capital, rumours of dazzling distribution arrangements and much name-dropping of celebrities from all spheres supposed to be behind the latest company, often followed by indignant denials. Studios were hastily built or acquired and described enthusiastically as the new British Hollywood. And before long potential shareholders were taking fright and the old contemptibles of British production, the hack professionals, were gathering like vultures.

1924 was a year of great difficulty in the British film industry. Appeals to book British films on patriotic grounds were accompanied by propaganda for the British National Film Weeks. Exactly a week after Palmer's published appeal for support for Hepworth, Bernerd of the Stoll company had an article in the same paper saying pointedly, 'We are running our business on a commercial basis, and we neither ask for sympathy nor expect it'.[5] These were brave words but not entirely fair, and Stoll himself already favoured protection for the film production industry.

To meet the slump some reorganization was necessary. Certain tentative links with production units in Europe were formed by Stoll in 1924. British Instructional, which had been using Stoll's Surbiton studio since 1923, was bought for £20,000, and Harry Bruce Woolfe from that company became a director on the Stoll board. But Stoll's own home output continued in the same unenterprising way. The production continued to be large, and returned to the attack on their many undistinguished literary properties. A. E. Coleby, after two films featuring the Japanese Hollywood star Sessue Hayakawa and his wife, *The Great Prince Shan* (Trade Show May 1924) and *Sen Yan's Devotion*, (Trade Show July 1925) left the company.* Elvey also left the company after

* Coleby's *The Flying Fifty-Five* which was released in 1928 seems to have been made in 1924. After being with Stoll he formed the F.H.C. Company—Faith, Hope and

Above: Ivor Novello in Cutts' *The Rat*, 1925.

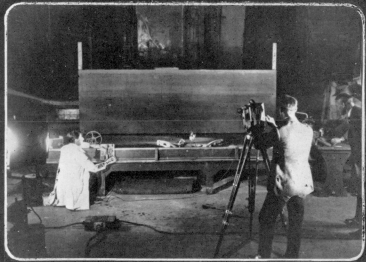

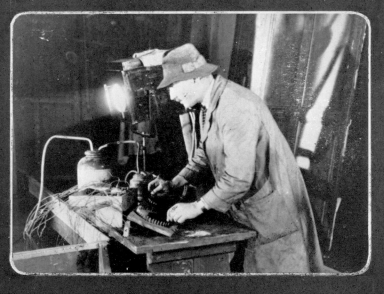

Top Left: Model shot from
British Instructional *Zeebr[ugge]*
1924.

Centre Left: Shooting model s[hot]
for *Zeebrugge*.

Bottom Left: At the explo[sion]
machine for *Zeebrugge*.

he had achieved some success with *The Love Story of Aliette Brunton* with Isobel Elsom (Trade Show August 1924), and found more scope later on with Gaumont. Sinclair Hill produced little of interest and Kellino continued to make small comedies of the type which had been so popular when he was with Gaumont: *His Grace Gives Notice* (Trade Show May 1924), *The Mating of Marcus* (Trade Show July 1924) and *Not for Sale* (Trade Show July 1924). On the other hand, shorts production, as in many British companies at this time, continued to flourish. Fred Paul's series of *Fu Manchu* stories, *Thrilling Stories from the Strand Magazine* by Bently, Hill and A. P. Wilson (Trade Show July 1924 and January 1925) and some two-reelers based on P. G. Wodehouse's stories (reviewed October 1924) by Wilson and starring Harry Beasley, all kept production alive in some form. Hugh Croise, who had recently made three short comedies based on stories by Pett Ridge, made a series based on *The Old Man in the Corner* stories by Baroness Orczy, starring Rolfe Leslie (12 two-reelers, Trade Show June 1924).

But from now on production began to decline in size. In 1925 Henry Edwards, after the Hepworth failure, started making films for the Stoll company with *King of the Castle* (Trade Show August 1925), *A Girl of London* (Trade Show October 1925) and *The Gold Cure* (Trade Show October 1925). These were more up to date and featured such rising players as Ian Hunter, Nora Swinburne and Brian Aherne. But apart from this, and a couple more comedies from Kellino before he left the company, the films began to look more and more old-fashioned. They were made by Hill and old hands like West, Paul, Malins and Bentley. Next year there were two more from Edwards before he also left, and a collection of foreign productions and oddities. *Boadicea* (Trade Show November 1926), a slow film made by Hill himself with a pleasingly statuesque performance by Phyllis Neilson-Terry, was an important production. In 1926 the cameraman who had been with the company since 1921, Jack Cox, left and joined the big new company British International Pictures. Ivor Novello was by now a big box-office star, and next year his early Mercanton film *Call of The Blood* (Trade Show January 1927), over which there had been disagreement was at last put out as a Stoll film. Hill seemed, in fact to be trying to keep output alive single-handed, but in vain. Floor space was soon being rented out, British Instructional was sold to E. A. Bundy, Bruce Woolfe left the Stoll Board in March 1927 and internal rifts and changes occurred after heavy losses. In the end it was stated by T. C. Elder that the company had lost £200,000 in the seven years of its existence.[6]

Sinclair Hill, the one constant factor in their production and one of the biggest operators in the sausage-machine type of film production, was now made managing director in an effort to save the situation. He attempted to modernize their film style and late in 1927 made an ambitious war film *Guns of Loos* (Trade Show February 1928). Despite some good notices for this, the attempt failed and production was abandoned at the very time when so many others, en-

Charity—with R. H. Cricks and the cameraman Stanley Mumford, late of the Progress Film Company. At Esher they made some interesting shorts and *The Inscrutable Drew* series of twelve short films featuring Henry Ainley.

couraged by the quota, were beginning or expanding production. By 1928 they were renting space to B. & D., British Instructional and Welsh–Pearson. A footnote was the offer for sale of the rights in 'Fifty-Three Books by Famous Authors', which must have been the unfilmable residue of their purchases. Owing to Sir Oswald Stoll's reluctance to install an American sound system and his efforts to promote an unsuccessful British invention, the studios were late in converting to sound, and Wilcox, who had been filming there, decided to build his own studio at Twickenham.

The company, with its large scale of operation and its mass production, did manage to weather the slump of the mid-twenties which ruined other and better producers and thus demonstrated the advantages of a large unit. It has also been said that they were among the earliest firms to realize the importance of editing and to employ specialist film editors, although this was surely due to size and the need to doctor and rehash poor productions rather than to any advanced understanding of film technique, and there is little to be said for most of the films from an artistic point of view. The majority of them, with their unreal appearance, their slowness, literariness and heavy dependence on titles were not very good.

Welsh–Pearson continued to produce in the later twenties and Pearson remained a highly respected figure in the industry. But like Stoll's, although for rather different reasons, this company did not survive unchanged. Pearson continued to be interested in mild developments of film narrative. But he had neither the creative brilliance of the Russians, essential to initiate a great change of outlook, nor on the other hand a grasp of business organization of a man like Wilcox. His tentative experiments with the film story lost him a great deal of support from the trade without putting him into the *avant-garde*, such as it was.

The next film he made without Betty Balfour, *The Little People* (Trade Show September 1926), was produced in France with a young assistant, Thorold Dickinson, who represented the new type of university-educated entrants to the industry. Together they devised a story:

'We are all, more or less, puppets unaware of the strings that pull us this way and that, creatures of circumstance. Tie that thought to the Italian puppets of Milan as similes of ourselves, and therein there is a film. . . .

'Gradually the theme broadened; the puppet strings could surely represent those restless desires that shape our lives in the constant search for happiness we all pursue. Love, wealth, fame, achievement, power, are the strings that pull us this way and that towards the goal, yet how many of us are truly happy?'[7]

They evolved a rather simple story about the errant daughter of a puppeteer family and with backing from Butcher they shot it in France, again with Mona Maris in the lead and with some designs by the young Cavalcanti. Once again Pearson was pursuing his elusive dream of changing the structure of film narrative, emphasizing theme rather than plot, and the publicity material spoke of the film as 'just a bit of life caught by the camera'. But the reception was very mixed and Pearson was labelled more firmly as a highbrow. Whilst the picturesque

Italian locations, scenes in the puppet theatre, the ballet school and Cavalcanti's modernist cabaret scene pleased the trade show audience and were
considered very artistic, mixed praise in the film trade, the fragile and unconventional story was savagely handled by some reviewers. Pearson suffered
the indignity of seeing a letter from his partner, Welsh, published in the press
in which he said that the company would 'call in an expert who has no prior
knowledge of the film to collaborate in its reconstruction, and revision of the
titling. . . .'[8] The film was re-edited and trade-shown again two months later,
although this is not mentioned in Pearson's reminiscences.

For a period now there was a curious situation, with Pearson still held in
high esteem as a leader of the industry but little practical respect accorded to
his actual work. The company was in a low state, the studio sold, and Pearson
himself seems to have lost heart in his experiments. Betty Balfour returned to
make the last film of her contract, *Blinkeyes* (Trade Show September 1926),
which was made at Cricklewood and handled by Gaumont's. Although she
played her usual rôle, the story was from an over melodramatic novel and the
old magic of their association was gone. To use Pearson's words in an interview
many years later, by the time they made *Satan's Sister* and *Blinkeyes* they had had
enough of each other. It was a disappointing finale.

The approaching quota legislation led to renewed activity in British production, much of it backed by American companies wishing to be sure of films to
fulfil their quota. In 1927 Pearson embarked on a film featuring the famous
music-hall performer Harry Lauder, *Huntingtower* (Trade Show February 1928),
from a book by John Buchan. Like many other films it had an American tie-up,
in this case with Paramount, which made its distribution secure; but in return
Pearson had to accept an American script-writer, co-star and cameraman. The
film, a conventional vehicle for Lauder, was shown early in 1928 and was a
reasonable success. The company was reorganized as Welsh–Pearson–Elder,
with R. C. Buchanan as Chairman and T. C. Elder, previously of Stoll's as
Joint Managing Director with Welsh. A company with a capital of £180,000
was floated, but being late in the investment boom was not fully subscribed.
There were plans for a new studio at Wembley. In the meantime one of the
floors at Cricklewood was hired and the unit was kept together with Bernard
Knowles as cameraman and Edward Carrick as designer.

In fact, however, all was far from well and the company, now apparently
treating Pearson as a slightly unreliable eccentric in artistic as well as in money
matters, was about to make a major miscalculation. For whilst Welsh–Pearson–
Elder had been laying plans for supposedly safe conventional film production
with their new capital backing, sound films had arrived. Pearson, quick and
enthusiastic, was immediately inspired by the new possibilities. His advice was
disregarded by the Board. Despite his vigorous support for the sound film an
ambitious programme of expensive but unimaginative silent films was planned.
Three old-fashioned directors were engaged. Geoffrey Malins was to do some
W. W. Jacobs' stories, Fred Paul and T. Hayes Hunter the melodramas *The
Broken Melody* (Trade Show October 1929) and *The Silver King* (Trade Show
June 1929). The last of these in particular was a major production costing,

according to Pearson, up to £60,000. But it was a Victorian melodrama dating from 1882 and Hayes Hunter, a spectacular personality from America who some ten years earlier had made *Earthbound*, a film described by *Close Up* as 'worthy', was in fact a dull director.

Ironically his old-fashioned film, *The Silver King*, was trade shown in the same month as the first successful British sound feature, *Blackmail*. It was, of course, a heavy financial loss to Welsh–Pearson. Meanwhile Pearson himself had made *Love's Option* (Trade Show September 1928) and a second Lauder film, this time an original story by Pat Mannock called *Auld Lang Syne* (Trade Show April 1929). The six songs sung by Lauder in this were originally meant to be accompanied by the cinema orchestras during exhibition, but so great was Pearson's frustration with his company's attitude to sound that with great technical difficulty and persistence the film was synchronized with existing records made by Lauder and recorded by R.C.A.

Shortly after this Pearson went to Hollywood to produce *Journey's End* in sound, but the new studios were never built and neither he nor the company ever regained their position as leading film makers. The way the company had ignored Pearson's advice is a particularly clear example of one of the major defects of British production, the undervaluing of the very people whose creative work the trade existed to handle, and the depressing lack of business support for originality.

This atmosphere was bound to thwart a man like Pearson, who was very conscious of the film's potential as an art. His experiments were perhaps not as daring as he fancied. He writes nostalgically of the rough and tumble of the film business but he was essentially gentle rather than daring, with an integrity rare in the film industry at the time. He retained the patient meticulousness of the former schoolmaster in his careful mounting of each production, and the fact that his origins were not in the theatre may have made him more receptive to the idea of film as a new medium. It was in *Love, Life and Laughter* that he first used a new form of narrative structure, and he speaks of his vague wish, by about 1923, for

'. . . nothing more than the capture of things seen, life in the living, and by selection and arrangement, a flow of the human tale, not the manufactured plot, that might carry feeling and understanding to an audience. . . .'[9]

He became obsessed with the need for a theme:

'The real value of the theme to the story is that, though stories may be themeless, with a thematic background the imaginative development, the dramatic force, and the vitality of the messages become all more powerful. At every stage of story construction, with the theme as background in conception, the author can solve each difficulty with ease by thinking back to his theme. Inspiration and illumination come readily to his aid.'[9]

In *Reveille*, with the victory of courage as his theme, he tested his theories:

'I knew that in *Reveille* I was risking all to test my belief that the silent film could be freer in structure, and more effective when loosely-knit scenes could capture Wordsworth's "homely sympathy that heeds the common life". . . . I spoke of my intention, warned them that *Reveille* was no well-carpentered story, merely the development of a theme. With a scrapbook of pictures of life caught in the living, no hero, no villain, no plot, no tying up of loose threads, I hoped future audiences would *feel* the things I wanted them to feel. . . .'[9]

Matters came to a head with *The Little People*, which was a far cry from the homely comedy which his public expected from him, and after this he received no support for such experiments.

Throughout the twenties he argued and lectured that the film was an art form, and tried to put his ideas into practice against heavy odds and a general lack of understanding. He never lost his enthusiasm, and his personal influence on film making was very great. A number of the better educated and more serious young entrants to the film industry passed through his hands or were encouraged by him, including Leslie Hiscott, Cedric Belfrage, Peter Le Neve Foster and later Thorold Dickinson and Edward Carrick. He was an early supporter of the Film Society. He argued passionately against the quota, maintaining that screen time was not the answer to Britain's problem, but help in achieving a higher quality of production. In practical matters he supported E. Beddington Behrens' plan to provide first-class studio accommodation. Of the older British film producers, it was only Pearson and perhaps Henry Edwards who approached film making with real imagination, and it was not only lack of resources that led him to use indirect suggestion as part of his technique but a positive pleasure in meeting the challenge of the film medium, limitations and all. He considered that a film should be conceived, written, directed and edited by one man and was keen to do this himself. Feeling that the film should grow out of the material at hand his own work was stongly influenced by the fact that in Betty Balfour he had found a star whose personality lent itself to cockney comedy. This was undoubtedly congenial to him also, and in his private notebooks Pearson wrote of

'Simple story, simple folk, utter sincerity, non-acting, non-theatricalism. . . . Character comedy concerning the "folk" they know.'

A Victorian sentimentality marked his work as it did that of D. W. Griffith, whom he greatly admired, and ultimately he underestimated the sophistication and modernity of the twenties. As an old man he himself wrote of this early naïve appeal to the emotions and said:

'The scenes I have described may seem naïve and over-melodramatic now, for in this present age, life is more controversial, less prone to outward emotional expression, a wiser and more critical age, though to my mind, a loser in some things that are born in the human heart.'[9]

A new type of man was needed for the post-war world, and these took over the production scene in the second half of the decade. Balcon had already laid his plans before 1924. His existence as a major producer began with the purchase of the Islington studios in 1924. J. C. Graham of Famous–Lasky announced in February of that year that they had abandoned production in England. Balcon was to write later:

'The negotiations which followed had an Alice in Wonderland quality. Baker and I went to see J. C. Graham, then in charge of Paramount here, and he agreed to part with the lease and equipment for a sum in excess of £100,000. We made a counter-offer of £14,000—which was accepted. Everything was fine except that we did not have £14,000 to back our offer and Mr Graham agreed it could be paid over four years on hire purchase.'[10]

Owing to the difficulty of getting adequate distribution advances in England until returns came in on the last picture, Balcon took to alternating work at home with work in Germany by means of an arrangement between W. & F. and U.F.A. The German side provided the backing, the English side supplied the production unit and handled distribution in the English speaking world. Their first Anglo-German venture, which was made at Neubabelsberg, was *The Blackguard* (Trade Show April 1925), made by Cutts from a novel, and featuring Jane Novak and a partly German cast with Walter Rilla and Bernhard Goetzke. It had a mixed reception. Then Cutts made *The Rat* (Trade Show September 1925) at Islington, and this had an outstanding success. It was shot by Hal Young and starred Ivor Novello and the American Mae Marsh, with Isabel Jeans, from a play written by Ivor Novello himself in collaboration with the stage actress Constance Collier. It was a ridiculous but romantic Apache story and both the film and Novello himself, with his wistful dark eyes, were very popular. Gainsborough put Novello under contract.

In 1926 Cutts' *Sea Urchin* (Trade Show February 1926) was again shot by Hal Young and starred Betty Balfour, in her third film made apart from Pearson. It was based on a recent stage play and showed Cutts in a happy light, moving easily through varied settings with a pleasing touch of comedy. W. & F. was as anxious as anyone to get hold of this popular British star, and also handled Mercanton's Anglo-French vehicle for her, *Cinders* (Trade Show September 1926). Her previous film, *Somebody's Darling* (Trade Show December 1925), had been made for Gaumont by George A. Cooper. Gainsborough, looking around for some extra talent, engaged Cooper early in 1926 to make *The Beautiful White Devil*, but the film was scrapped and he left.

Talent, however, was nearer home in Alfred Hitchcock, the most successful of all the film makers who started their careers in the British film industry during the twenties. Before Balcon took over Islington, Hitchcock, as a very young man, had been working there for Famous–Lasky writing and designing titles. He first tried direction when Hugh Croise was taken ill on a one-reeler called *Always Tell Your Wife* (Trade Show untraced), featuring Sir Seymour Hicks and his wife Ellaline Terriss. He tried independent production in 1922 with the

American star Clare Greet and Ernest Thesiger* but the film was not finished. He stayed with the studio when it was taken over by Balcon and acted as assistant on Cutts' early films, including the German production *The Blackguard*. He now, in 1925, started directing on his own for Gainsborough, making *The Pleasure Garden* (Trade Show March 1926) and *The Mountain Eagle* (Trade Show October 1926) in Germany as part of a W. & F. and Emelka deal. The first of these was a banal story, but Hitchcock's pace and technique were already evident and he was considered promising. Camerawork was by Baron Ventimiglia, the script by Eliot Stannard, and two American actresses, Virginia Valli and Carmelita Geraghty, played opposite Miles Mander and John Stuart. *The Mountain Eagle* was also scripted by Stannard and shot by Ventimiglia, and featured Nita Naldi and Bernhard Goetzke.

Meanwhile the company was reorganised. Piccadilly Pictures was formed in July 1926 with Cutts on a long contract and Woolf as chairman, and with Balcon and the actor Carlyle Blackwell as joint managing directors on the commercial and production sides respectively. The first two Piccadilly pictures were Hitchcock's *The Lodger* (Trade Show September 1926) and Cutts' sequel to his success *The Rat*, *The Triumph of the Rat* (Trade Show September 1926). Cutts' film was from an original story by himself and Reginald Fogwell, was shot by Hal Young and again starred Ivor Novello and Isabel Jeans. Cutts' technique was flexible and inventive and the film was hailed as his best so far. Nevertheless, things did not run smoothly for him, and by early 1927 he had left the company. Of his two films which were trade shown in 1927, *The Rolling Road* (Trade Show May 1927) had been shot by Hal Young and was an ingenuous desert island story, a vehicle for Carlyle Blackwell, and his highly praised *The Queen Was in the Parlour* (Trade Show April 1927) had been made in Germany for Fellner and Somlo with a German cast headed by Lili Damita.

From 1927 Cutts worked for First National–Pathé, making *Confetti* (Trade Show December 1927) with Jack Buchanan and Annette Benson and two films starring a young Czech actress, Anny Ondra, *God's Clay* (Trade Show August 1928) and *Glorious Youth* (Trade Show April 1929). Of these, the first was considered outstandingly good. Cutts was certainly one of the most interesting English directors of the twenties and his early importance to Balcon, and also to Wilcox (see page 132) should not be underestimated. Indeed, A. V. Bramble later went so far as to say that Gainsborough was founded on the work of Cutts; and other people, including Baynham Honri, confirmed the high regard in which he was held at the time. The characteristic difference between Balcon and the sausage-machine impresarios was always that talent came first with him. And until his discovery of Hitchcock, Cutts was the talent. Balcon recalled that Hitchcock, as a brilliant junior at the Islington studio when they took it over, attended the script discussions of Cutts' films and was always full of ideas. It may be that he contributed to these films. But some of Cutts' most successful and admired films, *The Triumph of the Rat*, *The Queen was in the Parlour* and *Confetti*, had nothing to do with Hitchcock, and the qualities for which Cutts was best known were quite different to those which later became characteristic

* Called variously *No. 13* by Peter Noble, or *Mrs Peabody* by Balcon.

of Hitchcock's work. But neither of them went in for introspection, theories and ideals. Both took pleasure in the 'little touches' which we have found earlier in Henry Edward's work. But whilst in Hitchcock's case these became integral to the development of the narrative and developed into fast, compelling visual story telling, in Cutts' work they tended to remain embellishments. He was an alive and attractive figure at this time, a showman interested in the mounting of films and exploring what the film medium could do. The big drama, tricky camerawork and particularly the mobile camera, were things that appealed to him, and his style and scale of production were modern and sophisticated. In the end, however, he seems to have had only a sketchy interest in film structure and he was, sadly, an uneven and unreliable film maker whose richness of imagination was not accompanied by discipline or control and whose work later fell off disappointingly.

Cutts was now supplanted at Gainsborough by Hitchcock. *The Lodger* (Trade Show September 1926), adapted by Hitchcock with Stannard from the novel by Mrs Belloc Lowndes, was shot by Ventimiglia at Islington and starred Ivor Novello and June. Distribution was held up.

'When *The Lodger* was cut and finished it was taken to Ivor Montagu, who was then running a company in association with Adrian Brunel. Montagu was asked to re-edit the film as C. M. Woolf of W. & F. Distributors was not particularly pleased with it. He re-cut some sequences, ordered some re-takes (which Hitchcock shot), wrote a new set of titles, reducing them to a sparse minimum, and commissioned McKnight Kauffer, the famous commercial designer, to design the titles and the backgrounds. *The Lodger* was then released, by W. & F., and was one of the biggest successes of the year. It established Hitchcock.'[11]

Of it, *The Bioscope* immediately said 'It is possible that this film is the finest British production ever made.'[12] The qualities later recognised as Hitchcock's trade marks were already being admired in this film: suspense, indirect suggestion, continuity and bridging devices of pleasing inventiveness. The map of crimes at the police station dissolving into the lodger's map in his room and many other smooth passages aroused great admiration and the film was felt to be a landmark in the history of British production.

Hitchcock made two more films for Gainsborough. *Downhill* (Trade Show May 1927) was scripted by Stannard from another ham romantic play by Ivor Novello and Constance Collier, this time about a public school boy who went to the dogs. It was shot by Claude McDonnell and again starred Ivor Novello, with Isabel Jeans and a large cast including Annette Benson, Ian Hunter and Lilian Braithwaite. Ivor Montagu, after his work on *The Lodger*, had joined Gainsborough as supervising editor and scenario chief and he edited *Downhill*, which included a flashy delirium sequence of mixes and dissolves. Next *Easy Virtue* (Trade Show August 1927) was adapted by the Hitchcock, Stannard, McDonnell and Montagu team from Noel Coward's play about a divorcée, featuring Isabel Jeans once more. Neither film was as good as his previous one and about the middle of the year Hitchcock left Gainsborough to join the new B.I.P. studios.

Meanwhile *The Ghost Train* (Trade Show September 1927) was another film made in Germany under the arrangement with Fellner and Somlo, directed in this instance by Geza von Bolvary and with a mainly German cast headed by Guy Newall. *One of the Best* (Trade Show November 1927), another vehicle for Carlyle Blackwell, was an unsophisticated costume drama, surprisingly enough made by the melodramatic and old-fashioned director T. Hayes Hunter. Adrian Brunel, already associated with Ivor Montagu in their editing firm, now also made a film for Gainsborough. His *Blighty* (Trade Show March 1927) was shown early in the year, and Balcon seemed for a while to have found another winner. It was a war story by Montagu, scripted by Stannard and with a large and excellent cast including Ellaline Terriss, Lillian Hall-Davis and a touching performance by the young Godfrey Winn. Extremely sentimental and coming at a time when war films were in fashion, it included a considerable footage of actuality film of the battlefields of France, soldiers marching, and Armistice rejoicings in London. This attempt to introduce realism, and at the same time save money, contrasted with some rather unrealistic sets, just as the understated playing of Nadia Sibirskaia emphasized the mouthing and gesticulating of some of the British players. It was, however, a very successful film.

After the quota legislation, a reorganization on a much bigger scale, Gainsborough Pictures (1928) Ltd, was registered with a capital of £262,500 in April 1928. Directors now included the Chairman C. M. Woolf, Maurice Ostrer and Balcon. A large part of the shares were held by the recently reorganized Gaumont–British Pictures Corporation, represented on the Board by Woolf and Ostrer. W. & F., who still handled all the Gainsborough pictures, had been acquired by Gaumont–British early in 1927, and Balcon's old colleague Saville was now working at Gaumont with Maurice Elvey.

1928 saw an attempt to promote Brunel as a leading director. The year opened with *The Constant Nymph* (Trade Show February 1928). A very successful recent play by Basil Dean and Margaret Kennedy, it had been based on the latter's novel about a young conductor and an eccentric and attractive family. Dean was made supervising producer on the film, but according to Brunel's autobiography the latter found him at this time inexperienced in the difference between film and stage production. A large cast was headed once more by Ivor Novello, with a charming performance by Mabel Poulton, and supported by Frances Doble, Dorothy Boyd and Benita Hume; camerawork was by the American cameraman Dave Gobbett, and much of it was shot on location in Switzerland. The film was a success, and Brunel went on to make *The Vortex* (Trade Show March 1928) from Noel Coward's notorious play. Ivor Novello, Willette Kershaw as his mother, and Frances Doble were in the cast; and the adaptation was again by Stannard. But as before the attempt to transfer Coward's essentially verbal style to a visual medium was difficult, and epigrams depending on a throw-away delivery looked merely facetious in the portentous pause of a title. In his autobiography Brunel attributes its failure to a bowdle-

F*   169

rized script of which Coward himself disapproved, and the fact that Brunel himself was switched to another production before being able to edit it in the way he had intended. At all events the loss of dialogue and the absence of action were fatal to the film. A third Brunel film shown this year was *A Light Woman* (Trade Show December 1928), which was scripted by Brunel and Angus Macphail from a novelettish story by Brunel's mother writing under the name of Dale Laurence, with Benita Hume and Gerald Ames, and shot by Claude McDonnell. This was liked for its locations in Malta and some Spanish dancing but considered weak in dramatic value and criticised for poor acting and characterization. It was the only Gainsborough film, apart from the first, which was not handled by W. & F. Brunel's last film for Gainsborough was *The Crooked Billet*, which he described as a silent film but which was trade shown in 1930 in a synchronized version.

Brunel was something of an enigma. He was in the forefront of the movement towards film art, a supporter of the Film Society, aware of the importance of editing, and had all the appearance of the *avant-garde*. The great success of *Blighty*, also, cannot be ignored. But despite a light wit and keen critical judgement, as a director he only made what Balcon later described as good little pictures. This assessment as an essentially light-weight talent was perhaps due to the fact that Brunel was working at this time as a director, whereas his talents were more those of a writer.

Other Gainsborough films shown in 1928 were another by Hayes Hunter, *The South Sea Bubble* (Trade Show July 1928), with Ivor Novello and Benita Hume in a story by Roland Pertwee, and another German production, von Bolvary's *The Gallant Hussar* (Trade Show September 1928), with Ivor Novello in a gaily irresponsible rôle at the head of a German cast. In December the last entirely silent film made at Islington, *The First Born* (Trade Show December 1928), directed by Miles Mander, was shown. This unusual film, although almost totally neglected by the public and the trade, received a tribute in Paul Rotha's *The Film Till Now*.

'Although Miles Mander has been connected principally with acting, he has made one film that provided evidence of his wit and intelligence in filmic expression. *The Firstborn*, made at Elstree two years ago, was almost entirely the product of Mander's creative mentality; the story, scenario, direction and principal rôle being his individual work, supported by Madeleine Carroll. In the copy of *The Firstborn* shown to the public, however, the merits of the direction and the continuity were rendered almost negligible by the poor assembling of the material by the distributing firm. It is understood that the film was edited without the control of the director by a professional cutter, hence much of Miles Mander's original conception was destroyed. As a light commentary on married life, flavoured with an environment of semi-political domestication, *The Firstborn* was conceived with a nice subtlety of wit. The treatment, especially of the eternal arguments and the dinner party, was sophisticated and clever. Mander has obviously a shrewd knowledge of feminine mentality and succeeded in transferring this into his handling of Madeleine

Carroll. Had the film been well assembled, according to the original manuscript, I believe that *The Firstborn* would have been a unique instance of an English domestic tragi-comedy in the cinema.'[13]

Meanwhile the sound film had arrived and everything else was secondary to the problem of converting the studios to sound production using British Acoustic, the Gaumont subsidiary's system. Work was started on the synchronization of sound effects and sound sequences for certain films released in 1929. An attempt was also made to reconcile Cutts with the company and in April 1929 the trade show was held of his film *The Return of the Rat* (Trade Show April 1929), written by Angus Macphail and shot by Roy Overbaugh, with Ivor Novello and Isabel Jeans, supported this time by Mabel Poulton. The spirit had gone, however, and the reconciliation was not a success. This year a number of films were made in Germany to take advantage of their sound facilities. The first sound trade show held by Gainsborough was the Fellner and Somlo film *The Wrecker* (Trade Show July 1929), made by von Bolvary with Carlyle Blackwell and Benita Hume, with sound effects synchronized by R.C.A., an unlikely story of a villainous railway manager who wrecked trains in order to benefit his bus business. In the same week *The Return of the Rat* was trade shown again with part dialogue synchronized by G.B.A. A number of synchronized films followed. A second version of *Woman to Woman* (Trade Show November 1929) made by Victor Saville with Betty Compson, and *Journey's End* (1930) directed by British actor James Whale but produced by George Pearson, were both produced in America. They were made under an arrangement of June 1929 with Tiffany-Stahl, and were Gainsborough's first full sound features. *Just for a Song* was the first full sound feature made at home in Islington.

Although Balcon had entered the industry early in the twenties he was the new style of producer and, representing a practical compromise between art and the box office, a beneficent influence. Although only interested in what he called the high-priced feature, his output was comparatively large for the hand-made film and he was able to maintain and encourage talent on a reasonable scale. The way in which he did this suggests that he had more than a businessman's appreciation of artistic talent when he found it, and besides Cutts, Hitchcock and Brunel he was able to provide opportunities to Ivor Montagu, Claude McDonnell, Hal Young, Angus Macphail, Arthur Tavares, Ian Dalrymple and Alma Reville. He avoided almost entirely the floaters, old reliables and professional hacks who were so numerous. One of the most important factors in the success of Gainsborough, of course, was the popularity of the velvet-eyed Novello, who appeared in film after film and was without doubt the biggest of all British stars. At first Balcon depended a great deal on the use of American leading players and hoped to secure American distribution by using them, even going to the United States to get distribution for *Woman to Woman*, but he soon became sceptical about the value of this. He continued to pay regard to adequate backing and distribution, however, and money was put, discriminatingly, into the behind-the-scenes value of good technicians and careful settings rather than in the so-called production values of enormous sets and high-priced stage actors or adaptations. The stories were mostly contemporary, many of them adaptations from plays and lesser novels, and although sometimes banal were chosen for their suitability for filming rather than, as was so often the case, for the publicity value attached to them. Although little mention was made of the fact for vicarious publicity, many of the films, from *Paddy-the-Next-Best Thing* onwards, were based on recent stage successes. Both *Paddy* and *The Prude's Fall* were staged in 1920, *Woman to Woman* in 1921, *The Rat* and *The Vortex* in 1924, *Ghost Train* in 1925, *Easy Virtue*, *The Constant Nymph*, *The Queen was in the Parlour* and *The Wrecker* in 1927.

Turning to Gaumont, in 1926 Maurice Elvey embarked on the transformation of the production side of this company. He had left Stoll's after his successful *Love Story of Aliette Brunton*, and made a few independent pictures. With *The Flag Lieutenant* (Trade Show October 1926), which was handled by Astra-National and starred Henry Edwards, he was to have another big popular success. He grasped the opportunity it gave him for some spectacular work with crowds, battles, sea planes and bombing, a large set of the fort in the desert, the landing of troops and battleships in action. He was promptly engaged by Gaumont, which was on the point of expansion. His first Gaumont picture was *Mademoiselle from Armentières* (Trade Show September 1926), starring Estelle Brody and John Stuart. Both this and *The Flag Lieutenant* were great box-office successes, and from now on Elvey's position as one of the most important film makers in England cannot be questioned, whatever the artistic quality of his films. The new production team of Elvey as director, Victor Saville as producer and Gareth Gundrey, who had joined Gaumont in 1921 as a scenario editor in charge of the scripts, were exactly attuned to the taste of the cinema audience. This winning combination was formed well before the quota legislation and owed little to it. Elvey was the only director who was able to make the transition from the very early days of the cinema to a leading, modern director ready at the end of this period to continue, still important, in the thirties and even the forties. Although not an originator himself, he was quick to adopt new ideas and to sense what the public liked. His discovery, Estelle Brody, became extremely popular and *Mademoiselle*, appearing in September 1926, followed the vogue for nostalgic and unrealistic war films started by *The Big Parade*, made in America in 1925 and reviewed in Britain in May 1926, and *What Price Glory*, made in 1926.

At the end of 1926 the Gaumont studio at Shepherd's Bush was closed while it was enlarged and improved at a reputed cost of £25,000. Victor Saville's *The Arcadians* (Trade Show November 1927), a woeful version of the musical comedy, was the first to be shot in the altered studios. Meanwhile, with the quota in sight early next year, there were drastic changes in the structure of the company. In March Gaumont–British Picture Corporation was registered, with the very large authorized capital of £2,500,000, and with the Bromheads, Simon Rowson of Ideal and the renter C. M. Woolf on the Board and with the financial backing of the Ostrer brothers. The company was to acquire the Bromhead's Gaumont company, with its old production and renting business and the large studios at Shepherd's Bush; Woolf's renting firm of W. & F., which handled the Gainsborough output; the renting firm of Ideal; and 21 cinemas. Thus were laid the foundations of a large combine with production, distribution and exhibition functions which would take advantage of the recent quota legislation and which was part of the growing move towards big business.

The next few years saw a run of Elvey films, not such outstanding financial successes as *The Flag Lieutenant* and *Mademoiselle* but most of them more or less doubling their costs. The first, *Hindle Wakes* (Trade Show February 1927), did much better than this. It was a remake of Elvey's own success of 1918 based on a pre-war play and starred Estelle Brody and John Stuart, with plenty of scope for modern production values in scenes of the mills and the Blackpool pleasure gardens. Then came *Roses of Picardy* (Trade Show April 1927) based on R. H. Mottram's novel *The Spanish Farm* and starring Lillian Hall-Davis and John Stuart. *The Glad Eye* (Trade Show July 1927), with Estelle Brody and John Stuart, was from a pre-war stage comedy. *The Flight Commander* (Trade Show September 1927), a silly story about the bombardment of a Chinese town which was specially built, with much publicity, at Hendon, featured the aviation celebrity Sir Alan Cobham to provide the aerial thrills, with Estelle Brody and John Stuart. This and *Quinneys* (Trade Show December 1927), with John Longden and Alma Taylor, were less remarkably successful at the box office. Camerawork on these films was by Basil Emmott and Percy Strong.

Elvey was the showman's friend and an admirable film maker for Gaumont's purpose. Practical and with more than half a glance towards the box office, he was nevertheless keen and shrewd about film technique and technically his films were better than average. He early realized the importance of editing and always worked with good cameramen. On the surface his films had a gloss of art and he diligently kept up to date with innovations in other people's work. But it was slickness rather than creative originality and his real flair was for understanding the cinema public's taste. In casting he was able to tell the type of player and the type of part that was liked, and repeat them, creating a sort of middle-class star of his own. He could find selling angles, see what was box office in either his own or other people's films, and do it again. *Mademoiselle Parley Voo* (Trade Show June 1928), with the same stars, and *Palais de Danse* (Trade Show 1928) with John Longden and Mabel Poulton, promised similar pleasures to *Mademoiselle from Armentières* and *Hindle Wakes* respectively, and enjoyed similar success.

Meanwhile the company had also begun to turn out films by Victor Saville as well as some by lesser film makers like Edwin Greenwood, Will Kellino, Sidney Morgan and Edwin Collins. At the end of 1927 a reciprocal scheme with the German U.F.A. company, whose films had previously been handled in Britain by W. & F., was announced whereby certain British films were to secure distribution in Germany. And in 1928 *The Physician* (Trade Show May 1928) was made as a joint Anglo-German production at Shepherd's Bush by Georg Jacoby and shot by Baron Ventimiglia with Miles Mander and Elga Brink.

Early in 1928 two large new exhibition combines were incorporated, Denman Picture Houses with a capital of £4,150,000 and 101 cinemas, and General Theatre Corporation with a capital of £2,000,000 and 55 cinemas. These companies, their Boards overlapping that of Gaumont–British, increased the latter's exhibition interests to 187 cinemas. In April 1928 Gaumont–British acquired a large holding in the new big Gainsborough Pictures (1928) Ltd, formed by Balcon, and were represented on the Board of the new company by Woolf and Maurice Ostrer. By June 1929 Gaumont's were installing their sound system, British Acoustic, which, unlike others, used a separate film and projector for the sound track. In February 1929 the Gaumont–British capital was increased to £3,750,000 and it acquired control of P.C.T., thus increasing its cinema interests to 287. The board consisted of the Bromhead brothers and Maurice and Isidore Ostrer, but in August 1929 the Bromheads resigned. The new board included the Osterers, C. M. Woolf and W. Evans.

By the end of the year Elvey, quick as usual, had turned out both sound and silent versions of *High Treason* (Trade Shows August 1929 and October 1929), a politically artless forecast of 1940 with Benita Hume and Jameson Thomas and some aggressively futuristic decor. It is significant of the naïvety of the film that in inventing a story of the future such familiar conceptions of the past as white feathers, 'conchies' and Zeppelins should have been used. The Full Talking version seems to have been trade shown first, in August. Blakeston spoke of 'the effect of actors in need of throat pastilles':

'We could go through this picture giving a documentation of the absurdities and failures in imagination of the art department and production staff, but we do not think *High Treason* is worth the space.

'There is one attempt to show that *Potemkin* has been heard of: the sequence of close-ups after the bombs have been let loose on the headquarters of the Peace Mission. Blood streaming from the mouths, and all the rest, but the same old extras instead of Mr Eisenstein's types.'[14]

One way and another Gaumont's had survived triumphantly from the earliest days of the commercial cinema in 1898 to the sound film. Kellino and Elvey, their chief directors in the twenties, were characteristic of the company both in being exceptionally competent and in their ability to find a successful formula and repeat it.

In 1919 Walter Forde, previously a young comedian in the music halls, was making short films called Zodiac comedies in a converted hangar at Kingsbury, Hertfordshire, and in 1921 he made 6 two-reelers at the Windsor studios at Catford (*Walter's Winning Ways* and *Walter Finds a Father*, reviewed in September 1921). Between 1923 and 1925 he gained experience in America, making films for Universal. In 1926 6 two-reelers with Forde and Pauline Peters made by James B. Sloane were shown in England.

A firm called Anglia Films had been registered in September 1923 with a capital of £20,000 and at Beaconsfield made a lamentable version of *The Fair Maid of Perth*, directed by Edwin Greenwood, which was not shown for several years. Meanwhile a film called *Human Desires* (Trade Show January 1925) featuring Clive Brook was only slightly more presentable. This latter was described as an Archibald Nettlefold film. Then in May 1926 it was announced that Nettlefold, of the Birmingham industrial family, had purchased the Walton studios from Hepworth. It seems possible that he expected to keep the studio going as before. Besides taking on Charles Bryce and Geoffrey Faithfull, Hepworth's former cameramen who were together responsible for much of the quality of Hepworth's and Edward's films respectively, and the cartoonist Anson Dyer, his first film was made by Hepworth himself with Alma Taylor and a number of their former colleagues. This was *The House of Marney* (Trade Show January 1927). But it was a hopelessly old-fashioned inheritance melo-drama, the falseness of which was emphasized rather than concealed by the realism and beauty of the locations on the Essex coast. It was re-edited to the satisfaction of Nettlefold by Harry Hughes, who had acted as Hepworth's assistant on the picture.

The film failed and after this Nettlefold pictures were made either by Harry Hughes or by Walter Forde. The Hughes pictures: *A Daughter in Revolt* (Trade Show May 1927), *Hell Cat* (Trade Show March 1928), *Virginia's Husband* (Trade Show May 1928), and *Troublesome Wives* (Trade Show August 1928) all featured Mabel Poulton, with many of the former stock company as supporting players. Hughes' work at this early period was in keeping with the characterless nature of the company, and *Close Up* wrote

'There is a British film going the rounds of the cinemas just now. It is called *Wild-Cat Hetty*, and it is one of the world's worst. Its story is as old and as hackneyed as the hills. There is not an original idea from the first reel to the last. The lighting and photography is dull; the direction despairing. Mabel Poulton, a capable actress, is utterly wasted.'[15]

The Walton studio was small and its productions had always been middle-class, mild and conventional. But the studio was to gain an entirely fortuitous significance now from the work of Walter Forde, who owed little to it and would have been his own likeable self wherever he worked. His first two feature films were *Wait and See* (Trade Show February 1928) and *What Next*[1] (Trade Show June 1928), both comedies directed and written by Forde and featuring himself with Pauline Johnson, who had been playing minor rôles since the early twenties. Then he was given a recent stage play to direct, *The Silent House* (Trade Show January 1929) which featured Mabel Poulton and was a chilling mystery with a horrible Chinaman played by one of the old standbys of English films, but it was not a success. His last silent comedy, *Would You Believe it!* (Trade Show May 1929), was directed and written by him, and this time reviewers, slow to recognize comic ability unless already established either in America or on the stage, at last began to take notice. But by this time sound film had become the fashion and even a Vocalian music recording could not save a comedy so essentially silent in technique. The films were slight comedies with a timidly daring style, dabbling politely in romantic farce, slapstick and a playful use of the medium. Forde himself appeared as a burly, amiable and innocent young man engaged in suburban misadventures, somewhat puzzled but hopefully dogged. He was too late for a career as a silent film comedian, but the direction and editing of the films showed a considerable talent, which was fortunately to find expression in the thirties.

Herbert Wilcox was more successful in becoming an important figure in the industry. Having formed his own company with Bundy in March 1925 he showed *The Only Way* in August. He decided that having an American star would make it easier to sell a film in America, and engaged Dorothy Gish at the high salary of £1,000 a week to make *Nell Gwynne* (Trade Show March 1926). The film was based on a book by Marjorie Bowen and not on a play, although José Collins had been playing in *Our Nell* in London in 1924. Antonio Moreno and the cameraman Roy Overbaugh also came from America and the film was shot at Islington. It seems to have been one of those grandiose costume pieces with no real period atmosphere or emotional meaning, a long cast with all personality stifled by the emphasis on fancy clothes. It cost £14,000[18] to make and Wilcox was eventually offered, by J. D. Williams, 50 per cent profit or £7,000 in addition to the whole production cost. According to the lawsuit reported in *Kine Year Book* for 1929, British National paid Wilcox £27,000 for the film. Wilcox went to America in January 1926 to arrange for its distribution there. It was given a special run in London early in 1926, opening what he describes as the first American-owned cinema in Great Britain, the London Plaza. This was owned by Famous Players, or Paramount as it was now called, and the film was exploited in America by the same company.

Wilcox had not yet discovered how to make an artistic success but *Nell Gwynne* did well at the box office and he had learnt the commercial value of big American stars, good technical standards and distribution tie-ups. J. D. Williams was now to play a considerable part in his career.

In the mid-twenties, as the old guard of producers disappeared, vertical integration and the new model businessman were gaining ground. The American J. D. Williams, who had earlier founded First National with Joseph Schenck, was busy in England at this time trying to create either a big company or a big combination of companies to secure the competitive advantages of large-scale operation for British production. This was in the air at the time and a trade scheme aiming at the same economy of overheads was also being considered. In September 1926 Williams, as managing director, formed British National with a capital of £50,000. He arranged to acquire the world rights of *Nell Gwynne* and sign up Dorothy Gish for three more Wilcox pictures, all to be backed by Paramount. According to the lawsuit later he arranged in July 1926 a remarkable contract by which Famous Players–Lasky agreed to finance each picture up to £45,000. Wilcox and Gish started on the first real British National picture, *London*, again shot by Overbaugh, which was from a story about a Limehouse waif by Thomas Burke. It was finished by August 1926, although not trade shown until January 1927.

Meanwhile British National had plans for a film city, or huge super-studio, partly for their own production and partly for hire. As usual, it was referred to as a British Hollywood. A forty-acre site near the old Neptune studio at Boreham Wood, Elstree, was bought and work started on the studio, later A.B.P.C., towards the end of 1926.

Wilcox began work on another Gish film, *Madame Pompadour*, at the unfinished Elstree studios. This had had a long run as a play at Daly's in 1923. It was shot by Overbaugh, and used the new Schufftan process, the English rights of which were held by the company. In December it was announced that the German director E. A. Dupont would be coming over to work for British National and there was talk of a fourth Wilcox film. Meanwhile Williams, who in Wilcox's words[17] had already been beaten in the battle of the American film giants before coming to this country, now became embroiled in more trouble with the other backers of British National, particularly the South African I. W. Schlesinger of I.V.T.A. and the Scottish renter John Maxwell. He was to be beaten again. Early in 1927 Maxwell and Schlesinger took over British National and the Elstree studios for British International Pictures (see page 186), and announced that British National would be replaced by B.I.P. when the assets of the four Wilcox pictures with Gish, *Nell Gwynne, London, Madame Pompadour* and one other called *Tip Toes*, were realized. The last two were in fact not trade shown until April and May 1928, and the company was wound up in March 1928.

In May of 1926, even before Hitchcock's Gainsborough film *The Lodger* (Trade shown September 1926) had been shown, B.I.P. had signed up this brilliant young director for £13,000 and were clearly pinning their hopes on him. Wilcox, on the other hand, broke away from them in 1927 and in June formed his own private company, British and Dominion, with his brother and the actor Nelson Keys, and with a capital of £55,000. Later in the year he showed *Mumsie* (Trade Show September 1927), which he had made at Twickenham from a successful play of 1920 by Edward Knoblock, a war story about a favourite son who turned out to be a coward. It was shot by Bernard Knowles and featured the American Pauline Frederick with Nelson Keys and Herbert Marshall. It was the first sign that Wilcox was abandoning the belief that to be big a film had to be spectacular.

British and Dominions Film Corporation became a public company and made a public issue in February 1928 with a total capital of £500,000. The issue was one of many during the quota rush, but in Wilcox's three films *The Only Way, Nell Gwynne* and *Mumsie* the company had something real to show the investors and the response was good. The prospectus stated that these three films had cost £70,000 to make and had so far grossed £180,000. They had plans for a large studio at Harrow but in the meanwhile were to use the Cricklewood studios, and had arranged distribution with W. & F.

The first film made under the new arrangement was *The Woman in White* (Trade Show January 1929), shot by David Kesson and directed by Wilcox at Cricklewood early in 1928 from the Wilkie Collins novel, and featuring Blanche Sweet from America. It was followed by *Dawn* (Trade Show April 1928), the film about Nurse Cavell. This was the film which caused such a censorship furore (see pages 66–8) but it was an outstanding film in other respects also, and was very successful. It was shot by Knowles and had an exceptional film performance by Sybil Thorndike. Wilcox had at last shaken off the idea that good showmanship meant the impersonal, spectacular drama or super with enormous casts, and was getting down to straightforward, credible narratives told with more pace. He continued to prefer high-class actors; production was still expensive although no longer ostentatious and he still liked to have a selling angle, but on the whole the stories were becoming simpler. *Dawn* was probably his best silent film and was respected even by many with comparatively high critical standards. Richard Watts wrote in *Close Up*:

'Now, it was not so surprising to find a Russian production an invigorating influence, but to see an English film also acting as pulmotor is surprising enough to deserve comment.

'The picture is, of course, that Herbert Wilcox production called *Dawn*, which deals with the wartime activities and execution of the nurse, Edith Cavell. In my opinion, *Dawn* is an interesting work because it tells a straightforward story straightforwardly, is beautifully acted by Sybil Thorndike, and, dealing with a theme still full of dynamite, it was thoroughly impartial and honourable in its treatment. But no one could say it was really important as a piece of cinema-making.'[18]

In his autobiography, Wilcox says that his company prospered and a series of unimportant but profitable films followed. But now the sound film was becoming increasingly attractive and in September he went to America to investigate. He saw the talkie *The Sidewalks of New York* while he was there and was much impressed. He stayed some time and produced there a sound film, *Black Waters* (British Trade Show May 1929), directed by Marshal Neilan for B & D. This was described as the first British full-talking film, but as it was made in Hollywood mainly by Americans it was not generally so regarded, and was of too poor a quality to create much interest. Wilcox came back convinced of the importance of the new development. In the meanwhile his last silent films were trade shown (*The Woman in White* and *The Bondman* in January 1929) and several indifferent films by various directors. One of these was *When Knights were Bold* (Trade Show February 1929), or 'when gags were old' according to Hugh Castle in *Close Up*, and featured Nelson Keys in a production by Tim Whelan, who had been one of Harold Lloyd's scriptwriters in America. But Wilcox himself, like Pearson, wished to start sound production. As there were delays in converting the Cricklewood studio to sound, British and Dominion decided to build a sound studio of their own at Elstree. This was the new Imperial Studio at Boreham Wood, near the old British National site. In May 1929 it was announced that B. & D. were the only European licensee of Western Electric sound recording, or Movietone, and this was eventually installed. The company got off to a very slow start in sound production in this country, however, with *Wolves* (Trade Show May 1930).

In some ways Wilcox, to whom film making still meant producing as well as direction, followed the same tortuous course as some of the business floaters, moving from set-up to set-up, film to film, constantly searching for finance and, having made or partly made his film often in hired studios, searching for secure distribution, particularly in America. But like Balcon, and unlike the small-timers, his plans were always on a grand scale. Each film was a major property, not a little commodity, still less one in a series or brand of commodity. Not well educated but much too intelligent to be ostentatious he kept his dignity, played it cool and learnt by experience. And by the end of the period he, like Balcon and Bruce Woolfe, was well established in a stable production organization of his own.

In this he was more successful than Henry Edwards, who had given up direction and turned to producing, writing or acting on a somewhat smaller scale. After the collapse of the Hepworth company, Henry Edwards continued for a while at the Walton studios and on location with his cameraman Charles Bryce, and made *Owd Bob* (Trade Show November 1924). This film, put out as an Atlantic Union production, carried on the tradition of rural English settings and good photography in an unusual country story about Lake District shepherds and their dogs, and was very highly praised. After this he directed four less distinguished films for Stoll in 1925, and in 1926 played the lead in Elvey's highly popular *The Flag Lieutenant* for Astra–National.

This film was exploited with great success by Julius Hagen. He and H. F. Double had begun as renters at the beginning of 1917 and later started the production of Kinekature Komedies in a converted shed at Eel Pie Island, Twickenham. These were to be a series featuring Lupino Lane, but only a few were made and by the middle of 1919 the company was bankrupt. Hagen, described in *The World Film Encyclopedia* as swarthy and jocose, then worked for various film companies including B. & C. and in 1926 was working as general manager of Astra–National. He was still looking for a way in to first-class production.

In April 1927, together with W. B. Williams, Hagen and Edwards broke away from Astra to form the W. P. Film Company to both produce and rent films. The production company was registered as Neo-Art in June 1927 with a capital of £1,000. Hiring the same Twickenham studios as had previously been used by Astra-National, they made two films, *The Fake* (Trade Show September 1927) and *Further Adventures of the Flag Lieutenant* (Trade Show November 1927). Both were adapted by George A. Cooper, shot by Horace Wheddon and William Shenton, and featured Henry Edwards. The former was directed by Georg Jacoby and was a dramatic story from a Lonsdale play about a girl married to a degenerate aristocrat to satisfy her father's ambition. The excellent cast was headed by Miles Mander and Edwards himself. *Further Adventures* was directed by Kellino and was a naval spy thriller by the same author, W. P. Drury, and with the same cast as *The Flag Lieutenant* of the year before; but the second film was not based on a successful play and was less well produced. Astra–National, moreover, brought an action for infringement of copyright in the summer of 1928, which was settled out of court with damages.

At the beginning of 1928 Hagen and Edwards left W.P., which made two further films without them, *The Rising Generation* (Trade Show September 1928) directed by Harley Knoles and George Dewhurst, and *White Cargo* (Trade Show May 1929). Both were made at Twickenham and the latter, made at the turn of the year, was later fitted with a sound track at the Whitehall studios at

Elstree and a sound version was trade shown in October 1929. Hagen, meanwhile, had formed the Strand Film Company in June 1928 with Cecil Cattermoul, a film agent, and the director Leslie Hiscott. Hiscott, who had worked for Famous Players in Britain and later for George Pearson, had recently made a series of two-reel comedies based on the Mrs May stories with Sydney Fairbrother, and was considered to be a director of great promise. *The Passing of Mr Quin* (Trade Show July 1928), produced by Cattermoul and directed by Hiscott with Stewart Rome, in a thriller by Agatha Christie, was put out as a Strand film. Later *S.O.S.* (Trade Show December 1928), produced by Hagen and directed by Hiscott, was made at Shepherds Bush from a current stage hit. Meanwhile Henry Edwards had written and acted in the British and Foreign Films' *Fear* (Trade Show September 1928) and *Three Kings* (Trade Show January 1929), made by Hans Steinhoff under an Anglo-German arrangement. He now joined Hagen again and Twickenham Film Studios was formed in January 1929.

Hagen, Hiscott and Edwards were among the directors of this private company, with a capital of £15,000, which took over the old studios at St Margaret's, Twickenham. The films continued to be known as Strand films. Their first was *Ringing the Changes* (Trade Show March 1929), a rather weak comedy directed by Hiscott and featuring Edwards. Early in 1929 they made *To What Red Hell,* scripted by Hiscott but directed by Edwin Greenwood, with a large cast headed by Sybil Thorndike, and Basil Emmott at the camera. Henry Edwards was largely responsible for the decision in April to install R.C.A. sound equipment, and the film was scrapped in June and re-made during the next two months as a sound film. It was taken by Tiffany as their first quota film. *The Feather,* also shot by Emmott and featuring Jameson Thomas, was the next directed by Hiscott and had songs recorded by R.C.A.

Meanwhile big changes had taken place in British Instructional Films. In 1926 Summers had made an important war film *Mons* (Trade Show September 1926), which was shot by Rodwell and Wheddon. But also trade shown in the same week were British Instructional's first ventures into drama, *Nelson* (Trade Show September 1926), also by Summers, and *Palaver* (Trade Show September 1926) by Barkas. *Nelson* was a stuffy public-career film, dignified and impressive in intention if not in execution. Cedric Hardwicke played Nelson and the film was shot by Jack Parker. Barkas' little film *Palaver* was more unusual. It was a story film shot and also written in Nigeria. Since joining British Instructional about 1924 Barkas had worked on the *Secrets of Nature* series and also filmed the Empire Tour, during which he visited Nigeria. He returned later with a small unit which included cameraman Rodwell, and they developed a story which would suit local conditions and use local people. His wife wrote:

'The general idea was to show the life of a British district officer in a remote part of the Empire, administering justice, building roads and bridges, teaching the natives to develop their country and live peaceably together.'[19]

There seems to have been no educational intention. It was simply a modest entertainment film which was given little exploitation, and although Rotha later dismissed it as ingenuous, it was a neat and fairly credible story which grew entirely out of the unit's experience of the place and was almost all shot there. It was a small step in an interesting direction. As Barkas said to the author many years later, it was a time when much ingenuity was being spent on ways of making studio work appear to have been shot out of doors and in unusual places, but he preferred the real thing. Charming, breezy, with shrewd and humorous observation of personality and dramatic detail, he was considered an excellent and original film maker by many of those in the industry at the time and might have achieved more during the twenties had he been working in a more vital milieu. As it was the film received little encouragement, and achieved neither box-office nor critical success. Barkas returned to straight actuality for the time being and was unable to exploit his taste for large-scale exterior filming until the thirties.

After this British Instructional gave up actuality in their feature work except for Summers' *Battles of the Coronel and Falkland Islands* (Trade Show September 1927) some time later and Barkas, who might have worked out some new fusion of drama and reality had he received any encouragement left British Instructional. In December 1925, the company's renter Craig with C. L. Buckle had started New Era Productions, which had a capital of £10,000, and they now began to produce a similar type of film. Barkas joined them to make their first, *The Somme* (Trade Show September 1927), which was shot by Sydney Blythe and Freddy Young. New Era was taking up the thread as British Instructional was letting it go, but they exercised less discrimination. When Barkas fell ill they engaged a man known as a fringe producer, M. A. Wetherell, who had a reputation for actuality work and camera adventuring superficially like that of Barkas. The film was later revised and edited by Barkas and Boyd Cable, although it was put out under Wetherell's name. *Q Ships* (Trade Show June 1928) was made by Barkas and Michael Barringer, and shot by Blythe, with studio work at Worton Hall. It dealt with the merchant ships used in the war to combat U-boats. Reviews were good and according to Honri the film was excellent, but the public may by now have been tiring of this type of film.

For British Instructional, meanwhile, Summers with Parker and Rodwell was making *The Battles of the Coronel and Falkland Islands*, the most famous of the war reconstructions. This was an ambitious, slow and impressive film made with ships lent by the Admiralty, and with the backing of the Federation of British Industries. For a few sequences studio sets, which struck rather a false note, were built at Cricklewood. It was more expensive than the other films, costing £18,000, but according to Bruce Woolfe grossed £70,000 in the United Kingdom alone. Besides being widely popular with the usual cinema public, and with many who normally found the cinema socially beneath them but were attracted by the serious and patriotic aspects of these films, they also extracted a grudging compliment from the cineaste. *Battles* was one of the very few British films thought worth reviewing in *Close Up*. The latter conceded that it, and also *The Somme*, were 'not bad' and managed to hold the attention, although it added that they were completely unreal and presented war from the 'romantic boy adventure book angle'.[20]

Close Up hardly ever mentioned a British film, so even this dubious compliment set the *genre* apart. Rotha in 1929 went so far as to describe the reconstructions as excellent examples of the documentary film.[21] In 1929, also, there was talk of a projected agreement between the Russian film industry and British Instructional. Whether true or not, the very existence of such a rumour is indicative of the position occupied by British Instructional. The films were technically up to date, realistic, and showed a new spirit in the cinema. They were slow and heavy, the acted sequences were somewhat stagey and the interpretation of events uncritically patriotic. But to put such serious material across at all was an impressive feat.

The quota legislation was now in sight, and big changes took place. The same E. A. Bundy who had backed Wilcox in early 1925 now bought British Instructional from Stoll's for £40,000, according to Bruce Woolfe, and turned it into a public company. Bruce Woolfe resigned from the Board of Stoll's in March 1927 and British Instructional Film (Proprietors) was registered in May. Bundy was Chairman, Bruce Woolfe was Managing Director and the writer John Buchan was a member of the Board. The prospectus was impressive, with its talk of contracts with the Admiralty and the War Office, projects in collaboration with the Air Ministry and plans for films written by John Buchan and Ian Hay. A public issue of £100,000 was made and, being one of the first to appeal for capital as a result of the quota and a firm with a high reputation, it was fully subscribed within a few hours.

The company apparently considered the vein of the war reconstructions to be played out and, apart from the *Secrets of Nature* films and some non-theatrical shorts, now turned exclusively to fiction. According to the prospectus the first production was to be a big film about the Gallipoli campaign. In fact this did not appear until 1930 (*Tell England*), but meanwhile production became more varied. It continued to be on a high technical standard and in addition the company now had one of the most promising of young British directors. As part of Bruce Woolfe's careful, dignified captaining of the company he had encouraged the entry of the new generation of well-connected, well-educated young men who, unlike their parents, were prepared to take films seriously. Working at British Instructional at this time were Arthur Woods, Ian Campbell-Gray, Frank Wells, John Amery, J. O. C. Orton and Mary Field. Another of the same generation was Anthony Asquith, the son of the former Liberal Prime Minister, who had worked on Sinclair Hill's film *Boadicea* which Bruce Woolfe had produced at Stoll's in 1926. Brilliant, cultured and sophisticated, he was entirely unlike earlier film makers. For one thing, he was familiar with the most advanced work abroad, especially the German fantasies and the work of Pudovkin and Eisenstein. At the age of twenty-six he made the film with which the reorganized company burst into true fictional drama in 1928, *Shooting Stars* (Trade Show February 1928), with Annette Benson, Brian Aherne and Donald Calthrop, shot by Rodwell and Harris at Cricklewood. A spectacularly brilliant film, it was an immediate success and in one move established Asquith as one of the most interesting people working in British production at the time.

As Asquith had very little experience of film production, especially of handling actors, the veteran A. V. Bramble had been made director, with Asquith nominally his assistant in addition to writing and editing the film. Throughout production the trade press, its snobbery greatly tickled, had been agog to see the famous Lady Asquith's son at work. Bramble had been producing mediocre films for years and was no match for this dazzling assistant, or indeed for the other members of the unit, Campbell-Gray and Orton. By most accounts he was a modest and helpful person, who co-operated as well as he could. As a result the film was Asquith's rather than his, and as this was widely known he received little credit for it. It was perhaps inevitable that he should end by feeling offended. He had left British Instructional and joined British Lion before the film was shown to the trade.

The British Instructional output was now handled by Pro Patria Films, except for those towards the end of the decade which were used as quota pictures by American companies, among whom they were much in demand. Pro Patria was registered in October 1927 with a capital of £60,000 by Bundy and Bruce Woolfe when New Era, now their rival, also turned to fiction production. The latter company were reorganized as New Era National Pictures in February 1928 with a capital of £136,000. Gordon Craig was knighted in 1929. They produced a few films in rented studios without much success and their first sound film was *The Co-optimists* (Trade Show November 1929), which had R.C.A. recording of dialogue and songs in a version of an annual stage review popular in the twenties. By this time Barkas was working with British Instructional again.

Asquith followed *Shooting Stars* with his first real solo, *Underground* (Trade Show July 1928), with Brian Aherne and the beautiful Elissa Landi, and shot by Rodwell. This, a thriller using the London Underground and the Battersea Power Station as backgrounds, was less well received. It was a time when low-life films in England were usually comedies, and the cinema public liked its drama in a high-class setting. It is ironical that this, which with *Shooting Stars* was one of the first British films to employ a lighting expert, the German Karl Fischer, should have angered some audiences not only by its 'distorted' angle shots but also by its 'murky' lighting. While the public was made uneasy by the traces of Russian and German influence, the highbrows were able to find other faults. Asquith was attacked by Harry Alan Potamkin, for example, for failing to portray the lives of the working classes properly:

'Mr Anthony Asquith determined to do a film of the lowly. . . . A hybrid film produced by a coincidence of absence of a precise cinema viewpoint and a remoteness from the lives of the protagonists of the narrative . . . unreal as the revelation of the people it purported to represent. There was no indication of the insinuation of their Underground existence in their lives. Just to have had certain adventures occur in the Underground does not allow you to offer your film as a document of the lives of the Underground people.'[22]

In fact there is no indication that this is what Asquith had intended, but the prejudice against his parentage seems to have been as great in some quarters as the prejudice in favour of it was in others. Rotha perhaps was nearer the truth in suggesting that Asquith had not as yet acquired maturity and still retained some of the brilliance for its own sake which had been so noticeable in *Shooting Stars*.

'He has certain ideas of cinematic representation, and he is happily able to put them into realization. . . . That he possesses a feeling for cinema was proved by all these films, but that he is still groping and undecided in his mind as to how to find expression for his ideas is equally plain. He has learnt varied forms of treatment from abroad, but has not as yet fully understood the logical reasons for using them. He has studied the Soviet and German cinema, but has failed to search deep enough. His technique still remains, after four productions, primitively on the surface. In his last picture, for example, there were several instances of quick cutting and symbolic reference, but they were employed because of themselves and not as a contributory factor to the film composition. For this reason, Asquith's work appears that of a virtuoso. . . .'[23]

Asquith's third film, *The Runaway Princess* (Trade Show March 1929), with Mady Christians, was an Anglo-German film made mostly in Germany in collaboration with Laenderfilm. Here Asquith was careful to avoid the charge of being arty and based the film on a romantic novel, but the result was considered disappointing.

The new company had announced the construction of a big new studio at Welwyn, at a cost of £60,000. This was started early in 1928 and was nearly finished by the end of the year. Meanwhile Summers had made *Bolibar* (Trade Show July 1928) at Cricklewood, starring Elissa Landi. A remarkable film in many ways, it was shown at the end of the Film Society season. But the appearance of this British film at the Film Society outraged Oswell Blakeston, writing in *Close Up* in May 1928, and it received surprisingly little attention. The photography by Jack Parker was pleasing, cutting and angles were spirited. But people were by now beginning to think only in terms of sound film. This may also explain the lack of interest in Summer's *The Lost Patrol* (Trade Show February 1929), a story of twelve men lost in the desert during the war and killed one by one by the Arab tribesmen surrounding them. Summers seemed to suffer from a certain outwardness in his treatment of the characters and this film was also critized for some long, sentimental flashbacks; but the highly critical Hugh Castle, not given to approving of British films, contrasted it favourably with *The Flag Lieutenant* 'and similar dither' and wrote in *Close Up* that

'. . . the memory of Clifford McLaglen as the Sergeant lingers. Not, I repeat, a great film. But very nearly.'[24]

Shiraz (Trade Show September 1929) by Franz Osten with an Indian cast was an Anglo-German film, one of three made by Osten partly in India. The others were *The Light of Asia* in 1926, and *A Throw of Dice* in 1929. The first film made entirely at the new studio at Welwyn was Orton's *The Celestial City*

(Trade Show March 1929). By the beginning of 1929 it was appreciated that sound production was bound to come, and a small sound studio was rapidly put up in the grounds. By April, when it was realized that the disc system originally favoured had become obsolete, the Klangfilm sound-on-film system was on order from Germany. The company's first part-sound feature was Asquith's *A Cottage on Dartmoor* (Trade Show January 1930), a joint Anglo-Swedish film which was originally planned as a silent film but which had a short dialogue sequence.

Some of the best technicians in the British film industry began at British Instructional and the artistic integrity of the company as a whole made it a contrast to much of the industry. But in some eyes nothing British could arouse much enthusiasm and Hugh Castle, writing in *Close Up*, was not thankful for small mercies:

'But the real cinema, the understanding cinema? . . . I once thought it would blossom at Welwyn, where British Instructional have their being. But if it has burst out, the frost nipped it badly in the bud.

'Bruce Woolfe, the head of that company, has certainly tried hard. He has given young men chances and has found that where two or three are gathered together in his name it pays to grant their request. Yet there is something lacking in what we have seen of their work. His young men suffer from family troubles. It must be a terrible thing to be the scion of a noble house. At Welwyn they have substituted for the brain bankruptcy of Wardour Street that intolerable and non-creative intellectual snobbery, the more vicious because it is unconscious, that characterizes that section of life which finds its way largely into the pictorial papers. If its men were drawn from the people they are supposed to represent on the screen, the Bruce Woolfe experiment might be more successful.'[25]

With British International Pictures we come to what must be regarded as a most important development in the production industry. By the end of the twenties it was the biggest and most successful producer in the country by far, and the most advanced example of vertical integration in the industry. It was led by the new type of businessman with ample finance, assured of distribution and sucking in talent from wherever it lay at home or abroad.

We have already seen that the American J. D. Williams, understanding the need for a larger scale of operation in British production and discovering Herbert Wilcox, who was at that time making *Nell Gwynne* with Dorothy Gish, had formed British National in September 1925 and set out to exploit Wilcox's films. After his trip to America in July 1926, and the contract he achieved by which Paramount agreed to pay up to £45,000 on Wilcox's films with Dorothy Gish, Williams became managing director of British National. His salary was to be £3,200 a year with £2,000 expenses and 10 per cent of the company's net profit.[26] A start was made on the new studio at Boreham Wood at Elstree, near the old Neptune studio, and Wilcox had begun work on two more Gish films, *London* (Trade Show January 1927) and *Madame Pompadour* (Trade Show April 1928).

Meanwhile, in March 1926, a private company for production had been registered under the name of M. E. Productions by John Maxwell. Maxwell, a Glasgow solicitor who had entered film exhibition in 1912 and acquired a small circuit, had moved over into the renting business and become chairman of Wardour Films about the beginning of 1923. A film made by Maurice Elvey at Cricklewood was put out by Wardour in June as an M. E. film, *The Woman Tempted* (Trade Show June 1926), but little was heard of it and Elvey joined Gaumont. Later in 1926 it was rumoured that Wardour had bought the Twickenham studios and would embark on production with *Tommy Atkins* and *Poppies of Flanders*.

By now all was not well with British National. Disagreements over finance came to a head when J. D. Williams was in America to raise money again towards the end of 1926, and these resulted in the cancellation of his contract. Williams later sued the company for wrongful dismissal and arrears of salary in March 1928 and the case was settled out of court.[26] The company meantime was taken over by Maxwell. Early in 1927 Maxwell's private company was renamed British International Pictures and refloated as a public company. Maxwell joined the Board of British National, and in March 1927 the manoeuvre was completed when British International acquired British National and their Elstree studio, and started production. Maxwell's colleagues from Wardour, Arthur Dent and J. A. Thorpe, joined the Board of B.I.P., and it was announced in April that B.I.P. would replace British National when the assets of the three Wilcox pictures, and one more called *Tip Toes*, were realized. Wardour was to have a five-year exclusive distribution contract, and the capital of B.I.P. was to be increased and underwritten by Wardour and the I. W. Schlesinger interests. Wilcox broke away from the company in June 1927 and went his own way (see page 177), and British National was finally wound up in March 1928. Schlesinger formed British International Film Distributors in December 1926 with a capital of £35,000, and later its subsidiary Tschechova Films for a separate brand of productions.

B.I.P. was the largest of the companies formed during this optimistic period and easily secured its capital before investors became wary. Maxwell rapidly became one of the most powerful figures in the British film industry and, expanding his interests in renting and exhibition, was to make his group one of the dominant factors in the film industry of the thirties. In November 1927 B.I.P. made a public issue of £312,500 out of its authorized capital of £600,000. The prospectus named the other directors as Sir Clement Kinloch-Cooke, Arthur Dent, John Thorpe, G. H. Gaunt and J. D. Bright. The issue was heavily oversubscribed. Later in the year Maxwell took a further step and formed Burlington, a private company with himself as Chairman and Victor Saville from Gainsborough as Managing Director, to make Saville's films at the B.I.P. studios. This was registered in January 1928 with a capital of £105,000. Maxwell, who was to exercise enormous influence over the course of British production, remained behind the scenes and had little of the impresario's personality.

Meanwhile B.I.P. had signed up as much talent as they could, including

Gainsborough's discovery Alfred Hitchcock, and production had started. Of four films, the only important one was Hitchcock's *The Ring* (Trade Show October 1927). This was a story of the fairgrounds and boxing rings written by Hitchcock himself with scenarist Eliot Stannard, another who had come from Gainsborough, and shot by the B.I.P. director of photography Jack Cox; it featured Carl Brisson, Lillian Hall-Davis, Ian Hunter and Gordon Harker. In this film Hitchcock was felt by many to have fulfilled his early promise. It showed his characteristic richness of detail and economy of means. *The Bioscope* called it 'the most magnificent British film ever made' and this was widely echoed, despite the rather trite triangle drama on which it was based. The other films, although well photographed by such cameramen as Cox, René Guissart and William Shenton, were by lesser directors and were undistinguished. They included *The Silver Lining* (Trade Show October 1927) by Thomas Bentley, who had been working briefly in Hollywood, Arthur Maude's *Poppies of Flanders* (Trade Show October 1927) with Jameson Thomas, and Harley Knoles' *The White Sheik* (Trade Show December 1927), also with Jameson Thomas and Lillian Hall-Davis.

In December 1927 Maxwell took another step and effected a merger between First National and Pathé. Since the war Pathé production had been confined to actuality and compilation films, but in 1927 a production-distribution-exhibition group involving First National, Pathé, P.C.T., United Artists and Lowes Inc. had been formed. As the quota came nearer, First National and Pathé began to back a certain amount of production. *Passion Island* (Trade Show June 1927) by Manning Haynes, with cameraman Percy Strong, was made at Rex Ingram's studio at Nice and on location in Corsica, and was adapted from a murky vendetta story by W. W. Jacobs. At this time Manning Haynes, who had started as an actor and had directed a number of films from stories by W. W. Jacobs for Artistic from 1922 to 1924, was regarded as a promising and even slightly highbrow director, and the film was greatly praised for such things as its mobile camera and a fight sequence which used superimposition of close ups of the participants instead of cutting. Other films were Jack Raymond's *Somehow Good* (Trade Show October 1927), made at Twickenham with Stewart Rome, Fay Compton and Dorothy Boyd, and Graham Cutts' *Confetti* (Trade Show December 1927) from an original scenario by Douglas Furber, with Jack Buchanan and Annette Benson. The latter, with a weak story, was mounted with Cutts' usual panache and some mildly cubist sets by designer Norman Arnold, shot by Roy Overbaugh, and was considered an outstanding, if showy, production. After the merger *The Ware Case* (Trade Show April 1928), directed by Haynes and shot by Shenton with Stewart Rome, was made at Twickenham, and *God's Clay* (Trade Show August 1928) was made by Cutts and Arnold again, featuring Anny Ondra, although this was not up to Cutts' earlier standard. *The Ware Case* was from a successful play which had enjoyed two long runs at Wyndham's Theatre in 1915 and 1924. In August 1928 the Maxwell group was further integrated when B.I.P. bought the 51 per cent interest in First National–Pathé held by P.C.T. Later First National–Pathé films were Raymond's *Zero* (Trade Show September 1928), with Fay Compton and Stewart Rome, and one of Cutts' last silent films, *Glorious Youth* (Trade Show April 1929), with Anny Ondra again, made this time at the B.I.P. studios at Elstree.

By now there had been further financial developments. In January 1928 Associated British Cinemas was incorporated. This company had twenty-nine cinemas in 1928 and was controlled by B.I.P. (see page 43). In February 1928 B.I.P. also acquired Sudfilm, the German distributing organization and it was announced that the German director Richard Eichberg would make four films for B.I.P. in German studios, films which would be distributed in England by Wardour and in Europe by Sudfilm. In March another deal was announced, this time with the Austrian Sascha Film Company, and the B.I.P. capital was increased to £750,000. In the middle of the year J. D. Williams was once more busy in America, this time for B.I.P., with big plans for the distribution of their pictures. B.I.P. made an arrangement in May 1928 to sell the first year's output of thirteen films in America, twelve of them to United Motion Picture Producers. And while in America Williams, with Maxwell and two others, floated World Wide Pictures Corporation in August, to handle fifty European pictures a year in America including the B.I.P. output. It was in this month, August 1928, that the P.C.T. holding in First National–Pathé was bought by B.I.P. and it was announced that in future B.I.P. would make the quota films required by them. Finally, in September the B.I.P. capital was increased to £1 million.

During 1928 the output was massive. During the first half of the year the last two of the British National pictures made by Wilcox in 1926 were shown at last, *Madame Pompadour* in April and *Tip Toes* in May. Both were based on stage successes, of 1923 and 1926 respectively. *Tip Toes* featured Dorothy Gish once more in the last of the quartet, with Will Rogers, Miles Mander and Nelson Keys, and was shot by Overbaugh at the Elstree studios. Three B.I.P. pictures started in 1927 and shown now were the comedy *A Little Bit of Fluff* (Trade Show May 1928) made by Jess Robins from America with the Hollywood comedian Syd Chaplin and the former Pearson star Betty Balfour, who had now completely abandoned her little *gamine* rôle: a back-stage drama called *Moulin Rouge* (Trade Show May 1928) by E. A. Dupont with Olga Tschechova, and a Hitchcock film called *The Farmer's Wife* (Trade Show March 1928) from the play by Eden Phillpotts, which had had a very long run at the Court Theatre in 1924. This featured Jameson Thomas, Lillian Hall-Davis and Gordon Harker. The Hitchcock film was very English in character but apart from this the international, or rather nationless, flavour of B.I.P. production began to be noticeable. There were a large number of films during the rest of the year, and although they were of high technical quality and drew on as many English top players, and as much foreign talent, as money could buy they were not particularly interesting. These were: *Tommy Atkins* (Trade Show May 1928) by Norman Walker, with Lillian Hall-Davis; *Toni* (Trade Show May 1928) by Arthur Maude, with Jack Buchanan and Dorothy Boyd; *Not Quite a Lady* (Trade Show July 1928) by Thomas Bentley, with Mabel Poulton; *Tesha* (Trade Show August 1928), the first Saville film, described by Hugh Castle, kind for once, as a 'sound dramatic subject,' starring Maria Corda and Jameson

Thomas, and with art director Hugh Gee and the German cameraman Werner Brandes; *Show Life* (Trade Show September 1928) by Richard Eichberg, a German production with Anna May Wong; *Paradise* (Trade Show September 1928) by Denison Clift, with Betty Balfour; *Adam's Apple* (Trade Show September 1928) with the comedian from America, Monty Banks, by the American director Tim Whelan; *Weekend Wives* (Trade Show November 1928) with Estelle Brody, Annette Benson, Jameson Thomas and Monty Banks again; and finally *Widecombe Fair* (Trade Show December 1928) by Norman Walker, with Violet Hopson and a large cast. *Widecombe Fair* also was treated kindly by Hugh Castle. Lachman's *Weekend Wives* was said by Oswell Blakeston to be 'as beautifully photographed, gowned and set as the average Paramount picture and as silly'.[27] Harry Lachman, who was an American, was not a Hollywood director but had made films at Nice with Rex Ingram in 1925. He had undoubted ability and a 'neat sense of camera'[28] and great things were expected of him at the time, but he could do little with a slick imitation-American bedroom farce. In addition Hitchcock made *Champagne* (Trade Show August 1928), a story by Walter Mycroft, with Gordon Harker, Jean Bradin and Betty Balfour, her silly but staunch femininity nicely brought out in her new flapper rôle. Despite the unmistakable Hitchcock touch and some good business the film was dismissed by Hugh Castle as champagne that had been left in the rain all night.[29]

It would probably be fair to say that the B.I.P. management saw themselves as being engaged in big business, not as nourishing and building up a team of creative artists in the way that Balcon, Bruce Woolfe and others had tried to do. They needed talent in large quantities and they needed it quickly. Much of it was creamed off the existing British companies, and doubtless glad to go, to a company where the opportunities must have seemed so much better. On the whole the company did manage to avoid the worst of the floaters and drifters who had such a gift for being on the spot when a new company was being formed, although the two pictures *Silver Lining* and *Tommy Atkins* were singled out by *Close Up* as particularly dreadful examples of the British film. But talent was so scarce in Britain that it was hardly possible for them to avoid the old reliables altogether, the mediocrities who were able to claim experience even if they had never made a good film in their lives. But from the beginning the company resorted to the importation of big names from abroad, directors, cameramen and stars. One result was that output, besides being very large, was extremely varied in character. But as is so often the case with imported celebrities, many came because they were already past their peak abroad, and the others were unable to do their best work after transplantation.

One thing the films had in common was that they were modern in conception and execution, and another was the absence of that old mean look that had plagued British production. Camerawork, especially by Cox and the Americans Guissart and Rosher and then the Germans Brandes, Sparkul and Püth, was excellent. The general appearance of the films was opulent and contemporary and sets were elaborate, using the new special processes for stages, night clubs, streets and big hotels. Even many outdoor scenes were shot in the studio and both sets and camerawork looked indoor and studio-bound, often dramatically and visually effective but lacking the realism of the old location work. In so far as stories and milieus had any common character they tended towards slightly sexy society or exotic glamour, but always glamour; comedy was of the mother-in-law, undressing, weekends at Deauville and 'taradiddles' type. The Syd Chaplin–Betty Balfour vehicle *A Little Bit of Fluff* (Trade Show May 1928) showed this pseudosophisticated world at its most tasteless, with night clubs and impersonal flats designed for bedroom farce rather than for living, with dislikeable people, smoothey men-about-town with oily hair and spats, the hen-pecked little husband on the loose behind mother-in-law's back and with ugly and cruel jokes like chucking ink at the latter's face, the bee inside the man's clothes, the midget embarrassingly mistaken for a child. Here was a company which did not even pay lip service to the idea of characteristically British films. The idea of forming a British Hollywood, however, was working out all too well, reproducing many of the less desirable features of large-scale production in meretricious films whose fluent and lavish production did not really obscure their banality. No one could say that *Moulin Rouge* was English in character, with Dupont as director, Werner Brandes as cameraman, Alfred Jünge as art director and Olga Tschechova and the French actor Jean Bradin in the leading parts of this story of Paris. Its story of a young man in love with his fiancée's mother was felt to be distasteful by some of the British press. But tripey nonsense that it was, it was remarkable compared with most British films of the time in its assured hold on the attention, and even *Close Up* objected only that it fell short of being a masterpiece.

Such films were apparently just what the British public wanted. In 1929 production continued to expand, as well it might, for in June it was announced that the company had made £200,000 profit in their first year, exactly the total sum lost by Stoll's in the seven years of their production. A.B.C.'s capital was increased to £2 million in January and their cinema holding in this year totalled 88. The films continued with Jean de Kucharski's *Emerald of the East* (Trade Show January 1929); Saville's second Burlington film *Kitty* (Trade Show January 1929), a capable version of a sentimental war novel by Warwick Deeping with John Stuart and Estelle Brody, designed by Hugh Gee and with some soft and romantic lighting and camerawork and real exteriors from Karl Püth; and Hitchcock's *The Manxman* (Trade Show January 1929) from the novel by Hall Caine, scripted by Stannard and shot by Cox once more. This featured Carl Brisson and Anny Ondra, and was another disappointing film for Hitchcock with an inferior subject. Dupont's *Piccadilly* (Trade Show January 1929) was from an original scenario by Arnold Bennett, shot by Werner Brandes, and featured Jameson Thomas as a night club proprietor, the American Gilda Gray as his *passé* mistress and Anna May Wong as the seductive young Chinese dancer. It was extravagantly admired by the press and the public, but Hugh Castle dissented. Listing the foreign names associated with it and describing it bitterly as a 'typical British film', he found it 'one of the world's worst'.[30] He wrote:

'. . . he might have been filming Timbuctoo for all the relation his picture bore its title. But that, of course, is the "international" note carried to perfection. Perhaps he left it so that they can call it "Broadway" in America.'[31]

Rotha was more charitable:

'Although not strictly the work of British technicians, Dupont's *Piccadilly* was undoubtedly the best film of its type to be made in this country. . . . The action was slow where it should have been fast, and fast where it should have been slow, but taking it as a whole, *Piccadilly* was the best film to be made by British International Pictures.'[32]

George Ridgwell's *The Lily of Killarney* (Trade Show February 1929) was from a play by Dion Boucicault. And under the Sascha arrangement Geza von Bolvary made *Bright Eyes* (Trade Show May 1929) with Betty Balfour, which was trade shown for a second time in October 1929 with songs synchronized by R.C.A. But without question the film of the year was Hitchcock's sound film *Blackmail* (Trade Show June 1929).

The Jazz Singer, the first sound feature seen in London, was shown at the Piccadilly Theatre on September 27, 1928. Many in the industry realized at once that a change to sound production was inevitable, and this included Maxwell, who had already returned in June from a visit to America full of enthusiasm for sound. But the British industry, already in a state of flux because of the quota legislation, was slow to pull itself together. As *The Bioscope* said.

'. . . continued silence was beginning to impose a strain, and as we waited for news of the first British feature length "talkie", the atmosphere grew thick with ugly signs.

'Fleet Street believed the bottom had fallen out of the British film business, and almost said so in as many words.'[33]

At last in April 1929 B.I.P. announced that they had a temporary sound studio fitted up with R.C.A. Phototone and that their forthcoming film *Blackmail* would have a dialogue sequence. In June the film was shown at a midnight *première* at the Regal Cinema, Marble Arch, with all the trimmings and proved to be a full talking film. It has been said that it was shot as a silent film and then reshot entirely as a sound film. But Hitchcock himself has written:

'It began as a silent picture, but I had made preparations so that dialogue could be added.

'The completed product proved a great surprise to the late John Maxwell, who was then the head of the Company. He had expected the dialogue to be confined to the last reel, as a "special added attraction". We used only incidental sound and music in the first reel, so that audiences would have that much more of a pleasant surprise when the characters on the screen began talking as the plot unfolded.

'I like to remember all the studio executives were pleased. They advertised it as a "99 per cent talking picture".'[34]

Scripted by Hitchcock, Benn Levy, and Charles Bennett from a play by Bennett, it was shot by Jack Cox, with Wilfred Arnold as designer. The cast included the foreign actress Anny Ondra, with the dubbed voice of Joan Barry, John Longden and Donald Calthrop. Besides being an exciting film in its own right, it was an intelligent approach to the use of sound and fully reinstated Hitchcock after the disappointment of *Champagne* and *The Manxman*.

Since his success with *The Lodger* in 1926 Hitchcock's films for Gainsborough and then B.I.P. had failed to advance his reputation as much as people had hoped. *The Ring* had received a lot of attention when put on at the Astoria in 1927 and had been greeted as a masterpiece by a public eager to find a British cinema genius. But the more serious critics maintained that it was a silly story treated without psychological insight and with an empty trickiness, although Hugh Castle did admit 'Hitchcock just missed great things in *The Ring*'.[35] Similarly *The Farmer's Wife* had failed to satisfy the harsher critics, and *Champagne* and *The Manxman* had offered him inferior material. But all these imperfect films are recognizably his, less from the angle work so often attributed to German influence than from his way of guiding the audience's thoughts by every indirect means at the cinema's disposal, including the continuity bridge that suggests some idea, the visual symbol, and the use of setting, lighting and pace to affect mood and understanding.

At last in this first sound film, a thriller which would have been congenial to him even as a silent film, Hitchcock had a conspicuous chance to display his talent. He did so with such striking effect that for a while any criticism of the British film was expected to collapse at the mention of *Blackmail*. He had with ease incorporated the new element of sound into his own individual approach to film narrative and used it like everything else indirectly as well as directly, creating sound images as full of meanings of their own as the literal words of dialogue. Such a passage was the famous knife sequence which was immediately singled out, and which has been quoted ever since, as a classic example of non-realistic sound:

'He has one sequence which, despite the way it has been glorified in the English press, gives one a clear idea of the potentialities of the medium. The girl over-hears a chatterbox discussing the murder, while the memory of the knife is still fresh in her penny-dreadful mind. The talk dies down and down until only the word "knife" emerges, stabbing, hurting.'[36]

At a time when the whole cinema world was uncertain, most film makers fumbling, the critics theorizing about counterpoint and the Soviet film makers as yet lacking the resources to put their ideas into practice, it was this shrewd and practical professional who unhesitatingly showed how sound could be made an integral part of film technique. Hugh Castle wrote somewhat grudgingly that it was 'a first effort of which the British industry has every reson to be proud' and even 'some of us already are beginning to say that talkies are an art'.[37] Rotha later wrote that it 'may not have been a particularly good film, but it was infinitely better than any American picture of the same time'.[38]

ove Top: New Guinea girl – *urley's Pearls and Savages,* *4.*

ove: Western actress – Hurley's *gle Woman,* 1926.

Right: Leslie Henson in *s of Money,* 1924.

tre Right: Alma Taylor and *yle Gardner in Hepworth's *nin' thro' the Rye,* 1923.

tom Right: Betty Blythe and *lyle Blackwell in Samuelson's *e,* 1925, directed by Leander *Cordova and with sets by *inrich Richter in a German *dio.

Top Left: Wetherell in his ow film *Livingstone*, 1925.

Centre Left: John Stuart, F Compton and Moore Marriott *London Love*, 1926.

Bottom Left: Henry Edwards Elvey's *The Flag Lieutena* 1926.

Various films under way at the time came out later in the year with some sort of sound added. *Under the Greenwood Tree* by Lachman (Trade Show September 1929) was 'jammed up with singing sequences', but Lachman tried to give these some reason for existence and *Close Up* wrote that the film 'has perhaps the best direction yet produced from a British studio'.[39] *Alf's Carpet* (Trade Show November 1929) by Will Kellino, with the foreign comedians Pat and Patachon, who were known in England as Long and Short, tried to recapture some of the earlier success of Darlington's *Alf's Button*. The important German director Arthur Robison made *The Informer* (Trade Show October 1929), which had been planned as a silent film but came out as part talking, with its foreign stars Lars Hanson and Lya de Putti, shot by Werner Brandes with careful German lighting and designed by Arnold. Finally Dupont made a spectacular film based on the sinking of the *Titanic* called *Atlantic* (Trade Show November 1929), which was full-talking and had a large cast including John Longden, Madeleine Carroll, Ellaline Terriss, Monty Banks, John Stuart and Donald Calthrop, and was shot by the American Charles Rosher. Of this film Rotha wrote:

'Dupont's first dialogue film, however, was an unprecedented example of wasted material. . . . It could have been one of the most powerful films ever made. It was one of the stupidest. First, the bathos of the dialogue was incredible; secondly, the acting was stage-like, stiff and unconvincing; thirdly, the actual shock of the collision was completely ineffectual. Technically, the photography was flat and uninteresting; the (unnecessary) model shots were crude and toy-like; and the mass of nautical errors was inexcusable; added to which there was a complete discrepancy of the water levels as the vessel sank.'[40]

Hitchcock was still only twenty-seven when he joined B.I.P. but he was already outstanding among British film makers. Like Asquith, he was of a generation that had grown up with the cinema and took it for granted as something quite different to the theatre. But unlike Asquith, who had an intellectual background and had studied the more advanced film techniques from abroad, he had an entirely empirical approach. He had started young and gained experience of every branch of film making. Five films for Gainsborough and five for B.I.P. now placed him at the top of British production, though still at the beginning of his long career. It was already clear that his use of the medium to catch and hold the attention was second to none. It was also evident that an attack upon the romantic emotions, or the significance of a theme such as preoccupied George Pearson, had no particular appeal for him and that he would stand or fall on having a credible, gripping story to tell. Like Elvey with his painstaking attention to detail, and a similar slickness and technical polish, he was unhampered by the older man's roots in the theatre and had an inventive imagination which unfailingly turned facts into film images. It was significant that this imagination was inventive rather than sympathetic, and that he did not appear to feel deeply with his characters. Critics were at pains to deny that he was a genius. But his mastery of film story-telling was great enough to compensate for this rather outward treatment and he was to become a great story teller.

One cannot avoid the suspicion that such a brilliant incorporation of the new element of sound into film technique might have been greeted with less condescension had it come from Germany, say, instead of Elstree. B.I.P. had the largest studio in England, and it was well equipped. They had capital and strong business leadership and assured distribution. But although many good film makers passed through the studio they rarely did their best work there. Dupont did nothing as outstanding as *Variety* (Germany 1926), nor Robison as *Warning Shadows* (Germany 1922). Hitchcock was the only first-class British director to work at B.I.P. at this time and most of his films there were a disappointment. B.I.P. came more and more to resemble its ideal, Hollywood. Aiming at sophistication and glossy, opulent production, they were ready to spend money on talent which had proved itself elsewhere, but lacked the artistic sympathy to encourage any development of the medium in their own studio. Strangely, what they did was to recreate in a wealthier and more sophisticated form the mass production or sausage-machine film making of the early Stoll and Ideal days. If Balcon was an artist's businessman and Wilcox a showman's businessman, Maxwell was a businessman's businessman.

Smaller companies were also formed to exploit the possibilities of the quota, and of these British Lion Film Corporation was one of the more successful. It was registered in December 1927 with an authorized capital of £210,000, large by the old standards but not by the new. The issue, however, was not fully subscribed although it was comparatively early in the field. Beaconsfield studio was bought from George Clark for £52,785,[41] a figure criticized later as too high. It owned film rights to the works of Edgar Wallace for seven years, and Wallace himself was made chairman of the company, of which the production manager was Percy Nash. The Canadian Sidney Olcott was brought over from America at a salary of £450 a week but later successfully sued the company on the grounds that the scenario for the first film he was to direct, *The Ringer*, was not suitable for the 'super-film' which by his contract he was entitled to have. Arthur Maude was engaged to complete *The Ringer* (Trade Show August 1928). Films were also put out during the year by A. V. Bramble (*Chick*, Trade Show August 1928) after his *Shooting Stars* débâcle, and by G. B. Samuelson (*The Forger*, Trade Show December 1928), both old-style directors, and the first year was one of very heavy losses. All the films were released by Ideal. In 1929 Maude's *The Flying Squad* (Trade Show January 1929) and *The Clue of the New Pin* (Trade Show March 1929) both featured Donald Calthrop, the first a Warner release and the second P.D.C. The latter was made for British Phototone and was described as the first all-talking British film, but aroused little interest, perhaps because it was on disc and technically rather unsatisfactory.

Edgar Wallace was personally interested in making films of his own works. During the twenties he enjoyed transferring his extremely popular stories to the theatre and it was to be expected that with his expansive temperament he should wish to fling himself into film making as well. Both *The Ringer* and *The Flying Squad* had run successfully as plays, at Wyndhams in 1926 and the Lyceum in 1928 respectively. The firm aimed at making straightforward mystery films and were not concerned with lavish production or emotional subtlety, but the rather old-fashioned directors employed got only fair results from their promising material. Meanwhile Wallace was preparing to take a more active part in production:

'It was because of the proven box-office appeal of the plays that Edgar was now approached to take the chairmanship of a film company which was about to be organized. In the first year of its existence the British Lion Film Corporation produced eight film versions of Edgar's plays.

'At the end of the year, and before the general release of any of these films, the talkie panic descended upon the film industry. Silent films were only just so much spoiled negative!

'It was a dreaful blow to the film company. It was a shock to Edgar. Everything had to be scrapped. The studio had to be wired for sound, virtually rebuilt.

'Meanwhile Edgar had tried his hand at directing.'[42]

It was after the arrival of sound that he went to Hollywood, where he died prematurely in 1932.

One of the more spectacular and, as it turned out, more lasting attempts to take advantage of the quota was that of Ludwig Blattner, around whom unfounded rumours began to circulate early in 1928, including one of a studio city at Elstree to be called Hollywood, England, a capital issue of £650,000, quota pictures for United Artists, sound-colour films and a new £60,000 studio. Blattner did in fact buy the old Neptune studios, and finally the Ludwig Blattner Film Corporation, with an authorized capital of £250,000, made a large public issue in May. This was considered somewhat speculative by *The Bioscope*, despite the promise of such foreign talents as Lupu Pick, Karl Freund, Lilian Harvey, Rex Ingram and Alice Terry, and an extremely inappropriate advertising slogan of 'British films for the world'. The first quota picture, *A Knight in London*, was trade shown in March 1929 and was much praised for Pick's direction and Freund's camerawork in an unworthy wrong-bedroom farce.

Even the old studio at Ealing, which was used in the mid-twenties for shorts production by Widgey Newman (Widgey R. Newman, registered September 1927, capital £100), was now rediscovered and brought back into use. It was bought by Union Studios in 1929, to be rebuilt and equipped for hire with R.C.A. sound at a cost of £250,000. This company failed but the site was later acquired by Associated Talking Pictures. This had been registered in May 1929 with a capital of £125,000 and with Basil Dean and Sir Gerald du Maurier on the Board, in an early attempt to unite stage and screen by means of the sound film.*

Later in 1927, as the quota rush gathered speed, some rather more doubtful propositions were put before the public. One of these was associated with the

* A bigger studio was subsequently put up at Ealing by A.T.P.

name of Adelqui Millar. When he had been with the Granger–Binger company as an actor during the early twenties he had been responsible for several scripts in which he wrote lush parts for himself to leer and lurch through some thick melodrama. On leaving Granger–Binger he had drifted from one more or less independent production to another for several years, some of them on the Continent. These included *Pages of Life* (Trade Show November 1922), distributed by Butcher's; *Pagliacci* (Trade Show August 1923); *The Apache* (Trade Show September 1925) and *The Blind Ship* (Trade Show May 1927), all by Napoleon. In addition he acted with Maria Corda in Michael Curtiz' Stoll–Sascha film made in Austria, *Moon of Israel* (Trade Show November 1924) and with Lillian Gish in Wilcox's British National film *London* (Trade Show January 1927). An adventurer of saturnine appearance, he had a leaning towards the exotic which sometimes slipped over into the absurd. The quota gave him a chance which he grasped energetically. At the end of 1927 Whitehall Films was formed with a capital of £200,000 and with Adelqui Millar, N. A. Pogson and Charles Lapworth on the Board. They planned to build a studio at Boreham Wood, Elstree, and make six films in the first year for only £10,000 each, spending £21,000 on the studio and £14,000 on equipment. Despite strong criticism in the trade press of this very over-optimistic prospectus, the issue was over-subscribed in a few hours, so accurately had Millar gauged the temper of the time. It was quite a new idea to advocate making films cheaply. Hitherto expensive production had been a mark of excellence, and in this new trend Whitehall showed a shrewd appreciation of the real meaning of the quota system. Construction began early in 1928 of what was eventually to be a well-built studio with a large stage. Meanwhile the company went abroad to start production and two films were made, *Life* (Trade Show January 1929), which was directed and acted by Millar, made in Spain and handled by New Era, and *The Inseparables*, which was directed by Millar with the assistance of John Stafford and had a better cast than usual, featuring Elissa Landi and Annette Benson, and with Pat Aherne instead of Millar himself. This was handled by Warner. There were rows early in 1928 and Millar was left in sole charge, but by early next year when the films were ready the company was in serious financial difficulty. Millar was removed from the Board in June 1929, and his contract cancelled.

Even more doubtful companies were formed in the name of the quota. George Banfield was another who had been trying to get into the mainstream of production from the middle twenties with shorts such as the *Haunted Houses* series of 1925, having actually entered the film industry in 1908. In August 1926 he acquired the Walthamstow studios from West and, forming a group with Leslie Eveleigh and cameramen Bert Ford and Phil Ross, registered British Filmcraft in September. During the quota discussions of the early part of the year some most ambitious plans were canvassed for a film to be written by Professor A. M. Low and the editor of the *Daily Sketch*, Ivor Halstead. This was to be called *Cosmos* and would show nothing less than

'The world from the beginning of time to the year 2,000. . . . The purpose of the film is to show that science has been responsible for the history of the world.'[43]

Nothing came of this extraordinary proposition, but later in the year it was said that the company had come down to earth and was contemplating building a new studio at Walthamstow and embarking on productions starring Matheson Lang. A public issue of £100,000 was made by British Filmcraft Productions in November 1927 and the opportunities offered by the quota were cited in the prospectus. *The Bioscope*, however, was critical:

'Among the list of successes claimed for Mr Banfield in the prospectus, only one is known to us.'[44]

There was unrest among the shareholders almost immediately. Apart from a *Sexton Blake* series of shorts, a *Dick Turpin* series featuring Matheson Lang and a series of shorts called *Ghosts of Yesterday,* they put out four features in late 1928 and early 1929. *Spangles* (Trade Show December 1928) was made by Banfield and shot by Ross, and was about a circus girl who leaves her wealthy lover and West End success to return to her faithful chum and the sawdust. It was handled by Paramount with fair success. *The Burgomaster of Stilemonde* (Trade Show January 1929), from the story by Maurice Maeterlinck about German atrocities in the treatment of hostages, was made by Banfield and featured Sir John Martin-Harvey in his stage part, and was much admired, although *The Bioscope* did admit to a doubt about the addition of a theme song:

> All that I long for, all that I love,
> Is stolen from my side.
> Hopes that were dearest fall on a sky
> Of shadows at eventide.
> I will be waiting and grieving
> As the sun goes down
> My heart is breaking: You're leaving
> As the sun goes down.[45]

Blue Peter (Trade Show February 1929) was made by A. H. Rooke and Leslie Eveleigh from a Temple Thurston story and featured Matheson Lang, and *Power Over Men* (Trade Show April 1929) was by Banfield and featured Jameson Thomas and Isabel Jeans.

British Screen Classics was registered by H. J. Whitcomb and H. S. Chambers in December 1925 with a capital of only £2,000 to acquire rights to some of Harry Parkinson's short films of London night life, and later also W. C. Jeapes' *Empire News Bulletin* from British Picture Productions, which was registered in March 1926 with a capital of £5,000. The distribution of both was taken over by J. V. Bryson of the European Motion Picture Company in November 1926, but during the next year the quota discussions became important and at the end of the year it was announced that British Screen Classics was to be taken over by a new company, British Screen Productions, which was to buy Worton Hall studios from Samuelson, and produce films by G. A. Cooper, Hugh Croise and Frank Miller. The company was registered in February 1928 with a capital of £250,000 and George W. Pearson, previously a renter, as managing director. Worton Hall was bought for £19,000. A public issue of the whole capital was made in March, but was considered another poor speculation by *The Bioscope*.[46] During 1928 and 1929 news, interest, travel and compilation films were made and a few extremely bad feature films which even the quota conditions could not make acceptable to the trade press. One of them, *Master and Man* (Trade Show February 1929), was summed up by Hugh Castle as 'really British. Another endurance test.'[47] Meanwhile the company, which was perhaps more interested in the ramifications of business than in actual film making, became involved in all sorts of other schemes. Towards the end of 1928 Lancashire Screen Productions was planned, with £200,000 capital, to use the aviation factory between Lytham and Blackpool for film production. A production and distribution tie-up with Rayart Pictures Incorporated of America was claimed and the acquisition through British Controlled Films* of big interests in the Emelka and Maxim film companies in Germany.[48] Finally, after the arrival of sound, International Talking Screen Productions was announced with the grandest plans of all, £850,000 capital and units in America, Germany and Britain which would make as many as 54 features a year, with British Screen Productions as the British link. However, by now the investors had learnt a little caution and the issue was heavily undersubscribed, *The Bioscope* in fact quoting City reports to the effect that 90 per cent of the issue was left with the underwriters.

British and Foreign Films, formed early in 1928 with a capital of £350,000, was also considered risky by *The Bioscope*. It showed several tendencies which were characteristic of the time, including international links and backing provided by renters from the provinces. British interests were represented by Booth Grainge of Leeds and Frederick White of Manchester, and German interests by Messtro and Orplid. Several films were made by Hans Steinhoff and other German directors with mixed casts which included Clifford Mc-Laglen, Lillian Hall-Davis and Mabel Poulton, Hans Schlettow and Elga Brink. The most notable film was *Three Kings* (Trade Show January 1929), a popular circus melodrama written and played by Henry Edwards with Warwick Ward also in the cast.

One of the strangest episodes centred round the activities of Edward Godal. Godal had, until the end of the war, run one of the so-called training schools for cinema actors, the Victoria Cinema Studios. After working from 1918 to 1924 as managing director of B. & C., he and his co-director Sir Berkeley Vincent formed Godal International Films in December 1924 with a capital of £2,000. *The Art of Love*, a series of two-reelers, was made by Edwin Greenwood (reviewed December 1925). By the end of next year Godal announced an astonishing plan for *The Peace of the World*, described as the first film to be especially

* Registered June 1927, with a capital £25,000; directors included A. Rassam and Gerald Malvern.

written by H. G. Wells. Wells had an on-and-off relationship with film writing throughout the twenties. He admired the work of Chaplin, and had allowed his *Kipps* and *The Wheels of Chance* to be filmed, but had resisted many attempts to persuade him to write original stories for the films. *Bluebottles, The Cure* and *Daydreams* were three short comedies directed by Ivor Montagu in 1928 for which Wells wrote the stories when his son Frank became involved in the film industry. In *The King Who Was A King* (1929), a novel presented as the synopsis for a film, he explained that 'a certain Mr Godal' had advertised *The Peace Of The World*, a title Wells had used for a series of wartime newspaper articles, as a film already in existence. It had aroused a good response and Godal had then, and only then, approached Wells to write a synopsis. Wells did so. The project came to nothing and the directors of the company quarrelled, to such an extent that counsel said of Sir Berkeley during the winding-up proceedings:

'I gather that he does not like Mr Godal . . . and desires rather to break him up. . . .'[49]

But strangely enough the rights in *The Peace Of The World* were stated to be an asset of £4,000. Mr Godal turned up again almost immediately as British Amalgamated Films in the company of Arthur Maude, fresh from making *Poppies in Flanders* and *Toni,* and Rudolph Solomon of Graham–Wilcox. There were plans to form a £230,000 company called British Multicolour Film Corporation, which would acquire both British Amalgamated and Graham–Wilcox and make colour films at Elstree. These came to nothing, like many other ambitious-sounding schemes at the time. The coincidence of the new quota laws and the conversion of the industry to sound production had indeed led to a period of rapid change. But by the end of 1929 the confidence of the public in the many new companies seeking capital had been considerably shaken.

CHAPTER SIX

The Arrival of the
Commercial Sound Film

The exhibition of films had always been accompanied by some form of sound, and silent film technique was developed because synchronization had not yet become reliable rather than because of any supposed virtue in silence. The invention of recording, reproducing, synchronizing and amplifying means was a tangle of patents, priorities and litigation, many of them concerned with some form of gramophone device. Lescarboura, writing at the beginning of this period and referring to sound film in general as 'cinephone', described not only attempts to synchronize the film and the phonograph, but also some successful efforts to produce sound-on-film, as well as experiments in electrical sound amplification. In 1921 *The Bioscope,* reporting a demonstration near Stockholm of a 'film-photophone' using sound-on-film and silenium for reconversion to sound, predicted a revolution in films.[1] The possibilities continued to intrigue technicians, and every now and then during the early twenties some hopeful inventor formed a company with yet another strange compound name, most of them concerned with some sort of synchronized disc.

Meanwhile the old substitutes for synchronized sound were in their heyday. By 1919 it was already fairly general for the better renters to supply cue sheets for musical accompaniment in the cinema, and compositions were advertised as 'suitable for picture fitting', 'Filmelodies' and 'Loose Leaf Cinema Incidentals'. 'Descriptive pieces suitable for kinema use have also been composed by Albert W. Ketelby.' Renters would either suggest the type of music suitable for different passages, or even suggest particular pieces of music, with title, composer and publisher, and indicate the exact sub-titles or incidents at which to put the music in question. General instructions might suggest tragic music, flowing, senti-mental, bright-lively, fox-trot, hymn, dramatic agitato, light intermezzo or very occasionally 'effect', or even 'silence'. Such romantic composers as Mascagni, Delibes, Massenet, Chaminade and Grieg were especially useful, with classical orchestral music coming into its own for tragic episodes and the lesser-known contemporary British composers for lighter stories. Cue sheets with exact instructions for particular pieces made difficulties for the musical directors of cinemas without large music libraries, but on the other hand such vague instruc-tions as 'flowing melody' set problems for those less well-versed in music, especially as few musical directors were able to see the films in advance, although the sameness of many films made their job easier. Very few films had music composed especially for them, although the film theme song, pioneered here by the music publishers Francis, Day Hunter, actually became popular before the arrival of the sound film. There were isolated cases of films with their own music such as *Berlin*, *Potemkin* and *Ten Days* by Edmund Meisel, and *L'Inhumaine* by Darius Milhaud. Edwin Evans, music critic of the *Pall Mall Gazette*, speaking at the Stoll Picture Theatre Club in 1923, said:

'My idea of cinema music is something evolved by the cinema itself, and so intimately bound up with the cinema that it would be out of place in the concert room. You will only get this if the music is written specially for the film. . . . There are only two possible means of approach—the Wagner way and the "episode" way. In the former case it is necessary to invent themes to suit the characters of the story; and, in the latter case, to treat episodes as complete in themselves, passing from one to another without a break.'[2]

But such a thoughtful attitude was rare. Betts wrote in despair:

'Not long ago when engaged in the bitter business of film criticism, I was given the task of finding out exactly what our directors of film music thought about its development and future. I now know that they thought nothing at all.'[3]

and Vachel Lindsay wrote:

'With fathomless imbecility, hoochey koochey strains are on the air while heroes are dying.'[4]

The writer Dorothy M. Richardson, writing in *Close Up* in 1927, preferred the flexibility of the pianist to an orchestral accompaniment unless the orchestra had rehearsed music written or arranged for the film in question, and described the typical cinema pianist:

'He could time a passage to culminate the break punctually on a staccato chord at a crisis. This is a crude example of his talent for spontaneous adaptation. As long as he remained with us music and picture were one. If the film were good he enhanced it, heightened its effect of action moving forward for the first time.'[5]

She contrasted the single piano player with his 'continuous improvisation varying in tone and tempo according to what was going forward on the screen' with an orchestra playing set pieces for each scene and thus killing the relationship between the onlooker and the film. She maintained that any music was better than no music, but that if synchronized sound effects were to become possible,

'. . . musical accompaniment will be superfluous whether as a cover for the sounds from the operator's gallery and the talking of the audience, or as a help to the concentration that is essential to collaboration between the onlooker and what he sees.'[5]

The cinema organ was coming into use by 1919, and even a crossbreed called the orgapian a few years later. The expensive Wurlitzer cinema organ was unknown in Britain in 1924, but in the next two years twelve were installed, including one at the Plaza which cost £15,000.[6] Other makes were the Mostel, which cost from 335 to 650 guineas, and the Christie orchestral unit organs at £1,400 to £12,000. The problem of effects also began to attract the ingenuity of the 'presentation expert' at the larger cinemas and led, for example, to the Vitasona effects machine, and ill-advised talk of noise music. Vivian Van Damm was criticized in *The Bioscope* for employing a crowd to provide mob noises for *Scaramouche* at the Tivoli in 1923, all of them, he assured the paper, Frenchmen from Soho and unable to talk English. *The Bioscope* also thought it wise to warn showmen that gunpowder would not be appropriate for *The Fall of Babylon*.[7] Such excesses brought too literal a use of sound effects into disrepute. A sensible suspicion arose that realism for its own sake was not always desirable. But then the sound film brought an even greater realism, with even less discrimination, into all types of film production.

For just as wireless had become a commercial proposition in the early twenties, the sound film experiments of the early twenties now bore fruit in 1926. The Vitaphone Corporation of America, controlled by Warners, put on a show of short films with sound on disc at the Warner Theatre in New York on August 6, 1926, and shortly afterwards came the American première of *Don Juan*, with effects and music. The Vitaphone system was a phonographic record made simultaneously with the film, reproduction taking place through a machine coupled to the motor drive of the projector; an electric pickup now transformed the sound into electrical voltage with the current in turn passing through an amplifying reproducer.[8] Almost immediately, in October 1926, an advertisement appeared in England for the Gaumont system British Acoustic. This was a sound-on-film system using a separate film for the sound which, according to Balcon, ran 50 per cent faster than the picture and through a separate projector. The company had been busy with the system for some time and claimed in its favour that it gave fidelity, volume, distinction, a wide range of production, and that it was practicable outdoors and unaffected by mixes, fades and chemical manipulation during development. No public demonstration took place at this date, however. At the same time the Phonofilm system, with sound on the side of the picture film, was demonstrated in a programme of shorts of British vaudeville artistes, the best known of whom was Billy Merson, at the Capitol, Haymarket, on September 27, 1926. Phonofilm had been invented by Dr Lee De Forest, and involved recording and reproduction by silenium and photo electric cell, the sound being recorded in synchronization with the picture on the edge of standard film. Reproduction required an attachment to the projector and electrical amplifiers. It had first been demonstrated in Britain in June 1923 at the Finsbury Park Cinema, when it was said the synchronization was perfect but articulation 'throaty'. The British rights had been secured by C. F. Elwell, and De Forest Phonofilms was registered in July 1923 with a capital of £50,000 to make British sound pictures. It had then been much improved and late in 1924 Elwell gave a show at the Royal Society of Arts. Throughout 1923 to 1926 the company had been experimenting at the Clapham studios, Cranmer Court, where the short films shown in 1926 were made.

Late in 1926 it was announced that the Vitaphone system would be available to producers in America through Western Electric, Bell Telephone Laboratories and the Vitaphone company, and there was said to be a big demand for it in the United States in 1927. Warner's *The Jazz Singer*, which was shown in America in 1927, was shown here in its synchronized, part-talkie version at the Piccadilly Theatre on September 27, 1928, and was followed closely by their film *The Terror* (October 1928). These pictures created a sensation, especially when it was heard later that Warner Brothers' profit for 1928 would be over £1,600,000. *The Jazz Singer* was a turning point. *The Bioscope* greeted it with, 'We are inclined to wonder why we ever called them Living Pictures'.[9] But Vitaphone's competitors were not idle. The British Acoustic system gave its first public show in September 1928 with some short films which included a speech by Ramsay MacDonald, Adrian Brunel's *In a Monastery Garden*, and *Life on H.M.S. Rodney*. It was later used by Gaumont for their first sound feature, Maurice Elvey's full-talking *High Treason* (Trade Show October 1929).

Phonofilm had also been busy, and in 1926 and 1927 G. A. Cooper, Thomas Bentley and others were producing shorts of various types at Clapham. These included the quarrel scene from *Julius Caesar* with Basil Gill and Malcolm Keen, made by Cooper; *His Rest Day*, a comedy sketch by Cooper; a song scene by Miles Mander called *Castles in the Air* and other song scenes and sketches such as *The Man in the Street* by Bentley; a turn by Nervo and Knox, made by Widgey Newman; more ambitious numbers such as a Grand Guignol short film called *The Antidote* by Bentley, and Mander's marital comedy *As We Lie*; and Edith and Sacheverell Sitwell reciting poems by Edith and Osbert. Late in 1927 there were changes in the composition of the company, which was taken over by I. W. Schlesinger and Harold Holt, who had plans for a studio at Wembley. By June 1928 it was reported that the studio was in use although not yet officially open. It was announced that forty cinemas had been fitted for Phonofilm at a cost to the company of £300 each, the cinema paying £16 10s a week for the hire and maintenance of the apparatus and a 3,000-foot programme.[10] Then came Warner's London triumph with *The Jazz Singer* and proof of the big commercial openings for sound features, and Phonofilms also seemed ready to move into big business. It was acquired in August 1928 by British Talking Pictures, a company formed with a capital of £500,000 to make and lease the equipment and rent the studio but not to produce films. Schlesinger and Holt were on the board. A subsidiary with a capital of £100,000, British Sound Films, was to produce and had a link with B.I.F.D., which was to provide the distribution outlet. At this time it was said that Henrik Galeen, who had previously produced for B.I.F.D., was to supervise production. It was claimed that all types of sound film used by leading American firms could be used on Phonofilm apparatus. It was at this time that De Forest sued Fox over Fox–Movietone, the sound-on-film process also being referred to as Movietone–Phonofilm. *The Crimson Circle*, a part-talking film shown in March 1929, was directed by F. Zelnik and was described in *Close Up* as a British sound film, although in fact it was largely German. But by mid-1929 it was said that sound film makers had not yet had facilities in England except for shorts production but that a big new studio was being built at Wembley. In October *Dark Red Roses*, made here, was shown. Others were planned, but in October 1929 the studio was burnt down.

By now other companies were appearing and the industry was alive with rumours. In June 1928 British Phototone was registered with a capital of £250,000 to exploit a system using twelve-inch discs and comparatively cheap reproduction equipment. The managing director was Dudley A. Bott, who was associated with the recording company British Brunswick and also with P.D.C. The firm was from the first connected with both Blattner and British Instructional. Asquith was rumoured to be 'musical consultant and adviser' and it was announced that British Instructional might make weekly one-reelers, and also that British Phototone would provide the music and effects background for three British Instructional films including Asquith's *Underground*. This was already being issued as a silent film. In June 1928 a sound film demonstration was held, which was not altogether successful, but nevertheless when an issue of £100,000 was made in July it was oversubscribed more than twenty-five times. At this time the recently formed Blattner Film Corporation, with which Ludwig Blattner, Karl Freund and Lupu Pick were associated, announced that they would also install British Phototone at their Elstree studio, the old Neptune one, and make sound shorts for P.D.C. release. The three made a sound film of the Kit Kat Restaurant in London. In September Blattner and Freund were said to be working in a German studio in which British Phototone had acquired an interest. In November some P.D.C. shorts made by Blattner Picture Corporation were shown at the Scala, but again were not entirely successful, although in this month also, according to the *Kine Year Book* of 1930, British Phototone signed a contract with British Instructional for three years. Early next year the Elstree studio and the British Instructional studio at Welwyn were nearly ready for sound production. Royalties were charged for the recording apparatus, and the reproduction apparatus was said to be interchangeable with other systems but not as cheap as it had been before. In March 1929 *The Clue of the New Pin*, made by British Lion for British Phototone and described as the first full-length British all-talkie, was trade shown as P.D.C.'s first quota film. This disc system was not very satisfactory and the company, with greatly expanded capital, was now involved in complicated negotiations involving various European companies and many patents, as a result of which their apparatus was superseded by normal sixteen inch records. Finally they had plans to make the longer feature films on sound-on-film and to distribute Klangfilm Tobis equipment in England. This was installed at the British Instructional studio at Welwyn and their first sound film, *A Cottage on Dartmoor*, was made by this system.

There were, of course, plenty of other attempts to take advantage of a rather confused situation. About August 1928 Electramonic, a gramophone grandly called a 'sound reproducing device', was oversubscribed ten times. The Celebritone Company, registered in October with a capital of £160,000, was also heavily oversubscribed; it seems to have been an amplifying system. Filmophone was registered at about the same time, with a capital of £225,000, to market a synchronization system for discs. And early in 1929 a studio in Leeds was said to be turning out Electrocord shorts which, again, sound like films with discs.

There was keen competition to be first with sound features and, with the added complication of the different systems, there were many conflicting claims. British Sound Films, using Phonofilm, trade showed their part-talkie *The Crimson Circle* in March 1929, and *Dark Red Roses* in October. British Lion's *The Clue of the New Pin* was also in March. But Hitchcock's very successful film *Blackmail*, in June, is usually regarded as the effective beginning of sound production in England. B.I.P., using R.C.A., followed *Blackmail* with Bentley's *The American Prisoner* and Harry Lachman's *Under the Greenwood Tree*, both in September, Arthur Robison's *The Informer* in October, and Dupont's *Atlantic* and Kellino's *Alf's Carpet* in November. The Burlington–B.I.P. film *Kitty*, made as a silent at Elstree by Victor Saville in 1928, was shown in June 1929 with part-talking sound recorded in America. Gainsborough began by experimenting with the cumbersome Gaumont–British system British Acoustic, and a sound version of Cutts' *The Return of the Rat* was synchronized by this system. *The Wrecker* by Bolvary, in July, had music and sound effects synchronized in New York by R.C.A. *Taxi for Two*, in November, and Clift's *The City of Play*, also in November, both had part-talking versions synchronized by R.C.A., and were followed in 1930 by *The Crooked Billet* and *Balaclava*. But the first full-sound feature actually made at Islington with the new R.C.A. equipment was *Just for a Song*, in the thirties. Meanwhile Victor Saville made a full-talking version of *Woman to Woman* in America as a joint Gainsborough Tiffany–Stahl production, and it was shown in November, followed in 1930 by the James Whale–George Pearson film *Journey's End*, also made in America. Welsh–Pearson themselves had shown a version of *Auld Lang Syne* with Lauder's songs on record synchronized by R.C.A., and their silent film *The Broken Melody* in October was also shown with a belatedly synchronized accompaniment, but no real conversion to sound was made. British Instructional showed *A Throw of the Dice* in October, a film with the Indian players Seeta Devi and Himansu Rao and synchronized with Breusing discs, but their first real sound production was Asquith's *A Cottage on Dartmoor* in 1930, the part-talking film recorded on Klangfilm Tobis equipment. New Era had Edwin Greenwood's full-talking R.C.A. *The Co-Optimists* in November; W.P. showed an R.C.A. full-talking version of their *White Cargo*, previously shown as a silent film, in October; Strand had Greenwood's full-talking R.C.A. *To What Red Hell* in October; and Gaumont–British, using their own system British Acoustic, showed Elvey's *High Treason* in August. B. & D. installed Western Electric, but were slow to make a sound film. So was Stoll, who wasted a couple of years on an embryonic British system, but as this was impossible to reproduce on either Western Electric or R.C.A. equipment, which was already being put into all the cinemas, the company eventually changed to Marconi Visatone.[11]

The situation by July 1928 seems to have been that R.C.A. Photophone, a sound-on-film system, was used for production in America by F.B.O., Pathé and First National, and was later installed in most British studios: Ealing, B.I.P., Twickenham, Islington and Walton. The installation of their reproduction equipment in the cinemas lagged behind that of Western Electric, but the R.C.A. system could be played off the Western Electric reproduction system.

Whereas by July 1928 Western Electric in America handled equipment for reproducing either disc or film of Western Electric type and had made enormous strides in installing reproduction equipment in the cinemas, in England it was installed only in the B. & D. studios. It covered the Vitaphone disc system of Warners and the Fox–Movietone sound-on-film system associated with Phonofilm.

The rivalry between sound-on-film and disc was by no means decided. At the time, the chief disadvantage of sound-on-film seems to have been that it gave only weak and poor sound, but to many this seemed of overriding importance. Discs gave better definition and volume. But on the other hand they were more trouble to transport and almost impossible on location, gave bad surface noise after wear, were more difficult to synchronize and made it harder to deal with accidental breaks or cuts in the film and incidentally more difficult for the censors.

By 1930 sound films had gained over silent to such an extent that out of some 717 films trade shown, 524 were sound films. Moreover 467 of the 524 sound films were listed as 'full-talking'. Only 82 of the 524 were British sound films.[12]

Western Electric was clearly gaining over R.C.A. in the cinemas, as 334 had Western Electric sound and only 145 R.C.A. But of the 82 British sound films, only 10 were recorded by Western Electric as against 56 R.C.A., by far the most common system in the British studios. In addition 6 British films had been made under the Gaumont system, British Acoustic. Other systems and anonymous films accounted for 357 of the combined Western Electric and R.C.A. output as against only 111 sound-on-disc, with another 17 of both systems being put out in both sound-on-film and disc versions. British studios showed little interest in disc sound. Of the 72 British films recorded by Western Electric, R.C.A., and British Acoustic together, only 2 were disc and 1 was done in both disc and sound-on-film versions; whereas of 413 foreign Western Electric and R.C.A. films, as many as 109 were disc, with 16 done in both disc and sound-on-film versions.

There was the problem of what to call this new thing. Phonie, phono-cinema, cinemalogue, cinelog, dramaphone, audies or outloudies, asked *The Bioscope*, considering talkie a 'poor, slangy word lacking in dignity'.[13]

Until sound proved itself as a commercial proposition, there were few to defend it except as a curiosity. During the early twenties isolated technical interest was inarticulate, commercial interest dormant, and anyone at all highbrow was hostile to the very idea. Even in so lowbrow an organ as *The Bioscope*, a writer in 1925 spoke of 'the language of the film—melting and mingling as it does in a kind of fluid eloquence', condemned 'literalists of the screen' and feared 'the silent drama is really to be shorn of its primal and essential attribute'.[14] But whilst the arguments proceeded in the mid-twenties on this high plane, many cinemas were quietly abandoning the pianist or the orchestra in favour of some form of mechanical reproduction system of gramophone and amplification, in the belief that they would later be able to adapt it.

There were two issues, whether the sound film would or would not last, and whether it was good or bad. Many thought it would prove to be a passing fashion like cine-variety. Michael Orme, writing in the *Illustrated London News* as early

as October 1927, was then a comparatively lonely voice predicting that sound
would take over from the silent film. The technical and financial barriers to its
widespread adoption seemed insuperable to some. Herbert Brenon was quoted
as saying that it was doomed to failure, John Maxwell of B.I.P. himself as calling
it a costly fad, and as late as May 1929 F. E. Adams rashly pronounced that

'Talkies are merely a temporary craze, like broadcasting and greyhound racing.'[15]

There was a body of opinion that held that sound would have lasting value only
for supporting films, novelties and topicals, and that the silent film would
continue to be the mainstay of the programme. Others, again, considered it
useful only for polemics, educational, political or advertising films. Even in
October 1928 *The Bioscope* technical section felt able to state:

'Thus it may be taken that the silent black and white film will remain the staple
product of the industry while sound, colour and stereoscopy will remain items
of novel appeal.'[16]

This idea persisted and as late as 1930 John Galsworthy, whose play *Escape*
was made into a talkie for A.T.P. by Basil Dean, maintained that there was still
a place for silent drama. Far from the silent film being doomed, there were
many who thought that to persist in the sound craze would kill the film industry
itself. 'The death-knell of the industry will be sounded through the amplifier
of a loud-speaker,' said one member of the industry in 1928. And an errata slip
attached to an attack on sound film in Betts' book *Heraclitus*, published in
1928, read:

'Since the above was written speaking films have been launched as a commercial
proposition, as the general pattern of the film of the future. As a matter of fact,
their acceptance marks the most spectacular act of self-destruction that has yet
come out of Hollywood, and violates the film's proper function at its source.
The soul of the film—its eloquent and vital silence—is destroyed. The film
now returns to the circus whence it came, among the freaks and fat ladies.'[17]

Actions spoke louder than words, silence was golden, films should be seen
and not heard, and in *Close Up* in April 1929 Betts headed his article 'Why
Talkies are Unsound'. But attacks were not confined to amiable puns. Miles
Mander, whose elegant silent film *The First Born* was unfortunately not trade
shown until the middle of the turmoil in 1928, said in October with a tinge of
bitterness:

'No one is going to persuade me that our public is going to tolerate for long an
entertainment which tends to eliminate any artistic merit which the silent
medium may possess.'[18]

Aldous Huxley, the American theatre critic George Jean Nathan, and Seymour

Stern were hostile. Cecil De Mille felt, according to *The Bioscope* in 1928, that talking pictures would tend to sacrifice the great pantomimic appeal of the screen and disillusion the patrons.[19] This was little advance on Denison Clift's position in 1922:

'I do not believe there is a future for "talking pictures" because the spectator can never forget the fact that he is watching photographs of people and not real people.'[20]

It was with some reason that people feared a return to stage actors in photographed versions of stage plays, from which the cinema had taken so long to break away. Theatre lovers, on the other hand, feared the effect it would have on the theatre itself, robbing it of both talent and audiences. There was anxiety about the future of cinema musicians and scorn for canned music. It was realized early that speech could be dubbed into foreign languages but, in view of the technical difficulty of this, it was felt that foreign markets would be lost and the international character of the cinema disappear. This consideration appeared very important to many people at the time. Nicholas Schenck was typical of those who foresaw only a limited future for sound, and said at a press conference in London that it might be useful for music, songs and effects like the roar of a football crowd, but that dialogue could not enhance the silent drama.[21] It was understandable that successful exponents of the silent film should continue to deplore its disappearance. Hal Roach, also, had reason to fear that it would retard comedy by requiring a pause for the laugh following every gag.[22] Harry Lauder, who had been interested in making sound pictures as early as 1920, had wanted sound primarily for his famous songs rather than for dialogue. It was well known that Chaplin took an extreme view. An open letter to him in *The Bioscope* in 1929 read:

'You have just stated, semi-officially, that you will never use dialogue in any film of yours and the decision is one which challenges approval. You say that though sound effects have come to stay you have no use for dialogue. "The art of pantomime is complete."

'Talking, you say, will not heighten illusion, but will destroy it. Films need dialogue about as much as Beethoven's Symphonies need lyrics, and you make a strong argument on art reaching perfection along the route of simplification. Speech, you say, will complicate what has taken years to simplify and you fear the process may set us back ten years.'[23]

On artistic grounds there was good reason to criticize the sound film as it then was, with the disadvantages of immobility, imperfect synchronization, poor dialogue, and actors and directors not yet used to the medium. It was reasonable, too, to regret the diminution of creative participation on the part of the audience. But it was a mistake to treat film itself as synonymous with silent film, and this was a mistake to which the more serious critics were particularly prone.

During the last ten or fifteen years some serious thought had been given to the essential nature of the film, and whereas one school of thought held that the important thing about it was light and movement, another considered that silence was the thing. Luigi Pirandello, it seemed, believed that

'The screen play should remain a wordless art because it is essentially a medium for the expression of the Unconscious.'[24]

At a lecture on *The Stage and the Cinema* Dr Percy Dearmer committed himself to the view that 'there was something about the film which required silence' and the speaker, Anthony Asquith, said

'. . . he hated to commit himself on such a new thing, but felt that the talking film might be a menace to the theatre. He did not think it had much to do with films proper, which expressed themselves in terms of pictures. . . .'[25]

The Russian film makers, not identifying film with silent film as so many others did, had already pointed out that the film's 'peculiar and individual function' was the juxtaposition of shots, rather than either silence or light and shade, and that the exercise of artistic selection lay in the rhythm and content of these juxtaposed shots. Yet many intellectuals, critics, literary people and creative film makers who of all people should have been familiar with this Russian message, had the greatest difficulty in applying it to the new situation and seeing how sound fitted without difficulty into this concept. It was almost as if their recent theorizing about silence had given them a vested interest in it. In Kenneth MacPherson's editorial of November 1927, *Close Up* dismissed sound as useful 'to lend atmosphere, and for a few necessary strident effects' but claimed that it would ruin the silent art and replace it with a stagey hybrid. Dorothy M. Richardson added more cautiously in another of her articles in *Close Up* that she thought the noises so far introduced were harmless and if used with discrimination all would be well, but that if on the contrary noises were used simply because they were now possible, and if more and more were to follow, it would be a 'blind move in a wrong direction, in the direction of the destruction of the essential character of the screenplay'.[26] Rotha, also, was careful:

'The act of recording dialogue is *not* a further resource, as some theorists like to imagine. The dialogue film at its best can only be a poor substitute for the stage. From an aesthetic point of view, sound can only be used to strengthen symbolism and emphasize dramatic action, and experiments on these lines will be successful and justified.'[27]

Ernest Betts, laying down laws and rationalizing things as they already were, was more dogmatic:

'The business of the film is to depict action, not to reproduce sound. It is not that one is opposed to something which is new, for the film itself is new and we would not be without it. But the spoken word, mechanically introduced, is not proper to the film medium, and tends to destroy the illusion which the film is trying to build up. . . . Moreover, it is axiomatic that the less said in a film by way of dialogue or explanation, the better. The immense magnification of people and things on the screen gives them a power which takes the place of speech, and in fact, nearly always results in too much being said. When a thing is larger than life, something must be taken away from it to give it proportion, and in the case of the screen, this thing is speech.'[28]

and later:

'The really anti-talkie argument is that speech attacks the film's peculiar and individual function, which is to imitate life in flowing forms of light and shade to a rhythmic pattern.'[29]

Critics might worry but the public wanted sound films and, therefore, so did the showmen. As might be expected, many theatre people were intrigued by its possibilities, and both the theatre critic Ivor Brown and the playwright Robert E. Sherwood showed interest. The theatrical producer Basil Dean formed Associated Talking Pictures in May 1929 to explore the possibilities. A few practicing film makers had something helpful to say. Carl Laemmle, for example, stressed the need for a new technique of direction, acting and cutting,[30] and Rex Ingram said:

'silent and sound pictures differed in temp and it was, therefore, essential that a film should be made in one or the other form. It was not merely a matter of stripping a sound film of the sound and leaving a silent picture.'[31]

A lyrical article by Pearson in the British Film Number of *The Bioscope* exclaimed:

'We shall bring a new force into cinema. . . . Ecstasy'!

and in his notebooks for 1930 he wrote:

'I think the secret is the thinking first in terms of the old technique . . . and using the new factors ONLY WHERE they supply something one could never entirely secure by the old way.'

He added some thoughts on dialogue, attempting an exact and fine parallel with pictures:

SCREEN DIALOGUE MUST BE FLEXIBLE . . . MOBILE . . . as is the CAMERA.

What one did with the *moving camera*, one *must do* with dialogue now . . . i.e. . . . with *sound*.
. . . PAN sound . . . move the mike *past* sound.
. . . MIX sound . . . run one sound *into* another.

. . . FADE sound . . . let sound *die* to nothing.
. . . IRIS sound . . . eliminate all sounds *but one*.
. . . RUN IN sound . . . let sound *increase* in volume.
. . . CUT sound . . . suddenly end sound . . .*drama*!
. . . C/U sound . . . vary *volume* of sound.
. . . L/S sound . . . ditto
. . . SOFT FOCUS sound . . . *blur* sound.
. . . STAB sound . . . *montage* . . . cross out . . . staccato.
. . . FLASH BACK sound . . . sound heard faintly in a *reminiscent* way.
. . . SYMBOLIC sound . . . not in actual relationship to scene, but by
        way of illustration. (Geese cackling at gossip scene, etc.)

Dogmatic hostility to sound on the part of the cineaste was abruptly silenced by an important joint statement by Eisenstein, Pudovkin and Alexandrov which *Close Up* printed in its issue of October 1928. This, while deploring literal and mechanical applications of sound, suggested its use as counterpoint to visual images.

'The cherished dream of a talking film is realized. . . . We who are working in the U.S.S.R. are fully conscious that our technical resources are not such as to enable us in the near future to achieve a practical success in this direction. For the rest, we judge it not inopportune to enumerate a number of preliminary considerations of a theoretical nature, the more so that, judging from the information that has reached us, attempts are being made to put this new perfection of the cinematographic art to a mistaken use.'

Not inopportune indeed. The manifesto reminded its readers that the characteristic which made the film unique was its shot construction, here translated as 'mounting'. It foresaw a period during which the most commercial films, ' "High cultural dramas" and other photographic performances of a theatrical nature' would be exploited and this construction would be disrupted; parts of the whole would be intensified, exaggerating their independent significance as distinct from the juxtaposition of the pieces, here translated as 'conjunction'.

'Only utilization of sound in counterpoint relation to the piece of visual mounting affords new possibilities of developing and perfecting the mounting.'

This would lead in time to 'the creation of a new *orchestral counterpoint* of sight-images and sound-images'. This was described as a 'natural outlet for the advance guard of cinematographic culture, by which they may escape from a number of seemingly blind alleys'. These blind alleys were the use of titles and elaborate visual reference shots or sequences interpolated into scenes, and were described as follows:

'The film text, and the countless attempts to include it in the scenic composition as a piece of mounting (breaking up of the text into parts, increasing or decreasing of the size of the type, etc.) . . . explanatory items, which overload the scenic composition and retard the tempo.'

After this clear-sighted, workmanlike and original attitude to sound film had been published, 'counterpoint' became the fashionable term and less was heard about the essential nature of silence.

Kenneth MacPherson in *Close Up* wrote of Hitchcock's *Blackmail*:

'I think Mr Hitchcock began to see, and is probably working it out in his mind now, and will use it well in his next film, that sound is not an accessory to lollop clumsily beside a film leashed in a twin harness, but a direct spur and aid to simplification, to economy. Acoustical montage, in short.'

He gave an example:

'You remember Anny Ondra after the murder pacing the streets. You remember her obsession with the flung back, trailing hand, of the murdered artist. At the end of her trudging, when she must have been, incidentally, very exhausted, the sight of a sleeping beggar with outflung, trailing hand, brings forth a scream. There is an immediate cut to the screaming face of the old woman who finds the artist's murdered body.'

He emphasized that sound was not just an accompaniment, 'and, if I may say so, neither do we want it solely as a counterpoint', but an integral part of the construction. In the example of the hand it was an economical way of showing a state of mind, and MacPherson quoted another example, when the father asked Anny Ondra if she was not well:

'A small screaming clang begins, which gets louder and louder, and bursts like a shell. Meanwhile you are watching Anny Ondra's face, very drawn, half stupified. Her father says "another customer". The clang-scream was the shop bell. Phobia has translated it thus to her, meaning psycho-analytically that through that door may come the police.'[32]

'Some of us', as Kenneth Macpherson had written, 'are beginning to say that talkies are an art.'

Meanwhile the commercial interests had never had any doubt about the desirability of the sound film and merely hesitated to commit themselves too quickly to any of the competing systems. Anyone clinging to silent films after the success of *The Singing Fool* was a Clinging Fool, and the industry was to be put on a Sound Basis.

The industry was back in the days of patent rights and interchangeability. But although the various systems might still struggle for survival, sound itself had definitely arrived. As well as the short films made in sound, the topicals and speeches and vaudeville turns and songs, many feature films already conceived and even made as silent films were hastily adapted by the addition of a sound accompaniment, part or whole, music and effects only or dialogue as well. Darlington related in his autobiography how *Alf's Carpet* was being made at Elstree:

'They began by making a silent film, but realizing suddenly that the future lay with talkies, they introduced a sound-track halfway through; so that at about the third reel the sub-titles ceased and the shadows on the screen began to speak, causing an effect as disconcerting as that made by Balaam's ass on an occasion equally unforeseen. Not only that, but as the two alleged funny men in the lead spoke no English their Cockney dialogue was "dubbed" and of course failed completely to synchronize with the movements of their Central European lips.'[33]

Balcon also recalled some Gainsborough films:

'They were half-mute, with the last reel or two suddenly becoming voluble. Peculiar hybrids, they were, but they were saved from the scrap heap and didn't fare badly with audiences.'[34]

Hugh Castle described the sound in *To What Red Hell*, directed by Edwin Greenwood, whom he described as showing 'no reason why he should ever make another picture':

'Nearly all the long-shots are silent picture material, and the "100 per cent dramatic dialogue" consists of close-up cuttings. The delicious way in which a noisy jazz band is synchronized with the inevitable long-shots, only to be completely cut out from talking close-ups of people supposed to be sitting on top of the dancers, is too funny to miss.'[35]

More lasting effects on work in the studio and methods of production began to show themselves at once. The equipment and additional skilled personnel made production more expensive, as did the intensified competition for stars, directors and, in time, orchestras. The camera, which had recently become so mobile, was now enclosed with the cameraman in a heavy soundproof box, so that camera mobility and location work ceased. The extreme sensitivity of the microphone, and the need to place it near the actors' voices, imposed a new rigidity on studio routine and on actors; the constant problem of where to put it, in order to pick up the voices and yet not show in the picture, affected both the size and character of the set and movement within it. There was a natural tendency to group the characters in front of the camera, with the microphone carefully out of sight, and keep them there. The minute-by-minute control the director used to have, with the studio orchestra to create mood, had gone and a new technique was necessary on the studio floor. Like camera movement, cutting had become very fluid by 1928. The more difficult cutting of sound with the picture checked this, and also had important repercussions on censorship (see page 58). Not only did cutting present new technical difficulties, but a new approach to film construction was required. Many isolated shots of significant objects or actions hitherto used for emphasis or reference, in so far as they had been substitutes for sound, were now redundant. A close shot of a person speaking, followed by a title or a shot suggesting the subject of his speech, now appeared absurdly mannered. In time the reaction shot was to provide an opportunity for variety here, but for the time being the change meant a simple reduction in the amount of cutting. Whilst variety of camerawork and editing were thus reduced to a minimum, acting and writing both took a step back towards the theatre. The new demands of elocution and memory made on actors were too much for many film stars and encouraged the use of stage actors; and the need for dialogue led to further specialization in script writing and an even greater resort to stage plays. The result was a vicious circle, for the renewed influence of stage ideas and stage people acted as a barrier to the discovery of new uses for the medium, and the static dialogue play once more became difficult to dislodge. The general effect was to elevate literal realism at the expense of the fluid impressionism which had at last emerged from over thirty years of largely empirical development. The increased expense and elaboration of production was going to circumscribe the film maker even further in future, and a new sort of superman was needed to impose any sort of creative individuality on a film.

Note: The link between Fox, Movietone and Phonofilm referred to on page 203 was through an inventor called Case, who was working along similar lines to De Forest. He joined forces with him for a while before 1925. After this he worked independently on innovations of his own; his system was bought by Fox about 1926, and used under the name of Fox-Case Movietone. As a result of the lawsuit brought by De Forest in the late twenties it was agreed that both groups were entitled to use the system.

CHAPTER SEVEN

Techniques of Film Production

(1) INTRODUCTION

It was widely accepted at the time, and has been so ever since, that few of the films made in England during the twenties were any good. Therefore, it is assumed, there is little to be learnt from studying them. This is difficult in any case since all but some two to three hundred, at most, of the eight or nine hundred feature films made in Britain between 1919 and 1929 were destroyed long ago, as indeed were most films all over the world. The desirability of preserving films or even the fact that they needed any special treatment to prevent physical deterioration (see page 35) was appreciated by few people at this time. Films which lay around in vaults after their commercial life was over, to be found with delight by later generations, did so mostly by accident and form a chance collection of very varied quality.

The history of film technique is usually told as a series of landmarks, with the peaks explained in detail and a general implication that the mass of other films improved as a result of the adoption of discoveries, inventions or revolutions introduced in these outstanding films. The commonplaces of film history in the twenties are the Westerns and the technical efficiency of America, its star system with giants like Douglas Fairbanks, Mary Pickford and Chaplin, and the later films of D. W. Griffith, the vamps and great lovers and the magnetic attraction Hollywood had for Continental stars and directors; the *avant-garde* and experimental films from France, and names like Bunuel, Renoir and Gance; German impressionism in the conception of films, in set design and camera angles, in the slow deliberate acting and soft, diffused lighting, and the names of Murnau, Lang and Pabst; realism, social purpose and constructive editing from Russia, with the pre-eminence of Eisenstein and Pudovkin; and the solitary, imaginative work of Flaherty. It is made to seem that other people simply adopted these inspired developments, and that as British film making contributed none of them there is no point in examining it further.

But the film was a new art form developing under continual scrutiny of civilized man, and as such is worth more than such a superficial look. Although it employed the arts of acting, the two-dimensional image and narrative, all of which had their origins in man's prehistoric past, it was beginning to be realized that film as such contained an element which made it an entirely new medium of artistic expression. The very cementing together of the celluloid images made it an organic combination of other arts, more than a simple sum of the other elements, by virtue of the selection and timing of these shots. This had not been appreciated by anyone when technical invention had first made cinematography possible. Unlike any other art form its primitive stage was still available for study, in fact was hardly over. The actual steps by which the basic techniques of the new medium emerged give us, in fact, a more interesting picture than is implied in the landmark theory. Even in British production they can be seen almost forcing themselves on their practitioners.

At first glance there seems to be little evidence, but when details are pieced together carefully like a jigsaw puzzle they can be surprisingly informative. Some idea of film making in Britain can be drawn from contemporary handbooks, reports, plans and documents and a few surviving film scripts; from reviews, news and comments about British films and film makers made at the time, especially in the trade papers, but also in yearbooks, fan papers, the national press and the few more serious critical magazines, books and articles; from the films which still exist; and from accounts and reflections made later, especially in the autobiographies and reminiscences of film makers and interviews with them or people who knew them.

In building up a picture of British films, the people who made them and how they set about it, common practice and their departures from it, we become more familiar with the problems which arose and the way in which they were solved. Except at first there seems to have been no real shortage in Britain of studios, some of which soon became larger, better equipped and more expensive after the war, although others lagged behind those of other countries in the quality of their equipment and technical skills. Costs of production went up, although slowly in comparison with those in America. The post-war heyday of location shooting died out as it became too expensive and later, with the special design processes, largely unnecessary; and finally with sound production it became, for a time, impossible. There was a growth of specialization of function within the studio, especially of production and direction, which diverged and attracted people of somewhat different types of ability. Screen writing drew heavily on novels and stage plays; and there was still some confusion between the job of providing plot content and that of putting on paper the film maker's working plan of how to visualize this on the screen, the latter still regarded by many as a literary function. Cameras, film stock and printing improved because of engineering and scientific advances abroad, especially in America and Germany; and in the work of the cameraman a greater variety of camera set-up and some camera mobility were significant, although perhaps less so than the new attention paid to lighting and its creative possibilities. Film players in England were still largely stage actors at the same time, but a more subtle style adapted to the silent film appeared as greater fluidity in writing, camerawork and editing diminished the physical and emotional distance between players and spectator. Set design made little progress in Britain owing to the cost of large or elaborately dressed sets but was transformed towards the end of the decade by the adoption of special technical processes from abroad. And editing, long regarded by most people as a combination of literary juggling and film doctoring, slowly developed more significant ways of assembling shots despite the widespread indifference to its true importance.

Exploring the details of run-of-the-mill filming confirms that the landmark theory is an over-simplification, which pays too little regard to the interrelation

between outstanding work by the exceptional innovator and the general development which gradually takes place in any technique in response to its inherent
needs. The same problems in the film medium faced all its exponents. Examination of ordinary film making shows that it is simply not true that genius discovered the way and the less gifted copied it. As in much scientific and technical
progress the same solutions, the logical outcome of the problems themselves,
often seem to have appeared to many people, not all of them equally gifted. The
difference between the genius and the rest lay in the effectiveness with which
he grasped and used the new ideas; and his influence lay in the new understanding
brought to others by his creative originality. The search for 'firsts' is of anti-
quarian interest only, except in so far as it refutes the belief that great developments appear as isolated inventions. As an example, it is absurd and irrelevant
to ascribe to D. W. Griffith the invention of the close-up or even the first use of
it cut into other shots. Certain trick cinematographers and producers much
inferior to him had used it from the earliest days of the cinema, indeed it was
as obvious a part of motion photography as the portrait. Even cutting had been
used by Hepworth as early as 1905. But the exceptional value of Griffith's work
was the effectiveness with which he used these and other basic elements of film
technique, thereby not so much introducing new devices as showing how much
could be done with them. The position of Eisenstein and Pudovkin and their
great contribution, creative editing, was similar. Their understanding of this
fundamental aspect of the film medium and their brilliant use of it illuminated
for other people the significance of the essential fact that a film was a sequence
of shots. Yet in British production during the twenties, before the great Soviet
films were seen or even discussed here, in fact even before they had been made,
film structure was being broken down into more and more shots of various types
and uses, and it is possible to trace the empirical development of a more complex
structure.

This was taking place in the work of people who, for the most part, had little
clear idea of what it meant but found that it solved day-to-day problems of film
story telling. Until the later twenties, with the foundation of the Film Society
and *Close Up* and the appearance of intellectual young film makers and critics,
there were few who showed any conscious interest in developments of film
technique abroad, and many a foreign film later regarded as a classic was just
one more commercial film at the time. Certainly there were few in Britain who
achieved anything outstanding in film making. But despite the scarcity of
exceptional talent the fundamentals of film technique were widely grasped and
used in Britain by the end of the twenties. This gradual progress was about to
receive a set-back in 1929, when the conversion to sound film production
brought about many changes. But in 1929 in the work of the best, here as
elsewhere, the moving picture after thirty years of existence had developed from
a realistic image recorded by a technician into a medium of artistic expression,
however naïve as yet, capable of communicating the personal vision of an artist.
In this chapter let us consider work in the British studios and some details of
production and direction, writing, design, camerawork, acting and editing, with
short sections on colour and animated films, a word about the cost of production

and finally about the making of actuality films. It may be that greater detail will explain why the achievement of the British film in the twenties was not more impressive than it was.

(2) THE STUDIOS

After the war of 1914–18 there were some 87,000 square feet of studio floor space available in Britain in twenty-three chief studios. Most were still partly daylight studios of glass with only auxiliary lighting, a handicap in a country with so little sunshine. They were of the primitive pre-war type, mostly conversions, and owing to the building restrictions few were expanded or improved immediately.

The largest was St Margarets, Twickenham, which had one large stage of 12,375 square feet and a small lot. It had been converted from a skating rink before the war by the London Film Company and had been a daylight studio until it was blacked out in 1916. The laboratories were burnt in 1918. It was taken over by Alliance from 1921 to 1924, used later by various homeless companies such as Astra–National, and then taken over by Hagen and Henry Edwards. The second in size was the early B. & C. studio at Hoe Street, Walthamstow, which had a partly glass stage of 9,000 square feet and had previously been a skating rink, and later was also used by Astra–National. The third in size was Welsh–Pearson's studio at Craven Park, Harlesden, which was converted from a school in 1918 and remained in their hands until it was closed in 1926. It had a large dark stage of 6,000 square feet and a lot, a carpenter's shop, scenic artists' dock, developing rooms, editing cubicles, projection theatre and its own electrical supply; the permanent staff consisted of two carpenters, two electricians, two scene painters, two handymen, a prop man, a cameraman, Pearson and his assistant, and a small orchestra.

There were five smaller studios of about 5,000 square feet each. The Catford studio at The Hall, Bromley Road, was used by Broadwest until they moved to Kew Bridge in 1922. This was an old daylight studio built on to a large house before the war when this way of using a mansion with its buildings and grounds as studio, processing and administrative departments and lot was the latest fashion. Barker's early studio at Ealing Green was similar in size and type, with three glass stages, a mansion and grounds. When Barker retired from production after the war it was used by Fred Paul, and in 1920 it was bought by General Film Renters who hoped to modernize it and let it out for hire, but soon went out of business. Various fringe and shorts producers such as Dallas Cairns, Beehive and later Widgey Newman used it during the twenties. In 1929 it was bought by Union Studios, equipped for R.C.A. sound, and later bought by Associated Talking Pictures with Basil Dean and Gerald du Maurier on the board. They finally put up another studio at the same site. Worton Hall, Kew Bridge, and Wood Street, Walthamstow, were also just over 5,000 square feet each. Worton Hall, Isleworth, consisted of two daylight stages in the large grounds of a mansion and had been converted by G. B. Samuelson before the war, and used by him until about 1921. After that it was hired out for the Malins–Sabatini films, among others, and sold in 1928 to British Screen Productions for £19,000 to be used for films by G. A. Cooper, Hugh Croise and Frank Miller. Princes Studio on the North side of Kew Bridge had one dark stage in a converted theatre which was later converted back, and was used during the early twenties by Lucky Cat, Lucoque and Walter West. 245 Wood Street, Walthamstow, was an early example of the specially built daylight studio, and was used during and after the war by Broadwest at the same time as the studios at Catford and Esher, and later was sold in 1926 to British Filmcraft for shorts production by Banfield.

Slightly smaller were the old Clarendon–Harma studios with two specially built daylight stages and lot at 16 Limes Road, Croydon, and a dark stage built after the war by Bertram Phillips in the grounds of a mansion at Thornton House, Clapham Park. Both studios fell into disuse. The Gaumont studio at Lime Grove, Shepherd's Bush, on the other hand, although it began life before the war as a daylight studio of only 3,600 square feet with no lot, flourished and was extensively altered in 1926 at a reputed cost of £25,000. It became the well-equipped G.B.P.C. studios in which, after 1928, the Gainsborough pictures were made.

There were some dozen other studios but they were comparatively small, from 1,300 to 2,400 square feet, and even included a converted boat builder's shed at Eel Pie Island, Twickenham, which was only a 750 square foot part-glass studio, used by Hagen and Double. The B.A.F.C. used a tiny pre-war daylight studio of 1,350 square feet in a mansion grounds at Bushey until the Alliance failure of 1921. After a period of hiring, this was bought by Randal Terraneau and G. Humphries in March 1927. Bertram Phillips, and later Quality Film Plays and G. A. Cooper's Screenplays, used a dark stage with no lot in converted railway arches at Cranmer Court, Clapham, until about 1923. A glass stage at Wadden New Road, Croydon, was converted to a garage in 1923 after being used for a while by Gaiety. A warehouse made a long, unusually shaped part-daylight studio in Ebury Street, London, for George Clark productions before the new Beaconsfield studio was ready in May 1922. A small glass stage specially built before the war in Portsmouth Road, Esher, was used at first by Broadwest and later by other producers. The old pre-war Neptune studio, a specially built dark stage of just over 2,000 square feet with a lot at Boreham Wood, Elstree, was owned by Ideal and used by them, by the first British Lion company and then by British Instructional before they moved to Surbiton, and was bought by Ludwig Blattner in 1927–28 for Phototone sound productions. The I. B. Davidson dark stage at 588 Lea Bridge Road, Leyton, was an early conversion of a horse-tram shed and was used by A. E. Coleby until about 1924. Regent House, Park Road, Surbiton, had a dark stage in another converted mansion, with grounds, and was Stoll's first studio in 1918; it continued to be used by Stoll until about 1923, and then by British Instructional. Weir House, Teddington, had a daylight stage in a converted mansion and was used by Master, H. B. Parkinson and Artistic. Even the well-known pre-war Hepworth studio at Hurst Grove, Walton-on-Thames, was quite small, being just over 2,000 square feet with two daylight studios and lot, and despite plans for a much improved and expanded establishment at Weybridge it was used until Hepworth's failure in 1924, and then bought by Archibald Nettlefold. Woodlands, Whetstone, had a small daylight studio and lot in a mansion grounds dating from before the war and was used for a while after the war by British Famous Films.

During the twenties some 200,000 square feet of new floor space was built or planned. Some 54,800 square feet of the old studios went out of use, but the potential floor space at the end of 1929 was considerable, although not all of it was in current use or even finished.* Early studios which continued in existence included Bushey, Ealing, Elstree (Neptune), Isleworth, Shepherd's Bush, Twickenham and Walton. The new ones were those at Beaconsfield, Cricklewood, three at Elstree (Imperial, Whitehall and B.I.P.), Islington, Southall, Welwyn and Wembley Park.

The studio at Beaconsfield was built by George Clark Productions to enable them to move out of Ebury Street and the London fog. It had one dark stage of 7,200 square feet and was opened for a few films in May 1922, after which it was derelict until bought by the second British Lion company for £52,785 in 1929,[1] A very big studio was opened by Stoll in 1919 to allow them to expand from their Surbiton base. This was a conversion of the Nieuport aeroplane works at Cricklewood. It had one L-shaped shooting stage of 20,000 square feet and two smaller ones totalling another 8,000 square feet, no grounds for a lot, but good equipment and an automatic developing plant. It was also let to other producers, and was expanded by another 9,000 square feet in 1927. The Islington studios, converted from a Metropolitan Railway power station in Poole Street in 1919 by Famous Players' British team on a lavish American scale were large by British standards just after the war, with their two dark stages totalling 13,000 square feet, and were taken over for £14,000 in 1924 by Balcon and his associates. Three new studios were built at Elstree, Imperial Studios built by Wilcox for his British and Dominion company in 1927 opposite the old Neptune studio; Adelqui Millar's Whitehall studios built near Elstree station in 1927 at a prospectus cost of £21,000 with another £14,000 for equipment; and the largest British studio, B.I.P., which was started at Elstree by British National in 1925 and taken over for £100,000 by B.I.P., was opened for filming in the autumn of 1927. This very large studio was to have two dark stages each of 30,000 square feet, a 40-acre lot, and lavish modern equipment and departments. An aeroplane hangar at Gladstone Road, Southall, was turned into one dark stage of 7,500 square feet by G. B. Samuelson about 1924. A small studio for De Forest Phonofilms was established at the site of the Wembley Exhibition by British Talking Pictures, but was burnt down in October 1929. A very big new studio only just coming into use at the end of the period was the British Instructional studio at Welwyn, which was built at a cost of £60,000 with one dark stage of 36,000 square feet.

Thus the new studios of the twenties were far larger than the old, but like them were concentrated around London. A few efforts were made to establish

* The Federation of British Industries figures for 1928 of nineteen stages and 105, 211 square feet presumably did not include those not actually in operation.

studios in other parts of the country. Right after the war the way for provincial production seemed open, and a hangar in Kingsbury, Hertfordshire, hangars and aerodrome buildings in St Anne's-on-Sea near Blackpool, and a drill-hall near Paignton in Devon were hopefully converted by Zodiac Comedies (Walter Forde), the Parkstone Film Company and the Torquay and Paignton Photoplay Company respectively. Hardly any production resulted from these companies, or from the Lancashire Film Studios which were founded at Rusholme, Manchester, in about 1921. Only little more successful was the mansion-type studio established by Raleigh–King Productions at Watcombe Hall, Babbacombe, Torquay, after the war. This had two small daylight stages built in the grounds and was intended for use by Dallas Cairns, who was making films at Ealing. By the time the studio was ready the company was in financial difficulties. The only provincial firm that was at all successful was the Progress Film Company at Shoreham-by-Sea, Sussex. Their studio was built before the war and was used by Sidney Morgan, who bought it after the war. It had a small output of feature films from the small daylight stage until it was burnt down in 1922.

The elaboration of work and lavish expenditure in these studios became so marked during the twenties that by 1928 Betts wrote in *Heraclitus*:

'Instead of asking: How can we most simply and faithfully and economically interpret such-and-such a theme? we ask: In how rich, costly, hair-raising, eye-watering and conventional a manner can this thing be done? Can we add to the list of directors, assistant directors, title-writers, camera-men, art directors, continuity men, publicity men, and even authors, whose totally uninteresting names flash on the screen as a preliminary to all "programme" or "feature" films, and from whose multiple authorship some sort of unity is supposed to emerge? Can we present a greater Flood than the original Flood, with more water and larger arks: a mightier fall of Rome, a more "miserable" version of *Les Miserables*? and the answer is always that we can.'[2]

Naturally the cost of all this had risen a great deal during the decade. *The Bioscope* remarked in 1928 that a fuse at Elstree from, say 11.30 a.m. to 2 p.m., might cost the company £300 to £400.[3] And in 1929 Arrar Jackson said that delays in production might cost the studio £500 a day.[4] A note on a K.M.A. scale of pay for a forty-hour week for some of the studio technicians in 1920 gives some indication of pay rates at the beginning of the period. Suggested rates ranged from £1 10s for secondary perforator minders, considered a suitable post for female labour, frame winders and secondary positive film joiners to £6 for judgement developers for negatives; other rates were £4 10s for negative film editors and assemblers, £5 5s for studio carpenters, £5 5s for scenic artists and modellers and £5 10s for electricians.[5]

Films took longer to produce. An inferior film like Ideal's *The Chinese Puzzle* was completed in eighteen days in 1919. Next year Kellino's *The Fordington Twins* took five weeks and, since some of the large cast were on the stage, required careful scheduling. *The Breed of the Treshams* in the same year took five weeks, with the expensive star Sir John Martin Harvey working for only three of them, whereas Samuelson's *All The Winners* took as long as nine weeks, possibly because much of it was shot on location. Companies with a studio and organization of their own were less pressed for time than people hiring studios and staff for short periods. Pearson was a producer who was reputed to take things more slowly, aiming at approximately four minutes of film in the can a day at the beginning of the twenties, according to his autobiography, against Kellino's record of ten. Even so an important film like *Nothing Else Matters* took only four weeks to film in 1920. But six years later *The Little People* took five weeks to shoot and another four to edit and title, although this was unusual.[6] Henry Edward's *Owd Bob* in 1924 took as long as eight weeks since much of it was shot on location in the Lake District, and location could and often did take longer than studio work.

It was normal now, moreover, to shoot a good deal of cover. English companies such as Stoll, Ideal and Gaumont had the reputation of being mean over this. Jeffrey Bernerd of Stoll took trouble to deny this in *Stoll's Editorial News* on the grounds that Plaisetty had taken 32,000 feet of negative in 1920 for *The Yellow Claw*, a six-reel film.[7] This extravaganza was scripted by Gerard Fort Buckle, as was *The Nighthawk*, a film which was never released but which, according to its producer, had consumed ten miles of negative.[8] Despite such flights L'Estrange Fawcett seems to have been exaggerating when he claimed in 1927:

'As much as 400,000 feet of negative, 200,000 from each of two cameras, may be shot to secure a final film 6,000 feet long.'[9]

In the case of *The Prodigal Son*, for which A. E. Coleby went to Iceland in 1922, no less than seventeen reels were actually used in the finished film.

After the war it was possible to get abroad again, and this was the golden age of location, enjoyed by many a lucky film unit. There were none of the special processes which later overcame the limitations in size and realism of studio sets so that the variety, beauty or realism of natural locations, and especially the better weather in other countries, encouraged travelling both here and abroad.

Louis Mercanton, who had worked in the theatre under Sir Herbert Tree but had a natural feeling for films, had unusual views about realism in production:

' "We are beginning to realize," Mr Mercanton told a *Bioscope* representative, "that the nearer we get to real life in making screen plays, the more convincing our results will be. . . . The logical consequence is, in my opinion, to dispense altogether with imitation settings and stage the action outside the studio amid scenes of real life.

"The 'mobile studio' which I am using in developing this policy consists, at present, of four motor lorries and two trailers, carrying a generating set (capable of developing 12,000 amps) and eighty lamps of all types, including a Sunlight arc. . . .

"So far as possible, I use real types for all smaller rôles. . . . Hitherto, my technical staff has consisted of two cameramen, five electricians, and an odd-job man . . . in six years time practically every important feature will be made entirely in 'real' interiors and exteriors." '[10]

But such developments were to take much longer than he expected. Meanwhile location finding and managing had become a special post. It included not only finding the right setting, but consideration of the light, architectural problems and transport. Home locations were many, and Pearson tells in his book of the shifts to which enterprising units might resort in their efforts to film the locations they wanted in a world that was frequently unco-operative. An Underground station was used in the middle of the night for scenes in Calvert's *Walls of Prejudice* of 1920. A *Kipps* unit, also in 1920, invaded the Savoy Restaurant, armed with arcs and spotlights and accompanied by H. G. Wells, who somewhat dryly

'. . . expressed delight in the portrayal of the personality of his creation. He never dreamed, he said, when he laid his little egg of a book, that it would hatch out anything so absolutely splendid.'[11]

Rob Roy was partly shot in the Trossachs, *Squibs Wins the Calcutta Sweep* in Piccadilly and Paris, *Wee McGregor's Sweetheart* in Scotland, *The Virgin Queen* at Beaulieu Abbey; *A Sporting Double* included scenes from a real Cup Final and the Derby, and *Don Quixote* was partly shot in the Lake District, which doubled for Spain. *Bonnie Prince Charlie* included a battle with 12,000 extras which was shot at Culloden. *The Passionate Adventure* had a post-war welcome home staged at Waterloo Station and contrasting, incidentally, with Brunel's economical use of actuality shots of armistic rejoicings in the London streets for *Blighty* several years later. And for the seaside resort scenes of *Hindle Wakes* in 1926 Elvey and his cameraman Basil Emmott filmed the Tower Ballroom at Blackpool with six Sunlight arcs, 20 to 30 spot lights and several mercury vapour lamps, and installed the camera in scenic railways and flying boats for the pleasure beach sequence.[12] By now the new special processes were making for greater flexibility in studio sets and the disadvantages of location work had come to the fore. In Honri's words:

'One can sympathize with the sensitive and mathematically minded F. Martin Thornton trying to cope with African desert scenes for *The River of Stars* in a gravel pit at Godstone; Australian bush scenes for *The Lamp in the Desert* on Berkhampstead Common or all-studio sets for the Canadian backwoods scenes in *The Little Brother of God*. But a cheeseparing policy as regards location had been the natural sequel of two Renee Plaisetty films made most expensively in North Africa: *The Broken Road* and *The Four Feathers*. The huge cost of these films virtually put an end to foreign locations, so far as Stoll was concerned.'[13]

Foreign locations were even more lavish than home ones and also more enjoyable, avoiding the grey skies and chill winds. Immediately after the war

Splendid Folly was shot at Capri; *The City of Beautiful Nonsense, Carnival* and *The Man Without Desire* were all partly filmed in Venice; *The Joyous Adventures of Aristide Pujol* in Paris; *The Black Spider, At The Villa Rose* and *The Persistent Lovers* at Nice; *Pillars of Society* went to Norway; *The Silver Bridge* to Switzerland and Italy; and *The Four Feathers* and *The Broken Road* were shot at great length in Algiers. At first location units had to pay import tax on all film material shot abroad. So little was the process of film editing understood at the time that in 1919 when A. E. Newbould tried in Parliament to get this import tax removed from footage shot by British film units, Mr Chamberlain suggested that material not to be used in the final film would avoid the tax if discarded in bond. But the *Kine Year Book* of 1923 was able to report:

'. . . but now the British producer has obtained considerable relief in this respect, as regulations have been framed by the Customs authorities permitting import into this country by payment of only one-third of a penny per foot, as against fivepence per foot, on negative film exposed by a British producing unit.'[14]

In the 1923 Finance Act this was changed to include not only films in which producer and all artists were British but those in which up to 25 per cent of the artists were foreign.[15]

Meanwhile a more international form of production had also appeared. G. B. Samuelson took a company to America in 1920 to make six films in a Californian studio. Interiors for Brunel's *The Man Without Desire* were shot in a Berlin studio and many location companies did some of their studio work in Nice. George Dewhurst, also, worked in a German studio about the same time as Brunel, and the exchange rates and excellent technical facilities encouraged a good deal of Anglo-German production in the middle of the twenties, including Samuelson's disastrous *She* in 1925 and Wilcox's *Chu Chin Chow* and *Decameron Nights*. Balcon, however, was the first producer to favour Anglo-German production as a regular procedure for films other than these spectacular productions involving enormous sets.

The elaboration of work in the studio produced the complicated structure to be found in the studios of the late twenties almost as soon as the war was over. At this early date the shortcomings of most British studios were that they were small, poorly equipped and meanly run, rather than that they lacked any of the necessary departments. Further progress during the twenties was largely a question of improving the facilities and learning to use them, rather than of greater elaboration. The arrival of sound film at the end of the decade did, of course, bring changes. But the British studio was already a very complex organization by 1920.

For although according to Boughey the studio in 1921 was still a 'large and lofty structure of glazed glass' [*sic*] with adjustable awnings and perhaps one end covered in, he already spoke of dark rooms, drying rooms, printing, chemical labs, scenery lofts, scene-painting studios, props departments, carpenters' rooms, dressing rooms, engine rooms, and grounds. Macbean, also, although he still classified studios in 1922 as daylight, mixed or dark, spoke of a desirable studio

John Stuart and Estelle Brody in Elvey's *Mademoiselle from Armentières*, 1926, with sets by A. Mazzci.

Top Left: Betty Balfour
Pearson's *Blinkeyes,* 1926.

Centre Left: Pearson on the
of *Reveille,* 1924, with Ste
Rome (centre), Betty Ba
and Frank Stanmore sitting,
Ralph Forbes and Walter
Tennyson.

Bottom Left: Anson Dyer's
toon for Hepworth, *Little*
Riding Hood.

size of at least 50 by 80 to 100 square feet, and listed scenery docks, paint and carpenters' shops, property rooms, dressing rooms and 'buffet and green rooms' and a photographic department with rooms for perforating film, loading cameras, developing, washing, printing, tinting, drying, cutting and editing. He spoke of general clerical work, scenario editing and literary work, producers' preparations, art direction and drafting, accountancy and costing, and projecting of the completed film. He pointed out how an expert scenario writer could put the story in the right form for costing and making the shooting plan. He described how things were shot out of sequence to use the sets to advantage and how it was for the producer [sic] to explain each shot to the actors; he must be free to concentrate on the acting, and the cameraman

. . . will instruct the studio electrician in placing the lamps in the position necessary to give the best illumination or afford the best lighting effects. Throughout the whole production it is essential that he should work in complete harmony and hand-in-hand with the producer.'[16]

The description of the new Stoll studio at Cricklewood[17] in 1920 under Jeffrey Bernerd and studio manager Sam Hardy also gives a picture of some complexity:

'There are two very large buildings, which adjoin. One of these is to be used as the studio, and the other will contain the factory plant, the producers' quarters, dressing rooms, restaurants, kitchen, developing and printing plant, safes, green-room, and all the other departments necessary for the equipment of modern picture making. . . . In this building there are five sets of apartments for producers, each of which consists of a producer's room . . . a typist's room . . . a projection room . . . a camera room, and a loading room.'

There were twelve dressing rooms and two stars' rooms; wardrobe departments, dressmaking and tailoring shops; general stores, factory stores, and safes for the negatives; there was a despatch department and a projection theatre, laboratories, negative development and printing rooms, and positive printing room; washing, tinting and toning department; and joining, drying and perforating rooms.

'The printing machines are De Brie Automatic, and an automatic developing plant is also being installed. . . . The big floor . . . is probably capable of accommodating the largest interior set likely to be necessary. Even then there would be room, in the remainder of the floor space available, for at least half a dozen ordinary sets, and there is actually room for the five producers, for whom quarters are provided on the "ground floor" to work simultaneously.'

There were large generators, and other departments including the title room, the stills photographic department, chemical mixing shop and property stores, offices, property shops, carpenters' shops and paint shops. The electrical equipment included such studio lighting from Lasky in America as 30 banks of

Cooper–Hewitt mercury vapour lamps, 4 Sunlight arcs, 24 Wohl broadsides, 14 Wohl duplex top-lights, 14 Wohl tilts, Kleigl spotlights and semi-indirect Wohl top-lights.

Amidst all this organization the function of the production head in obtaining finance, planning the use of facilities and assembling the unit was diverging from that of the director, who was responsible for the actual direction of actors and technicians. This distinction between the two spheres became clearer as the twenties proceeded. All the modern functions were emerging *ad hoc*, pushed forward by the pressure of experience. The director, still often called the producer, and the cameraman were the first whose creative importance became clear. That of the writer, the designer and the editor, and the share each of them had in the ultimate conception of the film, clarified more slowly. Meanwhile the functions, selection and training of the personnel in this fast-developing industry were haphazard. In this country it was too small for training schemes, and even training on the job was difficult to obtain. It was decided in October 1928 to start a British branch of the Society of Motion Picture Engineers for all workers connected with the film business, but even this hardly touched selection and training for the industry. Some Federation of British Industry Manufacturing Group proposals in 1927, designed to meet the greater need for British technicians expected after the quota, suggested combined action for training. It was suggested that the F.B.I. should approach the University Appointments Boards to arrange apprenticeships for directing, writing and editing; they were to approach a 'centre of dramatic instruction' for a special course for film acting, and various London institutions for training in photography and optical work.[18]

Unfortunately, entrance into the industry and training continued to be left to chance, and attention was focused instead on a supposed shortage of studio accommodation. The belief that there were not enough studio stages in England and a wistful but, in view of the weather, unrealistic search for a British Hollywood were persistent refrains in any consideration of the problems of British production. The head of an American firm in 1921 was even said to be hoping to found a British Los Angeles at Bournemouth. Some way to achieve the economies of large-scale production in a country with a small home market was sought every now and then, but the discussion usually turned on the sharing of studios rather than on training schemes or the provision of production finance.

In November 1925 an optimistic report prepared by E. Beddington Behrens and strongly supported by Welsh and Pearson was privately printed, entitled *A Project For Establishing National Film Studios*. Behrens, a wealthy finanncier with no personal experience of film production, had a 150-acre site at Brighton in mind for a studio company with 59,000 square feet of floor in four stages for hire, with electrical, chemical and design departments. The company 'would be responsible for building sets, supplying labour and material; in fact, everything short of actual production'. There would be about half a dozen trained staff 'in charge of electrical equipment, miniatures, the chemical laboratory for development, and a designer at the head of the scenic department'. It was expected that technical competence would be acquired by working with the foreign production companies who would hire the studio, although as the aim of the scheme was to build up the home industry it was perhaps naïve to expect French, German and American producers to co-operate. Behrens estimated that £200,000 capital was necessary, including £80,000 for building and £40,000 for electrical installation and equipment, and hoped to get £50,000 of government money under the Trade Facilities Act.

Early in 1927 an immediate result of the reference to the quota in the King's Speech was the announcement of a million-pound scheme to use the Palace of Engineering from the Wembley Exhibition as a British Hollywood. British Incorporated Pictures, registered in March 1927 as a private £100 company, was the result of months of planning by Ralph J. Pugh and his backer Rupert Mason, a Lancashire businessman. Illustrious names from the arts which were bandied about in connection with the plan included Oscar Ashe, Edmund Dulac, Galsworthy, Arnold Bennett, Eden Phillpotts, Hall Caine, Conan Doyle, Sabatini, Gordon Craig, Gerald du Maurier, Sybil Thorndike, Phyllis Neilson-Terry, Frank Brangwyn and Karsavina. Wembley Central Film Studios eventually acquired thirty-five acres for £147,500, with 277,200 square feet of potential floor space, but the backing fell through and a year later the Wembley property had been sold to an exhibitor who intended to form a studio for hire on somewhat less grandiose lines, called Wembley National Studios.[19]

The need for studio accommodation became a popular theme during quota negotiations. At a dinner at the Mayfair Hotel in June 1927 Thomas Welsh addressed members of the C.E.A. and K.R.S. on the need for a Central Film Studio. Pugh continued to advocate his idea of using the Wembley Exhibition grounds as a studio. At the same time the F.B.I. accompanied their proposals for training with suggestions for establishing an F.B.I. Clearing House for the hiring of supporting technical staff and sets. With the approach of sound in 1929 yet another large scheme was proposed. A couple of articles describing J. D. Williams's scheme for a huge twenty-stage studio near Elstree appeared in the summer of 1929.[20] A British film, with British director and leading players, would be filmed; before the sets were struck they would be used again by units of other nationalities shooting the same story. He estimated that 'for an increased cost of not more than 20 per cent on the English version, all the foreign versions will be made on the same scale and with the same excellence as the first one'. From the later article it appeared that each unit was to come to England in turn, so the re-use of sets before they were struck would imply a very large use of floor space. Such a system would discourage dialogue sequences and put a premium on crowd or other scenes which fitted all versions. Even so, Williams's claim that it would reduce the cost of talking pictures by 30 to 40 per cent seemed optimistic.

All these schemes ignored the importance of talent and professional training. Rotha complained of this widespread belief that all Britain needed was a studio city. He not only maintained that there was already sufficient studio space, but also vigorously defended the technical resources of Elstree, Welwyn, Islington and Walthamstow. The fact was that too much attention had been directed to the improvement of studios and equipment during the twenties, and too little to the people who were to use them.

(3) PRODUCTION AND DIRECTION

The producer's early task of directing all departments split during the twenties into two parts, production and direction. The terms producer and director were still used interchangeably in England from time to time throughout the decade. But the distinction was clear in America by the early twenties, and was gradually established in England also as the financial and administrative functions of production on the one hand and artistic direction on the other diverged and became more complex. A purely business head like that of Sir Oswald Stoll, who left the conduct of the studio to Jeffry Bernerd, was at first usually described as a managing director rather than as a producer. The first open acknowledgement that there were two functions involved in production appeared when a film was said to have been produced by one person, and the production 'supervised' by another. The job of studio manager, also, grew up to take over the detailed execution of administrative work, and both Boughey in 1921 and Speer in 1920 refer to his importance in the permanent studio companies. MacBean also mentions both the continuity girl and the producer's assistant, whom she helped:

'. . . with the help of a junior assistant (frequently and advantageously feminine), making notes of all details and artiste's dress, mode of entry, and description of sets for future reference when carrying out the connecting scenes.'[21]

In 1921 Boughey described the director, still often called the producer, as a commander-in-chief 'whose power rests far more on tact than on force':

'The director must be a man of very considerable experience, talent for organization, knowledge of human nature—especially semi-neurotic feminine human nature—critic of acting, artistic yet businesslike, and possess alongside a super-abundant vitality the god-given power to command without becoming a mere bully. To this list of talents and virtues many others, such as patience, quickness of perception, memory, creative ability, resource, and strong willpower might well be added. . . .'[22]

The work of this superman, according to Boughey, consists of choosing the scenario, staff, actors and actresses, co-ordinating their work, watching and approving rehearsals and set-building and choosing locations; on the set he 'exhorts, beseeches and inspires the actors, moves crowds of supers', directs the lighting, the cameras and the orchestra.

It was hardly surprising if the director developed into something of a personality to establish his position. Of Denison Clift, for example, it was said that he was 'an intensely vital man, he sizzles with efficiency'.[23] Frank Fowell painted an unattractive picture of one type of director:

'There is a certain type of producer who seems unable to avoid playing to the gallery of the studio staff. The cheap jest, the little semi-audible sneer followed by a Columbus-like gaze round the floor are part of his stock-in-trade. He will roar at the electricians, scream at the scene-shifters, howl if the camera man inadvertently "runs out", and proclaim his surprise that the Almighty has condemned him to work with such a crew of misbegotten cokeheads. When the "take" is over he becomes human again, pats the messenger-boy on the back and threatens to kiss the scrubber who brings him his tea. An electrician once said confidentially of one of this type, "You see, I daren't drop a spanner on him from the grid, I might hit the camera!" '[24]

Leading British film makers of the time like Hepworth and Pearson were of a gentler disposition and the many hacks in the industry could hardly afford such airs. Two of the more flamboyant personalities, G. B. Samuelson and Walter West, were among the first to recognize the separation of functions and readily handed over much of the more creative work on the studio floor to assistants, gradually confining themselves to supervision and the arrangement of finance and studio facilities. Hepworth also, although keenly aware of the film as an art form, and retaining tight control over stories, photography and his studio staff and stock company, seems to have had no objection to leaving much of the direction to juniors under his own supervision or, indeed, to leaving nearly half the output of his studios in the intensely creative hands of Henry Edwards, whose films were of a completely different character. Hepworth's personality, sensitive but somewhat austere, seems to have lacked an element of warmth and persuasive zeal helpful on the studio floor, and his views on the director's relation to the actors and editing (see pages 115–117) suggest the attitude of a producer rather than that of a director. Pearson, on the other hand, was able from the beginning to leave administrative matters to his business partner Tommy Welsh and concentrate on the film, showing a sympathetic and enthusiastic nature which encouraged and responded to talent and ideas in others.

The capacity to inspire was also, however, one of the attributes of a certain type of producer. As the old guard of producer-director withdrew between 1923 and 1925 the producer who arranged for others to make pictures took over. Michael Balcon was an early and outstanding example, who made possible the early work of Graham Cutts and later Hitchcock, besides that of many other directors, cameramen, designers, writers and editors. The new generation of directors, with a few exceptions like Wilcox, were not concerned with production at all. Maurice Elvey, who had been making films since before the war, achieved a marked improvement after the formation of a production team with Gareth Gundrey and Victor Saville in the mid-twenties left him free to concentrate on direction. Bruce Woolfe was another creative producer, contributing ideas as well as organization after he had established British Instructional as an important concern with a number of directors, and like Balcon he was a producer who found and nurtured new talent. Nettlefold, who had bought Hepworth's studio, proved to be a business head only. And John Maxwell was perhaps the nearest British approach to the high-powered Hollywood producer, providing production opportunities on such a scale that the director's individual style was not always able to survive.

To impose any individual style at all on the complicated and expensive film production machine of the late twenties, indeed, began to pose a problem, and there was considerable doubt as to how the film's existence as a creative art could be reconciled with increasingly factory-like methods of production. L'Estrange Fawcett wrote in 1927 of 'the committee producing scheme', and Betts wrote of the 'complex incubation in the studio of the film', and:

'Oh, the gregariousness, the popularity, the "all-togetherness" of the film business! How on earth has the creature journeyed so far and so featly at times, with its thousand drivers and sky-high baggage?'[25]

It was generally accepted that creative responsibility rested with the director, but there was a good deal of pretentiousness about this and few directors were known outside the trade apart from a small number of foreign celebrities. Rotha was to put in a strong plea for the director:

'Rare indeed is it to meet with an intelligent and sympathetic film producer; frequent indeed is it to meet upstart producers who make illegitimate claim to a knowledge of the film, riding roughshod over the conceptions of the director. If a film is to be a unity, clear-cut and single-minded, the director alone must preconceive it and communicate its content to the audience through groups of interpreters of his vision, under his supreme command. The construction of a film from the first conception to the final product must be under the absolute control of the director.'[26]

But to whom, if anybody, could this apply? It is a long way from a man with a camera selecting, filming and editing his own actuality material to even the creation of a factual film like *Drifters*, let alone a fiction film contrived with lights, sets, players and editors on the B.I.P. scale. To an ever increasing extent the director's capacity to express his own vision depended not only on how he visualized the finished film, but how far he was able to persuade or compel others to do what he wanted.

The film was in fact the work of a team and it was becoming increasingly difficult to locate the dominant creative influence. The extent of each person's imaginative contribution varied between individuals and studios. The director might conceive the original, or he might write it or share the writing, he might or might not edit it or influence the editing, or the editing might be more or less implicit in the film shot, or even in the script; he might have a greater or lesser share in the design and the types of lighting and camera angle. The reactions between people working on the same film played their part, and partnerships between two or more members of a team might generate creative ideas quite different to those of either individual alone. Clearly a certain type of producer, also, acted as a creative influence and cannot be dismissed from the process because he was not working on the studio floor.

Hitchcock and Asquith were outstanding among British directors of the twenties, but others also managed to achieve some sort of creative individuality.

Pearson, Henry Edwards, Graham Cutts, Walter Summers and Geoffrey Barkas, and more briefly Guy Newall and Miles Mander, all made films which had hopeful signs of a personal view. But as a general rule British directors lacked the support, financial and personal, necessary to overcome the deadening influence of the entrenched professional writers, designers, editors and cameramen, all possessing expertise but no imagination or interest in new ideas.

(4) WRITING

Film writing was a field particularly subject to the mediocre professional. The amateur photoplay submitted from outside the industry became a thing of the past during the early twenties, as did the popular handbook on how to write for the screen. By 1929, in America at any rate, the business had become highly organized, with a team of readers, adapters, continuity writers, gag men and title writers as well as the scenario editor and his assistants. *Close Up* in September 1929 claimed that solo scenario writing had disappeared a decade before.

All that Boughey[27] demanded of the scenario editor in 1921 was a rudimentary idea of how the camera was used to record a drama. He must read manuscripts, convert novels, alter them by adding or eliminating; he must know the technical possibilities of the studio and the type of parts suited to the various stars, and

'. . . must know what is novel in humorous situations, what is "good-form", non-libellous, technically correct, copyright and must himself be something of an author and playwright.'

Dealing with the mechanics of scenario writing Boughey was, after all, simply describing current practices. He defined the scenario as an 'elaboration of a plot or theme written in such a manner as to be the foundation of a photoplay'. He described the form liked by the studios of the time, with a cast plot, a synopsis, and a scene plot. He explained that scripts must be broken down into 'sets of instructions for the guidance of the different departments', or in other words production charts for lighting, sets, locations and actors. Above all, he emphasized the unsatisfied demand for good scripts.

Colden Lore's account of scenario work in 1923[28] goes into greater detail:

'. . . the story of a good Photoplay should, first of all, have a compelling central theme. The dramatic situations and incidents composing its plot should dovetail into each other and increase in marked stages in intensity up to the last crisis—the climax. They should be plausible, and contribute directly to the development of the plot. They should reveal the motives of the characters, and be portrayable by the manifestations of emotions. The characterisation should be consistent, and the play as a whole should have what is commonly known as "heart interest".'

231

First of all, the good writer should construct a plot based on a theme:

'Broadly speaking, the structure of a film story does not differ from that of a novel or drama. Each must have a central theme, and a plot by which this theme is propounded. . . .'

But these are of a strictly limited type. For both the synopsis and the scenario proper require

'. . . selecting and linking together in logical sequence a series of such incidents that, by their pictorial representation, the ideas and motives prompting the characters to action are at the same time revealed.'

The writer must remember, moreover, that there

'. . . are more people of untutored tastes than there are of education and accomplishment, but the former have as much right to entertainment adjusted to their capacity as the latter.'

and so

'The spectator is interested in people. . . .The film story must, therefore, constantly present conflicts of emotions, for their portrayal is the principal function of the Photoplay.'

and

'. . . the situations composing the plot . . . must be so selected that their causes and significance can be revealed by actions which must be photographically portrayable.'

In other words

'The photoplay in its present stage of evolution is not the medium for the fine delineation of character or for dealing with a person's great movements of introspection. The means at the disposal of the producer and artist alike are inadequate.'

It appeared, then, that emotional dramas likely to appeal to 'people of untutored tastes', and dealing with incident rather than character, were the best material for films. Colden Lore had some even more practical suggestions for the writer. He must sometimes adapt unsuitable stories because they are popular or fashionable, and they must then be 'built up' like an original story. He must remember costs when considering expensive artistes, crowd scenes, locations or the construction of large sets. When the synopsis had been accepted, he must write the scenario proper. This:

'. . . is a detailed description, in the proper chronological order in which the play is to be shown, of all the actions taking place in every scene, and of the effects to be presented. The directions, however, as to how these effects should be obtained do not fall within the province of the writer, but in that of the producer and the camera man.'

He emphasized that the scenario was not a literary work, but a 'carefully planned body of directions for the guidance of the producer'. He used the word continuity to signify the dovetailing of actions in logical time and place order and the use of explanatory titles or extra shots to bridge changes of time and place:

'The exercise of a certain amount of ingenuity is sometimes required to arrange the actions of the Photoplay so that complete continuity is maintained with only the most sparing use of scenes not absolutely essential to the story.'

He mentioned the use of 'double action' in this connection, and

'The words "meanwhile" and "meantime" are very frequently employed in Synopses to show that certain events are taking place simultaneously. This timing of incidents brings about "double action". . . .'

Other points of film technique which he singled out for mention were 'punch' and 'business'. The word punch was used variously for 'the dramatic meaning given to an act by certain facts previously revealed' or 'in place of the word "crisis", particularly the crisis demanded by some to mark the end of every reel in a multiple-reel photoplay', this being a survival from the days when it took some time to change the reels. The word 'business' was used in the theatrical sense:

'How, by what minor actions, facial expressions, byplay (all termed "business"), the thoughts and motives of the characters are portrayed is subject matter of the Scenario proper.'

In view of this, his previous remark that how effects be obtained must be left to the director and cameraman suggests that the dividing line between their functions was somewhat vague.

By 1929, when Arrar Jackson wrote,[29] there was a clear division between the synopsis, the treatment and the scenario or shooting script. According to him the ordinary film might now consist of some eight hundred shots and the way in which they were put together had evolved its own rules or rather common practices, which were understood by even the least original. In his Glossary, Jackson included not only the obvious terms like cut, scene, insert and iris view but iris-in and iris-out, mask view, slow motion, superimpose; and, of course, the distance denominations of long-shot, medium long-shot, medium mid-shot, mid-shot, medium close-up, close-up and big close-up. He had also terms for common techniques which had already been accepted into film making and must be familiar to any aspiring writer. Such were the Akeley shot:

'This is a shot taken of a rapidly moving object (like a train or a horse) where the object is held in the picture and the background can be seen flashing past.'

The use of mixing to denote a time lapse, and to introduce a memory or thought, was already hackneyed. The use of the Panoram or a tracking camera for what were later called establishing shots was also mentioned, and also their use to 'give an impression of immensity'. A vignette was

'A shot in which the edges are out of focus (taken through a special lens attachment). Thus in a big close-up of the heroine, it might be artistically more effective if the face was in focus and the hair vignetted out of focus.'

Perhaps the most interesting were descriptions of what were later called respectively the first-person camera and reaction shots:

'After a medium close-up establishing the movements of her head, we cut to the man's boots, slowly panoram up to his head, and then panoram down again to his boots. The effect is that the audience has looked that man up and down in in exactly the same manner as the woman did. . . .

'For example, two people are talking. The conventional place to put the camera is towards their sides, so that they will appear face to face on the screen. Now supposing in further action, one of the speakers has to see something happen which will cause him to assume an expression of annoyance. In the ordinary way, his face would be in profile, and the dramatic effect of his expression partly lost. If, however, the camera is placed so that the shot is taken over the shoulder of the other person, the main character's face is full to the lens, and his expression can be caught with proper significance. Such a shot would be an angle shot. . . . The use of the angle shot is unlimited. It can, by its effects, create greater realism than is ever possible on the stage, while as a variant to the conventional straight shot it has the highest possible value as an interest sustainer.'

Jackson noted an English practice of grouping shots into scenes in the script, giving the general location and estimated over-all time at the beginning and then numbering the shots Na, Nb and so on. By this time American writers usually numbered their shots consecutively right through the script. Perhaps the large number of bad British scripts which Jackson noticed may have been partly due to this habit, which put a premium on compact scenes in the stage manner. More important, British scenario preparation lacked foresight and left too much to the director:

'Observe how very carelessly the shots are described: distance denominations are almost ignored, camera angles do not appear to exist, and the things to be included within the range of the camera lens are left to the director. . . .'

But when Edward Dryhurst wrote about British scripts a little later he noted with relief that British scripts were beginning to be numbered in the American way.[30] He, a young film writer himself, was of the opinion that film writers should be trained in the cutting room if they were to master continuity.

The use of the title or sub-title was a branch of writing often seen at the time as a necessary evil. Macbean described how titles were made.[31] They were usually drawn in white on black paper and photographed on a black velvet table lit by mercury or half-watt lamps, with the camera vertically above them. It was also usual to photograph them on to the negative. The commonest method was 'to have the words printed in block letters on a card, which is then photographed with a cine-camera fitted with a *reversing lens*' or mirror effect. Titles could be mixed, faded or irised. Picture titles, with drawings or still photographs, were effective. Plate-titling was also used:

'. . . making, by ordinary photography, a transparent plate with the words of the title in black letters. This plate is then placed in a specially made optical apparatus somewhat resembling a magic lantern, and the letters on the plate, acting in the same way as a lantern slide, are projected *in miniature* direct on to positive film being passed through the gate of an ordinary film-printing machine.'

It was felt that the use of words was not strictly appropriate to the film but unavoidable when essential information could not be conveyed by images and action. But many companies were too ready to take this easy way out. *The Bioscope* said in 1919:

'Too many companies are using superfluous sub-titles in their pictures. Sub-titles do not belong primarily to screen subjects, and their primary use should be to cover the necessary breaks, and explain that which is incapable of being shown in action.
'An average of 100 sub-titles in a five-reel film is far too many.
'Every sub-title halts the action even when it does not confuse the mind. Motion pictures must be stories told in action.'[32]

And they repeated next year:

'Directors and scenario editors need to develop a greater sense of visual narrative.'[33]

There were attempts to make films without any titles at all. We have mentioned elsewhere Henry Edwards's early attempt to do this with *Lily of the Alley* shown in early 1923, and others made abroad about the same time. But at least one exhibitor denied that the public wanted the no-title film, claiming that it appealed to the intellect and

'There is little room in a showman's campaign for an appeal to the intelligence.'

In his opinion a real desire for dialogue existed and the no-title film was a freak. He referred to a 'recent admirable foreign production' which he had booked:

'. . . I can join the admirers of this clever divergence (not entirely novel, for in this field of experiment Henry Edwards, with *Lily of the Alley*, was a notable first) insofar as they congratulate the producer on having managed to tell a tale without words, but I submit that in both instances referred to the entertainment would have been heightened by a clear, unequivocal intimation of the conversation between the characters.'[34]

Certainly, the worse the film maker, the more heavily he relied on titles and the duller the film. The last reel of the copy of *Drifters* in the National Film Archive has a mere five titles and 160 shots, whilst the last reel of the Archive's *Comin' thro' the Rye* has 27 shots, with as many as 14 titles and one letter insert.[35] Four or five years apart in production, they were a generation apart in style. But Ivor Montagu had a word of warning for those eschewing titles at all costs:

'I am not one of those purists who believe that films should be made without titles, and I have no sympathy with directors who go any length to avoid titles for their own sake, and waste five hundred feet establishing a relationship that could be got over in ten with the title "So and so, now discarded friend of so and so—". The eye-strain of looking at moving visual images on a large screen is so considerable, that one must have titles if only to give the spectator the relief and interruption of the static breaks they form.

'On the other hand, it must be remembered that the title *is* static, and if held too long upon the screen, or brought in too often, it will hold up the movement and weaken the emotion of the scene. A scene may be shattered by an unnecessary title or a title in the wrong place, such as the title in the fight scene of *Vaudeville*. The Russians have the very good custom of splitting up the matter of one long spoken title into two or three short parts where necessary, for this holds up speed far less.'[36]

And *Close Up* was scathing about Hitchcock's film *The Ring*:

. . . Well, it *is* treated visually, but then its merit ends. Mr Hitchcock's method is to depict one simple fact, that a sub-title could have got over, by a long sequence, or a number of elaborate tricks. This is worse than a photographic rendering of a story, for it is pretentious. The way a boxer's name mounted to the top of the post before our eyes, for the time and expense were out of proportion to the effect.'[37]

But perhaps nothing could be as bad as a really unnecessary title. In *Laughter and Tears* in 1921 Adelqui Millar, from the context of the story quite obviously suffering the torments of jealousy, interrupts his violent gesticulations with the title

JEALOUSY!

and later, as he stands over the girl he thinks he has murdered, the film pauses for:

'Pierette! my little Pierette. Why won't you speak? . . . Tell me! . . . Tell me it is only a terrible dream! ! ! ! ! Wake up! . . . I love you—oh! for God's sake speak to me. . . . I cannot live without you!'

In general the frequency and length of the titles did hold the action up considerably. In the 1919 *Nelson*, a film of 8,000 feet, there were some 25 titles a reel. Even by 1928 it was estimated by Blakeston that a pot-boiler might contain some 80 titles. He also said that a normal length was 3 feet for the first word and one foot for every other two words, which prompts some distressing calculations. To take a title at random from a normal Stoll film of 1920, when titles might be a hundred or more in number, we find in *The Mystery of Mr Bernard Brown*:

'Helen, my greatest wish is to see Geoffrey married to someone who loves him. I wonder if you do?'

Even if there were only 85 titles in this early film, this would mean that about 1,000 feet, or a fifth of the film, would be written matter. Of course many titles were shorter, but many were also very much longer. Above all, the worse the film the more likely it was to have the longest, most closely packed explanatory titles bunched together at the beginning. On the other hand a long tense sex triangle scene in *Shooting Stars*, in 1928, for example, was played entirely without words, and there were only about six titles a reel in this film as a whole. By the end of the decade most titles were short spoken ones, which in fact did little to halt the film.

Mid-way between picture and titles was the insert, a letter or telegram, a sentence in a book, a teleprinter or some other device by which the written word might be introduced into the story as a picture. In all but the best films the titles, and sometimes the inserts were rather bad. There were many complaints about spelling, grammar and punctuation, as well as incomprehensible American slang or bad translations of foreign titles. Inserts were often made carelessly, the same handwriting appearing in letters written by different characters, telegrams in France arriving on English telegram forms and many similar lapses. Jarring results were found, also, in films which had been hacked about by renters or censors and patched together with titles of completely different appearance from those of the original ones.

A deliberate attempt to get visual value into the title was the art title, with a drawing or photograph or a symbolic design. Pearson, who started using them in *Garryowen* in 1920, and Guy Newall were two directors who were especially fond of art titles but many other makers also used them and McKnight Kauffer's designs for Hitchcock's *The Lodger* were even given some publicity of their own. In *Young Lochinvar* in 1923 some of the characters were introduced by short titles with pictorial symbols which made it unnecessary to give long verbal explanations, like the fox's head on the title introducing a cunning villain. Usually titles were decorated in an attempt to impart either beauty or humour, or possibly atmosphere, as in the funny-Chinese script used in Robey's *One Arabian Night* and the Gothic script in that part of *The Wandering Jew* which dealt with the Crucifixion. Like tinting and toning (see pages 279–280), the art titles were later described by a number of veteran film makers with a slightly apologetic affection. Like the former they were an artistic dead end, but a decorative and sometimes helpful embellishment.

More to the point were the efforts made by the Russian directors, and described above by Ivor Montagu, to get their titles down to the minimum and to keep them as near to pictures and to movement as they could, thus giving them an impact over and above their intellectual content. The slower and more literary the title, the less suitable to the audiences for whom the Russians were working. Consequently their short pithy titles were frequently broken into several parts, sometimes alternating with other shots, sometimes superimposed on them; sometimes the words moved, grew or diminished or even exploded on the screen. But the Russians were not the only ones to do this. It is interesting that a hum-drum director like Bentley in a film of 1920 called *General Post* experimented both with splitting titles into several shots and with superimposing them on the pictures.[38] There were many other British examples, which seem to have been quite spontaneous and not influenced in any way by the Russian experiments. Even in *Nelson* in 1919, an extremely primitive film, the famous last words were superimposed on the picture of Nelson's death. In *The Only Way* in 1925 the three words 'hanged', 'drawn' and 'quartered' were effectively separated by close shots of the lawyer's vicious face. In 1928 *Shooting Stars*, *First Born* and *Wait and See*, three highly imaginative later films, all contained examples of the superimposed title.

There was nevertheless an uneasy feeling that words delayed the action. An interesting way in which Hitchcock kept interest alive while conveying essential information was to be found in his first film, *Pleasure Garden*, in 1926. This contains a passage of some 34 shots and 6 titles which shows the two chorus girls chatting as they undress in their digs and go to bed. A great deal of background information and light on the girls' characters is inconspicuously fitted into a domestic scene of the girls' preparations for bed, which are interrupted by the playfulness of their small dog. This is very far from *Damaged Goods* in 1919, in which lengthy takes of people engaged in endless inaudible conversation alternate with equally long titles containing all the narrative.

Attempts to improve titles coincided with a growing awareness of the nature of film structure. Many steps in visual story-telling, indeed, were taken in the first place to avoid the need for a title. From early times these attempts were widely misunderstood, and seen as 'tricks' and 'deft touches', gimmicks of every type rather than the very fabric of visual narrative. Henry Edwards from the early twenties was in the habit of externalizing everything he could from character and emotions to the passage of time and place with symbolic shots, bridging passages or expressive interpolations. These were greatly admired, but as little touches and embellishments, or party tricks. Edwards himself was certainly aware of their meaning. With his stage background he referred to them as 'dramatization', and wrote an interesting article in *The Bioscope* called *The Language of Action*[39] at a time, 1920, when most of his colleagues from the theatre were still relying on exaggerated mime. The famous Hitchcock touch of later years, and many passages in Asquith's films, fulfilled the same function of saying much in little, and using the film's power of selection to bring associations and references to the spectator's mind.

A crude and incongruous example from Elvey's 1919 *Nelson* was the symbolic mixing of a shot of a peacock with one of the Kaiser. In Wilcox's *Decameron Nights* of 1924 when the Soldan is sitting on his throne gloomily thinking, according to the title, that Life's Ambition is but a bubble, a rather large bubble bounces surprisingly across the frame. *The Secret Kingdom*, a Stoll film of 1925, starts with the notion of swinging the camera in towards an actor's forehead and eyes and dissolving into a shot of what he is thinking about; unfortunately repetition makes this tedious and by the time the jury finally decides that the accused is innocent the difficulty of representing this abstraction seems to have been too much for the producer, and the word 'innocent' is flashed in illuminated letters over their heads.

Only a year later than this Hitchcock, in *Pleasure Garden*, was showing how visual embroidery or grace notes could be used to keep interest alive. In one example, the camera tracks along a theatre row of lascivious men's faces watching the show girls; at the end of the row our attention is given a nudge by a glimpse of a bored woman in the audience, dozing; as a fat old man picks his way along the row he treads on someone's feet, an apparently irrelevant detail which illuminates the relevant. But by the time he made his next film, *The Lodger*, Hitchcock had disciplined the profusion of his ideas to the service of the story. The lights of passing cars sweeping across the darkened room, for example, have a part to play in creating atmosphere and the world outside. In *Downhill*, when Ivor Novello is expelled from his public school and returns home, the tension is built indirectly as he waits for the inevitable uncomfortable interview with his father, the boy conversing politely with a friend of the family as his father looks, puzzled, at the calendar before his son is able to tell him privately why he is at home during term. It is one of Hitchcock's little jokes with the audience when we see Novello later, turned out of his home, wearing a dinner jacket; we pull back to see that this is because he is a waiter; then we observe that he is stealing; finally that it is taking place on a stage and that the boy has become an actor and is playing a thieving waiter.

In *Shooting Stars* in 1928 Asquith had several passages of ironic counterpoint in which details were built up to convey more than appeared on the surface. When the married film star, Annette Benson, is being interviewed by the fan paper's reporter we cut from the journalist's note 'Has found ideal mate' to a shot of her secret lover, the comedian, in his dressing room; then from 'loves all her fellow workers' to the chorus girls, whose reaction to her name proves her unpopularity. In another part of the film Annette Benson and her lover sign on the same page of an admirer's autograph book, leaving no room for her actor husband's signature, which is pushed on to another page. The comic's

239

own character and his contempt for her are shown when he is filming and finds that the prop man has forgotten the key which a coy little flapper is meant to give him; without scruple the comic lets her use the key which Annette Benson, with uncomfortably similar coyness, has just given to him in earnest.

Many different ways were found to bridge time and space. In *The Informer* in 1929, when the hero is on the run from the police he turns away from us looking his strong handsome self and then turns slowly back to us, unshaven and haggard. But soon many visual expressions for time were becoming hackneyed:

'That dreadful hour glass with the trickling sands; that bewitched calendar that jumps days with the brazen effrontery only comparable to that of the clock whose hands spin round in the most wanton way. . . .'[40]

This increasingly imaginative use of visual story-telling was not usually the work of the so-called scenarist. Films must have a story to tell, and a succession of images to tell it. The film industry attracted many who wished to create the succession of images, but few who had a story to tell. In this it differed from literary and stage creation, where the content did not appear as separable from the form. In almost all cases the person who thought of story-telling in visual terms was by inclination a director or editor, or both, and exercised his influence on the story structure from this vantage point. Creative directors who had a marked control over the script included Henry Edwards, Guy Newall, George Pearson, Graham Cutts and Cecil Hepworth, and later Hitchcock and Asquith as well as Brunel, Geoffrey Barkas and Walter Summers. Low pay and departmentalization combined to lower the status of the script writer. There were comparatively few people known by name as scenario writers in England at the time, and most of them were little more than hacks. R. Byron Webber, W. Courtenay Rowden, Alicia Ramsey of Gaumont, Kenelm Foss, Blanche MacIntosh of Hepworth's, L. H. Gordon at Stoll's, J. Bertram Brown, W. J. Elliott, Lydia Hayward, Frank Fowell, Benedict James, Harry Fowler Mear, Bannister Merwin and Frank Miller were names that appeared again and again. Later in the period more sophisticated and sometimes more creative writers were appearing, and names from the later twenties include Walter Mycroft at B.I.P., Angus Macphail at Gainsborough, Roland Pertwee at Gainsborough after leaving G. B. Samuelson, V. E. Powell of B.I.P. and Alma Reville, at first working with her husband Alfred Hitchcock and later on her own. But the biggest number of writing credits of all, over sixty, went to Eliot Stannard, as competent a professional as Murton was in art direction.

This low opinion of the script was a great weakness in the British industry. It underrated the importance of the story itself and seemed to justify partnerships like that of Elvey and Stannard, busily turning everything into the same formula stuff. Even by 1919 the way that every story was changed about and made uniform by the script department was the cause of much complaint. According to Honri, at one time almost half the scripts in the British film industry were being supplied by Stannard and Foss. The professionals turned up in company after company, 'knowing their craft' and imposing their second-rate conception of what a film should be on one hopeful new director after another.

It was widely assumed that stories must come from outside the industry. The publicity value of famous books and plays was realized, but the main reason for borrowing so heavily from them was that hardly anybody wrote directly for the screen. Right through the period the dearth of good stories and the imminent drying up of sources were frequently lamented, and attempts were made to persuade established novelists and dramatists to write original screen-plays. But their experiences in the studio did not encourage them. Temple Thurston, when addressing a C.E.A. Conference in 1921 after some unhappy experience with Hepworth's, complained that he had not been allowed any say in production. He recommended authors to give up taking any active interest in films and to take refuge in 'lucrative indifference'.[41] Many writers certainly felt like this. Hepworth's characteristic reply, courteous as ever, was that a writer could give as many instructions as he liked but that once he had handed over to the producer he must not interfere any more, an idea suggesting that the writer of the plot was really outside the process of creative film making. Robb Lawson's words were more apt:

'Certain novelists who are avaricious enough to desire to add to their incomes by receiving royalties for screen versions, have complained that the producer has maimed or mutilated their pet child. For these I have little sympathy. If the novelist is an artist, surely the medium in which he chose to express the idea was the final one. . . . If any novelist wants to write for the screen, let him be a true artist and invent his story, first of all, in terms of the screen.'[42]

H. G. Wells was contemptuous of the practices, if not the possibilities, of film making:

'Indeed, the idea that the film was just a way of telling stories in moving pictures dominated the cinema theatre entirely for nearly a couple of decades, and still dominates it. . . . It would be ungracious for a novelist to complain. Through a happy term of years "world cinema rights" distended the income of every well-known novelist and playwright. The deserving class of fiction writers was enriched even by the sale of "cinema rights" of tales quite impossible to put upon the films. . . . The industry . . . bought right and left; it bought high and low; it was so opulent it could buy with its eyes shut. It did. Its methods were simple and direct. It took all the stories it could get, and changed all that were not absolutely intractable into one old, old story, with variations of costume, scenery and social position.'[43]

Every possible or impossible play and novel, historical, classical, pot-boiling and contemporary, was wrung in to service and many second-rate writers enjoyed the lucrative indifference of which Temple Thurston spoke so bitterly. Some sixty of the hundreds of plays adapted in the decade were included in Parker's list of *Notable Productions on the London Stage*,[44] some forty of them as long

runs. Most of the plays were adapted only a year or two after their stage presenta-
tion, of which *Carnival* a year after the New Theatre presentation in 1920, *The
Constant Nymph* two years after being at the New Theatre in 1926 and *Easy
Virtue* a year after showing at the Duke of York's in 1926 were typical examples.
Alf's Button and *At the Villa Rose* were even filmed before they were put on as
plays. The early Balcon and Wilcox films, many B.I.P. ones, and the Edgar
Wallace films from British Lion were the most likely to be from recent productions, as prestige and money were needed to get them so quickly, whilst companies like Samuelson and Stoll acquired properties a little less desirable and
even humbler producers had to rely largely on old melodramas.

Some efforts were made to acquire good original screenplays but they were
not particularly successful. *The Rat* and its sequels were written with screen
possibilities in mind and Pearson tried his hand at original screenplays with
great idealism but varying results. A. A. Milne was associated with Brunel in
the production of some short comedies. Original stories written for the screen
were often even worse than the adaptations. Starting with a good idea, possibly
in an unfamiliar and interesting setting, the writers so often threw in too much,
too many characters and too much incident. Longing to reach great heights of
drama and wallow in emotion, but lacking the talent to create a credible situation
for it, they piled absurdity on absurdity, replacing plausibility with exaggeration.
The Triumph of the Rat is a perfect example of this from 1926. Films like Wilcox's
Dawn and Bruce Woolfe's *Boadicea* showed that simplicity in story outline and
acting was more effective. Temple Thurston's experiment has been mentioned
and it was announced towards the end of the period that an American company
hoped to interest Maeterlinck. Gerard Fort Buckle, who wrote the ambitious
theoretical dissertation on the film discussed earlier, also wrote two original scripts
himself which seem to have been somewhat unsuccessful, *The Yellow Claw* and
Nighthawk. Arnold Bennett wrote *Piccadilly* for B.I.P. in 1929. Persistent efforts
were made to draw H. G. Wells into films. He became interested at last with the
arrival of the sound film, which he described as the Art Form of the Future and
a form of 'spectacle-music-drama', and he wrote *The King Who Was A King*
in the form of a film. But his approach was highly intellectual and verbal, and
after outlining a veritable sermon of a story in the introduction he proceeded to
present it in such a way as to suggest that he had little understanding of film as
visual story-telling. His use of sound, also, was merely additional, and it is hard
to believe that with this attitude to it he could really have seen sound as a turning
point in the cinema. The action is designed throughout as a silent film with
montages and elaborate silent film symbols, packing the unwieldy message into
the many long, wordy and literary titles and the use of words superimposed on
pictures; faces and illustrative actions were to be incidental and the sound track
used only for music and effects.

In the end a competent hack seems to have had the best chance of survival
in the British script departments. But an industry which failed to bring to the
top people who approached visual story-telling with any originality could only be
second-rate. And if the designer was the assassin of the British film's appearance,
the hack scenarist was the assassin of its structure. British studios clung to the

idea of departmentalization and to the view expressed by MacBean at the beginning of the twenties. He felt that the 'creative ability', by which he apparently meant the facility of thinking of plots, had to be there in the first place, or borrowed from stage or novel, but that the technique of turning these into film scripts was something quite separate, and something which could easily be acquired; true, it was important to have a 'well-constructed and visualized series of scenes and actions which go to make the finished scenario'; but the real creative activity was literary or dramatic, whilst 'turning it into a scenario' was a mechanical matter which could soon be learned. For

'. . . it remains but to follow accepted lines and methods when drafting out the several scene-actions.'[45]

(5) DESIGN

Sets were built and dressed by someone at first loosely called the scenic artist, and later the designer or art director. The latter term became more general after the war. But as in so many other branches of film production the terminology was rather fortuitous. There was no clear idea that the designer, with the director and lighting cameraman, might be responsible for the total visual impact, or design, of the film. The importance of the designer's share in making the film look real, in establishing its moods, in implying the character and past lives of the people, and in giving the film a memorable image of its own, emerged very slowly. Techniques were often rudimentary, and in Elvey's *Nelson* of 1919 the polar landscape was even represented by the use of a slightly creased back-drop. In companies which had studios of their own, stocks of furniture and properties and parts of old scenes accumulated and were used again and again. The grand title of Art Director, and public recognition in the screen credits and publicity, were only considered appropriate by most firms when a 'spectacular' was mounted, and this happened rarely enough in England, where large sets and crowd scenes were too expensive for most studios and quite impossible for some.

It was when a specially artistic effect was sought that the art director came into his own. The dreary results of trying to be spectacular without spending much money can be seen in the thin theatrical trappings of such films as Robey's *One Arabian Night* and *The Wandering Jew*, both designed in 1923 by Walter Murton for Stoll. *The Only Way*, made at Twickenham and designed by W. G. Arnold, the John Stuart Blackton films made in 1921 and 1922 at Cricklewood, and Alliance's *Carnival* and *The Bohemian Girl*, made at Twickenham about the same time, were films with large sets and crowd scenes which managed to look solid, convincing and impressive. But three early spectaculars, Wilcox's *Chu Chin Chow* and *Decameron Nights*, designed by Arnold in 1923 and 1924, and G. B. Samuelson's *She* of 1925 were all made in the larger and better equipped studios of Germany. The facilities there attracted producers like Balcon, who embarked on a policy of Anglo-German production. Meanwhile some of the

243

most spectacular and visually pleasing films made in Great Britain were location films like *Young Lochinvar* in 1923, *Boadicea* in 1926, *Fox Farm* in 1922, and many others, and owed more to the location scout than to the designer.

Art was still considered a luxury in 1927, according to N. G. Arnold,[46] and in general the function of the designer was the humble one of providing, economically, a setting of reasonable verisimilitude. The designer was little more than a glorified set dresser in many studios and greatly hampered by lack of money. Such firms as Stoll, Ideal and Gaumont were notorious for this. One of the most noticeable things about the British films of the early twenties was the uniform appearance of the films of any one studio, and although this was partly due to the nature and use of its lighting and photographic equipment, it was also partly due to the unimaginative re-use of stock sets and props.

Stoll films had a characteristically dark brown appearance, peopled by bright white shirt collars and cuffs, moving as though disembodied through dark contemporary settings which were characterless and bare, their costume films dressed by theatrical costumiers on the level of an amateur show. If dark wooden panelling and dark leather upholstery appeared frequently in Stoll films, fabric panelling and spindly furniture were favoured in the lighter, but still impersonal home of the G. B. Samuelson world and the over-dressed, over-crowded costume plays of Ideal. Welsh–Pearson interiors were carefully dressed with signs of habitation and glowed with highlights like highly polished boots. Hepworth films had a paler look, with carefully chosen quaint rural exteriors, buildings not always very apt, and costumed when 'costume' was called for in unconvincing fancy dress. There was a discrepancy between the High Society British companies liked to portray and the appearance of most of the players. Perhaps the most pleasing image of all was that of Guy Newall's films which, designed by Charles Dalmon and at first affected by the shape of their long narrow studio at Ebury Street, had greater depth and a chintzy, white panelled, white painted-furniture look which soon developed into backgrounds which had some meaning for the story. Dalmon was reported in 1920 as saying that in Great Britain the art director 'scarcely exists at all'.[47] He was daringly publicized by this small company, but apart from him the only designers known at all widely in the early twenties were Willie Davies and Walter Murton. The former, who did comparatively little, had worked as a pageant master and then for D. W. Griffith before joining the British film industry. Murton, who was personally responsible for the sets of well over fifty films in this period, worked for Stoll and many other companies including British Instructional. One of the few entrenched professionals, he was responsible more than any other single person for the characteristic look of the British films of the early and middle twenties.

The technique of the time is described, again, by Boughey and MacBean. MacBean's chapter on art direction mentions flats, usually of three-ply on rigid timber frames as canvas was felt to be too flimsy, and

'It is not customary at the present time to *paint* mouldings on the flats; photographic excellence and public scrutiny make this method futile. All relief work should be *built* so that it actually stands out.'[48]

244

Most scene painting and costume design was limited to neutral colours, mainly in shades of grey and brown, and the designer must know how colours were affected by photography and different types of lighting. Boughey said the 'erection of an average set, or complete scene', might take from two to twenty days 'from the embryo sketch of the Art-Director to the final touches of carpenters and scene-painters', and he also, like MacBean, said in passing that the designer 'must know all about . . . light, shade . . .';[49] yet he was more interested in the art director having a wide knowledge of period, possession of 'special store-rooms fitted with antiques, Oriental weapons and curios, and objects of art'. MacBean recommended standardizing 'scene accessories' such as doors, windows, stairs and fireplaces. It was necessary for a competent designer to consider the position of lights and the movements of players, but not yet camera movement, at least not until the mid-twenties and then only rarely. As a result the sets still tended to be arranged as a stage, with space for movement in the middle and front and an open wall on one side, rather than having some part of the set in the foreground to create a feeling of depth. For a while, the bigger the set the more like a stage it was treated, with the camera set up to show as much as possible. A notable early exception to this was Davies's banquet scene in *The Bohemian Girl* of 1922, a very large set filmed at one part of the story from above, and at another point seen with two footmen and a table in the foreground used most effectively to give it depth.

On the whole the fashion for enormous sets passed the British producers by. *Chu Chin Chow* in 1923 was said in one of *Pictures and the Picturegoer*'s flights of fancy[50] to have gates of Baghdad as large as St Paul's Cathedral, and the occasional super film did break away from the small domestic backgrounds so popular here. But when British producers could not fit their stories into their small studios they preferred to go on location, or use their ingenuity to suggest what they could not show. Pearson's autobiography gives many instances of such imaginative suggestion, from the enlarged shadow of the works of a clock to convey the interior of a factory to the shadow of a bride cast on a single stone wall and pillar for a church wedding, or an overhead shot of one plaster lion and a small section of pavement to serve as Trafalgar Square. On the whole, however, British producers in the earlier part of the period avoided stories requiring ambitious scenery.

But even whilst sets were getting bigger and bigger in other countries, techniques were also being developed which in time were to make the erection of huge sets unnecessary. About 1919 F. P. Earle in America invented the glass shot, the first of a series of special processes which revolutionized the work of film design and extended the scope of the cinema. Seeking for a way in which a painter could influence the visual appearance of the film, he devised a way for the artist to paint the scene on to glass, leaving clear spaces here and there as required; the glass was supported in front of the camera in such a way that the actors could be seen through the clear spaces, at a correct distance to fit the perspective, and act in front of a neutral background which blended into the painted scene. This form of shot was later adapted to make it unnecessary to build ceilings or the upper parts of large sets, these being painted on to the glass and put in front of the camera so that the painted upper part and constructed lower part joined exactly. Considerable skill was needed to conceal the join.

These techniques were adapted to photographs, or to drawings or paintings on plywood, in Hall's Background Process. The American rights for this were held by Paramount and it was introduced into Britain by Benito Nichols of M.P. Sales.

'An artist's drawing, about 5 ft in length, is first prepared from a photograph of the scene it is wished to reproduce, omitting those sections in which it will be necessary to show movement of living players. This "cut out" is then suspended a few feet from the camera as a mask for the scene to be played on a real exterior some 60 ft behind. If necessary, the lower portion of the scene is solidly built to complete the drawing, which will appear on the screen in perspective.'[51]

Once more the principal was extended, this time to the model shot, in which a relief model was suspended in front of the camera and appropriately lighted. The next development was the Dunning Shot, patented by C. Dodge Dunning, also in America. This was a process by which the background was filmed first, and then run through the camera again to film the actions of the characters, who were superimposed. After this came the Schufftan Process, which was described in *The Bioscope* in January 1927. The British rights were bought by British National and used in 1927 first on *Madame Pompadour* after the system had been used in America and Germany. It was a more sophisticated development of the model shot. A mirror, a thin sheet of optical glass silvered on the surface, was placed just in front of the camera at an angle of 45 degrees to it. A model, photograph or diapositive lighted from behind was placed at right angles to the camera in such a way that it was reflected in the mirror. At appropriate places the silvering was scraped off the mirror to leave clear glass through which the camera could photograph the players performing in constructed portions of the set at the correct perspective. As in the glass shot the two combined to give a complete picture, and as before, skill was needed to get a good join, but according to Blakeston it was very realistic, especially when using a model.

Split matt shots, which had long been done in the camera, were made much easier when increased precision in optical printing made it possible to do them in the lab. Still photographic backgrounds, enlarged and pasted on canvas backing behind the actors, were followed by moving photographic backgrounds projected on to a sheet of glass or other transparent material behind the actors and the rest of the scene, the whole being filmed in synchronization with the speed of projection of the background. There was considerable difficulty in securing the synchronization, but an early attempt was made in England in the filming of a 'television screen' in Elvey's futuristic *High Treason* in 1929.

These developments revolutionized and greatly extended film production. Gone was the construction of yet more and more enormous sets. Gone also, unfortunately, at least for the time being, was the practice of shooting films other than documentary in their actual locations. Behren's project for establishing a national studio in 1925 had already laid great stress on the 'miniature department', and now the new processes were reinforced by the introduction of the heavy sound cameras in 1929. Everything combined to drive the film indoors. Now that the British film had at last raised adequate capital, the old mean appearance of the British high society film tended to be replaced by an artificial, indoor world of theatres, night clubs and wealthy, untenanted homes in a style of architecture unknown except on the screen, with hardly a glimpse of the real world outside.

There were exceptions, of course. The personnel of the art department began to improve, and the whole subject was taken more seriously. Early in 1928 even Stoll's announced as a studio revolution the fact that they would abandon the use of stock scenery. Theatrical design had been the centre of a creative upheaval in several countries for some time. Gordon Craig, son of Ellen Terry and godson of Henry Irving, had led a movement towards simplicity in theatrical design. *The Studio*, a magazine which frequently reviewed stage *décor*, occasionally included an article on film design and a little of the prevailing interest may have spread to the cinema. Pearson, who wrote in *The Bioscope* of meeting Craig and finding him not unsympathetic to the possibilities of the film, had engaged a most sophisticated designer for *The Little People* in the young Cavalcanti and from 1927 had Craig's son Edward Carrick working as his art director. Carrick was one of several more imaginative designers now finding their way into the British studios. Andrew Mazzei, Lancashire born, studied architecture and sculpture and worked for Famous Players in America, and then in Germany and Italy, before designing some of Elvey's later films. Ian Campbell-Gray, Clifford Pember, Arthur Woods and Hugh Gee were others, and B.I.P. engaged Alfred Jünge from Germany for *Moulin Rouge* and *Piccadilly*. Dupont's *Moulin Rouge*, shot by Werner Brandes, was perhaps the first film in Britain which could be said to have been designed with any distinction. The most prolific of the better designers at the time was Norman G. Arnold, who had worked on *Flames of Passion* for Balcon as early as 1922, and after that on many other large-scale productions by Cutts and Wilcox and later on B.I.P.'s *The Informer*. This film, which broke away from the current taste for high society, was designed with imagination and atmosphere, although the studio-made look of the street scenes and other exteriors set a new fashion for exteriors made indoors. C. W. Arnold, who designed Cutts' *The Rat* in 1925 with its modernist night-club scenes and mobile camera, worked on most of the Hitchcock films including *The Lodger*, in which the London streets if not realistic at least had a quality of foggy mystery which was of value to the film, and also made a very interesting experiment with a boxed-in set and a long travelling shot in *The Farmer's Wife*

'. . . a big "composite set" which includes the main entrance to a farmhouse, the large parlour, kitchen, farmyard and stairway leading up to a bedroom built in such a way as to enable shots to be taken from the bedroom into the parlour and *vice versa*. Incidentally the parlour "set", instead of being of the usual three-sided type, is completely boxed in.'[52]

Arnold also used the Schufftan process in *The Ring*, and designed Mander's interesting film *The First Born*. But the scarcity of original and inventive designers in the British film industry, and the stranglehold of competent hacks until the last few years, is one of the many sad features of the British silent film.

(6) CAMERAWORK

After the war MacBean wrote of the Bell and Howell, Cinchro, Darling, Debrie, Moy, Pathé, Vinten and Williamson cameras as well-known makes which were in use in England. Boughey described the 'professional camera . . . for both indoor and outdoor work, and in general design . . . similar to those in use by nearly all British and foreign film producers' as follows:

'The professional camera consists of a mahogany box measuring 14 ins in length, by $5\frac{1}{2}$ ins in width, and 15 ins in height, with brass protecting corners and leather carrying strap. The supply and take-up boxes, which are enclosed in the mahogany case, each hold 330 ft of film. There is a focusing tube from the exposure window to an aperature in the back of the case; and by means of a four-picture continuous movement sprockett, for both feed and take-up, with free loop on either side of pressure gate, a steady passing of the film is assured.

'This type of camera is fitted with every refinement, such as a *film-punch*, with which to mark the beginning and end of different subjects by punching a hole in the film; a *measurer*, showing at a glance the length of film exposed; a *two-speed device*, for eight pictures and one picture per turn of handle; a patent *claw movement*, turned at the rate of thirty-two pictures per second; a method whereby the film can be *reversed* and re-wound into the top or supply box for trick photography (such as the reversing of traffic in a street scene); a *speed indicator*, showing the feet per second at which the film is being exposed, a detachable box *view-finder*, two interchangeable *film masks* for trick work (such as a view through binoculars or keyhole); and a variety of tools and spare parts.'[53]

Elsewhere he mentioned other refinements, such as a camera with detachable turret and three lenses, each of which could be focused without disturbing the film; automatic dissolving accomplished by a shutter or iris-diaphragm or both simultaneously; telephoto lenses; an ultra-rapid camera for slow motion; and *revolving head* and *tilting table* for horizontal and vertical movements. Blakeston in 1928 gave a similar description of the popular Bell and Howell, Debrie and Mitchell cameras and the Eclair, Universal and Pathé, as well as the Akeley camera designed especially for travelling shots.*

* According to Blakeston, theoretically any number of copies of a film could be printed from one negative, but actually the base tended to become scratched after about 180. A positive deteriorated after being projected about twenty-one times. To make a negative from a positive, known as 'duping', tended to loose half tones and lead to a loss of photographic quality. Nevertheless, many films were duped, and Blakeston was very critical of the technical standard of mechanical printing.

Mechanical rather than hand turning of the camera became widespread during the decade. Lutz, in 1920, wrote that the cameraman must still learn 'to appraise time durations so accurately that he will turn the handle at this speed'[54] but Boughey wrote in 1921:

'For studio work the camera handle is turned by a small electric motor, of about one-sixth or one-eighth of a horse-power, possessing facilities for a very fine adjustment of the speed.'[55]

And the *Kine Year Book* of 1923 said:

'With the clockwork power drive on the 1922 French "Sept" camera, and the really light and portable electric drive on the 1922 Newman camera, where current can be taken from a three-cell wallet-size dry battery refill, power turning of intermittent motion and rewind enters upon a new phase.'[56]

All the same, according to Pearson's autobiography the automatic camera made only slow progress during the twenties and his own studio camera was hand operated, at 60 feet a minute, or 16 frames a second.

This seems to have been a normal speed, except for slow motion of up to about 32 frames a second, or fast motion photography of one to eight. Pathé were said to have an ultra-rapid camera taking 160 frames a second on a highly sensitized film.[57]

Nevertheless it seems to have been as normal for the cameraman to vary these speeds as it was for the hand projectionist to do so at his end of the process. In an article in 1921 the Pathé cameraman F. A. Bassill mentioned the manipulation of speeds in filming fights 'to brighten up the action of a particularly slow boxer' or the reverse.[58] A paper was read to the Society of Motion Picture Engineers late in 1926 from which it appears that there was a great deal of variation; comedy was expected to be projected at 90 to 95 feet a minute and slow drama at 80 to 85, respectively hastening or slowing down the action from the speed at which it had been shot; and it was suggested that speeds should be standardized at 60 feet for taking and 80 feet for projecting.[59] As late as 1928 Blakeston wrote:

'. . . a good cameraman changes his speed to suit the action. If he wants to slow up the action he turns faster. If he wants to quicken the action he turns slower.'[60]

Early film stock had been sensitive to blues, especially so to violet, partially sensitive to greens but not to reds. Orthochromatic stock was an improvement in that it was sensitive to greens as well as blues, and partially so to reds. Panchromatic stock, which was supposed to be equally sensitive to all and to give an accurate rendering of tone values, was common in America by the early twenties, but although available in England from about 1924 it was difficult to obtain and not in general use. Actuality cameramen were particularly anxious to get hold of the new stock, with its more realistic results. There was a marked difference in the appearance of films made with orthochromatic stock and mainly or

249

entirely arc lighting, hard and sharply contrasted, and later films shot on pan stock and lighted largely with incandescent lamps, softer and much more varied in tone.

One thing that continued to cause difficulty was the filming of night scenes. Night exteriors were being shot with the aid of Sunlight arcs in America by 1920, but despite isolated instances in England most night scenes were filmed by daylight and tinted dark blue or green. Even in 1928 Blakeston wrote that night scenes were shot before nightfall and that it was left to the developer to make them look dark, or that you could get 'beautiful night studies by repainting your scene a nocturnal shade'.[61]

Stock, lighting and the choice of camera angle occupied less of the early cinematographer's attention than camera design and photographic devices and tricks like fades, dissolves, slow and quick turning, reversing and model work. The professional card advertising the services of a first-class cameraman like J. J. Cox in *The Bioscope* in 1919 made a point of the fact that he was 'thoroughly experienced in Trick Work'. In MacBean's manual of 1922 he passes over the work of lighting the set and choosing the camera angle as a straightforward part of the cameraman's task requiring little consideration. And Boughey wrote of artificial lighting in 1921 only 'when the natural light of day is unsuitable'. But this was already out of date by the time he was writing and during the next few years the cinematographer who knew all about trick work was to be replaced by the lighting cameraman, whose art lay in choosing and lighting the camera set-up.

At the end of the war Shoreham was the only studio in Britain which still relied entirely on daylight, and many were entirely dark. The others were all lighted by Westminster arcs, varying in number from 15 to 20 in a small studio to 120 at Twickenham. Arcs, burning a carbon, were hot and intense and tended to flicker, needing continual adjustment as they burned down. As they were improved they could be adjusted to flood or spread, and to spot or concentrate; baby spots, domes or overhead lamps and Suns, very large and powerful arcs, became available. Characters had to be lit in such a way as to avoid the double shadows which tended to appear.

A number of studios also had banks of Cooper–Hewitt mercury vapour tubes, giving a softer light, an assortment of reflectors and diffusers, and supplementary lights such as Westminsters or the American Kleigl spots, Boardman Northlight lamps, Wohl broadsides, Wingfield Kerner lights, Jupiter sun arcs and Digby lamps. According to Honri, Barkay reflectors were used for the first time, with Westminster arcs, at the Bertram Phillips studio at Clapham in 1919. Blakeston speaks of diffusing strips of silk, linen or oil paper and also niggers, which were large, black boards in frames like easels, used to keep light from shining in the camera. MacBean also wrote of spotlighting:

'Spot-lights are now employed in nearly all studio scenes. The object is to throw a strong beam of light from a point high up and more or less opposite the camera, giving the halo effect on the hair and lighting up the face in a most satisfactory manner. These lights are used similarly to theatre spot-lamps, the beams being directed by hand to follow the movements of the artistes.'[62]

The newly equipped Islington and Twickenham studios were perhaps the most elaborately lighted, both of them importing the new powerful Sunlight arcs from America. Islington was reported to be spending up to £10,000 on lighting, which surprised British technicians not used to American standards. As *Pictures and the Picturegoer* puts it:

'Griffith employs a small army of skilled mechanics to operate the arc-lamps of many million candle-power which simulate sunshine, firelight, or moonbeams on the faces of his characters. The turning of a switch, and his light-beams can flood a scene with the chill winter twilight of Alaska, the blazing brilliance of the midday sun of the East, the soft glow of sunset; or invest a squalid attic with the dreary light of clouded dawn.'[63]

American cameramen, it seems, thought little of British equipment:

'. . . certain American cameramen insisting they could not do good work over here with our hitherto almost universal enclosed long arc. . . . American white flame studio arcs were imported, chiefly Wohl "broadsides" and Kleiglight side lamps. With these came large American-pattern double decker sixteen tube Cooper–Hewitt mercury vapour banks, and to cap the light there arrived last of all several examples of the Sun-Light arc, a monster photoplay production lamp taking one hundred and fifty amperes at one hundred and ten volts. These Sun-Light arc lamps burn carbons the positive of which has a core of the same sort of chemicals which make incandescent gasmantles glow. Actual crater light of a Sun-Light arc is no less than one hundred thousand candle-power, which can be amplified by means of a lens mirror to a concentrated three million candle-power beam. With Sun-Lights, arcs, Kleiglights, Wohls and mercury vapour banks all burning merrily together, reinforced with a half-dozen or so back spot lights, to say nothing of a few high candle-power half-watt lamps to brighten up dark corners. . . . '[64]

Boughey wrote that the Cooper–Hewitt mercury vapour tubes were in general use in America, sometimes in banks of as many as three hundred; mercury vapour lamps were cooler, softer and more diffused, but there were also special photographic arc-lights which were like them; lights were usually used in combination, frequently with mercury vapour frames over the top of the scene 'in the form of a glowing roof', with the addition of a few from the front and sides, suitably shielded.

Gradually the idea that lighting was not just necessary in order to see, but that it could contribute something of its own to the realism, the mood and the visual value of the film, forced itself on British producers. It was a sign of the times that Blakeston's book in 1928 had a separate chapter on lights. He spoke of water reflections on cabin walls, shafts of light in the fog, the firelight's flicker, the lighting of doors and windows. He referred to the two divergent types of lighting, the American school which was uniform and hard and was much copied in England, and the Continental school with its soft focus photography and eldritch half lights. An article in 1927 by Eveleigh pointing out that 'the heart of the studio is its lighting' had also distinguished the American and Continental styles:

'America proceeded along the lines of *mechanical* photography, using all kinds of cross lighting to get an excessive brilliance and snap, Germany employed more legitimate *photographic* methods, eschewing back-lighting almost altogether and generally proceeding along more artistic lines.'[65]

He also deplored the backwardness of British studios. With the arrival of pan stock came also incandescent lamps, which burned evenly without attention, giving a more diffused light, and fewer troublesome shadows. They required a new technique, and once again the British found themselves out of date. Incandescent lighting was finally made necessary by sound production:

'In the studio, technicians have turned their attention to the use of incandescent lighting units in place of or supplementing the usual arcs. Their use in America has now been well established especially in connection with the taking of sound films for which, of course, a silent illuminant is essential.'[66]

The importance of lighting was finally realized. Hitchcock's *Lodger* of 1926, for example, on which the cameraman was Baron Ventimiglia, had lighting effects which contributed greatly to the air of threatening mystery. The first important lighting credits in this country were those of the German technician Karl Fischer on *Shooting Stars* and *Underground* in 1928 for British Instructional, and from now on the key importance of lighting was inescapable.

Basil Emmott, who shared Grierson's responsibility for the lovely appearance of *Drifters* in 1929, was perhaps the most highly regarded of British cameramen:

'There is only one man, working in England, who is alive to the fact that each time the camera is moved there is a chance for a new lighting effect. . . .

'Maculose fragments of print, worn out by eager fingers, show some careful light-painting in close-up. The usual spotlight plays on the back of the hair, but not with that alarming halo effect, and a spotlight on the ground, screened by the back of the actress herself, catches a high light under a cheek bone. Another spotlight, covered with a silk, is trained on the right side of the face, and re-enforces with "inkies" spread in a semi-circle so that the intensity of light on the face becomes appreciably less towards the mouth and nose. To break up the shadows a fourth spotlight, also silked, shoots over the camera, catching the glint in the eyes of the woman and faintly illuminating the left side of the face, which, otherwise, is in shadow. . . .

'Emmott has studied it in America. He considers British laboratories bad, says "England's special failing is mental stinginess".

'He considers it good to go back to arcs; "Flood lighting and small effects, like splashing a small lamp across bricks to raise them from the wall, are the legitimate employment for the modern 'inkies', back lighting calls for economic arcs". He is using arcs on his next talkie and considers "the commutator hum, which occurs across an arc, can be removed by means of suitable chokes".[67]

It had always been realized that considerable technical skill was necessary for the cameraman, and there were at least forty of them working in Britain during the twenties whose names were widely known within the trade, and often credited on the film. Most were competent rather than imaginative, but among the best were many who stayed in the industry and became better known later, including Jack Cox, Bernard Knowles, Jack Parker, Stanley Rodwell, Desmond Dickinson and F. A. Young, as well as Emmott. The cameramen showed a greater consciousness of their existence as a professional group than other branches of the industry. The Kine Camera Men's Society was formed at the end of the war with 44 members out of a possible 60,[68] a London branch of the Society of Motion Picture Engineers in 1928. The British Association of Cinematographers and Allied Technicians formed early in 1928 was to include most other technicians as well.

Apart from lighting, the man wielding the camera was interested in broadly two aspects of what was in front of him, first what was to be included in the shot and secondly what sort of shot was to be used. In other words, the first meant the angle from which it was to be filmed; and this included both 'camera angle' as it was beginning to be called, although camera range, or distance, might have been clearer, as it referred to whether it was a long, mid or close shot or variant of these; and also 'angle' shots meaning low shots, overhead, slanted or any other unusual viewpoint. Secondly, consideration of what sort of shot was to be used concentrated not on the subject to be filmed, but on the camera itself—was it to be a masked shot, double exposure, split matt shot, was it to use an iris, fade, dissolve or wipe; and what form of change was to be used from one shot to the next, a fade, mix, cut or wipe?

In the early twenties the latter considerations, involving the devices of cinematography, seem to have been given more attention than the choice of camera angle. They were, indeed, the old tricks with which the early cinematographer had been accustomed to dazzle and mystify his audience. Although it was admitted that they must be justified by their function in the story, for some time they continued to be treated as a display of skill:

'. . . the villain of the picture, is seen coming along the road on a motor cycle, travelling at full pelt. Suddenly there appears on the screen just two white discs, representing the headlights of an approaching motor car. The discs grow larger as the lights approach and then switching back to a "close-up" of the motor cycle rider, trick photography is used to show that he is dazzled by the headlights of the approaching car. He is then seen to lose control of the cycle, which runs off the road, and throws him violently on to the back of his head. The screen then becomes perfectly black again, with the single exception of a small red dot, which is shown getting gradually smaller until it disappears altogether. Of course, the red dot represents the rear lamp of the motor. . . .'[69]

This description of a film of Calvert's in 1921 does not yet take such things for granted. Colden Lore in 1923 wrote of the fade:

'This effect is obtained by the use of the diaphragm between the lenses. (In the latest models a special shutter directly behind the lenses is employed for this purpose.) The diaphragm is a small device consisting of a number of thin discs so superimposed and connected with each other that, by a simple motion, they can be made to open evenly in circular form from almost complete closure to the fullest aperture of the lens. The amount of light to be admitted to the film can, therefore, be regulated to a nicety, and the diaphragm plays, consequently, an important part in photographic "tricks".

'When a picture is to be "faded in", the cameraman, while turning the film crank, gradually opens the diaphragm, admitting more and more light till the required amount is obtained and the picture is fully registered. In "fading out" the process is reversed. Either operation may, of course, be done slowly or quickly.'[70]

He also described the 'lap dissolve', taking place when the cameraman faded out, wound back, and faded in to another scene in such a way that

'. . . in the double exposure of a film, the actinic values of the light of the two different pictures are carefully graduated to complement each other so that the total amount of light permitted to act on the film remains constant throughout.'[70]

Visions, appearances and disappearances and transformation scenes could be made by simply stopping the camera, making the necessary changes and continuing filming:

'If, however, this vision is to appear gradually, the methods of double exposure will have to be applied, with this variation—that first of all, the furnishings of the set will be so arranged that the background against which this vision is to appear will be darkened. . . .'[70]

He mentioned the use of masks, shaped masks such as a keyhole or 'the binocular vignette', or filming with a corner of the picture masked and then using the film again with a complementary mask on the rest of the picture, the two being shown together. The iris 'is in front of the camera, intended to circumscribe the field that is to be photographed', and was effective at the beginning and end of scenes, to focus attention and act as a punctuation mark.

Hepworth was particularly fond of vignetting, and as we have seen (see page 114) he liked to use a discreet vignette for every shot. Masks of all shapes were very common in the early years, sometimes for a pretty effect, sometimes for a symbolic meaning, sometimes for emphasis of part of a long shot or of a big close-up, or even of a one-shot or two-shot. Another thing which Hepworth carried to extremes was the fading in and out of shots, in accordance with his belief that a sharp cut was disturbing to the spectator. Irising or fading were common ways to start or end a sequence, but many used them within sequences as well. *The Lure of Crooning Water*, a good example of 1920 film structure, has instances in which a shot is irised out, followed by a blackout, then a title, another blackout and the next shot irised in again. The result was rather leisurely. It was common to fade or dissolve even from long shots to close-ups within a conversation to avoid the supposed shock of cutting, yet the shot jarred far more because they were quite unmatched in appearance, as big close-ups were almost always taken against a dark background whatever the lighting of the rest of the sequence. It was Hepworth who carried this furthest, fading or irising in and out of every shot. Musical accompaniment in the cinema helped to keep his films alive, but this practice undeniably reduced their over-all pace. Yet even in 1927, when Manning Haynes featured a similar idea in *Passion Island*, *The Bioscope* treated it as something new:

'Your imposition of close-up upon long shot is an amazingly effective device which tomorrow will be adopted by the world.'[71]

Meanwhile the more discerning were finding ways of cutting from one shot to another which would really minimize the visual jump without implying a false time relationship such as that suggested by the fade or iris. Pearson's notes at the end of the period read:

'THE MOVING CAMERA SHOULD ONLY PHOTOGRAPH MOVING OBJECTS . . . remember this in *cutting* from C/U to L/S, etc. A moving camera is an EYE . . . the eye of the audience . . . and the eye sees no movement in static objects . . . to let the movement of the EYE become apparent rather than the movement of some *thing* is BAD TECNHIQUE.

'This applies to the RUN IN, *or* AWAY . . . it should only run parallel with some moving thing.'

Hepworth was an early enthusiast of double photography. His *Anna the Adventuress*, in which Alma Taylor played two parts, was shown in February 1920, a year before Mary Pickford played both mother and son in *Little Lord Fauntleroy*. In these films one player took two parts in the same scene by running the film through the camera twice, but each time with a different half masked by a shutter. To overcome difficulties in timing Hepworth used a phonograph geared to the camera, making a record of the producer's directions or commentary which could be played back when making the second half of the scene, to ensure perfect timing. Anything involving fades and dissolves, superimposition or double photography was at first done in the camera. Honri's notes point out that in the earliest days of the cinema R. W. Paul had obtained dissolve effects with double printing, but it was not until the mid-twenties that trick work began to return to the laboratory and the chemical fade process was introduced. Later, wipes and dissolves were to be done much more accurately on the optical printer, but he points out that for Elvey's second version of *Hindle Wakes* made in 1926 the elaborate montage sequence of the pleasure beach, with its complicated dissolves, was made by Basil Emmott entirely in the camera.

Blakeston described the iris, either in the centre or displaced to a corner, as a useful opening effect, like the curtain-off made by two plates opening horizontally, or the wipe-off made with a diagonal plate. The use of such things became more sophisticated during the twenties. But according to him they were still too prevalent. Writing in *Close Up* in April 1928 on the iris and other methods of film punctuation, he wrote:

'An iris appeared on the market which could be adjusted for twenty three, or possibly twenty-six, different opening effects. There was a pyrotechnic display of bursting stars; and of course wedding bells which grew in a second, like the fabulous fungus you see in the illustrations of fairy stories; even an inverted silhouette of a bridge was stretched across the screen to symbolize a clandestine meeting. . . .'[72]

and he complained that

'The average cameraman imagines that vignetting is artistic in itself.'[73]

Compared with the interest in vignetting, there was very little attention paid to camera angle as it was later understood. Colden Lore's account shows an extremely limited idea of the artistic possibilities inherent in the choice of camera distance. Being interested, apparently, only in the drama of emotional relationships, he saw the camera position as determined solely by the needs of visibility:

'The scenes are always taken at as close a range as possible, in order to permit the expressions of the emotions of the actors being clearly seen. For all practical purposes, therefore, the photographic "stage" is a space in the "set" severely circumscribed by these considerations, based on the size and power of the lens. The one in common use is a 2-inch lens, having, according to its make, an angle of from 28 to 35 degrees. Taking an angle of 30 degrees as an average, the "stage" has the shape of a trapezoid about 6 feet deep and 5 feet wide, the camera being usually 9 feet from the front or working line of this trapezoid. . . .

'In the scenario the distances between the camera and the object are roughly described as "Close Up", "Semi-Close Up", "Medium", "Semi-Long" and "Long" Shots, but no hard and fast distance definitions can be attached to these terms. Broadly speaking, the "Close Ups" are taken at from 5 to 9 feet from the working line, "Medium Shots" at from 9 to 15 feet, "Semi-Long Shots" at from 15 to 25 feet, and a "Long Shot" may be anything from 25 feet upwards. The "Close Up" is the photographic equivalent of the opera glass.'[74]

The run-of-the-mill English film of the early twenties showed this practical, unimaginative approach with very little variety of camera angle within the set, painfully emphasizing its stage-like construction with one open wall. Close shots

Right: Frank Stanmore in
son's *The Little People,* 1926.

re Right: Set designed by
lcanti for Pearson's *The
People,* 1926. Mona Maris
e centre.

om Right: Pearson directing
Little People in a French
o, Percy Strong at the
ra, Mona Maris and Gerald
s seated.

Top Left: Nora Swinburne in Kellino's *His Grace Gives Notice*, 1924.
Top right: Cedric Hardwicke in Summers' *Nelson*, 1926.
Bottom Left: Matheson Lang in *The Chinese Bungalow*, 1926.
Bottom Right: Phyllis Neilson-Terry as *Boadicea*, 1926.

were used only when they were inescapable. There was, in fact, widespread disapproval of any other method:

'As a producer, Mr Noy has been inclined to break up the continuity of his action unduly by constant changes of his camera range and unnecessary "cut-ins". The Americans inaugurated and developed this restless style of production in an effort, very often, to compensate poor acting and flaccid situations by feverish movement and variety. Such artifices are unnecessary with a really strong story and first-rate players. The frequent interpolation of close-ups in a big situation is irritating to the spectator and must be worrying to the actor.'[75]

An American wrote appreciatively of British restraint:

'. . . the absence of the many close-ups is welcome; American films contain always at least twenty of these near views, which, becoming merely pictures of enlarged pores and exaggerated mouths and eye-lids, are fast bringing fine photography into disrepute.'[76]

So suspicious were the ordinary film makers of the close-up that in the Robey film *One Arabian Night* in 1923, for example, there was only one close shot of this famous comedian's expressive face.

Among more enterprising film makers, however, a greater flexibility of camera angle and with it a certain advance in editing were beginning to appear. *The Lure of Crooning Water*, for example had a good deal of variety within sequences even in 1920, although it is true much of this seems fairly pointless. Sporting films were compelled by their very nature to develop greater fluidity. Rooke's *Sport of Kings* in 1922 showed its horse races with some variety of shots and masks; and in the boxing match the main long-shot camera set-ups could be interrupted by close-ups of the fighter's face when he was down for the count, and of faces in the audience, which would not have been possible in a news film of a real fight. In *The Bohemian Girl*, also in 1922, and in *Decameron Nights* of the year after, the presence of the principals in large crowd scenes was emphasized not only by close-ups, a fairly obvious way, but also by mid-close shots of them seen past other peoples' shoulders, giving a very satisfactory feeling of being in a crowd. In the former film, especially, the exchange of glances between Ivor Novello and Gladys Cooper from different positions in the crowd was managed with ease. In *Young Lochinvar* in 1923, a passage in which the four young people seated at a meal table exchange glances full of meaning explains their relationships in a businesslike sequence of close mid-shots completely without titles. Such passages contrast with crowd scenes in the lamentable *She* of 1925, in which the eye of the spectator must single the principals out of the tossing mob without any help from the camera. Even lesser film makers began to vary the angle within the sequence during the twenties and by the end of the silent film more subtle and significant choices were to be expected in the work of the best of them. In an opening passage in Mander's *First Born* in 1928 an overhead shot of four people at a round dinner table, gleaming with

I   257

candelabra, silver and glass in an otherwise dark screen, is followed by a mid-shot of each diner framed between two lamps in the surrounding darkness, talking and watching, which establishes the characters and their relationships in elegance and watchful isolation and suggests a combined achievement by writer, director, lighting cameraman and editor.

An overhead shot has an obvious charm and was perhaps the earliest form of self-consciously artistic angle shot. There was little attempt at such things at first. But large sets encouraged an overhead angle, as in the ball scene in *Damaged Goods* in 1919 and a high-beamed barn in *Marriage Lines* in 1921. Meal tables, like *First Born's*, also seemed to have asked for overhead shots and one occurred in *Lure of Crooning Water's* farmhouse supper; next year in *The Bohemian Girl* Knoles and his cameraman Guissart mounted an elaborate hunt luncheon in the castle, and its size and luxury were emphasized when it was seen from the gallery above. In this it contrasted with Stoll's *One Arabian Night* of the followng year, for although the enormous Stoll studio was used for a large set of the Emperor's throne room, so canvassy did it look that an overhead shot could emphasize only its empty and tawdry appearance. Brunel's *Man Without Desire*, shot partly in a German studio in 1923 by Henry Harris, was enterprising in the manner of the impressionist German films, with unexpected angles on the picturesque Venetian architecture, draped curtains, dwarfs and little negro slaves and with a touch of the macabre and mysterious in the magician's retorts and the sinister shadow of his hand weaving spells over the beautiful face of the sleeping hero. Graham Cutts started to play with the angle shot in *The Rat* in 1925 and *The Triumph of the Rat* next year. But angle shots for their own sake, which became so common in other countries, were a bit beyond most British studios and our cameramen hardly deserved such a stricture as that of Pommer, responsible in Germany for *The Last Laugh* (1924) and *Variety* (1926), who warned against freakish director's tricks and advised 'the camera must view the scene just as the natural spectator would see it.'[77] The overhead shot of Ivor Novello, as a youth crossing the large courtyard of the public school from which he has just been expelled in Hitchcock's *Downhill* (1927), suitably underlines his smallness and loneliness, and would satisfy even Asquith's demand for justification:

'. . . where the point of view of one of the characters is represented . . . to intensify a dramatic moment even if the "shot" represents no one's point of view . . . and to compose a good picture.'[78]

Camera mobility followed the same course. It first became popular as a virtuoso effect, and had later to be brought down to earth and used only when it had some significance in the film. At first the camera tilted and panned as needed, hovering uncertainly sometimes, as though unable to focus on its subject. Such small movements were used in preference to cutting. Cameras also tracked, as in the old phantom rides, where something like a racing horse made it a feature of the film. In *The Lady Owner* of 1923 there is a sequence where the camera, mounted on a car, follows beside the horses in the big race, but does not bother to do so when they are exercising on the Downs, which is only seen in long shots. There are many instances of the camera following people. In a short and unimportant comedy of the early twenties, Ivy Duke and Guy Newall's *Beauty and the Beast*, the camera tracks upstairs behind them, and in *Happy Ending* in 1924 it tracked down the garden after Fay Compton and Eric Lewis, pausing with them to emphasize points in the conversation. In 1922 in *The Bohemian Girl* the camera was moved to make the best of the size and splendour of the set in the dream sequence *I Dreamt that I Dwelt in Marble Halls*, and tracks slowly forward towards the throne through a large and magnificent marble hall. Mobility for more tricky purposes was very rare. The camera tilted this way and that to represent Robey's drunken view of the world in *One Arabian Night*; it viewed the garden from a moving swing in a self-conscious suggestion of Watteau in Cutts' *Triumph of the Rat*; and soared to and from the organ pipes in *Bolibar*, shot by Jack Parker in 1928, in a rather desperate attempt to get a visual representation of sound. In 1925 Cutts was the first to derive much glory from the travelling camera in this country. Under a *Bioscope* heading 'Graham Cutts, Inventor' it was described as a 'device' to avoid jumping from long shot to close shot and enabling actors to play scenes continuously.[79] He used it in *The Rat*, but many people claimed that it was tiring to the eye, although to later audiences his use of it would seem very mild, moving in from long to mid-close shot and following people about a little; in any case he modified it for *Triumph of the Rat*. Once more, when Hitchcock used the same device he proved to have a greater understanding of its possible significance. When Ivor Novello has to go and see the headmaster in *Downhill* the camera tracks with him through a very large study, making the witness feel small and apprehensive with him. Travelling establishing shots early in a film were used effectively in Hitchcock's *Farmer's Wife*, Walter Forde's *Wait and See*, and in *Kitty* and *Tesha* of 1928, the last two shot by Karl Püth. Georg Jacoby, in England to work on *The Physician* at about this time, believed in the mobile camera:

'. . . he does look forward to the day when it will be entirely practical to attain perfect continuity through a moving camera following the action and the players like a human eye, eliminating sudden jumps and mixes.

'The moving camera will travel round and about, over chairs and tables, through doorways and windows and so on. This can be done now with a camera on a crane, but the general awkwardness of such an apparatus and the necessarily frequent resort to a motor-driven camera, militate against its use for filming a picture in its entirety.'[80]

But it still did not receive universal favour. Writing of Werner Brandes' camera-work in Dupont's *Piccadilly* in 1929, Hugh Castle said:

'ART.
With a capital A. If Dupont wants to show two people in different rooms he pans from the attic, down the stairs, across the front room, through a brick wall or two, into the room, wanders around it and finally brings his camera to rest on his second character.'[81]

However, he need not have worried. Amongst the other effects of the sound film was the immobilization of the camera in its heavy sound-proof box. But by this time it was clearly understood that the choice of camera angle and type of shot, whether the contribution of the director or the cameraman or both, was an important part of the creative process.

(7) ACTING

Unlike the contribution of the writer or editor, the actor's work was conspicuous and his life seemed enviable to many. But players were badly paid in England compared to those in America, especially supporting players, and apart from the very few who regarded film acting as a career they had on the whole a low opinion of it and took their work on the stage more seriously. The small British studios were all in or near London. Because of this proximity to the West End theatre most supporting and many leading players remained primarily stage actors. This casual system impeded the development of a more suitable acting style, and enabled studios to go on paying low rates. Organization was slow. Gerald Ames wrote several articles in *The Actor* after the war was over advocating the unionization of film actors, and in September 1920 a mass meeting was held to discuss special arrangements for them at which it was resolved to form a cinema section of the Variety Artistes' Federation. But the Film Artistes' Guild was not formed until 1927, when there were enough established players acting either exclusively or chiefly in films to make such an organization worth while.

Some studios screened rushes to help the actors, director and cameraman to judge the results of the previous day's takes, and stars were believed by the public to take their acting very seriously. Music was provided in some studios to help them. Stage actors, working with no audience except the studio technicians, had to rely on the director to explain the continuity of production and character and to help them create the right mood. It was felt that a musical accompaniment would help them here and Pearson, for example, first used one in 1918, and had a permanent studio orchestra by the time he made *Nothing Else Matters* in 1920. Much publicity was devoted to showing how noble and important the stars' aspirations were. Malvina Longfellow was reported to have said that she thought Emma in the 1919 *Nelson* was her 'greatest screen achievement', and even to claim that she had made a point of studying Lady Hamilton's character, although this rudimentary film shows little sign of such study.

Large numbers of vaguely defined characters seen at a great distance, little more than walking names, trying to convey character and emotion by means of heavy make-up and exaggerated gestures, did much to justify the scorn in which film acting was held by the traditional theatre. Film acting seemed like slumming. The music-hall star Albert Chevalier, who had filmed with Hepworth before the war, wrote:

'. . . with Nature for scene painter, the cinema drama has a pictorial advantage which camouflages the inherent weakness of a dumb cast. To say that cinema acting is a new art is to talk nonsense . . . the actor in a film play need only be half-equipped.

'I can see the great possibilities of the cinema—its cheap prices and consequent wide appeal; its importance in connection with education; but I cannot believe a time will ever come when the most perfect machine will dethrone the living, breathing, human artist.

'I do not agree with Sir Oswald Stoll, who, writing recently in the *Daily Mail*, expressed the opinion that "the theatre could learn much from the cinema". The theatre has nothing to learn from its infant offshoot. The cinema play owes its existence to the theatre, and most of its popularity to the performances of experienced stage actors. By comparison with the flesh and blood reality of a spoken play, it is drama in cold storage. As such, it may continue to create a taste for the genuine thing.'[82]

A virtual pool of some two hundred bit players imbued with this spirit, readily available for film work, battened on one production outfit after another, imposing their own professional style on the most varied directors. English crowd work was particularly crude. It was easier to let the actors flutter and wring their hands, storm and stamp, clutch and gasp, than to work out incidents and shots which would convey feeling and thought with less absurdity. Even Pearson allowed the actor playing the part of the Weasel to lurch, wheel and stagger in long shot with ludicrous results in *Squibs Wins the Calcutta Sweep* in 1922. And in *Blighty* in 1927 the quiet stillness of Nadia Sibirskaia, an actress from France who had been in Kirsanov's haunting *Ménilmontant* in 1924, showed that a single movement of her eyes could be more telling than the gyrations of many British actresses.

During the next ten years there was to be a great change in all this. The alteration in the actors' appearance between 1919 and 1929, for one thing, was very marked. The actors of 1919 were heavily made-up, and the strangeness of film make-up was one of the most cherished legends of the silver screen. Yellow was much used in the days of orthochromatic stock. Boughey remarked that

'. . . a creamy screen-complexion is generally obtained by a coating of yellow grease-paint.'[83]

MacBean wrote that grease-paint had to be used to correct the distortions resulting from the film stock and lighting, particularly avoiding reds which photographed black, and that powder was necessary to conceal the shiny look of the grease-paint. The actor Rolfe Leslie was

'. . . one of the cleverest manipulators of make-up in movieland, and has often been engaged by producers specially to make up artistes for character roles.'[84]

C. Aubrey Smith advocated simplicity:

'What can I possibly say on such a limited subject as "Screen Make-Up". . . .

Armed with a stock of No. 5, another of No. 9, and some yellow powder, the artist may satisfy any producer in this country. . . . Very little make-up is really required by those playing ordinary parts. Just sufficient to counteract the effect of the strong artificial lighting which the actor or actress may be called upon to face and no more . . . the final word should rest with the cameraman.'[85]

But Steer gave the fans a lurid picture of the special make-up needed, with faces whitened and then tinted with yellow, lips and the part round the eyes shaded with bluish colours.[86]

Hepworth had strong and unusual views about make-up. He disapproved of it as much as he did of artificial lighting, and was proud that his star Alma Taylor used none, not so much because he admired realism as because he believed that make-up clogged the skin and prevented subtle nuances of expression. He was not, however, able to prevent his theatrical leading man Shayle Gardner from covering his face thickly with most unsuitable make-up. The stiffness and discomfort of stage grease-paint had persuaded Max Factor to develop a more flexible make-up in Hollywood by 1923, but this was not available in England during Hepworth's time even had he been the man to change his mind. In fact the nature of early film stock and lighting was such as to require some correction merely in order to achieve a natural appearance. But this was only one of the motives for its use. More important was the idea of character make-up, derived more or less unchanged from the theatre with all the traditional formulae for old age, villainy, comedy and national stereotypes. An extreme example was Matheson Lang's Chinese make-up in *Mr Wu* in 1919 and *The Chinese Bungalow* in 1926. Matheson Lang was one of the many actors particularly fond of the element of disguise and dressing-up in the theatre and he specialized in elaborate make-ups, which he brought virtually unchanged to the screen. Never for a moment did he look Chinese. This and other examples underlined a fact which was becoming more and more obvious. It was seen that making up an unsuitable person is no substitute, on the screen, for casting a suitable person in the first place. The actor occupied a rather different place in the two media of theatre and film, and whereas a sixty-year-old celebrity actor-manager might give a *tour-de-force* performance as Hamlet on the stage, a young and inexperienced amateur might well be more satisfactory as part of a film impression. As early as 1920 the Swedish director Mauritz Stiller was famous for casting appropriate types. The Russians' emphasis on using people of the right type as plastic material for the director, rather than employing professional actors to give a performance, was recognition of the same fact. In 1928 Dreyer's *Passion of Joan of Arc*, which was shot all in close-up and with no make-up at all, demanded an artist's selection of people with the right appearance. The growing importance of the casting director in the ordinary commercial cinema was tacit recognition of the same thing.

But one of the chief and most lasting reasons for screen make-up was glamour. People were learning how to use make-up, together with lighting, to suggest a beauty which did not exist in reality, or, at least, could not have been conveyed by the camera alone. This in turn created an ideal appearance which people came to expect from their stars, and which in time made great changes in the appearance acceptable in real life. When incandescent light and panchromatic film came into use it was thought by some that this meant the end of make-up. Blakeston, for example, said in 1928 that make-up was now 'unnecessary for men, although there is a special panchromatic foundation for women'.[87] But the glamorous appearance had by now established standards of its own which had nothing to do with realism, and Max Factor make-up was welcomed when it became available here at the end of 1927.

This was the great day of the Hollywood stars of the silent film, when Nazimova, Gloria Swanson and Rudolph Valentino brought dreams of sex and exotic glamour to millions, and Douglas Fairbanks, Mary Pickford and Charlie Chaplin were met by adoring crowds when they travelled abroad. The British film industry had made some attempt to create an aura of personal glamour like that of Hollywood and to manufacture stardom by publicity. But the British stars were somewhat homely in comparison with the legendary international figures. Ivy Close and Ivy Duke were half-heartedly referred to as flappers, and photographs of young actresses in swim suits appeared in the papers, although the home-grown vamp made comparatively little progress in this country—the young Joan Morgan was as pretty as the Gish sisters, but received little publicity. The first British actress to be systematically exploited as glamorous and well-dressed was Violet Hopson, and she did become quite well known as a local star despite a personality which made little real impact from the screen. The same company, Broadwest, tried similar methods with less success with another actress, Hilda Bayley, whose clothes were

'. . . le dernier cri, especially designed by a Russian artist to meet the demands of the camera.'[88]

But the dernier cri eluded British producers, not only because of its expense but because block booking held films up for many months after they were made. The mainspring of this type of star publicity was the emphasis on appearance. Beside the fashion pictures the fan magazines of the early twenties carried advertisements for perms, silk stockings and Helena Rubinstein make-up, interspersed with articles on the stars' most profound views on life. The public relations men fed the fan press with what they felt readers wanted, including all the clichés of enormous salaries, the stories of fantastic danger devotedly faced for the good of the film, figures of the yardage and cost of the cloth used in the latest spectacle, and above all the heart-warming stories of discovery. Monty Banks

'. . . was looking for a girl to portray his fiancée in the comedy, The Compulsory Husband. He had seen dozens of young actresses, and had selected from among them a few to whom he proposed giving a final test. But on the night before the test he visited a theatre, went into the bar during the interval, and there saw the ideal girl for the films. . . . Lilian Manton, programme girl and usherette, walked through those gates of hope with fame and fortune within her grasp.'[89]

The whole star complex, particularly the discovery stories, was a magnet to the screen-struck amateur, but neither training facilities nor a regular entry system existed and they had to be content with daydreams and fan activities. The publicity departments may have felt they could turn anybody into a star, but they found this was not so in 1928 when vigorous promotion of a gorgeous Franco-Spanish actor, Alexander D'Arcy, as the new Valentino was a total failure. Something, at least, was required from the intending star, though no one seemed very sure what it was. It was hard to pin down the ability to project a personality on the screen, but a very small number of people seemed able to create a clear, compelling presence which had nothing to do with publicity. Betty Balfour and Ivor Novello, and to a lesser extent Alma Taylor, were the only early British stars comparable in popularity to the Hollywood favourites, but although other players such as Stewart Rome, Joan Morgan, Lillian Hall-Davis, Chrissie White and Mabel Poulton achieved considerable local popularity, it was in unexpected performances from a very few people like Victor McLaglen, Guy Newall and Ivy Duke that a vivid impression of a real person suddenly appeared, less because of exceptional acting than because of some personal quality which was hard to define.

Early British production relied almost entirely on the stage for actors. Visiting celebrities from the stage and music hall tried the new medium. Sir John Martin Harvey and Sir Frank Benson continued what Benson himself and Forbes Robertson had tried earlier, a recording of the *fin de siècle* actor-manager in one of his favourite rôles, giving dominating and killing performances in films of monumental boredom. Martin-Harvey was nearly sixty when he played Sidney Carton for Wilcox, Benson already sixty-five when he made *Becket* for Stoll. The great Ellen Terry in her seventies made several small, graceful appearances in unworthy films and in one, *The Bohemian Girl* of 1922, of better quality. Seymour Hicks and Ellaline Terriss, who were in their late fifties, experimented modestly. Sybil Thorndike appeared as Edith Cavell in *Dawn*, at forty-six putting regular film actresses to shame with the calm authority of her performance, and Phyllis Neilson-Terry, considerably younger, was a noble embodiment of Boadicea. The great music-hall performers Harry Lauder and George Robey were both in their fifties when they tried the cinema, following the earlier efforts of Billy Merson. Merson, who did not follow up his early experiment until he ventured a short sound film later, seems to have realized how much even a slapstick music-hall comic actually relied on words. Robey's song titles suggest a largely verbal style: 'He'll get it where he's gone to, now', 'Touching that little affair', 'Oh! how rude!', 'I had to be cruel to be kind', 'Say no more about it'!, 'Archibald! certainly not!'. His comic style depended heavily on the pedantic prim absurdity of the songs and patter and, despite his mastery of facial expression, the eyebrows, the waddling walk, his style was hardly visual at all. Lauder was more fortunate than Robey in his director, Pearson, who provided him with comedy situation stories, but he also was very largely a singer with comic patter rather than a visual comic. His songs were sometimes lyrical, sometimes humorous: 'I love a lassie', 'Stop yer tickling, Jock', 'We parted on the shore', 'Roamin' in the gloamin' ', 'Just a wee Deoch-an-Doris'. But most of his laughs came from gags and patter and he also, on film, was reduced to little more than a 'funny' lovable appearance and joke titles. Nellie Wallace (*Why Men Leave Home*, 1922) and Harry Tate (*Motoring*, 1929) were both filmed in characteristic sketches by inferior companies, and Fred Karno and company were filmed in his sketch *Early Birds* in 1923. Other comedians who tried the medium were Leslie Henson in *Alf's Button* in 1920, and his stage success *Tons of Money* in 1924, and less successfully Rebla (*Forty Winks* and *Who Laughs Last* in 1920), Grock (*What for?* in 1927), Jack Hulbert and Cicely Courtneidge (*Told in a Two-Seater* in 1921) and Lupino Lane (*Who's Afraid* in 1927). The British cinema was badly in need of comedy, relying largely on Betty Balfour, Will Kellino, Walter Forde and later the imported slickness of Syd Chaplin and Monty Banks. But of the established stage comics who experimented with the cinema none seem to have understood the different style needed.

Leading men were particularly likely to come from the stage, although there were a few cases of the successful outsider like Victor McLaglen, described in *Pictures and the Picturegoer* as 'farmer, miner, globe-trotter, soldier, boxer'.[90] Most of the early leading men were stage veterans sadly lacking in romance and noticeably older than the girl film stars. Men who were in the twenty-five to thirty-five age group during the early twenties had suffered the heaviest casualties during the war and most leading actors at this time were somewhat older. Like Matheson Lang himself, Milton Rosmer, James Carew, Gerald Ames, Carlyle Blackwell, Fred Paul, Fred Groves, Stewart Rome and even Henry Edwards were all in their forties and lacked youth, dash or sex appeal. Many of the leading ladies who specialized in films, such as Evelyn Brent, Flora le Breton, Ivy Close, Mary Odette, Madge Stuart and Marjorie Hume, although young, had little to distinguish them from each other. Lillian Hall-Davis, a beauty queen who entered films in 1921 and appeared in many films throughout the twenties, was beautiful but typical in her reliability and lack of personality, and was described by *Close Up* as 'an actress of hard efficiency and no charm'.[91] There were also a number of director-star partnerships which owed nothing to acting talent. To these the Hepworth–Alma Taylor, Guy Newall–Ivy Duke, Henry Edwards–Chrissie White and Pearson–Balfour teams were honourable exceptions.

Apart from these, players of distinctive personality did not appear until the later twenties, when a marked change occurred. In the case of the girls this meant the departure of the producers' girl friends and the arrival of a new generation of young actresses born around 1900 and equally at home on the screen and on the stage. These included Edna Best, Nora Swinburne, Norah Baring, Chili Bouchier, Dorothy Boyd, Madeleine Carroll, Joan Barry, Eve Gray and such occasional visitors from the theatre as June. Meanwhile Betty Balfour, Annette Benson and Estelle Brody continued to be kept busy. Of the men, most of the fortyish heroes of the early twenties were gradually replaced after 1925 by heroes of twenty-five to thirty who were young enough to have escaped the brunt of the war. Ian Hunter, John Stuart, John Longden, Carl Harbord, Carl Brisson and Brian Aherne were some of those who brought a welcome sign of virility and youth. Nevertheless an article in *The Bioscope* as late as 1928 complained that Ivor Novello and Betty Balfour were still the only players with real star quality and drawing power.[92]

By now the whole appearance of the films and the actors was different. Improvements in lighting and make-up had been accompanied by a greater intimacy of camera position, and a development of character delineation by the selection of incident and detail. The younger and more intelligent players had observed the German examples in films like *Decameron Nights*, a British production which had been made in a German studio with a partly German cast, and had adopted a slower, more deliberate style, full of pregnant pauses, long looks and deep breathing. But both leading and supporting players of both sexes in England continued to come largely from the stage and to keep a foot in both camps. Ivor Novello, Fay Compton, Owen Nares and Jack Buchanan were among the stage players well known for their film work who yet remained essentially of the theatre. In one way this was very necessary, for success in British films was neither secure nor profitable and was regarded by many merely as a step up to greater success either on the stage or in Hollywood. Many other successful stage players, like Lilian Braithwaite, Laddie Cliff, Constance Collier, Gladys Cooper and others merely dabbled in films. It would probably be fair to say that all the older supporting players in small, medium and character parts were semi-successful stage players, still getting as much stage work as they could and in many cases not mentioning their cinema work in their directory entries later in life, even when they had been regular standbys of the film producer. For example, Matheson Lang starred in many films and was well known in the trade, which was extremely proud of his connection with it, but he did not care to mention this in Parker's *Who's Who in the Theatre*. Thus, despite a gradual improvement in film acting, the British cinema continued to be very closely tied to the stage, and there were few exclusively film stars.

There continued to be some who disliked the star system. With cries of 'Wake up, England!' Tom Terriss in a bitter letter[93] had described it as a cancerous growth, and its imminent death was often predicted. Over-frequent use of the large close-up made this, also, an object of great suspicion. It is hard to realize now the frequency and anger with which the close-up was attacked, and the passion with which people who regarded it as an odious fad hoped that it would soon disappear. The star system did substitute the promotion and glorification of personality for real advances in film technique, but it was never very highly developed in England. The few early stock companies were too small and too poor, and the most important, Hepworth's, was opposed to the system. The sophisticated modern producers, from Balcon and Wilcox to B.I.P. in the second half of the period, were largely content to borrow glamour that had been created elsewhere, whether on the stage, in America or in other countries.

Of course, a major reason for the scarcity of home-grown film stars was the vicious circle of economic and artistic poverty. Anyone who appeared to have star quality was tempted to try Hollywood or some other place where not only pay but opportunities were so much better. Not all of them achieved success there. Walter Forde, Evelyn Brent and Hayford Hobbs were in Hollywood by

1923, and Flora le Breton and Madge Stuart were making plans to go. Lupino Lane and Peggy Hyland made films there. G. K. Arthur, after making a hit in Stoll's *Kipps* of 1921, went to America and eventually starred in von Sternberg's *The Salvation Hunters* in 1925. Percy Marmont, although British, starred in American films. Stewart Rome went in 1925 and Warwick Ward, after working quietly on many British films, rose to stardom in German films after 1925. Herbert Marshall was well known on the British stage but went to America soon after his important starring part in Wilcox's *Mumsie* in 1927, at about the same time as Clive Brook, who had successfully appeared in many British films without becoming a star in the early twenties. Ronald Colman also appeared in a number of British films without recognition and departed for America fairly early. Basil Rathbone was well known on both the British and the American stage and quickly went to America after starting his film career with Stoll's. Many others who later achieved world stardom in America included Brian Aherne, Madeleine Carroll, Cedric Hardwicke, Ian Hunter, C. Aubrey Smith, Victor McLaglen, Ralph Forbes, John Loder and Ray Milland.

The traffic was not all one way. Wilcox, Balcon and B.I.P. all felt at one time or another that the only way to make production economic was to secure distribution abroad, and used American and to a smaller extent German stars to give their films an international appeal. British and Colonial had announced that they would try to capture the American market by using American stars as early as 1919. Gertrude McCoy, working for British Actors in 1919, did not think much of English studio methods and equipment. This critical attitude was often found among visiting stars although, as many of them were somewhat past their peak, they were in no position to be particular. Balcon brought Betty Compson over at a high salary for his first productions, Wilcox imported Betty Blythe, Dorothy Gish and Will Rogers, and both Balcon and Wilcox later used German stars in Anglo-German productions. When the quota was announced later on it was felt that Britain lacked enough top level talent to fulfil the new production opportunities and there were many visitors, especially at B.I.P., from Tallulah Bankhead, Lionel Barrymore, Anna May Wong and Jean Bradin to Monty Banks, Syd Chaplin, Antonio Moreno and Olga Tschechova, Maria Corda, Lya de Putti and Gilda Gray and many others. Britain appeared to have moved into the world of the stars, but this appearance was an illusion as long as it was necessary for the stardom to be created elsewhere.

(8) EDITING

Possibly the greatest development in film technique during the twenties was that of editing. If we consider the cinema in general, and the Russian cinema in particular, this is certainly true. If we consider only the practice of editing in British production many changes certainly took place, but they were empirical, imperfectly understood and very slow. This contrast between the intellectual appreciation of film assembly by the Russians, and the slow, blind steps by which British studios fumbled their way forward, is the most depressing aspect of

British production. The number of shots in a reel increased greatly and their length decreased correspondingly. But the underlying significance of this change was only dimly appreciated by all except a small number of film makers.

As in other branches of film technique, the name by which the technician came to be known helped to confuse the issue. We have seen the functions of the lighting cameraman develop somewhat unexpectedly out of the work of the 'photographer'; the distinction of producer and director appear spontaneously when the work of the early 'producer' grew too heavy; and the term art director reflected the fact that design had only been considered in spectacle or art films. In the same unpremeditated way the word 'editor' emerged from an uneasy shuffling of the functions of editing the script, writing the titles, sticking the film together, and doctoring an unsatisfactory film with scissors and cement. In the end the term editor, and cutter even more so, unfortunately suggested cutting out rather than putting together.

This might have been fair enough had editing been confined to the technical job of choosing takes and trimming the ends to fit them together smoothly, exactly as indicated in the script or by the director. But there was no clear dividing line between this trimming and the much more basic job of deciding the very framework of the film. Had editing been called film assembly or construction, this title, although clumsy, might have been a more useful indication of its function. The word 'montage' became current with news of the new Russian technique, but it soon became associated with the idea of a montage sequence, or flashy set piece of impressionism in the middle of an otherwise literally cut film, further confused by the fact that in Britain this usually took the form of double exposure rather than of quick cutting, and was alternatively called an impressionistic mix.

In short it was not felt that the exact order and timing of the shots was an important matter and it was usually left to a subordinate technician. Consequently little development took place. In the early twenties takes were long, variety of camera angle within set-ups was the exception, and reference shots relating to anything outside the literal narrative were rare indeed. Cutting was taken to mean simply the physical work of cutting and sticking bits of film more or less closely according to instructions, and customs and rules were evolved from experience to make the shots move smoothly into each other. But as doctoring the film by rearrangement or retitling was still part of it there was no formal distinction between the subordinate job and that of determining the structure of the film, and the guiding influence on the latter depended on the personalities involved. The editor was usually a poor last. There was little idea that editing was an integral part of the whole conception of the film as an assembly of shots until this was introduced by the Russian films, or by accounts of them, in the later twenties.

At the beginning of the twenties, with one reel of 1,000 feet taking 16 minutes 40 seconds at a projection speed of 60 feet a minute, a feature film as a rule was 5 or 6 reels, or an hour and 20 to 40 minutes. Boughey said in 1921 that, with retakes, the total amount of film shot to get a film of this length might amount to 10,000 to 15,000 feet. This was printed, and the editor 'cuts, arranges, transposes, deletes, and finally re-assembles' down to perhaps 6,000 feet; he could finally shorten or remove episodes or cover them 'by a short descriptive title' and reduce it to 4,000 or 5,000 feet. This was rather more wasteful than many small companies could afford, but there was always some selection. Hepworth took a low view of the importance of this part of film production and left it to 'the girl' to follow the script and get the pieces stuck together, with as few cuts as possible. A. E. Coleby and Walter West, neither of them interested in art or theories, were both concerned with action stories of horse racing or crime in which the action moved rapidly from place to place, and were thus drawn into a consideration of the duration and alternation of shots, becoming aware as a result that their final format could rarely be visualized in exact detail at scenario stage. Many directors did, and were proud of doing, their own 'assembling'. George Ridgwell cut his own films when he was at Stoll's. Challis Sanderson and G. A. Cooper both edited their own modest films and both later became editors. Elvey was a director who realized the importance of editing although he did not do it himself. The professional cutter existed early in the large, factory-like American studios, and Brenon brought one over from the States for *12.10* in 1919. Stoll, with its similar structure, was one of the first British companies to employ specialized film editors, among them Billy Williams, Challis Sanderson, Leslie Brittain and Sam Simmons.

The theory after the war was fairly simple. In 1922 MacBean devoted little of his book to what he called 'piecing together the scenes'. He implied that the scenario was to be a shot-by-shot plan of the final film. Under 'Cutting and Joining'[94] he wrote

'The first print (or producer's copy) is carried out under the supervision of the producer by girls trained to the work. . . .'

but conceded

'After projecting the first copy, due alterations are made and when a satisfactory result is obtained. . . '.

Boughey went into it in somewhat greater detail[95] but showed an even more limited idea of film structure. He identified shot with scene:

'Each scene contains only one main incident having a direct bearing on the story, for it must be remembered that every time the camera is moved there is a fresh scene. . . .

'This makes a comparatively large number of scenes in a long play, such as a five-reel drama, unavoidable and vitally necessary.'

and even

'Tests have proved conclusively that in the case of the screen the human eye tires after about three or four minutes, which compels a change of scene in, at least, every 150 to 200 ft of film. . . .'

Exercised about the strain on the eye of shots of more than this length he suggested that they should be

'. . . broken either by titles or by *collateral* scenes (i.e. those which carry on the collateral action)'.

Thus he approached film structure from an exactly opposite position from that of the Russians. To him it was not a structure built up out of shots, but a long photograph in which cuts unfortunately had to be made for various reasons. Changes of scene-shot were made to follow the geographical movement of the action: to relieve eye-strain; to introduce 'deft touches' which conveyed details of character, time and place; and finally 'psychological cuts' were made for purposes such as emphasis.

With cutting used in each case to overcome some difficulty, no wonder the editor or cutter seemed like a doctor, and his work, often a 'very difficult and trying operation',[96] remedial rather than creative. Rules were evolving from experience. Honri tells how, at Stoll in the early twenties, he learnt simple rules from Ridgwell: to cut from long shot to close shot at the point of maximum movement; to synchronize movements when cutting from one shot of movement to another; and to have movement at the beginning and end of an insert.

So far so good. But by now the whole idea of editing was fortuitously mixed up with film doctoring. A small company in difficulties with an intractable film might call in an independent editor. Indeed, perhaps Stoll itself had specialized editors earlier than most firms less because of its concern for film technique than because the dullness of some of the filmed results of its bulk purchase of unsuitable stories required desperate remedies. Some films were cut and recut by several people before they were finished. Charles Barnett wrote proudly of his 'Fourteen Years with the Scissors' and how he had changed stories, shortened them, lengthened them by reprinting passages or adding titles and scenic shots, and even turned a serious film into a burlesque.[97] In some cases new shots were provided, especially close-ups, which at this time were always shot with a dark background and therefore did not need to be matched. Moreover the very word editing was connected with titling and literary chopping and changing, and miracles were expected from an outsider shifting the pieces around as he added his titles. Nor was it only the production firms who did this. Much early editing was an attempt by renters to pep up a dragging film or to adapt imported films to what they felt British audiences, and the British censors, required in the way of length, moral and social outlook and titles. American titling came in for much criticism and an item in 1923 estimated that an average of some 500 feet was cut from American negatives, including 'scenic cuts and irrelevant titling'. A more serious, and very well known, undertaking was that formed by Adrian Brunel and Ivor Montagu, which adapted many famous foreign films from the middle twenties onwards and shepherded them through their censorship difficulties in this country. No better way of learning about film structure could have been devised and this firm introduced many later editors to the film industry.

Sadly, such outside professionals were on occasion called in to alter films, and make them palatable to the trade, which talented directors had made a little more adventurous than usual. In 1926 neither Hitchcock's *The Lodger* nor Pearson's *The Little People* were acceptable at first to timid renters. The whole idea of such tampering was beginning to upset serious film makers.

The finished film was now a most complex assembly of shots, and for an outsider to interfere with this was more and more objectionable. Yet at the same time it was becoming less easy for one ordinary person to handle the whole thing as well as direct, and the position of the professional editor within the production firm became more important. The sheer physical bulk of celluloid grew, and the amount of film cover which was shot grew in some cases to inordinate length. Blakeston said in 1928 that directors 'sometimes run to over a hundred takes of one shot' and mentions 60,000 feet for a 'coherent seven thousand feet'. The total footage shot for Jacoby's *The Physician* made in England in 1928 was said to be 90,000 feet,[98] and as much as 900,000 for Carl Laemmle's *Uncle Tom's Cabin*, made in America in 1927.[99] The best takes had to be selected and the 'chief editor begins to alter sequences, eliminate and cross-cut action'. Blakeston said in 1928:

'Before the Russians one could say that a fade was four feet, short scenes six feet, action scenes fifteen feet, and a close-up a single foot.'[100]

But now it could be said that 'when others had worked with feet the Russians had worked with frames'. Others were slow to follow the Russian example. By 1928 an ordinary scenario for a one and a quarter hour film might have about 400 scene-shots, but such a structure was hopelessly inadequate 'even for the old-fashioned picture' and according to the degree of development of the producing company this structure was further broken down during shooting and editing. According to Arrar Jackson in 1929 the ordinary film might have about 800 shots. A great film like G. W. Pabst's *The Love of Jeanne Ney*, made in Germany in 1927, was even said to have some 2,000 cuts.

In the older style of film making Hepworth's *Comin' thro' the Rye* of 1923 makes much of the heroine's walk in the sunny field of ripening grain, which was to be accompanied in the cinema by the music of the song. Yet despite excellent photography the few straightforward long takes of this field, seen without the music, lack anything to sustain the interest. It is interesting to imagine Eisenstein's handling of such a scene at the same date, with a multitude of shots of the rye field, the sunny sky and the birds, the grain, shadows and all the background of changing nature which is implicit in the heroine's memory of meeting her lover, in the same field, at a different time of the year. Hepworth's treatment of continuity was rough in the extreme. A scene of intense drama when Paul's engagement is broken is to be followed by a different 'chapter' in the book, in which the young Alma Taylor is playing happily, so the mood is abruptly switched by the perfunctory title: 'Naturally the tragedy makes no lasting impression on those not nearly concerned.'

To illustrate how far story-telling through a series of images had advanced by 1928, a 95-foot sequence of 20 shots and a single word from Mander's *First Born* is interesting because it ingeniously conveys an incident which is essentially non-visual. In this passage Madeleine Carroll wishes to show her devoted admirer that all is well with her marriage and that she can easily phone her husband Hugo; when she tries to do so, however, a crossed wire leads to her overhearing her husband's phone conversation with his girl friend. Earlier film makers, daunted by such a problem, might well have resorted to an explanatory title. Here, using three telephonists and some parallel by-play with them absorbed in their books as they carelessly attend the switchboards, glances exchanged between Madeleine Carroll and her admirer, small insets of Hugo and the girl friend in the corners of the screen with some large close-ups and a single title: 'Hugo!' the film in just over a minute and a half turns this into a visual incident.

It was realized by only a few in this country that it was here, in the question of film structure, that they had found the key to the art of the film. The old-fashioned film maker, starting with one long scene, had been induced by one reason and another to cut and cut it until even hack production had reached the stage where one film might contain some hundreds of shots. But the Russians, starting from Kuleshov's view of the film as a structure built up by sticking shots together, had produced works with thousands of shots, some only a few frames in length, using the juxtaposition of their content and the rhythm of their presentation to produce a total impression. The only silent film made in England entirely on this model was Grierson's *Drifters* in 1929, although Anthony Asquith and a few others were also strongly influenced by the Russian conception towards the end of the period.

The comedian Walter Forde was no *avant-garde* theorist, but in his film *Would You Believe It?* of 1928 an ingenious half-reel with some 95 shots shows Walter being chased up and down the spiral staircase of an underground station by a gang who are anxious to steal his attaché case. The setting consists chiefly of the top and bottom entrances to the stairs and a single section of the spiral. All are seen from a single, simple camera angle, but by rapid cutting of repeat shots of this section with the hero, the villains, and then the case itself sliding down on its own, the illusion of a chase up and down the stairs is created, alternating with incidents at the top and the bottom. The comedy effect of this simple sequence is successfully created by using the juxtaposition of shots to suggest an incident which in fact never took place. Much more sophisticated use of both camera angle and length of shot is to be found in Asquith's first film, *Shooting Stars*, in 1928. In this film, about 27 shots from 1 to 10 feet in length in a dazzling passage of about 90 feet, show a film comedian clowning on the film set, swinging on the chandelier; among the artistes and technicians below a fat man, intending to shoot him with a property gun, accidentally picks up a real, loaded gun and kills the comedian, who falls from the chandelier. The angles chosen, from a very large close-up of the dying comic's astonished eyes and grotesque eyebrows, to overhead shots of the crowd, shots of the swinging chandelier from below and its swinging shadow get variety, giddy movement and shock into this brief sequence. Another passage, of the trick cyclist's crash over a cliff, was equally intricate. Asquith's second film later in the year, *Underground,* used quick cutting and a variety of camera angle with less obtrusive brilliance but to surer effect in over 40 shots in 180 feet.* Brian Aherne chases the murderer over the roof of the Battersea Power Station, down to the wharf by means of a crane, beside the canal and up to the mouth of the Underground tunnel, in a variety of shots and angles which make dramatic use of height and the industrial background.

It was evident that by this stage the idea of an editor following a simple A.B.C. of smooth cutting to join shots as indicated in the shooting script could no longer be the whole story in fact, even if it were so in theory. Carried to its logical conclusion Blakeston's view implied that if a film was going to have some thousand cuts they should be at least generally indicated in the scenario and the film should be written, directed and cut by one person. In reality very few people were capable of such a feat with a full-length studio film, although a short actuality film such as *Drifters* could still be almost a solo. An article by Harry Hughes, an editor himself, showed that he believed that the film should be the product of one mind, but indicated that in practice editing in the British studios was the responsibility variously of the editor alone, of the editor under the direction of the director, or of the director. Ivor Montagu, also an editor, did not feel that the director was the best person to do the editing. In the end the question of who took the greatest share of the creative process was to depend on the people involved in any particular film, the scenario writer usually being the originator of virtually the outline only. Named editors slowly began to appear in the British film industry, although very few, among them Angus Macphail, H. Leslie Brittain, P. L. Mannock, Ivor Montagu, Alma Reville, Challis Sanderson and Emile de Ruelle were credited on the screen.

Dupont was said to be doing the assembling, titling and cutting of *Moulin Rouge* himself in 1928,[101] and in America von Stroheim made no secret of his anger when his extravagant footage for *Wedding March* was handed to other people to make into two films. In 1927 *The Bioscope* had said:

'I understand that largely owing to the efforts of Marcel l'Herbier, the French producer, an organization of European film directors is to be formed with a view to preserving their productions from mutilation when in the hands of film editors. Fritz Lang and Karl Grune are mentioned as the German representatives concerned in this new association, and Geo. Pearson and Alfred Hitchcock have, I hear, accepted invitations to become members.'[102]

Close Up, showing rare approval of a British film, maintained in 1929 that *Under the Greenwood Tree* had shown signs of a 'rhythmic flow' butchered by the cutter, and deduced:

'It proves, first and foremost, the imbecility of letting one man make a picture

* The length and number of shots given in these examples are those in the copies of the films in the National Film Archive, but it is impossible to say if they are exactly as in the finished trade show copies.

and another cut it. The day will come when the professional editor is unknown in our studios.'[103]

(9) COSTS

The cost of the work of all these specialists rose steeply during the ten years from 1919 to 1929. At the end of the war British film companies were still producing at the same level of cost and technical competence as before 1914. Reliable figures of production cost are rare but it is possible to form some idea of it from occasional books and trade journals of the time, reminiscences both published and unpublished, and court cases. It was in a court action that Bentley's 1919 film *The Lackey and the Lady*, strongly criticized for its poor quality, was stated to have cost about £4,000. *The Home Maker* of the same year, a film on the semi-amateur fringe of production, may have cost as little as £1,500. The A.E.F.C. prospectus of 1921 quoted a number of post-war films made by Harma costing from £3,000 to £8,000 each, and according to A. V. Bramble his own *Wuthering Heights*, a 1920 film of which in his old age he remained extremely proud, had cost £6,000. In the same year Pearson's *Nothing Else Matters*, which he likewise continued to regard as one of his best films, had cost £7,000. And the 1919–20 prospectus of even the ambitious new firm Alliance planned 26 five-reelers at £4,750 each, 26 one-reelers at £1,000 each and four supers at £7,425 each.

In reality the Alliance films proved to be much more expensive than this and by 1921 or 1922 it was no longer really possible to produce a feature film of tolerable quality for £1,000 a reel. H. W. Thompson was only a little more realistic when, in 1922, he budgeted £120,000 for twelve films. According to Boughey[104] a five-reel film which had cost £4,000 to £5,000 before the war should have cost £15,000 to £20,000 by 1921. But for most British firms this was still an unattainable standard, and Michael Balcon has said that by the early twenties the normal British film still cost less than £1 a foot, or about £6,000 to £7,000, and not many British films were to be found among the high-priced features of £10,000 to £25,000.

The rise in costs was partly due to inflation. But it was very largely a real increase due to the elaboration of equipment and methods and the use of specialized technicians. Another factor was the rivalry of stars and later, to some extent, of directors also, although this was less so in England than in America. It was also beginning to be seen that high costs carried their own prestige, and the trade press was used for announcements like Gaumont's that they would make films costing £12,000 which would be 'good enough for distribution abroad'.

There are few figures of the actual pay of staff, and companies and individuals differed widely. Boughey said grandly in 1921 that a well-known director, in America at least, could earn more than any Prime Minister in the world, and Steer[105] said in 1920 that a good studio manager in Britain would get up to £1,000 or even £2,000 and the casting manager up to £1,000. Bentley, a director of undeservedly high standing at the time, was offered £750 a film by British

Actors according to his own claim after the unfortunate case of *The Lackey and the Lady*, and regarded it as an indignity when reduced to £20 a week and commission. By the mid-twenties, according to Balcon, a first-class director in Britain might receive £1,000 a film and an average one £500 to £750.

The rise in actors' pay was more marked. Arthur Walcott, a regular supporting player, was to get only £10 a week with expenses for two months at Pathé in 1919, according to a later court case, and an unknown actress was promised a mere £6 a week for playing in *Unmarried* in 1920. According to Honri, Hepworth was paying Stewart Rome a modest £10 a week for leading rôles at the end of the war and Rome was glad to accept the offer of £20 a week from West, by no means a lavish producer. Hepworth, who was very critical of the excesses of the star system, said in an interview that he never paid Alma Taylor more than £60 a week, but this was unusually low for an acknowledged star by 1924. A fan book of 1920 stated that a young acress might earn some £400 a year, 'equivalent to what an infantry sergeant-major will make per year under the new pay regulations'.[106] Aurèle Sydney was reported to have signed a contract with Gaumont in 1919 'approaching three figures a week', which was said to be the highest contract salary in Britain at the time. At the other end of the scale, the Variety Artiste's Federation negotiated an agreement for crowd workers in 1920 at a minimum of £1 1s a day. Visiting stars, whether from America or from the stage, earned or were reputed to earn fabulous sums and these rose steeply. Sir John Martin-Harvey was paid £1,000 for appearing in *The Breed of the Treshams* in 1920, but on receiving only £7,300 as combined fee and royalty from *The Only Way* five years later he was able to sue the producers. In 1919 Stoll, it was said, offered the boxer Georges Carpentier £6,000 for a single film, beside which the £700 a week offered to George Robey in 1923 by the same company seems surprisingly little. The American actress Betty Compson was brought over to England by Balcon in 1923 at £1,000 a week for *Woman to Woman* and *The White Shadow*, and Betty Blythe was promised, but did not get, £2,000 a week salary and expenses for appearing in *She*, G. B. Samuelson's disastrous attempt to follow the fashion for high-priced foreign stars. The British feature player could, however, according to Balcon, expect only about £70 to £100 a week by the mid-twenties, which compared even less favourably than directors' pay with standards in Hollywood where, according to the publicity, Pola Negri signed a contract for 18 films in three years at more than £50,000 a year in 1920, and Mary Pickford earned £260,000 in the next two years.

The pay of cameramen, designers and editors is harder to discover. A. V. Bramble said to the author that a professional cameraman like Horace Wheddon at Ideal was paid about £15 a week in 1920 but that a top job might be worth about £60 a week. The Alliance cameraman René Guissart seems to have earned £90 a week, in keeping with the rather lavish standards of this company. Balcon has said that by the middle of the twenties a first-class cameraman could reasonably expect £50 a week. The importance of the story was recognized and the value of film rights to books and plays, both for practical and for publicity reasons, rose quickly. As early as 1919 *The Bioscope* complained of rapacious writers demanding from £500 to £1,000 for screen rights with 10 per cent royalties. Rowson said that a good original screen story would soon be worth £500 to £600, and a slightly later report that W. J. Locke was writing an original story for £10,000 for Norma Talmadge was considered by *The Bioscope* to be a typical piece of American absurdity. The pay of the scenario writers themselves seems to have been very variable. American salaries were certainly higher, and when Eve Unsell arrived to write scripts for Famous Lasky in 1919 her pay of £250 surprised British writers. Rowson said he could foresee a future in which good scenario writers would earn £6,000 a year but, meanwhile, to come down to earth, an anonymous writer complained that he received an average fee of £3 10s a script. By 1923 Frank Fowell maintained that a good continuity writer might get from £1,000 to £5,000 for a script in America, but according to Balcon an average British script writer might still only expect from £25 to £30 a week. In general, the British film industry paid very little for its scripts and as a result was extremely short of good writers.

The rise in production costs continued through the twenties. West, with his bare-bones production, would still risk a contract for twelve films at up to £4,000 each as late as 1924. But even the British Instructional war reconstructions, a relatively cheap form of production, rose from £3,000 for *Armageddon* in 1923 to £8,000 for *Zeebrugge* next year, and up to some £12,000 the year after that for *Ypres*. Pearson's *Love, Life and Laughter* in 1923 cost £18,000 and Henry Edwards' *Owd Bob* next year £12,000, both films of some merit, whilst Coleby's *The Prodigal Son*, which was inordinately long and was shot on location with a reckless disregard for footage, cost as much as £37,000. Sir John Martin-Harvey's vehicle *The Only Way* cost £24,000. There were exaggerated rumours about the cost of *Chu Chin Chow*, and it was even reported by *Pictures and the Picture-goer* in a mad moment that it had cost a million pounds.

Despite the publicity value of fan figures like this many producers remained cautious. Adelqui Millar's prospectus of November 1927 planned six films at £10,000 each. According to Balcon, Brunel's *Blighty*, by no means an unambitious picture, cost only about £10,000. *Mons* cost £12,000, and Pearson's much loved film *The Little People* cost only £9,000. An extremely popular and profitable group of pictures by Elvey continued to be modestly priced through the late twenties. *Mlle from Armentières*, *The Flag Lieutenant*, *Hindle Wakes*, *The Glad Eye*, *Mlle Parley-Voo* and *Palais de Danse* all cost between £8,000 and £11,000 and *Roses of Picardy* about £15,000, grossing anything from £4,000 to £56,000.

Meanwhile American extravagance astounded us. As early as 1920 Laemmle mentioned six recent pictures costing between £14,000 and £31,000, while Carmine Gallone announced in 1926 that the new version of *The Last Days of Pompeii* was to cost £100,000.[107] The President of the Federation of British Industries estimated that whilst ordinary American six-reelers might cost from £8,000 to £20,000, a super might well cost from £100,000 to as much as £300,000.[108] L'Estrange Fawcett wrote in 1927 that an average American feature cost £30,000 whilst one made in Great Britain would be nearer £17,000, but that *The Big Parade* had cost £100,000, and *Ben Hur* £800,000. There were frequent complaints about American costs, however, both here and in America itself, where many were critical of the high labour costs and general extravagance.

It was difficult for the small British companies to emulate this but by the later twenties salaries and other costs had risen noticeably. Hitchcock, at twenty-eight the highest paid British director, signed a B.I.P. contract in 1927 for twelve pictures in three years at £13,000 a year, and as B.I.P. expanded their directors, usually foreign, were being offered from £10,000 to £15,000 a year. Dupont, making *Madame Pompadour* for British National in 1926, was reported to have a contract for £12,000, and Sidney Olcott, known chiefly for much earlier American pictures and no longer at the top of his form, was brought over by British Lion for 10 weeks at £450 a week in 1928. L'Estrange Fawcett in 1927 pointed to directors in America getting £6,000 to £14,000 a picture and there had even been talk of Lubitsch having a five-year contract with Warners for 3 films a year at a guaranteed minimum of £30,000 a film. £10,000 to £15,000 a year, however, was probably the upper limit in Britain. Producers on the whole did not have the same prestige value as stars and directors. A producer like Balcon, however, would receive more than just a salary. Stars presented perhaps the greatest contrast to Hollywood. In 1927 L'Estrange Fawcett could write of ordinary American stars earning £400 to £800 or more a week and it was said that actor-director Emil Jannings had a new three-year contract with Paramount increasing from £1,600 to £2,000 a week. British standards were low in comparison. Harry Lauder, faring better than Robey a few years earlier, was said to have been offered £10,000 for his work in *Huntingtower* and Ivor Novello to receive £3,000 to £4,000 a film when his film reputation was at its height. But this was exceptional. According to a court action Marjorie Hume, an average leading player, received only £40 a week from British Filmcraft in 1928. Other technicians were also unlucky. In 1927 L'Estrange Fawcett said that £150 to £200 a week would be normal pay for a cameraman in America, and as there was a growing awareness of the importance of camerawork and lighting in the British studios it seems likely that British rates were gradually forced up from Balcon's figure of £50 from the middle of the period, but designers and editors were only slowly being recognized as skilled creative workers and approximately £15 a week may be regarded as good average pay for either of them about the middle of the twenties. L'Estrange Fawcett suggested a possible £150 a week for scenario writers but this is probably too high. More was paid for film rights. According to *The Bioscope*

'An average price paid today for the rights of an average play or novel is between £1,000 to £3,000. The work of a comparatively unknown writer commands, generally speaking, between £400 to £1,500, and may be had, on occasions, for as little as £100. . . . In the past, the limit for the British producer, with his restricted film market, has been in the neighbourhood of £5,000, though £8,000 was paid for *Chu Chin Chow* and £7,000 for Galsworthy's *Loyalties*.'[109]

In 1929 Arrar Jackson gave other figures: a story in treatment form might fetch from £150 to £500; scenarios from £150 to £400, £50 being an average price for the scenario alone; the combined return for an original story and scenario being from £350 upwards.[110]

By 1920 box office takings in Britain might be £40,000 to £50,000 on a very successful high-priced feature, but it was extremely rare for a British film to do as well as this (see pages 52–53). Balcon said in his paper to the British Kinematograph Society that a British film of 1920 could normally expect to make only about £12,000 for the renter. Even as late as 1925 an American, Joe May, said that no European producer should normally spend more than about £10,000 on a film if dependent on his home market alone. Production was not an attractive investment and there was a chronic shortage of capital. Much British production was conducted on a hand-to-mouth basis with an advance here and an advance there until the film was completed somehow. Capital increased gradually but it was argued that production companies in this country got, and indeed asked for, too little capital in the first place. In 1925 Sir John Ferguson, President of the Institute of Bankers, spoke with guarded approval of investment in production:

'The British Banks, though seemingly holding aloof from all interest in the cinematograph trade, had for a long time been watching its development with keen interest. The position had now been reached when the Banks could express every confidence in the cinema industry, and were prepared to give such expression to that confidence as circumstances warranted and deserved.'[111]

But the vicious circle of capital shortage, poor quality production and small returns was not to be broken so easily and the scarcity of production capital on a modern scale continued to be acute. It was Commander Kenworthy who, in a far-seeing analysis of the problem before the quota legislation and legal abolition of block-booking, suggested cheap government lending of some £20,000,000 of production finance. No attention seems to have been paid to the idea.

We have seen that what finally brought capital into the industry in a significant quantity was the approach of quota legislation in about 1927 and, a little later, the commercial possibilities of the sound film. In early 1927 the President of the Board of Trade stated in reply to a question that about £4,000,000 was invested in production, and by the end of the twenties a number of production companies were quoted on the Stock Exchange. Yet according to some observers even after the quota legislation British production was still conducted largely on the basis of grudging and inadequate advances from renters, who strengthened their hold on the industry and claimed any credit that was going. Nevertheless prices could now go up, which they did, although not always wisely. Wilcox was ahead of the quota and one of the first of the big spenders. *The Only Way* in 1925, *Nell Gwynne* in 1926 and *Mumsie* in 1927 together cost £70,000. B.I.P. spent money in something like the Hollywood manner and *The Ring*, *Poppies of Flanders*, *The White Sheik* and *The Silver Lining* in 1927 and *A Little Bit of Fluff* and *Moulin Rouge* in 1928 cost £150,000 altogether. Brunel claimed in his memoirs that his film *The Constant Nymph* in 1928 cost £30,000 and *A Light Woman* in the same year £17,000. *The Burgomaster of Stilemonde*, shown in 1929, cost some £20,000, and even *If Youth But Knew*, by the old-fashioned producer G. B. Samuelson, was planned at a cost of £25,000. It was reported in June 1929 that *To What Red Hell* was to be re-made as a sound film at a cost of £50,000. Sound was to bring a steep rise in costs. There was even a rumour in 1928 that a Blattner film was to cost £100,000. But by the end of the twenties, according to Balcon, a normal cost of £30,000 to £35,000 was reasonable. Maxwell, less cautious, was quoted as saying that producers could spend £50,000 on a film now even if it was not specially designed for American distribution.

(10) COLOUR

Colour in films was not a great issue in the twenties. A number of people were trying to perfect true-colour systems, and demonstrations were held from time to time, but to most people colour in films meant tinting and toning and this was taken for granted.

To tint a film, the positive was dipped into a bath of aniline dye whilst still on the frame; this dyed the gelatine and gave an even tint all over the picture, and would wash out in water. In toning, the film was immersed in a bath of chemical which discoloured the silver composing the image, and then washed in water; the darker parts of the image received the greater depth of tone. Many films were sepia throughout, but most used colours only for certain scenes, and tints mentioned by Boughey in 1921 included blue-green, orange-brown, crystal violet, brilliant yellow and rose bengal. Blakeston later described a similar range. More elaborate combinations of tinting and toning in one image were also possible.

Most firms tinted and toned their films in the early twenties for visual pleasure as much as anything, with varying degrees of subtlety. Often it was used as a way of suggesting mood or atmosphere, from the sentimental blue tone on pink tint used for the sylvan love scenes in *The Lure of Crooning Water* in 1920 to the sudden burst of passionate red on Mary's wedding night in Elvey's *Passionate Friends* in 1922. Very often, also, it was used to indicate something which the very simple film technique employed was otherwise unable to convey. The most common example of this was the use of blue or green to suggest that the scene was taking place at night or in darkness. This was an almost universal practice before improvements in lighting and stock made night filming possible. The contrast of black-and-white or sepia shots with the blue or green stressed the alternation of light and darkness, or outdoors and indoors, and was even used in mid-take to suggest the sudden switching on or off of a light. Red for firelight and conflagrations was similar in its narrative function although not essential, as a shot of the flames or smoke could easily be used to convey information. These two uses were by far the most common and occurred frequently even in other-wise colourless films.

Tinting continued throughout the twenties and in the middle of the period was still being used in up-to-date pictures such as *The Rat* in 1925, *The Flag Lieutenant* and *Boadicea* in 1926, *Hindle Wakes* in 1927 and the early Hitchcock films including *The Lodger*. Hitchcock cut green shots into sepia in *Downhill* in 1927, in a sequence showing Ivor Novello's delirium, using sepia for reality and green for what he imagined was happening. But as a rule tinting began to disappear as night filming spread and as constructive editing took over its story function. The cheerful firesides, bleak days, dawn and even night were increasingly shown by the selection of suitable images. B.I.P., for example, does not seem to have used colour at all. Yet perhaps the finest examples of all are to be found in *Drifters*, although both pan stock and advanced editing methods were used in this film. The exquisitely beautiful cold, green-grey gleam of a fisherman's glass float on the night swell, the deep green under-water shots and the palest lavender grey of dawn in the white-housed village on the shore show what could be done with tinting, and justify the nostalgic affection with which many early film makers looked back on it. Brunel wrote in his autobiography:

'. . . as we were photographing black and white, we achieved something of the colourful quality of Morocco by having our prints tinted and toned various colours—which can be as dreadful as some modern "natural colour" films, but with discretion, can be very attractive and suggestive of the natural colour scheme.'[112]

This is characteristic of the almost apologetic way in which many early film makers late spoke of tinting and toning. It is true that much of it was crude, and the instances mentioned in *The Passionate Friends* and *The Lure of Crooning Water* would seem quaint and largely irrelevant, even distracting, once audiences were used to the technique of story telling by the selection of significant images. Nevertheless, although a blind alley as far as film technique was concerned, tinting could be a charming embellishment when it was used with skill.

At the same time there was a persistent desire for realistic colour. Some people, like Cecil B. De Mille, were doubtful:

'From a long study of the matter, I have come to the conclusion that a rapidly changing colour reflected in the screen is one of the most trying experiences which the human eye can be subjected to.'[113]

But this attitude was rare. Generally the desirability of realism in colour, as in sound and to a lesser extent stereoscopy, was taken for granted.

True colour film processes meanwhile were the subject of experiments in several parts of the world. The broad issues were whether a two- or three-colour process would be used, whether a special camera and projector would be necessary, how fast the film would need to be exposed and projected, and of course the cost.

The most notable British inventor was William Friese-Greene, whose two-colour system Biocolour and the law suit with Urban's and G. A. Smith's Kinemacolor Company belong to an earlier period. In the early twenties Smith used a system now called Kinechrome, but Friese-Greene had already taken out four new patents in 1918 and 1919, and Colour Photography was registered with a capital of £25,000 early in 1920, with his son Claude and O. Humphrey as directors. They were using a two-colour additive process with alternating red-orange and blue-green filters and a projection speed of 1,000 feet in 10 minutes, or 22 to 24 pictures a second compared with the usual 16. William Friese-Greene died in 1921 but his work was carried on by his son, and a new company was formed in 1923, in which the latter was technical director. For a time Felix Orman, previously with Prizma Colour, was production manager and W. Vinten his adviser. The *première* of their Spectrum films was held in March 1924, with various split-reel subjects including shots of William Friese-Greene, *Moonbeam Magic* made at Twickenham, *The Dance of the Moods* with the Margaret Morris Dancers, and *Quest of Colour*. In May Claude Friese-Greene addressed the Royal Photographic Society Kinematograph group. In December 1925 a series of 26 one-reelers in colour called *The Open Road* was shown. The films were little more than elementary scenics. Drawbacks to the system were the projection speed and the extra cost of using panchromatic stock and the more elaborate processing. The system worked in a fashion and the trade, still feeling guilty after Friese-Greene's tragic death, was ready to praise if not to buy. A footnote to this was an exchange of letters in *The Bioscope*[114] between Claude Friese-Greene and a Dr John Campbell. The latter, disputing the new invention, claimed that he himself had more or less perfected an alternating system at 24 to 32 frames a second as early as 1911, but that an alternating system would never in fact be good enough as it could succeed only where movement was in nearly parallel lines. Friese-Greene, replying that invention was in fact never an individual achievement, maintained:

'I claim to have effected improvements which have been patented, and are being patented, such improvements having put our company into such a position that we are able to show colour on the screens of the world at a price well within the reach of any producer and exhibitor.'[115]

The films, however, were more successful with reds than with other colours, which tended to merge into a yellow-green even though there was little movement within the frame, and the system was not taken up by the film industry.

Others were also at work. F. W. Donisthorpe was said to be conducting experiments from about 1916 onwards and in 1921 was mentioned in connection with the Clerk–Maxwell two-colour additive process, two pictures taken simultaneously and projected through two projection lenses fitted to a normal projector, at half the normal speed, but the results were said to be crude.[116] Professor Gorsky, experimenting in France on a three-colour process with the colours on the film positive showed some results at the Windmill Street Kinema.[116] M. Herault, after many years work, showed some film in 1921 based on a three-colour system of Cros and Ducos du Hauron.[117] This took three images through violet, green and orange screens and projected them on a normal projector with a stronger light and at three times the normal speed; the film had to be chemically treated to sensitize it sufficiently for the greater speed.

More important commercially was Prizma Colour.* A two-colour system, its

* This was American in origin and the fact that Blackton came to England to produce, together with the name "Prizma", suggests some similarity to Technicolor, which used light split up by a prismatic mirror.

281

invention in America was ascribed to William Kelley and by 1920 was being used in Selznick pictures, and in 1921 in D. W. Griffith's *Dream Street*. At first, two negatives sensitized to red-orange and blue-green were taken successively and superimposed on the positive; later they were taken simultaneously in a two-lens camera and superimposed on a double-sided positive, each frame coated red on one side and green on the other. The improved system was brought to Britain by John Stuart Blackton with W. T. Crespinal as Prizma specialist in charge of the camera. The printing was to be done in America. *The Glorious Adventure* was described as the first important fiction film all in a colour process other than Kinemacolor, and was trade shown in January 1922. Great interest was aroused, but the colour was far from perfect.

Meanwhile Technicolor was pursuing its own development. This was at first a two-colour process, based on red and blue, the colour being split by a prismatic mirror to take two pictures simultaneously on special panchromatic stock and printed on two positives stuck together and screened in the normal way. The system, invented by C. Comstock and H. D. Kalmus, had been in existence since 1917. In 1921 it was used in America in *The Toll of the Sea*, which was not shown in Britain until 1923, well after Blackton's film. *Wanderer of the Wasteland* was made in U.S.A. in 1923 and shown in Britain in February 1925, and parts of a couple of First National Films were also made in colour. The turning point in colour production, however, was *The Black Pirate*, which was made in the U.S.A. and shown in Britain in March 1926. Leslie Eveleigh addressed the Royal Photographic Society on Technicolor in 1926, and announced that the Technicolor experts were at work on a three-colour method. This was described by Colin Bennett in *The Bioscope* as 'The lineal descendant of Chronochrome', Gaumont's three-colour process of earlier years.[118]

Technicolor continued to produce and improve, and renewed interest in colour on a commercial scale was shown in the late twenties. A large company was formed in June 1928 as British Multicolour Film Corporation.[119] T. A. Mills, working in London in 1926 on a three-colour process, red blue and green, brought out Zoechrome.[120] This was described later as follows:

' "Zoechrome" is an invention of a Londoner, T. A. Mills, which was demonstrated early in the year, and is the result of four consecutive printing operations from one negative of double lengths. The taking attachment consists of four lenses in one mount, one of which takes a complete black-and-white image every eight perforations, the space between being occupied by three-quarter size images of the same subject. The latter are obtained by taking through a colour screen which cuts out its equivalent of the visible spectrum. The black-and-white negative is taken on a 3-in lens, the colour selective negative on three lenses of shorter focus.'[121]

The Keller–Dorian three-colour system used red, green and blue-violet sections on a disc in an ordinary camera with 'panchromatic stock that has been specially embossed on the sutone with a number of minute cylindrical lens elements'. At first connected with Kodacolor for amateur photographers, this was adopted by

Blattner towards the end of 1928. Other systems mentioned from time to time included Pathechrome, Photocolor, Busch and Raycol.[122]

The success of the sound film coincided with Technicolor's *Black Pirate*. Many regarded the two as similar revolutions in film technique, expecting colour to transform film production as sound did. There was a lot to learn. When the common technical difficulties of fringing, especially of moving objects, the predominance or distortion of certain colours and the unlikely-looking bluish fleshtones had been overcome it was still some time before people realized that literal naturalness or crowded, aggressively 'colourful' film subjects such as costume dramas gave only a very limited idea of the possibility of colour composition. It was necessary to relearn the subtle use of colour for mood or over-all effects as in the old tinted and toned films, of which H. G. Wells had written:

'Colour in the films is no longer as it is in real life, a confusing and often unmeaning complication of vision. It can be introduced into the spectacle for effect, slowly flushing the normal black and white with glows of significant hue, chilling, intensifying, gladdening. It can be used to pick out and intensify small forms. It can play gaily or grotesquely over the scene with or without reference to the black-and-white forms.'[123]

More fundamental, the analogy with sound was false. Colour was a new artistic element in film making but would not affect the narrative structure of the film itself as sound had done.

(II) ANIMATION

By the beginning of the twenties the technique of animation was well understood. It was clearly set out in a book by W. G. Lutz published in America and England in 1920 and called *Animated Cartoons*.

Lutz was an artist, who had previously published books on anatomy and drawing, and he approached animation from the artist's standpoint rather than as an easy way to make money. He seems also to have been impressed by its possibilities for education and explanation. Along with some rather commonplace guidance to the wham-bang clichés of strip humour he devoted much attention to anatomical studies and the analysis of human and animal movement. It is evident from his description that although not as large or complex as contemporary feature-film studios, animated cartoon production had reached the stage of a cottage-industry, with a small staff of animators, tracers and camera and laboratory technicians. It was still possible to embark on it on a very small scale, however.

Lutz pointed out that a half-reel cartoon required 8,000 pictures, with 16 frames a foot for 500 feet. The skill of the animator lay in getting sufficient illusion of movement from a minimum of drawing. Considerable judgement was needed to calculate how many frames of each stage in a movement, at any particular speed and in any particular direction, were necessary to give verisimilitude of both movement and perspective. For this a detailed knowledge of how living things moved was essential, experience in timing and spacing it, and experience of how far short-cuts like whirling lines were convincing.

In his practical guide to production Lutz indicated the need to plan a story suitable for animation and the amount of movement necessary to convey each action. The chief animator then lay down the visual appearance, character and behaviour traits of the protagonists and planned the film's execution. Lutz described the use of what was later called a light box, with its pegs and sheets of paper with accurate registering holes to fit them. Using this it was possible to trace those parts of the picture which were not moving, which considerably cut down the work of fresh drawing, and divided the work between a few highly skilled animators and the more numerous unskilled tracers. The work could be further reduced by the use, firstly, of cells. These were sheets of celluloid with the same registering holes, on which would be drawn those parts of the action which had not moved, and which could then be superimposed on the background as many times as necessary in combination with new drawings of only the moving parts. Secondly, in the panorama, more of the landscape than could be seen in any one part of the action was drawn in one long picture, which could be moved along in relation to the camera and provided with new cells and drawings of the moving parts. The drawings and cells assembled on the registering pins, held down by a sheet of glass and lighted from above, were finally photographed from above. One photograph of each picture was taken when ready, and when the frames were projected one after another at the usual speed they gave the illusion of movement, more or less smooth according to the skill of the animator. Lutz also mentioned the use of titles and animated words, balloons of speech and other visual symbols from the world of the strip cartoon such as ZZZZZ! for snoring, and the usual assortment of Bangs and Whacks; 'cut-outs' or flat cut-out models with jointed parts; 'animated sculpture' or flexible models which were changed in shape from picture to picture; and silhouette drawings.

There were a number of cartoon series from America, where according to Lo Duca[124] the cell had been introduced by Earl Hurd in 1914 and the panorama by Nolan in 1916. After the war Phillips's half-reel Film Fables were made in England by the English animators Dudley Buxton, Anson Dyer, the newspaper cartoonist 'Poy' and others. Dyer, who also made advertising films, joined the Hepworth company in July 1919 and made a number of film skits and other films for them including *Othello* (Trade Show July 1920), *Merchant of Venice* (Trade Show August 1919), *Romeo and Juliet* (Trade Show October 1919), *Bobby the Scout* (Trade Show October 1921), *'Amlet* (Trade Show December 1919) and a delightfully drawn *Little Red Riding Hood* (1922) and others. He also made animated sequences for a number of British Instructional films and, later, a 3,600-foot patriotic film *The Story of the Flag* (Trade Show November 1927) for Nettlefold at the old Hepworth studio. Other cartoonists included Lancelot Speed, who with A. B. Payne adapted the latter's *Daily Mirror* strip *Pip, Squeak and Wilfred* for film (Trade Show January 1921), and the newspaper sports cartoonist Tom Webster in 1923 (*Tishy*, film reviewed in February 1923, and

Alfred and Steve one-reelers in 1926). Dudley Buxton's Miffy films started in 1921 and Studdy's *Bonzo the Dog* in 1924.

Dudley Buxton's films of 1921 were very elementary, with separate gags rather than a story, plenty of footage used up by titles and the repetition of sequences, and with simplified backgrounds and the movement taking place in otherwise empty parts of the picture. The Bonzo films drawn by George Ernest Studdy for W. A. Ward in 1924 (first Trade Show October 1924) were more advanced, with anthropomorphized animal characters worked out with considerably more characterization. The story line, instead of playing for violence, used the medium's ability to draw processes which could not be represented by photography: the little dog sniffed up the smell of the rabbit and visibly developed physically rabbit-like traits; he was transformed in turn into an egg, a bird-like creature and a sausage which all, however, were still recognizably Bonzo. Pictorially, the films were more complicated and the animation was · smoother. More interesting technique than usual included ideograph-captions like the dotted lines shooting from Bonzo's eyes to the thing he was looking at, words reproduced on the picture and becoming bigger or smaller, and whirling stars, lines and clouds.

The earliest moving pictures, the optical toys, had of course been drawings rather than photographs. By the twenties animated drawing, apart from sections of documentary or teaching films and animated maps, existed only in the form of these short comic films and was not taken seriously as an art. There was little fundamental change in technique until the thirties when sound, colour, the mixture of drawn and live action, and abstract or poetic drawings and designs drawn straight on to film introduced new ideas. The Australian artist Len Lye's abstract film *Tusalava*, which had musical accompaniment, was shown at the London Film Society, which had assisted in its production, at the very end of this period in December 1929. But such change as there was in the twenties consisted mainly of increasing smoothness in the work of the best animators as they gained experience of their medium.

(12) FILMS OF FACT

Films made outside the studio included everything from simple records of events as they happened to the most elaborate recreation of events for the camera. Films of fact may be taken as a loose term indicating a connection with reality somewhat closer than that found in theatrical representations. There are four ways in which each of the many categories of factual film may be considered. Firstly, the motives for which they were made, whether to record, to persuade, to amuse or to teach, differed widely; secondly, so did the degree to which they were specially filmed or compiled from library material; thirdly, if specially filmed, the extent to which the subject had been specially arranged for shooting ranged from the spot record film to careful rehearsals of invented situations; and fourthly, it is illuminating to consider the degree to which the material was expected to speak for itself or whether attention was paid to the film technique employed.

285

The weekly recording of 'spot' news without interpretation was provided by the *Pathé Gazette* and *Pathé Weekly Pictorial*, the *Topical Budget* and the *Gaumont Graphic*. Their aim was simply to cover all suitable events clearly and get the film to the cinemas quickly. The news reels were available for three-day runs at a graduated series of charges, the price decreasing each fourth day. According to Boughey in 1921:

'Editions and separate publications in the principal capitals of the world, and the interchange of topical films between one country and another forms the special feature of all screen-newspapers.'[126]

It would seem that very roughly a sixth of the film shot, sometimes by a large number of cameras if the event were important, was used in the newsreel. From time to time, however, material that lent itself to one- or two-reel compilations was used more fully and in particular big fights and horse races, which were always the occasion for keen rivalry between the companies, were sometimes made into longer films.

Extended coverage of fights, the Derby, the Cup Final and such events as the Wembley Exhibition of 1924 retained the superficial character of the record film, and attempted no background explanation or editorial viewpoint. They were essentially spot news extended in length solely because of the long duration of the 'event'. Pathé was particularly active in this field with such films as *The Wembley Exhibition* (Trade Show August 1924, five reels), *Wembley by Night* (released October 1924, two reels), *Great Moments of Big Fights* (Trade Show January 1925, two reels), *Look Back on 1924* (reviewed January 1925, one reel), *Who's Who in our Test Team* (reviewed April 1926, one reel) and *Our Prince* (reviewed July 1927, one reel). The Prince of Wales' many tours of the Empire in the early twenties were recorded in a number of staid films, and *Across India With the Duke of Connaught* (Trade Show April 1921) was taken for the Topical Film Company by two official cinematographers. Similar, too, was *Britain's Birthright* (Trade Show March 1925), an excruciatingly dull six and a half reels by British Instructional of the Empire Tour of the Special Service Squadron of the Royal Navy in 1923–24. The essential information was crammed into long indigestible factual titles accompanying visual material as simple as that of an early scenic. The type continued in existence and even in 1928 a *Tour of the Dominions by the Right Honourable L. S. Amery, MP* was duly recorded in the same fashion.

Almost as simple in structure and aim were the very few scientific record films. There were few examples. Dr John Russell Reynolds used experimental cine radiographs from 1921 onwards for clinical diagnosis, and by 1921 Kodak was building up a library of medical films. But *The Film in National Life* found that film had been little used in Britain for scientific record and research. Percy Smith's work, and indeed that of the other cameramen working on the *Secrets of Nature* series for British Instructional, was scientific in the broadest sense, but the films were much more than records and have been discussed in another chapter. They had shown how valuable the film camera could be in recording natural processes, and the same Report pointed out:

'Accelerated photography (very slow mechanical exposure) has given a new significance to the gradual processes of plant growth and decay. Micro-cinematography joins the perception of a microscope to that of the film camera.'[126]

A simple form of record film which had always been popular was the scenic. Hepworth, always slow to change and always in love with the beauty of the English countryside, showed many of these in the early twenties. Claude Friese-Greene made a series of one-reelers for Humfriese Films in 1920, *The Beauty of Britain* (Trade Show August 1920), which included some aerial film, and his series of 1925, *The Open Road* (Trade Show December 1925), was also of special interest as it was made in his colour process; but both series were otherwise extremely conventional. Amongst the programme fillers of the mid-twenties were many films such as Harry B. Parkinson's 15 one-reelers *Wonderful Britain* (Trade Show 1926) and Gaumont's *Here and There in the British Isles*. The photography improved but the film technique hardly changed, and several British Instructional travel series about the Empire from 1925 to 1927 were little more sophisticated.

The scenic made in a foreign country, with shots of the local population and occupations thrown in, had been the early travel film. Travel and news event now combined in a number of full-length expedition films. These followed the example of Ponting, who had brought back a vast amount of film from Scott's last Polar expedition and used it with great success for a form of illustrated lecture. The first of these was *South*, shown at the end of 1919, a film of Sir Ernest Shackleton's trip to the Antarctic in 1914–17 on the *Endurance*, shot by the Australian Frank Hurley. The film did well and the same cameraman, with Claude McDonnell and J. C. B. Mason, went again with Shackleton in 1921–22 on his third trip, on which he died, and brought back *Southward on the 'Quest'*. These two films were a strange contrast. The earlier had a more eventful story to tell as the ship had been crushed by ice and sunk, leaving part of the expedition to survive on a block of ice for several months. Not only does the film show the ship being crushed and its masts toppling, but it uses a greater variety of shots, close shots, pans, still shots by flashlight of the ship at night, and in general has a brighter appearance, more interesting titles and every sign of a cameraman who went everywhere and wanted to know about everything. The later film used a more primitive technique, training the camera on a long shot of some object of interest and letting it turn. The shots of penguins, albatross and other wild life were of interest to naturalists at home, but as a piece of film-making it was strangely lacking in the verve of the earlier one.

Next there were films of the two Everest expeditions. *Climbing Mount Everest* (first shown December 1922) was filmed by J. B. L. Noel for the Royal Geographical Society on the second climb in 1922, *The Epic of Everest* (Trade Show December 1924) by the same cameraman on the third climb in 1924, with laboratory work by Arthur Pereira. In the latter film the rescue of the marooned men was watched by a 'telescopic lens' described in the titles as 'enormously high-powered', and the final climb was watched from Eagle's Nest Point and claimed to be the 'longest view' ever taken. Mallory and Irvine were seen from two miles away, at a height of over 26,000, followed by an iris of the summit, after which they vanished. The emotional impact of this historic material fights to get through the antiquated technique, the long informative titles, the interminable takes, the vistas of snowy peaks with no movement to be seen except the occasional drift of a wispy cloud.

In the same year H. G. Ponting released *The Great White Silence* (Trade Show May 1924). He had taken a couple of years to edit the original 40,000 feet of film from which he had compiled his early film lectures of Scott's last expedition, and had now produced a long feature film. Ponting, who was a friend of Meares, had shown unusual enterprise in taking a film camera on this early expedition, and another member of the team told in later years how keen he had been, and how members of the expedition were always being asked to act for the camera or 'pont' as they called it, and how they had sailed close to an iceberg 'for the benefit of the cinematograph.'[127] The beautiful photography and the fascinating subject were there, on celluloid, and could not be destroyed. But the heavy and old-fashioned construction of the film, the long titles, the inverted commas equating every sub-title to the lecturer's commentary, the perfunctory uplift passage at the end, failed to involve the spectator in any way.

After these five snowy heavyweights there were a few more modest expedition films, including two of long flights over Africa with pioneer aviator Alan Cobham, *With Cobham to the Cape* (Trade Show June 1926), filmed by Basil Emmott when Cobham flew from Cairo to Cape Town, and *Round Africa with Cobham* (shown November 1928). Rosita Forbes' *From Red Sea to Blue Nile* (first run July 1925) and Sir Curtis Lampson's *From Senegal to Timbuctu* (reviewed December 1924) were others, and the Algarsson–Worsley British Arctic Expedition brought home a two-reeler of their 1924–25 trip, *Under Sail in the Frozen North* (Trade Show June 1926).

After the explorer who agreed to take a film cameraman along on the easier parts of the trip, came the enterprising spirit who arranged a trip of his own in order to bring back a commercially viable film of it. The early twenties saw a number of these travellers' tales, which overlapped the true expedition films but might be better described as camera expeditions. The titles suggest the exotic worlds revealed for the first time, living and moving, to the eyes of the industrialized West: *Wonderland of Big Game* and *The Vast Sudan* (1923 and 1924, by A. Radcliffe Dugmore), *Wildest Africa* and *To Kilimanjaro* (February 1923 and December 1924, by Ratcliffe Holmes), *To Lhasa in Disguise* (January 1924, Dr McGovern), and *Crossing the Great Sahara* (1924, Angus Buchanan).

Cherry and Richard Kearton had pioneered unfaked animal photography and cinematography in Africa and other places before the war. During the twenties Cherry Kearton put out a few films, e.g. *Wild Life Across the World* (Trade Show June 1923), *Toto's Wife* (July 1924), *With Cherry Kearton in the Jungle* (March 1926), but these do not seem to have been from new expeditions and Kearton rapidly lost his reputation for genuine actuality work. *Toto's Wife* caused

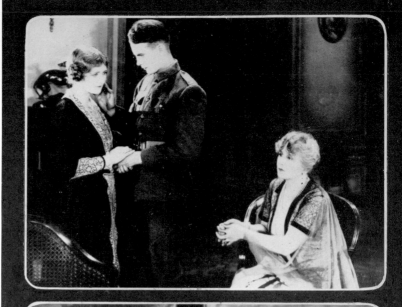

Right: Lillian Hall-Davis,
frey Winn and Ellaline
iss in Brunel's *Blighty*,

re Right: Elvey's *Mademoi-
Parley Voo*, 1928.

m Right: Estelle Brody in
y's *Hindle Wakes*, 1927,
sets by Mazzei and Basil
not at the camera.

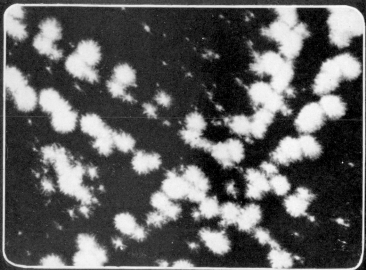

Top Left: Alma Taylor and J[
Longden in *Quinney's*, 1927.

Centre Left: Mould growing f[
a fly's footprints in the *Se[
of Nature* film by Percy Sm[
Plants of the Pantry, 1927.

Bottom Left: Jack Buchanar[
Cutts' *Confetti*, 1927, with [
by Norman G. Arnold.

such an uproar at the Trade Show with some outrageously false sequences that it was finally put out with this ingenuous title:

'At this stage Sally and I met red-hot adventure. For obvious reasons it was impossible to photograph at the time, but when all danger had passed, the episode was reconstructed as faithfully as possible to enable you to visualize some of the perils suffered by travellers in the great sand wastes of the Sahara.'[128]

Two of these films suggested to their producers a new possibility in film making. One was *Pearls and Savages* (Trade Show October 1924), for which the same Frank Hurley who had made the two Shackleton films travelled to New Guinea. Once again, despite a limited idea of film structure, his lively curiosity brought back some fascinating material, rare in the twenties when such anthropological material as tribal dancing and the living conditions of primitive societies had only been seen in the remoteness of the still picture. *Cape to Cairo* (Trade Show April 1926) was a film record of a car journey made by Major and Mrs C. Court Treatt. Both Hurley and the Court Treatts realized that these exotic lands could be used as a real setting for film dramas growing out of local conditions.

So far all the factual films we have discussed have been more or less straight recording. But the idea of a narrative thread which would sustain the natural interest of strange and exotic environments through a full-length film had appeared early in the twenties. It led to a *genre* which is loosely described as the exotic, in which a more or less dramatic narrative film was made in some distant land, with the local people taking all or most of the parts, and the story more or less truthfully based on the actual life of those people. One of the few great film makers, the American Robert Flaherty, had made *Nanook of the North* and shown it in 1922. This is described in the Museum of Modern Art *Film Index* as

'. . . a pictorial record of the struggles of an Eskimo and his family to preserve life against the rigors of their climatic environment.'[129]

But the idea of going to remote areas and giving an account of the unfamiliar life there, like so many other ideas in the cinema, was a logical development which was reached by a number of people independently. An anonymous Stoll film made in East and Central Africa, *Nionga* (Trade Show May 1925), bears an introductory title which states that it took three years to 'rehearse', which means that the work must have begun in 1922 and is most unlikely to have been influenced by Flaherty. But whereas the latter's films were simple unforced accounts growing naturally out of the real lives of the people he studied, British examples range from little more than narrative travel films to extreme cases of the location filming of ordinary dramas, and in any case can hardly bear comparison with the work of an exceptional film maker like Flaherty. The story of *Nionga* was of a young betrothed couple and how, when the young man was killed, the bride was burnt in her hut in accordance with the local practice. It suggested an interest in the local customs and was told at leisure with scenes of the 'savages', as the titles called them, fishing and dancing and otherwise going about their business. But the long explanatory titles, the long shots, pans, 'phantom rides' in boats and all the paraphernalia of the primitive travel film, told the story without the smallest trace of visual or dramatic imagination.

The formula varied according to the film maker. An interesting camera adventurer was Wetherell, who had worked for I.V.T.A. in South Africa and who made his *Livingstone* (Trade Show September 1925) in Africa as early as 1923, with Gustav Pauli as cameraman and with English players in the leading parts. His *Robinson Crusoe* (Trade Show May 1927) was made partly in Tobago. Pauli later made a film of his own in New Zealand, *The Romance of Hine Moa* (Trade Show December 1926), with a Maori cast and a story based on old Maori legends.* *Palaver* (Trade Show September 1926) was made by Barkas for British Instructional. With cameraman Rodwell and three English leading players, Barkas, who had been to Nigeria whilst filming one of the Royal tours, returned to write a story on the spot which would incorporate local material and people. The result was an unpretentious but nicely made film which received less credit than it deserved. Frank Hurley now made *Jungle Woman* (Trade Show December 1926) and *Pearl of the South Seas* (Trade Show April 1927), which he wrote, directed and shot independently with white leading players and local extras, but his good intentions resulted only in ludicrous 'Colonial' stories and disastrous acting, with some crude editing of studio sequences different in tint and lighting to the rest of the film and with ill-matched sets. Ben R. Hart and St J. Clowes made *Northwards* in the North of Norway in 1928, with a Lapp cast, for British Screen Productions. And in 1929 the Court Treatts used their previous experience of Africa to make *Stampede* (Trade Show January 1930), a film with an entirely African cast which was highly regarded by the critics although in fact its artistic and technical mediocrity did not live up to the vitality of its conception.

During the twenties the Americans Merian C. Cooper and Ernest B. Shoedsack showed *Grass*, made in Persia in 1925, *Chang*, made in Siam in 1927 and *The Four Feathers*, made in 1929; Flaherty made *Moana* in Samoa in 1925 and Brückner made *Samba* in South Africa, which was shown in Britain in May 1928. In all these 'natural resource' films, as Rotha called them, the narrative thread was so slender that they were in fact documentary rather than drama, and in technique and maturity of outlook they left their British counterparts far behind. But it is a sad sidelight on the disadvantages under which British film makers now suffered that *Close Up* of May 1928 wrongly assumed that *Samba* was 'the first actual "scenario" with negros (*sic*) as players', *Nionga* quite forgotten. The British film makers had little ability to create memorable images, and were less interested in a film study of real life than in telling a story which grew out of the foreign environment. Nevertheless they shared with the foreign film makers a desire to create a narrative art which would open more windows on the world, enlarging our experience of the geographical and ethnic environment, and their work helped to consolidate the growing interest of a more serious and discriminating audience.

* *Under the Southern Cross* (Trade Show March 1929) may have been a later version of the same material.

Meanwhile an entirely different branch of actuality filming flourished at home, the short interest or magazine film. It is hard to believe that the makers of these trivial films had any interest in them except as cheap programme fillers, but it is a branch of British production which prospered while the rest slumped. It seems to have been more or less self-contained. The practitioners were not as a rule technicians from the feature world taking shelter during a time of difficulty, nor did those trained in shorts production usually graduate to features.

From the beginning of the period the *Pathé Pictorial*, and later Pathé's *Eve's Film Review*, regularly covered personalities, fashions and social events, and Gaumont's *Around the Town* had short items about the shows, restaurants and cabarets. Both the Hepworth and Gaumont companies put out short interest films from time to time such as Gaston Queribet's *Q'riosities* made for Hepworth, and in 1922 Grangers began a series of *Marvels of the Universe*. The name of John Betts appeared in November 1920 with 12 one-reel *Turf Favourites*. In 1923, besides a longer *Fox-Hunting Pageant* (Trade Show April 1923), he had another series of one-reelers called *Pillars of the Turf*. By 1924 these films were appearing in great numbers and Betts was doing one-reelers for Stoll, *Racing Outlook* and '*Sporting Life*' and a series of *What Not to Do But How to Do It* on all kinds of sports. In addition Geoffrey Benstead and Harry B. Parkinson appeared, with *Hints of Horsemanship* from the former and two series made for Graham–Wilcox by the latter, *Wonderful London* and *London's Famous Cabarets*. Many firms produced occasional items of this type but John Betts, Geoffrey Benstead and Harry B. Parkinson, and later Widgey Newman, dominated the field and continued a stream of routine films about show business, sports, dogs and horse racing or 'curiosities', and occasionally fiction (e.g. Harry B. Parkinson's *London's Famous Cabarets*, 1925, *Across the Footlights*, the *Bindle* series of comedies, *Romances of the Prize Ring* and 6 two-reel fight dramas by Andrew Soutar in 1926; Widgey Newman's *Off the Beaten Track*, 1925, and *This Year's Derby's Secrets*, 1927; John Betts' *Sport and Interest in a Fresh Light*, 1927). If news reels were newspapers without editorials, the interest films were magazines devoted to trivialities. Most of them were handled by Butcher's, Phillip's, Pioneer, Stoll's and Moss and they enabled exhibitors to build up what had come to be regarded as an acceptable programme. It is difficult to say whether they had any positive popularity with audiences except as make-weights.

The interest film presented information frivolously, simply to pass the time. A different motive was to be found in both the advertising and the advice or propaganda films, both of which presented facts in order to persuade people to action. Commercial advertising films, like interest films, had existed from the very early days of the cinema. Like them in being sponsored, and in being films of persuasion, were a number of films made during the twenties for various official or voluntary social service organizations. These included the Local Government Board, the L.C.C., the Ministry of Agriculture and Fisheries, Bermondsey Borough Council Health Propaganda Department and the Dental Board of the U.K.; and Save the Children Fund, the Society of Friends, the Salvation Army and the National Councils for combating Venereal Diseases and for the Prevention of Tuberculosis. Such films aimed to persuade for the good of the spectator rather than for the good of the sponsor, and had their antecedents in the many official short films made during the war.

Other films with a social purpose were educational films. All factual films could be described loosely as educational, and had long been so regarded, and the usual educational film show of the time consisted of a mixture of such travel, natural history, interest and even 'industrial' films as were available and seemed to fit in with traditional patterns of education. But people gradually recognized that this, although interesting and even stimulating, was not education in the school sense. The special production of teaching films, however, hardly existed. Makes such as Urban's Movie Chats provided suitable items compiled from the work of many film makers, and Visual Education handled a number of specially made films. But it was British Instructional which first had a consistent policy in this country of producing academically accurate short films of high quality, with their *Secrets of Nature* series (see pages 130–131). From 1922 onwards these outstanding films played a versatile rôle, as works of art and scientific record to their makers, entertainment to the cinemas, and teaching to the educational film enthusiasts. The impetus came in the first place from the film makers themselves. Pike, Knight and Higham all made bird films for other firms and most of the group of film makers were cameraman-naturalists who were lucky to find under Bruce Woolfe's leadership an opportunity to make their work economically viable. British Instructional did more, and branched out into other educational films. In 1926 a two-reel *Naval Warfare, 1789–1805* was an offshoot of their Nelson film, and next year a two-reel *Roman Britain* followed the production of *Boadicea*. In addition several series of short films about various parts of the world appeared from 1925 onwards and in 1928 two longer films called *The Benguela Railway* and *The Opening of Takoradi Harbour*. Superficially, indeed, these films were little different from simple travel films, but the care with which they were made, and above all the intention with which they were made, put them in a class of their own.

Parallel with this development of the educational film were a series of war films made by British Instructional, from *The Battle of Jutland* shown in 1921 to *The Battles of the Coronel and Falkland Islands*, which was shown in 1927. These films were, indeed, the reason for Bruce Woolfe's entry into film production and were his original contribution to the development of the cinema.

During the first world war large archives of actuality film, mainly of the battlefields, had been built up by the official cameramen, but little had been done to convert this raw material into a coherent picture of the war. After the armistice a few film people had tried to follow them with factual films about world events. Nash's *Women Who Win*, about the women's services, appeared in 1919, and Elvey's *Victory Leaders*, which in later years he optimistically referred to as a documentary, appeared in the same year. In March 1920 came *The World's Greatest Story*, 15 two-reelers (Trade Show March 1920), a series by Fred Paul in which actuality material was cursorily linked by florid titles, and which was strongly criticized in the daily papers for its crudity.

It was the outsider, Bruce Woolfe, working quietly on his own in 1919, who first found a satisfactory way to make a factual film study of aspects of the war.

This he did by a combination of actuality material and animated maps and diagrams in *The Battle of Jutland*, a dignified account of the battle which scored a somewhat unexpected critical and popular success. He was encouraged by this to supplement actuality material with re-enacted incidents in his next two films, *Armageddon* (Trade Show November 1923), which was about Allenby's campaign in Palestine, and *Zeebrugge* (Trade Show October 1924). Then followed *Ypres* (Trade Show October 1925), *Mons* (Trade Show September 1926) and finally the most important of them all, *The Battles of the Coronel and Falkland Islands* (Trade Show September 1927), all three directed for him by Walter Summers. By now British Instructional had turned most of its attention to fiction films, but two more of the same type, *The Somme* (Trade Show September 1927) and *Q Ships* (Trade Show June 1928), were made for New Era largely by Barkas, who had been one of the former British Instructional team.

These films gained a great deal of prestige for British films and even for the cinema itself. The more demanding critics, like Bryher, were prepared to consider them seriously, if not to approve:

'I was not hopeful about "Mons" because my experience of English films had not been encouraging. But I went prepared to admire at least an attempt at a good picture. I thought even that as it was historical reconstruction, a sort of document, we should have achieved a possibly ponderous, but correct transcription of the early days of the war, photographed with a dull but scientific accuracy similar to the scientific films in which English photography has achieved a reputation. But it was disappointing from every point of view.

'It was so badly photographed. . . . But beyond the photography was the film itself—full of the kind of sentimentality that makes one shudder, a sentimentality that Hollywood even would not dare offer to a Middle Western audience. . . mixture of a Victorian tract for children and a cheap serial in the sort of magazines one finds discarded on a beach. . . .

'There was no central idea back of the picture. The whole theme was "we are English making an English picture, therefore be good to us". And that will not make either a commercial or an artistic success of British films.'[130]

Battles fared little better at her hands, and she pointed out that once again the film was merely an outward chronicle, lacking the imaginative use of significant detail; once again it took a romantic boys' adventure view of war as 'an elaborate and permissible adventure', failing to suggest its horror, waste and stupidity. Her concession that 'the *Battle of the Falklands* is not a bad film' sums up the critical standing of these films as a serious effort to use the cinema medium for a worth-while purpose, worthy of critical attention, but in the end disappointing.

Nevertheless a few years later, when the word documentary had become fashionable, Rotha himself referred to them as excellent examples of the documentary film, and they did have some of the characteristics of the latter. The intention and seriousness of purpose were typical, and the preference for recreated reality rather than spot record. *Battles*, for example, had a cast list of ships playing the parts of those which had taken part in the actual incidents, supplemented with some rather unfortunate studio and trick work. The use of real settings and non-professional players was characteristic of the work of the Soviet directors and of Flaherty and others working at the same time, but the technique did have disadvantages which were not always overcome in the British films. A real army on the move, as the wartime records had poignantly shown, stared idly or cheerfully at the camera or were too tired to bother; but in *Mons*, their uniforms either too clean or too theatrically tattered they uncomfortably avoided looking at it, and the staggering and tottering with which they conveyed fatigue were reminiscent of the melodramas of 1910. But although inferior to the work of the few great film makers abroad, the films were an intelligent attempt to use the cinema for a new purpose and seem to have owed nothing to foreign example. Summers' *Battles*, with its impersonal mass hero, its angle and overhead shots of decks and companionways and swivelling guns bears a strange superficial resemblance to *Potemkin*. Even its cutting, superimposed titles and multiple images were more advanced than the technique found in the usual British film of the time. But *Potemkin*, although made in 1925, was not shown in England until 1928 and it would seem that the achievements of the British film makers, such as they were, were completely independent.

The war reconstruction films were commercial entertainment, but they also had a form of sponsorship in that they received official assistance. Other uses of sponsored films for the creation of a favourable image or climate of opinion increased throughout the twenties. Nash's series *Our National Industries*, which were deliberately non-technical and avoided the direct advertising of particular firms, were made in co-operation with the Federation of British Industries for the Wembley Exhibition of 1924. In the same year the Air Ministry sponsored a film on the work of the British airways called *The Imperial Airways*. More directly commercial films were made, like a Vickers-Aviation film of their aircraft and a long film made for I.C.I. about the construction of the new I.C.I. House in 1928. The content of films like *West Africa Calling* (one reel, 1928), made by British Instructional for the Conservative and Unionist Central Office, *The Union of Post Office Workers* (four reels, 1927) made independently, and *Arise and Walk* (three reels, 1929) produced for the Central Council for the Care of Cripples, read like the documentaries of the thirties as far as intentions went and clearly sought to give a full and coherent account of their subjects.

They fell short of what was later known as documentary cinema, however, in their relatively unsophisticated film technique. The term documentary was coined by John Grierson in a 1926 review of Flaherty's *Moana* in America and was later defined by him as the 'creative treatment of reality'. And it was Grierson who, in 1929, made for the Empire Marketing Board what was perhaps the only landmark film in the whole of the British silent cinema, and the beginning of the documentary school of film making in England, *Drifters*.

An article in the *Westminster Gazette* had called for a Government Film Department soon after the war,[131] and the idea of using official films for information and propaganda, especially about the Empire, recurred every now and then. Little had been done, however. In the end it was Imperial sentiment which led to the foundation of a school of film making of great importance to Britain, as it also did to the quota legislation. In May 1926 the Empire Marketing Board was set up to further the marketing of Empire produce in Britain by means of all the publicity media. John Grierson was described in an American periodical at this time as an

'English publicist who has been engaged for several months in a study of the American motion picture industry, under the authorization of the British Government.'[132]

In February 1927 he returned to England and went to see the head of the Empire Marketing Board, Sir Stephen Tallents, and was appointed Films Officer. Walter Creighton was also engaged and sent to Hollywood towards the end of 1927 to study film production. Meanwhile the only activity of the Board in relation to the film was to run cinema shows of interest shorts at the Imperial Institute, and questions were asked in Parliament in late 1928 and early 1929 about the work of the Empire Marketing Board Cinema Officer. To the great amusement of the film trade the latter was admitted to have no technical experience. Creighton finally made an ambitious full-length film called *One Family*. It was not a success, but the situation was saved in late 1929 when a three-reeler about the herring fleet made by Grierson was given the unusual honour of a showing at the Film Society.

Drifters was immediately accepted by the serious film public, such as it was, with an enthusiasm quite unknown for a British film. In the book *Grierson on Documentary*, Forsythe Hardy wrote:

'*Drifters* aroused immediate interest because of both its subject-matter and its technique. In the studio-bound British cinema, whose most daring expedition was into a West End theatre to photograph an Aldwych farce or a Co-optimists' show, a film which drew its drama at first-hand from real life was something revolutionary . . . Here was workaday Britain brought to the screen for the first time; what has become familiar today through a thousand documentary films had then the impact of startling discovery. In technique also *Drifters* struck a note which was new in Britain. Grierson had studied the work of the Russian directors—had indeed helped to prepare the version of *Potemkin* shown in America—and he applied to his own film the principles of symphonic structure and dynamic editing evolved by Eisenstein and Pudovkin. *Drifters* might have broken new ground in its theme and remained technically dull; in fact, its form was little less exciting than its content.'[133]

It is difficult to overestimate the importance of this film. All the same it is misleading to place so much emphasis on the novelty of its subject matter. Although the current trend led by such companies as B.I.P. was certainly indoors, to an elaborate and unreal studio-created world, the British had not been as tightly tied to the stage or as studio-bound as Forsythe Hardy has suggested. Even in entertainment films there had always been a tradition of low-life stories and outdoor work, and the many locations and expeditions, the

Secrets of Nature, the war reconstructions and the small but constant output of industrial and sponsored films of all types had always been well liked. As in so many other cases, it was not the idea which was new so much as the skill with which it was done. It would be difficult to tell from a précis of three films about the herring fleets, those of 1922 and 1925 and this one, that there was any marked difference between them.[134] But one look at the films themselves leaves no doubt about what makes the last of them revolutionary.

In the enthusiasm of the moment the new documentary films were to be described as films of social purpose, or even of social analysis,[136] but Grierson's own definition, the creative treatment of reality, remains the best. It may be that most of the film makers who were to go in for documentary tended to be interested in current affairs and to have broadly liberal sympathies, but it is not true that an essential characteristic of the documentary was social purpose, or even that it should be a film of social analysis. It was not the subject which made *Drifters* remarkable, or even the viewpoint expressed. There was already a long tradition of films about life and industry in everyday Britain, but what distinguished this one, and what continued to make the documentary a separate *genre* whether the subject was mail trains, gun dogs or tea plantations was their impact on the spectator. *Drifters* conveys the beauty and strangeness of the sea, the gulls, the fish, boats and the cold light of dawn in the fishing village as vividly as it follows the starting of the engine or the return to the busy quay. It, and every other good documentary, was to involve the spectator in a facet of real life by its creative use of the film medium, and it is this alone which makes Grierson's achievements a turning point in the British cinema.

Grierson himself said[135] that he had learnt from the Russians, the American Western and from Flaherty, and *Drifters* was in fact a faithful exercise in some of the Russian editing methods. Rotha called it

'. . . the only film produced in this country that reveals any real evidence of construction, montage of material, or sense of cinema as understood in these pages . . . the theme of *Drifters* was pure in filmic textures.'[137]

At last Britain had a factual film which made a complete break with the old illustrated lecture. Impressions were built up by the cutting, sometimes very rapid, of a multitude of selected images superly photographed by Basil Emmott, who was himself no stranger to actuality filming. The old belief of pioneers like Hepworth that all cutting jarred the spectator was refuted. For the visual and intellectual content were so selected that far from checking attention they led the spectator irresistibly onwards, to an understanding that was both intellectual and emotional.

The characteristics of what was later to be called the documentary movement were already present. The serious and often poetic approach to the real world, usually but not always the activities of mankind, and the use of advanced techniques of film construction amounted to a style of film making which was new in both spirit and method. Real people and real surroundings were shown without the use of professional actors, sets or fictional stories. But the realism was not that of the record film, being a combination of actual events and of situations recreated for the camera, and at their best the films were creative works of art. It was essential that they be specially shot and not, as with many interest films, compiled from library material. Such was their prestige that finance for this was to become available during the thirties from a number of official organizations and large commercial firms willing to sponsor them as a form of public relations, and this sponsorship, also, became one of the characteristics of the documentary movement. As Rotha said,[138] the Empire Marketing Board Film Unit under Grierson acted during the next few years as the first real *avant-garde* in this country, and

'. . . laid in Britain the seeds of documentary; which was to become . . . this country's most important contribution to cinema as a whole.'[139]

CHAPTER EIGHT

The Quality of British Production

The previous chapters hardly suggest a high level of artistic awareness in the British film industry during the twenties. There is considerable evidence that British films were generally felt to be bad even at the time. Production became accustomed to being called a Cinderella industry, and to such blistering attacks as this one from Joseph Schenck:

'British producers . . . do not consider what the public requires. They do not produce good pictures. They have never produced good pictures. They simply produce pictures and shove them out into the world . . . you have no personalities to put on the screen. The stage actors and actresses are no good on the screen. Your effects are no good, and you do not spend nearly so much money.'[1]

Next year Marcus Loew was even more unkind at a lunch given in his honour:

'Not even on the horizon can I see even the nucleus of a British film producing industry.'[2]

In 1927 *Close Up*, which at one point referred to British production as muck, rarely mentioned British films by name and then only with contempt, asserting:

'We know that an announcement "British Film" outside a movie theatre will chill the hardiest away from its door. . . .'[3]

This was an overstatement. Some of the more popular Hepworth, Pearson and British Instructional Films among others, as well as the films of Elvey, Wilcox and Balcon, had enjoyed considerable local success. Nevertheless it was near enough to the truth, and so was their sneering reference after quota legislation had led to a burst of activity:

'England on the upgrade. Money being thrown about. Determined on efficient mediocrity.'[4]

The habit of ascribing to Britain qualities which are in some mystical way inimical to the cinema persisted for many years. Truffaut, in his important book on Hitchcock,[5] in 1968 used the word 'uncinematic' about England. But mysterious generalizations cannot explain the standard of British film making during the twenties; instead, it would be well to take a look at some of the hard facts underlying it.

But first it is necessary to distinguish two different aspects of quality. L'Estrange Fawcett wrote in 1927:[6]

'It is certainly a great pity that we cannot produce satisfactory films.'

but, whilst wishing that Britain, like America, could turn out a large number of money-making films, he also longed for an occasional film which would

'. . . stamp our producing centres as capable of the finest individualist work known.'

The existence of a large body of conventional entertainment films of high professional and commercial quality is not the same thing as outstanding creative activity, but the conditions which permit the one may well form a basis for the other. The situation is not peculiar to films. Bertrand Russell, discussing men of rare or exceptional greatness has written:

'In the ages in which there were great poets, there were also large numbers of little poets, and when there were great painters there were large numbers of little painters. The great German composers arose in a milieu where music was valued, and where numbers of lesser men found opportunities.'[7]

It was particularly so in the cinema because of the nature of the medium. The industrial structure provided the creative artist's tools. An economically stable industry could keep in existence a body of experienced technicians with the physical equipment of production, and also the ability and willingness of management to risk capital on new ideas and inventiveness. Within this structure a more imaginative individual or group than usual could sometimes flourish. It was, in fact, during the twenties that the dual nature of the film became evident, and with it the problem of reconciling the creative intention of the artist and the extremely complex economic framework within which he must operate. There are, therefore, two questions to consider, the trade and public ideal of quality, the commercially successful film; and the intellectual's ideal of quality, outstanding creative activity and artistic leadership.

The size of the country, its climate and its previous history were unalterable facts which were to affect the course of British film making. The climate, of comparatively little importance in later years, gave film making a bad start in this country. In the early days films were made by sunlight, at first in the open air and then in glass-covered stages; even when auxiliary lighting was introduced the amount of sunlight still mattered. More sophisticated dark stages became normal after the war but location shooting was of great importance. Much has been said about the magnificent scenery of California, but it was the sunshine rather than the scenic possibilities which gave it an advantage. There were several companies after the war which bravely announced their intention to make films with a 'very English' setting but failed to take the weather into account, and gradually had to give up the attempt. And even at the end of the period when location shooting was made less important by the introduction of new photographic and design processes, filming on the studio lot was still handicapped in this country.

An early disadvantage like this can easily have a cumulative effect by limiting profits and hence the capital and size of the earliest firms. An even more important difficulty of the British film makers was the size of the home market in comparison with that of America, which by the twenties had roughly five times as many cinemas. The competitive advantages of mass production, including the spread of overheads like studios and equipment, high salaried staff and publicity organizations, were acquired earlier and more easily where there was ready access to a large home market. Such advantages, after all, are not peculiar to the film industry.

Beginning as they had in fairground shows, penny gaffs and lantern lectures, films had everywhere attracted the type of enterprise which was out to make a fast return, and had only taken up production to supply their own exhibition needs. A film costing a similar amount to make could bring in money more easily in a country with a big home market and, when it had done so, there was more to spend on the next production. More ambitious schemes, the latest and best equipment, full and continuous use of large studios and finally the most demanding talent, were soon within reach. Not only that, but it became possible to spend large sums on promotion, and even before 1914 the money spent on publicity for American brands of film, and then for individual American stars, built up a demand for American pictures not only at home but in other countries too. England, importing films freely before the war as part of a flourishing *entrepôt* trade, was peculiarly vulnerable because of language and cultural ties to the appeal of the American film.

London's position as the centre of the world's film trade did not survive the war. Relatively unaffected, the big American companies were able to develop their own contacts with other countries. But although the war may have accelerated the British decline, it certainly was not its root cause, which was the disparity of size. By the early twenties the process was far advanced. Well-made, lavish and highly publicized American films were available for lower individual prices than the meagre, mean, little known British ones. Big amalgamations of production, distribution and exhibition interests in America had already formed powerful combines in the face of which the English market was helpless. The various booking practices tied the market up neatly. The big companies offered commercial advantages for booking their large blocks of films; this led naturally to advance booking, because of the size of the blocks; and this led as inevitably to blind booking, since dates were so far ahead that films were not always available for viewing. These practices were often abused, and incidentally left exhibitors with few dates free for the occasional product of small British firms. But the high moral tone in which they were condemned was somewhat insincere. Essentially they were as convenient to exhibitors as to renters and American producers, and moreover the few English production firms which were big enough were only too glad to do the same thing, although as inconspicuously as possible.

It was hardly surprising that this booking situation helped to kill the small, old-fashioned British producer. The companies which suffered were those unable to realize how much films had changed, and in all probability would have disappeared anyway. There were signs throughout the twenties of attempts to reconcile the naturally small scale of the industry in Britain with the economies of large-scale production. There were several schemes for a shared 'national studio' and various forms of co-operation such as the British Film Weeks; also plans for vertical integration like backing and distribution agreements between producers and renters, and the plan for an exhibitors' co-operative to finance production. It was dimly realized that some form of compromise between large- and small-scale operation was desirable. But the film industry was part of the general economic picture of the country, and in addition to its own difficulties was subject to the same economic depression which affected other industries. By the time the quota was passed in 1927 the cumulative effect was so great that it was hardly likely to be overcome by the means proposed. All the same it is very noticeable that the companies which failed were those which were still living in the past. The post-war economic difficulties had not prevented the successful appearance of a new type of film entrepreneur.

There were other direct results of being a small country. One was the influence on film making of the London theatre. Film makers, huddling in the South for the available sunshine, were within reach of the capital, and indeed this very centralization may well have helped to make London the pre-war world film market. But because the studios were so near the centre of the English theatrical world, players came and went freely between studios and theatre. Film companies, moreover, were able to borrow from the theatre important players who had no intention or need of becoming successful in the cinema itself. The interchange may have been necessary, as British film production was so small and precarious that comparatively few could live entirely on their earnings from it. But it meant that there was neither motive nor opportunity for actors to adapt themselves to the silent screen and discover a suitable style, nor for companies to turn them into film stars. Much has been made of Hepworth's stock company, but it consisted mostly of experienced second-class stage actors. Hepworth, with Chrissie White and Alma Taylor, and to a lesser extent Samuelson, tried to popularize their own film stars, but many members of the large, undisciplined casts in British films in the early twenties continued to regard themselves as stage actors first and foremost, reduced from time to time to a little slumming on the film. With the outstanding exception of Betty Balfour, an actress who became an extremely popular star in England by her film work, this continued to be true in the mid-twenties, and changed only gradually as a new generation of young actors born since the beginning of the film industry and equally at home on both stage and screen became popular after about 1924–25. The only other British star of a popularity equal to that of Betty Balfour was Ivor Novello, and he preferred the stage and eventually gave up film work. As for the bit players and extras, there was an army of variously unsuccessful stage actors who flocked to each studio in turn and did much to give British films their name for deplorable crowd work. Stories and script-writing, also, showed far greater dependence on the theatre and its ways than they did in

America. But the social traditions which had by now relaxed sufficiently to accept certain leading members of the theatrical profession as respectable members of society stood fast when it came to the cinema, and many actors regarded their film work simply as an embarrassing necessity.

The country was not only small, it was also old. Or rather, its long history of social and economic development had reached a stage where existing patterns of activity and thought were firmly established, and somewhat inflexible in the face of change. The industrial revolution was over. It had left us running out of steam in some respects, with an already ageing structure of industrial production and commerce which, once impressive, now seemed small and tame in comparison with the more recently emerged economies of other countries. The bustling enterprise which had once led the world was also the first to become set in its ways. There was a strong class structure, in which those who succeeded in industry and trade tended to become traditionalists themselves, and adopt the ways of the upper classes. Because of the extra economic difficulties, far more capital and salesmanship would have been needed than in America to make the film industry a success; whereas in fact capital and enterprise on the grand scale were less ready to be attracted to the cinema in this country. Film adventurers in America might make their fast buck, put it back into films and proudly graduate to being film tycoons. But in England big business did not consider the film industry as a suitable field of activity until the twenties, when it was represented first by Lord Beaverbrook and Sir Edward Hulton. By then production was already in trouble, and their interest in it was shortlived; they soon realized that the profits lay in film distribution, especially in the distribution of American films. By the time John Maxwell put production on a big business footing at the end of the twenties a new situation had been created by the quota legislation. Nevertheless two more enlightened producers, Balcon and Bruce Woolfe, had entered the film industry when things were at their worst and in their very different ways had kept afloat by intelligent business methods and a genuine feeling for the film medium until things improved. Wilcox, acting as his own film maker as well as producer, took somewhat longer to acquire financial stability. But with these exceptions the British film industry was not so much short of potential film makers as of managerial talent to back them.

The vicious circle of bad quality and lack of money resulting from the basic conditions of the country's climate, size and history made the British film industry less and less able to stand up to American competition. There was a chronic shortage of capital. From the old companies, unconsciously hampered by the possession of little antiquated studios and little antiquated ideas of finance, to such ambitious new companies as Alliance, requests for capital were pitched too low and the cost of modern production was seriously underestimated. The resulting parsimony in salaries, equipment and mounting was fatal to the films. The reluctance of banks to finance production, frequently deplored and contrasted with the happy situation in America, was hardly unreasonable in view of the poor prospects of the investment. Most of the companies were run by men of little imagination, who were reluctant to back anything unusual or unproved. This even extended to a lack of confidence in such talented members of the industry as Hitchcock or Pearson, whose work was on occasion shelved or cavalierly recut. It was several years before Balcon and Wilcox, who obtained capital film by film on a more realistic scale, were to acquire an adequate financial basis. Once the quota was law, capital flowed readily into the industry for a while and a number of other companies were also able to achieve financial security, but the habit of encouraging artistic inventiveness was not so easy to acquire.

Paul Rotha wrote as an impatient young man:

'The root of the trouble in this country lies in the conservative and narrow-minded outlook of the producing executives.'[8]

A little later even the sober report *The Film in National Life* was to agree:

'Much of the British industry has been in the hands of men of little vision, who sought a quick return for their money. If they failed to hit their mark, they were apt to aim lower instead of higher.'[9]

Pusillanimous management was accompanied by a preference for trivial and inoffensive film content. Possibly this standard was a fair reflection of the tastes of the mass audience of the time. But the Victorian spirit of the early film makers lingered in the front offices to such an extent that a version of *Maria Marten* was made in 1928, and an important firm like Welsh–Pearson actually embarked on a programme of silent melodramas in 1928 in defiance of the advice of its own film director, George Pearson, who already saw that the silent film was finished. In a series of booklets on the general theme of the future Betts wrote in despair of *The Future of the Film*:

'When the Future of Hell is written in this series, a large number of pages will have to be reserved for the Americans who make films. (Our chaste, timid, honest, respectable, patriotic, provincial English film directors will of course go to Heaven.)'[10]

But then, the British public's preference for society drama was well known. It was appropriate that Goldwyn, searching politely for a tribute, could find nothing better to say than that

'. . . no actor . . . can enter a drawing room like an Englishman.'[11]

One of the disadvantages of small scale is the inability to attract the very talented or to retain them once they have proved their ability. This was most noticeable in the case of star quality, that mysterious and essential ingredient of the commercial film, which was increasingly subject to the pull of Hollywood unless it was firmly anchored on the London stage. Victor McLaglen, C. Aubrey Smith, Ronald Colman, Basil Rathbone, Clive Brook and others went to Hollywood, whilst Leslie Howard and Jack Buchanan were two of the many actors who found little scope in films at this time and preferred the stage. It seemed impossible to stop the drain of talent. Early producers, on the other hand, tried to borrow foreign stars, and this became even more important when production expanded suddenly at the end of the decade. The large, modern output of B.I.P. depended heavily on it, and also on foreign technicians and directors. The international appeal of the film medium, which had been seen as a universal language, was a matter of pride to film enthusiasts in the early days. But the new internationalism of the late twenties was different, reflecting only the universal appeal of profit. The joint foreign productions, usually German or Austrian, of Stoll, Gainsborough and British Instructional, gained finance, distribution and technical experience but could do little towards forming a genuinely national school of film making. This was true also of the large number of European and American directors, stars and technicians who were brought here after the quota. And the difficulties experienced by transplanted foreign talent, especially with a language difficulty to overcome, can be seen clearly in the case of Robison and Dupont whose films for B.I.P., if remarkable for this British studio, were considered far from their own best work. It was suspected by some that the characterless amalgam of styles in a so-called international production was in fact less likely to make a film attractive to other countries than a strongly national style of film making, however foreign, which expressed qualities of universal human concern.

The sporadic and unenterprising salesmanship of British producers abroad, also, was notorious. After the war it almost seemed as if British producers expected the world to come to them, rather than that they should go out and sell. The few who went abroad early with their little films, including Hepworth, Stoll's and the London Film Company, found it harder than they had expected and were soon discouraged. Here again, the new generation of businessmen were prepared to take more trouble and their efforts to promote individual films abroad, as well as to secure joint foreign backing, were partly successful. But there was a widespread lack of interest in foreign markets, a failure to find out what they wanted or to make a consistent and well-publicized effort to provide it. To many abroad it must have seemed as if British film production did not exist. Here again, as with timid management, the many adverse comments on this unadventurous export policy could have been applied to other industries besides that of film production. Appeals to the Empire as a natural extension of the home market, frequently heard outside the industry, were unrealistic.

If the British film industry did not have the natural, economic and social advantages of the American film industry, nor did it get the official help and encouragement given to films in Germany and Soviet Russia. Although, or perhaps indeed because, they suffered far greater disruption as a result of war and revolution, both these countries experienced greater changes in theatre, writing, painting, music and architecture as well as film, and both were prepared to take the cinema seriously from the end of the war onwards. France also was a centre of artistic experiment and several important exponents of the traditional fine arts there were not ashamed to be involved in experimental film making. The intellectual life of Europe had been in a state of creative ferment for some time. Great Britain was only on the fringe of these movements. It is in keeping with the general picture that the great revolutionary of stage design in Britain before the war, Edward Gordon Craig, had found little understanding in his own country and left it to live abroad. In Germany, where the problems of a limited home market were similar to those of Britain, the government early passed the Kontingent laws and persuaded the Deutsches Bank to back Ufa, thus providing not only a quota system but also direct financial help for production. An industry was able to exist which made screen history, even if it did not make money. In Russia, where the vast market was potential rather than actual, film makers depended not on box-office success but on official patronage, and this at a time when change and experiment were at a premium. In 1919 these countries had found themselves with an urgent need to rebuild and think anew. The paradox of winning the war for Britain was that by encouraging complacency it put the country at a psychological disadvantage. The development of the film industry was left, like so many other things, to chance. Sidney Morgan had suggested a quota system in 1917, but so great was the inertia that national measures to help the industry did not come into operation until the end of the twenties.

Moreover it was not only the government which failed to support and encourage the film. Writing of the conditions under which great artists flourish, Bertrand Russell says:

'In those days poetry, painting, and music were a vital part of the daily life of ordinary men, as only sport is now.'[12]

Close-Up, in its own characteristic style, had made a similar point in its day:

'The truth is that the average attitude of England and the English to art is so wholly nonchalant and clownish that it is quite useless to expect any art to indigenously flower there. Isolated instances may here and there crop up, but REALLY the Englishman can only be roused to enthusiasm on the football field.'[13]

Far from valuing the film, the cultural and academic élite was either hostile or indifferent to it and, being ignorant of its nature, quite unaware of its potential as an art.

The reaction to this came when some slightly rebellious or non-conforming younger members of the same social class, too young to regard the cinema as a new phenomenon, began about the middle of the twenties to form a coterie taking serious, even rather pretentious, notice of the film. At the same time similar young people were beginning to enter film production itself, especially under the auspices of George Pearson and Bruce Woolfe. Gordon Craig's own son was one of them. Both groups wished to raise the artistic standard of the cinema and did succeed in doing so to some extent. But it is also likely that because of their background and upbringing they tended to have a certain veneration for abroad as the natural home of taste and culture, and an attitude of condescension to the predominantly lower and lower middle-class British film industry. It was easier for a highbrow critic to overlook the absence of refinement in American film makers than in British ones. Much of the industry at home deserved their contempt, no doubt, but the sneering fast became a prejudice. Once the idea of British inferiority was fashionable, few were brave enough to praise anything British without hedging. One could safely admire European films, or be politically bold and admire those from Soviet Russia; one could even be roguish about the enjoyable vulgarity and sentimentality from Hollywood; but to mention the good qualities of a British film maker without qualification might give the wrong impression. The new young upper or upper-middle class entrants to the industry at the end of the decade, sons of the establishment themselves, received some favourable attention. Most of them, in any case, acknowledged their debt to German and Russian influences, and were thus doubly acceptable. But Grierson's *Drifters*, a meticulous adaptation of Russian techniques in the highly respectable category of the factual film, was the first British production to arouse unreserved admiration from these circles.

This attitude requires examination because it was significant of the status of the British film and the artistic snobbery which deprived it of support at home. It was as if, in order to prove what good sports they were, the more cultivated critics would put their standards in abeyance for an American film: but for a British one of similar quality they would insist on gravely measuring it by the very highest standards and finding it wanting. When writing of an Elvey or Squibs film no *Close Up* writer would have adopted their otherwise jolly pose that

'. . . really good art IS commercial, and the mob has a curious nose for what is good. . . .'[14]

Many of the American films they praised so whimsically have stood the test of time no better than the British ones, and to later tastes appear naïve in conception and boring in execution. Yet the extremely popular Elvey or Saville films, for example, were not given the same tolerant treatment as enjoyable hokum. Above all, this trait led to a belittling of the work of Alfred Hitchcock which is absolutely central to the question of artistic quality in the British film.

The public and the trade had been in no doubt as to Hitchcock's exceptional gifts as a story teller from the first film he directed in 1925, and after *The Lodger* in 1926 he had received considerable praise from the more serious critics also. They, wrestling at the time with various theories as to the essence of film art, were much preoccupied with light, silence, rhythm and finally the magic word from Russia, montage. Meanwhile Hitchcock, whose imagination had been fired by American rather than by Continental films, was developing a compelling narrative technique by the assembly of a highly individual choice of shots which led the spectator irresistibly onwards. The relation of this to the Russian preoccupation with film construction went unnoticed. Later, when the sound film arrived, many intelligent people at first condemned it as a death blow to film art and then, enlightened by the famous Russian manifesto, hastily adopted the fashionable word counterpoint as the key to the proper use of sound. Again

Hitchcock had worked along his own lines, and without bothering about pronouncements made a first sound film which suggested how the new element could be used as an integral part of film technique. Had Hitchcock been German, Russian or French, had he even presented himself as a more conventionally bohemian figure, he would almost certainly have been taken more seriously. As it was the rather ordinary looking young man, working first in humdrum Islington and later at Elstree, seems to have been absorbed in his own work and quite uninterested in highbrow reaction. He was tagged with a grudging label 'very clever entertainer, but not an artist. . . .' This reputation remained unchanged for many years until his work was revalued by the younger French cineastes after the second world war, by which time he was, understandably, no longer working in England. The question of whether he was indeed an artist and why he left England is thus of great significance to an understanding of the British film.

For the purposes of this discussion and to avoid misunderstanding it is advisable to define the word artist in some more useful sense than merely as a practitioner of one of the traditional fine arts. It is more helpful to think of a creative artist as one who uses his medium of expression, whatever it is, in such a way as to impart something of his own vision to others, something which would not have been there without the exercise of his own imaginative understanding in the selection of the means at his disposal. An art then becomes more readily explicable as a medium which permits a high degree of this choice. To take a commonplace example, the carving of traditional figures and objects in wood, ivory or stone in a way laid down in great detail, as it usually is in what is loosely called folk art, is essentially a craft inasmuch as the possibilities for choice, the individual's selection expressing his own vision, are extremely limited and the demands of custom very strong; whereas in sculpture the possibilities of selection, although still perhaps within a broad framework of convention, are far more free and permit a wide range of choice to the individual. Just as there are craft workers with more than the usual imaginative flexibility who may be described as artists, the traditional fine arts can be practised with partial success by people who, lacking any real imaginative understanding but having an ability to follow conventional methods, or even to imitate others, are in a deeper sense craftsmen rather than artists. Painting, 'art' in its most obvious sense, is absurdly reduced to a craft in painting-by-numbers, where the exponent need exercise no selection whatever.

The film had already shown itself to have very wide possibilities for the exercise of choice, above all in the juxtaposition of shots of different content and duration. It was in this area in which it was unique, and in which it presented the creative imagination with an artistic medium of enormous possibility. It would not be fair to conclude, because the achievement of the British film was so small at this time, that there were no artists at work in it. On the contrary, there were a number who showed imagination in the use of the medium. Had they worked in a more vital milieu they would probably have been more clearly recognizable as artists. Asquith, who in time was to mature into a film maker with integrity and a style of his own, had not yet outgrown a precocious and rather derivative brilliance. But Hitchcock had already developed a strongly individual style simply by using the resources of film construction as such. He had done this quite independently and out of his own intuitive feeling for the medium, yet his flexible and inventive handling of film structure was regarded merely as ingenious continuity, and not seen for what it was, the exploration of the film's unique quality. It was said by people who appreciated him simply as an entertainer that his use of the medium was instinctive, that he was fascinated with the means of expression to the exclusion of what was expressed, that he had nothing to say and that his preoccupation with provoking an audience reaction was unworthy of a serious artist. Like many artists in other fields he had a spontaneous, indeed almost obsessive, fascination with the use of his medium; but he was highly conscious of the meaning for every nuance in it and the word instinctive, with its suggestion of lucky blundering, was quite unsuitable. Like most artists, also, his conscious objective was not to express himself, an objective which, like happiness, is rarely attained by direct pursuit, but to express something to others. In his case the desire to hold the attention of the spectator matured into the famous suspense story in which the audience is riveted with apprehension. And it was this, in fact, which with remarkable consistency over his long career was to prove the vehicle of his self-expression, the something he had to say, the personal vision of a hostile external world in which the innocent are constantly threatened by involvement in dangers not of their making. This *genre*, which he was to make his own, can be seen from the long series of conversations with Truffaut to be far from accidental, but deeply rooted in his background and character. Yet few of his contemporaries saw in him an artist of outstanding quality.

As for genius, the world is so emotive and so liable to individual interpretation that it is probably better to refer simply to the exceptional creative artist, using this term in line with Russell's definition of the exceptional man in a broader sense as having

'. . . a quality of energy and personal initiative, of independence of mind, and of imaginative vision.'[15]

And the exceptional creative artist must surely be not the most skilful but the most creative, not the artist who produces the most perfect work but he who by his imaginative insight effectively gives the medium a push along his own line of development. Such creative transformation of the silent cinema can perhaps at its best claim only two influences, that of D. W. Griffith and what we may sum up as the Soviet influence associated with Kuleshov, Eisenstein and Pudovkin. But on any wider definition, one for example which would include Chaplin, Flaherty, Pabst and others who extended the medium by their own effective use of it, Hitchcock should certainly be included. It would seem to be as a result of his own class background and lack of pretension, occurring in a society where the popular entertainment film was taken seriously only if it was American, that he was greatly underestimated by the very people who should have been most delighted to find him in their midst. One sad lesson of the British film in the twenties was the ease with which our institutions and patterns of thought could belittle our creative individuals.

The economic, social and cultural conditions were hardly likely to foster many men of exceptional, or even ordinary, originality in the cinema. But although exceptional talent may not flourish without the right conditions, its actual incidence depends on the unique interaction of heredity and environment in each individual. To find environmental causes for the actual incidence of creative talent would be difficult. All that we can say is that because of the poor quality of commercial leadership in the film industry at this time the surrender to mediocre professionalism was widespread, and many of those who were allowed to play the largest part in making the British films of the day were hacks. But even the society which does not value its creative talent will have some might-have-beens. The wonder is not that there was so little inventive and creative talent as that, in an industry which did so little to search for it or promote it, there was so much.

By 1929 the elements of silent film technique were familiar, in one way or another, and although most serious art critics were still firmly prejudiced against the cinema in this country, artistic talent had begun to enter the industry. In the early or middle twenties Henry Edwards, Guy Newall, Graham Cutts, Adrian Brunel, George Pearson and Geoffrey Barkas had all, to a greater or less extent, brought something new and imaginative to their film making. Later Walter Summers, Walter Forde and Miles Mander showed unusual promise in their handling of the silent film medium, unfortunately just before it was superseded by sound film. Turning to the frankly commercial entertainment film, Maurice Elvey, Victor Saville and Herbert Wilcox managed to make satisfactory films despite the unfavourable conditions. Elvey, in particular, was an extremely adaptable worker who made typical Stoll films when he worked for Stoll, better films for a better company, and would certainly have made films of a good Hollywood standard had he had access to comparable resources. Finally, Hitchcock, John Grierson in his enigmatic fashion, and Anthony Asquith had already made outstanding films. Among players, Betty Balfour and Ivor Novello were the only real stars but many others, as soon as they had any small success here, left for Hollywood. On the whole, this seems quite a fair amount of talent to appear in ten years in a depressed and despised industry in a small country. How much outstanding native-born talent appeared in the film industry of a country the size of America, with its favourable conditions? It is significant that Chaplin himself was English, and that his art flourished in the social climate and commercial opportunities of Hollywood in a way that it probably could not have done at home. Sweden, also, which figures in many an account of world cinema simply on the strength of Sjöstrom, Stiller and Greta Garbo, lost all of them to Hollywood during the twenties. The mysteriously uncinematic nature of Britain was, in fact, antipathetic not so much to the appearance of creative and inventive film talent as to its encouragement and practical support by society and commerce.

In the end, of course, an attempt was made to alter the unfavourable conditions by means of the quota legislation of 1927. But this was the result of some confusion between the aims of exhibitors, producers and patriotic people outside the industry. It failed to distinguish between the two different types of quality, the mass of popular entertainment films and the rarer works of artistic leadership. The many motives behind this legislation did include a desire to see Britain take its place with work of creative imagination. But what the actual mechanism of the Act was framed to produce was a large output of films of roughly British origin. It ignored the fact that whilst poor quality may have been due to small markets, providing a large market would not necessarily improve that quality. It was assumed that economic prosperity would be followed by better production or rather, those who cared about artistic quality allowed themselves to be persuaded by those whose main object was quantity. The small producer's classic answer to the competitive advantages of mass production is an output which although small is of very high quality and prestige, enabling it to survive without being swamped by a large output of cheaper goods. Some British makes of car, French couturier clothes and many other luxuries are well-known instances of this. Such industries are typically a matter of national pride, but in the case of the British film its very character as a national product was about to be undermined. It may have been true that there was no real, widespread and deeply felt national preoccupation or theme seeking expression, despite the lip service paid to the ideal of the Empire, which so many had unsuccessfully tried to wish upon the film maker. But the final failure of the quota legislation was to define satisfactorily what, in fact, constituted a British film.

The result was more complex than those who framed the Act had expected. For one thing, the accumulated advantage of America enabled it to profit further from the new situation. Above all it did nothing to solve the underlying problem of the cinema, of how an artist could survive in, and use, an industrial structure. From now on film makers were face to face with the difficulty of reconciling the cinema's existence as an industry, with a fairly large economic optimum size, with its existence as a form of artistic expression, the personal optimum of which was necessarily much smaller. This dichotomy of scale was felt in all countries. And it was this dual nature of the film, perhaps more than anything else, which made the intellectual establishment in Britain so reluctant to admit its artistic existence. How could the organization of so much equipment and so many people contain an art? Speaking of Gordon Craig's struggle to establish his form of theatrical production as a work of art, his son has written:

'It was obvious to him that it must be conceived by one person, and even if it was dependent, like music, on others for its execution, those others must be controlled by one artist throughout the whole performance.'[15]

If an artist like Craig, well connected and working in a respectable sphere like the theatre, had found little response to such ideas in England, how much less likely it was that the possibility of artistic expression through the brash new industrial apparatus of the film should be taken seriously here.

The serious younger critics' theoretical attempts to define and locate the element of artistic creation in the film, and the practical changes within the studios as the various functions diverged and were defined and graded, were aspects of the film's puzzling existence as a form of artistic creation by a group.

Characteristically, this was to be partly resolved in Britain during the next decade by the documentary movement, where the domination of one mind over a comparatively small and simple group could be clearly seen. But even if the film was dominated by the creative imagination of one person, it was still the organic result of the fusion of the work of the individuals, sparking off each other's imagination and implementing the results through each other's work. In this it was a true part of the modern world and manifested one of its most fundamental problems, the reconciliation of the individual's initiative and independence of action with the ever larger groups brought about by technical change.

NOTES TO CHAPTERS

CHAPTER ONE (pages 15–31)

References are to works listed in the Bibliography on page 322.

[1] *Bioscope*, May 22, 1924, page 18.
[2] *Anatomy of Motion Picture Art* by Eric Elliott, page 142.
[3] *Bioscope*, March 6, 1919, page 76.
[4] *Op. cit.*, October 9, 1919, page 46.
[5] *The Mind and the Film* by Gerard Fort Buckle, page xii.
[6] *The Film in National Life*, page 10.
[7] *Bioscope*, August 21, 1919, page 8.
[8] *Heraclitus, or the Future of Films* by Ernest Betts, pages 44–6.
[9] *Bioscope*, January 19, 1922, page 20.
[10] *Op. cit.*, February 9, 1922, page 7.
[11] *Op. cit.*, April 12, 1923, page 37.
[12] *Op. cit.*, April 3, 1923, page 13.
[13] *Op. cit.*, January 30, 1919, page 4.
[14] *My Life and Times, Octave Five 1915–1923* by Compton Mackenzie, page 193.
[15] *Close Up*, December 1927, pages 27–32.
[16] *Op. cit.*
[17] *Bioscope*, April 10, 1929, page 23.
[18] *Let's Go to the Pictures* by Iris Barry, page ix.
[19] *Heraclitus, or the Future of Films* by Ernest Betts, page 9.
[20] *Op. cit.*
[21] *Close Up*, January 1929, page 76.
[22] *The Mind and the Film* by Gerard Fort Buckle, page xiv.
[23] *Anatomy of Motion Picture Art* by Eric Elliott, page 42.
[24] *Op. cit.*, page 43.
[25] *Op. cit.*, pages 49–50.
[26] *Op. cit.*, page 31.
[27] *Op. cit.*, page 113.
[28] *Op. cit.*, page 151.
[29] *Bioscope*, April 3, 1929, page 23.
[30] *The Modern Photoplay and its Construction* by Colden Lore, page 14.
[31] *Films: Facts and Forecasts* by L'Estrange Fawcett, page 217.
[32] *Op. cit.*, page 270.
[33] *Close Up*, August 1927, page 35.
[34] *Op. cit.*, October 1927, pages 15–16.
[35] *Heraclitus, or the Future of Films* by Ernest Betts, pages 14–16.
[36] *Films of the Year 1927–1928*, page 3.
[37] *Parnassus to Let* by Eric Walter White, pages 34–5.
[38] *Pudovkin on Film Technique,* edited by Ivor Montagu, page vii.
[39] *Op. cit.*, pages 139–41.
[40] *Op. cit.*, page 93.
[41] *Let's Go to the Pictures* by Iris Barry, page ix.

CHAPTER TWO (pages 32–70)

[1] *Bioscope*, February 9, 1922, page 5.
[2] *Op. cit.*, June 14, 1923, page 62.
[3] *Op. cit.*, March 3, 1927, page 38.
[4] *Writing for the Screen* by Arrar Jackson, page 16.
[5] *Bioscope*, April 17 1924, page 14.

[6] *Bioscope*, June 18, 1927, page 50.
[7] *Op. cit.*, December 31, 1925, page 25.
[8] *Op. cit.*, August 4, 1927, page 20; and April 3, 1929, page 21.
[9] *Op. cit.*, January 23, 1919.
[10] *Close Up*, August 1927, pages 15–17.
[11] *Bioscope*, February 27, 1929, page 25.
[12] *Op. cit.*, May 27, 1920, page 29.
[13] *Op. cit.*, January 4, 1923, page 34.
[14] *Kine Year Book*, 1927, page 134.
[15] *Bioscope*, March 4, 1926, page 30.
[16] *Close Up*, September 1927, page 67.
[17] *The Film in National Life.*
[18] *Close Up*, October 1927.
[19] *Bioscope*, April 24, 1929, page 15.
[20] *Op. cit.*, October 23, 1919, page 25.
[21] *Op. cit.*, July 12, 1923, page 15.
[22] *Op. cit.*, June 10, 1920, page 26.
[23] *Op. cit.*, March 11, 1920, page ii.
[24] *Op. cit.*, June 10, 1920, page 26.
[25] *Op. cit.*, November 15, 1923, page 27.
[26] *Op. cit.*, March 22, 1928, page 31.
[27] *Op. cit.*, March 18, 1920, page 17.
[28] *Op. cit.*, February 10, 1927, page 23.
[29] *The Theatre, Music Hall & Cinema Companies Blue Book.*
[30] *Bioscope*, March 31, 1927, page 33.
[31] *Op. cit.*, May 3, 1928, page 32.
[32] *Op. cit.*, January 16, 1919, page 16; and March 8, 1928, page 52.
[33] *Op. cit.*, February 6, 1919, page 6.
[34] *Op. cit.*, February 19, 1920, page 4.
[35] *Op. cit.*, November 6, 1924, page 29.
[36] *The Factual Film.*
[37] *A Statistical Survey of the Cinema Industry in Great Britain in 1934.*
[38] *Bioscope*, January 21, 1927, page 22.
[39] *Op. cit.*, August 4, 1927, page 20; and April 3, 1929, page 21.
[40] *Op. cit.*, May 8, 1929, page 23.
[41] *Op. cit.*, December 4, 1919, page 7.
[42] *Op. cit.*, October 22, 1925, page 24.
[43] *Op. cit.*, February 17, 1927, pages 4–5.
[44] *The Film in National Life*, page 43.
[45] *Bioscope*, March 13, 1919, page 5; December 4, 1919, page 7; and March 17, 1921, pages 5–6.
[46] *The Film Industry* by Davidson Boughey, page 92.
[47] *Bioscope*, January 10, 1925, page 25.
[48] *Op. cit.*, June 26, 1924, page 21.
[49] *Op. cit.*, December 9, 1926, page 30.
[50] *Op. cit.*, January 27, 1927, page 22.
[51] *The Cinema in Education*, page 88.
[52] *The Film in National Life*, page 6.
[53] *Op. cit.*, page 6.
[54] British Board of Film Censors Annual Report, 1921, page 5.
[55] *Op. cit.*, 1929, page 10.
[56] *Op. cit.*, 1919, pages 3–4.
[57] *Op. cit.*, 1919, page 5.
[58] *Do We Need a Censor?* by Viscount Brentford, page 21.
[59] Museum of Modern Art *Film Index*, page 529.
[60] *Bioscope*, February 12, 1925.

[61] *Bioscope*, February 16, 1928, pages 33, 38.
[62] *Motion Picture Problems* by W. Marston Seabury, pages 104–5.
[63] *Op. cit.*, pages 98–9.
[64] *The Political Censorship of Films* by Ivor Montagu, pages 13–14.
[65] *Op. cit.*
[66] *Bioscope*, October 24, 1928, page 29.
[67] *The Political Censorship of Films* by Ivor Montagu, page 11.
[68] *Do We Need a Censor?* by Viscount Brentford, page 23.
[69] *The Freedom of the Movies* by Ruth Inglis.
[70] *Parnassus to Let* by Eric Walter White, page 48.
[71] *The Political Censorship of Films* by Ivor Montagu, page 21.
[72] *The Film in National Life*, page 28.

CHAPTER THREE (pages 71–106)

[1] *Bioscope*, September 29, 1927, page 43.
[2] *Op. cit.*, April 5, 1923, page 23.
[3] *Op. cit.*, February 12, 1920, page 18.
[4] *Op. cit.*, July 31, 1919, page 49 and September 18, 1919, page 43.
[5] *Op. cit.*, October 2, 1919, page 22.
[6] *Op. cit.*, February 13, 1919, page 6, 22.
[7] *Op. cit.*, May 8, 1924, page 31.
[8] *Cinematograph Films Act, 1927: Moyne Report*, page 5.
[9] *Bioscope*, July 12, 1923, page 16.
[10] *Op. cit.*, May 7, 1925, page 44.
[11] *Op. cit.*, April 1, 1926, page 18.
[12] *Op. cit.*, June 10, 1926, page 18.
[13] *Kine Year Book*, 1924, page 162; 1921, pages 13–14; and *Bioscope*.
[14] *Bioscope*, June 10, 1920, page 5.
[15] *Op. cit.*, January 18, 1923, page 60; August 23, 1923, page 29.
[16] *Thirty Years of Film Production* by Michael Balcon.
[17] *Films: Facts and Forecasts* by L'Estrange Fawcett, page 48.
[18] *Bioscope*, June 10, 1920, page 5.
[19] *Op. cit.*, January 18, 1923, page 60.
[20] *Op. cit.*, September 13, 1923, page 49.
[21] *Op. cit.*, November 20, 1924, page 45.
[22] *Op. cit.*, August 28, 1919, page 5.
[23] *Op. cit.*, September 23, 1920, pages 10, 31.
[24] *Kine Year Book*, 1922, pages 2–3.
[25] *Op. cit.*, 1928, pages 13, 18.
[26] *Bioscope*, December 1st, 1927, page 36; December 8, 1927, page 31.
[27] *Films: A Report on the Supply of Films: Monopolies Commission Report*, page 56.
[28] *Bioscope*, February 16, 1928, pages 67–8.
[29] *Op. cit.*, August 7, 1919, page 8.
[30] *Op. cit.*, August 28, 1919, page 8.
[31] *Op. cit.*, October 16, 1919, page 10; January 8, 1920, page 23.
[32] *Kine Year Book*, 1921, pages 12–13; *Bioscope*, October 28, 1920, pages 4, 24.
[33] *Bioscope*, May 12, 1921, page 8.
[34] *Op. cit.*, September 29, 1921, page 5.
[35] *Op. cit.*, July 12, 1923, page 43.
[36] *Op. cit.*, November 8, 1923, page 40.
[37] *Op. cit.*, November 29, 1923, page 39.
[38] *The Film Till Now* by Paul Rotha, page 313.
[39] *Op. cit.*, pages 81–2.
[40] *Bioscope*, December 10, 1923, page 34.

[41] *Bioscope*, June 26, 1924, page 35.
[42] *Op. cit.*, April 12, 1923, page 4.
[43] *Op. cit.*, October 6, 1921, page 61.
[44] *Op. cit.*, September 6, 1923, page 36.
[45] *Op. cit.*, September 18, 1924, page 51.
[46] *The Times*, May 15, 1925.
[47] *Bioscope*, June 25, 1925, page 16.
[48] *Kine Year Book*, 1926, pages 7–15.
[49] *Bioscope*, November 5, 1925, page 23 *et al.*, *Kine Year Book*, 1926, pages 7–15.
[50] *Op. cit.*, November 19, 1925, page 46.
[51] *Op. cit.*, February 11, 1926, pages 31, 36; and *Kine Year Book*, 1927, pages 9–15.
[52] *Kine Year Book*, 1927, pages 9–15.
[53] *Bioscope*, July 15, 1926, page 11; August 19th, 1926, page 40.
[54] *Cinematograph Films Act, 1927: Moyne Report*, page 7.
[55] *Bioscope*, November 25, 1926, pages 32–3; and *The Film in National Life*, pages 1–9.
[56] *Op. cit.*, January 12, 1928, page 28.
[57] *Op. cit.*, March 17, 1927.
[58] *Film Renter and Moving Picture News*, January 1, 1927.
[59] *Bioscope*, December 17, 1925, page 24.
[60] *Op. cit.*, September 22, 1927, page 24.
[61] *Op. cit.*, January 28, 1926, page 46.
[62] *Op. cit.*, June 11, 1925, page 12.
[63] *Cinematograph Films Act, 1927: Moyne Report*, page 30.
[64] *A Competitive Cinema* by Terence Kelly, page 76.
[65] *Films: A Report on the Supply of Films: Monopolies Commission Report*, page 61.
[66] *A Statistical Survey of the Cinema Inustry in Great Britain in 1934.*
[67] *The Factual Film*, by the Arts Enquiry, page 58.
[68] *Cinematograph Films Act, 1927: Moyne Report*, page 20.
[69] *The Film in National Life*, page 45.
[70] *Kine Year Book*, 1928, pages 9–11.
[71] *Cinematograph Films Act, 1927: Moyne Report*, page 30.
[72] *Close Up*, November 1927, page 52.
[73] *Bioscope*, June 13, 1928, page 34.
[74] *Op. cit.*, March 13, 1929, page 31.
[75] *Cinematograph Films Act, 1927: Moyne Report*, page 14.
[76] *A Statistical Survey of the Cinema Industry in Great Britain in 1934.*
[77] *Thirty Years of Film Production*, by Michael Balcon.

CHAPTER FOUR (pages 107–155)

[1] *Bioscope*, February 1, 1923, page 39.
[2] *Op. cit.*, January 5, 1922, page 6.
[3] *Op. cit.*, November 11, 1919, page 62.
[4] *Came the Dawn* by Cecil Hepworth; much of this section is based on this work.
[5] *I do What I Like* by W. A. Darlington, page 277.
[6] *Bioscope*, October 16, 1919, page 67.
[7] *Op. cit.*, March 20, 1919, page 68.
[8] *The Secrets of the Cinema* by Valentia Steer, page 70.
[9] *Bioscope*, May 31, 1923, page 57.
[10] *My Wonderful Visit* by Charles Chaplin, pages 142–3.
[11] *My Autobiography* by Charles Chaplin, page 295.
[12] *Secrets of Nature* by Mary Field and Percy Smith, page 10.
[13] Most of this information is based on the account given in *Secrets of Nature*.
[14] *The Film Till Now* by Paul Rotha, page 322.
[15] *Bioscope*, April 15, 1920, page 60.

[16] *Bioscope*, July 1, 1920, page 10.
[17] *Twenty-Five Thousand Sunsets* by Herbert Wilcox, page 59.
[18] *Bioscope*, April 30, 1925, page 30; December 3, 1925, page 47.
[19] Information from *Thirty Years of Film Production* and from *Michael Balcon Presents . . . a Lifetime of Films*, both by Michael Balcon.
[20] *Bioscope*, November 24, 1921, page 74.
[21] *Picturegoer*, August 1922, page 34.
[22] *Kine Year Book*, 1929, pages 223 and 225.
[23] *Op. cit.*, 1927, page 167.
[24] *Bioscope*, October 31, 1928, page 32.
[25] *Op. cit.*, February 7, 1924, page 29.
[26] *Op. cit.*, February 27, 1919, page 8.
[27] *Op. cit.*, March 13, 1919, page 7.
[28] Information for this paragraph is partly from *Bioscope* April 28, 1921, page 5; December 2, 1920, page 7; May 5, 1921, page 7; June 26, 1924, page 22; and April 28, 1921, page 8.
[29] *Nice Work* by Adrian Brunel, page 57.
[30] *Bioscope*, April 15, 1920, pages 78–9.
[31] Information from *Nice Work* and *Close Up*, October 1928, pages 43–6.
[32] *Bioscope*, December 18, 1919, page 14; *Kine Year Book*, 1921, page 140.
[33] *Op. cit.*, December 8, 1921, page 70.
[34] *Op. cit.*, September 29, 1921, page 13; and October 13, 1921, page 45.
[35] *Op. cit.*, March 18, 1926, page 61. Walter West in an interview put the figure at £8,000.
[36] *Op. cit*, March 18, 1926, page 61.
[37] *Close Up*, July 1929.
[38] *Kine Year Book*, 1921, page 194.

CHAPTER FIVE (pages 157–199)

[1] *Bioscope*, February 26, 1925, page 31; July 8, 1926, page 30; and June 2, 1927, page 24.
[2] *Op. cit.*, August 19, 1926, page 19.
[3] *Cinematograph Films Act, 1927: Moyne Report*, page 187.
[4] *The Film Till Now* by Paul Rotha, page 315.
[5] *Bioscope*, July 17, 1924, page 30.
[6] *Op. cit.*, August 4, 1927, page 21.
[7] *Flashback* by George Pearson, page 141.
[8] *Bioscope*, May 20, 1926, page 30.
[9] *Flashback* by George Pearson, page 125.
[10] *Thirty Years of Film Production* by Michael Balcon.
[11] *Index to the Work of Alfred Hitchcock* by Peter Noble, page 8.
[12] *Bioscope*, July 16, 1926, page 39.
[13] *The Film Till Now* by Paul Rotha, page 319.
[14] *Close Up*, September 1929.
[15] *Op. cit.*, April 1929.
[16] *Twenty-five Thousand Sunsets* by Herbert Wilcox.
[17] *Op. cit.*, by Herbert Wilcox, page 69.
[18] *Close Up*, August 1928.
[19] *Behind the Camera* by Natalie Barkas, page 15.
[20] *Close Up*, October 1927.
[21] *The Film Till Now* by Paul Rotha, page 322.
[22] *Close Up*, March 1929.
[23] *The Film Till Now* by Paul Rotha, page 320.
[24] *Close Up*, July 1929.
[25] *Op. cit.*, April 1929.

[26] *Kine Year Book*, 1929, page 202.
[27] *Close Up*, May 1929.
[28] *Op. cit.*, July 1929.
[29] *Op. cit.*, March 1929.
[30] *Op. cit.*, July 1929.
[31] *Op. cit.*, March 1929.
[32] *The Film Till Now* by Paul Rotha, pages 321–2.
[33] *Bioscope*, April 10, 1929, page 21.
[34] *Elstree Story*, page 81.
[35] *Close Up*, March 1929.
[36] *Op. cit.*, August 1929.
[37] *Op. cit.*, August 1929.
[38] *The Film Till Now* by Paul Rotha, page 83.
[39] *Close Up*, October 1929.
[40] *The Film Till Now* by Paul Rotha, pages 321–2.
[41] *Bioscope*, April 14, 1929, page 30.
[42] *Edgar Wallace* by his wife, page 65.
[43] *Bioscope*, May 19 1927, page 20.
[44] *Op. cit.*, November 24, 1927, pages 24, 61.
[45] *Op. cit.*, February 27, 1929, page 31.
[46] *Op. cit.*, March 22, 1928.
[47] *Close Up*, July 1929.
[48] *Bioscope*, November 7, 1928, page 26.
[49] *Op. cit.*, February 9, 1928, page 50.

CHAPTER SIX (pages 200–214)

[1] *Bioscope*, September 29, 1921, page 6.
[2] *Op. cit.*, April 5, 1923, page 22.
[3] *Close Up*, July 1928, page 46.
[4] *The Art of the Moving Picture* by Vachel Lindsay, page 192.
[5] *Close Up*, August 1927, pages 58–62.
[6] *Kine Year Book*, 1927, page 211.
[7] *Bioscope*, February 21, 1924, page 51.
[8] See *Kine Year Book*, 1927, page 215.
[9] *Bioscope*, October 3, 1928.
[10] *Op. cit.*, June 13, 1928, page 54.
[11] According to Baynham Honri.
[12] Figures compiled fom *Kine Year Book*, 1931; figures relate to films reviewed up to November 27, 1930.
[13] *Bioscope*, January 2, 1929, page 40.
[14] *Op. cit.*, January 15, 1925, page 45.
[15] *Op. cit.*, May 8, 1929, page 28.
[16] *Op. cit.*, October 17, 1928, page i.
[17] *Heraclitus, or the Future of Films* by Ernest Betts.
[18] *Bioscope*, October 31, 1928, page 21.
[19] *Op. cit.*, August 15, 1928, page 26.
[20] *Op. cit.*, January 26, 1922, page 20.
[21] *Op. cit.*, August 1, 1928, page 27.
[22] *Op. cit.*, August 22, 1928, page 32.
[23] *Op. cit.*, January 23, 1929, page 29.
[24] *Op. cit.*, October 31, 1928, page 21.
[25] *Op. cit.*, February 6, 1929, page 26.
[26] *Op. cit.*, October 1927, page 64.
[27] *The Film Till Now* by Paul Rotha, page 110.

[28] *Heraclitus, or the Future of Films* by Ernest Betts.
[29] *Close Up*, April 1929.
[30] *Bioscope*, August 8, 1929, page 21.
[31] *Op. cit.*, April 24, 1929, page 12.
[32] *Close Up*, October 1929.
[33] *I Do What I Like* by W. A. Darlington, page 283.
[34] *Thirty Years of Film Production* by Michael Balcon.
[35] *Close Up*, October 1929.

CHAPTER SEVEN (pages 215–297)

The Studios
[1] *Bioscope*, April 14, 1929, page 30.
[2] *Heraclitus, or the Future of Films* by Ernest Betts, page 19.
[3] *Bioscope*, May 30, 1928, page 25.
[4] *Writing for the Screen* by Arrar Jackson, page 72.
[5] *Bioscope*, July 29, 1920, page 50.
[6] Information from Baynham Honri, and *Flashback* by George Pearson.
[7] *Stoll's Editorial News*, October 14, 1920, page 10.
[8] *Bioscope*, September 15, 1921, page 41.
[9] *Films: Facts and Forecasts* by L'Estrange Fawcett, page 161, etc.
[10] *Bioscope*, March 24, 1921, page 7.
[11] *Op. cit.*, November 11, 1920, page 51.
[12] *Op. cit.*, October 28, 1926, page 67.
[13] Notes to the author.
[14] *Kine Year Book*, 1923, page 23.
[15] *Bioscope*, July 5, 1923, page 22.
[16] *Kinematograph Studio Technique* by L. C. MacBean, page 15.
[17] *Stoll's Editorial News*, October 14, 1920, pages 5–6.
[18] *Bioscope*, June 23, 1927, page 24.
[19] *Op. cit.*, June 16, 1927, page 18; May 30, 1928, page 17.
[20] *Op. cit.*, May 29, 1929, and June 19, 1929.

Production and Direction
[21] *Kinematograph Studio Technique* by L. C. MacBean, page 16.
[22] *The Film Industry* by Davidson Boughey, pages 52–3.
[23] *Bioscope*, February 24, 1921, page 6.
[24] *Op. cit.*, July 1, 1919, page x.
[25] *Heraclitus, or the Future of Films* by Ernest Betts.
[26] *The Film Till Now* by Paul Rotha, pages 110–11.

Writing
[27] *The Film Industry* by Davidson Boughey.
[28] *The Modern Photoplay and its Construction* by Colden Lore.
[29] *Writing for the Screen* by Arrar Jackson.
[30] *British Film Number*, 1928, page 225.
[31] *Kinematograph Studio Technique* by L. C. MacBean.
[32] *Bioscope*, October 30, 1919, page 29.
[33] *Op. cit.*, January 15, 1920, page 23.
[34] *Op. cit.*, June 4, 1923, page 25.
[35] Information from Harold Brown at the National Film Archive.
[36] *British Film Number*, 1928, page 79.
[37] *Close Up*, January 1928.
[38] *Bioscope*, March 11, 1920, page 50.
[39] *Op. cit.*, July 1, 1920, page 4.

⁴⁰ *Through a Yellow Glass* by Oswell Blakeston.
⁴¹ *Bioscope*, July 28, 1921, page 33; August 18, 1921, page 6.
⁴² *Op. cit.*, January 19, 1922, page 21.
⁴³ *The King Who Was a King* by H. G. Wells, pages 10–11.
⁴⁴ *Who's Who in the Theatre*, 1925 edition.
⁴⁵ *Kinematograph Studio Technique* by L. C. MacBean.

Design
⁴⁶ *Bioscope*, June 18, 1927, page 171.
⁴⁷ *Op. cit.*, July 1, 1920, page 15.
⁴⁸ *Kinematograph Studio Technique* by L. C. MacBean.
⁴⁹ *The Film Industry* by Davidson Boughey.
⁵⁰ *Picturegoer*, October 1923, page 17.
⁵¹ *Bioscope*, February 16, 1922, page 20.
⁵² *Op. cit.*, November 10, 1927, page 36.

Camerawork
⁵³ *The Film Industry* by Davidson Boughey, page 12.
⁵⁴ *Animated Cartoons—How they are Made* by E. G. Lutz, page 57.
⁵⁵ *The Film Industry* by Davidson Boughey, page 46.
⁵⁶ *Kine Year Book*, 1923, page 219.
⁵⁷ *Bioscope*, December 11, 1919, page 14.
⁵⁸ *Op. cit.*, December 15, 1921, page 24.
⁵⁹ *Op. cit.*, December 16, 1926, page 22.
⁶⁰ *Through a Yellow Glass* by Oswell Blakeston, page 72.
⁶¹ *Op. cit.*, by Oswell Blakeston, page 50.
⁶² *Kinematograph Studio Technique* by L. C. MacBean, page 100.
⁶³ *Picturegoer*, March 1923, page 19.
⁶⁴ *Kine Year Book*, 1921, pages 84–5.
⁶⁵ *Bioscope*, June 18, 1927, page 173.
⁶⁶ *Kine Year Book*, 1929, page 244.
⁶⁷ *Close Up*, December 1929, page 468.
⁶⁸ *Bioscope*, November 20, 1919, page 18c.
⁶⁹ *Op. cit.*, September 15, 1921, page 41.
⁷⁰ *The Modern Photoplay and its Construction* by Colden Lore, pages 19–21.
⁷¹ *Bioscope*, June 2, 1927, page 21.
⁷² *Close Up*, April 1928.
⁷³ *Through a Yellow Glass* by Oswell Blakeston, page 100.
⁷⁴ *The Modern Photoplay and its Construction* by Colden Lore, pages 17–18.
⁷⁵ *Bioscope*, May 6, 1920, page 60.
⁷⁶ *Op. cit.*, October 25, 1923, page 48.
⁷⁷ *Op. cit.*, January 27, 1927, page 26.
⁷⁸ *Close Up*, May 1929, page 27.
⁷⁹ *Bioscope*, May 7, 1925, page 50.
⁸⁰ *Op. cit.*, February 23, 1928, page 41.
⁸¹ *Close Up*, July 1929, page 45.

Acting
⁸² *Bioscope*, July 22, 1920, page 14.
⁸³ *The Film Industry* by Davidson Boughey, page 46.
⁸⁴ *Bioscope*, June 10, 1920, page 23.
⁸⁵ *Op. cit.*, July 1, 1920, page vii.
⁸⁶ *The Secrets of the Cinema* by Valentia Steer, pages 20–21.
⁸⁷ *Through a Yellow Glass* by Oswell Blakeston, page 17.
⁸⁸ *Bioscope*, March 20, 1919, page 51.
⁸⁹ *Elstree Story*, page 61.
⁹⁰ *Picturegoer*, February 1923, page 24.
⁹¹ *Close Up*, May 1928, page 34.

[92] *Bioscope*, July 4, 1928, page 28.
[93] *Op. cit.*, February 6, 1919, page 8.

Editing
[94] *Kinematograph Studio Technique* by L. C. MacBean.
[95] *The Film Industry* by Davidson Boughey.
[96] *Op. cit.*, pages 65–66.
[97] *Bioscope*, January 31, 1924, page 35.
[98] *Op. cit.*, April 5, 1928, page 27.
[99] *Op. cit.*, September 1, 1927, page 60.
[100] *Through a Yellow Glass* by Oswell Blakeston.
[101] *Bioscope*, March 8, 1928, page 54.
[102] *Op. cit.*, April 28, 1927, page 31.
[103] *Close Up*, October 1929.

Costs
[104] *The Film Industry* by Davidson Boughey.
[105] *The Secrets of the Cinema* by Valentia Steer.
[106] *Op. cit.*, page 25.
[107] *Bioscope*, January 1, 1920, page 11; January 28, 1926, page 42.
[108] *Op. cit.*, January 28, 1926, page 47.
[109] *Op. cit.*, June 18, 1927, page 153.
[110] *Writing for the Screen* by Arrar Jackson, page 134.
[111] *Bioscope*, December 10, 1925, page 19.

Colour
[112] *Nice Work* by Adrian Brunel page 76.
[113] *Bioscope*, October 14, 1920, page 35.
[114] *Op. cit.*, October 2, 1924, page 33; October 9, 1924, page 37.
[115] *Op. cit.*, October 9, 1924, page 37.
[116] *Kine Year Book*, 1922, page 212.
[117] *Bioscope*, January 27, 1921, page 5; February 17, 1921, page 25.
[118] *Op. cit.*, April 1, 1926, page iii.
[119] *Op. cit.*, June 27, 1928, page 17.
[120] *Kine Year Book*, 1927, pages 207–8.
[121] *Op. cit.*, 1930, page 268.
[122] *Op. cit.*, 1929, page 445; *Bioscope*, November 14, 1928, page 27; *Kine Year Book*, 1930, page 268.
[123] *The King Who Was a King* by H. G. Wells, page 16.

Animation
[124] *Le Dessin Animé* by Lo Duca.

Films of Fact
[125] *The Film Industry* by Davidson Boughey, page 75.
[126] *The Film in National Life*, page 112.
[127] *With Scott: the Silver Lining* by Griffith Taylor, page 59.
[128] *Bioscope*, August 7, 1924, page 12.
[129] The Museum of Modern Art *Film Index*, page 579.
[130] *Close Up*, July 1927.
[131] *Bioscope*, February 20, 1919, page 7.
[132] *Motion Picture News*—see *Bioscope*, November 25, 1926, page 30.
[133] *Grierson on Documentary* by Forsythe Hardy.
[134] *National Film Archive Catalogue*, Part II, pages 63, 74 znd 104.
[135] *Grierson on Documentary* by Forsythe Hardy, page 1.
[136] *Close Up*, November 1929.
[137] *The Film Till Now* by Paul Rotha.
[138] *Op. cit.*, page 314.
[139] *Documentary Film* by Paul Rotha, page 104.

ove: George Pearson directing.

p Right: Sybil Thorndike in Wilcox's *wn,* 1928

ttom Right: Anna May Wong in Dupont's *cadilly,* 1929, with sets by Alfred Jünge d Werner Brandes as lighting camera-n.

Top Left: Gordon Harker
Carl Brisson in Hitchcock's
Ring, 1927, with sets by C.
Arnold and camerawork by
Cox.

Bottom Left: Walter Ford
his own film *Would You Be*
it!, 1929.

NOTES TO CHAPTERS

CHAPTER EIGHT (pages 298–311)

[1] *Bioscope*, January 8, 1925, page 54.
[2] *Op. cit.*, June 24, 1926, page 23.
[3] *Close Up*, July 1927.
[4] *Op. cit.*, January 1928.
[5] *Hitchcock* by François Truffaut.
[6] *Films: Facts and Forecasts* by L'Estrange Fawcett, page 20.
[7] *Authority and the Individual* by Bertrand Russell, pages 58–59.
[8] *The Film Till Now* by Paul Rotha, page 319.
[9] *The Film in National Life*, page 43.
[10] *Heraclitus, or the Future of Films* by Ernest Betts, page 40.
[11] *Bioscope*, January 8, 1925, page 54.
[12] *Authority and the Individual* by Bertrand Russell, pages 58–59.
[13] *Close Up*, July 1927, pages 8–10.
[14] *Op. cit.*, July 1927.
[15] *Authority and the Individual*, page 57.
[16] *Gordon Craig* by Edward Craig, page 209.

BIBLIOGRAPHY

Anatomy of Motion Picture Art by Eric Elliott, published by Pool in 1928.

Animated Cartoons—How they are Made: their Origin and Development by E. G. Lutz, published by Chapman and Hall in 1920.

Anthony Asquith, New Index Series No. 5, edited by Peter Noble, published by the British Film Institute in 1952.

Art and Design in the British Film by Edward Carrick, published by Dennis Dobson in 1949.

The Art of Photoplay Writing by Stuart Woodley, published by Azure Film Productions in 1921.

The Art of the Moving Picture by Vachel Lindsay, published by Macmillan in 1922, a revised edition of the book first published in 1915.

Authority and the Individual by Bertrand Russell, first Reith Lectures published by Allen & Unwin in 1949.

Behind the Camera by Natalie Barkas, published by Geoffrey Bles in 1934.

Behind the Motion Picture Screen by A. C. Lescarboura, published by the Scientific American Publishing Company in 1919.

The Bioscope, weekly from 1919 to 1929, published by Ganes.

The British Board of Film Censors' *Annual Reports* for 1919, 1921, 1923, 1925, 1926, 1928 and 1929.

Camera House Cinematograph Journal, published by Butcher's Film Service, 1919–1922.

Came the Dawn by Cecil Hepworth, published by Phoenix House in 1951.

The Cinema in Education, Report by the Psychological Research Committee of the National Council of Public Morals, published by Allen & Unwin in 1925.

Cinematograph Films Act, 1927, published by His Majesty's Stationery Office in 1927.

Cinematograph Films Act, 1927: Report of a Committee appointed by the Board of Trade (Moyne Report), published by His Majesty's Stationery Office in 1936.

Close Up, numbers from July 1927 to December 1929, published by Pool.

A Competitive Cinema by Terence Kelly, published by the Institute of Economic Affairs in 1966.

Designing for Moving Pictures by Edward Carrick, published by The Studio Publications.

Le Dessin Animé by Lo Duca, published by Prisma in 1948.

Documentary Film by Paul Rotha, published by Faber and Faber in 1936.

Do We Need a Censor? by Viscount Brentford, published by Faber and Faber in 1929.

Edgar Wallace by his wife, published by Hutchinson in 1932.

The Elstree Story, published by Clerke and Cockeran in 1948.

The Factual Film, a survey by The Arts Enquiry published by P.E.P. and Oxford University Press in 1947.

Filmed Books and Plays, 1928–1967, by A. G. S. Enser, published by Andre Deutsch.

The Film Index, Volume I, The Film as Art, published by the Museum of Modern Art Film Library in New York in 1941.

The Film Industry by Davidson Boughey, published by Sir Isaac Pitman and Sons in 1921.

The Film in National Life, the Report of the Commission on Educational and Cultural Films, published by Allen & Unwin in 1932.

Films: A Report on the Supply of Films for Exhibition in Cinemas (Monopolies Commission Report), published by Her Majesty's Stationery Office in 1966.

Films: Facts and Forecasts by L'Estrange Fawcett, published by Geoffrey Bles in 1927.

Film Society Programmes for seasons 1925/6, 1926/7, 1927/8 and 1928/9.

Films of the Year 1927–28 by Robert Herring, published by The Studio in 1928.

Film Technique by V. I. Pudovkin, enlarged version published by Newnes in 1933 of book published by Gollancz in 1929.

The Film Till Now by Paul Rotha and Richard Griffith, and published in 1951 by Vision—revised edition of book by Paul Rotha, published originally in 1930.

Film World by Ivor Montagu, published by Pelican Books in 1964.

Flashback by George Pearson, published by Allen & Unwin in 1957.

The Freedom of the Movies by Ruth Inglis, Report from the Commission on the Freedom of the Press, published by the University of Chicago Press in 1947.

Friese-Greene, Close-up of an Inventor by Ray Allister, published by Marsland Publications in 1948.

Gordon Craig by Edward Craig, published by Victor Gollancz in 1968.

The Great White South by Herbert Ponting, published by Duckworth in 1921.

Grierson on Documentary by Forsythe Hardy, published by Collins in 1946.

The Hepworth Magazine, published by the Hepworth Film Company in 1921.

Heraclitus, or the Future of Films by Ernest Betts, published by Dutton in 1928.

Hitchcock by François Truffaut, published by Secker and Warburg in 1968.

How I Filmed the War by Geoffrey Malins, published by Herbert Jenkins in 1919.

I Do What I Like by W. A. Darlington, published by Macdonald and Company in 1947.

Index to the Work of Alfred Hitchcock by Peter Noble, published by the British Film Institute in 1949.

Ivor Novello by Peter Noble, published by the Falcon Press in 1951.

Kinematograph Monthly Record, published by Odham's Press.

Kinematograph Studio Technique by L. C. MacBean, published by Sir Isaac Pitman and Sons in 1922.

The Kine Weekly, weekly from 1919 to 1929, published by Odham's Press.

Kine Year Book, published by Odham's Press.

The King Who Was a King by H. G. Wells, published by Ernest Benn, 1929.

Let's Go to the Pictures by Iris Barry, published by Chatto and Windus in 1926.

Michael Balcon Presents . . . A Lifetime of Films by Michael Balcon, published by Hutchinson in 1969.

Michael Balcon's Twenty-five Years in Films by M. Danischewsky, published by World Film Publications in 1947.

The Mind and the Film by Gerard Fort Buckle, published by Routledge in 1926.

The Modern Photoplay and its Construction by Colden Lore, published by Chapman and Dodd in 1928.

The Monthly Film Record, published by Odham's Press.

Motion Picture Problems—the Cinema and the League of Nations by William Marston Seabury, published by Avondale Press in New York in 1929.

Moving Pictures, How they are Made and Worked by F. A. Talbot, new edition published by Lippincott in 1923 of a book previously published in 1912.

Mr Wu Looks Back by Matheson Lang, published by Stanley Paul in 1941.

My Autobiography by Charles Chaplin, published by The Bodley Head in 1964.

My Life and Times, Octave Five, 1915–23 by Compton Mackenzie, published by Chatto and Windus in 1966.

My Wonderful Visit by Charlie Chaplin, published by Hurst and Blacket in 1922.

National Film Archive Catalogue, Part II, Silent Non-Fiction Films 1895–1934, published by the British Film Institute in 1960.

National Film Archive Catalogue, Part III, Silent Fiction Films 1895–1930, published by the British Film Institute in 1966.

Nice Work by Adrian Brunel, published by Forbes Robertson in 1949.

Parnassus to Let by Eric Walter White, published by the Hogarth Press in 1928.

The Picturegoer, and *Pictures and the Picturegoer*, published by Odham's Press.

Picturegoer's Who's Who and Encyclopaedia, 1933, published by Odham's Press.

The Picture Palace, and other Buildings for the Movies by Dennis Sharp, published by Hugh Evelyn in 1969.

The Political Censorship of Films by Ivor Montagu, published by Gollancz in 1929.

Project for Establishing National Film Studios—a Report by E. Beddington Behrens, privately printed in November 1925.

Pudovkin on Film Technique, translated by Ivor Montagu and published by Gollancz in 1929, reprinted in 1933, with additional material.

The Secrets of the Cinema: Your Favourite Amusement from Within by Valentia Steer, published by C. Arthur Pearson in 1920.

The Seven Lively Arts by Gilbert Seldes, published by Harper in 1924.

Stars of the Screen, 1932, edited by Cedric Osmond Birmingham and published by Herbert Joseph.

A Statistical Survey of the Cinema Industry in Great Britain in 1934 by Simon Rowson, a paper read before the Royal Statistical Society on December 17, 1935, and printed in the Journal XCIX, part I, 1936.

Stoll's Editorial News, published by the Stoll Film Company.

The Studio, numbers from 1919 to 1929, published by The Studio.

The Theatre, Music Hall and Cinema Companies Blue Book, 1927/8, edited by T. G. Hatherill-Mynott, published by Redway, Mann & Company.

Thirty Years of Film Production, a paper delivered by Sir Michael Balcon to the British Kinematograph Society in 1949.

This Film Business by Rudolf Messel, published by Ernest Benn in 1928.

Through a Yellow Glass by Oswell Blakeston, published by Pool in 1928.

The Times Film Number, March 19, 1929.

Twenty-five Thousand Sunsets by Herbert Wilcox, published by The Bodley Head in 1967.

Twenty Years of British Film, 1925–1945 by Balcon, Lindgren, Manvell and Hardy, published by the Falcon Press in 1947.

Walturdaw Releases, 1919 to 1923, published by the Walturdaw Company.

Who's Who in the Theatre, edited by John Parker, published by Pitman and Sons, 5th edition for 1925 and 11th edition for 1952.

With Scott: the Silver Lining by Griffith Taylor, published by Smith, Elder and Company in 1916.

The World Film Encyclopedia, 1933, edited by Clarence Winchester and published by the Amalgamated Press.

Writing for the Screen by Arrar Jackson, published by A. & C. Black, 1919.

This list includes feature films, that is to say films of five reels in the early years but longer in the later years, as well as a few shorter productions and some factual films which are of unusual interest. It accounts for the bulk of British production, some of it carried out with foreign collaboration, between the end of the first world war in November 1918 and the beginning of sound production in British commercial feature films in the middle of 1929, with a certain amount of overlap at both ends. All the films except one are reasonably sure to have been finished and shown, although not necessarily booked. The date given is that of the first or trade show, as neither the beginning nor the end of production can usually be dated with any precision. The intervals between production and showing varied, and were especially long in the early years.

Details include some or all of the following: the title: production company: length: date: details of reissues, alternative titles, sound, colour, and foreign collaboration if any: director, cameraman, scenarist and original source, art director and editor, and most of the players. This list is the index to a history, not an archive or a casting directory. I have therefore included the names of about a thousand players and have excluded those, otherwise unknown, whose few appearances I consider of no interest for the purposes of this history.

T.S. indicates Trade Show date.

ACROSS INDIA WITH THE
DUKE OF CONNAUGHT

Topical Film Co.
6,400 ft
T.S. 4.21

P.   U. K. Whipple and H. C. Jeapes

ADAM'S APPLE

British International Pictures
7,200 ft
T.S. 9.28

D.   Tim Whelan
C.   René Guissart and C. W.
     Pocknall
Sc. Tim Whelan and Rex Taylor
Art J. E. Wills

     Monty Banks
     Gillean Dean

Judy Kelly
Colin Kenny

ADVENTURE

Hero
T.S. 5.25

P.   M. A. Wetherell

ADVENTURES OF CAPTAIN
KETTLE, THE

Austen Leigh
5 reels
T.S. 10.22

D.   Meyrick Milton
Sc. Cutcliffe Hyne

     Charles Kettle
     E. L. Frewin
     A. Austin Leigh

ADVENTURES OF MR PICKWICK, THE

Ideal
6,000 ft
T.S. 11.21

D. Thomas Bentley
Sc. E. A. Baughn and Eliot Stannard from novel by Charles Dickens

Fred Volpe
Arthur Cleave
Ernest Thesiger
Bransby Williams
Mary Brough
Joyce Dearsley

ADVENTURES OF SHERLOCK HOLMES, THE

Stoll
Series, 15 2-reelers
T.S. 3.21

D. Maurice Elvey
C. Germaine Burger
Sc. W. J. Elliott from stories by A. Conan Doyle. With Eille Norwood

A Case of Identity
The Copper Beeches
The Beryl Coronet
The Devil's Foot
The Dying Detective
The Empty House
The Man with the Twisted Lip
The Noble Bachelor
The Priory School
The Redheaded League
The Resident Patient
Scandal in Bohemia
The Solitary Cyclist
Tiger of San Pedro
The Yellow Face

ADVENTUROUS YOUTH

Pall Mall
4,868 ft
T.S. 2.29

Derrick de Marney
Dino Galvani
Rene Clama

AFRAID OF LOVE

Britannia
7,000 ft
T.S. 3.25

D. Reginald H. West
C. Horace Wheddon
Sc. Walter Summers, from story by Hon. Mrs John Russell

Hon. Mrs John Russell
Juliette Compton
Adeline Hayden-Coffin
Moore Marriott
Mickey Brantford
Jameson Thomas
Leslie Faber

AFRICA TODAY

Missionary Film Co.
T.S. 10.27

D. T. H. Baxter
C. Joseph Best

AFTERGLOW

Samuelson
6,000 ft
T.S. 9.23

British Film Week
D. Walter Summers

Minna Grey
Lillian Hall-Davis
Simeon Stuart
James Lindsay

AFTER MANY DAYS

Progress
6 reels
T.S. 1.19

D. Sidney Morgan
Sc. Sidney Morgan

Bruce Gordon
Alice Russon
Adeline Hayden-Coffin

AFTER THE VERDICT

B.I.F.D.
9,370 ft
T.S. 1.29

D. Henrik Galeen
C. Theodor Sparkhul
Sc. Alma Reville from novel by Robert
Hichens

Olga Tschechova
Warwick Ward
Malcolm Tod
Betty Carter
Daisy Campbell
Henry Victor

AFTERWARDS

A.P.D.
6,500 ft
T.S. 11.28

D. Lawson Butt
C. A. Frenguelli
Sc. R. Byron Webber from novel by
Kathlyn Rhodes

Marjorie Hume
Julie Suedo
Cecil Barry
J. R. Tozer
Dorinea Shirley
Jean Jay
Fewlass Llewellyn
Frank Parfitt

ALF'S BUTTON

Hepworth
7 reels
T.S. 5.20

British Film Week 1924
D. C. M. Hepworth
Sc. Blanche MacIntosh from novel by
W. A. Darlington

Leslie Henson
John MacAndrews
Alma Taylor
James Carew
Eileen Dennes
Gerald Ames
Gwynne Herbert
Jean Cadell

ALF'S CARPET

British International Pictures
5,500 ft
T.S. 11.29

Part talking, R.C.A.
D. Will Kellino
Sc. Val Valentine from story by W. A.
Darlington

Long and Short

ALLEY CAT

British and Foreign
7 reels
T.S. 3.29

P. Sidney Morgan
D. Hans Steinhoff
C. N. Farkass
S. Joan Morgan from novel by
Anthony Carlyle

Mabel Poulton
Jack Trevor
Shayle Gardner
Clifford McLaglen
Marie Ault

327

ALLEY OF THE GOLDEN
HEARTS, THE

Bertram Phillips
6,290 ft
T.S. 10.24

D. Bertram Phillips
C. Percy Anthony
Sc. Harry Engholme, from story by
E. P. Kinsella and Frank Miller

John Stuart
Queenie Thomas
Frank Stanmore
Cecil Morton York
Judd Green
Adeline Hayden-Coffin
Pollie Emery
Mary Brough
Nigel Barrie
Bernard Vaughan

ALL MEN ARE LIARS

Progress
4,800 ft
T.S. 1.19

Sc.
from novel by Joseph Hocking

George Harrington
Bruce Gordon
Jennie Earle
Alice de Winton
Alice Russon

ALL ROADS LEAD TO
CALVARY

H. W. Thompson
5 reels
T.S. 12.21

D. Kenelm Foss   Asst. John Miller
C. Jack Parker
Sc. Kenelm Foss from story by Jerome
K. Jerome

Minna Grey
Mary Odette
Bertram Burleigh

ALL SORTS AND CONDITIONS
OF MEN

Ideal
5,000 ft
T.S. 7.21

D. Georges Tréville
Sc. Colden Lore from novel by Walter
Besant

Renée Kelly
Rex Davis

ALL THE SAD WORLD
NEEDS

B.A.F.C.
5,000 ft
Release 1.19

New title of PEEP O' DAY

P. Hubert Herrick
Sc. Kenelm Foss

Lauri de Frece
Joan Legge
Adelaide Grace
Lennox Pawle

ALL THE WINNERS

Samuelson
6,000 ft
T.S. 10.20

D. Geoffrey Malins
Sc.
from novel by Arthur Applin
(*Wicked*)

Owen Nares
Maudie Dunham

Sam Livesey
Maidie Hope
Ena Beaumont
Dora Lennox

ALWAYS TELL YOUR WIFE

1923

D. Hugh Croise, Alfred Hitchcock

Seymour Hicks
Ellaline Terriss

AMATEUR GENTLEMAN, THE

Stoll
6 reels
T.S. 3.20

D. Maurice Elvey
C. Paul Burger
Sc.
    from novel by Jeffrey Farnol

Langhorne Burton
Dalton Summers
Madge Stuart
Sydney Seaward
Pardoe Woodman
E. Vivian Reynolds
Cecil Humphreys
Will Corrie
Judd Green
Gerald McCarthy
Edward Arundel
Geoffrey Wilmer
Sinclair Hill

AMAZING PARTNERSHIP, THE

Stoll
5,153 ft
T.S. 6.21

D. George Ridgwell
Sc.
    from story by E. Phillips Oppen-
    heim

Gladys Mason
Milton Rosmer
Temple Bell
Edward Arundel
Robert Vallis
Arthur Walcott
Charles Barratt
Harry Worth

AMAZING QUEST OF ERNEST BLISS, THE

Hepworth
(1) 5 episodes   (2) 6,000 ft
(1) T.S. 7.20   (2) T.S. 9.21

D. Henry Edwards
C. Charles Bryce
Sc. Henry Edwards from novel by E.
    Phillips Oppenheim

Henry Edwards
Chrissie White
Mary Brough
Douglas Munro
Henry Vibart
Esme Hubbard
Gerald Ames

AMERICAN PRISONER, THE

British International Pictures
6,666 ft
T.S. 9.29

    Full talking, R.C.A.
D. Thomas Bentley
C. René Guissart
Sc. Eliot Stannard from novel by
    Eden Phillpotts

Carl Brisson
Madeleine Carroll
A. Bromley Davenport
Cecil Barry
Nancy Price
Carl Harbord
Reginald Fox

ANGLE, ESQUIRE

Gaumont
5 reels
T.S. 11.19

D. Will Kellino
C. A. St Aubyn Brown

> Aurèle Sydney
> Gertrude McCoy
> George Traill
> Cecil du Gué

ANNA THE ADVENTURESS

Hepworth
6,000 ft
T.S. 2.20

D. C. M. Hepworth
Sc.
> from novel by E. Phillips Oppenheim

> Alma Taylor
> James Carew
> Gwynne Herbert
> James Annand
> Jean Cadell
> Ronald Colman
> Christine Rayner
> Gerald Ames

APACHE, THE

Millar-Thompson
7,400 ft
T.S. 9.25

D. Adelqui Millar
Sc. Michael Allard

> Adelqui Millar
> Mona Maris
> Jerrold Robertshaw
> Jameson Thomas

APPEARANCES

Famous Players–Lasky British

5,374 ft
T.S. 6.21

D. Donald Crisp
C. Hal Young
Sc. Margaret Turnbull from play by
Edward Knoblock

> Mary Glynne
> David Powell
> Langhorne Burton
> Marjorie Hume
> Mary Dibley
> Percy Standing

APRÈS LA GUERRE

(1927) See under BLIGHTY

ARCADIANS, THE

Gaumont–British
7,000 ft
T.S. 11.27

D. Victor Saville
Sc.
> from play by Mark Ambient and
> Alex M. Thompson

> Ben Blue
> H. Humberston Wright
> Gibb McLaughlin
> Cyril McLaglen
> Jeanne de Casalis
> Vesta Sylva
> John Longden

ARISE AND WALK

Oxford Films, for the Central Council
for the Care of Cripples
2,715 ft
1929

D. John Greenidge
C. Randal Terraneau and Frank Canham
Sc. John and Terence Greenidge

ARMAGEDDON

British Instructional Films
6 reels
T.S. 11.23

British Film Week 1924

D. H. Bruce Woolfe

AS GOD MADE HER

Anglo–Hollandia
6,000 ft
T.S. 5.20 and 9.20

D. Maurice H. Binger and B. E.
Doxat-Pratt
Sc. B. E. Doxat-Pratt from story by
Helen Protheroe Lewis

Mary Odette
Adelqui Migliar
Henry Victor
Lola Cornero

AS HE WAS BORN

Butcher's
4,865 ft
T.S. 1.19

D. Wilfred Noy
Sc. Leon M. Lion from novel by
Tom Gallon

Odette Goimbault
Will Corrie
Jeff Barlow
A. B. Imeson
Athol Forde
Mary Dibley

ATLANTIC

British International Pictures
8,213 ft
T.S. 11.29

Full talking, R.C.A.

D. E. A. Dupont
C. Charles Rosher
Sc.

from novel by Ernest Raymond
(*The Berg*)

John Longden
Madeleine Carroll
Ellaline Terriss
Franklin Dyall
Arthur Hardy
Monty Banks
Donald Calthrop
Francis Lister
Joan Barry
John Stuart

AT THE MERCY OF TIBERIUS

Samuelson
6 reels
T.S. 5.20

D. G. B. Samuelson

Peggy Hyland

AT THE VILLA FALCONER

British and Foreign
6,100 ft
T.S. 12.28

D. Richard Oswald

Eve Gray
Clifford McLaglen
Maria Jacobini

AT THE VILLA ROSE

Stoll
6 reels
T.S. 4.20

D. Maurice Elvey
C. Paul Burger
Sc. Sinclair Hill from novel and play
by A. E. W. Mason
Art Walter Murton

Langhorne Burton
Edward Arundel
Norman Page
Eva Westlake
Manora Thew
Kate Gurney

331

AUCTION MART, THE

B.A.F.C.
6 reels
T.S. 2.20

D. Duncan McRae
Sc. Adrian Brunel from novel by
    Sidney Tremayne

Gertrude McCoy
Moya Nugent
Charles Quartermaine
Simeon Stuart
Minnie Rayner

AUDACIOUS MR. SQUIRE THE

British and Colonial
5,000 ft
T.S. 10.23

D. Edwin Greenwood
Sc. Eliot Stannard, turned into play
    by Eliot Stannard and Sidney
    Bowkett

Jack Buchanan
Sydney Paxton
Valia
Russell Thorndike
Malcolm Tod
Dorinea Shirley
Fred Rains

AULD LANG SYNE

Welsh–Pearson–Elder
6,800 ft
T.S. 4.29

With 6 songs synchronised with
earlier records and recorded by
R.C.A.
D. George Pearson
Production Manager Denis Ship-
    wright. Asst. Thorold Dickinson
C. Bernard Knowles Asst. Fred Ford
Sc. P. L. Mannock
Art Walter Murton
Co-editor Thorold Dickinson

Harry Lauder
Dorothy Boyd
Pat Aherne
Hugh E. Wright
Dodo Watts

AUNT RACHEL

Samuelson
5,500 ft
T.S. 7.20

D. Albert Ward
Sc.
    from novel by David Christie
    Murray

Haidee Wright
Isobel Elsom
Tom Reynolds
Lionelle Howard
James Lindsay
Leonard Pagden

AUTOCRAT, THE

New Regal
6 reels
T.S. 7. 19

D. Tom Watts
C. J. C. Bee Mason
Sc. Tom Watts

William Brandon
Reginald Fox

AUTUMN OF PRIDE, THE

Gaumont
6,000 ft
T.S. 7.21

D. Will Kellino
C. A. St Aubyn Brown
Sc. Paul Roof from story by E.
    Newton Bungaye

Nora Swinburne
David Hawthorne

Cecil Morton York
Mary Dibley
Cecil du Gué
C. H. Mansell
Clifford Heatherley

AYLWIN

Hepworth
5,485 ft
T.S. 7.20

D. Henry Edwards
C. Charles Bryce
Sc.
    from novel by Theodore Watts-
    Dunton

    Chrissie White
    Henry Edwards
    Gwynne Herbert
    Mary Dibley
    Henry Vibart
    Gerald Ames

BACHELOR HUSBAND, A

Astra
5,000 ft
T.S. 11.20

D. Kenelm Foss
Sc. Kenelm Foss from story by Ruby
    M. Ayres in *Daily Mirror*

    Lyn Harding
    Renée Mayer
    Hayford Hobbs
    Phyllis Joyce
    Irene Rooke
    Lionelle Howard
    Will Corrie
    Gordon Craig
    Eva Westlake

BACHELOR'S BABY, A

Granger–Davidson
5 reels

T.S. 6.22

    British Film Week 1924

D. A. H. Rooke
Sc. Lydia Hayward from novel by
    Rolf Bennett

    Tom Reynolds
    Haidee Wright
    Malcolm Tod
    Constance Worth

BACHELOR'S CLUB, THE

Ideal
5,500 ft
T.S. 6.21

D. A. V. Bramble
Sc. Eliot Stannard from novel by
    Israel Zangwill

    Ben Field
    Mary Brough
    Arthur Cleave
    Sydney Paxton
    Sydney Fairbrother
    Ernest Thesiger
    Dora Lennox
    Jack Denton
    James Lindsay
    A. G. Poulton
    Alice de Winton

BALL OF FORTUNE, THE

7,000 ft
T.S. 6.26

D. Hugh Croise
Sc.
    from novel by Sydney Horler

    James Knight
    Mabel Poulton
    Dorothy Boyd
    Billy Meredith

BARGAIN, THE

Hepworth
5,800 ft
T.S. 11.21

D. Henry Edwards
C. Charles Bryce
Sc. Henry Edwards from play by Henry Edwards and Edward Irwin

Henry Edwards
Chrissie White
Henry Vibart
Rex McDougall
Mary Dibley
James Annand
John MacAndrews
John East

BARS OF IRON

Stoll
5 reels
T.S. 11.20

D. F. Martin Thorton
Sc.
from novel by Ethel M. Dell

Madge White
J. Edwards Barber
J. R. Tozer
Roland Myles

BARTON MYSTERY THE

Stoll
6,000 ft
T.S. 2.20

D. Harry Roberts
C. E. H. Harrison
Sc. R. Byron Webber from play by Walter Hackett

Lyn Harding
Edward O' Neil
Hilda Bayley
Arthur Pusey

Eva Westlake
Maud Cresall

BATTLE OF JUTLAND, THE

British Instructional Films
3 reels
T.S. 9. 21

D. H. Bruce Woolfe
Sc. Major-General Sir George Aston

BATTLES OF THE CORONEL AND FALKLAND ISLANDS, THE

British Instructional Films
8,300 ft / 8,000 ft
T.S. 9.27

P. H. Bruce Woolfe
D. Walter Summers Asst. J. O. C. Orton
Sc. Harry Engholme and Capt. Frank C. Bowen
C. Jack Parker and Stanley Rodwell

BEAUTIFUL KITTY

Walter West
5 reels
T.S. 7.23

British Film Week 1924

D. Walter West

Violet Hopson
James Knight
Arthur Walcott

BECAUSE

5 reels
T.S. 12.21

P. Edith Mellor

334

BECKET

Stoll
6,540 ft
T.S. 11.23

British Film Week 1924

D. George Ridgwell
C. J. Rosenthal Jnr.
Sc. Eliot Stannard from play by Lord Tennyson
Art Walter Murton

Sir Frank Benson
A. V. Bramble
Mary Clare
William Lugg
Percy Standing
C. H. Mansell
Gladys Jennings
Bertram Burleigh
Sydney Paxton
Harry Worth
Sidney Folker
Alex G. Hunter
Bert Darley

BEETLE, THE

Barker Motion Photography
5 reels
T.S. 11.19

D. Alexander Butler
Sc.
from novel by Richard Marsh

Maudie Dunham
Fred Morgan

BELOVED VAGABOND, THE

Astra–National
7,500 ft / 9,000 ft

D. Fred Leroy Granville
C. Walter Blakeley

Sc. S. K. Winston from novel and play by W. J. Locke
Art E. P. Kinsella

Carlyle Blackwell
Phyllis Titmuss
Madge Stuart
Mrs Hubert Willis
Sydney Fairbrother
Cameron Carr
Irene Tripod
Hubert Carter

BELPHEGOR THE MOUNTEBANK

Ideal
5,500 ft
T.S. 4.21

D. Bert Wynne
Sc. Eliot Stannard from play by Charles Webb, from the French

Milton Rosmer
Margaret Dean
Warwick Ward
Peter Coleman
A. Harding Steerman
H. Heaton Grey
Nancy Price
Kathleen Vaughan
Leal Douglas

BENTLEY'S CONSCIENCE

Ideal
4,150 ft
T.S. 2.22

D. Denison Clift
Sc.
from novel by Paul Trent

Robert Loraine
Betty Faire
Ivo Dawson
J. Fisher White
Henry Victor

BESIDE THE BONNIE BRIAR BUSH

Famous Players–Lasky British
4,500 ft
T.S. 11.21

D. Donald Crisp
C. Hal Young
Sc. Margaret Turnbull from novel by
    Ian Maclaren and plays by James
    McArthur and Augustus Thomas

    Donald Crisp
    Mary Glynne
    Alec Fraser
    Dorothy Fane
    Langhorne Burton
    Jerrold Robertshaw

BETTA THE GYPSY

Famous Pictures
5 reels
T.S. 3.19

D. Charles Raymond
C. E. L. Groc
Sc. Edith Mellor from operetta by
    Edward Waltyre (Edith Mellor)

    Marga la Rubia
    Malvina Longfellow
    George Foley
    Frank Dane
    Charles Raymond
    Edward Combermere
    Barbara Gott

BEYOND THE DREAMS OF AVARICE

Ideal
6 reels
T.S. 8.20

Sc.
    from novel by Walter Besant

    Joyce Dearsley
    Henry Victor

Adelaide Grace
A. Harding Steerman

BIGAMIST, THE

George Clark
9,000 ft
T.S. 8.21

Sc. Guy Newall from novel by F. E.
    Mills Young

    Julian Royce
    Ivy Duke
    Guy Newall
    A. Bromley Davenport
    Barbara Everest
    Douglas Munro

BILL OF DIVORCEMENT, A

Ideal
6 reels
T.S. 8.22

    British Film Week 1924

D. Denison Clift
Sc.
    from play by Clemence Dane

    Constance Binney
    Fay Compton
    Malcolm Keen
    Henry Victor
    Henry Vibart
    Fewlass Llewellyn

BLACKGUARD, THE

Gainsborough, with U.F.A. of Germany
9,200 ft
T.S. 4.25

P. Michael Balcon Asst. Erich
    Pommer
D. Graham Cutts Asst. Alfred Hitch-
    cock
C.
Sc. Alfred Hitchcock from novel by
    Raymond Paton
Art Alfred Hitchcock

336

Walter Rilla
Bernhard Goetzke
Jane Novak
Frank Stanmore
Martin Hertzberg
Rosa Valetti
Dora Bergner
Fritz Alberti

BLACKMAIL

British International Pictures
8 reels
T.S. 6.29

Full talking, R.C.A.

P. John Maxwell
D. Alfred Hitchcock   Asst. Frank Mills
C. J. J. Cox
Sc. Alfred Hitchcock, Ben Levy and Charles Bennett from novel by Charles Bennett
Art Norman G. Arnold, Wilfred Arnold
Ed. Emile de Ruelle
Music. Campbell and Connely

Anny Ondra (voice of Joan Barry)
John Longden
Sara Allgood
Donald Calthrop
Cyril Ritchard
Hannah Jones
Harvey Braban
Phyllis Monkman

BLACK SHEEP

Progress
5 reels
T.S. 3.20

D. Sidney Morgan
Sc. Sidney Morgan from serial by Ruby M. Ayres in *Daily Mirror*

Marguerite Blanche
Eve Balfour
George Bellamy

George Keene
Arthur Lennard

BLACK SPIDER, THE

British and Colonial
5 reels
T.S. 5.20

D. George Edwardes Hall
Sc. Carlton Dawe

Lydia Kyasht
Sam Livesey
Ronald Colman
Bertram Burleigh
Mary Clare
Adeline Hayden-Coffin
C. Hayden-Coffin
Betty Hall

BLACK TULIP, THE

Granger–Binger
5,500 ft
T.S. 9.21

D. Frankland A. Richardson
C. F. Boersma
Sc.
from novel by Alexander Dumas

Zoe Palmer
Gerald McCarthy
Edward Verkade
Coln Hissing

BLACK WATERS

British and Dominion, American production
7,182 ft
T.S. 5.29

Full talking, made in U.S.A.

P. Herbert Wilcox
D. Marshall Neilan

Mary Brian
John Loder
James Kirkwood

BLADYS OF THE STEWPONEY

Ben Priest Films
5 reels
T.S. 12.19 and 12.21

D. L. C. MacBean
Sc.
from novel by S. Baring Gould

Marguerite Fox
S. J. Cauldwell
Arthur Chisholm
Adeline Hayden-Coffin
Wyndham Guise

BLAZING THE AIRWAY TO INDIA

Geoffrey Malins
6,000 ft
T.S. 1.23

BLEAK HOUSE

Ideal
6,000 ft
T.S. 1.20

D. Maurice Elvey
Sc. W. J. Elliott from novel by Charles Dickens

Constance Collier
Edward Arundel
Clifford Heatherley
William Burchill
A. Harding Steerman
Norman Page
E. Vivian Reynolds
Ion Swinley
Helen Haye

BLIGHTY

Gainsborough
8,603 ft / 8,400 ft
T.S. 3.27

New title of APRÈS LA GUERRE

P. Michael Balcon and Carlyle Blackwell
D. Adrian Brunel Asst. Norman Walker
C. J. J. Cox
Sc. Eliot Stannard from story by Ivor Montagu
Art Bertram Evans
Supervising editor Ivor Montagu

Ellaline Terriss
Lillian Hall-Davis
Godfrey Winn
Nadia Sibirskaia
Jameson Thomas
Wally Patch
Dino Galvani
Seymour Hicks
Houston Sisters

BLIND SHIP, THE

Millar, Anglo–French production
7,100 ft
T.S. 5.27

P. Adelqui Millar
D. J. Glavani and A. Frenguelli Asst. Douglas Elder
Sc.
from novel by Jean Barreyre

Adelqui Millar
Collette Darfeuil
Jerrold Robertshaw

BLINKEYES

Welsh–Pearson
7,300 ft
T.S. 9.26

D. George Pearson
Sc.
from novel by Oliver Sandys

Betty Balfour
Frank Stanmore
J. Fisher White

338

Pat Aherne
Dorothy Seacombe
Frank Vosper
Mary Dibley
Tom Douglas

BLOOD MONEY

Granger–Binger
5,000 ft
T.S. 2.21

D. Fred Goodwins
Sc.
  from novel by Cecil Bullivant

Arthur Cullin
Adelqui Millar
Dorothy Fane
Fred Goodwins
Frank Dane
Colette Brettel
Harry Ham

BLUE BOTTLES

Angle Pictures
1,934 ft
1928

P. Lionel Rich
D. Ivor Montagu
C. Lionel Rich
Sc. Frank Wells from story by H. G. Wells
Art Frank Wells

Elsa Lanchester
Dorice Fordred
Marie Wright
Charles Laughton
Joe Beckett
Norman Haire

BLUE PETER

British Filmcraft
7,665 ft
T.S. 2.29

D. A. H. Rooke   Asst. Leslie Eveleigh
Sc.
  from play by E. Temple Thurston

Matheson Lang
Gladys Frazin
Mary Dibley
Cameron Carr
A. Bromley Davenport.

BLUFF

Hardy
6,240 ft
T.S. 11.21

British Film Week 1924

D. Geoffrey Malins
C. Germaine Burger
Sc. Rafael Sabatini from his novel

Lewis Willoughby
Laurence Anderson
Majorie Hume
Sydney Paxton

BOADICEA

Stoll
8,000 ft
T.S. 11.26

P. H. Bruce Woolfe
D. Sinclair Hill
C. Jack Parker
Sc.
Art W. Murton

Phyllis Neilson-Terry
Lillian Hall-Davis
Clifford McLaglen
Edward O' Neill
Fred Raynham
Humberston Wright
Cyril McLaglen
Sybil Rhoda
Ray Raymond
Clifford Heatherley

BODEN'S BOY

Hepworth
7,500 ft / 5,135 ft
T.S. 10.23

D. Henry Edwards
Sc. Henry Edwards from novel by
    Tom Gallon

    Henry Edwards
    Chrissie White
    Stephen Ewart
    Francis Lister
    Henry Vibart
    Judd Green

BOHEMIAN GIRL, THE

Alliance
7,800 ft
T.S. 5.22

D. Harley Knoles
C. René Guissart
Sc.
    from opera by Balfe
Art Willie Davies

    Gladys Cooper
    Ivor Novello
    Constance Collier
    C. Aubrey Smith
    Ellen Terry
    Henry Vibart
    Gibb McLaughlin

BOLIBAR

British Instructional Films
8,000 ft
T.S. 7.28

    New title of THE MARQUIS
    OF BOLIBAR

D. Walter Summers Asst. J. O. C.
    Orton
C. Jack Parker
Sc. Walter Summers and J. O. C.
    Orton from novel by Leo Perutz
    (*Marquis de Bolibar*)

Art Arthur Woods
Ed. Adrian Brunel and Ivor Montagu
Titles   Adrian   Brunel   and   Ivor
    Montagu

    Jerrold Robertshaw
    Elissa Landi
    Cecil Barry
    Carl Harbord
    Hubert Carter

BONDMAN, THE

British and Dominion
8,660 ft
T.S. 1.29

P. Herbert Wilcox
D. Herbert   Wilcox   Asst.   Robert
    Harwood
C. David Kesson
Sc. T. A. Innes from novel and play
    by Sir Hall Caine
Art Clifford Pember

    Frances Cuyler
    Norman Kerry
    Donald McCardle
    Dora Barton
    Edward O'Neill
    Florence Vie
    Judd Green
    Henry Vibart

BONNIE MARY

Master
5 reels
T.S. 12.18 and 3.19

D. A. V. Bramble
C. A. G. Frenguelli
Sc. Eliot Stannard from story by
    Herbert Pemberton based on ballad
    (*Bonnie Mary of Argyle*)

    Arthur Cullin
    Jeff Barlow
    Miriam Ferris

BONNIE PRINCE CHARLIE

Gaumont
6,540 ft
T.S. 11.23

    British Film Week 1924

D. C. C. Calvert
C. A. St Aubyn Brown and H. W. Bishop
Sc. Alicia Ramsey

    Ivor Novello
    Gladys Cooper
    Hugh Miller
    Sydney Seaward
    A. B. Imeson
    Lewis Gilbert
    Arthur Wontner
    Nancy Price
    Adeline Hayden-Coffin
    A. Bromley Davenport

BOUNDARY HOUSE

Hepworth
5 reels
T.S. 12.18

D. C. M. Hepworth
Sc.
    from novel by Peggy Webling

    Alma Taylor
    Gwynne Herbert
    Gerald Ames
    Victor Prout
    John MacAndrews

BOY WOODBURN, THE

George Clark
5 reels
T.S. 5.22

D. Guy Newall
C. H. Harris
Sc.
    from novel by Alfred Olivant
Art titles Alex Scruby

    A. Bromley Davenport
    Guy Newall
    Ivy Duke
    Cameron Carr
    Douglas Munro
    Mary Rorke

BRANDED

Gaumont
6 reels
T.S. 9.20

D. C. C. Calvert
Sc.
    from novel by Gerald Biss

    Josephine Earle
    Dallas Anderson
    Nora Swinburne
    Francis Lister

BRED IN THE BONE

(1920) See under INHERITANCE

BREED OF THE TRESHAMS, THE

Astra
6,000 ft
T.S. 9.20

D. Kenelm Foss
C. Frank Canham
Sc. B. M. Dix and E. G. Sutherland from play by John Rutherford (B. M. Dix and E. G. Sutherland)

    Sir John Martin-Harvey
    Mary Odette
    Hayford Hobbs
    Charles Vane
    A. B. Imeson
    Philip Hewland
    J. Nelson Ramsaye
    Gordon Craig
    Will Corrie

BRENDA OF THE BARGE

Harma
4,639 ft
T.S. 4.21

D.   A. H. Rooke
C.   Leslie Eveleigh

    Majorie Villis
    James Knight
    Bernard Dudley
    Blanche Stanley
    Tom Coventry

BRIDAL CHAIR, THE

Samuelson
6 reels
T.S. 7.19

Sc. Roland Pertwee and G. B. Samuelson

    Miriam Sabbage
    C. M. Hallard
    Daisy Burrell
    Mary Rorke

BRIGHT EYES

British International Pictures–Sascha,
Anglo-Continental production
6,000 ft
T.S. (1) 5.29   (2) 10.29

    Sound version T.S. 10.29 with
    sychronised Songs, R.C.A.

D.   Geza von Bolvary
Sc.
    from story by F. Schutz

    Betty Balfour
    Jack Trevor
    Marcel Vibert

BRITAIN'S BIRTHRIGHT

British Instructional Films
6,200 ft / 6,500 ft
T.S. 3.25

'Arranged' by Professor Arthur Percival
Newton

    (The Empire tour of the Special
    Service Squadron of the Royal
    Navy, 1923–4.)

BROKEN BOTTLES

Gaumont
2 reels
T.S. 7.20

    Leslie Henson

BROKEN MELODY, THE

Welsh–Pearson–Elder
6,414 ft
T.S 10.29

    Synchronised

D.   Fred Paul
C.   Bernard Knowles   Asst. Eric Gray
Art Edward Carrick

    Georges Galli
    Cecil Humphreys
    Audrée Sayre
    Enid Stamp-Taylor
    Mary Brough
    Albert Brouett

BROKEN ROAD, THE

Stoll
5,000 ft
T.S. 6.21

D.   René Plaisetty
C.   J. J. Cox
Sc. Daisy Martin from novel by A. E.
    W. Mason

    June Putnam
    Mary Massart
    Harry Ham
    Tony Fraser
    Maresco Marisini
    Harry Worth

Robert English
Cyril Percival
Gwen Williams

BROWN SUGAR

Samuelson
5,600 ft
T.S. 7.22

D. Fred Paul
Sc. Walter Summers from play by Lady (Arthur) Lever

Owen Nares
Lillian Hall-Davis
Margaret Halstan

BUILD THY HOUSE

Ideal
5,200 ft
T.S. 10.20

D. Fred Goodwins
Sc. Eliot Stannard from story by S. Trevor Jones

Henry Ainley
Jerrold Robertshaw
Ann Trevor

BULLDOG DRUMMOND

Hollandia
6 reels
T.S. 11.22

D. Oscar Apfel
Sc.
 from play by 'Sapper'

Evelyn Greeley
Carlyle Blackwell
Dorothy Vane
Warwick Ward

BULLDOG DRUMMOND'S THIRD ROUND

Astra–National
7,300 ft

T.S. 10.25

New title of THE THIRD ROUND

D. Sidney Morgan Asst. Jack Raymond
C. Bert Cann
Sc.
 from story by 'Sapper'

Jack Buchanan
Betty Faire
Juliette Compton
Allan Jeayes
Austen Leigh
Frank Goldsmith
Edward Sorley

BURGOMASTER OF STILEMONDE, THE

British Filmcraft
8 reels
T.S. 1.29

D. George Banfield
Sc.
 from story and play by Maurice Maeterlinck
Art R. Byron Webber

Sir John Martin-Harvey
Fern Andra
John Hamilton
Robert Andrews
J. Nelson Ramsaye
A. B. Imeson
Mickey Brantford
Wilfred Shine
Fred Raynham
Adeline Hayden-Coffin

BURIED CITY, THE

S. African production
5,800 ft
T.S. 3.21

M. A. Wetherell
Mabel May

343

BURNT IN

B.A.F.C.
5 reels
T.S. 7.20

D. Duncan McRae
Sc. S. H. Herkomer from story by
S. B. Hill

Henry Vibart
Sam Livesey
Bertram Burleigh
Gertrude McCoy
Adelaide Grace

BY BERWYN BANKS

Progress
5 reels
T.S. 11.20

D. Sidney Morgan
C. S. J. Mumford
Sc.
from novel by Allen Raine

Langhorne Burton
Arthur Lennard
Eileen McGrath
Judd Green

CALL OF THE BLOOD, THE

Mercanton. French production of 1920
bought by Stoll
6,321 ft
T.S. 4.20 and 1.27

D. Louis Mercanton
Sc. Louis Mercanton from novel by
Robert Hichens

Phyllis Neilson-Terry
Ivor Novello

CALL OF THE EAST

International Artists Films
T.S. 10.22

Reissued in 1927 as HIS
SUPREME SACRIFICE

D. Bert Wynne

Doris Eaton
Dorinea Shirley
Walter Tennyson
Warwick Ward

CALL OF THE ROAD, THE

I. B. Davidson
6,000 ft
T.S. 10.20

D. A. E. Coleby
C. D. P. Cooper
Sc. A. E. Coleby

Victor McLaglen
Phyllis Shannaw
H. Nicholls Bates
A. E. Coleby
Geoffrey Benstead
Adeline Hayden-Coffin
Warwick Ward

CALL OF YOUTH, THE

Famous Players–Lasky British
4,400 ft
T.S. 11.20

D. Hugh Ford
C. Hal Young
Sc. Eve Unsell from story by Henry
Arthur Jones

Mary Glynne
Ben Webster
Jack Hobbs
Malcolm Cherry
Marjorie Hume

CALVARY

Master
5,200 ft
T.S. 2.20

D. Edwin J. Collins
C. Jack Parker
Sc.
from novel by Rita

344

Henry Victor
Malvina Longfellow
Wallace Bosco
Dorothy Moody
Barbara Everest
Charles Vane
Fred Goodwins

CANDYTUFT, I MEAN VERONICA

5,000 ft
T.S. 6.21

Mary Glynne
Daisy Markham
George Relph
Leslie Faber
Ena Grossmith

CAPE TO CAIRO

T.S. 4.26

P. Major C. Court Treatt
C. T. A. Glover

CARD, THE

Ideal
5,000 ft
T.S. 4.22

D. A. V. Bramble
Sc.
   from novel by Arnold Bennett

Laddie Cliff
Norman Page
Sydney Paxton
Hilda Cowley
Mary Dibley
Arthur Cleave
Jack Denton
Joan Barry
Arthur McLaglen
Bob Vallis

CARNIVAL

Alliance

6,500 ft
T.S. 2.21

D. Harley Knoles
C. Philip Hatkin
Sc. Adrian Johnson and Rosina Henley
   from play by H. C. M. Hardinge
   and Matheson Lang

Matheson Lang
Hilda Bayley
Ivor Novello
Maria de Bernaldo

CARRY ON

Britannia
7,050 ft
T.S. 12.27

D. Dinah Shurey
C. Randal Terraneau and Desmond
   Dickinson
Sc. Lydia Hayward from story by
   'Taffrail'

Moore Marriott
Wyndham Guise
Cynthia Murtagh
Pat Aherne
Trilby Clark
C. M. Hallard
Alf Goddard

CASE OF LADY CAMBER, THE

Broadwest
6 reels
T.S. 8. 20

D. Walter West
Sc. Benedict James from play by
   H. A. Vachell

Violet Hopson
Gregory Scott
Stewart Rome
Mercy Hatton
C. M. Hallard
Pollie Emery

345

CASTLES IN SPAIN

Lucoque–Taylor
5,000 ft
T.S. 6.20

D. H. Lisle Lucoque
C. I. Roseman
Sc. Nellie E. Lucoque

Bertie Gordon
Jeff Barlow
R. Heaton Grey
C. Aubrey Smith
Lilian Braithwaite
Maud Yates
Hayford Hobbs
Charles Vane

CELESTIAL CITY, THE

British Instructional Films
8,768 ft
T.S. 3.29

D. J. O. C. Orton
C. Jack Parker
Sc. J. O. C. Orton, from novel by
Baroness Orczy
Art Frank Wells

Norah Baring
Rebla
Cecil Fearnley
Malvina Longfellow
Henri de Vries
Lewis Dayton

CHAMBER OF HORRORS

British Instructional Films
5,014 ft
T.S. 3.29

D. Walter Summers

Frank Stanmore

CHAMPAGNE

British International Pictures
8,038 ft

T.S. 8.28

Prod. John Maxwell
D. Alfred Hitchcock   Asst. Frank
Mills
C. J. J. Cox
Sc. Eliot Stannard and Alfred Hitch-
cock, from story by Walter C.
Mycroft
Art C. W. Arnold
Ed. Alfred Hitchcock

Betty Balfour
Ferdinand von Alten
Jean Bradin
Gordon Harker
Jack Trevor
Marcel Vibert

CHANNINGS, THE

5 reels
T.S. 11.20

D. Edwin J. Collins
Sc.
from novel by Mrs Henry Wood

Dorothy Moody
Dick Webb
Charles Vane
Frank Arlton
Lionelle Howard
Diana Morrow

CHAPPY—THAT'S ALL

Stoll
4,800 ft
T.S. 7.24

D. Thomas Bentley
C.
Sc. Eliot Stannard, from story by
Oliver Sandys

Lewis Gilbert
Gertrude McCoy
Francis Lister
Edwin Greenwood
Joyce Dearsley

346

CHERRY RIPE

H. W. Thompson
5,000 ft
T.S. 8.21

D. Kenelm Foss   Asst. John Miller
C. Frank Canham
Sc. Kenelm Foss from story by Helen
    Mathers
Art Titles T. C. Gilson

Mary Odette
Lionelle Howard

CHICK

British Lion
7,215 ft
T.S. 8.28

D. A. V. Bramble
Sc.
    from novel by Edgar Wallace

Bramwell Fletcher
Trilby Clark
Chili Bouchier
Edward O'Neill

CHILDREN OF GIBEON, THE

Progress
5 reels
T.S. 11.20

D. Sidney Morgan
C. S. J. Mumford
Sc. Irene Miller and Sidney Morgan
    from novel by Walter Besant

Langhorne Burton
Sydney Fairbrother
Barbara MacFarlane
Eileen McGrath
Alice de Winton
Arthur Lennard
J. Denton Thompson
Joan Morgan

CHINESE BUNGALOW, THE

Stoll
6,700 ft
T.S. 5.26

D. Sinclair Hill
C. J. J. Cox
Sc.
    from play by Marion Osmond and
    James Corbet

Matheson Lang
Genevieve Townsend
Juliette Compton
Shayle Gardner
Clifford McLaglen

CHINESE PUZZLE, A

Ideal
5 reels
T.S. 9.19

D. Fred Goodwins   Asst. Challis N.
    Sanderson
Sc.
    from play by Leon M. Lion and
    Marian Bower

Sybil Arundale
Lilian Braithwaite
Sam Livesey
Milton Rosmer
Leon M. Lion
Charles Rock

CHRISTIE JOHNSTON

Broadwest
6 reels
T.S. 10.21

P. Walter West
D. Norman McDonald
Sc. G. W. Clifford from novel by
    Charles Reade

Stewart Rome
Gertrude McCoy
Clive Brook
Gordon Craig

CHU CHIN CHOW

Graham–Wilcox
9,000 ft
T.S. 9.23

D. Herbert Wilcox
C. René Guissart
Sc. Herbert Wilcox from play by Oscar Asche with music by Frederick Norton
Art Norman Arnold

Betty Blythe
Herbert Langley
Randle Ayrton
Judd Green
Eva Moore
Jameson Thomas
Jeff Barlow
Olaf Hytten
Dacia

CIGARETTE MAKER'S ROMANCE, A

5 reels
T.S. 6.20 and 2.21

D. Tom Watts
C. J. C. Bee Mason
Sc. E. Ross from novel by F. Marion Crawford and play by Charles Hannan

R. Henderson Bland
Tom Coventry

CINDERS

W. and F. Anglo-French production
7,180 ft
T.S. 9.26

D. Louis Mercanton
C. Percy Strong
Sc. Fred Wright and Louis Mercanton

Betty Balfour
Fred Wright
Irene Tripod

A. G. Poulton
André Roanne

CIRCUS JIM

Granger–Binger
5 reels
T.S. 1.22

D. B. E. Doxat-Pratt and Adelqui Millar
Sc. Adelqui Millar

Evelyn Brent
Adelqui Millar
Norman Doxat-Pratt
William Vanderveer

CITY OF BEAUTIFUL NONSENSE, THE

Hepworth
5 reels
T.S. 11.19

D. Henry Edwards
C. Charles Bryce
Sc.
from novel by E. Temple Thurston

Henry Edwards
Chrissie White
Gwynne Herbert
Henry Vibart
Douglas Munro
Teddy Taylor
Stephen Ewart
James Lindsay

CITY OF PLAY, THE

Gainsborough
7 reels
T.S. 11.29

Part talking, R.C.A.

D. Denison Clift   Asst. L. B. Lestocq
C. Claude McDonnell
Sc. Angus Macphail

Chili Bouchier
Pat Aherne
Lawson Butt
James Carew
Rene Clama
Olaf Hytten
Harold Huth

CLASS AND NO CLASS

Gaumont
6,207 ft
T.S. 12.21

British Film Week 1924

D. Will Kellino
C. A. St Aubyn Brown
Sc.
from story by E. Newton Bungaye

Judd Green
Pauline Johnson
David Hawthorne
Tom Coventry
Cecil du Gué
Cyril Smith
Marie Ault

CLAUDE DUVAL

Gaumont-Westminster
9,180 ft
T.S. 4.24

D. G. A. Cooper
C. Henry Harris

Fay Compton
Nigel Barrie
James Lindsay
Betty Faire
A. B. Imeson
Stella St Audrie
James Knight
Dorinea Shirley
Tom Coventry
Hugh Miller

CLIMBING MOUNT EVEREST

Captain J. B. L. Noel
4,945 ft
First show December 1922

C. Capt. J. B. L. Noel

(2nd Everest expedition of 1922)

CLUE OF THE NEW PIN, THE

British Lion
7,292 ft
T.S. 3.29

British Phototone

D. Arthur Maude
C. Horace Wheddon
Sc. Kathleen Hayden from novel by
Edgar Wallace

Donald Calthrop
Benita Hume
Kim Peacock
Caleb Porter
Fred Rains
John Gielgud

COCAINE

(1922) See under WHILE LONDON SLEEPS

COCKTAILS

British International Pictures
6,236 ft and 6,100 ft
T.S. 12.28

D. Monty Banks
Sc.
from story by S. Sydney and Rex
Taylor

Long and Short
Enid Stamp-Taylor
Nigel Barrie

COLLEEN BAWN, THE

Stoll
6,400 ft
T.S. 1.24

D. W. P. Kellino
C. William Shenton
Sc. Eliot Stannard from play by Dion
Boucicault from novel (*The Colle-gians*)

    Stewart Rome
    Henry Victor
    Colette Brettel
    Marie Ault
    Gladys Jennings

COLLEEN BAWN, THE

(1929) See under LILY OF KIL-LARNEY, THE

COLONEL NEWCOME (THE PERFECT GENTLEMAN)

Ideal
5,000 ft
T.S. 7.20

D. Fred Goodwins
Sc. W. J. Elliott from novel by
William Thackeray (*The New-comes*)

    May Whitty
    Haidee Wright
    Milton Rosmer
    Lewis Willoughby
    Temple Bell
    Bobby Andrews

COMIN' THRO' THE RYE

Hepworth
6 reels
T.S. 11.23

    British Film Week 1924

D. C. M. Hepworth
C. Geoffrey Faithfull

Sc.
from novel by Helen Mathers

    Alma Taylor
    James Carew
    Shayle Gardner
    Gwynne Herbert
    Eileen Dennes
    Henry Vibart
    Francis Lister
    Ralph Forbes
    John MacAndrews
    Nancy Price
    Christine Rayner

COMRADESHIP

Stoll
6,000 ft
T.S. 1.19
New title of COMRADES IN ARMS

D. Maurice Elvey   Asst. Challis N.
Sanderson
C. Paul Burger
Sc. Jeffrey Bernerd from original story
by Louis N. Parker

    Gerald Ames
    Lily Elsie
    Guy Newall
    Peggy Carlisle
    Edward Arundel
    Dallas Cairns
    Kate Gurney

COMRADES IN ARMS

(1919) See under COMRADESHIP

CONFESSIONS

Stoll
6,200 ft / 6,000 ft
T.S. 5.25

D. W. P. Kellino
C. J. J. Cox
Sc. Lydia Hayward from magazine
story by Baillie Reynolds, *Con-fession Corner*

Art Walter Murton

Ian Hunter
Joan Lockton
Gladys Hamer
Fred Raynham
Eric Bransby Williams
W. Saunders
Moore Marriott

CONFETTI

First National
6,183 ft
T.S. 12.27

D. Graham Cutts
C. Roy Overbaugh
Sc. Douglas Furber
Art Norman G. Arnold
Ed. Arthur Ellis

Jack Buchanan
Annette Benson
Sydney Fairbrother
Robin Irvine
Audrée Sayre

CONSCRIPTS OF MISFORTUNE

(1924) See under WOMEN AND
DIAMONDS

CONSPIRATORS, THE

Stoll
5 reels
T.S.6.25

D. Sinclair Hill
C. Horace Wheddon
Sc. Sinclair Hill from story by E.
Phillips Oppenheim
Art Walter Murton
Ed. Challis N. Sanderson

David Hawthorne
Betty Faire
Moore Marriott
Fred Rains
Edward O'Neill
Margaret Hope

CONSTANT NYMPH, THE

Gainsborough
10,600 ft
T.S. 2.28

P. Basil Dean
D. Adrian Brunel
C. Dave Gobbett
Sc. Adrian Brunel, Margaret Kennedy
and Alma Reville from novel and
play by Margaret Kennedy and
Basil Dean

Mabel Poulton
Ivor Novello
Benita Hume
Frances Doble
Dorothy Boyd
Mary Clare

CONTRABAND

(1925) See under FORBIDDEN
CARGOES

CONVICT 99

Samuelson
5,800 ft
T.S. 4.19

Sc.
from novel by Marie Connor and
Robert Leighton

Daisy Burrell
C. M. Hallard
Wee Georgie Wood

CO-OPTIMISTS, THE

New Era
7,000 ft
T.S. 11.29

Full talking and songs, R.C.A.

D. Edwin Greenwood
C. Sydney Blythe and Basil Emmott

CORINTHIAN JACK

Master
5 reels
T.S. 6.21

D. W. Courtenay Rowden
Sc. W. Courtenay Rowden from novel
by Charles E. Pearce

Victor McLaglen
Warwick Ward
Dorothy Fane
Kathleen Vaughan

COTTAGE ON DARTMOOR, A

British Instructional Films
7,528 ft
T.S. 1.30

Part talking, Klangfilm

P. H. Bruce Woolfe
D. Anthony Asquith   Asst. F. Bundy
C. Stanley Rodwell and M. Lind-
hölm
Sc. Anthony Asquith from story by
Herbert Price
Art Arthur Woods

Uno Henning
Hans Schlettow
Norah Baring

COUPLE OF DOWN-AND-
OUTS, A

Napoleon
5/6 reels
T.S. 11.23

British Film Week 1924

P. G. B. Samuelson
D. Walter Summers
Sc.
from story by W. Townend

Rex Davis
Edna Best
George Foley

CRIMSON CIRCLE, THE

Kinema Club
5,300 ft
T.S. 10.22

British Film Week 1924

D. George Ridgwell
C. Joe Rosenthal Jnr., Phil Ross,
Arthur Kingston
Sc. P. L. Mannock from novel by
Edgar Wallace

Madge Stuart
Eva Moore
Rex Davis
Fred Groves
Sydney Paxton
Clifton Boyne
Robert English
Mary Odette
Victor McLaglen
Flora le Breton
Henry Victor
Henry Vibart
Jack Hobbs

CRIMSON CIRCLE, THE

British Sound Films; Anglo-German
production
7 reels
T.S. (1) 3.29   (2) 8.29

Part talking, B.T.P. disc, in version
shown 8.29

D. Friedrich Zelnik (silent), Sinclair
Hill (sound)
Sc.
from novel by Edgar Wallace
Musical effects by Edmund Meisel

Lya Mara
Stewart Rome

CROOKED BILLET, THE

Gainsborough
7 reels
T.S. 3.30

Top Right: Brian Aherne in Asquith's *Underground*, 1928. Lighting by Karl Fischer.

Bottom Right: Asquith directing Cyril McLaglen (on the floor) on the set of *Underground*, 1928, watched by his mother Lady Asquith and, at left, Bruce Woolfe.

Top Left: Grierson and
Emmot shooting Drifters.

Centre Left: Estelle Broc
Victor Saville's Kitty, 1929

Below Left: Tallulah Bank
in His House in Order, 1928

Below Centre: Lya de Putt
Warwick Ward in The Info
1929, by Robinson.

Below Right: Harry Laud
Pearson's Auld Lang Syne,

Part talking, R.C.A.

D. Adrian Brunel
C. Claude McDonnell
Sc. Angus Mcphail from play by Dion Titheradge

Carlyle Blackwell
Miles Mander
Madeleine Carroll
Gordon Harker
Kim Peacock
Raymond Massey
Margaret Yarde

CROOKED STAIRCASE, THE

(1929) See under RINGING THE CHANGES

CROXLEY MASTER, THE

British Exhibitors Films
5 reels
T.S. 9.21

D. Percy Nash
C. S. L. Eaton
Sc. Harry Engholme from book by Sir Arthur Conan Doyle

Dick Webb
Dora Lennox
Joan Ritz
Louis Rihll
Cecil Morton York
George Turner

CRUCIFIXION

(1919) See under SOUL'S CRUCI-FIXION, A

CRY FOR JUSTICE, THE

Vanity
5 reels
T.S. 7.19

D. A. G. Frenguelli

Mary Glynne
Geoffrey Wilmer

CUPID IN CLOVER

British Screen Productions
6,481 ft
T.S. 2.29

D. Frank Miller
Sc.
from novel by Upton Gray (*Yellow Corn*)

Betty Siddons
James Knight
Wyndham Guise

DAMAGED GOODS

Samuelson
6,500 ft
T.S. 12.19

D. Alexander Butler
Sc.
from play by Eugene Brieux

Bassett Roe
J. Fisher White
Marjorie Day
Campbell Gullan
Annie Esmond
Rita Ricardo
James Lindsay

DANGEROUS LIES

Famous Players–Lasky British
7,000 ft
T.S. 9.21

D. Paul Powell
Sc. Mary O'Connor from story by E. Phillips Oppenheim

Mary Glynne
Minna Grey
David Powell

M

353

DANIEL DERONDA

Master
5,500 ft
T.S. 5.21

D. W. Courtenay Rowden
Sc. W. Courtenay Rowden from novel
by George Eliot

Reginald Fox
Clive Brook
Dorothy Fane
Ann Trevor

DARBY AND JOAN

Master
6,500 ft
T.S. 10.19

D. Percy Nash
C. S. L. Eaton
Sc.
from story by Sir Hall Caine

Derwent Hall Caine
Ivy Close
Edward O'Neill
Leal Douglas
Douglas Munro
Meggie Albanesi
Edward Craig
Ernest Douglas
Joan Ritz
George Wynne

DARK RED ROSES

British Sound Films
6,000 ft
T.S. 10.29

Full talking and songs, B.T.P.

Sc.
from story by Stacey Aumonier

Frances Doble
Stewart Rome

DAUGHTER IN REVOLT, A

Nettlefold
7,300 ft
T.S. 5.27

D. Harry Hughes   Asst. W. G.
Saunders
C. Charles Bryce
Sc. Harry Hughes from novel by
Sidney Gowing

Mabel Poulton
Marie Ault
Edward O'Neill
Pat Aherne
Lilian Oldland
Daisy Campbell
Hermione Baddeley
Ena Grossmith
Gertrude Sterroll

DAUGHTER OF EVE, A

Broadwest
5 reels
T.S. 8.19

D. Walter West

Violet Hopson
Stewart Rome
Cameron Carr
Vesta Sylva

DAUGHTER OF LOVE, A

Stoll
5,500 ft
T.S. 2.25

D. Walter West
C. Phil Ross
Sc. Lucita Squires from novel by
Mrs K. J. Key
Art Walter Murton

Violet Hopson
Jameson Thomas
Arthur Walcott
Minna Grey

354

Madge Tree
John Stuart
Fred Raynham
Gladys Mason

DAVID AND JONATHAN

Samuelson
6 reels
T.S. 7.20

P.   G. B. Samuelson
D.   Alexander Butler
Sc.
    from novel by E. Temple Thurston

    Madge Titheradge

DAWN

British and Dominion
7,300 ft
T.S. 4.28

P.   Herbert Wilcox
D.   Herbert Wilcox
C.   Bernard Knowles
Sc. Reginald Berkeley

    Sybil Thorndike
    Mary Brough
    Marie Ault
    Dacia Deane
    Haddon Mason
    Cecil Barry
    Edward O'Neill
    Maurice Braddell
    Mickey Brantford
    Ada Bodart
    Gordon Craig
    Edward Sorley

DAWN OF TRUTH, THE

Diamond Super
5 reels
T.S. 5.20

D.   L. C. MacBean
C.   Lucien Egrot
Sc. L. C. MacBean

H. R. Hignett
John Gliddon
Bernard Vaughan
Helga Jerome

DEAD CERTAINTY, A

Broadwest
5 reels
T.S. 4.20

D.   Walter West
Sc. P. L. Mannock from story by
    Nat Gould

    Poppy Wyndham
    Cameron Carr
    Gregory Scott

DEAD MAN'S LOVE, A

5,500 ft
T.S. 5.22

D.   Maurice de Marsan
Sc.
    from novel by Tom Gallon

    Bertram Burleigh
    Amy Verity

DEAR FOOL, A

Stoll
5,000 ft
T.S. 7.21

D.   Harold Shaw
C.   Jack Coward
Sc. Frank Miller
Art Walter Murton

    George K. Arthur
    Edna Flugrath
    Edward O'Neill
    C. Tilson-Chowne
    Bertie Wright
    Mabel Archdale

355

DEBT OF HONOUR, A

Stoll
5 reels
1922

D. Maurice Elvey
C. J. J. Cox
Sc.
    from novel by E. M. Dell
Art Walter Murton

Isobel Elsom
Hilda Sims
Lionelle Howard
Clive Brook
Sydney Seaward
Frank Goldsmith
Lewis Gilbert

DECAMERON NIGHTS

Graham–Wilcox and Universum Film
8,940 ft
T.S. 9.24

D. Herbert Wilcox
C. Theodor Sparkhul
Sc. Herbert Wilcox, from play by
    Robert McLaughlin adapted from
    Boccaccio by Boyle Lawrence
Art Norman G. Arnold

Lionel Barrymore
Werner Krauss
Bernhard Goetzke
Hannah Ralph
Randle Ayrton
Xenia Desni
Jameson Thomas
Ivy Duke
Albert Steinruck

DEMOS

Ideal
5,700 ft
T.S. 4.21

D. Denison Clift

Sc. Denison Clift from novel by
    George Gissing

Milton Rosmer
Gerald McCarthy
Mary Brough
Haidee Wright
Warwick Ward
Evelyn Brent
Olaf Hytten
J. G. Butt
Daisy Campbell

DESIRE

(1920) See under MAGIC SKIN,
THE

DIAMOND MAN, THE

I. B. Davidson
5,800 ft
T.S. 10.24

D. A. H. Rooke
C. Leslie Eveleigh
Sc. Eliot Stannard, from News of the
    World serial by Edgar Wallace

Gertrude McCoy
Mary Odette
Arthur Wontner
Reginald Fox
Philip Hewland

DIAMOND NECKLACE, THE

Ideal
5,900 ft
T.S. 1.21

D. Denison Clift
Sc. Denison Clift from story by Guy
    de Maupassant

Milton Rosmer
Jessie Winter
Mary Brough
J. G. Butt
Warwick Ward

DIANA OF THE CROSSWAYS

Ideal
5,000 ft
T.S. 5.22

D. Denison Clift
Sc.
  from novel by George Meredith

  Fay Compton
  Henry Victor
  J. Fisher White
  Ivo Dawson
  J. R. Tozer
  A. Harding Steerman

DIANA OF THE ISLANDS

George Clark
Unfinished?

D. F. Martin Thornton
C. Emile Lauste
Sc.
  from novel by Ben Bolt

  Walter Tennyson
  Nigel Barrie
  Cecil du Gué
  G. Clifton Boyne

DICK'S FAIRY

Seal
5,000 ft
T.S. 10.21

  C. H. Mansell
  Gordon Craig
  Eva Westlake
  Albert Brantford
  Joan Griffith

DICK TURPIN'S RIDE
TO YORK

Stoll
7,500 ft
T.S. 9.22

  British Film Week 1924

D. Maurice Elvey

Sc. L. H. Gordon from novel by
  Harrison Ainsworth (*Rookwood*)

  Matheson Lang
  Isobel Elsom
  Norman Page
  Lewis Gilbert
  Cecil Humphreys
  James English
  Madame d'Esterre
  Malcolm Tod
  Tony Fraser

DICKY MONTEITH

H. W. Thompson
5 reels
T.S. 2.22

D. Kenelm Foss   Asst. John Miller
C. Jack Parker
Sc. Kenelm Foss from story by Leon
  M. Lion and Tom Gallon

  Joan Morgan
  Stewart Rome
  J. Nelson Ramsaye

DON QUIXOTE

Stoll
5 reels
T.S. 12.23

  British Film Week 1924

D. Maurice Elvey
C. J. J. Cox
Sc. Sinclair Hill from novel by Cer-
  vantes
Art Walter Murton
Ed. H. Leslie Brittain
Titles Arthur Wimperis

  George Robey
  Jerrold Robertshaw
  Marie Blanche
  Sydney Fairbrother
  Frank Arlton
  Bertram Burleigh
  Minnie Leslie
  Adeline Hayden-Coffin

357

DOOR THAT HAS NO KEY, THE

Alliance
6,150 ft
T.S. 3.21

P. Harley Knoles
D. Frank Crane
Sc.
from novel by Cosmo Hamilton

Evelyn Brent
Betty Faire
George Relph
Olive Sloane

DOUBLE EVENT, THE

H. W. Thompson
5,000 ft
T.S. 7.21

D. Kenelm Foss
Sc. Kenelm Foss from play by Sidney Blow and Douglas Hoare

Mary Odette
Lionelle Howard
Tom Coventry

DOUBLE LIFE OF MR. ALFRED BURTON, THE

Lucky Cat
5 reels
T.S. 8.19

D. A. H. Rooke
C. Joe Rosenthal Jnr.
Sc. Kenelm Foss from story by E. Phillips Oppenheim

Kenelm Foss
Gordon Craig
Ivy Duke
James Lindsay

DOWNHILL

Gainsborough
8,635 ft
T.S. 5.27

P. Michael Balcon
D. Alfred Hitchcock Asst. Frank Mills
C. Claude McDonnell
Sc. Eliot Stannard from play by David L'Estrange (Ivor Novello and Constance Collier)
Art Bertram Evans
Ed. Ivor Montagu, Lionel Rich

Ivor Novello
Isabel Jeans
Ben Webster
Robin Irvine
Lilian Braithwaite
Violet Farebrother
Norman McKinnell
Jerrold Robertshaw
Annette Benson
Ian Hunter
Barbara Gott
Sybil Rhoda
Hannah Jones
Alf Goddard

DRIFTERS

New Era for Empire Marketing Board
3,631 ft
First show 11.29

D. John Grierson
C. Basil Emmott
Ed. John Grierson

DUCHESS OF SEVEN DIALS, THE

London Film Co.
5,400 ft
T.S. 1.20

D. Fred Paul
Sc. Harry Engholme

Majorie Hume
Adelaide Grace
Hubert Willis
Edward Arundel
Cecil Mannering
Harry Paulo

DUKE'S SON

George Clark
6,000 ft
T.S. 6.20

D. Franklin Dyall
C. Bert Ford
Sc. Guy Newall from novel by Cosmo Hamilton
Art Charles Dalmon
Art titles Alex Scruby

Ivy Duke
Guy Newall
Edward O'Neill
Hugh C. Buckler
Philip Hewland
Lawford Davidson
Douglas Munro

EARLY BIRDS

Brouett-Egrot
3 reels
T.S. 12.23

D. Albert Brouett
C. Lucien Egrot
Sc. P. L. Mannock from music hall sketch

Fred Karno

EASY VIRTUE

Gainsborough
7,300 ft
T.S. 8.27

P. Michael Balcon
D. Alfred Hitchcock
C. Claude McDonnell
Sc. Eliot Stannard from play by Noel Coward
Art Clifford Pember
Ed. Ivor Montagu

Isabel Jeans
Franklin Dyall
Eric Bransby Williams

Ian Hunter
Robin Irvine
Violet Farebrother
Dacia Deane
Dorothy Boyd
Enid Stamp-Taylor

EDGE O' BEYOND, THE

Samuelson
6 reels
T.S. 10.19

Sc. Irene Miller from novel by Gertrude Page

Isobel Elsom
Owen Nares
Minna Grey
C. M. Hallard
Mary Rorke
Ruby Miller

EDGE OF YOUTH, THE

Gaumont
6 reels
T.S. 6.20

D. C. C. Calvert
Sc. Paul Rooff

Josephine Earle
Dallas Anderson
Cecil du Gué
George Bellamy

EDUCATION OF NICKY, THE

Harma
4,200 ft
T.S. 4.21

D. A. H. Rooke
C. Leslie Eveleigh
Sc. May Wynne

James Knight
Constance Worth
Majorie Villis
Mary Rorke

EILEEN OF THE TREES

(1929) See under GLORIOUS YOUTH

ELEVENTH COMMANDMENT, THE

Gaumont
7 reels
T.S. 9.24

D. G. A. Cooper
C. Basil Emmott
Sc.
    from play by Brandon Fleming, and his novel *Pillory*
Art Stephen Reid

    Fay Compton
    Stewart Rome
    Lillian Hall-Davis
    Jack Hobbs
    Dawson Milward
    Charles Quartermaine
    Brian Aherne

ELEVENTH HOUR, THE

Stoll
5 reels
1922

D. George Ridgwell
C. Alfred H. Moses
Sc. L. H. Gordon from novel by E. M. Dell
Art Walter Murton

    Dennis Wyndham
    Madge White
    M. Gray Murray
    Charles Barratt

ELUSIVE PIMPERNEL, THE

Stoll
5 reels
T.S. 1.20

D. Maurice Elvey
C. Paul Burger

Sc. Frederick Blatchford from novel by Baroness Orczy
Art Barry Barnard

    Cecil Humphreys
    Marie Blanche
    Norman Page
    Edward Arundel
    A. Harding Steerman

EMERALD OF THE EAST

British Instructional Pictures
5,600 ft
T.S. 1.29

D. Jean de Kucharski
C. M. Planner, J. Rive, George W. Pocknall
Sc.
    from story by Mrs Jerbanu Kothawala
Ed. Emile de Ruelle

    Frank Dane
    Mary Odette
    Jean de Kucharski
    Joshua Kean
    Maria Forescu
    Promotha Rive
    Kenneth Rive
    Gillian Dean
    Lya Delvelez

ENCHANTMENT

London Film Co:
6 reels
T.S. 4.20

D. Einaar Bruun
Sc. Frank Fowell from novel by E. Temple Thurston

    Mary Odette
    Henri Krauss
    Edward O'Neill
    George Bellamy
    Henry Vibart
    Eric Barclay

ENGLISH ROSE, THE

Fred Paul
T.S. 11/12.23

D.   Fred Paul
Sc.
    from play by G. R. Sims and
    Robert Buchanan

    Sidney Folker
    Amy Brandon Thomas
    Fred Paul
    Humberston Wright
    Jack Raymond

EPIC OF EVEREST, THE

Explorers' Films
6,000 ft
T.S. 12.24

P.   Captain J. B. L. Noel
C.   Captain J. B. L. Noel
Lab. work Arthur Pereira

(3rd Everest Exped. in 1924)

EUGENE ARAM

Granger–Davidson
8,000 ft
T.S. 3.24

D.   A. H. Rooke
C.   S. J. Mumford
Sc.
    from novel by Bulwer Lytton
Art   Willie Davies

    Mary Odette
    Walter Tennyson
    James Carew
    A. Bromley Davenport
    Lionel d'Aragon
    Arthur Wontner
    Barbara Hoff

EVER OPEN DOOR, THE

Ideal

4,850 ft
T.S. 7.20

D.   Fred Goodwins
Sc.   W. J. Elliott from play by G. R.
    Sims

    Hayford Hobbs
    Terence Cavanagh
    Margaret Hope
    Daphne Glenn

EVERY MOTHER'S SON

Britannia Films
8,000 ft
Special run: 2.26

D.   Reginald H. West

    Rex Davis
    Haddon Mason
    Marie Ault
    Gladys Hamer
    Moore Marriott
    Johnny Butt
    Alf Goddard
    Jean Jay
    Mrs Hubert Willis
    Leal Douglas

EVIDENCE ENCLOSED

(1925) See under SETTLED OUT
OF COURT

EVIL THAT MEN DO, THE

Dewhurst
5 reels
T.S. 8.23 and 5.24

    New title of THE LITTLE
    DOOR INTO THE WORLD

D.   George Dewhurst
C.   Gustav Pauli
Sc.   George Dewhurst

    Lawford Davidson
    Olaf Hytten

EXPERIMENT, THE

Stoll
5 reels
T.S. 1922

D. Sinclair Hill
C. Adolph Burger
Sc. W. J. Elliott from novel by
Ethel M. Dell
Art Walter Murton

Clive Brook
Evelyn Brent
Hilda Sims
Norma Whalley

EXPIATION

Stoll
T.S. 1922

D. Sinclair Hill
Sc.
from novel by E. Phillips Oppenheim

Ivy Close
Fred Raynham
Lionelle Howard
Malcolm Tod
Fred Rains

FACE AT THE WINDOW, THE

B.A.F.C.
6 reels
T.S. 4.20

D. Wilfred Noy
C. Jack Christian
Sc.
from novel by F. Brooke Warren

C. Aubrey Smith
Charles Quartermaine
Gladys Jennings
Jack Hobbs
Simeon Stuart
Ben Field
Kathleen Vaughan

Kinsey Peile
Michelin Potous
Adrian Brunel
Jeff Barlow

FAIR MAID OF PERTH, THE

Anglia
6 reels
T.S. 10.25

D. Edwin Greenwood
Sc. Eliot Stannard from novel by Sir
Walter Scott

Russell Thorndike
Lionel d'Aragon
Sylvia Caine

FAITHFUL HEART, THE

Samuelson
5 reels
T.S. 8.22

Sc. Walter Summers from play by
Monckton Hoffe

Owen Nares
Lillian Hall-Davis
Cathleen Nesbitt

FAITH HOPE & CHARITY

(1919) trilogy
FAITH—IN BONDAGE (q.v.)
HOPE—SWEETHEARTS (q.v.)
CHARITY—SOME ARTISTS (q.v.)

FAKE, THE

Neo-Art
8,500 ft
T.S. 9.27

D. Georg Jacoby
C. William Shenton and Horace
Wheddon
Sc. G. A. Cooper from play by
Frederick Lonsdale
Ed. Ivor Montagu

Henry Edwards
Norman McKinnell
Elga Brink
Miles Mander
Juliette Compton
A. Bromley Davenport
J. Fisher White
Ursula Jeans
Julie Suedo
Ivan Samson

FAKE SPIRITUALISM EXPOSED

F.H.C.
4 reels
T.S. 6.26

D. A. E. Coleby

Arthur Prince
Yvonne Thomas

FALL OF A SAINT, THE

Gaumont
6,000 ft
T.S. 1.20

D. Will Kellino
Sc.
from novel by Eric Clement Scott

Josephine Earle
Gerald Lawrence
H. Heaton Grey
Dallas Anderson

FANCY DRESS

Lucky Cat
5 reels
T.S. 9.19

D. Kenelm Foss
C. Joe Rosenthal Jnr. and Bert Ford
Sc. Kenelm Foss

Godfrey Tearle
Guy Newall
Ivy Duke
Will Corrie
Frank Miller

FARMER'S WIFE, THE

British International Pictures
8,775 ft
T.S. 3.28

P. John Maxwell
D. Alfred Hitchcock Asst. Frank Mills
C. J. J. Cox
Sc. Eliot Stannard from play by Eden Phillpotts
Art C. W. Arnold
Ed. Alfred Booth

Jameson Thomas
Lillian Hall-Davis
Gordon Harker
Gibb McLaughlin
Louise Pounds
Olga Slade
Antonia Brough

FATE'S PLAYTHING

Anglo–Hollandia
5,650 ft
T.S. 5.20

Sc.
from novel by Mrs D. C. F. Harding (*Oranges and Lemons*)

Constance Worth
Adelqui Migliar
Hector Abbas
Frank Dane
Master Doxatt-Pratt
Bruce Gordon

FEAR O' GOD

(1926) Title of THE MOUNTAIN EAGLE in U.S.A.

363

FEATHER, THE

Strand
8,000 ft
T.S. 11.29

Synchronized songs, R.C.A.

D. Leslie Hiscott
C. Basil Emmott
Sc. C. M. Matheson

Jameson Thomas
Vera Flory
Randle Ayrton
Mary Clare
John Hamilton
James Reardon
Irene Tripod
W. Cronin Wilson

FETTERED

Walturdaw
T.S. 1919

D. A. Bocchi
Sc. Kenelm Foss from book by Joan
Sutherland

Manora Thew
Hayford Hobbs
Bert Wynne
Peggy Patterson
Evelyn Harding
Charles Vane
George Butler

FIFTH FORM AT ST DOMINIC'S, THE

Granger–Davidson
7,000 ft
T.S. 11.21

Reissued 1923. British Film Week
1924

D. A. E. Coleby
Sc.

from story by Talbot Baines Reed
William Freshman
Ralph Forbes

FIFTY THOUSAND MILES WITH THE PRINCE OF WALES

5,897 ft
T.S. 11.20

FIRES OF FATE

Gaumont
7,200 ft
T.S. 7.23

British Film Week 1924

D. Tom Terriss
C. A. St Aubyn Brown and H. W.
Bishop
Sc. Alicia Ramsey from book by Sir
Arthur Conan Doyle (*The Tragedy
of the Korosko*) and his play (*The
Fires of Fate*)

Wanda Hawley
Nigel Barrie
L. de Cordova
Edith Craig
Arthur Cullin
Stewart Rome
Douglas Munro
Percy Standing
Cyril Smith

FIRES OF INNOCENCE

Progress
5,000 ft
T.S. 9.22

New title of A LITTLE WORLD
APART

D. Sidney Morgan
C. S. J. Mumford
Sc.

from novel by George Stevenson
(*A Little World Apart*)

Joan Morgan
Marie Illington
Arthur Lennard

364

Nell Emerald
Bobby Andrews

FIRST BORN, THE

Gainsborough
7,786 ft
T.S. 12.28

P. Michael Balcon
D. Miles Mander   Prod. Man. Harry Ham
C. Walter Blakeley
Sc. Miles Mander and Alma Reville from play *The Common People*
Art C. W. Arnold
Ed. Arthur Tavares
Titles Ian Dalrymple

Miles Mander
Madeleine Carroll
Ivo Dawson
John Loder
Naomi Jacobs
Bernard Vaughan
Theodore Mander

FLAG LIEUTENANT, THE

Barker Motion Photography
5 reels
T.S. 9.19

D. Percy Nash
Sc.
    from play by Lt. Col. Drury and Leo Trevor

Ivy Close
George Wynne

FLAG LIEUTENANT, THE

Astra–National
8,900 ft
T.S. 10.26

D. Maurice Elvey
C. W. Shenton, Leslie Eveleigh, F. Young
Sc. P. L. Mannock
Art A. L. Mazzei

Henry Edwards
Lilian Oldland
Fred Raynham
Fewlass Llewellyn
Lionel d'Aragon
Hayford Hobbs
Humberston Wright
Dorothy Seacombe
Forrester Harvey
Frank Dane

FLAME, THE

Stoll
6,300 ft
T.S. 7.20

D. F. Martin Thornton
C. Percy Strong
Sc. F. Martin Thornton from novel by Olive Wadsley

Reginald Fox
Evelyn Boucher
Fred Thatcher
Dora de Winton
Frank E. Petley
William Lenders

FLAMES OF PASSION

Graham Wilcox Productions
9,000 ft
T.S. 11.22

Part Prizma colour

D. Graham Cutts
C. René Guissart
Sc. Herbert and M. V. Wilcox
Art Norman G. Arnold

Mae Marsh
Herbert Langley
Allan Ainsworth
Eva Moore
A. G. Poulton
C. Aubrey Smith
Henry Vibart

365

FLIGHT COMMANDER, THE

Gaumont
8,000 ft
T.S. 9.27

P. Elvey–Saville–Gundrey production
D. Maurice Elvey
C. Percy Strong, Basil Emmott
Sc. Eugene Clifford from story by John Travers
Art Andrew Mazzei

Sir Alan Cobham
Estelle Brody
Vesta Sylva
John Stuart
Humberston Wright
Edward O'Neill
Alf Goddard
Cyril McLaglen
A. Bromley Davenport
William Pardoe
John Longden

FLYING FIFTY-FIVE, THE

Stoll
5,600 ft
T.S. 9.28

D. A. E. Coleby
Sc.
from novel by Edgar Wallace

Annie Esmond
Adeline Hayden-Coffin
Lionelle Howard
Johnny Butt
Lionel d'Aragon
Stephanie Stevens
Frank Perfitt
Bert Darley

FLYING SCOTSMAN, THE

British International Pictures
5,502 ft
T.S. 2.20

Part talking, R.C.A.

D. Castleton Knight
Sc. Joe Grossman

Moore Marriott
Pauline Johnson
Cyril McLaglen
Raymond Milland

FLYING SQUAD, THE

British Lion
7,572 ft
T.S. 1.29

D. Arthur Maude
C.
Sc. Kathleen Hayden and Arthur Maude from play by Edgar Wallace

Donald Calthrop
Wyndham Standing
Henry Vibart
John Longden
Dorothy Bartlett

FORBIDDEN CARGOES

6,235 ft
T.S. 8.25

New title of CONTRABAND

D. Fred Leroy Granville

Peggy Hyland
James Lindsay
Clifford McLaglen
Robert Vallis

FORDINGTON TWINS, THE

Gaumont
6 reels
T.S. 8.20

D. Will Kellino
Sc.
from story by E. Newton Bungaye

Dallas Anderson

366

The Terry Twins
Mary Brough
Whimsical Walker
Cecil du Gué
Cyril Smith

FOREST ON THE HILL, THE

Hepworth
6,000 ft
T.S. 12.19

D. C. M. Hepworth
Sc. Blanche MacIntosh from novel by
Eden Phillpotts

Alma Taylor
James Carew
Gerald Ames
Eileen Dennes
Stephen Ewart
Gwynne Herbert
John MacAndrews
Judd Green
Lionelle Howard

FORGER, THE

British Lion
7,305 ft
T.S. 12.28

D. G. B. Samuelson
Sc.
from *Daily Mail* serial by Edgar
Wallace

Lillian Rich
Nigel Barrie
Sam Livesey
Winter Hall
Ivo Dawson

FORGIVE US OUR TRESPASSES

Mary Marsh Allen
T.S. 1919

D. L. C. MacBean

Mary Marsh Allen

Joyce Templeton
Booth Conway
George Bellamy
Marsh Allen
H. R. Hignett
Bernard Vaughan

FOR HER FATHER'S SAKE

Samuelson
4,983 ft
T.S. 5.21

D. Alexander Butler
Sc.
from play by Alfred Sutro (*The
Perfect Lover*)

Isobel Elsom
Owen Nares
James Lindsay

FORTUNE OF CHRISTINA M'NAB, THE

Gaumont
6,200 ft
T.S. 4.21

D. Will Kellino
Sc. Paul Roof from novel by Sarah
MacNaughton

Nora Swinburne
David Hawthorne
Francis Lister
Eva Westlake

FORTUNE'S FOOL

Hardy
6,650 ft
T.S. 7.25 and 5.27

New title of THE SCOURGE

D. Geoffrey Malins
Sc. Rafael Sabatini

Madge Stuart
J. R. Tozer

FOR VALOUR

G. B. Samuelson
6,120 ft
T.S. 10.28

D. G. B. Samuelson

Mary Rorke
Dallas Cairns

FOUL PLAY

Master
4,800 ft
T.S. 6.20

D. Edwin J. Collins
C. J. Parker
Sc. Walter Courtenay Rowden from
novel by Charles Reade

Renée Kelly
Cecil Morton York
C. H. Mansell
Charles Vane
Henry Hallatt

FOUR FEATHERS, THE

Stoll
5,000 ft
T.S. 5.21

D. René Plaisetty
C. J. J. Cox
Sc. Daisy Martin from novel by A. E.
W. Mason

Henry Vibart
Mary Massart
Roger Livesey
Harry Ham
Robert English
Harry Worth

FOUR JUST MEN, THE

Stoll
5,000 ft
T.S. 5.21

Reissued 1929

D. George Ridgwell
C. Alfred Moses
Sc. George Ridgwell from novel by
Edgar Wallace

Cecil Humphreys
George Bellamy
C. H. Croker King
C. Tilson-Chowne
Robert Vallis
Edward Arundel

FOUR MEN IN A VAN

Direct
7,000 ft
T.S. 12.21

D. Hugh Croise
C. Frank Grainger
Sc. Hugh Croise from novel by R.
Andom

Manning Haynes
Donald Searle
Gordon Hopkirk
Johnny Butt
Moore Marriott

FOX FARM

George Clark
6,000 ft
T.S. 7.22

D. Guy Newall
C. Hal Young
Sc.
from novel by Warwick Deeping
Art titles Alex Scruby

Ivy Duke
Guy Newall
A. Bromley Davenport

FRAILTY

Stoll
5,966 ft
T.S. 7.21

D. F. Martin Thornton

C. Percy Strong
Sc. L. H. Gordon from novel by Olive
Wadsley

Madge Stuart
Paulette del Baye
H. Agar Lyons
Sidney Lewis Ransom
J. Edwards Barber
Roland Myles
Frank Petley

FROGGY'S LITTLE BROTHER

Stoll
5,750 ft
T.S. 11.21

D. A. E. Coleby
C. D. P. Cooper
Sc. A. E. Coleby from story by
Brenda (Mrs G. Castle-Smith)
Art Walter Murton

Maurice Thompson
Agnes Poulton
James English

FROM RED SEA TO
BLUE NILE

Britannia
6,000 ft
First run 7.25

C. Harold J. Jones

Rosita Forbes

FROM SENEGAL TO
TIMBUCTU

6 reels/11,000 ft
Reviewed 12.24

Presented by Sir Curtis Lampson
C. Arthur Pereira

FRUITFUL VINE, THE

Stoll
7,000 ft
T.S. 9.21

D. Maurice Elvey
C. Germaine Burger
Sc. Leslie H. Gordon from novel by
Robert Hichens
Art Walter Murton
Ed. H. Leslie Brittain

Valia
Robert English
Basil Rathbone
Edward Arundel
Fred Raynham
Mary Dibley
Irene Rooke
Paulette del Baye
Peter Dear
Mme. d' Esterre

FURTHER MYSTERIES OF
DR. FU-MANCHU

Stoll
Series, 8 2-reelers
T.S. 8.24

D. Fred Paul
C. Frank Canham
Sc. Fred Paul from stories by Sax
Rohmer
Art Walter Murton

H. Agar Lyons

The Coughing Horror
Cragmire Tower
The Golden Pomegranates etc.

FURTHER EXPLOITS OF
SEXTON BLAKE

Gaumont
T.S. 8.19

D. Harry Lorraine

Douglas Payne
Jeff Barlow
Majorie Villis
Frank Dane
William Brandon

FURTHER ADVENTURES OF SHERLOCK HOLMES

Stoll
Series, 15 2-reelers
T.S. 1922

D.   George Ridgwell
C.   Alfred H. Moses
Sc. George Ridgwell from stories by A. Conan Doyle
Art Walter Murton with Eille Norwood

Abbey Grange
Black Peter
The Boscombe Valley Mystery
The Bruce Partington Plans
Charles Augustus Milverton
The Golden Pince-Nez
The Greek Interpreter
The Musgrave Ritual
The Naval Treaty
The Norwood Builder
The Red Circle
The Reigate Squires
The Second Stain
The Six Napoleons
and one other

FURTHER ADVENTURES OF THE FLAG LIEUTENANT

Neo–Art
8,500 ft
T.S. 11.27

D.   W. P. Kellino
C.   Horace Wheddon, W. Shenton
Sc. G. A. Cooper from story by W. P. Drury

Henry Edwards
Isabel Jeans
Lyn Harding
Fewlass Llewellyn
Lilian Oldland
Fred Raynham

GALLANT HUSSAR, THE

Gainsborough, Anglo-German film
6,666 ft
T.S. 9.28

D.   Geza von Bolvary

Ivor Novello
Evelyn Holt
Ernest Verebes
Paul Otto

GAMBLE IN LIVES, A

British and Colonial
5,000 ft
T.S. 11.20

D.   George Ridgwell
Sc.

from play by Frank Stayton (*The Joan Danvers*)

Norman McKinnell
Malvina Longfellow
Molly Adair
Alec Fraser

GAMBLERS ALL

Samuelson
5 reels
T.S. 10.19

D.   Dave Aylott
Sc.

from play by Mrs Martindale

Madge Titheradge
Ruby Miller
C. M. Hallard
Henry Vibart
Owen Nares

GAMBLE WITH HEARTS, A

Master
5 reels
T.S. 1923

D. Harry B. Parkinson
Sc.
    from story by Anthony Carlyle

    Olaf Hytten
    Milton Rosmer
    Cecil Morton York
    Valia
    Madge Stuart

GAME OF LIFE, THE

Samuelson
10,000 ft
T.S. 6.22

D. G. B. Samuelson
Sc. G. B. Samuelson and Laurie
    Wylie

    Isobel Elsom
    James Lindsay
    Campbell Gullan
    Tom Reynolds
    Dorothy Minto
    Wyndham Guise
    Fred Lewis
    Lillian Hall-Davis

GARDEN OF RESURRECTION, THE

George Clark
5,000 ft
T.S. 12.19

D. A. H. Rooke
C. Joe Rosenthal Jnr.
Sc. Guy Newall from novel by E.
    Temple Thurston
Art Charles Dalmon

    Guy Newall
    Ivy Duke
    Franklin Dyall
    Mary Dibley
    Douglas Munro
    Hugh C. Buckler
    Humberston Wright
    Madge Tree
    Lawford Davidson
    Winifred Sadler

GARRYOWEN

Welsh–Pearson
5,900 ft
T.S. 1.20

D. George Pearson
C. Emile Lauste
Sc. George Pearson from novel by H.
    de Vere Stacpoole
Art titles Ernest Jones

    Moyna MacGill
    Hugh E. Wright
    Fred Groves
    Arthur Cleave
    Bertram Burleigh
    Alec Thompson
    Leo Carelli

GAY CORINTHIAN, THE

I. B. Davidson
5,500 ft
T.S. 7.24

    2-reel version issued in 1926

D. A. H. Rooke
C. Leslie Eveleigh
Sc.
    from novel and *News of the
    World* Serial by Ben Bolt

    Victor McLaglen
    H. Humberston Wright
    Cameron Carr
    Betty Faire
    Jack Denton
    Donald McCardle
    George Turner
    Exguardsman Penwell

GAYEST OF THE GAY, THE

(1924) See under HER REDEMPTION

GENERAL JOHN REGAN

Stoll
6,000 ft
T.S. 10.21

D. Harold Shaw
C. J. J. Cox
Sc. W. J. Elliott from novel and play by George A. Birmingham (Rev. James O. Hannay)
Art Walter Murton

Milton Rosmer
Edward O'Neill
Bertie Wright
Edward Arundel
Judd Green
Madge Stuart
Robert Vallis
Wyndham Guise
Mabel Archdale

GENERAL POST

Ideal
5,000 ft
T.S. 3.20

Reissued as 2-reeler in 1923
D. Thomas Bentley
Sc. Eliot Stannard from play by J. E. Harold Terry

Dawson Milward
R. Henderson Bland
Lilian Braithwaite
Joyce Dearsley
C. H. Mansell
Adelaide Grace
Edward Arundel
Douglas Munro
Rachel de Solla

GENTLEMAN OF FRANCE, A

Stoll
5,900 ft
T.S. 6.21

D. Maurice Elvey
Sc.
from novel by S. J. Weyman

Eille Norwood
Allan Jeayes
Hugh C. Buckler
William Lenders
Faith Bevan
Sydney Seaward
Madge Stuart
Pardoe Woodman
Mme. d'Esterre
Harvey Braban
Edward Arundel

GENTLEMAN RIDER, THE

Violet Hopson
5 reels
T.S. 9.19

D. Walter West

Violet Hopson
Stewart Rome
Gregory Scott

GHOST TRAIN

Gainsborough; Anglo-German production
6,500 ft
T.S. 9.27

D. Geza von Bolvary
Sc.
from play by Arnold Ridley

Guy Newall

GIRL OF LONDON, A

Stoll
6,406 ft
T.S. 10.25

D. Henry Edwards
C. D. P. Cooper
Sc.
from story by Douglas Walshe
Art Walter Murton

Genevieve Townsend
Ian Hunter
Nora Swinburne
George Mulcaster

Bernard Dudley
Harvey Braban
Nell Emerald
Kiyoshi Takase

GIRL OF TODAY, A

(1928) See under LOVE'S OPTION

GLAD EYE, THE

Reardon–British
6,000 ft
T.S. 5.20

D. Kenelm Foss
C. Leslie Reardon
Sc. Kenelm Foss from play by José G. Levy from story by Paul Armont and Nicholas Nancey (*Le Zèbre*)

Dorothy Minto
James Reardon
Hayford Hobbs
Kenelm Foss
Pauline Peters
Will Corrie
George Bellamy
Douglas Munro

GLAD EYE, THE

Gaumont–British
7,700 ft
T.S. 7.27

P. Elvey–Saville production
D. Maurice Elvey
C. Percy Strong, Basil Emmott
Sc.
from play by José G. Levy from story by Paul Armont and Nicholas Nancey (*Le Zèbre*)

Estelle Brody
John Stuart
H. Humberston Wright
Mabel Poulton
Jeanne de Casalis
A. Bromley Davenport
John Longden

GLORIOUS ADVENTURE, THE

Stuart Blackton Productions
9 reels
T.S. 1.22

Prizma colour

D. John Stuart Blackton
C. Nicholas Musurca
Sc. Felix Orman
Art Walter Murton
Art titles Nicholas Musurca

Lady Diana Manners
Gerald Lawrence
Cecil Humphreys
William Luff
Lennox Pawle
Elizabeth Beerbohm
Victor McLaglen
Flora le Breton
Tom Haselwood
Haidee Wright
Fred Wright
Rosalie Heath

GLORIOUS YOUTH

First National-Pathé
7,146 ft
T.S. 4.29

New title of EILEEN OF THE TREES

D. Graham Cutts
Prod. Manger Harry Ham
Sc. Reginald Fogwell and Maclean Rogers from novel by H. de Vere Stacpoole (*Eileen of the Trees*)

Anny Ondra
William Freshman
Gibb McLaughlin
Forrester Harvey
Randle Ayrton
Dora Barton
Barbara Gott
Jerrold Robertshaw
A. Bromley Davenport
J. R. Tozer

GOD IN THE GARDEN, THE

Master
5,500 ft
T.S. 10.21

D. Edwin J. Collins
Sc.
from novel by Keble Howard

Edith Craig
Arthur Pusey
Mabel Poulton
James English
Cecil Morton York
A. Harding Steerman
Mabel Archdale

GOD'S CLAY

T.S. 11.19

D. A. H. Rooke
C. Joe Rosenthal Jnr.
Sc.
from novel by Claude and Alice
Askew

Janet Alexander
Maud Yates
A. H. Rooke
Humberston Wright
Adeline Hayden-Coffin
J. H. Batson

GOD'S CLAY

First National–Pathé
6,301 ft
T.S. 8.28

D. Graham Cutts
Sc. Maclean Rogers from novel by
Claude and Alice Askew
Art Norman G. Arnold

Anny Ondra
Haddon Mason
Trilby Clark
Marie Ault
Annie Esmond

GOD'S GOOD MAN

Stoll
7 reels
T.S. 8.19

D. Maurice Elvey
C. Paul Burger
Sc.
from novel by Marie Corelli

Basil Gill
Peggy Carlisle
Edward Arundel
Kate Gurney

GOLD CURE, THE

Stoll
5,700 ft
T.S. 10.25

D. Will Kellino
C. J. J. Cox
Sc. Lydia Hayward from story by
Sara Jeanette Duncan
Art Walter Murton

Queenie Thomas
Eric Bransby Williams
Jameson Thomas
Moore Marriott
Nell Emerald
A. E. Raynor
Gladys Harmer

GOLDEN BUTTERFLY, THE

Stoll–Sascha; Austrian production
7,500 ft
T.S. 7.26

D.
Sc.
from book by P. G. Wodehouse

Lili Damita
Niels Astur
Jack Trevor

374

GOLDEN DAWN, THE

R. D. Independent Productions
5,000 ft
T.S. 9.21

D. Ralph Dewsbury
C. Sylvano Balboni
Sc. Bannister Merwin

Gertrude McCoy
Warwick Ward
Sydney Fairbrother
Mary Brough
Charles Vane
Frank E. Petley
Philip Hewland

GOLDEN WEB, THE

Garrick
5 reels
T.S. 9.20

D. Geoffrey Malins
C. S. J. Mumford
Sc. from novel by E. Phillips
Oppenheim

Milton Rosmer
Ena Beaumont
Nina Munro

GOOD FOR NOTHING

Hollandia
5 reels
T.S. 2.23

Carlyle Blackwell
Evelyn Greeley

GOODWIN SANDS, THE

(1930) See under
LADY FROM THE SEA, THE

GRASS ORPHAN, THE

Ideal

6 reels
T.S. 2.23

British Film Week 1924

D. Frank Crane
Sc. from novel by I. A. R. Wylie
(*Paupers of Portman Square*)

Reginald Owen
Margaret Bannerman
Douglas Munro
Peter Dear

GREAT COUP, A

Broadwest
5 reels
T.S. 11.19

P. Walter West
D. George Dewhurst
Sc. J. Bertram Brown from story by
Nat Gould

Poppy Wyndham
Gregory Scott
Stewart Rome
Cameron Carr

GREAT DAY, THE

Famous Players-Lasky British
3,700 ft
T.S. 11.20

D. Hugh Ford   Asst. J. E. Boyle
C. Hal Young
Sc.
from play by G. R. Sims and
Louis N. Parker

Marjorie Hume
Arthur Bourchier
Bertram Burleigh
Adeline Hayden-Coffin
Meggie Albanesi
Percy Standing
Geoffrey Kerr
Lewis Dayton

375

GREAT GAME, THE

I. B. Davidson
6 reels
T.S. 12.18

New title of THE STRAIGHT GAME

D. A. E. Coleby
Sc. A. E. Coleby from novel by Andrew Soutar

Bombardier Billy Wells

GREAT GAY ROAD, THE

Broadwest
5,600 ft
T.S. 10.20

D. Norman McDonald
Sc. Norman McDonald from novel and play by Tom Gallon

Stewart Rome
Ernest Spalding
A. Bromley Davenport
Ralph Forster
John Stuart
Pauline Johnson

GREATHEART

Stoll
5,000 ft
T.S. 6.21

D. George Ridgwell
Sc. Mrs Sydney Groom from novel by Ethel M. Dell

Madge Stuart
Cecil Humphreys

GREAT PRINCE SHAN, THE

Stoll
6 reels
T.S. 5.24

D. A. E. Coleby
C. D. P. Cooper
Sc.

from novel by E. Phillips Oppenheim

Sessue Hayakawa
Tsuru Aoki
A. E. Coleby
Henry Vibart
David Hawthorne
Fred Raynham
Ivy Duke
Valia
H. Nicholls Bates

GREAT TURF MYSTERY, A

Walter West
5,250 ft
T.S. 1.24

D. Walter West

Violet Hopson
Warwick Ward
James Knight
Arthur Walcott
Marjorie Benson

GREAT WELL, THE

Ideal
6,400 ft
T.S. 4.24

D. Henry Kolker
Sc.

from play by Alfred Sutro

Seena Owen
Joan Morgan
Dora de Winton
Cameron Carr
Eva Moore
Simeon Stuart
A. V. Bramble
Lawford Davidson
Thurston Hall
Harvey Braban

376

GREAT WHITE SILENCE, THE

7,300 ft
T.S. 5.24

P.   H. G. Ponting

GREEN CARAVAN, THE

Granger-Master
5,000 ft
T.S. 11.22

British Film Week 1924

D.   Edwin J. Collins
Sc.
    from novel by Oliver Sandys

    Catherine Calvert
    Valia
    Gregory Scott
    Ivo Dawson
    Wallace Bosco
    Sunday Wilshin

GREEN TERROR, THE

Gaumont
6 reels
T.S. 7.19

Sc.   G. W. Clifford from serial in *News of the World* by Edgar Wallace

    Aurèle Sydney
    Heather Thatcher
    Cecil du Gué

GRIP OF IRON, THE

Famous Pictures
5 reels
T.S. 1.20

D.   Bert Haldane
Sc.
    from play by Arthur Shirley

    Malvina Longfellow
    George Foley
    James Lindsay

GUNS OF LOOS

Stoll
7,900 ft
T.S. 2.28

P.   Oswald A. Mitchell
D.   Sinclair   Hill   Asst. Harcourt Templeman
C.   D. P. Cooper, Desmond Dickinson, Sydney Eaton
Sc. Reginald Fogwell and Leslie H. Gordon
Ed. H. Leslie Brittain
Titles Edward Strong

    Madeleine Carroll
    Bobby Howes
    Henry Victor
    Donald McCardle
    Hermione Baddeley
    Adeline Hayden-Coffin
    Tom Coventry
    William Freshman
    Wally Patch
    Philip Hewland
    Jeanne le Vaye
    Frank Goldsmith

GUY FAWKES

Stoll
6,000 ft
T.S. 9.23

British Film Week 1924

D.   Maurice Elvey
C.   J. J. Cox
Sc. Alicia Ramsey
Art. Walter Murton
Ed. Challis N. Sanderson

    Matheson Lang
    Jerrold Robertshaw
    Lionel d'Aragon
    Robert English
    Hugh C. Buckler
    Edward O'Neill
    Pino Conti
    Shayle Gardner
    Dallas Cairns
    Peter Dear
    Nina Vanna

GWYNETH OF THE WELSH HILLS

Stoll
6,000 ft
T.S. 11.21

D. F. Martin Thornton
C. Percy Strong
Sc.
   from story by Edith Nepean

Madge Stuart
Mrs Hubert Willis
Lewis Gilbert
J. R. Tozer
Gladys Jennings
Harvey Braban
R. Henderson Bland
Robert Vallis
Eille Norwood

GYPSY CAVALIER, A

Stuart Blackton Production
6,740 ft
T.S. 8.22

New title of MY LADY APRIL
British Film Week 1924

D. John Stuart Blackton
C. Nicholas Musurca
Sc.
   from novel by John Overton
   (*My Lady April*)

Georges Carpentier
Flora le Breton
William Luff
Simeon Stuart
Mary Clare
Rex McDougall
Norma Whalley
Nell St John Montague
Hubert Carter
Percy Standing
A. B. Imeson
Henry Latimer

Charles Stuart Blackton
Rosalie Heath
Ursula Jeans

HANDY ANDY

Ideal
5,900 ft
T.S. 2.21

D. Bert Wynne
Sc. Eliot Stannard from novel by Samuel Lover

Kathleen Vaughan
Fred Morgan
Wallace Bosco
Warwick Ward
Peter Coleman

HAPPY ENDING

Gaumont
8,100 ft
T.S. 2.25

D. G. A. Cooper
Sc. P. L. Mannock from play by Ian Hay

Jack Buchanan
Fay Compton
Gladys Jennings
Joan Barry
Jack Hobbs

HARBOUR LIGHTS, THE

6 reels
T.S. 2.23

British Film Week 1924

D. Tom Terriss
C. William Shenton
Sc. Eliot Stannard from play by G. R. Sims and H. Pettitt

Tom Moore
Isobel Elsom

Gerald McCarthy
Judd Green
Gibson Gowland
Mary Rorke
Annette Benson
Percy Standing

HARD CASH

Master
5,150 ft
T.S. 1.21

D. Edwin J. Collins
Sc. W. Courtenay Rowden from novel by Charles Reade

Frank Arlton
Cecil Morton York
Dick Webb
Alma Green

HAVEN, THE

(1922/3) See under NIGHTHAWK

HAWK, THE

(1923 and 1924) See under HUTCH STIRS 'EM UP

HEADMASTER, THE

Astra
5,500 ft
T.S. 1.21

D. Kenelm Foss
Sc. Kenelm Foss from play by Wilfred T. Coleby and Edward Knoblock

Cyril Maude
Miles Malleson
Simeon Stuart
Lionelle Howard
Will Corrie
Gordon Craig
J. H. Batson
Margot Drake

HEAD OF THE FAMILY

Artistic
5,300 ft
T.S. 6.22

D. Manning Haynes
C. Frank Grainger
Sc. Lydia Hayward from story by W. W. Jacobs

Cynthia Murtagh
Johnny Butt
Charles Ashton
Daisy England

HEART OF A ROSE

Union Photoplays
5,600 ft
T.S. 7.19 and 10.19

D. Jack Denton
Sc. Langford Reed from story by Grenville Taylor

Stella Muir
Douglas Payne
Henry Victor

HEART OF THE MOOR

(1919) See under SECRET OF THE MOOR, THE

HEARTSTRINGS

British and Colonial
5,200 ft
T.S. 10.23

Sc. Eliot Stannard from novel by Mrs Gaskell (*The Manchester Marriage*)

Gertrude McCoy
Edith Bishop
Victor McLaglen
Kate Gurney
Russell Thorndike
Sydney Fairbrother

379

HELEN OF FOUR GATES

Hepworth
5,880 ft.
T.S. 9.20

D. C. M. Hepworth
Sc. Blanche MacIntosh from novel by
Mrs. E. Holdsworth

Alma Taylor
James Carew
George Dewhurst
John MacAndrews
Gwynne Herbert
Gerald Ames

HELL CAT

Nettlefold
6,700 ft
T.S. 3.28

D. Harry Hughes
Sc. Harry Fowler Mear from play by
Florence A. Kilpatrick (*Hell Cat
Hetty*)

Mabel Poulton
Eric Bransby Williams
Pauline Johnson
Frank Stanmore
John Hamilton
Marie Ault
Mary Dibley

HENRY, KING OF NAVARRE

Stoll
6 reels
T.S. 3.24

D. Maurice Elvey
C. J. J. Cox

Matheson Lang
H. Humberston Wright
H. Agar Lyons
Gladys Jennings
Henry Victor
Stella St. Audrie
Mme. d'Esterre

HER BENNY

Diamond Super
6,000 ft
T.S. 1.20

D. George Dewhurst
Sc. George Dewhurst from novel by
Silas K. Hocking

Anthony Johnson
Robert Vallis
C. H. Mansell
Peggy Patterson
Babs Reynolds
Sydney Wood

HER HERITAGE

5 reels
T.S. 3.19

D. Bannister Merwin
Sc. Arthur Weigall

Phyllis Monkman
Jack Buchanan
E. Holman Clark

HER LONELY SOLDIER

Barker Motion Photography
5 reels
T.S. 2.19

D. Percy Nash
Sc. Irene Miller

Daphne Glenn

HER PENALTY

Broadwest
4,700 ft
T.S. 1.21

New title of PENALTY

P. Walter West
D. Einaar Bruun
C. Benedict James

Pauline Peters
Clive Brook
Stewart Rome
Philip Hewland

HER REDEMPTION

Bertram Phillips
5 reels
T.S. 10.24

Known also as GAYEST OF THE
GAY, THE

D. Bertram Phillips
Sc.
from play by Arthur Shirley

John Stuart
Queenie Thomas
Frank Stanmore
Cecil Humphreys
Wyndham Guise
Arthur Cleave
Juliette Compton

HER SON

Broadwest
6 reels
T.S. 6.20

D. Walter West
Sc. Bertram Jacobs from play and book
by H. A. Vachell

Violet Hopson
Stewart Rome
Mercy Hatton
John Stuart
Cameron Carr

HER STORY

Samuelson
5 reels
T.S. 6.20

P. G. B. Samuelson

D. Alexander Butler
Sc. Dion Titheradge

Madge Titheradge
C. M. Hallard
Campbell Gullan

HIDDEN HAND, THE

Laurence Cowen
5 reels
T. S. 11.18

D. Lawrence Cowen
Sc. Lawrence Cowen from his own
film *It is for England* (1916) and
play

HIDDEN LIFE

Anglo-Hollandia
5,000 ft
T.S. 1920

Sc.
from novel by Robert Hichens

Anna Bosilova
Adelqui Migliar

HIGH TREASON

Gaumont
8,263 ft (sound): 7,046 ft (silent)
T.S. (1)8.29 and (2)10.29

Full talking version, British
Accoustic

D. Maurice Elvey
Sc.
from play by Pemberton Billing

Benita Hume
Jameson Thomas
Humberston Wright
Kiyoshi Takase
Basil Gill

381

HINDLE WAKES

Gaumont-British
8,800 ft
T.S. 2.27

P. Elvey–Saville–Gundrey production
D. Maurice Elvey
C. Basil Emmott
Sc.
   from play by Stanley Houghton
Art A. L. Mazzei

Estelle Brody
John Stuart
Marie Ault
Irene Rooke
Gladys Jennings
H. Humberston Wright
Alf Goddard
Cyril McLaglen
Norman McKinnell

HINE MOA

(See under ROMANCE OF HINE MOA, THE)

HIS DEAREST POSSESSION

Hepworth
5 reels
T.S. 1.19

D. Henry Edwards
C. Charles Bryce
Sc. E. Temple Thurston

Chrissie White
Henry Edwards
Esme Hubbard
John MacAndrews

HIS GRACE GIVES NOTICE

Stoll
5,900 ft
T.S. 5.24

D. W. P. Kellino
Sc.
   from play by Lady Troubridge

Henry Victor
Nora Swinburne
John Stuart
Eric Bransby Williams
Mary Brough
Gladys Hamer
Robert English

HIS HOUSE IN ORDER

Ideal
7,400 ft
T.S. 2.28

P. Meyrick Milton
D. Randle Ayrton
Sc. P. L. Mannock from play by Sir Arthur Pinero

Tallulah Bankhead
Ian Hunter
David Hawthorne
Mary Dibley
Wyndham Guise
Nancy Price

HIS LAST DEFENCE

Vanity
5 reels
T.S. 11.19 and 7.20

D. Geoffrey Wilmer
C. Phil Ross
Sc. R. Byron Webber from play by Dion Titheradge (*The K.C.*)

Mary Glynne
Dennis Neilson-Terry
Helen Haye

HIS OTHER WIFE

British Exhibitors Films
5 reels
T.S. 9.21

Sc.
   from story by George R. Sims

Marie Minetti
Eileen McGrath
Jack Raymond

HIS SUPREME SACRIFICE

(1927) See under CALL OF THE EAST

HIS WIFE'S HUSBAND

Quality
4 reels
T.S. 12.22

D. G. A. Cooper
Sc. Adrian Johnson

 Madge Stuart
 Olaf Hytten

HOBSON'S CHOICE

Master
6,000 ft
T.S. 4.20

D. Percy Nash
C. S. L. Eaton
Sc. W. Courtenay Rowden from play
 by Harold Brighouse

 Joan Ritz
 Joe Nightingale
 George Wynn
 Charles Heslop
 Ada King
 Louis Rihll

HOME MAKER, THE

George Dewhurst
5,000 ft
T.S. 1.19 and 4.20

D. George Dewhurst
Sc. Donovan Bayley

 Basil Gill
 Gwynne Herbert
 Manora Thew
 Peggy Patterson
 Jeff Barlow
 C. H. Mansell
 Lottie Blackford
 Nessie Blackford
 Trevor Bland

HONEYPOT, THE

Samuelson
6,000 ft
T.S. 10.20

 For sequel, see LOVE MAGGIE
 (1921)

D. Fred Leroy Granville
Sc.
 from novel by Countess Barcynska

 Peggy Hyland
 James Lindsay
 Campbell Gullan
 Alfred Drayton
 Lilla Laverne
 Maidie Hope
 Lillian Hall-Davis

HONOUR

Ideal
6 reels
T.S. 5.23

 Meggie Albanesi

HORNET'S NEST

Walter West
6,102 ft
T.S. 3.23

 British Film Week 1924.
 Reissued 1926 in 2-reel version

P. Walter West
Sc.
 from novel by Andrew Soutar

 Fred Wright
 Florence Turner
 James Knight
 Lewis Gilbert
 Kathleen Vaughan
 Cecil Morton York
 Nora Swinburne
 Jeff Barlow
 Arthur Walcott

HOTEL MOUSE, THE

Samuelson
6,500 ft
T.S. 7.23

D. G. B. Samuelson
Sc. Walter Summers
from play by M. Gerbidon and
M. Armont

Lillian Hall-Davis
Campbell Gullan
Josephine Earle
Warwick Ward

HOUND OF
THE BASKERVILLES

Stoll
5,000 ft
T.S. 7.21

D. Maurice Elvey
C. Germaine Burger
Sc. W. J. Elliott from story by Sir
Arthur Conan Doyle
Art. Walter Murton

Eille Norwood
Hubert Willis
Allan Jeayes
Rex McDougall
Lewis Gilbert
Fred Raynham
Mme. d'Esterre
Robert English
Robert Vallis

HOUP-LA

British Screen Productions
6,722 ft
T.S. 6.28

D. Frank Miller
Sc. Arthur Phillips from play by
Hugh E. Wright and Fred Thompson

Frank Stanmore
George Bellamy
Peggy Carlisle
James Knight

HOUR OF TRIAL, THE

I. B. Davidson
5,000 ft
T.S. 1.20

Janet Alexander
Cecil Humphreys
Maud Yates

HOUSE OF MARNEY, THE

Nettlefold
6,600 ft
T.S. 1.27

D. C. M. Hepworth
Sc. Harry Hughes, from story by
John Goodwin

Alma Taylor
John Longden
James Carew
Gibb McLaughlin
Cameron Carr
John MacAndrews
Patrick Susands
Stephen Ewart

HOUSE OF PERIL, THE

H. W. Thompson
5 reels
T.S. 2.22

D. Kenelm Foss   Asst. John Miller
C. Jack Parker
Sc. Kenelm Foss from play by H. A.
Vachell based on novel by Mrs
Belloc Lowndes (*The Chink in the
Armour*)

Fay Compton
Flora le Breton
Roy Travers
A. B. Imeson
J. Nelson Ramsaye
Irene Tripod
Wallace Bosco

Right: Elvey's forecast of lon in 1949 in *High Treason*,

re Right: Maria Corda in le's *Tesha*, 1928. Set by n Gee, lighting cameraman her Brandes.

m Right: Dupont's *Atlantic*,

Top Left: Brunel's *The Cons[tant] Nymph*, 1928, showing M[abel] Poulton on the left, Ivor Nov[ello] at the head of the table and M[ary] Clare to the right of him.

Centre Left: Isabel Jeans [in] Hitchcock's *Easy Virtue*, 1[927] with sets by Clifford Pember[ton].

Bottom Left: Stage number [with] set by Alfred Junge in Dupo[nt's] *Moulin Rouge*, 1928.

HOUSE ON THE MARSH, THE

London Film Co.
5,250 ft
T.S. 3.20

D. Fred Paul
Sc.
from novel by Florence Warden

Cecil Humphreys
Peggy Patterson
Harry Welchman

HOW LORD KITCHENER WAS BETRAYED

Screenplays
6,000 ft
T.S. 11.21

D. Percy Nash
Sc. from account for *John Bull* by John Ramsay

Fred Paul

HUMAN DESIRES

Anglia
6,789 ft
T.S. 1.25

D. Burton George
C. Bert Cann

Marjorie Daw
Clive Brook
Juliette Compton
Warwick Ward

HUMAN LAW

Astra-National
7,000 ft
Premiere 5.26

D. Maurice Elvey

Isobel Elsom
Paul Richter

HUNDREDTH CHANCE, THE

Stoll
5,000 ft
T.S. 6.20

D. Maurice Elvey
C. Paul Burger
Sc. Sinclair Hill from novel by Ethel M. Dell

Mary Glynne
Sydney Seaward
Edward Arundel
Dennis Neilson-Terry
Eille Norwood

HUNTING TOWER

Welsh-Pearson
7,192 ft
T.S. 2.28

D. George Pearson   Asst. James Reardon
C. Roy Overbaugh and Bert Ford
Sc. Charles Whittaker from story by John Buchan

Sir Harry Lauder
Vera Voronina
Pat Aherne
Nancy Price
John Manners
Moore Marriott
W. Cronin Wilson

HURRICANE HUTCH IN MANY ADVENTURES

Ideal
5 reels
T.S. 3.24

D. Charles Hutchison
Sc. Eliot Stannard

Charles Hutchison
Malcolm Tod
Lionelle Howard
Warwick Ward
Daisy Campbell
Robert Vallis

HUSBAND HUNTER, THE

Samuelson
6,000 ft
T.S. 1.20

Sc.
    from novel by Olivia Roy

    Madge Titheradge
    C. M. Hallard
    Tom Reynolds
    Minna Grey

HUTCH STIRS 'EM UP

Ideal
5,200 ft
T.S. 8.23

    New title of THE HAWK
    British Film Week 1924

D. Frank Crane
Sc. Eliot Stannard

    Charles Hutchison
    Joan Barry
    Aubrey Fitzgerald
    Malcolm Tod
    Sunday Wilshin
    Gibson Gowland

HYPOCRITES, THE

Granger-Binger
6,000 ft
T.S. 2.23

D. Charles Giblyn
C. F. Boersma
Sc. Eliot Stannard from play by Henry Arthur Jones

    Wyndham Standing
    Sydney Paxton
    Gertrude Sterroll
    Harold French
    Roy Travers
    Lilian Douglas
    Mary Odette

IF FOUR WALLS TOLD

Samuelson
6,000 ft
T.S. 9.22

D. Fred Paul
Sc. Walter Summers from play by Edward Percy

    Minna Grey
    Campbell Gullan
    Fred Paul
    Lillian Hall-Davis
    John Stuart

IF YOUTH BUT KNEW

G. B. Samuelson
8,000 ft
T.S. 8.26

D. G. A. Cooper
C. Sydney Blythe
Sc.
    from story by K. C. Spier

    Lillian Hall-Davis
    Godfrey Tearle
    Mary Odette
    Wyndham Standing
    Mary Rorke
    Forrester Harvey
    Minnie Rayner

IMPERFECT LOVER, THE

Broadwest
6,000 ft
T.S. 10.21

D. Walter West
C.
Sc. P. L. Mannock from story by Andrew Soutar

    Violet Hopson
    Stewart Rome
    Cameron Carr
    Simeon Stuart
    Pauline Johnson

IMPOSSIBLE WOMAN, THE

Ideal
5 reels
T.S. 9.19

D. Meyrick Milton
Sc. from play by Haddon Chambers
from story by Anna Douglas
Sedgwick (*Tante*)

Constance Collier
Langhorne Burton
Edith Craig
Christine Rayner

IN BONDAGE

Samuelson
T.S. 8.19

'FAITH', of trilogy, FAITH,
HOPE AND CHARITY, q.v.

D. Rex Wilson
Sc. Roland Pertwee and G. B.
Samuelson

Sydney Fairbrother
Haidee Wright
C. M. Hallard

INDIAN LOVE LYRICS, THE

Stoll
6,920 ft
T.S. 7.23

British Film Week 1924

D. Sinclair Hill
C. D. P. Cooper
Sc. Sinclair Hill from poems by
Lawrence Hope (*The Garden of
Kama*) and song cycle by Amy
Woodford-Finden
Art Walter Murton
Ed. H. Leslie Brittain

Owen Nares
Catherine Calvert
Malvina Longfellow

J. Nelson Ramsaye
Pino Conti
Roy Travers
Fred Rains
Shayle Gardner
Daisy Campbell
Fred Raynham
Arthur McLaglen

INFAMOUS LADY, THE

New Era
7,500 ft
T.S. 11.28

New title of MAYFAIR

D. Geoffrey Barkas and Michael
Barringer   Asst. Roy Travers
C. Sydney Blythe   Asst. G. Drisse
Sc. Geoffrey Barkas and Michael
Barringer

Arthur Wontner
Walter Tennyson
Ruby Miller
Muriel Angelus

INFORMER, THE

British International Pictures
7,688 ft
T.S. 10.29

Part, talking, R.C.A.

D. Arthur Robison   Asst. J. Harlow
C. Werner Brandes and L. Rodgers,
T. Sparkhul
Sc. Benn Levy from novel by Liam
O'Flaherty
Art Norman Arnold   Asst. J. E. Wills
Ed. Emile de Ruelle

Lars Hanson
Lya de Putti
Dennis Wyndham
Carl Harbord
Mickey Brantford
Warwick Ward
Daisy Campbell

IN FULL CRY

Broadwest
5,000 ft
T.S. 3.21

P. Walter West
D. Einaar Bruun
Sc. Benedict James and Frank Fowell from novel by Richard Marsh

Pauline Peters
Stewart Rome
Cecil Mannering
Philip Hewland
C. Tilson-Chowne

INHERITANCE

B.A.F.C.
5,000 ft
T.S. 10.20

New title of BRED IN THE BONE

D. Wilfred Noy
Sc. S. H. Herkomer from story by H. Pullein-Thompson

Mary Odette
Jack Hobbs
Ursula Hughes
Simeon Stuart

IN HIS GRIP

Gaumont
5,900 ft
T.S. 6.21

British Film Week 1924

D. C. C. Calvert
Sc.
from novel by David Christie Murray

Cecil Morton York
Netta Westcott
David Hawthorne
Cecil du Gué
George Bellamy

INNOCENT

Stoll
5,000 ft
T.S. 2.21

D. Maurice Elvey
C. Germaine Burger
Sc. W. J. Elliott from story by Marie Corelli

Madge Stuart
Basil Rathbone
Laurence Anderson
Edward O'Neill
W. Cronin Wilson
Frank Dane
Annie Esmond
Mme d'Esterre
M. Gray Murray

INSEPARABLES, THE

Whitehall
6,586 ft
T.S. 3.29

D. Adelqui Millar Asst. John Stafford

Jerrold Robertshaw
Pat Aherne
Elissa Landi
Annette Benson
Fred Rains
Gabriel Gabrio

IN THE BLOOD

Walter West
6,000 ft
T.S. 11.23

British Film Week 1924

D. Walter West
C. G. Toni
Sc. J. Bertram Brown from novel by Andrew Soutar

Victor McLaglen
Cecil Morton York
Mrs Hayden-Coffin
John Gliddon
Lilian Douglas
Arthur Walcott
Valia
Humberston Wright
George Foley
Fred Percy
Judd Green
Clifford McLaglen
Kenneth McLaglen
Guardsman Penwell

IN THE GLOAMING

Broadwest
5,000 ft
T.S. 19.19

Sc. J. Bertram Brown from the ballad

Violet Hopson
Cameron Carr

IN THE NIGHT

Granger–Binger
5,000 ft
T.S. 1.21

D. Frankland A. Richardson
Sc.
from play by Cyril Harcourt

Dorothy Fane
Adelqui Millar
Hayford Hobbs
C. M. Hallard
Frank Dane
Gladys Jennings

IRISH MOTHER, AN

5,508 ft
T.S. 9.28

Denis O'Shea

IRON STAIR, THE

Stoll
5,000 ft
T.S. 5.20

C. Percy Strong
Sc.
from novel by Rita

Reginald Fox
Madge Stuart
Frank E. Petley
H. Agar Lyons
J. Edwards Barber

IRRESISTIBLE FLAPPER, THE

Broadwest
3,300 ft
T.S. 2.19

D. Frank Wilson

Violet Hopson
Ivy Close
Ruby Belasco
Basil Gill
Gerald Ames
Charles Vane
Mme. d'Esterre

ISLAND OF DESPAIR, THE

Stoll
6,200 ft
T.S. 5.26

D. Henry Edwards
C. D. P. Cooper
Sc. Margot Neville
Art Walter Murton

Matheson Lang
Marjorie Hume
J. Fisher White
Jean Bradin
Gordon Hopkirk
Clifford McLaglen

389

ISLAND OF WISDOM

Cairo
5,000 ft
T.S. 7.20

D. Anthony Keith
C. Walter Blakeley
Sc. Anthony Keith

Margaret Hope
Percy Standing

IT HAPPENED IN AFRICA

(1924) See under WOMEN AND
DIAMONDS

I WILL

Lucky Cat
5 reels
T.S. 7.19

D. Hubert Herrick and Kenelm Foss
Sc. Kenelm Foss

Guy Newall
Ivy Duke
Dorothy Minto
Cyril Raymond
Wallace Bosco
Bernard Vaughan

I WILL REPAY

Ideal
6,500 ft
T.S. 2.24

D. Henry Kolker

Flora le Breton
Lewis Gilbert
L. de Cordova
Georges Tréville
A. B. Imeson
Ivan Samson

JACK, SAM AND PETE

Pollock–Daring
5 reels
T.S. 11.19

Sc.
from stories by S. Clarke Hook

Manning Haynes

JOHN FOREST FINDS HIMSELF

Hepworth
5,035 ft
T.S. 11.20

D. Henry Edwards
C. Charles Bryce
Sc. H. Fowler Mear from story by
Donovan Bayley

Henry Edwards
Chrissie White
Gerald Ames
Gwynne Herbert
Henry Vibart
Eileen Dennes
Mary Brough
John MacAndrews
Hugh Clifton
Victor Prout
'MacEdwards'

JOHN HERIOT'S WIFE

Anglo–Hollandia
5,000 ft
T.S. 7.20

D.
Sc.
from novel by Claude and Alice
Askew

Mary Odette
Henry Victor
Adelqui Migliar
Anna Bosilova
Lola Cornero

JOYOUS ADVENTURES OF ARISTIDE PUJOL, THE

Kenelm Foss
5,000 ft
T.S. 3.20

P. Kenelm Foss
D. Frank Miller
Sc. Frank Miller from novel by W. J. Locke and his play (*An Adventure of Aristide Pujol*)

Kenelm Foss
Barbara Everest
Bryan Powley
Pauline Peters
Irene Drew

JUAN JOSE

(1929) See under LIFE

JUDGE NOT

London Film Co.
5,000 ft
T.S. 9.20

D. Einaar J. Bruun
Sc.
    from story by Holger Madsen

Fay Compton
Chappell Dosset
Fred Groves
Christine Silver
Mary Brough
George Bellamy
Henry Vibart
Eric Barclay
Adeline Hayden-Coffin

JUNGLE WOMAN, THE

Hurley–Stoll
6,000 ft
T.S. 12.26

D. Frank Hurley
C. Frank Hurley

Sc. Frank Hurley

Eric Bransby Williams
Grace Savieri
Jameson Thomas
Lilian Douglas
W. G. Saunders

KEEPER OF THE DOOR

Stoll
5 reels
T.S. 19.19

D. Maurice Elvey
Sc.
    from novel by Ethel M. Dell

Peggy Carlisle
Basil Gill

KILIMANJARO

(1924) See under TO KILIMANJARO

KILTIES THREE, THE

Gaiety
5,819 ft
T.S. 11.18

Bob Reed

KING OF THE CASTLE

Stoll
6,000 ft
T.S. 8.25

D. Henry Edwards
C. D. P. Cooper
Sc.
    story by Keble Howard

Marjorie Hume
Brian Aherne
Dawson Milward
Moore Marriott
Albert E. Raynor
Adeline Hayden-Coffin

391

KING'S HIGHWAY, THE

Stoll
7,500 ft
T.S. 10.27

D. Sinclair Hill   Asst. Victor Peers
C. D. P. Cooper, Desmond Dickinson
Sc. Sinclair Hill from novel by Lord
   Lytton (*Paul Clifford*)
Art Walter Murton
Titles L. H. Gordon

Matheson Lang
Joan Lockton
James Carew
Gerald Ames
Clifford Heatherley
Mark Lupino
Frank Goldsmith
Nell Emerald
George Butler
Sydney Seaward
Aubrey Fitzgerald
Gladys Crebbin
Tom Coventry
Wally Patch
Henry Latimer

KING'S MATE

(1927) See under WHITE SHEIK,
THE

KINSMAN, THE

Hepworth
5 reels
T.S. 7.19

D. Henry Edwards
C. Charles Bryce
Sc. Henry Edwards from novel by
   Mrs Alfred Sidgwick

Henry Edwards
Chrissie White
James Carew
Gwynne Herbert
Victor Prout
Judd Green

John MacAndrews
Marie Wright
Christine Rayner

KIPPS

Stoll
6,139 ft
T.S. 1.21

D. Harold Shaw
C. Silvano Balboni
Sc. Frank Miller from novel by H. G.
   Wells

George K. Arthur
Edna Flugrath
Edward Arundel
Christine Rayner
John East
Annie Esmond
Judd Green

KISSING CUP'S RACE

Broadwest
6,000 ft
T.S. 1.21

2-reel version reissued 1927

D. Walter West
Sc. Benedict James from poem by
   Campbell Rae-Brown

Violet Hopson
Gregory Scott
Clive Brook
Joe Plant
Adeline Hayden-Coffin

KITTY

British International Pictures
8,100 ft
T.S. 1.29 (silent),   6.29 (sound)

Sound parts made in U.S.A.

D. Victor Saville   Asst. M. Gaffney
C. Karl Püth

Sc. V. E. Powell from novel by
Warwick Deeping
Art Hugh Gee
'technical director': G. Burgal

Estelle Brody
John Stuart
Marie Ault
Moore Marriott
Winter Hall
Olaf Hytten
Charles Ashton
Charles Levey
Gibb McLaughlin
Jerrold Robertshaw

KITTY TAILLEUR

Granger–Binger
5 reels
T.S. 4.21

D. Frankland A. Richardson
Sc. Frank Fowell from novel by May
Sinclair

Marjorie Hume
Lewis Dayton
Nora Hayden
Ivo Dawson

KNAVE OF DIAMONDS, THE

Stoll
5,500 ft
T.S. 7.21

D. René Plaisetty
C. J. J. Cox
Sc. L. H. Gordon from novel by Ethel
M. Dell
Art Walter Murton

Mary Massart
Alec Fraser
Olaf Hytten
Cyril Percival
Annie Esmond

KNAVE OF HEARTS

Harma
5 reels
T.S. 7.19

D. F. Martin Thornton
C. Phil Ross

Evelyn Boucher
James Knight
J. Edwards Barber
H. Agar Lyons
Frank E. Petley
Jeff Barlow
Adeline Hayden-Coffin
Nessie Blackford
Lottie Blackford

KNIGHT IN LONDON, A

Blattner
6,750 ft
T.S. 3.29

D. Lupu Pick
C. Karl Freund
Sc. Charles Lincoln from story by
Mrs Horace Tremlett
Music by Edward Kunneke

Lilian Harvey
Ivy Duke
Bernard Nedell
Robin Irvine
Robert English

KNOCK-OUT, THE

Samuelson
6 reels
T.S. 5.23

P. G. B. Samuelson
D. Alexander Butler
C. Sydney Blythe
Sc. Walter Summers

Rex Davis
Lillian Hall-Davis
Tom Reynolds
Josephine Earle
Julian Royce

N*   393

LACKEY AND THE LADY, THE

B.A.F.C.
T.S. 3.19

D. Thomas Bentley
Sc.
    from novel by Tom Gallon

    Violet Graham
    Odette Goimbault
    Adelaide Grace
    Pope Stamper
    Roy Travers
    Jeff Barlow
    A. E. Matthews
    Leslie Howard
    Athol Forde

LADDIE

Master
5,000 ft
T.S. 9.20

D. Bannister Merwin
Sc. Bannister Merwin

    Sydney Fairbrother
    C. Jarvis Walter

LADY AUDLEY'S SECRET

Ideal
5,150 ft
T.S. 10.20

D. Jack Denton
C. Claude McDonnell
Sc. Eliot Stannard from novel by Mary
    Braddon and play by George
    Roberts

    Margaret Bannerman
    Hubert Willis
    Betty Farquhar
    Manning Haynes
    William Burchill
    Wallace Bosco

LADY CLARE

B.A.F.C.
6 reels
T.S. 11.19

D. Wilfred Noy
Sc. Dale Laurence (Adey Brunel)
    from poem by Tennyson

    Simeon Stuart
    Mary Forbes
    Mary Odette
    Barbara Everest
    Gladys Jennings
    Fewlass Llewellyn
    Jack Hobbs
    Charles Quartermaine
    Arthur Cleave
    Athol Forde

LADY FROM THE SEA, THE

British International Pictures
T.S. 4.30

    New title of THE GOODWIN
    SANDS

D. Castleton Knight
C. Theodor Sparkhul
Sc. Joe Grossman

    Raymond Milland
    Moore Marriott

LADY NOGGS

Progress
5,000 ft
T.S. 1.20

D. Sidney Morgan
Sc. Sidney Morgan from novel by
    Edgar Jepson and story in *Windsor*
    Magazine, and play by Cicely
    Hamilton

    Joan Morgan
    George Keene

LADY OWNER, THE

Walter West
5,750 ft
T.S. 4.23

British Film Week 1924

D. Walter West
C. G. Toni
Sc. J. Bertram Brown

Violet Hopson
James Knight
Warwick Ward
Arthur Walcott
Jeff Barlow
Fred Rains
Marjorie Benson

LADY TETLEY'S DECREE

London Film Co.
4,800 ft
T.S. 5.20

D. Fred Paul
Sc.
from play by W. E. and Sybil
Downing

Marjorie Hume
Hamilton Stewart
Sidney Lewis Ransome

LAND OF HOPE AND GLORY

G. B. Samuelson
8,700 ft
T.S. 11.27

P. G. B. Samuelson
D. Harley Knoles
C. René Guissart
Sc. Adrian Brunel from story by
Valentine Williams based on Elgar's
Anthem of Empire

Ellaline Terriss
Lyn Harding
Robin Irvine

Ruby Miller
Enid Stamp-Taylor
Henry Vibart
Daisy Campbell
Kenneth McLaglen

LAND OF MY FATHERS

Glen
5,000 ft
T.X. 9.21 and 4.23

D. Fred Rains
C. Lucien Egrot
Sc. Diana Torr

John Stuart
Edith Pearson
Yvonne Thomas
Fred Rains

LAND OF MYSTERY, THE

6,000 ft
T.S. 7.20

D. Harold Shaw
Sc. Bannister Merwin

Edna Flugrath
Fred Morgan
John M. East
Lewis Gilbert
Norman Thorp
Christine Rayner
Phyllis Bedells

LAST ADVENTURES OF
SHERLOCK HOLMES

Stoll
Series, 15 2-reelers
T.S. 3.23

D. George Ridgwell
C. Alfred Moise
Sc. George Ridgwell from stories by
A. Conan Doyle
Art Walter Murton

With Eille Norwood

The Carbuncle
The Cardboard Box
The Crooked Man
The Dancing Men
The Disappearance of Lady Carfax
The Engineer's Thumb
The Final Problem
The Gloria Scott
His Last Bow
The Mazarin Stone
The Missing Three-Quarter
The Mystery of Thor Bridge
The Silver Blaze
The Speckled Band
The Three Students

LAST POST, THE

Britannia
8,000 ft
T.S. 1.29

D. Dinah Shurey
C. D. P. Cooper
Sc. Lydia Hayward from story by Dinah Shurey

Trilby Clark
John Longden
Frank Vosper
J. Fisher White
A. B. Imeson
Alf Goddard
Johnny Butt
Cynthia Haynes

LAST ROSE OF SUMMER, THE

Samuelson
5,000 ft
T.S. 2.20

Sc. Roland Pertwee from novel by Hugh Conway

Minna Grey
Owen Nares
Tom Reynolds
Daisy Burrell

LAST WITNESS, THE

Stoll
5,960 ft
T.S. 8.25

New title of THE WITNESS

D. Fred Paul
C. J. J. Cox
Sc.
from story by F. Britten Austin
Art Walter Murton

Isobel Elsom
Fred Paul
Stella Arbenina
John Hamilton
Queenie Thomas
Aubrey Fitzgerald

LAUGHTER AND TEARS

Granger–Binger
6,000 ft
T.S. 9.21

D. B. E. Doxat–Pratt
Sc. Adelqui Millar

Adelqui Millar
Maudie Dunham
Evelyn Brent
Dorothy Fane
E. Story Gofton
Bert Darley

LAUNDRY GIRL, THE

Hooper–Mellor
5 reels
T.S. 19.19

D. A. G. Frenguelli
Sc.
from story by Edith Mellor

John Gliddon
Geoffrey Wilmer

LAW DIVINE, THE

Master
5,000 ft
T.S. 11.20

D. Challis N. Sanderson and Harry B. Parkinson
Sc. Frank Miller from story by H. V. Esmond

H. V. Esmond
Eva Moore
John Reid
Evelyn Brent
Mary Brough

LIFE

Whitehall
7,147 ft
T.S. 1.29

New title of JUAN JOSE

D. Adelqui Millar
Sc.
from play by Joachim Dicenta (*Juan Jose*)

Adelqui Millar
Marie Ault
Marcel Vibert
Manuelito del Rio

LIFE OF LORD BYRON, THE

(1922) See under PRINCE OF LOVERS, A

LIFE OF ROBERT BURNS, THE

Burns-Scott
T.S. 10.26

D. Maurice Sandground

LIFE ON THE OCEAN WAVE

British Instructional Films
5,000 ft
T.S. 4.26

LIGHTS OF HOME, THE

British Exhibitors Films
5,000 ft
T.S. 12.20

D. Fred Paul
Sc.
from play by G. R. Sims and Robert Buchanan

George Foley
Nora Hayden
Jack Raymond
Cecil Morton York
John Stuart

LIGHTS O' LONDON

Gaumont
7,386 ft
T.S 9.23
British Film Week 1924

D. C. C. Calvert
Sc.
from play by G. R. Sims

Cecil Morton York
Nigel Barrie
H. R. Hignett
Mary Brough
James Lindsay
Mary Clare
Wanda Hawley

LIGHT WOMAN, A

Gainsborough
7,300 ft
T.S. 12.28

D. Adrian Brunel
C. Claude McDonnell
Sc. Adrian Brunel and Angus Macphail from story by Adey Brunel ('Dale Laurence')

Benita Hume
C. M. Hallard
Gerald Ames
Donald McCardle

LIKENESS OF THE NIGHT, THE

British Exhibitors Films
5,000 ft
T.S. 2.21

D. Percy Nash
Sc.
    from play by Mrs W. K. Clifford

    Renée Kelly
    Minna Grey
    Hubert Willis
    Arthur Cullin

LILAC SUNBONNET

Progress
5,250 ft
T.S. 7.22

D. Sidney Morgan
C. S. J. Mumford
Sc.
    from story by S. R. Crockett

    Joan Morgan
    Warwick Ward
    Pauline Peters
    Arthur Lennard
    Arthur Walcott
    Forrester Harvey

LILY OF KILLARNEY, THE

British International Pictures
6,100 ft
T.S. 2.29

    New title of THE COLLEEN BAWN

D. George Ridgwell
Sc.
    from play by Dion Boucicault (*The Colleen Bawn*) from novel *The Collegians*

    Gillean Dean
    Barbara Gott
    Dennis Wyndham

    J. Fisher White
    Wilfred Shine
    Janet Alexander
    Edward O'Neill
    Pamela Parr

LILY OF THE ALLEY

Hepworth
7,000 ft
T.S. 2.23

    British Film Week 1924

D. Henry Edwards
C. Charles Bryce

    Henry Edwards
    Chrissie White
    Frank Stanmore
    Campbell Gullan
    Lionel d'Aragon
    Mary Brough

LINKED BY FATE

Samuelson
6 reels
T.S. 8.19

D. Albert Ward
Sc.
    from novel by Charles Garvice

    Malcolm Cherry
    Isobel Elsom
    Esme Hubbard
    Bernard Vaughan
    E. A. Douglas
    Manning Haynes
    George Goodwin
    Barbara Gott

LION'S MOUSE, THE

Granger–Binger
5 reels
T.S. 4.23

D. Oscar Apfel

Sc.
from novel by C. N. and A. M.
Williamson

Wyndham Standing
Mary Odette
Rex Davis

LITTLE BIT OF FLUFF, A

Kew Films
5 reels
T.S. 1919

D. Kenelm Foss
C. Lucien Egrot
Sc. Kenelm Foss from play by Walter
W. Ellis

Ernest Thesiger
Alfred Drayton
Bertie Wright
Esme Hubbard
James Lindsay
Dorothy Minto
Gladys Jennings

LITTLE BIT OF FLUFF, A

British International Pictures
7,900 ft
T.S. 5.28

D. Jess Robins
C. René Guissart and G. W. Pocknall
Sc. Wheeler Dryden from play by
Walter W. Ellis
Art C. W. Arnold
Ed. Ben Travers and Syd Chaplin
Titles Ben Travers and Ralph Spence

Syd Chaplin
Betty Balfour
Clifford McLaglen
Annie Esmond
Enid Stamp-Taylor
Cameron Carr
Plaza Tiller Girls

LITTLE BROTHER OF GOD

Stoll
6,000 ft
T.S. 4.22

D. F. Martin Thornton
C. Percy Strong
Sc. L. H. Gordon from novel by L. H.
Gordon
Art Walter Murton

Victor McLaglen
Alec Fraser
Fred Raynham
Valia
Bert Wright
Lionelle Howard
Bob Vallis
J. Edwards Barber

LITTLE CHILD SHALL LEAD THEM, A

Bertram Phillips
5 reels
T.S. 7.19

D. Bertram Phillips
C. Percy Anthony
Sc. Bay Rothe

Queenie Thomas
Bruce Gordon
Adeline Hayden-Coffin
Alice de Winton

LITTLE DEVIL-MAY-CARE

Gaumont, Anglo–French production
7 reels
T.S. 9.27

D. Marcel l'Herbier

Betty Balfour
Jacques Catelaine

LITTLE DOOR INTO THE WORLD, THE

(1923) See under EVIL THAT MEN DO, THE

LITTLE DORRIT

Progress
6,250 ft
T.S. 8.20

D. Sidney Morgan
C. S. J. Mumford
Sc.
　　from novel by Charles Dickens

　　Lady Tree
　　Langhorne Burton
　　Joan Morgan

LITTLE HOUR OF PETER WELLS, THE

Granger–Binger
5,000 ft
T.S. 8.20

Sc. Eliot Stannard from novel by David Whitelaw

　　Heather Thatcher
　　O. B. Clarence

LITTLE MISS LONDON

6,912 ft
T.S. 3.29

D. Harry Hughes

　　Pamela Parr
　　Frank Stanmore
　　Reginald Fox
　　Pauline Johnson
　　Eric Bransby Williams

LITTLE MISS NOBODY

5,500 ft
T.S. 6.23

　　British Film Week 1924

D. Wilfred Noy
Sc.
　　from play by H. Graham

　　Flora le Breton
　　Aubrey Fitzgerald
　　Ben Field
　　Sydney Paxton
　　Donald Searle
　　Gladys Jennings
　　John Stuart
　　Eva Westlake
　　James Reardon

LITTLE MOTHER

Ideal
5,700 ft
T.S. 3.22

D. A. V. Bramble
Sc. May Wynne

　　Florence Turner
　　John Stuart
　　Lilian Douglas
　　Harvey Braban

LITTLE PEOPLE, THE

Welsh–Pearson
7,500 ft
T.S. 4.26 and 6.26

D. George Pearson Asst. James Reardon
C. Percy Strong
Sc. George Pearson and Thorold Dickinson
Art Cavalcanti
Ed. Fred Pullin
Puppet craft Henri Gad

Mona Maris
Frank Stanmore
Gerald Ames
Randle Ayrton
James Reardon
Barbara Gott
Harry Furniss

LITTLE WELSH GIRL, THE

5,250 ft
T.S. 4.20

Christine Silver
Humberston Wright

LITTLE WORLD APART, A

(1922) See under FIRES OF
INNOCENCE

LIVINGSTONE

Hero
6,500 ft
Premiere 9.25

Reissued as 6 shorts of 1,050 ft
each in 1927–8

D. M. A. Wetherell
C. Gustav Pauli

M. A. Wetherell

LODGER, THE

Gainsborough
7,685 ft
T.S. 9.26

P. Michael Balcon
D. Alfred Hitchcock   Asst. Alma
Reville
C. Baron Ventimiglia

Sc. Eliot Stannard and Alfred Hitch-
cock from novel by Mrs. Belloc
Lowndes
Art Bertram Evans and C. W. Arnold
Ed. Ivor Montagu (and subtitles)
Art titles McKnight Kauffer

Ivor Novello
June
Marie Ault
Malcolm Keen
Arthur Chesney

LONDON

British National
5,581 ft
T.S. 1.27

D. Herbert Wilcox
Sc.
from story by Thomas Burke

Dorothy Gish
Margaret Yarde
Adelqui Millar
John Manners
Adeline Hayden-Coffin

LONDON LOVE

Gaumont
7,560 ft
T.S. 7.26

D. Manning Haynes
C. W. Shenton
Sc. Lydia Hayward

Fay Compton
John Stuart
Miles Mander
Moore Marriott
A. B. Imeson
Humberston Wright
Arthur Walcott
Leal Douglas

LONDON PRIDE

London Film Co.
5,000 ft
T.S. 2.20

D. Harold Shaw
Sc. Bannister Merwin from play by
Gladys Unger and Neil Lyons

Fred Groves
Edna Flugrath
Frank Stanmore
O. B. Clarence
Edward Arundel
Mary Brough
Douglas Munro
Mary Dibley
Cyril Percival
Constance Backner
Lottie Blackford
George Turner

LONELY LADY OF GROSVENOR
SQUARE, THE

Ideal
4,600 ft
T.S. 3.22

D. Frank Crane
Sc. Sinclair Hill and Arthur Walton
from novel by Mrs Henry de la
Pasture

Betty Faire
Gertrude Sterroll
Mrs Hubert Willis
Arthur Pusey
Dorothy Fane
Daisy Campbell
Eileen McGrath
Ralph Forster
A. Harding Steerman
Jack Hobbs

LONG ODDS

Stoll
5 reels

T.S. 5.22

D. A. E. Coleby
Sc. A. E. Coleby

A. E. Coleby
H. Nicholls Bates
Edith Bishop

LORNA DOONE

Lucoque
5,000 ft
T.S. 2.20

D. H. Lisle Lucoque
Sc. Nellie Lucoque from novel by R.
D. Blackmore

Gordon Craig
Dennis Wyndham
Bertie Gordon
George Bellamy
Cecil Morton York
Frank Dane

LOST LEADER, THE

Stoll
T.S. 1922

D. George Ridgwell
Sc.
from novel by E. Phillips Oppenheim

LOST PATROL, THE

British Instructional Films
7,250 ft
T.S. 2.29

D. Walter Summers
Sc.
from novel by Philip MacDonald
(*Patrol*)

Cyril McLaglen

LOUDWATER MYSTERY, THE

Broadwest
4,800 ft
T.S. 2.21

P. Walter West
D. Norman McDonald
Sc. Benedict James from novel by
Edgar Jepson

Cameron Carr
Gregory Scott
Pauline Peters
Clive Brook
Arthur Walcott
C. Tilson-Chowne

LOVE AND THE WHIRLWIND

Alliance
6 reels
T.S. 3.24

D. Harold Shaw
Sc.
from novel by Helen Prothero
Lewis

Clive Brook
Marjorie Hume
Arthur Cullin
Edward O'Neill
Frank Goldsmith
Reginald Fox

LOVE AT THE WHEEL

Master
5,500 ft
T.S. 9.21

D. Bannister Merwin
Sc. Harry B. Parkinson

Pauline Johnson
Victor Humphreys
Clare Greet
Annette Benson
A. Harding Steerman

LOVE IN THE WELSH HILLS

Regent
5,800 ft
T.S. 1.24

D. Bernard Dudley
C. John Mackenzie

Marjorie Villis
James Knight
Constance Worth

LOVE IN THE WILDERNESS

Samuelson
5,000 ft
T.S. 5.20

P. G. B. Samuelson
D. Alexander Butler
Sc.
from novel by Gertrude Page

Madge Titheradge
C. M. Hallard
Campbell Gullan
Maudie Dunham

LOVE, LIFE AND LAUGHTER

Welsh–Pearson
6,300 ft
T.S. 5.23 and 5.27
New title of TIP TOES
British Film Week 1924
Reissued in 1927 as 6,500 ft

D. George Pearson Asst. Leslie
Hiscott
C. Percy Strong (London night photo-
graphy by A. H. Blake)
Sc. George Pearson

Betty Balfour
Harry Jonas
Frank Stanmore
Annie Esmond
Nancy Price
Sydney Fairbrother
A. Harding Steerman
Gordon Hopkirk
Dacia

LOVE MAGGIE

Samuelson
6,000 ft
T.S. 2.21

Sequel to THE HONEYPOT
(1920)

D. Fred Leroy Granville
Sc. Colden Lore

Peggy Hyland
James Lindsay
Campbell Gullan
Maudie Dunham
Maidie Hope
Lillian Hall-Davis

LOVERS IN ARABY

Atlas–Biocraft
5,200 ft
T.S. 5.24

D. Adrian Brunel

Annette Benson
Adrian Brunel
Miles Mander
Norman Penrose

LOVES OF MARY QUEEN OF SCOTS, THE

Denison Clift Art Productions
8 reels
T.S. 11.23

New title of MARIE, QUEEN
OF SCOTS
British Film Weeks 1924

D. Denison Clift
C. William Shenton
Sc. Denison Clift

Gerald Ames
Lionel d'Aragon
Fay Compton
Ellen Compton
Irene Rooke
Betty Faire
Nancy Kenyon

Dorothy Fane
Julie Hartley-Milburne
Donald McCardle
E. A. Douglas
Harvey Braban
Ivan Samson
John Stuart
Sydney Seaward

LOVE'S OPTION

Welsh–Pearson–Elder
5,980 ft
T.S. 9.28

New title of A GIRL OF TODAY

D. George Pearson Asst. Denis
Shipwright
C. Bernard Knowles Asst. Fred Ford
Sc.
from novel by Douglas Newton
(*The Riddle*)
Ed. Asst. Thorold Dickinson

James Carew
Henry Vibart
Pat Aherne
Dorothy Boyd

LOVE STORY OF ALIETTE BRUNTON, THE

Stoll
7,450 ft
T.S. 8.24

D. Maurice Elvey
C. J. J. Cox
Sc. Alicia Ramsey, from novel by
Gilbert Frankau
Art W. Murton
Ed. H. Leslie Brittain

Isobel Elsom
Henry Victor
James Carew
Adeline Hayden-Coffin
Lewis Gilbert
H. Humberston Wright
Minnie Leslie
Robert Vallis

LOWLAND CINDERELLA, A

Progress
5 reels
T.S. 12.21

D. Sidney Morgan
C. S. J. Mumford
Sc.
 from novel by S. R. Crockett

 Joan Morgan
 Ralph Forbes
 George Foley
 Mavis Clare

LUCK OF THE NAVY, THE

Graham–Wilcox
8,000 ft
T.S. 11.27

D. Fred Paul
C. Claude McDonnell
Sc.
 from play by Mrs Clifford Mills

 Evelyn Laye
 Henry Victor
 Robert Cunningham
 Hayford Hobbs
 Norma Whalley
 H. Agar Lyons
 William Freshman
 Zoe Palmer
 Wally Patch

LUNATIC AT LARGE, THE

Hepworth
5,800 ft
T.S. 3.21

D. Henry Edwards
C. Charles Bryce
Sc. George Dewhurst from novel by J.
 Storer Clouston

 Henry Edwards

 Chrissie White
 Gwynne Herbert
 George Dewhurst
 Buena Bent
 James Annand
 John MacAndrews

LURE OF CROONING WATER, THE

George Clark
5,000 ft
T.S. 1.20

D. A. H. Rooke
C. J. Rosenthal
Sc. Guy Newall from novel by Marion
 Hill
Art Charles Dalmon

 Ivy Duke
 Guy Newall
 Mary Dibley
 Hugh C. Buckler
 Douglas Munro
 Arthur Chesney
 Lawford Davidson
 Winifred Sadler
 Chun Ah Moy

MADAME POMPADOUR

British International Pictures
9,200 ft
T.S. 4.28

D. Herbert Wilcox
C. Roy Overbaugh
Sc.
 from play by Frederick Lonsdale
 and Harry Graham

 Dorothy Gish
 Antonio Moreno
 Henri Bosc
 Gibb McLaughlin
 Nelson Keys
 Marie Ault
 Cyril McLaglen

MADEMOISELLE FROM ARMENTIÈRES

Gaumont
7,900 ft
T.S. 9.26

P.   A. C. and R. C. Bromhead
D.   Maurice Elvey
C.   W. Shenton
Sc. Victor Saville and V. G. Gundrey
Art A. L. Mazzei

    Estelle Brody
    John Stuart
    Marie Ault
    Alf Goddard
    Humberston Wright
    John Hamilton
    Clifford Heatherley
    Albert Raynor
    Gabriel Rosca

MADEMOISELLE PARLEY VOO

Gaumont
7,300 ft
T.S. 6.28

D.   Maurice Elvey
Sc. F. V. Merrick and Jack Harris

    Estelle Brody
    John Stuart
    Alf Goddard
    Humberston Wright
    Wallace Bosco
    John Longden

MAGIC SKIN, THE

British and Colonial
6,000 ft
T.S. 1.20

    New title of DESIRE

D.   George Ridgwell

Sc.
    from novel by Balzac (*La Peau de Chagrin*)

    Yvonne Arnaud
    Dennis Neilson-Terry
    Austen Leigh
    Christine Maitland
    Saba Raleigh
    Pardoe Woodman

MAGISTRATE, THE

Samuelson
5,400 ft
T.S. 5.21

D.   Bannister Merwin
Sc. Bannister Merwin from play by Sir Arthur Pinero

    Tom Reynolds
    Roy Royston
    Dawson Milward
    Maudie Dunham

MAID OF THE SILVER SEA, THE

George Clark
5,000 ft
T.S. 11.22

D.   Guy Newall
Sc. Guy Newall from novel by John Oxenham

    Guy Newall
    Ivy Duke
    A. Bromley Davenport

MAISIE'S MARRIAGE

(1923) See under MARRIED LIFE

MANCHESTER MAN, THE

Ideal
5,000 ft
T.S. 10.20

D. Bert Wynne
Sc. Eliot Stannard from novel by
    Mrs Linnaeus Banks

    Hubert Willis
    Hayford Hobbs
    William Burchill
    A. Harding Steerman
    Dora de Winton
    Warwick Ward
    Aileen Bagot

MAN FROM HOME, THE

Famous–Lasky
6,800 ft
T.S. 6.22

D. George Fitzmaurice
C. A. Miller
Sc. Ouida Bergere from play by Booth
    Tarkington and Harry Leon Wilson

    Anna Q. Nilsson
    James Kirkwood

MAN'S SHADOW, A

Progress
5,510 ft
T.S. 12.20

D. Sidney Morgan
C. S. J. Mumford
Sc. Sidney Morgan from play by
    Robert Buchanan from the French

    Langhorne Burton
    Violet Graham
    Gladys Mason
    Arthur Lennard
    J. Denton Thompson
    Sydney Paxton
    Babs Reynolds

MAN WHO FORGOT, THE

Harma
6 reels
T.S. 9.19

D. F. Martin Thornton
Sc. F. Martin Thornton from story
    by Reuben Gilmer

    Marjorie Villis
    Bernard Dudley
    James Knight
    H. Agar Lyons
    James Barber
    Evelyn Boucher

MAN WHO WON, THE

Samuelson
6 reels
T.S. 1.19

D. Rex Wilson

    Isobel Elsom
    Owen Nares
    C. M. Hallard
    Minna Grey

MAN WITHOUT DESIRE, THE

Atlas Biocraft
7,000 ft
T.S. 12.23

D. Adrian Brunel
C. Henry Harris
Sc. Frank Fowell from idea by Monck-
    ton Hoffe

    Ivor Novello
    Nina Vanna
    Sergio Mari
    Adrian Brunel
    Jane Dryden (Babs Brunel)

MANXMAN, THE

British International Pictures
8,163 ft
T.S. 1.29

P. John Maxwell
D. Alfred Hitchcock Asst. Frank Mills
C. J. J. Cox
Sc. Eliot Stannard from novel by Sir Hall Caine
Art C. Wilfred Arnold
Ed. Emile de Ruelle

Carl Brisson
Malcolm Keen
Anny Ondra
Randle Ayrton
Kim Peacock
Clare Greet

MARCH HARE, THE

Lucky Cat
5 reels
T.S. 8.19

D. Frank Miller
C. Bert Ford
Sc. Frank Miller from story by Guy Newall

Guy Newall
Ivy Duke
Will Corrie
Lewis Gilbert
Philip Hewland

MARIA MARTEN

Ideal
7,430 ft
T.S. 3.28

D. Walter West
C. Phil Ross

Warwick Ward
Trilby Clark
Dora Barton

Frank Parfitt
James Knight
Chili Bouchier
Judd Green
Vesta Sylva

MARIE, QUEEN OF SCOTS

(1923) See under LOVES OF MARY QUEEN OF SCOTS, THE

MARQUIS OF BOLIBAR, THE

See under BOLIBAR

MARRIAGE LINES, THE

Master
5,750 ft
T.S. 11.21

D. Wilfred Noy
Sc. Wilfred Noy from novel by J. S. Fletcher

Sam Livesey
C. Tilson-Chowne
Barbara Hoffe
Lewis Dayton
Arthur Walcott

MARRIED LIFE

Ideal
5,000 ft
T.S. 10.21

D. Georges Tréville
Sc. Adrian Johnson from play by J. B. Bucktone

Gerald McCarthy
Hilda Anthony
Peggy Hathaway

MARRIED LIFE

Napoleon
6,200 ft
T.S. 5.23

New title of MARRIED LOVE or MAISIE'S MARRIAGE

P. G. B. Samuelson
D. Walter Summers
C. Sydney Blythe
Sc. Marie C. Stopes and Walter Summers

Lillian Hall-Davis
Sam Livesey
Sydney Fairbrother
Rex Davis
Mary Brough
Bert Darley

MARRIED LOVE

(1923) See under MARRIED LIFE

MARRIED TO A MORMON

6,000 ft
T.S. 4.22

Evelyn Brent
Clive Brook

MARY FIND THE GOLD

Welsh–Pearson
6,400 ft
T.S. 3.21

D. George Pearson
C. Emile Lauste
Sc. George Pearson
Art titles Ernest Jones

Betty Balfour
Hugh E. Wright
Arthur Cleave
T. Weguelin
Tom Coventry
Mabel Poulton
Gladys Hamer
Mary Dibley

MASTER AND MAN

British Screen Productions
8,700 ft
T.S. 2.29

D. G. A. Cooper
C. Gustav Pauli
Sc. G. A. Cooper from play by Henry Pettitt and G. R. Sims
Art James Carter

Henri de Vries
Anne Grey
Humberston Wright
Betty Siddons
Maurice Braddell
Frank Stanmore
Olaf Hytten
Mary Brough

MASTER OF CRAFT, A

Ideal
4,700 ft
T.S. 4.22

D. Thomas Bentley
Sc. Eliot Stannard from story by W. W. Jacobs

Fred Groves

MATING OF MARCUS, THE

Stoll
6,000 ft
T.S. 7.24

D. W. P. Kellino
Sc.
from story by Mabel Barnes Grundy

Moore Marriott
David Hawthorne
George Bellamy
Billie and Dollie
Mme. d'Esterre

MAYFAIR

(1928) See under INFAMOUS LADY, THE

MAYOR OF CASTERBRIDGE, THE

Progress
5,500 ft
T.S. 11.21

D. Sidney Morgan
C. S. J. Mumford
Sc. Sidney Morgan from novel by Thomas Hardy

Fred Groves
Mavis Clare
Pauline Peters
Warwick Ward

MEG

5,000 ft
T.S. 10.27

C. W. H. Shaw
Sc. Arnold Tolson

Yorkshire cast

MELODY OF DEATH, THE

Stoll
5 reels
1921

D. F. Martin Thornton
C   Percy Strong
Sc. L. H. Gordon from story by Edgar Wallace
Art Walter Murton

Hetta Bartlett
Philip Anthony
H. Agar Lyons

MEMBER OF TATTERSALLS, A

Samuelson
6 reels
T.S. 10.19

D. Albert Ward
Sc. Albert Ward from play

Tom Reynolds
Campbell Gullan
James Lindsay
Isobel Elsom
Malcolm Cherry

MIRAGE

George Clark
5 reels
T.S. 1.23

D. A. H. Rooke
Sc. Ivy Duke from story by E. Temple Thurston

Edward O'Neill
Douglas Munro
Blanche Stanley
Dorothy Holmes-Gore
Geoffrey Kerr
Guy Newall
Ivy Duke

MIRANDA OF THE BALCONY

(1924) See under SLAVES OF DESTINY

MIRIAM ROZELLA

Astra–National
7,500 ft
T.S. 3.24

D. Sidney Morgan
C. S. J. Mumford
Sc.
    from serial by B. L Farjeon

Owen Nares

Gertrude McCoy
Moyna MacGill
Mary Brough
Sydney Paxton
Ben Webster
Russell Thorndike
Nina Boucicault
Gordon Craig

MISS CHARITY

Master
5,000 ft
T S. 9.21

D. Edwin J. Collins
Sc.
from novel by Keble Howard

Joan Lockton
Dick Webb

MIST IN THE VALLEY

Hepworth
6,820 ft
T.S. 3.23

British Film Week 1924

D. C. M. Hepworth
Sc.
from novel by Dorin Craig

Alma Taylor
G. H. Mulcaster
Gwynne Herbert
James Carew
Lionel d'Aragon
Douglas Munro
Charles Vane
John MacAndrews
Fred Rains
Esme Hubbard
Maud Cressall

M'LORD OF THE WHITE ROAD

Granger–Davidson

6,800 ft
T.S. 11.23

D. A. H. Rooke
C. Leslie Eveleigh
Sc. Kinchen Wood from novel by
Cedric D. Fraser

Victor McLaglen
Majorie Hume
James Lindsay
Mary Rorke

MONEY

Ideal
5,400 ft
T.S. 6.21

D. Duncan McRae
Sc. Eliot Stannard from play by
Lord Lytton

Henry Ainley
Sydney Paxton
Margot Drake
Ethel Newman
James Lindsay
Olaf Hytten
Faith Bevan

MONEY HABIT, THE

Granger–Commonwealth
6,200 ft
T.S. 1.24

D. Walter Niebuhr
C. Baron Ventimiglia
Sc. Alicia Ramsey from story by
Paul Potter

Nina Vanna
Clive Brook
Warwick Ward
Annette Benson
Fred Rains
Eva Westlake

MONEY ISN'T EVERYTHING

Stoll
5,000 ft
T.S. 2.25

D. Thomas Bentley
Sc.
from story by Sophie Cole

Olive Sloane
Lewis Gilbert
Gladys Hamer
John Hamilton

MONKEYNUTS

Gaumont (French film)
7,500 ft
T.S. 5.28

D. Louis Mercanton
Sc.
Edited and titled P. L. Mannock

Betty Balfour
Walter Butler

MONKEY'S PAW

Artistic
5,700 ft
T.S. 2.23

British Film Week 1924

D. Manning Haynes
C. Frank Grainger
Sc. Lydia Haywood and Manning Haynes from story by W. W. Jacobs

Moore Marriott
A. B. Imeson
Marie Ault
Charles Ashton
Johnny Butt
George Wynne
Tom Coventry

MONS

British Instructional Films
7,500 ft
T.S. 9.26

New title of THE RETREAT FROM MONS

P. Walter Summers
C. Stanley Rodwell and Horace Wheddon

MONTE CARLO

Gaumont–Phocea (Anglo–French film)
8,750 ft
T.S. 9.25

D. Louis Mercanton

Betty Balfour
Carlyle Blackwell
Robert English

MONTY WORKS THE WIRES

Artistic
5,000 ft
T.S. 6.21

P. George E. Redman
D. Challis N. Sanderson and Manning Haynes
C. Frank Grainger
Sc. Lydia Hayward and Manning Haynes
Ed. Challis N. Sanderson

'Montmorency'
Manning Haynes
Mildred Evelyn
Eva Westlake
Gladys Hamer

MOON OF ISRAEL

Stoll–Sascha (Anglo–Austrian production)
10 reels
T.S. and first run 11.24

D. Michael Curtiz
Sc.
    from novel by Sir H. Rider Haggard

    Adelqui Millar
    Maria Corda

MOORS AND MINARETS

Novello–Atlas Renters
6 1-reelers
T S. 12.23

D. Adrian Brunel

MORD EM'LY

Welsh–Pearson
6 reels
T.S. 1.22

D. George Pearson
C. Emile Lauste
Sc. Eliot Stannard from story by Pett Ridge

    Betty Balfour
    Fred Groves

MOTH AND RUST

Progress
5,000 ft
T.S. 11.21

D. Sidney Morgan
C. S. J. Mumford
Sc.
    from story by Mary Cholmondeley

Sybil Thorndike
Malvina Longfellow
Langhorne Burton
George Bellamy

MOTHERLAND

Samuelson
7.002 ft
T.S. 10.27

D. G. B. Samuelson

    Rex Davis
    A. Harding Steerman
    Eva Moore
    James Knight

MOTORING

International Ciné
5,506 ft
T.S. 3.29

D. George Dewhurst

    Harry Tate

MOULIN ROUGE

British International Pictures
10,500 ft
T.S. 5.28

D. E. A. Dupont
C. Werner Brandes, James Rogers
Art Alfred Jünge

    Olga Tschechova
    Eve Gray
    Jean Bradin
    Forrester Harvey
    Georges Tréville
    Marcel Vibert
    Blanche Bernis

MOUNTAIN EAGLE, THE

Gainsborough–Emelka
7,503 ft
T.S. 10.26

    Called FEAR O'GOD in U.S.A.

P. Michael Balcon
D. Alfred Hitchcock Asst. Alma Reville
C. Baron Ventimiglia
Sc. Eliot Stannard and Charles Lapworth
Art Willy and Ludwig Reiber

    Nita Naldi
    Bernhard Goetzke
    John Hamilton
    Malcolm Keen
    Ferdinand Martini

MR GILFIL'S LOVE STORY

Ideal
5,400 ft
T.S. 4.20

D. A. V. Bramble
C. Horace Wheddon
Sc. A. Weiner from story by George Eliot (in *Scenes of Clerical Life*)

    Mary Odette
    R. Henderson Bland
    John Boella
    A. Harding Steerman
    Dora de Winton
    Peter Upcher
    Aileen Bagot
    Norma Whalley
    Irene Drew

MR JUSTICE RAFFLES

Hepworth
6 reels
T.S. 10.21

P. C. M. Hepworth
D. Gerald Ames and Gaston Queribet
Sc. Blanche MacIntosh from novel by E. W. Hornung

    Gerald Ames
    Eileen Dennes
    James Carew
    Hugh Clifton
    Gwynne Herbert
    Henry Vibart

MR PIM PASSES BY

Samuelson
6,077 ft
T.S. 4.21

D. Albert Ward
Sc.
    from play by A. A. Milne

    Peggy Hyland
    Campbell Gullan
    Maudie Dunham
    Henry Kendall
    Wyndham Guise
    Tom Reynolds
    Hubert Harben
    Annie Esmond

MR PREEDY AND THE COUNTESS

Welsh–Pearson
1925

D. George Pearson
C. Percy Strong
Sc.
    from play by R. C. Carton

    Mona Maris
    Frank Stanmore
    Buena Bent
    Gladys Hamer
    Gibb McLaughlin
    A. Harding Steerman
    Annie Esmond

MRS ERRICKER'S REPUTATION

Hepworth
5,780 ft
T.S. 12.20

D. C. M. Hepworth

Sc. Blanche MacIntosh from novel by
Thomas Cobb

Alma Taylor
Gerald Ames
Gwynne Herbert
James Carew
Eileen Dennes

MRS THOMPSON

Samuelson
5,000 ft
T.S. 12.19

D. Rex Wilson
Sc.
from novel by W. B. Maxwell

Minna Grey
Isobel Elsom
Wyndham Guise
Bertram Burleigh
Marie Wright
C. M. Hallard
James Lindsay
Tom Reynolds

MR WU

Stoll
T.S. 10.19

D. Maurice Elvey
C. Paul Burger
Sc. Frederick Blatchford from play by
Harry M. Vernon and Harold
Owen
Art W. Murton

Matheson Lang
Lillah McCarthy
Meggie Albanesi
Edward Arundel
Roy Royston

MUMSIE

Herbert Wilcox
6,858 ft
T.S. 9.27

D. Herbert Wilcox   Asst. Robert
Cullen

C. Bernard Knowles
Sc.
from play by Edward Knoblock

Pauline Frederick
Herbert Marshall
Nelson Keys
Frank Stanmore
Donald McCardle

MY LADY APRIL

(1922) See under GYPSY CAVALIER,
A

MY LORD CONCEIT

Stoll
6,000 ft
T.S. 2.21

D. F. Martin Thornton
Sc.
from novel by Rita

Evelyn Boucher
Maresco Marisini
J. Edwards Barber
Frank E. Petley

MYSTERY OF DR
FU-MANCHU, THE

Stoll
Series, 15 2-reelers
T.S. 5.23

D. A. E. Coleby
C. D. P. Cooper
Sc. A. E. Coleby and Frank Wilson
from stories by Sax Rohmer
Art Walter Murton
With: H. Agar Lyons

The Cry of the Nighthawk
The Fiery Hand
The Fungi Cellars
The Miracle
The Queen of Hearts
The Sacred Order
The Shrine of Seven Lamps
The Silver Buddha, etc.

415

MYSTERY OF MR BERNARD BROWN, THE

Stoll
5 reels
T.S. 1920

D. Sinclair Hill
C. John Mackenzie
Sc. Mrs Sidney Groom from story by
E. Phillips Oppenheim

Edward Arundel
Pardoe Woodman
Clifford Heatherley
Norma Whalley
Frank E. Petley

MYSTERY ROAD, THE

Famous Players–Lasky British
6,800 ft
T.S. 10.21

D. Paul Powell
C. Claude McDonnell
Sc.
from novel by E. Phillips
Oppenheim

Mary Glynn
David Powell
Ruby Miller
Irene Tripod
Percy Standing
Lewis Gilbert
Pardoe Woodman
Arthur Cullin

NAKED MAN, THE

Hepworth
5,500 ft
T.S. 11.23

British Film Week 1924

D. Henry Edwards
C. Charles Bryce
Sc.
from play by Leon M. Lion and
Tom Gallon (*Felix Gets a Month*)

Henry Edwards
Chrissie White
Stephen Ewart
Gwynne Herbert
Maud Cressall
James Carew
E. Holman Clark
Henry Vibart
Frank Stanmore
Jean Cadell

NANCE

Samuelson
5,000 ft
T.S. 7.20

D. Albert Ward
Sc.
from novel by Charles Garvice

Isobel Elsom
Mary Forbes
James Lindsay
Ivan Samson
Bassett Roe

NARROW VALLEY, THE

Hepworth
5,000 ft
T.S. 6.21

D. C. M. Hepworth
Sc. George Dewhurst

Alma Taylor
George Dewhurst
James Carew
Gwynne Herbert
Hugh Clifton
Lottie Blackford
Nessie Blackford

NATURE OF THE BEAST, THE

Hepworth
T.S. 1919

D. C. M. Hepworth
C. C. M. Hepworth
Sc. E. Temple Thurston

Alma Taylor
Gerald Ames
James Carew
Gwynne Herbert
Stephen Ewart
Mary Dibley
Victor Prout
Christine Rayner
John McAndrews

NAVAL WARFARE, 1789–1805

British Instructional Films
1,528 ft
1926

Cedric Hardwicke

NELL GWYNNE

British National
7,760 ft
Special run 3.26

D. Herbert Wilcox   Asst. Arthur
   Barnes
C. Roy Overbaugh
Sc. Herbert Wilcox from story by
    Marjorie Bowen
Art N. G. Arnold

Dorothy Gish
Randle Ayrton
Sydney Fairbrother
Juliette Compton
Judd Green
Gibb McLaughlin
Fred Rains
Forrester Harvey
Aubrey Fitzgerald
Booth Conway
Edward Sorley
Hilda Cowley
Dorinea Shirley
Johnny Butt
Tom Coventry
Donald McCardle
Rolfe Leslie

NELSON

International Exclusives
7 reels
T.S. 12.18 and 1.19

D. Maurice Elvey
C. A. Frenguelli
Sc. Eliot Stannard
Animation Anson Dyer

Malvina Longfellow
Donald Calthrop
Ivy Close
Ernest Thesiger
Edward O'Neill
Allan Jeayes

NELSON

British Instructional Films
8,000 ft
T.S. 9.26

D. Walter Summers
C. Jack Parker and E. Warneforde
Art Walter Murton

Gertrude McCoy
Cedric Hardwicke
Frank Arlton

NETS OF DESTINY

I. B. Davidson
5,600 ft
First run 11.24

D. A. H. Rooke
C. Leslie Eveleigh
Sc. Eliot Stannard from novel by
    Maurice Drake, *The Salving of a
    Derelict*

Stewart Rome
Gertrude McCoy
Mary Odette
Judd Green
Cameron Carr
Reginald Fox
Robert English

NIGHTHAWK, THE

Gliddon d'Eyncourt
Finished 1922/3

New title of THE HAVEN

D. John Gliddon
C. W. H. Howse
Sc. Gerard Fort Buckle from story by
Eden Philpotts (*The Haven*)

Malvina Longfellow
Henri de Vries
Sydney Seaward
Nadia Ostrovska
Caleb Porter
Mary Brough

NIGHT RIDERS, THE

Samuelson
5,000 ft
T.S. 7.20

D. Alexander Butler
Sc.
from novel by Ridgwell Callum

Maudie Dunham
Albert Ray

NIONGA

Stoll
5 reels
T.S. 5.25

NOBODY'S CHILD

British and Colonial
5 reels
T.S. 10.19

D. George Edwardes Hall
Sc. George Edwardes Hall from the
play (*The Whirlpool*)

José Collins

Godfrey Tearle
Mrs Saba Raleigh
J. Fisher White
Ben Webster

NO. 5, JOHN STREET

H. W. Thompson
5,300 ft
T.S. 12.21

D. Kenelm Foss   Asst. John Miller
C. Frank Canham
Sc. Kenelm Foss from story by Richard Whiteing
Art titles T. C. Gilson

Zena Dare
Roy Travers
Randle Ayrton
Mary Odette
Lionelle Howard

NON-CONFORMIST PARSON, THE

British Lion
5 reels
T.S. 3.19

D. A. V. Bramble
Sc. Eliot Stannard from novel by Roy Horniman

George Keene
Constance Worth
Gwen Williams
Evan Thomas
Arthur Cullin
Annie Esmond
George Goodwin
Rachel de Solla

NORTHWARDS

British Screen Productions
Ben Hart and St John Clowes

NO. 7 BRICK ROW

Harma
5 reels
T.S. 1921/22

D. Fred W. Durrant
Sc.
from novel by William Riley

Constance Worth
Marjorie Villis
James Knight
J. G. Butt

NOT FOR SALE

Stoll
6,460 ft
T.S. 11.24

D. W. P. Kellino
C. Percy Strong
Sc. Lydia Hayward from novel by Monica Ewer
Art W. Murton
Ed. Challis N. Sanderson

Gladys Hamer
Ian Hunter
Mary Odette
Edward O'Neill
Mary Brough
Mickey Brantford
Lionelle Howard
Jack Trevor
Minnie Leslie
W. G. Saunders
Robert Vallis
Moore Marriott
George Bellamy

NOT GUILTY

Windsor
5,427 ft
T.S. 3.19

D. A. Bocchi
C. Randal Terraneau

Sc. Kenelm Foss

Kenelm Foss
Charles Vane
Hayford Hobbs
Philip Hewland
Evelyn Harding
Barbara Everest
Bert Wynne

NOTHING ELSE MATTERS

Welsh–Pearson
6,400 ft
T.S. 7.20

D. George Pearson
C. Emile Lauste
Sc. George Pearson and Hugh E. Wright
Art titles Ernest Jones

Betty Balfour
Hugh E. Wright
Moyna MacGill
Leal Douglas
Arthur Cleave
Mabel Poulton
Alec Thompson
George Keene
Pollie Emery
The Stedman Dancers

NOTORIOUS MRS CARRICK, THE

Stoll
4,450 ft
T.S. 7.24

D. George Ridgwell
Sc.
from novel by Charles Proctor (*Pools of the Past*)

Disa
A. B. Imeson
Cameron Carr
Sidney Folker

NOT QUITE A LADY

British International Pictures
7,250 ft
T.S. 7.28

D. Thomas Bentley
C. James Rogers
Sc. Eliot Stannard from play by St John Hankin (*The Cassilis Engagement*)
Art J. E. Wills

Mabel Poulton
Barbara Gott
Maurice Braddell
Janet Alexander
Dorothy Bartlam
George Bellamy

NUMBER 13

W. and F.
Made 1922
Unfinished

D. Alfred Hitchcock
C. J. Rosenthal

Clare Greet
Ernest Thesiger

ODDS AGAINST HER

Barker Motion Photography
5 reels
T.S. 11.19

D. Alexander Butler

Milton Rosmer
George Foley

ODDS ON

6,129 ft
T.S. 2.29

Phyllis Gibbs

OLD ARMCHAIR, THE

British Exhibitors' Films
5,200 ft
T.S. 11.20

D. Percy Nash
C. S. L. Eaton
Sc. George Pickett

Joan Ritz
Cecil Morton York
Frank Tennant
Cecil Manning
Manora Thew

OLD BILL THROUGH THE AGES

Ideal
6,600 ft
T.S. 3.24

British Film Week 1924

D. Thomas Bentley
C. Horace Wheddon
Sc. Eliot Stannard

Syd Walker
Arthur Cleave
Jack Denton

OLD COUNTRY, THE

Ideal
5,000 ft
T.S. 4.21

D. A. V. Bramble
Sc. Eliot Stannard from play by Dion Clayton Calthrop

Haidee Wright
Gerald McCarthy
George Bellamy
Sidney Paxton
Ethel Newman
Kathleen Vaughan

OLD CURIOSITY SHOP, THE

Welsh–Pearson
7,000 ft
T.S. 4.21

D. Thomas Bentley
C. E. E. Warneforde and Emile Lauste
Sc. G. A. Atkinson from novel by Charles Dickens

    Mabel Poulton
    William Lugg
    Pino Conti
    Barry Livesey
    Hugh E. Wright
    Bryan Powley
    Minnie Rayner
    A. Harding Steerman

OLD MAN IN THE CORNER, THE

Stoll
Series, 12 2-reelers
T.S. 6.24

D. Hugh Croise
C. D. P. Cooper
Sc. Hugh Croise from stories by Baroness Orczy
Art Walter Murton
    With: Rolf Leslie

    The Kensington Mystery
    The Tragedy of Barnsdale Manor
    The York Mystery, etc.

OLD WIVE'S TALE, THE

Ideal
5 reels
T.S. 12.21

D. Denison Clift
C. Geoffrey Barker
Sc.
    from novel by Arnold Bennett

    Fay Compton
    Florence Turner
    Mary Brough
    Norman Page
    Henry Victor
    Karsavina

ONCE ABOARD THE LUGGER

Hepworth
5,250 ft
T S 10.20

P. C. M. Hepworth
D. Gaston Queribet and Gerald Ames
Sc. Blanche MacIntosh from novel by A. S. M. Hutchinson

    E. Holman Clark
    Eileen Dennes
    Evan Thomas
    Fred Lewis
    Gwynne Herbert
    Winifred Sadler
    John MacAndrews

ONE ARABIAN NIGHT

Stoll
4,500 ft
T.S. 12.23

    New title of WIDOW TWANKEE
    British Film Week 1924

D. Sinclair Hill
C. D. P. Cooper
Sc. Sinclair Hill
Art Walter Murton
Ed. H. Leslie Brittain and Rupert Hazell
Art titles Edward Strong

    George Robey
    Lionelle Howard
    Edward O'Neill
    W. G. Saunders
    H. Agar Lyons
    Julie Suedo

ONE COLOMBO NIGHT

Stoll
5,000 ft
T.S. 2.26

D. Henry Edwards
C. D. P. Cooper
Sc. Alicia Ramsey from story by
Austen Phillips
Art Walter Murton
Ed. H. C. Hoagland

Marjorie Hume
Godfrey Tearle
James Carew
Nora Swinburne
J. Fisher White
Julie Suedo
Dawson Milward
William Pardoe
Annie Esmond

ONE OF THE BEST

Gainsborough
8,000 ft
T.S. 11.27

D. T. Hayes Hunter
C. James Wilson
Sc. P. L. Mannock from play by
Seymour Hicks and George
Edwards
Art Clifford Pember

Carlyle Blackwell
Walter Butler
Randle Ayrton
James Carew
Eve Gray
Julie Suedo
Simeon Stuart
James Lindsay
Elsa Lanchester
Cecil Barry
Harold Huth

ONLY A MILL GIRL

Foxwell
5,000 ft
T.S. 12.19

Harry Foxwell
Betty Farquhar

ONLY WAY, THE

Graham–Wilcox
10,075 ft
T.S. 8.25

D. Herbert Wilcox   Asst. Arthur
Barnes
C. Claude McDonnell
Sc. Freeman Wills from novel by
Charles Dickens (*A Tale of Two
Cities*) and play by Rev. Freeman
Wills and Frederick Langbridge
Art Norman J. Arnold

Sir John Martin-Harvey
Ben Webster
J. Fisher White
Madge Stuart
Frank Stanmore
Betty Faire
Mary Brough
Gibb McLaughlin
Judd Green
Fred Rains
Jean Jay
Margaret Yarde
Michael Martin-Harvey

ONWARD, CHRISTIAN SOLDIERS

Samuelson
5 reels
T.S. 12.18

D. Rex Wilson

Minna Grey
Isobel Elsom
Owen Nares
Tom Reynolds

OPEN COUNTRY

Stoll
4,696 ft
T.S. 1922

D. Sinclair Hill
C. Alfred H. Moise
Sc. Sinclair Hill from novel by Maurice Hewlett
Art Walter Murton

Bertram Burleigh
Bryan Powley
Daisy Campbell
Dorinea Shirley
Norma Whalley
George Bellamy
Miles Mander
David Hawthorne

OPEN ROAD, THE

Claude Friese–Greene
26 1-reelers
T.S. 12.25

C. Claude Friese–Greene

OTHER PERSON, THE

Granger–Binger
5 reels
T.S. 4.21

D. B. E. Doxat-Pratt
Sc. Benedict James from novel by Fergus Hume

Adelqui Millar
E. Story Gofton
Ivo Dawson
Arthur Walcott
Arthur Pusey
Zoe Palmer

OUT TO WIN

Ideal
7,000 ft/6 reels
T.S. 8.23

British Film Week 1924

D. Denison Clift
Sc.
from play by Roland Pertwee and Dion Clayton Calthrop

Clive Brook
Cameron Carr
Olaf Hytten
Daisy Campbell
E. A. Douglas
Robert English
A. B. Imeson
Ivo Dawson
Catherine Calvert

OWD BOB

Atlantic Union
6,300 ft
T.S. 11.24

D. Henry Edwards
C. Charles Bryce and Bert Ford
Sc. Hugh Maclean from novel by Alfred Oliphant

J. Fisher White
James Carew
Ralph Forbes
Frank Stanmore
Robert English
John M. East

OXFORD

1,256 ft
1928

P. Bernice de Bererac
D. Charles Calvert
C. Basil Emmott
Ed. Thorold Dickinson

PACE

(1928) See under SMASHING THROUGH

PADDY-THE-NEXT-BEST-THING

Graham–Wilcox
7,200 ft
T.S. 1.23

D. Graham Cutts
C. René Guissart
Sc.
from novel by Gertrude Page and play by W. Gayer-Mackay and Robert Ord (Mrs Gayer-Mackay)

Mae Marsh
Lilian Douglas
Darby Foster
G. K. Arthur
Haidee Wright
Nina Boucicault
Tom Coventry
Simeon Stuart
Mildred Evelyn

PAGES OF LIFE

Adelqui Millar
5,500 ft
T.S. 11.22

D. Adelqui Millar
C. Bert Ford
Sc. Adelqui Millar

Adelqui Millar
Evelyn Brent
Jack Trevor
Gertrude Sterroll
Sunday Wilshin
Luis Hidalgo

PAGLIACCI

6 reels
T.S. 1923

British Film Week 1924

D. Adelqui Millar
C. Sydney Blythe

Sc.
from opera by Leoncavallo

Lillian Hall-Davis
Campbell Gullan
Adelqui Millar
Frank Dane

PALAIS DE DANSE

Gaumont
7,697 ft
T.S. 7.28

P. Maurice Elvey and V. Gareth Gundrey
D. Maurice Elvey
C. Percy Strong
Sc. Jean Jay
Art Andrew Mazzei

John Longden
Mabel Poulton
Robin Irvine
Hilda Moore
Chili Bouchier
Jerrold Robertshaw

PALAVER

British Instructional Films
7,500 ft
T.S. 9.26

D. Geoffrey Barkas
C. Stanley Rodwell
Sc. Geoffrey Barkas

Haddon Mason
Hilda Cowley
Reginald Fox

PALLARD, THE PUNTER

Gaumont
6 reels
T.S. 1.19

Sc.
from novel by Edgar Wallace (Grey Timothy)

424

J. L. V. Leigh
Heather Thatcher
Lionel d'Aragon
C. Morton York
Cyril Smith

PARADISE

British International Pictures
7,246 ft
T.S. 9.28

D. Denison Clift
C. René Guissart
Sc.
    from story by Sir Philip Gibbs
Art J. E. Wills

Betty Balfour
Alexandre d'Arcy
Winter Hall
Joseph Striker
Barbara Gott
Dino Galvani
Boris Ranevsky
Albert Brouett
Ena de la Haye
Jack Manners

PASSING OF MR QUIN, THE

Strand
8,259 ft
T.S. 7.28

P. C. Cattermoul
D. Leslie Hiscott
C. Horace Wheddon
Sc.
    from story by Agatha Christie
Art J. T. Garside

Stewart Rome
Clifford Heatherley
Trilby Clark
Mary Brough
Ursula Jeans

PASSIONATE ADVENTURE, THE

Gainsborough
8,000 ft
T.S. 8.24

P. Michael Balcon
D. Graham Cutts Asst. Alfred Hitchcock
C. Claude McDonnell
Sc. Michael Morton and Alfred Hitchcock from novel by Frank Stayton
Art Alfred Hitchcock

Alice Joyce
Clive Brook
Marjorie Daw
Victor McLaglen
Lillian Hall-Davis
J. R. Tozer
Mary Brough
John Hamilton

PASSIONATE FRIENDS, THE

Stoll
6,300 ft
T.S. 12.21

D. Maurice Elvey
C. J. J. Cox
Sc. L. H. Gordon from novel by H. G. Wells
Art Walter Murton

Madge Stuart
Valia
Milton Rosmer
Frederick Raynham
Ralph Forster
Edward Arundel
Lawford Davidson
Annie Esmond

PASSION ISLAND

Pathé
7,500 ft
T.S. 6.27

D. Manning Haynes Asst. Jack Raymond
C. Percy Strong
Sc. Lydia Hayward from story by W. W. Jacobs

Moore Marriott
Randle Ayrton
Lilian Oldland
Walter Butler
Dacia Deane
Gladys Hamer
Johnny Butt
Jack Raymond
Cynthia Murtagh

PATRICIA BRENT, SPINSTER

Garrick
5,000 ft
T.S. 12.19

D. Geoffrey Malins
C. S. J. Mumford
Sc. Eliot Stannard from novel

Ena Beaumont
Lawrence Leyton

PAUPER MILLIONAIRE, A

Ideal
5 reels
T.S. 6.22

D. Frank Crane
Sc. Eliot Stannard

C. M. Hallard

PEACEMAKER, THE

Stoll
5,600 ft
T.S. 3.22

D. A. E. Coleby
C. D. P. Cooper
Sc. A. E. Coleby
Art Walter Murton

A. E. Coleby
Minnie Leslie
Sam Austin
Frank Wilson
H. Nicholls Bates
Robert Vallis
Humberston Wright
Maud Yates
George Bellamy

PEARL OF THE SOUTH SEAS

Stoll
5,000 ft
T.S. 4.27

D. Frank Hurley
C. Frank Hurley
Sc. Frank Hurley

Eric Bransby Williams
Jameson Thomas
W. G. Saunders
Lilian Douglas
James English
Dallas Cairns

PEARLS AND SAVAGES

Stoll
6,000 ft
T.S. 10.24

P. Frank Hurley

PEEP BEHIND THE SCENES, A

Master
5 reels
T.S. 12.18

D. Geoffrey Malins
Sc.
    from story by Mrs O. F. Walton

    Ivy Close
    Gerald Ames

PEEP BEHIND THE SCENES, A

British and Dominion
7,372 ft
T.S. 1.29

D. Jack Raymond
Sc.
    from story by Mrs O. F. Walton

    Frances Cuyler
    Haddon Mason
    Johnny Butt

PEEP O'DAY

(1919) See under ALL THE SAD WORLD NEEDS

PENALTY

(1921) See under HER PENALTY

PENNILESS MILLIONAIRE

Broadwest
4,900 ft
T.S. 9.21

Sc. Frank Fowell from novel by David Christie Murray

    Stewart Rome
    Gregory Scott
    Cameron Carr
    George Foley

PERPETUA

Famous Players–Lasky British
6,200 ft
T.S. 5.22

D. John S. Robertson
C. Roy Overbaugh
Sc.
    from novel by Dion Clayton Calthrop

    Ann Forrest
    Percy Standing
    David Powell
    Geoffrey Kerr

PERSISTENT LOVERS, THE

George Clark
6,420 ft
T.S. 4.22

D. Guy Newall
C. Bert Ford
Sc. Guy Newall from story by A. Hamilton Gibbs

    Guy Newall
    Ivy Duke
    E. A. Douglas
    Douglas Munro
    A. Bromley Davenport
    Lawford Davidson
    Julian Royce
    Barbara Everest
    Winifred Sadler

P. G. WODEHOUSE STORIES

Stoll
Series, 2-reelers
T.S. 10.24

D. Andrew P. Wilson
Sc.
    from stories by P. G. Wodehouse
    With: Harry Beasley

    Chester Forgets Himself
    The Clicking of Cuthbert
    The Long Hole
    Ordeal by Golf
    Rodney Fails to Qualify

PHYSICIAN, THE

Gaumont
8,260 ft
T.S. 5.28

P. Elvey–Gundrey productions
D. Georq Jacoby
C. Baron Ventimiglia
Sc. Edwin Collins from play by
Henry Arthur Jones

    Miles Mander
    Elga Brink
    Ian Hunter
    Lissi Arne
    Humberston Wright
    Julie Suedo
    Henry Vibart
    Mary Brough
    A. Bromley Davenport

PICCADILLY

British International Pictures
9,763 ft
T.S. 1.29

D. E. A. Dupont Asst. Rona D.
Goetz
C. Werner Brandes
Sc. Arnold Bennett
Art Alfred Jünge
Ed. J. N. McConaughty
Music Eugene Contie

    Jameson Thomas
    Gilda Gray
    Anna May Wong
    King Ho Chang
    Cyril Ritchard
    Hannah Jones
    Charles Laughton

PILLARS OF SOCIETY

R. W. Syndicate
6,000 ft
T.S. 9.20

D. Rex Wilson

Sc. W. Courtenay Rowden from play
by Henrik Ibsen

    Norman McKinnell
    Ellen Terry
    Irene Rooke
    Pam Neville
    Joan Lockton
    Hayford Hobbs

PIPES OF PAN, THE

Hepworth
6 reels
T.S. 2.23

    British Film Week 1924

D. C. M. Hepworth
Sc. George Dewhurst

    Alma Taylor
    G. H. Mulcaster
    Lawrence Hanray
    James Annand
    Hugh Clifton
    Buena Bent
    John MacAndrews
    Eileen Dennes

PLACE OF HONOUR, THE

Stoll
5.050 ft
T.S. 6.21

D. Sinclair Hill
Sc.
from story by Ethel M. Dell

    Madge White
    Hugh C. Buckler

PLAYTHING, THE

5,837 ft
T.S. 9.29

    Part talking, R.C.A.

    Nigel Barrie
    Estelle Brody

PLEASURE GARDEN, THE

Gainsborough–Emelka
7,508 ft
T.S. 3.26

P. Michael Balcon
D. Alfred Hitchcock   Asst. Alma
   Reville
C. Baron Ventimiglia
Sc. Eliot Stannard from novel by
   Oliver Sandys
Art C. W. Arnold, Ludwig Reiber

Virginia Valli
Carmelita Geraghty
Miles Mander
John Stuart
Nita Naldi
George Schnell
Carl Falkenberg
Ferdinand Martini
Florence Helminger

POLAR STAR, THE

T.S. 1919/20

D. A. Bocchi

Manora Thew
Bert Wynne
Evelyn Harding
Peggy Patterson
Charles Vane
Hayford Hobbs

POPPIES OF FLANDERS

British International Pictures
8,700 ft
T.S. 10.27

D. Arthur Maude   Asst. W. W.
   Bowden
C. G. W. Pocknall

Sc. V. E. Powell from story by 'Sapper'
Art J. E. Wills
Ed. S. Simmonds

Jameson Thomas
Eve Gray
Malcolm Tod
Gibb McLaughlin
Henry Vibart
Daisy Campbell
Cameron Carr

POSSESSION

Hepworth
5 reels
T.S. 9.19

D. Henry Edwards
C. Charles Bryce
Sc.
   by Olive Wadsley

Henry Edwards
Chrissie White
Bubbles Brown
Gerald Ames
Gwynne Herbert
Annie Esmond
Stephen Ewart

POTTER'S CLAY

Big Four Famous Productions
6 reels
T.S. 3.22

D. Grenville Taylor
C. Robert Dykes
Sc. Langford Reed

Ellen Taylor
Peggie Hathaway
Douglas Payne
Dick Webb
Wallace Bosco

POUPÉE, LA

5,200 ft
T.S. 12.20

D. Meyrick Milton
Sc.
from comic opera by Edmund
Audrien

Flora le Breton
Richard Scott
William Farren
Fred Wright

POWER OVER MEN

British Filmcraft
6,918 ft
T.S. 4.29

D. George Banfield
Sc. George Banfield from story by
Denison Clift

Jameson Thomas
Isabel Jeans
Gladys Frazin
Franklyn Bellamy
Wyndham Standing
Gibb McLaughlin
Jerrold Robertshaw
Judd Green
James Knight
Reginald Fox
Frank Dane

PREHISTORIC MAN, THE

Stoll
5 reels
Release 4.24

D. A. E. Coleby
C. D. P. Cooper
Sc. A. E. Coleby
Art Walter Murton
Ed. Leslie Brittain
Titles H. Leslie Brittain and Edward
Strong

George Robey
Marie Blanche
H. Agar Lyons
W. G. Saunders
Johnny Butt

PRESUMPTION OF STANLEY HAYE, M.P., THE

Stoll
5,500 ft
T.S. 4.25

D. Sinclair Hill

David Hawthorne
Betty Faire
Fred Raynham
Kinsey Peile
Dora de Winton

PRICE OF SILENCE, THE

(1922) See under SHIFTING SANDS

PRIDE OF THE FANCY, THE

Sameulson
5,000 ft
T.S. 12.20

D. Albert Ward
Sc.
from novel by George Edgar

Daisy Burrell
Tom Reynolds
Rex Davis
Dorothy Fane
Wyndham Guise
Pope Stamper
Fred Morgan

PRIDE OF THE NORTH, THE

I. B. Davidson
5,700 ft
T.S. 1.20 and 2.20

D. A. E. Coleby

Cecil Humphreys
Richard Buttery
Nora Royland
H. Nicholls Bates
Blanche Kellino
James English

PRINCE AND THE BEGGARMAID, THE

Ideal
4,600 ft
T.S. 5.21

D. A. V. Bramble
Sc. Eliot Stannard from play by Walter Howard

Henry Ainley
Kathleen Vaughan
Harvey Braban
Sydney Paxton

PRINCE OF LOVERS, A

Gaumont
7,850 ft
T.S. 6.22

New title of THE LIFE OF LORD BYRON

British Film Week 1924

D. C. C. Calvert
C. A. St Aubyn Brown and Basil Emmott
Sc. Alicia Ramsey from her play

Howard Gaye
Mary Clare
R. H. Hignett
Marjorie Day
David Hawthorne
Wyndham Guise
George Foley
Saba Raleigh
Marjorie Hume

PRINCESS OF NEW YORK, THE

Famous Players–Lasky British
6,400 ft
T.S. 6.21

D. Donald Crisp
C. J. Rosenthal Jnr.
Sc. Margaret Turnbull from story by Cosmo Hamilton

Mary Glynne
David Powell
Ivo Dawson
Dorothy Fane
George Bellamy
Philip Hewland
Saba Raleigh

PRINCESS PRISCILLA'S FORTNIGHT

(1929) See under RUNAWAY PRINCESS, THE

PRODIGAL SON, THE

Stoll
17 reels
T.S. 2.23 and 4.29

British Film Week 1924
Reissued as 6,500 ft in 1929 re-edited by Charles Barnett
D. A. E. Coleby
C. D. P. Cooper
Sc.
from novel and play by Sir Hall Caine

Henry Victor
Stewart Rome
Colette Brettel
Edith Bishop
Frank Wilson
Adeline Hayden-Coffin
H. Nicholls Bates
Louise Conti
Peter Upcher

431

PRUDE'S FALL, THE

Balcon–Saville–Freedman
1925

P. Michael Balcon
D. Graham Cutts   Asst. Alfred
    Hitchcock
C. Hal Young
Sc. Alfred Hitchcock from play by
    May Edgington and Rudolph
    Besier
Art Alfred Hitchcock

    Jane Novak
    Julanne Johnstone
    Warwick Ward
    Henry Vibart
    Marie Ault
    Edith Craig

PUPPET MAN, THE

British and Colonial
5,000 ft
T.S. 8.21

D. Frank Crane
C. I. Roseman
Sc. Cosmo Gordon Lennox

    Molly Adair
    Hilda Anthony
    Hugh Miller
    Marie Belocci
    Harry Paulo
    John Reid

PURSUIT OF PAMELA, THE

London Film Co.
5,000 ft
T.S. 1.20

D. Harold Shaw
Sc. Bannister Merwin from play by
    C. B. Fernald

    Edna Flugrath
    Douglas Munro
    Hubert Willis
    Wyndham Guise
    Ma Fu

QUALIFIED ADVENTURER, THE

Stoll
6,700 ft
T.S. 8.25

D. Sinclair Hill
C. D. P. Cooper
Sc.
    by Selwyn Jepson

    Matheson Lang
    Genevieve Townsend
    Cameron Carr
    Wyndham Guise
    J. Nelson Ramsaye
    Fred Rains
    Moore Marriott

QUEEN'S EVIDENCE

British and Colonial
6,000 ft
T.S. 12.19

D. James McKay
Sc. George Edwardes Hall from novel
    by Louisa Parr and C. E. Munro
    (*Adam and Eve*)

    Godfrey Tearle
    Unity Moore
    Janet Alexander
    Lauderdale Maitland
    Edward Sorley

QUEEN WAS IN THE PARLOUR, THE

Gainsborough
7,250 ft
T.S. 4.27

D. Graham Cutts
Sc. Graham Cutts from play by Noel
Coward

Lili Damita
Paul Richter
Harry Liedtke
Klein Rogge

QUESTION OF TRUST, A

Stoll
6,000 ft
T.S. 8.20

D. Maurice Elvey
C. Paul Burger
Sc. Sinclair Hill from novel by Ethel
M. Dell

Madge Stuart
C. H. Croker King
Harvey Braban
Edward Arundel

QUINNEYS

Gaumont–British
8,600 ft
T.S. 12.27

D. Maurice Elvey
Sc.
from book and play by H. A.
Vachell

John Longden
Alma Taylor
Henry Vibart
Francis Cuyler
Ursula Jeans
Cyril McLaglen
Judd Green
Lionel d'Aragon
Wallace Bosco

"Q" SHIPS

New Era Productions
7,800 ft
T.S. 6.28

D. Geoffrey Barkas and Michael
Barringer
C. Sydney Blythe
Sc.
Adviser: Lt Com. Auten

RACING DRAMAS

Gainsborough
2 reels each
1925

D. Walter West

Steve Donoghue
Miles Mander
Carlyle Blackwell
June

Riding for a King
Dark Horses
A Knight of the Saddle
Beating the Book
Come on, Steve
The Golden Spurs

RAINBOW CHASERS, THE

Educational Film Company
T.S. 9.19

D. Geoffrey Malins

RANK OUTSIDER, A

Broadwest
6,000 ft
T.S. 11.20

P. Walter West
D. Richard Garrick
Sc. P. L. Mannock from novel by Nat
Gould

Gwen Stratford
John Gliddon
Cameron Carr
Lewis Dayton
Joe Plant
A. Jassawalla

433

RAT, THE

Gainsborough
7,323 ft
T.S. 9.25

P. Michael Balcon
D. Graham Cutts
C. Hal Young
Sc. Graham Cutts from play by Ivor Novello and Constance Collier ('David L'Estrange')
Art C. W. Arnold

Ivor Novello
Mae Marsh
Isabel Jeans
James Lindsay
Marie Ault
Julie Suedo

RECOIL, THE

Hardy
5,000 ft
T.S. 3.22

D. Geoffrey Malins
Sc. Rafael Sabatini

Phyllis Titmuss
Eille Norwood
Laurence Anderson
Dawson Milward

RED HEELS

Stoll–Sascha (Austrian production)
7,900 ft
T.S. 1.26

D. Michael Curtiz
Sc.
from novel by Margery Lawrence

Lili Damita
Eric Barclay

REMEMBRANCE

British Independent Productions
(British Legion)
7,500 ft
T.S. 9.27

D. Bert Wynne
C. Horace Wheddon
Sc. George King

Rex Davis
Violet Hopson
Alf Goddard
Hayford Hobbs
Enid Stamp-Taylor
Gladys Hamer

REPENTANCE

Brand Z
5 reels
T.S. 9.22

D. E. R. Gordon
C. Harold Bast
Sc. E. R. Gordon

Peggy Hathaway
Ray Raymond

REST CURE, THE

Stoll
4,700 ft
T.S. 11.23

D. A. E. Coleby
C. D. P. Cooper
Sc. George Robey and A. E. Coleby
Art Walter Murton
Ed. H. Leslie Brittain

George Robey
Sydney Fairbrother

RETREAT FROM MONS, THE

(1926) See under MONS

RETURN OF THE RAT, THE

Gainsborough
7,612 ft
T.S. 4.29

Synchronized, GBA

D. Graham Cutts

434

C. Roy Overbaugh
Sc. Angus Macphail
Art Alan McNab

Ivor Novello
Isabel Jeans
Gordon Harker
Bernard Nedell
Marie Ault
Mabel Poulton
Gladys Frazin

REVEILLE

Welsh–Pearson
8,000 ft
T.S. 6.24

D. George Pearson Asst. Robert Cullen
C. Percy Strong Asst. Bernard Knowles
Sc. George Pearson
Art Leslie Dawson and Harry Jonas
Effects by Charles Penley

Betty Balfour
Frank Stanmore
Stewart Rome
Ralph Forbes
Sydney Fairbrother
Simeon Stuart
Walter Tennyson
Buena Bent
Gertrude Sterroll

RIGHT ELEMENT, THE

Samuelson
5,000 ft
T.S. 12.19

D. Rex Wilson
Sc. Roland Pertwee

Campbell Gullan
Miriam Ferris
Mary Rorke
Annie Esmond
Tom Reynolds

RIGHT TO LIVE, THE

Granger–Davidson
6,000 ft
T.S. 6.21

D. A. E. Coleby
Sc. A. E. Coleby

A. E. Coleby
H. Nicholls Bates
Phyllis Shannaw
Peter Upcher

RIGHT TO STRIKE, THE

British Super
5 reels
T.S. 7.23

P. G. B. Sameulson
D. Fred Paul
Sc. Walter Summers from play by Ernest Hutchinson

Fred Paul
Lillian Hall-Davis

RING, THE

British International Pictures
8,400 ft
T.S. 10.27

P. John Maxwell
D. Alfred Hitchcock Asst. Frank Mills
C. Jack Cox
Sc. Alfred Hitchcock and Eliot Stannard
Art C. W. Arnold
Continuity Alma Reville

Carl Brisson
Lillian Hall-Davis
Ian Hunter
Gordon Harker
Forrester Harvey
Billy Wells
Harry Terry

435

RINGER, THE

British Lion
7,150 ft
T.S. 8.28

D. Arthur Maude
Sc.
    from play by Edgar Wallace

    Leslie Faber
    Lawson Butt
    Nigel Barrie
    Hayford Hobbs
    John Hamilton
    Muriel Angelus
    Annette Benson

RINGING THE CHANGES

Strand
6.915 ft
T.S. 3.29

    New title of THE CROOKED
    STAIRCASE

D. Leslie Hiscott
C. Walter Blakeley
Sc.
    from novel by R. Raleigh King
    (*Jix*)
Art James Carter

    Henry Edwards
    Margot Landa
    Barbara Gott
    Philip Hewland
    Forrester Harvey

RISING GENERATION, THE

W–P
7,000 ft
T.S. 9.28

D. Harley Knoles
Sc.
    from play by Wyn Weaver and
    Laura Leycester
Ed. George Dewhurst

    Jameson Thomas
    Alice Joyce
    William Freshman
    Joan Barry
    Betty Nuthall
    Robin Irvine
    Gerald Ames
    Clare Greet

RIVER OF LIGHT, THE

Brilliant
5,000 ft
T.S. 2.21

D. Dave Aylott
Sc. Dave Aylott

    Jack Jarman
    Dave Aylott
    Phyllis Shannaw

RIVER OF STARS, THE

Stoll
5 reels
1921

D. F. Martin Thornton
C. P. Strong
Sc. L. H. Gordon from story by Edgar
    Wallace
Art Walter Murton

    Edward Arundel
    W. Dalton Summers
    H. Agar Lyons
    Faith Bevan
    Fred Thatcher
    Philip Anthony
    J. E. Barber

ROAD TO HAPPINESS, THE

Stoll–Sascha (Austrian production)
6,700 ft
T.S. 7.26

D. Michael Curtiz

    Lili Damita

Jack Trevor
Walter Rilla
Carl Ebert

ROAD TO LONDON, THE

Associated Exhibitors
5 reels
T.S. 11.21

P. Bryant Washburn

Bryant Washburn
Joan Morgan
Mrs Saba Raleigh
George Foley
Gibb McLaughlin

ROBINSON CRUSOE

Epic
6,500 ft
T.S. 5.27

D. M. A. Wetherell Asst. Denis Shipwright
C. Joe Rosenthal
Sc.
from novel by Daniel Defoe

M. A. Wetherell
Fay Compton

ROB ROY

Gaumont
6,100 ft
T.S. 9.22

D. Will Kellino
C. A. St Aubyn Brown and Basil Emmott
Sc. Alicia Ramsey

David Hawthorne
Gladys Jennings
Wallace Bosco
Alec Hunter
Roy Kellino
Simeon Stuart

ROCK OF AGES

Bertram Phillips
5 reels
T.S. 2.19

D. Bertram Phillips

Queenie Thomas
Lottie Blackford
Bernard Vaughan
Ernest Douglas

ROCKS OF VALPRÉ, THE

Stoll
6 reels
1919

D. Maurice Elvey
C. Paul Burger
Sc. Byron Webber from novel by Ethel M. Dell
Art Dallas Cairns

Peggy Carlisle
Cowley Wright
Basil Gill
Winifred Sadler

RODNEY STONE

British Exhibitors Films
6,500 ft
T.S. 8.20

D. Percy Nash
C. S. L. Eaton
Sc. W. Courtenay Rowden from novel by Sir Arthur Conan Doyle

Lionel d'Aragon
Cecil Morton York
Frank Tennant
Fred Morgan
Douglas Payne
Rex Davis
Joan Ritz
Ethel Newman

437

ROGUE IN LOVE, A

Diamond Super
5,400 ft
T.S. 9.22 and 5.23

D. Albert Brouett
C. Lucien Egrot
Sc. Harry Hughes from novel by Tom
Gallon

    Frank Stanmore
    Betty Farquhar
    Fred Rains
    Ann Trevor
    Gregory Scott

ROGUES OF THE TURF

5,800 ft
T.S. 1.23

    British Film Week 1924

D. Wilfred Noy
C. S. J. Mumford
Sc.
    from play by John F. Preston

    Mavis Clare
    Olive Sloane
    Dora Lennox
    James Lindsay
    Fred Groves
    Robert Vallis
    James Reardon

ROLLING ROAD, THE

Gainsborough
7/8 reels
T.S. 5.27

D. Graham Cutts Asst. Robert
Cullen
C. Hal Young
Sc.
    from story by Boyd Cable
Art Bertram Evans

    Carlyle Blackwell
    Flora le Breton
    Clifford Heatherley

Marie Ault
A. V. Bramble
Cameron Carr
Mickey Brantford

ROMAN BRITAIN

British Instructional Films

1,860 ft
T.S. 1.27

ROMANCE OF A MOVIE STAR,
THE

Broadwest
5,500 ft
T.S. 8.20 ft

D. Richard Garrick
Sc. J. Bertram Brown from serial by
Coralie Stanton and E. Hoskin in
Evening News (*The World's Best
Girl*)

    Violet Hopson
    Stewart Rome
    Gregory Scott
    Cameron Carr
    Mercy Hatton

ROMANCE OF HINE-MOA, THE

Sphere (New Zealand film)
5,500 ft
T.S. 12.26

D. Gustav Pauli
C. Gustav Pauli
Sc.
    based on Maori legends

    All-Maori cast

ROMANCE OF LADY
HAMILTON, THE

Famous Pictures
6 reels
T.S. 7.19

D. Bert Haldane
Sc. Kenelm Foss
Art Willie Davies

Malvina Longfellow
Barbara Gott
Frank Dane
Maud Yates
H. Humberston Wright
Will Corrie

ROMANCE OF MAYFAIR, A

Stoll
5,000 ft
T.S. 4.25

D. Thomas Bentley
Sc.
from story by J. C. Smith (*The Crime of Constable Kelly*)

Betty Faire
Henry Victor
Edward O'Neill
Fred Raynham
Gertrude Sterroll
George Foley
Temple Bell
Eva Westlake
Minna Grey

ROMANCE OF OLD BAGHDAD, A

H. W. Thompson
6 reels
T.S. 3.22

D. Kenelm Foss   Ass. John Miller
C. Jack Parker
Sc. Kenelm Foss from novel by Jessie
Douglas Kerruiel (*Miss Haroun-al-Raschid*)
Art T. C. Gilson

Matheson Lang
Manora Thew
Douglas Munro
Dacia

Victor McLaglen
A. Harding Steerman
Henry Victor

ROMANCE OF POSTAL TELEGRAPHY, THE

Gaumont
1 reel
First show 1.22

P. C. C. Calvert
C. Basil Emmott

ROMANCE OF WASTEDALE, A

Stoll
6,000 ft
T.S. 11.21

D. Maurice Elvey
C. J. J. Cox
Sc.
from novel by A. E. W. Mason

Milton Rosmer
Fred Raynham
Irene Rooke
Valia

ROMANY, THE

Welsh–Pearson
5,700 ft
T.S. 1.23

D. F. Martin Thornton
C. Percy Strong
Sc. Eliot Stannard

Victor McLaglen
Hugh E. Wright
Irene Norman
Peggie Hathaway
Minna Grey
Harvey Braban
Malcolm Tod
H. Agar Lyons
John M. East

ROSES IN THE DUST

Gaumont
6,050 ft
T.S. 10.21

British Film Week 1924

D. C. C. Calvert
C. Basil Emmott
Sc. L. de Cordova

Gladys Mason
Iris Rowe
David Hawthorne
Gordon Craig

ROSES OF PICARDY

Gaumont–British
8,500 ft
Première 4.27

P. Elvey–Saville–Gundrey production
D. Maurice Elvey
Sc. F. V. Merrick and Jack Harris from novels by R. H. Mottram (*Spanish Farm* and *Sixty-four, Ninety-four*)

Lillian Hall-Davis
John Stuart
Jameson Thomas
A. Bromley Davenport
Clifford Heatherley
Marie Ault
H. Humberston Wright

ROTTERS, THE

Ideal
5,000 ft
T.S. 8.21

D. A. V. Bramble
Sc.
from play by H. F. Maltby

Sydney Fairbrother
Sydney Paxton
Stanley Holloway

ROUGH SEAS

(1929) See under YOU KNOW WHAT SAILORS ARE

ROUND AFRICA WITH COBHAM

8,155 ft
T.S. 11.28

C. S. R. Bonnett

ROYAL DIVORCE, A

Napoleon
11,000 ft
T.S. 1.23

British Film Week 1924

P. G. B. Samuelson
D. Alexander Butler
C. Sydney Blythe
Sc. Walter Summers from play by W. G. Wills and C. G. Collingham

Gwilym Evans
Gertrude McCoy
Mary Dibley
Lillian Hall-Davis
Gerald Ames
Jerrold Robertshaw
Tom Reynolds

ROYAL OAK, THE

Stoll
6,170 ft
T.S. 11.23

D. Maurice Elvey
Sc.
from play by W. Dimond

Henry Victor
Henry Ainley
Clive Brook
Thurston Hall
Peter Dear
Bertie Wright
Betty Compson

ROYAL REMEMBRANCES

Gaumont
4,906 ft
T.S. 11.28

P.   Will Day from material by Louis Lumière, R. W. Paul and C. M. Hepworth

---

RUGGED PATH, THE

T.S. 7.25

D.   W. Richard Hall

Stewart Rome
Mary Odette

RUNAWAY PRINCESS, THE

British Instructional Films and Lända-Film
7,053 ft
T.S. 3.29

New title of PRINCESS PRISCILLA'S FORTNIGHT

P.   H. Bruce Woolfe
D.   Anthony Asquith Asst. Victor Peers
C.   Arpad Viragh, Henry Harris
Sc. Anthony Asquith from novel by Elizabeth Russell (*Princess Priscilla's Fortnight*)
Art Ian Campbell-Gray, Hermann Warm
German supervision: Fritz Wendenhausen

Mady Christians
Paul Kavanagh
Fred Rains
Claude H. Beerbohm
Norah Baring

RUNNING WATER

Stoll
5 reels
T.S. 10.22

British Film Week 1924

D.   Maurice Elvey
Sc.
from novel by A. E. W. Mason

Madge Stuart
Julian Royce
Lawford Davidson
Edmund Lewis Waller

RUSSIA—THE LAND OF TOMORROW

Gaiety
5 reels
T.S. 2.19

D.   Maurice Sandground
Sc. Captain Merivale. Research E. Esdaile

Eve Balfour
A. B. Imeson
Bob Read

SACRIFICE, THE

British Instructional Films
6,602 ft
T.S. 3.29

D.   Victor Peers
Sc.
from play by Tennyson Jesse and H. M. Harwood

Audrée Tourneur
G. H. Mulcaster
Lewis Dayton

SAFETY FIRST

Stoll
6,000 ft
T.S. 10.26

D. Fred Paul
C. J. J. Cox
Sc. Margot Neville

Queenie Thomas
Brian Aherne
Mary Brough
Patrick Susands
Humberston Wright
Johnny Butt
Fred Morgan

SAHARA LOVE

Stoll (Anglo–Spanish production)
7,000 ft
T.S. 3.26

D. Sinclair Hill
Sc.
from story by A. L. Vincent

Marie Colette
Edward O'Neill
Gordon Hopkirk
John Dahelly

SAILORS DON'T CARE

Gaumont British
7,500 ft
T.S. 3.28

P. Elvey–Gundrey production
D. W. P. Kellino
C. Baron Ventimiglia and Basil Emmott

Estelle Brody
John Stuart
Alf Goddard
Humberston Wright
Gladys Hamer
Wallace Bosco
Shayle Gardner
Mary Brough

SAILOR TRAMP, A

Welsh–Pearson
5,800 ft
T.S. 7.22

D. F. Martin Thornton
Sc. Eliot Stannard from story by Bart Kennedy

Victor McLaglen
Hugh E. Wright
Pauline Johnson
Ambrose Manning
Mrs Hubert Willis

SALLY BISHOP

Stoll
8,000 ft
T.S. 12.23

D. Maurice Elvey
C. J. J. Cox
Sc.
from novel and play by E. Temple Thurston
Art Walter Murton
Ed. H. Leslie Brittain

Marie Doro
Henry Ainley
Dallas Cairns
Maie Hanbury
Florence Turner
A. Bromley Davenport
Sydney Fairbrother
Stella St Audrie
Valia
Mary Dibley
H. Humberston Wright
George Turner
Bunty Fosse

SAM'S BOY

Artistic
5 reels
T.S. 2.22

D. Manning Haynes

C. Frank Grainger
Sc. Lydia Haywood from story by W.
     W. Jacobs (in *Footlights*)

    Johnny Butt
    Tom Coventry
    Mary Braithwaite
    Kate Gurney
    Bobbie Rudd

SAM'S KID

5 reels
T.S. 4.22

    Hayford Hobbs
    Gertrude McCoy

SANDS OF TIME

Harma
5 reels
T.S. 8.19

D. Randle Ayrton
C. Frank Canham
Sc. Reuben Gilmer

    Bertram Burleigh
    John Gliddon
    Mercy Hatton
    Jeff Barlow
    Adeline Hayden-Coffin

SATAN'S SISTER

Welsh–Pearson
7,800 ft
T.S. 5.25

D. George Pearson Asst. Robert
    Cullen
C. Percy Strong Asst. Desmond
    Dickinson
Sc.
    from novel by H. de Vere Stacpoole

    Betty Balfour
    James Carew
    Frank Perfitt

    Frank Stanmore
    Caleb Porter
    Jeff Barlow

SAVED FROM THE SEA

Gaumont
6,000 ft
T.S. 10.20

D. Will Kellino
Sc. Will Kellino from play by Arthur
    Shirley and Ben Landeck

    Nora Swinburne
    Philip Anthony
    C. C. Calvert
    Wallace Bosco
    Terence Cavanagh

SCALLYWAG, THE

Master
5,000 ft
T.S. 3.21

D. Challis N. Sanderson
Sc. W. Courtenay Rowden from novel
    by Grant Allen

    Hubert Carter
    Cecil Morton York
    Fred Thatcher

SCANDAL, THE

Granger–Davidson
6,300 ft
T.S. 5.23

D. A. H. Rooke
C. Leslie Eveleigh
Sc. Kinchen Wood from play by Henri
    Bataille

    Henry Victor
    Vanni Marcoux
    Hilda Bayley
    Edward O'Neill

SCARLET LADY, THE

Violet Hopson
6 reels
T.S. 3.22

D. Walter West
Sc. J. Bertram Brown

Violet Hopson
Lewis Willoughby
Gertrude Sterroll
Adeline Hayden-Coffin
Cameron Carr
Arthur Walcott

SCARLET WOOING, THE

Progress
5 reels
T.S. 4.20

D. Sidney Morgan
Sc. Sidney Morgan

George Keene
Eve Balfour
Joan Morgan
Marguerite Blanche
Arthur Walcott
George Bellamy

SCHOOL FOR SCANDAL, THE

Bertram Phillips
6,350 ft
T.S. 9.23

British Film Week 1924

D. Bertram Phillips
Sc.
from play by R. B. Sheridan

Queenie Thomas
Frank Stanmore
Sydney Paxton
Basil Rathbone
John Stuart

A. G. Poulton
Mary Brough

SCIENTIST, THE

(1922) See under SILENT
EVIDENCE

SCOURGE, THE

(1921) See under FORTUNE'S
FOOL

SEA URCHIN

Gainsborough
7,954 ft
T.S. 2.26

P. Michael Balcon
D. Graham Cutts Asst. Leslie
Hiscott
C. Hal Young
Sc. Graham Cutts from play by John
Hastings Turner
Art C. W. Arnold

Betty Balfour
George Hackathorne
Haidee Wright
Clifford Heatherley
Cecil Morton York
A. G. Poulton
Marie Wright
W. Cronin Wilson
Irene Tripod

SECOND TO NONE

Britannia
7,674 ft
Premiere 11.26

D. Jack Raymond
C. Sydney Blythe and Percy Strong
Sc. Lydia Haywood from stories by
'Bartimeus'

Benita Hume

Moore Marriott
Mickey Brantford
Daisy Campbell
A. B. Imeson
Johnny Butt
Alf Goddard
Ian Fleming
Tom Coventry

SECRET KINGDOM, THE

Stoll
5,600 ft
T.S. 8.25

D. Sinclair Hill
C. Percy Strong
Sc. Alicia Ramsey
Sc. Alicia Ramsey from story by
    Bertram Atkey (*Forbidden Fires*)
Art Walter Murton

Matheson Lang
Stella Arbenina
Genevieve Townsend
Eric Bransby Williams
Lilian Oldland
Frank Goldsmith
Robin Irvine
L. de Cordova
Charles Barratt
A. Harding Steerman
George Bellamy

SECRET OF THE MOOR, THE

British Lion
5 reels
T.S. 9.19

Sc.
    from novel by Morice Gerard

Philip Hewland
Gwen Williams
George Goodwin

SECRETS OF NATURE

British Instructional Films
1 reel each
From August 1922

Set 1
The Cuckoo's Secret
The Lair of the Spider
The Evolution of the Caddis Fly
Skilled Insect Artisans
Hands Versus Feet
Infant Welfare in the Bird World

Set 2
The Sparrow Hawk
Fathoms Deep Beneath the Sea
Frocks and Frills
Studies in Animal Motion
The Seashore
Children of Nature

Set 3
The Battle of the Ants
Nature's Gliders
Story of the Buzzard
Story of the River
Tragedy of the Sea
Story of Peter the Raven

Set 4
White Owl
The Sea
Nature's Armour
The Rook
The Labyrinth Spider
Water Babies

Set 5
The Common Butterfly
The Diver
Marine Parade
Spring
The Path through the Wood
Where Flies go in the Winter

SECRETS OF NATURE

British Instructional Films
1 reel each
1923

Set 1
> The May-Fly
> Battles with Salmon
> The Stickleback
> Story of Westminster Hall
> Robin
> Giant Snails

Set 2
> Cabbages and Things
> A Fly Fisher's Festival
> Crabs and Camouflages
> The Gannet
> Hunting Spider
> Fear

Set 3
> The Tale of a Dog Fish
> Fowl Story
> Summer
> Tiger-Beetle
> Wasp
> Dinner-time at the Zoo

Set 4
> Sea Breezes
> Jack Daw
> Concerning Bills
> The Stream
> Humble Friends
> Strange Friendships

Set 5
> Tiger of the Stream
> The Grouse
> The Pond
> Zoo Babies
> Autumn
> Betty's Day at the Zoo

SECRETS OF NATURE

British Instructional Films
1 reel each
1924

Set 1
> Paws and Claws

> Swallow Tail Butterfly
> The Dipper
> Vapourer Moth
> Swallows
> Strange Courtship

SECRETS OF NATURE

British Instructional Films
1 reel each
1926

Set 1
> Puss Moth
> Seed Time
> Golden Eagle
> The Gnat
> Round the Empire at the Zoo
> Life of a Plant

Set 2
> Emperor Moth
> Magpie
> Phantoms (gnats)
> Battle of the Plants
> An Aquarium in a Wine Glass
> Busy Bees

SECRETS OF NATURE

British Instructional Films
1 reel each
1927

Set 1
> Plants of the Pantry
> Nursery of the Cormorant
> Story of Cecropia
> Romance of the Flowers
> Denizens of the Garden
> Story of the Leaf

Set 2
> Story of the Grasses
> Ant Lion
> Floral Co-operative Society
> Story of the Glass of Water
> Praying Mantis
> Plant Magic

SECRETS OF NATURE

British Instructional Films
1 reel each
1929

Set 1
The Frog
Springtime at the Zoo
The Iris Family
Scarlet Runner and Co.
Honey Bee
Home Wrecker

SENEGAL TO TIMBUCTU

(1925) See under FROM SENEGAL TO TIMBUCTU

SEN YAN'S DEVOTION

Stoll
5,400 ft
T.S. 7.24

D. A. E. Coleby
C. D. P. Cooper
Sc. A. E. Coleby
Art Walter Murton
Ed. H. Leslie Brittain

Sessue Hayakawa
Tsuru Aoki
Fred Raynham
H. Agar Lyons
H. Nicholls Bates
Tom Coventry
Jeff Barlow
Johnny Butt

SETTLED OUT OF COURT

Gaumont
8,500 ft
T.S. 10.25

New title of EVIDENCE ENCLOSED

D. G. A. Cooper
C. William Shenton
Sc. Eliot Stannard

Fay Compton
Jack Buchanan
Jeanne de Casalis
Leon Quartermaine
Kinsey Peile

SHADOW BETWEEN, THE

Ideal
5,000 ft
T.S. 6.20

D. George Dewhurst
C. Silvano Balboni
Sc. George Dewhurst from novel by Silas K. Hocking

Doris Lloyd
Lewis Dayton
Gertrude Sterroll
Wallace Bosco
Simeon Stuart
Sydney Paxton

SHADOW OF EGYPT, THE

Astra–National
7,600 ft
T.S. 11.24

D. Sidney Morgan Asst. Robert Cullen
C. Claude McDonnell
Sc. Sidney Morgan from novel by Norma Lorimer
Art E. P. Kinsella

Carlyle Blackwell
Milton Rosmer
Alma Taylor
Joan Morgan
John Hamilton
Arthur Walcott

447

SHADOW OF EVIL

5,700 ft
T.S. 5.21

Cecil Humphreys
Mary Dibley

SHADOW OF THE MOSQUE, THE

Richard Hall Productions
6,500 ft
T.S. 2.24

D. W. Richard Hall
Sc.
from novel by Maurice McDogail

Stewart Rome
Mary Odette

SHE

G. B. Samuelson
8,250 ft
T.S. 5.25

P. G. B. Samuelson
D. Leander de Cordova
C. Sydney Blythe
Sc. Walter Summers from novel by Sir H. Rider Haggard
Art Heinrich Richter

Betty Blythe
Carlyle Blackwell
Jerrold Robertshaw
Mary Odette
Tom Reynolds

SHEBA

Hepworth
5 reels
T.S. 10.19

D. C. M. Hepworth
Sc. Blanche MacIntosh from novel by Rita

Alma Taylor

James Carew
Gerald Ames
Eileen Dennes
Lionelle Howard
Mary Dibley
Eric Barker
Ronald Colman

SHEER BLUFF

Granger–Binger
5 reels
T.S. 12.21

D. Frankland A. Richardson
Sc. Benedict James

Maudie Dunham
Henry Victor
Percy Standing

SHIFTING SANDS

6 reels
T.S. 12.22

New title of THE PRICE OF SILENCE

D. Fred Leroy Granville
C. Silvano Balboni
Sc. R. C. Wells

Peggy Hyland
Lewis Willoughby
Valia

SHIPS THAT PASS IN THE NIGHT

British Exhibitors Films
5,400 ft
T.S. 9.21

D. Percy Nash
C. S. L. Eaton
Sc. Percy Nash from novel by Beatrice Harraden

Irene Rooke
Arthur Vezin
Daisy Markham

SHIRAZ

British Instructional Films
8,065 ft
T.S. 9.28

Supervisor in India: Himansu Rai
D. Franz Osten Asst. Victor Peers
C. Henry Harris, E. Schunemann
Sc. Naranjan Pal, W. Burton

Seeta Devi
Himansu Rai
Charu Roy
Enakshi Rama Rau

SHIRLEY

Ideal
5,400 ft
T.S. 4.22

D. A. V. Bramble
Sc.
from novel by Emily Brontë

Carlotta Breeze
Elizabeth Irving
Clive Brook

SHOOTING STARS

British Instructional Films
7,200 ft
T.S. 2.28

P. H. Bruce Woolfe
D. A. V. Bramble Asst. Anthony Asquith
C. Stanley Rodwell and H. Harris. Lighting: Karl Fischer
Sc. Anthony Asquith and J. O. C. Orton
Art Ian Campbell-Gray, Walter Murton

Annette Benson
Brian Aherne
Donald Calthrop
Chili Bouchier
Wally Patch

SHOULD A DOCTOR TELL?

Napoleon
6,800 ft
T.S. 11.23

British Film Week 1924

P. G. B. Samuelson
D. Alexander Butler
C. Sydney Blythe
Sc. Walter Summers

Henry Vibart
Lillian Hall-Davis
Francis Lister

SHUTTLE OF LIFE, THE

B.A.F.C.
5,256 ft
T.S. 11.20

D. D. J. Williams
Sc. S. H. Herkomer from story by Isobel Bray

C. Aubrey Smith
Evelyn Brent
Gladys Jennings
Jack Hobbs
Bert Darley
Rachel de Solla

SIGN OF FOUR, THE

Stoll
6,500 ft
T.S. 5.23

D. Maurice Elvey
C. J. J. Cox
Sc. Maurice Elvey from stories by Sir Arthur Conan Doyle
Art Walter Murton

Isobel Elsom
Fred Raynham
Norman Page
Eille Norwood
Humberston Wright
Arthur Cullin
Mme. d'Esterre

SILENT EVIDENCE

Gaumont
5,500 ft
T.S. 12.22

New title of THE SCIENTIST
British Film Week 1924

D. C. C. Calvert
C. Basil Emmott

David Hawthorne
Marjorie Hume
Frank Dane
Cecil du Gué
H. R. Hignett

SILENT HOUSE, THE

Nettlefold
9,376 ft
T.S. 1.29

D. Walter Forde
Sc. H. Fowler Mear from play by J. G.
Brandon and George Pickett

Mabel Poulton
Gibb McLaughlin
Albert Brouett
Kiyoshi Takase
Frank Parfitt
Arthur Stratton

SILVER BRIDGE, THE

Cairns–Torquay
5,000 ft
T.S. 9.20

D. Dallas Cairns
Sc. Eliot Stannard from novel by
Helen Prothero Lewis

Dallas Cairns
Betty Farquhar
H. Humberston Wright
J. H. Batson
Madge Tree

SILVER GREYHOUND

Harma
5 reels
T.S. 2.19

P. F. Martin Thornton
D. Bannister Merwin
Sc. Bannister Merwin

Marjorie Villis
James Knight
Mary Dibley
Frank E. Petley
Jeff Barlow
Dallas Cairns

SILVER KING, THE

Welsh–Pearson–Elder
8,462 ft
T.S. 6.29

D. T. Hayes Hunter
C. Bernard Knowles Asst. Fred
Ford
Sc. Fern Sherie from play by Henry
Arthur Jones and Henry Herman
Art Walter Murton

Percy Marmont
Bernard Nedell
Jean Jay
Hugh E. Wright
Harold Huth
Chili Bouchier

SILVER LINING

I. B. Davidson
6 reels
T.S. 11.19

D. A. E. Coleby

Bombardier Billy Wells

SILVER LINING, THE

British International Pictures
7,400 ft
T.S. 10.27

D. Thomas Bentley
C. William Shenton, G. W. Pocknall
Sc. V. E. Powell from story by Bai
    David
Art C. W. Arnold
Ed. J. Hayden

Marie Ault
Pat Aherne
John Hamilton
Eve Gray
Sydney Fairbrother
Moore Marriott
Mrs Fred Emney

SIMPLE SIMON

Hepworth
5,450 ft
T.S. 2.22

D. Henry Edwards
C. Charles Bryce
Sc. Henry Edwards and W. Courtenay
    Rowden

Henry Edwards
Henry Vibart
Hugh Clifton
Mary Dibley
Esme Hubbard
'MacEdwards'
Chrissie White

SINGLE LIFE

Ideal
4,750 ft
T.S. 10.21

D. Edwin J. Collins
Sc.
    from play by J. B. Buckstone

Campbell Gullan
Sydney Paxton
Cyril Raymond
Kathleen Vaughan

SINGLE MAN, A

British Lion
6 reels
T.S. 19.19

D. A. V. Bramble
Sc. Hubert Henry Davies

Irene Drew
Cecil Mannering
Alice de Winton

SINISTER STREET

Ideal
4,980 ft
T.S. 1.22

D. George Béranger
Sc.
    from novel by Compton Mackenzie

Maudie Dunham
Marjorie Day
John Stuart
Amy Verity
A. Tilson-Chowne
A. G. Poulton

SINLESS SINNER, A

British and Colonial
6 reels
T.S. 8.19

D. James McKay

Marie Doro
Mary Jerrold
Sam Livesey
Christine Maitland
Godfrey Tearle

451

SINS YE DO, THE

Stoll
6,800 ft
T.S. 11.24

D. Fred Leroy Granville
C. J. E. Rogers
Sc. Mary Murillo from novel by Emmeline Morrison
Ed. H. Leslie Brittain

Joan Lockton
Henry Victor
Eileen Dennes
Jerrold Robertshaw
Jameson Thomas
Eric Bransby Williams
Edward O'Neill
Frank Parfitt
Maie Hanbury
Annie Esmond

SISTER OF SIX, A

W and F with Isepa, Anglo–German production
7,196 ft
T.S. 6.27

D. Carl Hoffman
Sc.
from novel by H. Ferenc (*The Daughters of Madame Guyrkovica*)

Betty Balfour
Willy Fritsch

SISTER TO ASSIST 'ER, A

Baron
5,200 ft
T.S. 9.22

British Film Week 1924

D. George Dewhurst
C. Gustav Pauli
Sc. George Dewhurst from Fred Emney's sketch based on John le Breton's 'Mrs May' series

Mary Brough
Pollie Emery
Billie Baron
Cecil Morton York

SISTER TO ASSIST 'ER, A

6,000 ft
T.S. 9.27

D. George Dewhurst
C. Percy Strong
Sc. from F. Emney's sketch based on 'Mrs May' series by John le Breton

Mary Brough
Pollie Emery
A. Bromley Davenport
Alf Goddard
H. Humberston Wright

SKIN GAME, THE

Granger–Binger
6,000 ft
T.S. 1.21

D. B. E. Doxat-Pratt
Sc.
from play by John Galsworthy

Edmund Gwenn
Helen Haye
Meggie Albanesi
Dawson Milward
Mary Clare
Malcolm Keen
Jack Hobbs

SKIPPER'S WOOING, THE

Artistic
5,400 ft
T.S. 9.22

D. Manning Haynes
C. Frank Grainger
Sc. Lydia Hayward from story by W. W. Jacobs

Bobbie Rudd
Johnny Butt
Tom Coventry
Cynthia Murtagh
Gordon Hopkirk
Ernest Hendrie
Moore Marriott
Roy Travers
Charles Levey

SLAVES OF DESTINY

Stoll
5,100 ft
T.S. 5.24

New title of MIRANDA OF THE BALCONY

D. Maurice Elvey
Sc.
from novel by A. E. W. Mason (*Miranda of the Balcony*)

Matheson Lang
Valia
Henry Victor
H. Agar Lyons
H. Humberston Wright

SMART SET, THE

British Lion
5,000 ft
T.S. 12.19

D. A. V. Bramble
Sc. Eliot Stannard from story by Neville Percy

Neville Percy
Gwen Williams

SMASHING THROUGH

Gaumont
7,098 ft
T.S. 9.28

New title of PACE

D. W. P. Kellino
C. Baron Ventimiglia
Sc. John Hunter and William Leas

John Stuart
Eve Gray
Hayford Hobbs
Alf Goddard
Julie Suedo
Gladys Hamer

SNOW IN THE DESERT

Broadwest
5,000 ft
T.S. 12.19

P. Walter West
Sc.
from serial by Andrew Soutar in *Daily Sketch*

Violet Hopson
Stewart Rome
Ronald Colman
Simeon Stuart

SOME ARTIST

Samuelson
T.S. 8.19

'CHARITY' of trilogy FAITH, HOPE AND CHARITY, q.v.

D. Rex Wilson

Campbell Gullan

SOMEBODY'S DARLING

Gaumont
8,800 ft
T.S. 12.25

D. G. A. Cooper
C. William Shenton
Sc.
    from story by Sidney Morgan

    Betty Balfour
    J. Fisher White
    Fred Raynham
    Forrester Harvey
    G. Clifton Boyne
    A. Bromley Davenport
    Minna Grey
    Jack Harris
    Rex O'Malley

SOMEHOW GOOD

Pathé
7,973 ft
T.S. 10.27

D. Jack Raymond
C. Hal Young
Sc. Lydia Haywood from novel by
    William de Morgan

    Fay Compton
    Dorothy Boyd
    Stewart Rome
    J. Fisher White

SOMME, THE

New Era
8,100 ft
T.S. 9.27

D. M. A. Wetherell
C. Sydney Blythe, F. A. Young
Sc. Revised and edited by Boyd Cable
    and Geoffrey Barkas

SONIA

Ideal
6,000 ft
T.S. 9.21

D. Denison Clift
Sc.
    from novel by Stephen McKenna

    Evelyn Brent
    Clive Brook
    Cyril Raymond
    Henry Vibart
    Olaf Hytten

SON OF DAVID, A

Broadwest
5,000 ft
T.S. 1.20

P. Walter West
D. E. Hay Plumb
Sc. Charles Barnett

    Arthur Walcott
    Poppy Wyndham
    Vesta Sylva
    Constance Backner
    Robert Vallis
    Ronald Colman
    Harry Royston

SON OF KISSING CUP

Walter West
6,000 ft
T.S. 8.22

    British Film Week 1924

D. Walter West
Sc. J. Bertram Brown from novel by
    Campbell Rae–Brown

    Violet Hopson
    Stewart Rome
    Cameron Carr
    Judd Green
    Adeline Hayden-Coffin

SONS OF THE SEA

British Instructional Films
6,000 ft
T.S. 9.25

D. H. Bruce Woolfe
C. Jack Parker

S.O.S.

Strand
7,250 ft
T.S. 12.28

P. Julius Hagen
D. Leslie Hiscott
Sc.
    from play by Walter Ellis

    Robert Loraine
    Ursula Jeans
    Lewis Dayton
    Bramwell Fletcher
    Audrée Sayre

SOUL OF GUILDA LOIS, THE

(1919) See under SOUL'S
CRUCIFIXION, A

SOUL'S AWAKENING, A

Gaumont
6,000 ft
T.S. 7.22

    New title of WHAT LOVE
    CAN DO

    British Film Week 1924

D. Will Kellino

    Flora le Breton
    David Hawthorne
    Ethel Oliver

SOUL'S CRUCIFIXION, A

Broadwest
5,500 ft
T.S. 1.19

    New title of CRUCIFIXION or
    THE SOUL OF GUILDA LOIS

P. Walter West
D. Frank Wilson
Sc.

    from novel by Newman Flower

    Violet Hopson
    Basil Gill
    Cameron Carr
    Hilda Bayley
    J. H. Batson

SOUTH

I.T.A. Film Syndicate
4,494 ft
1919

C. Frank Hurley

    Sir Ernest Shackleton's Antarctic
    expedition, 1914–17, on 'Endur-
    ance'

SOUTHERN LOVE

Graham–Wilcox
7,500 ft
T.S. 1.24

    New title of SPANISH PASSION

D. Herbert Wilcox
C. René Guissart

    Betty Blythe
    Herbert Langley
    Warwick Ward
    Liane Haid
    Randle Ayrton

SOUTH SEA BUBBLE

Gainsborough
8,302 ft
T.S. 7.28

D. T. Hayes Hunter Asst. John Chandos
C. Walter Blakeley
Sc.
from novel by Roland Pertwee
Ed. Arthur Tavares

Ivor Novello
Benita Hume
S. J. Warmington
Ben Field
Annette Benson
Sydney Seaward
Alma Taylor
Mary Dibley
John Hamilton
Harold Huth

SOUTHWARD ON THE 'QUEST'

4,602 ft
1922

C. Frank Hurley and Claude McDonnell

Shackleton's third expedition, the Shackleton–Rowett Antarctic expedition of 1921

SPANGLES

British Filmcraft
7,425 ft
T.S. 12.28

D. George Banfield Asst. Leslie Eveleigh
C. Phil Ross
Sc. Fred Raynham

Fern Andra
Gladys Frazin
Forrester Harvey
A. B. Imeson
James Knight
Lewis Dayton

SPANISH JADE, A

Paramount (Famous–Lasky)
6,700 ft
T.S. 8.22

D. John S. Robertson
C. Roy Overbaugh
Sc.
from novel by Maurice Hewlett

David Powell
Evelyn Brent
Marc MacDermott
Harry Ham
Frank Stanmore

SPLENDID FOLLY, THE

Walturdaw
6,000 ft
T.S. 12.19

D. A. Bocchi
Sc. Hegley Sedgwick from novel by Margaret Pedlar

Manora Thew
Evelyn Harding
Hayford Hobbs
Charles Vane
George Butler
Peggy Patterson
Bert Wynne
Eileen McGrath
James English

SPORTING DOUBLE, A

Granger–Davidson
5,000 ft
T.S. 7.22

D. A. H. Rooke
C. Leslie Eveleigh

John Stuart
Douglas Munro
Terry Cavanagh
Tom Coventry
Myrtle Vibart
Lilian Douglas

SPORTING INSTINCT, THE

Granger–Davidson
5,200 ft
T.S. 9.22

D. A. H. Rooke
C. Leslie Eveleigh

    Lilian Douglas
    J. R. Tozer
    Mickey Brantford

SPORT OF KINGS

Granger–Davidson
5,200 ft
T.S. 1.22

    Reissued as 2-reeler

D. A. H. Rooke
Sc. A. H. Rooke

    Victor McLaglen
    Douglas Munro
    Phyllis Shannaw
    Cyril Percival

SPORTSMAN'S WIFE, A

Broadwest
6,000 ft
T.S. 6.21

D. Walter West
Sc. J. Bertram Brown

    Violet Hopson
    Mercy Hatton
    Adeline Hayden-Coffin
    Clive Brook
    Gregory Scott

SQUIBS

Welsh–Pearson
5,750 ft
T.S. 9.21

D. George Pearson
C. Emile Lauste
Sc. Eliot Stannard and George Pearson
    from one-act play by Clifford
    Seyler

    Betty Balfour
    Mary Brough
    Fred Groves
    Hugh E. Wright
    W. Cronin Wilson
    Annette Benson

SQUIBS' HONEYMOON

Welsh–Pearson
4,800 ft
T.S. 12.23

    British Film Weeks 1924

D. George Pearson
C. Percy Strong, Bernard Knowles

    Hugh E. Wright
    Fred Groves
    Frank Stanmore
    Robert Vallis
    Irene Tripod
    Betty Balfour

SQUIBS, M.P.

Welsh–Pearson
6 reels
T.S. 9.23

    British Film Week 1924

D. George Pearson
C. Percy Strong
Sc. George Pearson, Leslie Hiscott,
    Will Dyson

    Betty Balfour
    Hugh E. Wright
    Fred Groves
    Frank Stanmore
    Irene Tripod

P*

SQUIBS WINS THE CALCUTTA SWEEP

Welsh–Pearson
5,300 ft
T.S. 9.22

D. George Pearson
C. Emile Lauste
Sc. Hugh E. Wright and George Pearson

Betty Balfour
Fred Groves
Hugh E. Wright
Annette Benson
Bertram Burleigh
Ambrose Manning
Mary Brough

SQUIRE OF LONG HADLEY, THE

Stoll
6 reels
T.S. 5.25

D. Sinclair Hill
Sc. Eliot Stannard, from novel by E. Newton Bungaye

Marjorie Hume
Brian Aherne
G. H. Mulcaster
Humberston Wright
Eileen Dennes
A. E. Raynor
Tom Coventry

STABLE COMPANIONS

Samuelson
5,960 ft
T.S. 5.22

D.
Sc. Walter Summers

Lillian Hall-Davis
Robert English
Clive Brook

STAMPEDE

Pro Patria
7,200 ft
T.S. 1.30

D. C. Court Treatt and Stella Court Treatt   Asst. Errol Hinds
C. C. Court Treatt and Errol Hinds
Sc. Stella Court Treatt
Asst. Ed. John Orton

STARLIT GARDEN, THE

George Clark
6,400 ft
T.S. 7.23

D. Guy Newall
C. Harry Rendall
Sc.
from story by H. de Vere Stacpoole
Art titles Alex Scruby

Ivy Duke
Guy Newall
Cecil Morton York
Mary Rorke
Valia
A. Bromley Davenport
Lawford Davidson
Marie Ault
Irene Tripod

STELLA

Master
5,500 ft
T.S. 4.21

D. Edwin J. Collins
Sc. from novel by Sir H. Rider Haggard

Molly Adair
Manning Haynes
Charles Vane

STIRRUP CUP SENSATION, THE

West
5,500 ft
T.S. 9.24

D. Walter West
Sc. Campbell Rae–Brown

Stewart Rome
Violet Hopson
Judd Green
Cameron Carr
Robert Vallis
Gertrude Sterroll

STORY OF THE ROSARY, THE

Master
5,000 ft
T.S. 1.20

D. Percy Nash
Sc. Walter Courtenay Rowden from play by Walter Howard

Charles Vane
Marjorie Day
Malvina Longfellow
Dick Webb
Frank Tennant
Cameron Carr
Irene Rooke

STRAIGHT GAME, THE

(1919) See under GREAT GAME, THE

STRANGLING THREADS

Hepworth
6,600 ft
T.S. 9.23

Remake of THE COBWEB, 1917

D. C. M. Hepworth
Sc.
from play by Leon M. Lion and Naunton Davies (*The Cobweb*)

Alma Taylor
James Carew
Gwynne Herbert
Campbell Gullan
Mary Dibley
Eileen Dennes
John MacAndrews

STRAWS IN THE WIND

Bertram Phillips
6,320 ft
T.S. 3.24

New title of WHY

D. Bertram Phillips
Sc.
from story by Burton George

Queenie Thomas
Fred Paul

STREET OF ADVENTURE, THE

H. W. Thompson
5,000 ft
T.S. 8.21

D. Kenelm Foss
Sc. Kenelm Foss from story by Sir Arthur Conan Doyle

Lionelle Howard
H. V. Tollemache
Will Corrie
Roy Travers
Irene Rooke

SUMMER LIGHTENING

(1928) See under TROUBLESOME WIVES

SUNKEN ROCKS

Hepworth
5 reels
T.S. 8.19

D. C. M. Hepworth
Sc.
    from story by E. Temple Thurston

    James Carew
    Alma Taylor
    Gerald Ames
    Nigel Playfair
    John MacAndrews

SWALLOW

I.V.T.A.—South African production
4,000 ft
T.S. 12.22

    Joan Morgan
    Hayford Hobbs

SWEENEY TODD

Ideal
6,500 ft
T.S. 9.28

D. Walter West

    Moore Marriott
    Zoe Palmer
    Judd Green
    Harry Lorraine

SWEET AND TWENTY

Progress
5 reels
T.S. 11.19

D. Sidney Morgan
Sc.
    from play by Basil Hood

    Marguerite Blanche
    Langhorne Burton
    George Keene

    Arthur Lennard
    George Bellamy

SWEETHEARTS

Samuelson
T.S. 8.19

    'HOPE' of trilogy FAITH, HOPE AND CHARITY, q.v.

D. Rex Wilson
C. Sydney Blythe
Sc. G. B. Samuelson and Roland Pertwee from story by W. S. Gilbert

    Isobel Elsom
    Malcolm Cherry
    Wyndham Guise

SWINDLER, THE

Stoll
5,000 ft
T.S. 12.19

D. Maurice Elvey
Sc.
    from novel by Ethel M. Dell

    Marjorie Hume
    Cecil Humphreys
    Edward Arundel
    Neville Percy

SWORD OF DAMOCLES, THE

British and Colonial
5,000 ft
T.S. 8.20

D. George Ridgwell
Sc.
    from play by H. V. Esmond (Leonie)

    José Collins
    H. V. Esmond
    Bobby Andrews

SWORD OF FATE

British Exhibitors Films
5,000 ft
T.S. 1.21

D. Frances Grant
Sc. Frances Grant and Kate Gurney
from novel by Henry Herman

Lionel d'Aragon
David Hawthorne
Simeon Stuart
Charles Vane
Kate Gurney
Judd Green
Dorothy Moody

SYBIL

Ideal
5,000 ft
T.S. 6.21

D. Jack Denton
C. Horace Wheddon
Sc. Colden Lore from novel by Disraeli

Evelyn Brent
F. Cowley Wright

TANGLED HEARTS

6,000 ft
T.S. 5.21

Sc.
from novel by C. H. Bullivant

G. H. Mulcaster
Gertrude McCoy

TANSY

Hepworth
5,610 ft
T.S. 12.21

D. C. M. Hepworth
Sc. George Dewhurst from novel by
Tickner Edwards

Alma Taylor
James Carew
Gerald Ames
George Dewhurst
Hugh Clifton
Rolf Leslie
Eileen Dennes
Teddy Royce

TAVERN KNIGHT, THE

Stoll
6,659 ft
T.S. 9.20

D. Maurice Elvey
C. Paul Burger
Sc. Sinclair Hill from novel by Rafael
Sabatini

Eille Norwood
Cecil Humphreys
C. H. Croker King
Madge Stuart
Edward Arundel
Conway Booth
Clifford Heatherley

TAXI FOR TWO

Gainsborough
6,785 ft
T.S. 11.29

Part talking, R.C.A.
D. Alexander Esway (silent), Denison
Clift (sound)
C. Jimmy Wilson
Sc. dialogue—Ian Dalrymple and
Angus Macphail

Mabel Poulton
Gordon Harker
John Stuart

TELL YOUR CHILDREN

Donald Crisp Production
5,532 ft
T.S. 9.22

> British Film Week 1924

D. Donald Crisp

> Doris Eaton
> Walter Tennyson
> Margaret Halstan
> Mary Rorke
> Adeline Hayden-Coffin

TEMBI

7,825 ft
T.S. 7.29

P. and D. Cherry Kearton

TEMPORARY GENTLEMAN, A

Samuelson
6,000 ft
T.S. 6.20

Sc.
    from play by H. F. Maltby

> Owen Nares
> Madge Titheradge
> Sydney Fairbrother
> Arthur Vezin
> Alfred Drayton
> Maudie Dunham
> Tom Reynolds

TEMPORARY VAGABOND, A

Hepworth
5,050 ft
T.S. 1.20

D. Henry Edwards
C. Charles Bryce
Sc. Henry Edwards from story by
    Stuart Woodley

> Henry Edwards
> Chrissie White
> Stephen Ewart
> Gwynne Herbert
> Douglas Munro
> John MacAndrews

TEMPTATION OF CARLTON EARLE, THE

Phillips
6,000 ft
T.S. 3.23

D. Wilfred Noy
Sc. Wilfred Noy from novel by Stella
    M. During

> C. Aubrey Smith
> Gertrude McCoy
> James Lindsay
> Simeon Stuart

TEMPTRESS, THE

British and Colonial
5,000 ft
T.S. 11.20

D. George Edwardes Hall
Sc. George Edwardes Hall from play
    by T. W. Robertson (from Balzac's
    play *L'Aventurière*)

> Yvonne Arnaud
> Langhorne Burton
> Austen Leigh
> John Gliddon
> Saba Raleigh
> Christine Maitland
> Lennox Pawle

TESHA

British International Pictures
7,826 ft
T.S. 8.28

D. Victor Saville Asst. Basil Roscoe
C. Werner Brandes

462

Sc. Victor Saville and Walter Mycroft
from novel by Countess Barcynska
Art Hugh Gee
Titles Arthur Wimperis

Maria Corda
Jameson Thomas
Paul Kavanagh
Clifford Heatherley
Daisy Campbell
Espinosa
Bunty Fosse
Mickey Brantford
Boris Ranevsky

TESTIMONY

George Clark
7,189 ft
T.S. 10.20

D. Guy Newall
C. Bert Ford
Sc. Guy Newall from novel by Claude
and Alice Askew

Ivy Duke
Mary Rorke
David Hawthorne
Barbara Everest
Douglas Munro
Lawford Davidson

THIRD EYE, THE

Graham Wilcox
7,200 ft
T.S. 1.29

D. P. MacLean Rogers
Sc. P. MacLean Rogers

Dorothy Seacombe
John Hamilton
Hayford Hobbs
Cameron Carr
Ian Harding
Jean Jay

THIRD ROUND, THE

(1925) See under BULLDOG
DRUMMOND'S THIRD ROUND

THIS FREEDOM

Ideal
7,300 ft
T.S. 4.23

British Film Week 1924

D. Denison Clift
C. Horace Wheddon
Sc. Denison Clift from novel by A. S.
M. Hutchinson

Fay Compton
Clive Brook
Adeline Hayden-Coffin
Gladys Hamer
Gladys Hamilton
Charles Vane
Julie Hartley-Milburne
Athene Seyler
Robert English
John Stuart
Fewlass Llewellyn
Bunty Fosse

THIS MARRIAGE BUSINESS

Enders–Hiscott
6,206 ft
Reviewed 12.27

Produced, directed, written and edited
by F. A. Enders and Leslie Hiscott

Owen Nares
Estelle Brody
Marjorie Hume
Jeff Barlow

THOROUGHBRED, THE

London Screen Plays
5,608 ft
T.S. 12.28
D. Sidney Morgan

Ian Hunter
Louise Prussing
H. Agar Lyons

463

THOSE WHO LOVE

7,929 ft
T.S. 11.29

Part talking, R.C.A.

William Freshman
Blanche Adele

THOU FOOL

Stoll
5,100 ft
T.S. 9.28

D. Fred Paul
Sc. J. J. Bell from story by J. J. Bell

Stewart Rome
Wyndham Guise
J. Fisher White
Mickey Brantford
Marjorie Hume
Mary Rorke
Darby Foster
Nelson Ramsaye
Adelaide Grace

THOU SHALT NOT

(1922) See under WAS SHE
GUILTY?

THREE KINGS

British and Foreign
6,824 ft
T.S. 1.29

D. Hans Steinhoff
Sc. Henry Edwards

Henry Edwards
Warwick Ward
John Hamilton
Clifford McLaglen
Evelyn Holt

THREE LIVE GHOSTS

Famous Players–Lasky British
6,600 ft
T.S. 3.22

D. George Fitzmaurice
C. A. Miller
Sc. Ouida Bergere from play by
    Frederick S. Isham

Anna Q Nilsson
Edmund Goulding
Norman Kerry
Clare Greet
Annette Benson
Dorothy Fane
Wyndham Guise

THREE MEN IN A BOAT

Artistic
5,000 ft
T.S. 11.20

D. Hugh Croise
Sc. Hugh Croise from novel by Jerome
    K. Jerome

Lionelle Howard
Johnny Butt
Manning Haynes

THREE PASSIONS, THE

St Georges
8 reels
T.S. 12.28

D. Rex Ingram
C. L. H. Burel
Sc.
    from story by Cosmo Hamilton
Art Heinrich Kleys
Ed. Arthur Ellis

Alice Terry
Ivan Petrovitch
Shayle Gardner
Leslie Faber

THRILLING STORIES FROM THE 'STRAND MAGAZINE'

Stoll
Series, 5 2-reelers
T.S. 7.24 and 1.25

THROUGH FIRE AND WATER

Ideal
6,188 ft
T.S. 2.23

British Film Week 1924

D. Thomas Bentley
C. Horace Wheddon
Sc. Eliot Stannard from novel by Victor Bridges (*Greensea Island*)

Flora le Breton
Clive Brook
Lawford Davidson
Jerrold Robertshaw
Edward Arundel
M. A. Wetherell
Esme Hubbard

THROUGH STORMY WATERS

5,000 ft
T.S. 8.20

Eileen Bellamy
George Keene

THROUGH THREE REIGNS

Hepworth
3,000 ft
T.S. 7.22

THROW OF DICE, A

British Instructional Films–U.F.A.
8 reels
T.S. 10.29

Breusing discs

D. Franz Osten   Alan Campbell
C. E. Schunemann
Sc. W. Burton

Seeta Devi
Himansu Rai
Charu Roy
Kanwa

TIDAL WAVE

Stoll
6,000 ft
T.S. 8.20

D. Sinclair Hill
C. John Mackenzie
Sc. Sinclair Hill from novel by Ethel M. Dell

Poppy Wyndham
Judd Green
Annie Esmond
Dora Lennox
Pardoe Woodman
Sydney Seaward

TILLY OF BLOOMSBURY

Samuelson
5,400 ft
T.S. 9.21

D. Rex Wilson
Sc.
from novel (*Happy-Go-Lucky*) and play by Ian Hay

Edna Best
Tom Reynolds
Helen Haye
Fred Lewis
Henry Kendall
Isabel Jeans
Leonard Pagden
Campbell Gullan
Lottie Blackford

465

TINTED VENUS, THE

Hepworth
5,000 ft
T.S. 4.21

D. C. M. Hepworth
Sc. Blanche MacIntosh from novel by
F. Anstey

Alma Taylor
George Dewhurst
Eileen Dennes
Gwynne Herbert
Hugh Clifton
Maud Cressall

TIP TOES

British National
6,286 ft
T.S. 5.28

D. Herbert Wilcox
C. Roy Overbaugh
Sc.
from play by Guy Bolton and Fred
Thompson

Dorothy Gish
Nelson Keys
Will Rogers
Miles Mander

TIT FOR TAT

Hepworth
5,200 ft
T.S. 8.22

D. Henry Edwards
C. Charles Bryce
Sc. Jessie J. Robertson

Henry Edwards
Chrissie White
Eileen Dennes
Gwynne Herbert
Christine Rayner
Annie Esmond
Mary Brough

TOILERS, THE

Neville Bruce
5,200 ft
T.S. 3.19 and 6.20

C. Lucien Egrot
Sc. Eliot Stannard from song by
Piccolo Mini

Manora Thew
Gwynne Herbert
George Dewhurst
Ronald Colman
Will Corrie
Eric Barker

TO KILIMANJARO

Ratcliffe Holmes
7,000 ft
T.S. 12.24

D. Ratcliffe Holmes
C. George A. Plowman

TOMMY ATKINS

British International Pictures
9,550 ft
T.S. 5.28

D. Norman Walker   Asst. F. C. Ewin
C. René Guissart and Claude Friese-
Greene
Sc. Ian Hay and Eliot Stannard from
play by Ben Landeck and Arthur
Shirley
Art J. E. Wills
Ed. S. Simmonds

Henry Victor
Walter Butler
Lillian Hall-Davis
Jerrold Robertshaw
Shayle Gardner
Cyril McLaglen
Eric Wison
Leslie Tomlinson

466

TONI

British International Pictures
6,000 ft
T.S. 5.28

D. Anthony Maude
C. George W. Pocknall
Sc. V. E. Powell from play by Douglas
   Furber and Harry Graham
Art J. E. Wills

   Jack Buchanan
   Dorothy Boyd
   Henry Vibart
   Moore Marriott
   Forrester Harvey
   Hayford Hobbs
   Lawson Butt
   Frank Goldsmith

TONS OF MONEY

Stoll
5 reels
T.S. 3.24

D. Frank Crane
C. Bert Cann
Sc. Lucita Squiers from play by Will
   Evans and Valentine
Titles by Tom Webster

   Leslie Henson
   Flora le Breton
   Mary Brough
   Jack Denton
   Douglas Munro
   Elsie Fuller

TORN SAILS

Ideal
5,000 ft
T.S. 10.20

D. A. V. Bramble
Sc. Eliot Stannard from novel by
   Allen Raine

   Milton Rosmer
   Mary Odette
   Geoffrey Kerr

TOTO'S WIFE

Cherry Kearton Films
6,500 ft
T.S. 7.24

P. Cherry Kearton

TO WHAT RED HELL

Strand
8,000 ft
T.S. 10.29

   Full talking, R.C.A.

D. Edwin Greenwood
C. Basil Emmott
Sc. Leslie Hiscott from play by Percy
   Robinson

   Sybil Thorndike
   Bramwell Fletcher
   John Hamilton

TOWN OF CROOKED WAYS, THE

A.R.T. Films
5,200 ft
T.S. 1.21

D. Bert Wynne
C. Randal Terraneau
Sc.
   from novel by J. S. Fletcher
Art J. A. Williamson

   Edward O'Neill
   Cyril Percival
   Bert Wynne
   Poppy Wyndham
   Charles Vane
   Judd Green
   Eileen McGrath
   Arthur Cullin
   George Bellamy
   Arthur Walcott
   Fred Rains
   Wallace Bosco

467

TRAINER AND TEMPTRESS

Walter West
7,500 ft
T.S. 9.25

D. Walter West
Sc.
from novel by Atty Persse and A. J. Russell

Juliette Compton
James Knight
C. Morton York
Judd Green
Sydney Seaward

TRAPPED BY THE MORMONS

Master
6 reels
T.S. 3.22

D. Harry B. Parkinson
C. Theodore Thumwood
Sc. Frank Miller

Evelyn Brent
Lewis Willoughby
Olaf Hytten
Cecil Morton York
Ethel Newman
George Wynne
Olive Sloane

TRENT'S LAST CASE

Broadwest
5,500 ft
T.S. 10.20

D. Richard Garrick
Sc. P. L. Mannock from story by E. C. Bentley

Gregory Scott
George Foley
Clive Brook
Cameron Carr
Pauline Peters

TRIUMPH OF THE RAT, THE

Gainsborough
7,550 ft
T.S. 9.26

P. Michael Balcon and Carlyle Blackwell
D. Graham Cutts
C. Hal Young
Sc. Graham Cutts and Reginald Fogwell
Art Bertram Evans
Titles Roland Pertwee

Ivor Novello
Isabel Jeans
Nina Vanna
Julie Suedo
Marie Ault
Adeline Hayden-Coffin
Mickey Brantford
Gabriel Rosca
Charles Dormer

TRIUMPH OF THE SCARLET PIMPERNEL, THE

British and Dominion
7,946 ft
T.S. 11.28

D. T. Hayes Hunter
C. W. Shenton
Sc.
from novel by Baroness Orczy
Art Clifford Pember

Matheson Lang
Marjorie Hume
Nelson Keys
Juliette Compton
Haddon Mason
Harold Huth

TROUBLESOME WIVES

Nettlefold
5,870 ft
T.S. 8.28

New title of SUMMER LIGHTENING

P. Archibald Nettlefold
D. Harry Hughes
C. Charles Bryce
Sc. Harry Hughes from play by Ernest Denny (*Summer Lightening*)

    Mabel Poulton
    Eric Bransby Williams
    Marie Ault
    Reginald Fox
    Lilian Oldland

TROUSERS

Bertram Phillips
5,000 ft
T.S. 4.20

D. Bertram Phillips

    Queenie Thomas
    Bernard Vaughan
    Fred Morgan
    Lottie Blackford
    Nessie Blackford

TRUANTS, THE

Stoll
T.S. 19.22

D. Sinclair Hill
C. Adolph Burger
Sc.
    from novel by A. E. W. Mason
Art Walter Murton

    Joan Morgan
    Robert English
    Lawford Davidson
    George Bellamy
    Lewis Gilbert

TRUE TILDA

London Film Co.
4,650 ft
T.S. 4.20

D. Harold Shaw
Sc.
    from story by Sir Arthur Quiller-Couch

    Edna Flugrath
    Edward O'Neill
    Douglas Munro
    George Bellamy
    Gordon Craig
    Simeon Stuart

TUSALAVA

Len Lye for London Film Society
1929 (shown at Film Society 12.29)
Made by Len Lye
Music Jack Ellit

TWELVE POUND LOOK, THE

Ideal
5,000 ft
T.S. 9.20

D. Jack Denton
Sc. Eliot Stannard from play by Sir James Barrie

    Milton Rosmer
    Jessie Winter
    Aileen Bagot
    J. Nelson Ramsayc
    E. Story Gofton
    Athalie Davis
    José Shannon

TWELVE-TEN

British and Colonial
6,000 ft
T.S. 19.19

D. Herbert Brenon

    Marie Doro
    Ben Webster
    James Carew

469

TWENTY YEARS AGO

British Screen Classics
1,420 ft
T.S. 6.28
Ed. Ben R. Hart and St J. Clowes

TWO LITTLE DRUMMER BOYS

Blakely
7,500 ft
T.S. 10.28

D.   G. B. Samuelson
Sc.
    from play by Walter Howard

    Wee Georgie Wood
    Alma Taylor
    Walter Butler
    Alf Goddard

TWO LITTLE WOODEN SHOES

Progress
3,525 ft
T.S. 9.20

D.   Sidney Morgan
C.   S. J. Mumford
Sc. Sidney Morgan from novel by
    Ouida

    Joan Morgan
    Langhorne Burton
    J. Denton Thompson
    Constance Backner

UGLY DUCKLING, THE

Samuelson
6,000 ft
T.S. 5.21

D.   Alexander Butler

    Maudie Dunham
    Florence Turner
    Albert Ray

UNCLE DICK'S DARLING

Fred Paul
5 reels
T.S. 6.22

D.   Fred Paul
Sc. R. Byron Webber from play by
    H. J. Byron

    Athalie Davis
    George Bellamy
    Humberston Wright
    Frank Dane
    Sidney Folker

UNDERGROUND

British Instructional Films
7,282 ft
T.S. 7.28

P.   H. Bruce Woolfe
D.   Anthony Asquith   Asst. Hal
    Martin
C.   Stanley Rodwell Lighting: Karl
    Fischer
Sc. Anthony Asquith
Art Ian Campbell-Gray

    Elissa Landi
    Norah Baring
    Brian Aherne
    Cyril McLaglen

UNDER SAIL IN THE FROZEN NORTH

Gaumont
2,109 ft
T.S. 6.26

C.   J. C. Bee Mason
    Algarsson–Worsley British Arctic
    Expedition, 1925

UNDER THE GREENWOOD TREE

British International Pictures
8,386 ft
T.S. 9.29

    Full talking and songs, R.C.A.

D. Harry Lachman
Sc.
    from the book by Thomas Hardy
Art C. W. Arnold

    Marguerite Allen
    John Batten

UNDER THE SOUTHERN CROSS

New Zealand film
5,606 ft
T.S. 3.29

UNINVITED GUEST, THE

5,000 ft
T.S. 7.23

D. George Dewhurst
C. Gustav Pauli
Sc. George Dewhurst

    Madge Stuart
    Stewart Rome
    Cecil Morton York
    Cameron Carr
    Leal Douglas
    Arthur Walcott

UNION OF POST OFFICE WORKERS, THE

Union of P.O. Workers
3,709 ft
rev. 2.27

Sc. Horace Nobbs

UNMARRIED

Granger–British
6,000 ft
T.S. 4.20

D. Rex Wilson for National Council for the Unmarried Mother and her Child
Sc. Arthur Backer

    Gerald du Maurier
    Malvina Longfellow
    Mary Glynne
    Edmund Gwenn
    Mary Rorke
    Annie Esmond

UNREST

Cairns–Torquay
6,000 ft
T.S. 4.20 and 8.21

Sc. R. Byron Webber from novel by Warwick Deeping

    Mary Dibley
    Dallas Cairns
    Maud Yates
    Edward O'Neill

UNSLEEPING EYE, THE

Seven Seas
6,450 ft
T.S. 5.28

P. Alexander Macdonald
D. Alexander Macdonald
C. Walter H. B. Sully
Sc. Alexander Macdonald
Ed. Adrian Brunel and Ivor Montagu

    Wendy Osbourne

UNWANTED, THE

Napoleon
7 reels
T.S. 4.24

D. G. B. Samuelson
D. Walter Summers

    C. Aubrey Smith
    Mary Dibley
    Nora Swinburne
    Lillian Hall-Davis
    Francis Lister

UNWRITTEN LAW, THE

3 reels
T.S. 6.29

    Full talking, R.C.A.

    Ion Swinley
    Rosalie Fuller

USURPER, THE

B.A.F.C.
6 reels
T.S. 9.19

D. Duncan McRae
Sc. Adrian Brunel from novel by W. J. Locke

    Gertrude McCoy
    Stephen Ewart
    Geoffrey Kerr
    Fred Volpe

VICTORY

7 reels
T.S. 3.28

D. M. A. Wetherell
C. F. A. Young and Joe Rosenthal

    Moore Marriott
    Walter Butler
    Julie Suedo
    Marie Ault

VICTORY LEADERS, THE

Stoll
1,757 ft
T.S. 6.19

D. Maurice Elvey
C. Paul Burger and Lt Tong

VI, OF SMITH'S ALLEY

Broadwest
5,585 ft
T.S. 9.21

D. Walter West
C. A. G. Frenguelli
Sc. Charles Barnett

    Violet Hopson
    Amy Verity
    George Foley
    Sidney Folker
    Peter Upcher
    Cameron Carr

VIRGINIA'S HUSBAND

Nettlefold
6,300 ft
T.S. 5.28

D. Harry Hughes
C. Charles Bryce
Sc. Harry Hughes from play by Florence A. Kilpatrick

    Lilian Oldland
    Mabel Poulton
    Marie Ault
    Pat Aherne
    Ena Grossmith

VIRGIN QUEEN, THE

John Stuart Blackton Productions
7 reels
T.S. 1.23

    Partly in Prizma colour

472

D. John Stuart Blackton
C. Nicholas Musurca
Sc. Harry Pirie Gordon

Lady Diana Manners
Carlyle Blackwell
Norma Whalley
William Luff
Hubert Carter
Bernard Dudley
Lionel d'Aragon
Walter Tennyson
A. B. Imeson
Marian Blackton
Violet Virginia Blackton
Tom Haselwood
Ursula Jeans

VORTEX, THE

Gainsborough
6,281 ft
T.S. 3.28

P. Michael Balcon
D. Adrian Brunel Asst. Chandos Balcon
C. Jimmy Wilson
Sc. Eliot Stannard from play by Noel Coward
Art Clifford Pember
Titles Roland Pertwee

Ivor Novello
Willette Kershaw
Frances Doble
Simeon Stuart
Kinsey Peile
Julie Suedo
Dorothy Fane

VULTURE'S PREY, THE

I.V.T.A.—South African film
5,100 ft
T.S. 2.22

M. A. Wetherell

WAIT AND SEE

Nettlefold
6,352 ft
T.S. 2.28

P. Archibald Nettlefold
D. Walter Forde Asst. James Reardon
C. Geoffrey Faithfull Asst. Fred Ford
Sc. W. G. Saunders

Walter Forde
Pauline Johnson
Frank Stanmore
Sam Livesey
Charles Dormer
Mary Brough

WALLS OF PREJUDICE

Gaumont
5,200 ft
T.S. 4.20

D. C. C. Calvert
Sc.
from play by Mrs Alexander Gross (*Break Down the Walls*)

Josephine Earle
Dallas Anderson
Pat Somerset
Cecil du Gué
Zoe Palmer

WANDERING JEW, THE

Stoll
8,300 ft
T.S. 6.23

British Film Week 1924

D. Maurice Elvey
C. J. J. Cox
Sc. Alicia Ramsey from play by E. Temple Thurston based on play by Eugene Sue
Art Walter Murton

473

Matheson Lang
Hutin Britton
Lewis Gilbert
Isobel Elsom
Gordon Hopkirk
Hubert Carter
Lionel d'Aragon
Malvina Longfellow
Shayle Gardner
Hector Abbas
Louise Conti
Fred Raynham
Jerrold Robertshaw
Peter Dear

WARE CASE, THE

First National-Pathé
7,689 ft
T.S. 4.28

D. Manning Haynes Asst. L. F. Pridmore
C. W. Shenton, Paul Lambert
Sc. Lydia Hayward from play by George Pleydell
Art Hugh Gee

Stewart Rome
Betty Carter
Ian Fleming
Cynthia Murtagh
Cameron Carr

WAS SHE GUILTY?

Granger–Binger
5 reels
T.S. 8.22

New title of THOU SHALT NOT

D. George Béranger
C. F. Boersma

Gertrude McCoy
Zoe Palmer
William Freshman

WAS SHE JUSTIFIED?

Walter West
5,500 ft
T.S. 11.22

D. Walter West
Sc.

from play by Maud Williamson and Andrew Soutar (*The Pruning Knife*)

Florence Turner
Lewis Gilbert
Ivy Close
John Reid
George Bellamy
Arthur Walcott

WAY OF A MAN, THE

Gaumont
6,500 ft
T.S. 1.21

D. C. C. Calvert
Sc. H. V. Bailey

Josephine Earle
Cecil du Gué
Lewis Dayton
Philip Anthony
George Bellamy
Cyril Smith

WAY OF THE WORLD, THE

I. B. Davidson
5,000 ft
T.S. 6.20

D. A. E. Coleby
Sc. A. E. Coleby

A. E. Coleby
Capt. Gordon Coghill
Charles Kane
Babs Ronald

WEAVERS OF FORTUNE

Granger–Davidson
5,500 ft
T.S. 12.22

British Film Week 1924

D. A. H. Rooke
C. Leslie Eveleigh

Henry Vibart
Dacia
Myrtle Vibart
Mrs Hubert Willis
Derek Glynne

WEEKEND WIVES

British International Pictures
7,226 ft
T.S. 11.28

D. Harry Lachman
C. J. J. Cox
Sc. Victor Kendall and Rex Taylor
Art Hugh Gee
Ed. Emile de Ruelle

Estelle Brody
Annette Benson
Jameson Thomas
Monty Banks
George Gee
Ernest Thesiger
Koko Arrah

WEE MACGREGOR'S SWEETHEART, THE

Welsh–Pearson
5,600 ft
T.S. 6.22

D. George Pearson
C. Emile Lauste
Sc. George Pearson and J. J. Bell from stories by J. J. Bell

Betty Balfour
Bunty Fosse

M. A. Wetherell
Mabel Archdale
Bryan Powley
Minna Grey
Cyril Percival
J. Denton Thompson
Nora Swinburne
Marie Ault
Donald McCardle

WEMBLEY EXHIBITION, THE

Pathé
5,000 ft
T.S. 8.24

WESTWARD HO!

British Exhibitors' Films
6 reels
T.S. 11.19

D. Percy Nash
Sc. Walter Courtenay Rowden from novel by Charles Kingsley
Art Seymour Lucas

Renée Kelly
Charles Quartermain
Irene Rooke

WE WOMEN

Stoll
5,100 ft
T.S. 2.25

D. W. P. Kellino
C. William Shenton
Sc. Lydia Hayward from novel by Countess Barcynska
Art W. Murton
Ed. Challis N. Sanderson

Billie and Dollie
John Stuart
Nina Vanna
Minnie Leslie
Cecil du Gué
Charles Ashton

475

WHAT LOVE CAN DO

(1922) See under SOUL'S
AWAKENING, A

WHAT MONEY CAN BUY

Gaumont
6,400 ft
T.S. 7.28

D. Edwin Collins
Sc.
    from play by Arthur Shirley and
    Ben Landeck

    Madeleine Carroll
    Cecil Barry
    Humberston Wright
    Alf Goddard
    John Longden
    Maudie Dunham
    Judd Green

WHAT NEXT?

Nettlefold
6,170 ft
T.S. 6.28

D. Walter Forde

    Walter Forde
    Pauline Johnson
    Frank Stanmore
    Douglas Payne
    Charles Dormer
    Frank Parfitt

WHAT PRICE 'LOVING CUP'?

Walter West
5,750 ft
T.S. 10.23

    British Film Week 1924

D. Walter West

    Violet Hopson
    James Lindsay
    James Knight
    Cecil Morton York
    Marjorie Benson

WHAT THE BUTLER SAW

Gaumont
5,855 ft
T.S. 10.24

D. George Dewhurst
Sc.
    from play by E. F. Parry and
    Frederick Mouillot

    Guy Newall
    Irene Rich
    A. B. Imeson
    John MacAndrews
    A. Bromley Davenport
    C. Morton York
    Pauline Garon
    Drusilla Wills
    Hilda Anthony

WHEELS OF CHANCE, THE

Stoll
5 reels
1922

D. Harold Shaw
C. A. R. Terraneau
Sc. Frank Miller from novel by H. G.
    Wells
Art Walter Murton

    George K. Arthur
    Bertie Wright
    Mabel Archdale
    Judd Green
    Clifford Marle
    Wallace Bosco

WHEN GREEK MEETS GREEK

Violet Hopson
5,500 ft
T.S. 6.22

D. Walter West
Sc.
from novel by Paul Trent

Violet Hopson
Stewart Rome

WHEN IT WAS DARK

Walturdaw
5 reels
T.S. 10.19

D. A. Bocchi
Sc. Kenelm Foss from novel by Guy
Thorne

Hayford Hobbs
Charles Vane
George Butler
Evelyn Harding
Bert Wynne
Peggy Patterson
Manora Thew
Judd Green
Arthur Walcott

WHEN KNIGHTS WERE BOLD

British and Dominion
7,213 ft
T.S. 2.29

D. Tim Whelan
Sc.
from play by Charles Marlow

Nelson Keys
Eric Bransby Williams
Harold Huth

WHERE THE RAINBOW ENDS

British Photoplay Productions
5,000 ft
T.S. 11.21

D. H. Lisle Lucoque
Sc. from children's play by Mrs
Clifford Mills and Reginald Owen

Roger Livesey
Vesta Sylva

WHILE LONDON SLEEPS

5 reels
T.S. 7.22

New title of COCAINE, T.S. 5.22
and rejected by Censor

D. Graham Cutts
C. Theodore Thumwood

Hilda Bayley
Tony Fraser
Flora le Breton

WHITE CARGO

W and P
7,965 ft
T.S. 5.29 (silent), 10.29 (sound)

Full talking, R.C.A.

D. J. B. Williams and Arthur Barnes
C. Karl Püth
Sc.
from novel by Vera Simonton
(*Hell's Playground*) and play by
Leon Gordon

Gipsy Rhouma
Leslie Faber
Humberston Wright
Maurice Evans
John Hamilton
Henri de Vries

WHITE HEAT

Graham–Wilcox
7,000 ft
T.S. 9.26

D. Thomas Bentley
C. W. Shenton
Sc. Eliot Stannard from novel by 'Pan'

    Walter Butler
    Juliette Compton
    Wyndham Standing
    Vesta Sylva
    George Bellamy
    Estelle Brody
    Bertram Burleigh

WHITE HEN, THE

Zodiac
5,000 ft
T.S. 1.21

D. Frankland A. Richardson
Sc.
    from novel by Phyllis Campbell

    Mary Glynne
    Leslie Faber
    Pat Somerset
    Cecil Humphreys

WHITE HOPE, THE

Walter West
6,000 ft
T.S. 10.22

D. Walter West
Sc.
    from novel by W. R. H. Trow-bridge

    Violet Hopson
    Stewart Rome
    John MacAndrews
    Lionelle Howard
    Frank Wilson

WHITE SHADOW, THE

Balcon–Saville–Freedman
5,047 ft
T.S. 2.24

P. Michael Balcon
D. Graham Cutts   Asst. Alfred Hitchcock
C. Claude McDonnell
Sc. by Michael Morton
Art Alfred Hitchcock
Ed. Alfred Hitchcock

    Betty Compson
    Clive Brook
    Henry Victor
    Daisy Campbell
    A. B. Imeson
    Olaf Hytten

WHITE SHEIK, THE

British International Pictures
8,980 ft
T.S. 12.27

    New title of KING'S MATE

D. Harley Knoles
C. J. J. Cox, René Guissart
Sc. V. E. Powell from novel by Rosita Forbes (*King's Mate*)
Ed. Joseph Hayden

    Jameson Thomas
    Lillian Hall-Davis
    Warwick Ward
    Forrester Harvey
    Gibb McLaughlin
    Julie Suedo
    Clifford McLaglen

WHITE SLIPPERS

Stoll
6,180 ft
T.S. 8.24

D. Sinclair Hill
C. J. J. Cox
Sc. Mary Murillo

478

Matheson Lang
Joan Lockton
J. Nelson Ramsaye
Arthur McLaglen
Adeline Hayden-Coffin
Charles Barratt
Albert Raynor
Irene Tripod

WHO IS THE MAN?

G. B. Samuelson
6,000 ft
T.S. 9.24

D. Walter Summers

Isobel Elsom
Lewis Dayton
Langhorne Burton
Henry Vibart
Mary Rorke
John Gielgud

WHOSOEVER SHALL OFFEND

Windsor
6 reels
T.S. 2.19

D. A. Bocchi
Sc. Kenelm Foss from novel by F. Marion Crawford

Kenelm Foss
Mary Marsh Allen
Charles Vane
Barbara Everest
Evelyn Harding
Philip Hewland
Hayford Hobbs
Mary Odette

WHY?

(1924) See under STRAWS IN THE WIND

WHY MEN LEAVE HOME

4,000 ft
T.S. 9.22

Nellie Wallace

WIDECOMBE FAIR

British International Pictures
6,800 ft
T.S. 12.28

D. Norman Walker
C. Claude Friese-Greene
Sc. Eliot Stannard from novel by Eden Phillpotts
Art J. E. Wills
Ed. Emile de Ruelle

Wyndham Standing
Violet Hopson
Moore Marriott
Judd Green
William Freshman
Marguerite Allen
George Cooper

WIDOW TWANKEE

(1923) See under ONE ARABIAN NIGHT

WILD HEATHER

Hepworth
5,000 ft
T.S. 9.21

D. C. M. Hepworth
Sc.
from play by Dorothy Brandon

Chrissie White
Gwynne Herbert
James Carew
Gerald Ames
George Dewhurst
G. H. Mulcaster
Hugh Clifton
James Annand
Eileen Dennes

479

WILL, THE

Ideal
5,000 ft
T.S. 2.21

D. A. V. Bramble
Sc. Eliot Stannard from play by Sir
James Barrie

Milton Rosmer
J. Fisher White
Pam Neville
Mary Brough

WILL AND A WAY, A

Artistic
4 reels
T.S. 2.22

D. Manning Haynes
C. Frank Grainger
Sc. Lydia Hayward from story by W.
W. Jacobs

Ernest Hendrie
Pollie Emery
Cynthia Murtagh
Johnny Butt
Charles Ashton
John Braithwaite
Agnes Brantford

WINDING ROAD, THE

British Famous Films
5,000 ft
T.S. 9.20

Edith Pearson
Cecil Humphreys

WINDOW IN PICCADILLY, A

7,500 ft
T.S. 1.28

D. Sidney Morgan

De Groot

Joan Morgan
Maurice Braddell
James Carew
Julie Suedo
John Hamilton
Olga Lindo

WINE OF LIFE, THE

I. B. Davidson
5,600 ft
T.S. 5.24

D. A. H. Rooke
C. Leslie Eveleigh
Sc.
from novel by Maud Annesley

Juliette Compton
Clive Brook
James Carew
Betty Carter
Gertrude Sterroll
Mildred Evelyn

WINNING GOAL, THE

Samuelson
5,000 ft
T.S. 8.20

Sc.
from novel by Harold Brighouse
(*The Game*)

Maudie Dunham
Haidee Wright
Tom Reynolds
Harold Walden
Alfred Drayton

WISP O' THE WOODS

British Lion
5 reels
T.S. 8.19

D. Lewis Willoughby
Sc.
from story by Norman Macdonald

Constance Worth
Arthur Cullin
Gwen Williams
Evan Thomas
S. J. Warmington

WITH ALL HER HEART

I. B. Davidson
5,000 ft
T.S. 6.20

D.   Frank Wilson
Sc.
>   from novel by Charles Garvice

>   Milton Rosmer
>   Mary Odette
>   J. H. Batson

WITH CHERRY KEARTON IN THE JUNGLE

Cherry Kearton
5,000 ft
Reviewed 3.26

P.   Cherry Kearton

WITH COBHAM TO THE CAPE

Gaumont
8 1-reelers or 7 reels
T.S. 6.26

C.   Basil Emmott

WITHIN THE MAZE

Films Legrand, Anglo-French production
6,300 ft

T.S. 4.23
Sc.
>   from novel by Mrs Henry Wood

>   Constance Worth
>   Gerald Ames

WITNESS, THE

(1925) See under LAST WITNESS, THE

WOMAN AND THE MAN, THE

5,000 ft
T.S. 5.25

Sc.
>   from story by Robert Buchanan

>   Milton Rosmer

WOMAN IN PAWN, A

Gaumont
6,845 ft
T.S. 10.27

P.   Victor Saville
D.   Edwin Greenwood
C.   Baron Ventimiglia
Sc.
>   from play by Frank Stayton (*In Pawn*)

>   John Stuart
>   Gladys Jennings
>   Chili Bouchier

WOMAN IN WHITE

British and Dominion
6,702 ft
T.S. 1.29

D.   Herbert Wilcox   Asst. Robert Cullen
C.   David Kesson
Sc.
>   from novel and play by Wilkie Collins

>   Blanche Sweet
>   Haddon Mason
>   Louise Prussing
>   Cecil Humphreys
>   Frank Parfitt
>   Minna Grey

WOMAN OF HIS DREAMS, THE

Stoll
4,320 ft
T.S. 7.21

D. Harold Shaw
C. J. Coward
Sc. Leslie H. Gordon from novel by Ethel M. Dell

Mary Dibley
Sydney Seaward
Alec Fraser
Edward Arundel
Fred Thatcher

WOMAN OF NO IMPORTANCE, A

Ideal
5,250 ft
T.S. 6.21

D. Denison Clift
Sc.
from play by Oscar Wilde

Fay Compton
Milton Rosmer
M. Gray Murray
Henry Vibart
Daisy Campbell

WOMAN OF THE IRON BRACELETS, THE

Progress
5,000 ft
T.S. 9.20

D. Sidney Morgan
Sc.
from novel by Frank Barrett

Eve Balfour
Arthur Walcott
Alice de Winton
George Bellamy
George Keene
Marguerite Blanche

WOMAN REDEEMED, A

Stoll
8,200 ft
T.S. 8.27

P. Victor Peers
D. Sinclair Hill
C. D. P. Cooper, Desmond Dickinson
Sc. Mary Murillo from story by F. Britten Austin (*The Fining Pot is for Silver*)
Art W. Murton
Ed. H. L. Brittain

Joan Lockton
Stella Arbenina
Brian Aherne
James Carew
Robert English
Gordon Hopkirk

WOMAN TEMPTED, THE

M.E.
7,500 ft
Premiere 6.26

D. Maurice Elvey
Sc.
from novel by Countess of Cathcart

Juliette Compton
Nina Vanna
Joan Morgan
Warwick Ward
Adeline Hayden-Coffin
Malcolm Tod
Judd Green

WOMAN TO WOMAN

Balcon–Saville–Freedman
7,455 ft
T.S. 11.23

British Film Week 1924
Remade in 1929

P. Michael Balcon

D. Graham Cutts Asst. Alfred Hitchcock
C. Claude McDonnell
Sc. Alfred Hitchcock and Graham Cutts from play by Michael Morton
Art. Alfred Hitchcock
Ed. Alma Reville

Betty Compson
Josephine Earle
Marie Ault
Clive Brook
Henry Vibart

WOMAN TO WOMAN

Gainsborough and Tiffany Stahl,
Anglo–American production
8,039 ft
T.S. 11.29

(Remake of 1923 WOMAN TO WOMAN)
Full talking, R.C.A.

D. Victor Saville

Juliette Compton
George Barraud

WOMAN WHO OBEYED, THE

Astra
6,700 ft
T.S. 9.23

D. Sidney Morgan
C. S. J. Mumford
Sc. Sidney Morgan

Stewart Rome
Hilda Bayley
Henri de Vries
Gerald Ames
Valia
Ivo Dawson
Peter Dear

WOMAN WITH THE FAN, THE

Stoll
4,890 ft
T.S. 7.21

D. René Plaisetty
Sc. Leslie H. Cox from novel by Robert Hichens

Mary Massart
Alec Fraser
Cyril Percival
Paulette del Baye

WOMEN AND DIAMONDS

George Clark Productions
5,200 ft
T.S. 6.24

New title of CONSCRIPTS OF MISFORTUNE or IT HAPPENED IN AFRICA

D. F. Martin Thornton
C. Emile Lauste
Sc.

from story by G. Clifton Boyne

Florence Turner
Madge Stuart
M. A. Wetherell
Victor McLaglen
Walter Tennyson
Simeon Stuart
Cecil du Gué
Norma Whalley

WOMEN OF THE EMPIRE

Hagen
5 reels
T.S. 3.19

P. Rev. A. J. Waldron

WOMEN WHO WIN

Trans–Atlantic
5 reels
T.S. 1919

Produced under the auspices of the Women's Service
D. Percy Nash and Fred Durrant
C. J. C. Bee Mason
Sc. E. Alma Stout

WON BY A HEAD

British Exhibitors' Films
5,000 ft
T.S. 7.20

D. Percy Nash
Sc. John Gabriel

Rex Davis
Frank Tennant
Douglas Payne
Vera Cornish

WONDERFUL STORY, THE

Graham–Wilcox
5 reels
T.S. 5.22

D. Graham Cutts
Sc. P. L. Mannock, Herbert Wilcox and Graham Cutts from story by I. A. R. Wylie

Herbert Langley
Lillian Hall-Davis
Olaf Hytten
Bernard Vaughan

WONDERFUL WOOING, THE

Stoll
6,300 ft
T.S. 9.25

D. Geoffrey Malins
C. D. P. Cooper
Sc. from story by Douglas Walshe
Art Walter Murton

Marjorie Hume
Genevieve Townsend
Daisy Campbell
Eric Bransby Williams
George Mulcaster
Tom Coventry

WONDERFUL YEAR, THE

H. W. Thompson
6,000 ft
T.S. 9.21

D. Kenelm Foss   Asst. John Miller
C. Frank Canham
Sc. Kenelm Foss from novel by W. J. Locke and story in *Nash's Magazine*
Art titles T. C. Gilson

Margot Drake
Lionelle Howard
Randle Ayrton
Mary Odette
Hubert Carter
Frank Stanmore
Gwen Williams

WORLDLINGS, THE

(1) 6,000 ft (2) 5,000 ft
T.S. (1) 2.20 (2) 8.21

D. Eric Harrison
C. J. C. Bee Mason
Sc. Eric Harrison from novel by Leonard Merrick

Margaret Halstan
Ivy Close
Edward O'Neill
Basil Gill

WORLD OF WONDERFUL REALITY

Hepworth–Edwards
5 reels
T.S. 3.24

D. Henry Edwards
C. Charles Bryce

484

Sc.
from novel by E. Temple Thurston

Chrissie White
Henry Edwards
Gwynne Herbert
James Lindsay
Stephen Ewart

WOULD YOU BELIEVE IT!

Nettlefold
5,015 ft
T.S. 5.29

Music on Vocalion recording

P. Archibald Nettlefold
D. Walter Forde
C. Geoffrey Faithfull
Sc. Walter Forde and H. Fowler Mear
Art W. G. Saunders
Ed. Adeline Culley
Music Paul Mulder

Walter Forde
Pauline Johnson
Arthur Stratton
Albert Brouett

WRECKER, THE

Gainsborough, Anglo–German
production
6,705 ft
T.S. 7.29

Sound effects, R.C.A.

D. Geza von Bolvary   Asst. Chandos Balcon
C. Otto Kanturek
Sc. Angus Macphail from play by Arnold Ridley and Bernard Meri-vale
Art O. F. Werndorff   Asst. Alan McNab

Carlyle Blackwell
Benita Hume
Gordon Harker
Winter Hall

WUTHERING HEIGHTS

Ideal
6,200 ft
T.S. 7.20

Reissued in 2 reels in 1923

D. A. V. Bramble
Sc. Eliot Stannard from novel by Emily Brontë

Milton Rosmer
Warwick Ward
Ann Trevor
Cyril Raymond
Colette Brettel
Cecil Morton York
Dora de Winton
Aileen Bagot
George Traill

W. W. JACOBS PRODUCTIONS

Artistic
Series, 6 2-reelers
T.S. 10.23 and 1.24

D. Manning Haynes
Sc. Lydia Hayward from stories by W. W. Jacobs

The Constable's Move
An Odd Freak
The Convent
Lawyer Quince
The Boatswain's Mate
Dixon's Return

YELLOW CLAW, THE

Stoll
6,200 ft
T.S. 1.21

D. René Plaisetty
C. J. J. Cox
Sc. Gerard Fort Buckle from story by Sax Rohmer
Art Walter Murton

485

Fotheringham Lysons
Norman Page
Arthur Cullin
Mary Massart
June
Cyril Percival
Sydney Seaward
Kiyoshi Takase
Kitty Fielder
Annie Esmond
Geoffrey Benstead
Harvey Braban
George Harrington

YOU KNOW WHAT SAILORS ARE

Gaumont–British
7,598 ft
T.S. 12.28

New title of ROUGH SEAS

D. Maurice Elvey
Sc.
from novel by W. E. Townend (*A Light for his Pipe*)

Chili Bouchier
Matilde Comont
Cyril McLaglen
Alf Goddard
Jerrold Robertshaw

YOUNG LOCHINVAR

Stoll
5,500 ft
T.S. 10.23

British Film Week 1924

D. Will Kellino
C. Basil Emmott
Sc. J. Preston Muddock from poem by Sir Walter Scott. Alicia Ramsey
Art Walter Murton
Ed. Challis N. Sanderson

Owen Nares
Bertie Wright
Cecil Morton York
Charles Barratt
J. Nelson Ramsaye
Dick Webb
Gladys Jennings

YPRES

British Instructional Films
8,000 ft
T.S. 10.25

P. H. Bruce Woolfe
D. Walter Summers

ZEEBRUGGE

British Instructional Films
7 reels
T.S. 10.24

Made with assistance of the Admiralty and the Belgian Government

P. H. Bruce Woolfe and A. V. Bramble
C. Jack Parker
From material supplied by Cmdr. K. M. Bruce

ZERO

First National-Pathé
8,159 ft
T.S. 9.28

D. Jack Raymond
Sc. Lydia Hayward from novel by Collinson Owen
Art W. Murton

Fay Compton
Stewart Rome
Jeanne de Casalis
Sam Livesey
Dorinea Shirley
J. R. Tozer

INDEX